**ontents**

ORGANIZATION THEORY AND DESIGN

SEVENTH EDITION

Richard L. Daft
Vanderbilt University

SOUTH-WESTERN
— ✦ —™
THOMSON LEARNING

Australia · Canada · Mexico · Singapore · Spain · United Kingdom · United States

Organization Theory and Design, 7e by Richard L. Daft
Vice President/Publisher: Jack W. Calhoun
Executive Editor: John Szilagyi
Developmental Editor: Denise Simon
Marketing Manager: Rob Bloom
Production Editor: Kelly Keeler
Manufacturing Coordinator: Sandee Milewski
Internal Design: A Small Design Studio/Ann Small
Cover Design: Paul Neff Design
Cover Image: © Josef Beck/FPG
Photo Manager: Cary Benbow
Production House: DPS Associates, Inc.
Printer: R.R. Donnelley

Printed in the United States of America
3 4 5 03 02

For more information contact South-Western Publishing, 5191 Natorp Blvd.,
Mason, Ohio, 45040 or find us on the Internet at http://www.swcollege. com
For permission to use material from this text or product, contact us by
• **telephone: 1-800-730-2214**
• **fax: 1-800-730-2215**
• **web: http://www.thomsonrights.com**

Library of Congress Cataloging-in-Publication Data

Daft, Richard L.

   Organization theory and design / Richard L. Daft.—7th ed.
     p. cm.
   Includes bibliographical references and index.
   ISBN 0-324-02100-3
   1. Organization. 2. Organizational sociology—Case studies. I. Title.

HD31 .D135 2000
658.4—dc21

00-027139

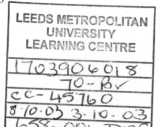

Preface

My vision for the seventh edition of *Organization Theory and Design* is to integrate the most recent thinking about organization design with classic and traditional ideas and theories in a way that is interesting and enjoyable for students. This edition has undergone a transformation. Significant changes have been made in many areas, including a new chapter, major revisions of several chapters to incorporate the most recent ideas, new case examples, new examples of e-commerce organizations, new book reviews, new end-of-chapter cases, and new end-of-book integrative cases. The research and theories in the field of organization studies are insightful, rich, and help students and managers understand their organizational world and solve real-life problems. My mission is to integrate the concepts and models from organizational theory with changing events in the real world to provide the most up-to-date view of organization design available.

FEATURES NEW TO THE SEVENTH EDITION

Many students in a typical organization theory course do not have extensive work experience, especially at the middle and upper levels, where organization theory is most applicable. To engage students in today's world of organizations, the seventh edition adds or expands significant features: a new chapter that discusses the important concept of knowledge management and the impact of new information technology, a feature called Taking the Lead that focuses on companies that are on the cutting edge of today's rapidly changing business world, student experiential activities that engage students in applying chapter concepts, new Book Marks, new In Practice examples, and new end-of-chapter and integrative cases for student analysis. The total set of features substantially expands and improves the book's content and accessibility.

TAKING THE LEAD

The Taking the Lead boxes describe companies that have undergone a major shift in organization design, strategic direction, values, or culture as they strive to become learning organizations and be more competitive in today's turbulent global environment. Many of these companies are applying new ideas to compete in the world of e-commerce. The Taking the Lead examples illustrate company transformations toward knowledge sharing, empowerment of employees, new structures, new cultures, the breaking down of barriers between departments and organizations, and the joining together of employees in a common mission.

Examples of Taking the Lead organizations include Cisco Systems, SOL Cleaning Service, Rowe Furniture Company, Deere & Company, Novartis, Trilogy Software, and the U.S. Department of Agriculture.

NEW CHAPTER

The new chapter, Chapter 7, describes the growing impact of information technology and the emphasis on knowledge management in today's organizations. The Internet and the information revolution are changing practically everything about doing business. Information technology and knowledge management have become crucial weapons for companies in all industries. More than facilities, equipment, or even products, it is a company's information and knowledge resources and how they are used that define organization success. These changes are having a tremendous impact on organization design as managers look for ways to enable employees to build and share information and knowledge throughout the organization. The chapter discusses mechanisms for both *explicit* and *tacit* knowledge management.

NEW CONCEPTS

Many concepts have been added or expanded in this edition. New material has been added on the horizontal organization structure, e-commerce, the balanced scorecard, enterprise resource planning, intranets and extranets, strategies for competing globally, the large-group intervention approach to organization development, culture strength and organizational subcultures, mass customization in manufacturing and service firms, and the shift from organizations designed for efficiency toward those designed for learning and change. In addition, the new concept of knowledge management is described thoroughly in Chapter 7.

NEW BOOK MARKS

Book Marks, a unique feature of this text, are book reviews that reflect current issues of concern to managers working in real-life organizations. These reviews describe the varied ways companies are dealing with the challenges of today's changing environment. New Book Marks in the seventh edition include *New Rules for the New Economy*, *Business @ the Speed of Thought*, *The Innovator's Dilemma*, *The Trillion-Dollar Enterprise*, *The Living Company*, *The 48 Laws of Power*, *The Alchemy of Growth*, *Open Boundaries*, and *Competing on the Edge*.

NEW CASE EXAMPLES

This edition contains numerous new examples to illustrate theoretical concepts. Many examples are international, and all are based on real organizations. New chapter opening cases include Weyerhaeuser Company, Barnes & Noble, Danone Group, SAS Institute, White Rose Nursery and Crafts, and Oxford Health Plans. New In Practice cases used within chapters to illustrate specific concepts are Xerox, Cementos Mexicanos (Cemex), Aluminum Company of America/ International Association of Machinists, Toyota Motor Corporation, Starbucks Coffee, the Holt Companies, American Standard Companies, Wal-Mart, TNT UK, Tommy Hilfiger, Charles Schwab Corp., Turner Industries, Biogen, Inc., Encyclopaedia Britannica, and Progressive Corporation.

NEW INTEGRATIVE CASES

In addition, several new integrative cases have been added to encourage student discussion and involvement. New integrative cases include Custom Chip, Inc., Microsoft, Dowling Flexible Metals, and XEL Communications.

STUDENT APPLICATIONS

Student application exercises are included at the end of every chapter. Each chapter contains a Workbook—an exercise through which students gain more experience with chapter concepts. Selected chapters also have a Workshop exercise that engages a student group in a larger learning experience. In addition, several challenging new end-of-chapter cases have been added. These include Southern Discomfort, Implementing Change at National Industrial Products, The Daily Tribune, Does This Milkshake Taste Funny?, Cracking the Whip, Airstar Inc., Century Medical, and W.L. Gore & Associates: Entering 1998.

OTHER FEATURES

Many of the features from previous editions have been so well received that the general approach has been retained.

1. Multiple pedagogical devices are used to enhance student involvement in text material. A Look Inside introduces each chapter with a relevant and interesting organizational example. In Practice cases illustrate theoretical concepts in organizational settings. Frequent exhibits are used to help students visualize organizational relationships, and the artwork has been redone to communicate concepts more clearly. The Summary and Interpretation section tells students which points are important in the broader context of organizational theory. The Briefcase feature tells students how to use concepts to analyze cases and manage organizations. Cases for Analysis are tailored to chapter concepts and provide a vehicle for student analysis and discussion.

2. Each chapter is highly focused and is organized into a logical framework. Many organization textbooks treat material in sequential fashion, such as Here's View A, Here's View B, Here's View C, and so on. *Organization Theory and Design* shows how they apply to organizations. Moreover, each chapter sticks to the essential point. Students are not introduced to extraneous material or confusing methodological squabbles that occur among organizational researchers. The body of research in most areas points to a major trend, which is reported here. Several chapters develop a framework that organizes major ideas into an overall scheme.

3. This book has been extensively tested on students. Feedback from students and faculty members has been used in the revision. The combination of organization theory concepts, book reviews, examples of leading organizations, case illustrations, experiential exercises, and other new teaching devices is designed to meet student learning needs, and students have responded very favorably.

SUPPLEMENTS

Instructor's Resource Guide with Test Bank (ISBN: 0-324-02101-1)

Written by Karen Dill Bowerman of California State University, Fresno. The resource guide contains chapter overviews, chapter outlines, lecture enhancements, discussion questions, discussion of workbook activities, discussion of chapter cases, Internet activities, case notes for integrative cases, and a guide to the videos available for use with the text. The test bank consists of multiple-choice, true/false, and essay questions.

A computerized version of the test bank is available upon request. ExamView® Pro (ISBN: 0-324-02105-4), an easy to use test-generating program, enables instructors to create printed tests, Internet tests, and online (LAN-based) tests quickly. Instructors can enter their own questions, using the software provided, as well as customize the appearance of the tests they create. The QuickTest wizard permits test generators to use an existing bank of questions to create a test in minutes, using a step-by-step selection process.

PowerPoint Presentation Slides (ISBN: 0-324-02102-X)

Developed by Charlene L. Coe with Karen Dill Bowerman, both of California State University, Fresno, and prepared in conjunction with the text and instructor's resource guide, more than 150 PowerPoint slides are available to supplement course content, adding structure and visual dimension to lectures.

Video

A new video library is available to users of the seventh edition to show how organizations and leaders apply organization theory to the real world. A tape of Video Examples (ISBN: 0-324-02104-6) examines a range of issues. Critical thinking questions appear at appropriate intervals in the 10- to 15-minute segments.

Product Support Web Site

A rich Web site at http://daft.swcollege.com complements the text, providing many extras for students and instructors.

ACKNOWLEDGMENTS

Textbook writing is a team enterprise. The seventh edition has integrated ideas and hard work from many people to whom I am very grateful. The reviewers and focus group participants of the sixth edition made an especially important contribution. They praised many features, were critical about things that didn't work well, and offered several suggestions. I thank the following individuals for their significant contributions to this text.

David Ackerman
University of Alaska, Southeast

Michael Bourke
Houston Baptist University

Jo Anne Duffy
Sam Houston State University

Patricia Feltes
Southwest Missouri State University

John A. Gould
University of Maryland

Bruce J. Hanson
Pepperdine University

Guiseppe Labianca
Tulane University

Jane Lemaster
University of Texas-Pan American

Steven Maranville
University of Saint Thomas

Rick Martinez
Baylor University

Julie Newcomer
Texas Woman's University

Asbjorn Osland
George Fox University

Laynie Pizzolatto
Nicholls State University

Samantha Rice
Abilene Christian University

Richard Saaverda
University of Michigan

W. Robert Sampson
University of Wisconsin, Eau Claire

W. Scott Sherman
Pepperdine University

Jack Tucci
Southeastern Louisiana University

I especially thank and acknowledge Karen Dill Bowerman, California State University, Fresno, for her terrific contribution to the *Instructor's Resource Guide* that accompanies *Organization Theory and Design*. Karen did a superb job developing new questions for the test bank, creating new teaching ideas and auxiliary lectures, and writing teaching notes for the cases. Karen's work provides many additional resources for instructors to use in class. In addition, Charlene Coe worked with Karen to develop an excellent set of PowerPoint slides to supplement the text.

Among my professional colleagues, I owe a special debt to Arie Lewin, who over the last few years has made excellent suggestions for new material about international structures, advanced information technology, and top-management direction. I appreciate, too, the intellectual stimulation from friends and colleagues at the Owen School: Bruce Barry, Ray Friedman, Rich Oliver, David Owens, and Bart Victor.

I want to extend special thanks to my editorial associate, Pat Lane. Pat provided outstanding help throughout the revision of this text. She skillfully drafted materials on a variety of cases and topics, found resources, and did an outstanding job with the copyedited manuscript, page proofs, and ancillary materials. Pat's personal enthusiasm and care added to the high level of excellence in the seventh edition. I am also grateful to Denise Simon and Linda Roberts. Denise took over as development editor and did everything right to keep the project and me on track, and she handled the permissions in record time. Linda took responsibility for the completion of several projects that provided me time to focus on revising this book.

The team at South-Western also deserves special mention. John Szilagyi, executive editor, did a superb job of moving the project forward while offering ideas for improvement. Kelly Keeler, production editor, provided extraordinary project coordination and used her creativity and management skills to facilitate the book's on-time completion. In addition, Crystal Chapin and the team at DPS Associates helped to guide me through the details of the production process.

Finally, I want to acknowledge the love and contributions of my wife, Dorothy Marcic. Dorothy was very supportive and has helped me grow emotionally during our time together. She took the book a giant step forward with her creation of the Workbook and Workshop student exercises, which are a significant addition to the text. I also want to acknowledge the love and support of all my daughters, who make my life special during our precious time together.

Introduction to Organizations

Organizations and Organization Theory

CHAPTER 1

A LOOK INSIDE

International Business Machines Corporation

*O*wning stock in IBM was like owning a gold mine. The overwhelming success of the IBM PC sent the company's already high profits soaring, and IBM was ranked as the world's largest company in terms of stock market value. Big Blue, as the company was known, was creating jobs around the world, its workforce ultimately swelling to 407,000.

A decade later, those who had invested their lives—or their money—in a company they thought could never fail watched long-cherished dreams go down the drain. The company went from earning a $6 billion profit to reporting a whopping $5 billion loss two years later. IBM stock lost more than $75 billion in value, an amount equal to the gross domestic product of Sweden. Everyone associated with the once-great company suffered.

- More than 140,000 IBM workers lost their jobs. Entire towns that sprang up because of IBM watched their economies disappear. New York's middle Hudson Valley was devastated, and when IBM announced layoffs in 1993, local officials requested that gun shops close for the day.
- As IBM stock fell from $176 to the low $40s, so did the retirement hopes of hundreds of thousands of investors, from IBM executives to the small-town grandmother who thought she'd made the safest investment in the world.
- By the time IBM gave up its no-layoffs policy, damaged employee morale was re-inforced by former employees who sold T-shirts with the IBM logo spelling out "I've Been Misled."
- After a long career of rising to the top of one of the world's greatest companies, the chairman of IBM, John Akers, resigned under heavy pressure, taking other top executives with him. But more than careers were tarnished that day. On the same day, the company shook the financial world by announcing that for the first time in history, it was slashing its quarterly dividend from $1.21 to $.54 a share.

The fall of IBM, the giant of the computer industry for eighty years, is a classic story of organizational decline. The company went from literally being at the top of the world to fighting for its life. How did it happen? Just as importantly, what changes have current IBM executives implemented to bring new life to the company and regain status as a leader in the computer industry?

Background

IBM grew out of a conglomerate formed in 1911 that primarily made scales, coffee grinders, cheese slicers, and time clocks. The so-called "Computer-Tabulating-Recording" component of the conglomerate grew quickly, and the 1924 name change to International Business Machines Corporation signaled a significant shift in focus.

For fifty-seven years, until 1971, IBM was led by the Thomas Watsons (senior and junior). The leaders who followed them were not as forceful or visionary as the Watsons, but they inherited a strong company that clearly dominated the computer market. In the mid-1960s, IBM introduced the System/360 family of mainframe computers—six models launched simultaneously, requiring five new factories and creating thousands of new jobs. An outstanding success, the 360 sealed IBM's leadership in the computer industry. Some think it may have marked another turning point as well.

"Bureaucracy Run Amok"

Retired IBM executive Malcolm Robinson, who rose to a senior post in IBM Europe, said, "The scale of the [System/360 project] created a complexity in the business that almost couldn't be handled. It was chaos for a while. So an organization had to be created to bring things under control and make sure that kind of breakdown never happened again. And that really may have been what made the bureaucracy take off."[1] Statistics indicate that Robinson was right. IBM's personnel count went up almost 130 percent between 1963 and 1966, while sales rose about 97 percent.

Too many people and too many meetings caused IBM executives to make mistakes. Decisions that should have been made quickly in response to changes in the computer market were delayed or ignored because of the cumbersome management system that demanded everything be done "the IBM way." For one thing, the IBM way demanded consensus through meetings, so any time a participating staff member "nonconcurred," in the jargon of the company, decisions were referred to another meeting. IBM choked on the bureaucratic culture. When IBM's new chairman took over after the resignation of John Akers, he said of the troubled company, "It was bureaucracy run amok."

The IBM culture led to such things as the ridiculous—but relatively harmless—file of IBM-approved jokes for executives to tell at luncheons or other speaking engagements. But it also led to disaster.

"The Times They Are A-Changin'"

Around the time IBM introduced its 360 line of computers in the mid-1960s, folk singer Bob Dylan's song "The Times They Are A-Changin'" was released. Unfortunately, IBM didn't change with the times. The company staked its claim in the world of multimillion-dollar mainframes. It was late getting into the personal computer market, choosing to steer what company leaders in the 1970s thought was a safe course—preserving the company's mainframe profits.

By the time IBM decided to enter the personal computer game in earnest, the death knell was already starting to toll on the profits from mainframes. The values that guided IBM and its mainframe leadership—the caution, the obsessive training of employees, a focus on following rather than anticipating customer needs, and a guarantee of lifetime employment to its workers—didn't work when IBM moved into the fast-paced, ever-changing, competitive world of personal computers.

It's Not What They Did; It's What They Didn't Do

The IBM PC was an instant success for IBM, but the PC war was already lost. It's what the company *didn't* do, both before and after the introduction of the PC, that ultimately caused its downfall.

The first big mistake IBM made was in not taking advantage of a new technology the company itself invented in the mid-1970s. The reduced instruction-set computing (RISC) microprocessor offered simplified, faster computing, well-suited to the minicomputers that were gaining popularity. But the new technology threatened the huge profits from the company's mainframe business. The decision to develop smaller, less expensive machines with new technology kept getting delayed until the competition stepped way ahead of IBM at its own game.

At least as damaging to IBM's future was its subsequent failure to grab a larger share of PC profits when it had the opportunity. The company signed on with Microsoft for the PC's software and Intel for the microprocessor. IBM might, at the time, have purchased all or part of both of these companies, allowing Big Blue to cash in on the huge profits that are now accruing to the two smaller firms. Several years later, Bill Gates again encouraged IBM to purchase around 10 percent of Microsoft, believing it would be beneficial to his own company as well as to IBM. Again, IBM declined—a very expensive mistake. If IBM had bought 10 percent of Microsoft then, the company would today have turned a $100 million investment into more than $3 billion.

Another thing IBM didn't do quickly was accept that its no-layoffs policy was no longer working in the fast-paced computer business. As one former manager put it, the policy was defended "like virginity." Rather than admitting the organization needed to be streamlined and the workforce cut, IBM began several years of "reorganizing"—eliminating positions here, firing employees there for the slightest infractions of the rules. The company gradually increased the pressure for workers to accept severance offers. All the time, IBM's then-Chairman John Akers kept insisting that no one was being laid off. Though some championed Akers's efforts to maintain this distinctive piece of IBM's culture, employee morale and company image were severely damaged by these word games by the time IBM finally gave up its sacred no-layoffs policy.

IBM Today

In 1993, Louis V. Gerstner, Jr., stepped into this mess with the determination to shine up IBM's image and create a culture in which IBM people waste fewer opportunities, minimize bureaucracy, and put the good of the company ahead of their separate divisions. In his first year as chairman and CEO, he revamped IBM's finances, brought in outsiders to head up several critical divisions, and dramatically altered financial incentives for top executives, basing about 75 percent of their variable pay on the overall performance of the company. Today, sweaters, chinos, and loafers have replaced starched white shirts and blue suits in many IBM offices, an outward symbol that the company's stiff, bureaucratic culture has given way to a more relaxed, adaptable one. Gerstner, known for his sometimes lightning-quick decisions, dismantled a top-management committee that often stifled action and began talking to employees and customers directly through e-mail.

IBM suffered by missing opportunities and delaying action; Gerstner wants to make sure the same thing doesn't happen in the new networking era. He has pulled together resources from all over the giant company and focused them on the goal of bringing customers all sorts of e-business solutions. When Gerstner announced recently that IBM earns more money from Internet business than the top 25 Internet companies combined, Big Blue's stock prices soared. Rather than trying to compete with computer companies such as Dell, which can offer cheaper, customized machines by streamlining supply chains and bypassing traditional distribution channels, Gerstner decided to tap into the gold mine created by overwhelmed executives seeking to gain control over their increasingly complex information systems. Thus, IBM is pursuing the fastest growing segment of the information technology marketplace—the demand for electronic business services—by selling services, hardware, software and know-how that can address virtually any IT dilemma. IBM has more than 10,000 e-business customers; its products and services link businesses' internal networks to the World Wide Web and help them order supplies, work with distributors, analyze sales projections, and manage business intelligence.

Gerstner came to IBM with a vision of a future in which major corporations will buy computing power and applications software the way they buy electric service, never even knowing or caring where the computer that does the work is located. As that vision becomes a reality, IBM is poised at the forefront to reap the benefits. Gerstner's strategies have combined the IBM name, a hip advertising campaign, and the widest range of products, services, and experts in the information services industry to bring about one of the most remarkable turnarounds in corporate America.[2]

Welcome to the real world of organization theory. The shifting fortunes of IBM illustrate organization theory in action. IBM managers were deeply involved in organization theory each day of their working lives—but they never realized it. Company managers didn't fully understand how the organization related to the environment or how it should function internally. Familiarity with organization theory helps managers such as Lou Gerstner analyze and diagnose what is happening and the changes needed to keep the company competitive. Organization theory gives us the tools to explain the decline and turnaround of IBM. It helps us understand and explain what happened in the past, as well as what may happen in the future, so that we can manage our organizations more effectively.

ORGANIZATION THEORY IN ACTION

TOPICS

Each of the topics to be covered in this book is illustrated in the IBM case. Consider, for example, IBM's failure to respond to or control such elements as customers, suppliers, and competitors in the fast-paced external environment; its inability to coordinate departments and design control systems that promoted efficiency; slow decision making, such as delaying action on exploiting the potential of new technology; handling the problem of large size; the absence of a forceful top management team that allowed IBM to drift further and further into chaos; and an outmoded corporate culture that stifled innovation and change. These are the subjects with which organization theory is concerned. Organization theory can also explain how Lou Gerstner and his top managers found the right structure and strategies that helped revitalize the giant company.

Of course, organization theory is not limited to IBM. Every organization, every manager in every organization, is involved in organization theory. Johnsonville Foods, a Sheboygan, Wisconsin, sausage maker, turned a floundering family business into a dynamic fast-growing company by reorganizing into self-directed teams. Hewlett-Packard Company—which was suffering from some of the same problems as IBM in the 1980s—went through a major, highly successful reorganization, using concepts based in organization theory.

Today, H-P is one of the fastest-growing companies in the computer industry. Xerox Corporation has gone through a similar transformation. Chairman and CEO Paul Allair's turnaround plan for Xerox included slashing costs, selling off the company's financial services divisions, streamlining the supply chain, and reducing product development time. And Xerox continues to restructure to meet changing competitive conditions. The company recently announced that it will cut 10 percent of the workforce, close factories, and hire outside companies to handle storage and distribution. Xerox plans to use the savings to build up high-margin businesses such as servicing equipment and creating computer networks, as well as increase marketing efforts to compete with Hewlett-Packard in lower-cost office machines.[3]

Organization theory draws lessons from these organizations and makes those lessons available to students and managers. The story of IBM's decline is important because it demonstrates that even large, successful organizations are vulnerable, that lessons are not learned automatically, and that organizations are only as strong as their decision makers. The stories of Johnsonville Foods, Hewlett-Packard, Xerox, and IBM also illustrate that organizations are not static; they continuously adapt to shifts in the external environment. Today, many companies are facing the need to transform themselves into dramatically different organizations because of new challenges in the environment.

CURRENT CHALLENGES

Research into hundreds of organizations provides the knowledge base to make IBM and other organizations more effective. For example, challenges facing organizations at the beginning of the twenty-first century are quite different from those of the 1970s and 1980s, and thus the concept of organizations and organization theory is evolving. For one thing, the world is changing more rapidly than ever before. In a survey of top executives, coping with rapid change emerged as the most common problem facing managers and organizations today.[4] Some specific challenges facing IBM and other organizations are competing globally, embracing change, competing through e-commerce, managing knowledge and information, supporting diversity, and maintaining high standards of ethics and social responsibility.

Global Competition. The cliché that the world is getting smaller is dramatically true for today's organizations. With rapid advances in technology and communications, the time it takes to exert influence around the world from even the most remote locations has been reduced from years to only seconds. Business is becoming a unified global field as trade barriers fall, communication becomes faster and cheaper, and consumer tastes in everything from clothing to cellular phones converge. Thomas Middelhoff of Germany's Bertelsmann AG, which bought the U.S. publisher Random House, put it this way:"There are no German and American companies. There are only successful and unsuccessful companies."[5] In the twenty-first century, organizations will have to feel "at home" anywhere in the world. Companies can locate different parts of the organization wherever it makes the most business sense; top leadership in one country, technical brainpower and production in other locales. For example, Canada's Northern Telecom selected a site in the southwest of England as its world manufacturing center for a new fixed-access radio product. Siemens of Germany moved its electronic ultrasound division to the United States, while the U.S. company DuPont shifted its electronics operations headquarters to Japan.[6]

Although this growing interdependence brings many advantages, it also means that the environment for companies is becoming extremely complex and extremely competitive. Organizations have to learn to cross lines of time, culture, and geography in order to survive. Every company, large and small, faces international competition on its home turf at the same time it confronts the need to be more competitive in international markets. Rising managers today need to know a second or third language and develop cross-cultural understanding. Large companies such as IBM and Ford are working to globalize their management structures to remain competitive internationally, while even the smallest companies are searching for structures and processes that help them reap the advantages of global interdependence and minimize the disadvantages.

Organizational Turbulence. For much of the twentieth century, organizations operated in a relatively stable business environment, so managers could focus on designing structures and systems that kept the organization running smoothly and efficiently. There was little need to search for new ways to cope with increased competition or shifting customer demands. All that began to change in the 1980s, and today's organizations are struggling to catch up with the changes that have proliferated since then. Advances in computers and information technology are driving many of these changes at the same time they provide ways to cope with them. This chapter's Book Mark examines how technology is transforming the world of business. Customers expect new products and services developed more

ℬook ℳark 1.0

New Rules for the New Economy: 10 Radical Strategies for a Connected World

By Kevin Kelly

Our organizations, as well as our everyday lives, have been engulfed by technology. In *New Rules for the New Economy*, Kevin Kelly points out that the entire economic order is being reshaped by "shrinking computers and expanding communications." He outlines three distinguishing characteristics of the new economy: it is global; it favors ideas, information, and relationships over tangible products; and it is intensely interconnected. Taken together, these characteristics produce an economy and a society that is rooted in the concept of the network. *New Rules for the New Economy* outlines ten strategies for thriving in today's networked world.

NEW RULES FOR SUCCESS

Kelly believes the "networked" world is the prime force that managers must focus on to help their organizations thrive. His new rules for the new economy include the following:

- *Embrace the swarm.* A trillion tiny parts, Kelly says, can yield brilliant, massive results if they are properly connected into a swarm. By connecting people from the bottom up in a network, organizations can achieve superior performance in a turbulent environment. This means not only using networking technology but finding ways to tap into the collective mindpower of everyone in the organization. He uses the example of Cementos Mexicanos (Cemex), which thrives on the chaos of delivering cement in rural Mexico and other developing regions. Cemex transformed the industry by using extensive networking technology and giving drivers and dispatchers the information and authority they needed to make decisions and act quickly.
- *Feed the web first.* Organizations maximize the value of their networks by making it easy for others to participate—employees, customers, suppliers, and even competitors. Those who thrive in the new economy focus not on maximizing their own value but on maximizing the value of the network. A complex web of interrelationships helps everyone become stronger and more powerful. The software industry provides an example. The programmers who created the game Doom deliberately made it easy to modify. Therefore, hundreds of other companies issued games that were superior to the original but that ran on the Doom system. Everyone profited from the expansion.

- *Move from places to spaces.* The boundaries of distance and geography are becoming increasingly irrelevant as more and more economic activity takes place electronically. As Kelly puts it, "As the economy infiltrates each network medium, it trades a physical marketplace for a conceptual marketspace." One result is the trend toward *disintermediation*, which means consumers can bypass the traditional middleman and buy directly from the manufacturer. Today, anyone can log onto the Internet and shop for the lowest-priced refrigerator directly from the manufacturer rather than shopping in a retail store.
- *Embrace opportunities before efficiencies.* Productivity and efficiency are the wrong things to care about in the new economy. Measuring efficiency requires a uniform output, which is becoming increasingly rare in an economy that emphasizes customization and creative innovation. Machines have taken over routine and uniform work, enabling human beings to focus on opportunities rather than efficiencies. Opportunities require flexibility, creativity, exploration, and curiosity, qualities that thrive in a network. Kelly goes so far as to argue that "any job that can be measured for productivity probably should be eliminated from the list of jobs that people do." Everyone today, he says, should be focused on opportunities—on doing the right thing rather than doing things right.

CONCLUSION

Kelly believes the networked economy opens up never-before-imagined worlds of opportunity for individuals and organizations. Thanks to networks, he says, the "new global economic culture is characterized by decentralized ownership and equity, by pools of knowledge instead of pools of capital, by an emphasis on an open society, and, most important, by a widespread reliance on economic values as the basis for making decisions in all walks of life." *New Rules for the New Economy* has much to say about how to manage knowledge, communication, and information in today's complex, interconnected, and turbulent world.

New Rules for the New Economy is published by Viking Penguin, a member of Penguin Putnam Inc.

often and delivered more rapidly, and they often want them customized to their exact needs. Mass production and distribution techniques are being replaced with new computer-aided systems that can produce one-of-a-kind variations and streamlined distribution systems that deliver products directly from the manufacturer to the consumer. Another shift brought about by technology is that the financial basis of today's economy is *information* rather than the tangible assets of land, buildings, and capital. In this new era, the primary factor of production becomes knowledge rather than machines, increasing the power of employees. Today's knowledge workers want more than a paycheck; they expect interesting work and opportunities to participate and learn.

The mindset needed by organizational leaders is to expect the unexpected and be prepared for constant change. One of the hottest trends in recent years is the use of *enterprise resource planning* (ERP). These complex information systems collect, process, and provide information about an organization's entire enterprise, including identification of customer needs, orders, product design, production, purchasing, inventory, distribution, human resources, receipt of payments, and forecasting of future demand. These and other new types of information systems have a profound impact on the design of organizations. In addition, because ERP systems integrate the whole organization, managers and employees can use the information to adjust plans and respond to opportunities at a moment's notice.

The challenge for managers and organizations in most countries is not just to cope with change but to embrace it, even create it. The organizational forms and patterns of behavior that were once successful no longer work, yet new patterns are just emerging. As stated in one management article, "Most managers today have the feeling that they are flying the airplane at the same time they are building it."[7]

E-commerce. One area in which many traditional managers feel particularly awkward is the new world of e-business or e-commerce. Within just a few years, the Internet has been transformed from a "toy" used by a few computer nerds to a broad communications and trade center where more than 90 million people exchange information or close deals around the world.[8] Most executives know that the Internet could, over the next few years, change almost everything in every industry, but many of them don't know how to transform their organizations to fit into this new world. IBM, as discussed in the opening case, is thriving again by using its know-how to help other organizations compete in the e-business era. Although business on the Internet is booming, the United States and Canada are barely in the infancy of this trend, while countries in Europe, Latin America, and Asia are still in the embryonic stage.[9] One organization that has made the transition to an Internet-based, thoroughly digitized business is Dell Computer Corp. Dell has pioneered the use of end-to-end digital networks to keep in touch with customers, take orders, pull together components from suppliers, and ship customized products directly to consumers. This trend toward *disintermediation*— eliminating the middleman—will ultimately affect every industry. In a meeting of executives, consultants, and professors at Harvard University, participants concluded that businesses today must either "Dell or be Delled."[10]

Companies embracing the new world of e-business, whether to sell products, streamline operations, or improve communications with customers and partners, are thriving. Those that ignore the trend do so at their own peril. Even today's industry leaders will not survive if they can't compete in an Internet-driven economy.

The Internet tears down boundaries of time and space, enabling organizations to create entirely new businesses and reach markets they never could have before.

For example, Byers Chrysler Plymouth Dodge in Columbus, Ohio, hooked up with Autoweb.com, a Net car-buying service, and is now selling twelve more cars per month, including some to buyers hundreds of miles away. By enabling businesses to link directly to suppliers, factories, distributors, and customers, the Internet breaks down boundaries between organizations and enables partnership and collaboration on a previously unheard-of scale. As one e-commerce entrepreneur put it, "If you remain insular in this business, you'll get eaten alive."[11]

Managing Knowledge and Information. Technology also plays a key role in the trend toward knowledge management and the sharing of information across and between organizations. Recognizing that intellectual capital—what employees know—matters more than any other asset today, companies seek to manage knowledge just as they manage cash flow, human resources, or raw materials. New positions such as chief information officer, chief knowledge officer, director of knowledge management, and chief learning officer reflect the importance of information and knowledge in today's organizations. Daniel Holtshouse, director of knowledge initiatives at Xerox, estimates that about a fifth of *Fortune* 500 companies have someone who serves in the capacity of a chief knowledge officer, and the number is growing.[12]

Information technology, including the Internet, supports knowledge management and the broad sharing of information and is generally related to changes in how organizations are designed and managed. In the past, organizational hierarchies developed in part to move information up and down the system. The guiding assumption of many companies was that key ideas and decisions originated at the top and were channeled downward. Competitive companies today, though, are guided by the assumption that the organization needs ideas from everyone, and that the role of managers is to find ways to open channels of communication to allow ideas, information, and knowledge to flow throughout the organization. Thus, an emphasis on knowledge management and information sharing often leads to a flattening of organization structures and greater empowerment and involvement of employees. In addition, some thriving companies, including Andersen Windows, Chevron, and Springfield Remanufacturing, share knowledge such as best practices not only across functions but also with other companies, including partners, suppliers, and even competitors, based on the belief that a mutual sharing of good ideas is the best way to keep their organizations competitive.[13]

Diversity. Diversity is a fact of life that no organization can afford to ignore. The workforce—as well as the customer base—is changing in terms of age, gender, race, national origin, sexual orientation, and physical ability. The average worker is older now, and many more women, people of color, and immigrants are entering the workforce. Immigration accounted for nearly half of the increase in the U.S. labor force in the 1990s, and immigrants will likely constitute a growing share of workers in the twenty-first century. By the year 2020, it is estimated that women will comprise fully half of the total U.S. workforce and that Asian Americans, African Americans, and Hispanics will make up more than 30 percent. People of Asian, African, and Hispanic descent are expected to comprise about 35 percent of the U.S. population by 2020.[14] The growing diversity of the workforce brings a variety of challenges, such as maintaining a strong corporate culture while supporting diversity, balancing work and family concerns, and coping with the conflict brought about by varying cultural styles. For example, at the DaimlerChrysler plant in western Alabama, managers have struggled to blend German and American workers' cultural styles. While the Germans consider most of their Alabama colleagues lax, too talkative, and somewhat superficial, the American workers find the Germans to be rigid, formal, even humorless. "The Germans are very blunt," said one worker. "You don't get politeness out of them about work."[15]

People from diverse ethnic and cultural backgrounds offer varying styles, and organizations must learn to welcome and incorporate this diversity into the upper ranks. For example, recent research has indicated that women's style of doing business may hold important lessons for success in the emerging world of the twenty-first century. Yet the glass ceiling persists, keeping women from reaching positions of top leadership.[16]

Ethics and Social Responsibility. Ethics and social responsibility have become hot topics in corporate America. Companies of all sizes are rushing to adopt codes of ethics, and most are also developing other policies and structures that encourage ethical conduct. Organizations get into trouble when they fail to pay attention to ethical issues in the blind pursuit of making money. In recent years, numerous companies, including Archer-Daniels-Midland, Baker & Taylor Books, Prudential Insurance, and Columbia/HCA, have been charged with serious breaches of ethical or legal standards. And the problem is not limited to U. S. companies. Two giant pharmaceutical companies, Hoffman-LaRoche, a Swiss firm, and Germany's BASF AG, recently pleaded guilty to charges that they plotted to raise and fix the prices of vitamins used in virtually every American home and added to bread, milk, and breakfast cereal. For their role in the conspiracy, BASF AG will pay a $225 million fine, and Hoffmann-LaRoche will pay $500 million, the largest federal criminal fine ever imposed on a company.[17]

On the other hand, a growing number of companies are demonstrating their commitment to high standards of ethics and social responsibility. Marriott Corporation tries to help build healthy communities through its "Pathways to Independence Program," which targets welfare recipients. Program candidates go through dozens of hours of rigorous training and then "graduate" to a job in the company. Microboard Processing Inc. frequently hires high-risk workers, from welfare recipients to felons and former drug addicts, based on the belief that everyone deserves a chance to turn their lives around.[18] The Gap's Community Action Program allows headquarters employees to take paid time off to become involved in volunteer activities.

PURPOSE OF THIS CHAPTER

The purpose of this chapter is to explore the nature of organizations and organization theory today. Organization theory has developed from the systematic study of organizations by scholars. Concepts are obtained from living, ongoing organizations. Organization theory can be practical, as illustrated in the IBM case. It helps people understand, diagnose, and respond to emerging organizational needs and problems.

The next section begins with a formal definition of organization and then explores introductory concepts for describing and analyzing organizations. Next, the scope and nature of organization theory are discussed more fully. Succeeding sections examine the history of organization theory and design, the development of new organizational forms in response to changes in the environment, and how organization theory can help people manage complex organizations in today's rapidly changing world. The chapter closes with a brief overview of the themes to be covered in this book.

WHAT IS AN ORGANIZATION?

Organizations are hard to see. We see outcroppings, such as a tall building or a computer workstation or a friendly employee; but the whole organization is vague and abstract and may be scattered among several locations. We know organizations are there because they touch us every day. Indeed, they are so common that we take them for granted. We hardly notice that we are born in a hospital, have our birth records registered in a government agency, are educated in schools and universities, are raised on food produced on corporate farms, are treated by doctors engaged in a joint practice, buy a house built by a construction company and sold by a real estate agency, borrow money from a bank, turn to police and fire departments when trouble erupts, use moving companies to change residences, receive an array of benefits from government agencies, spend forty hours a week working in an organization, and are even laid to rest by an undertaker.[19]

DEFINITION

Organizations as diverse as a church, a hospital, and IBM have characteristics in common. The definition used in this book to describe organizations is as follows: **organizations** are (1) social entities that (2) are goal directed, (3) are designed as deliberately structured and coordinated activity systems, and (4) are linked to the external environment.

The key element of an organization is not a building or a set of policies and procedures; organizations are made up of people and their relationships with one another. An organization exists when people interact with one another to perform essential functions that help attain goals. Recent trends in management recognize the importance of human resources, with most new approaches designed to empower employees with greater opportunities to learn and contribute as they work together toward common goals. Managers deliberately structure and coordinate organizational resources to achieve the organization's purpose. However, even though work may be structured into separate departments or sets of activities, most organizations today are striving for greater horizontal coordination of work activities, often using teams of employees from different functional areas to work together on projects. Boundaries between departments as well as those between organizations are becoming more flexible and diffuse as companies face the need to respond to changes in the external environment more rapidly. An organization cannot exist without interacting with customers, suppliers, competitors, and other elements of the external environment. Today, some companies are even cooperating with their competitors, sharing information and technology to their mutual advantage.

IMPORTANCE OF ORGANIZATIONS

It may seem hard to believe today, but "organizations" as we know them are relatively recent in the history of humankind. Even in the late 19th century there were few organizations of any size or importance—no labor unions, no trade associations, few large businesses, non-profit organizations or governmental departments. What a change has occurred since then! The Industrial Revolution and the development of large organizations transformed all of society. Gradually, organizations became central to people's lives and today they exert a tremendous influence in our society.[20]

Organizations are all around us and shape our lives in many ways. But what contributions do organizations make? Why are they important? Exhibit 1.1 lists

EXHIBIT 1.1   *Importance of Organizations*

1. Bring together resources to achieve desired goals and outcomes
2. Produce goods and services efficiently
3. Facilitate innovation
4. Use modern manufacturing and computer-based technology
5. Adapt to and influence a changing environment
6. Create value for owners, customers, and employees
7. Accommodate ongoing challenges of diversity, ethics, and the motivation and coordination of employees

seven reasons organizations are important to you and to society. First, organizations bring together resources to accomplish specific goals. Consider MaMaMedia Inc. (*www.mamamedia.com*), founded by Irit Harel. To accomplish the goal of providing an entertaining children's Web site based on the educational research of the legendary MIT Media Lab, Harel had to raise more than $11 million; negotiate alliances with partners such as Scholastic, Inc., Netscape Communications, America Online, and General Mills; recruit quality employees who believed in the theory that interactive play promotes learning; develop activities that promote constructive creativity; and line up advertisers and sponsors for the site.[21]

Organizations also produce goods and services that customers want at competitive prices. Companies look for innovative ways to produce and distribute goods and services more efficiently. One way is through e-commerce, as discussed earlier, and through the use of computer-based manufacturing technologies. Redesigning organizational structures and management practices can also contribute to increased efficiency. Organizations create a drive for innovation rather than a reliance on standard products and outmoded ways of doing things. The trend toward the learning organization reflects the desire to improve in all areas. Computer-aided design and manufacturing and new information technology also help promote innovation.

Organizations adapt to and influence a rapidly changing environment. Some large companies have entire departments charged with monitoring the external environment and finding ways to adapt to or influence that environment. One of the most significant changes in the external environment today is globalization. Organizations such as Coca-Cola, AES Corporation, Heineken Breweries, and Xerox are involved in strategic alliances and partnerships with companies around the world in an effort to influence the environment and compete on a global scale.

Through all of these activities, organizations create value for their owners, customers, and employees. Managers need to understand which parts of the operation create value and which parts do not; a company can be profitable only when the value it creates is greater than the cost of resources. McDonald's made a thorough study of how to use its core competencies to create better value for customers. The study resulted in the introduction of Extra Value Meals and the decision to open restaurants in different locations, such as inside Wal-Mart and Sears stores.[22] Finally, organizations have to cope with and accommodate today's challenges of workforce diversity and growing concerns over ethics and social responsibility, as well as find effective ways to motivate employees to work together to accomplish organizational goals.

Organizations shape our lives, and well-informed managers can shape organizations. An understanding of organization theory enables managers to design organizations to function more effectively.

ORGANIZATIONS AS SYSTEMS

OPEN SYSTEMS

One significant development in the study of organizations was the distinction between closed and open systems.[23] A **closed system** would not depend on its environment; it would be autonomous, enclosed, and sealed off from the outside world. Although a true closed system cannot exist, early organization studies focused on internal systems. Early management concepts, including scientific management, leadership style, and industrial engineering, were closed-system approaches because they took the environment for granted and assumed the organization could be made more effective through internal design. The management of a closed system would be quite easy. The environment would be stable and predictable and would not intervene to cause problems. The primary management issue would be to run things efficiently.

An **open system** must interact with the environment to survive; it both consumes resources and exports resources to the environment. It cannot seal itself off. It must continuously change and adapt to the environment. Open systems can be enormously complex. Internal efficiency is just one issue—and sometimes a minor one. The organization has to find and obtain needed resources, interpret and act on environmental changes, dispose of outputs, and control and coordinate internal activities in the face of environmental disturbances and uncertainty. Every system that must interact with the environment to survive is an open system. The human being is an open system. So is the planet earth, the city of New York, and IBM. Indeed, one problem at IBM was that top managers seemed to forget they were part of an open system. They isolated themselves within the IBM culture and failed to pay close attention to what was going on with their customers, suppliers, and competitors. The rapid changes over the past few decades, including globalization and increased competition, the explosion of the Internet and e-business, and the growing diversity of the population and workforce, have forced many managers to reorient toward an open-systems mindset and recognize their business as part of a complex, interconnected whole.

To understand the whole organization, it should be viewed as a system. A **system** is a set of interacting elements that acquires inputs from the environment, transforms them, and discharges outputs to the external environment. The need for inputs and outputs reflects dependency on the environment. Interacting elements mean that people and departments depend on one another and must work together.

Exhibit 1.2 illustrates an open system. Inputs to an organization system include employees, raw materials and other physical resources, information, and financial resources. The transformation process changes these inputs into something of value that can be exported back to the environment. Outputs include specific products and services for customers and clients. Outputs may also include employee satisfaction, pollution, and other by-products of the transformation process.

A system is made up of several **subsystems**, as illustrated at the bottom of Exhibit 1.2. These subsystems perform the specific functions required for organizational survival, such as production, boundary spanning, maintenance,

EXHIBIT 1.2   *An Open System and Its Subsystems*

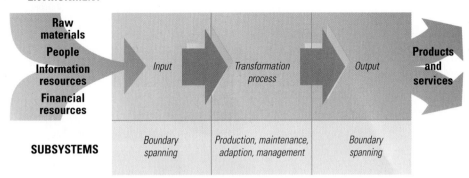

adaptation, and management. The production subsystem produces the product and service outputs of the organization. Boundary subsystems are responsible for exchanges with the external environment. They include activities such as purchasing supplies or marketing products. The maintenance subsystem maintains the smooth operation and upkeep of the organization's physical and human elements. The adaptive subsystems are responsible for organizational change and adaptation. Management is a distinct subsystem, responsible for coordinating and directing the other subsystems of the organization.

ORGANIZATIONAL CONFIGURATION

Various parts of the organization are designed to perform the key subsystem functions illustrated in Exhibit 1.2. One framework proposed by Henry Mintzberg suggests that every organization has five parts.[24] These parts, illustrated in Exhibit 1.3, include the technical core, top management, middle management, technical support, and administrative support. The five parts of the organization may vary in size and importance depending on the organization's environment, technology, and other factors.

Technical Core. The technical core includes people who do the basic work of the organization. It performs the production subsystem function and actually produces the product and service outputs of the organization. This is where the primary transformation from inputs to outputs takes place. The technical core is the production department in a manufacturing firm, the teachers and classes in a university, and the medical activities in a hospital. At IBM, the technical core produces hardware, software, and e-business services for clients.

Technical Support. The technical support function helps the organization adapt to the environment. Technical support employees such as engineers and researchers scan the environment for problems, opportunities, and technological developments. Technical support is responsible for creating innovations in the technical core, helping the organization to change and adapt. Technical support at IBM is provided by departments such as technology, research and development, and marketing research.

Administrative Support. The administrative support function is responsible for the smooth operation and upkeep of the organization, including its physical and human elements. This includes human resource activities such as recruiting and hiring, establishing compensation and benefits, and employee training and

EXHIBIT 1.3   *Five Basic Parts of an Organization*

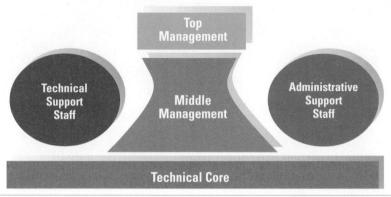

Source: Based on Henry Mintzberg, *The Structuring of Organizations* (Englewood Cliffs, N.J.: Prentice-Hall, 1979), 215–297; and Henry Mintzberg, "Organization Design: Fashion or Fit?" *Harvard Business Review* 59 (January-February 1981): 103-116.

development, as well as maintenance activities such as cleaning of buildings and service and repair of machines. Administrative support functions in a corporation such as IBM might include the human resources department, organizational development, the employee cafeteria, and the maintenance staff.

Management. Management is a distinct subsystem, responsible for directing and coordinating other parts of the organization. Top management provides direction, strategy, goals, and policies for the entire organization or major divisions. Middle management is responsible for implementation and coordination at the departmental level. In traditional organizations, middle managers are responsible for mediating between top management and the technical core, such as implementing rules and passing information up and down the hierarchy.

In real-life organizations, the five parts are interrelated and often serve more than one subsystem function. For example, managers coordinate and direct other parts of the system, but they may also be involved in administrative and technical support. In addition, several of the parts serve the *boundary spanning* function mentioned in the previous section. For example, in the administrative support realm, human resources departments are responsible for working with the external environment to find quality employees. Purchasing departments acquire needed materials and supplies. In the technical support area, research and development departments work directly with the external environment to learn about new technological developments. Managers perform boundary spanning as well, such as when Lou Gerstner of IBM works directly with major customers. The important boundary spanning subsystem is embraced by several areas, rather than being confined to one part of the organization.

DIMENSIONS OF ORGANIZATION DESIGN

The systems view pertains to dynamic, ongoing activities within organizations. The next step for understanding organizations is to look at dimensions that describe specific organizational design traits. These dimensions describe organizations much the same way that personality and physical traits describe people.

Organizational dimensions fall into two types: structural and contextual, illustrated in Exhibit 1.4. **Structural dimensions** provide labels to describe the internal characteristics of an organization. They create a basis for measuring and comparing organizations. **Contextual dimensions** characterize the whole organization, including its size, technology, environment, and goals. They describe the organizational setting that influences and shapes the structural dimensions. Contextual dimensions can be confusing because they represent both the organization and the environment. Contextual dimensions can be envisioned as a set of overlapping elements that underlie an organization's structure and work processes. To understand and evaluate organizations, one must examine both structural and contextual dimensions.[25] These dimensions of organization design interact with one another and can be adjusted to accomplish the purposes listed earlier in Exhibit 1.1.

STRUCTURAL DIMENSIONS

1. *Formalization* pertains to the amount of written documentation in the organization. Documentation includes procedures, job descriptions, regulations, and policy manuals. These written documents describe behavior and activities. Formalization is often measured by simply counting the number of pages of documentation within the organization. Large state universities, for example, tend to be high on formalization because they have several volumes of written rules for such things as registration, dropping and adding classes,

EXHIBIT 1.4   *Interacting Contextual and Structural Dimensions of Organization Design*

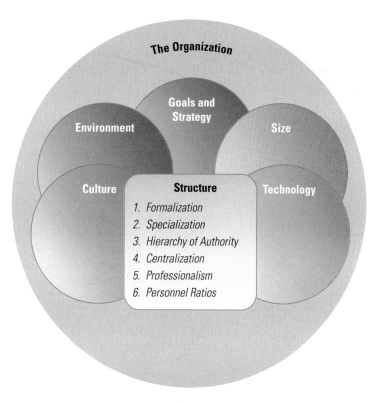

student associations, dormitory governance, and financial assistance. A small, family-owned business, in contrast, may have almost no written rules and would be considered informal.

2. *Specialization* is the degree to which organizational tasks are subdivided into separate jobs. If specialization is extensive, each employee performs only a narrow range of tasks. If specialization is low, employees perform a wide range of tasks in their jobs. Specialization is sometimes referred to as the *division of labor.*

3. *Hierarchy of authority* describes who reports to whom and the span of control for each manager. The hierarchy is depicted by the vertical lines on an organization chart, as illustrated in Exhibit 1.5. The hierarchy is related to *span of control* (the number of employees reporting to a supervisor). When spans of control are narrow, the hierarchy tends to be tall. When spans of control are wide, the hierarchy of authority will be shorter.

4. *Centralization* refers to the hierarchical level that has authority to make a decision. When decision making is kept at the top level, the organization is centralized. When decisions are delegated to lower organizational levels, it is decentralized. Organizational decisions that might be centralized or decentralized include purchasing equipment, establishing goals, choosing suppliers, setting prices, hiring employees, and deciding marketing territories.

5. *Professionalism* is the level of formal education and training of employees. Professionalism is considered high when employees require long periods of training to hold jobs in the organization. Professionalism is generally measured as the average number of years of education of employees, which could be as high as twenty in a medical practice and less than ten in a construction company.

6. *Personnel ratios* refer to the deployment of people to various functions and departments. Personnel ratios include the administrative ratio, the clerical ratio, the professional staff ratio, and the ratio of indirect to direct labor employees. A personnel ratio is measured by dividing the number of employees in a classification by the total number of organizational employees.

CONTEXTUAL DIMENSIONS

1. *Size* is the organization's magnitude as reflected in the number of people in the organization. It can be measured for the organization as a whole or for specific components, such as a plant or division. Because organizations are social systems, size is typically measured by the number of employees. Other measures such as total sales or total assets also reflect magnitude, but they do not indicate the size of the human part of the social system.

2. *Organizational technology* refers to the tools, techniques, and actions used to transform inputs into outputs. It concerns how the organization actually produces the products and services it provides for customers and includes such things as computer-aided manufacturing, advanced information systems, and the Internet. An automobile assembly line, a college classroom, and an overnight package delivery system are technologies, although they differ from one another.

3. The *environment* includes all elements outside the boundary of the organization. Key elements include the industry, government, customers, suppliers, and the financial community. Environmental elements that affect an organization the most are often other organizations.

EXHIBIT 1 . 5   Organization Chart Illustrating the Hierarchy of Authority for a Community Job Training Program

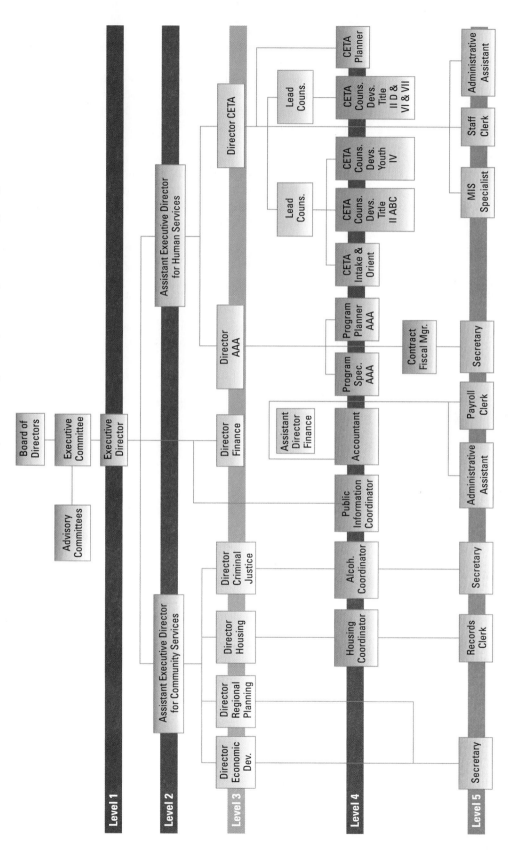

4. The organization's *goals and strategy* define the purpose and competitive techniques that set it apart from other organizations. Goals are often written down as an enduring statement of company intent. A strategy is the plan of action that describes resource allocation and activities for dealing with the environment and for reaching the organization's goals. Goals and strategies define the scope of operations and the relationship with employees, customers, and competitors.

5. An organization's *culture* is the underlying set of key values, beliefs, understandings, and norms shared by employees. These underlying values may pertain to ethical behavior, commitment to employees, efficiency, or customer service, and they provide the glue to hold organization members together. An organization's culture is unwritten but can be observed in its stories, slogans, ceremonies, dress, and office layout.

The eleven contextual and structural dimensions discussed here are interdependent. For example, large organization size, a routine technology, and a stable environment all tend to create an organization that has greater formalization, specialization, and centralization. More detailed relationships among the dimensions are explored in later chapters of this book.

These dimensions provide a basis for the measurement and analysis of characteristics that cannot be seen by the casual observer, and they reveal significant information about an organization. Consider, for example, the dimensions of W. L. Gore & Associates compared with those of Wal-Mart and a governmental agency.

In Practice 1.1

W. L. Gore & Associates

When Jack Dougherty began work at W. L. Gore & Associates, Inc., he reported to Bill Gore, the company's founder, to receive his first assignment. Gore told him, "Why don't you find something you'd like to do." Dougherty was shocked at the informality but quickly recovered and began interrogating various managers about their activities. He was attracted to a new product called Gore-Tex, a membrane that was waterproof but breathable when bonded to fabric. The next morning, he came to work dressed in jeans and began helping feed fabric into the maw of a large laminator. Five years later, Dougherty was responsible for marketing and advertising in the fabrics group.

Bill Gore died in 1986, but the organization he designed still runs without official titles, orders, or bosses. People are expected to find a place where they can contribute and manage themselves. The company has some 4,200 associates (not employees) in twenty-nine plants. The plants are kept small—up to two hundred people—to maintain a family atmosphere. "It's much better to use friendship and love than slavery and whips," Bill Gore said. Several professional employees are assigned to develop new products, but the administrative structure is lean. Good human relations is a more important value than is internal efficiency, and it works. New plants are being built almost as fast as the company can obtain financing.

Contrast that approach to Wal-Mart, where efficiency is the goal. Wal-Mart achieves its competitive edge through employee commitment and internal cost efficiency. A standard formula is used to build each store, with uniform displays and merchandise. Wal-Mart operates about 1,850 discount stores, as well as 600 Supercenters, 453 Sam's Clubs, and 700 international stores. Its administrative expenses are the lowest of any chain. The distribution system is a marvel of efficiency. Goods can be delivered to any store in less than two days after an order is placed. Stores are controlled from the top, but store managers are also given some freedom to adapt to local conditions.

Performance is high, and employees are satisfied because the pay is good and more than half of them share in corporate profits.

An even greater contrast is often seen in government agencies or not-for-profit organizations that rely heavily on public funding. Most state humanities and arts agencies, for example, are staffed by only a small number of employees, but workers are overwhelmed with rules and regulations and swamped by paperwork. Employees who have to implement rule changes often don't have time to read the continuous stream of memos as well as keep up with their daily work with community arts organizations. Employees must require extensive reporting from their clients in order to make regular reports to a variety of state and federal funding sources. Agency workers are frustrated and so are the community-based organizations they seek to serve. These organizations often refuse assistance because of the extensive paperwork involved.[26]

Exhibit 1.6 illustrates several structural and contextual dimensions of Gore & Associates, Wal-Mart, and the state arts agency. Gore & Associates is a medium-sized manufacturing organization that ranks very low with respect to formalization, specialization, and centralization. A number of professional staff are assigned to nonworkflow activities to do the research and development needed to stay abreast of changes in the fiber industry. Wal-Mart is much more formalized, specialized, and centralized. Efficiency is more important than new products, so most activities are guided by standard regulations. The percentage of nonworkflow personnel is kept to a minimum. The arts agency, in contrast to the other organizations, reflects its status as a small part of a large government bureaucracy. The agency is overwhelmed with rules and standard ways of doing things. Rules are dictated from the top. Most employees are assigned to workflow activities, although in normal times a substantial number of people are devoted to administration and clerical support.

Structural and contextual dimensions can thus tell a lot about an organization and about differences among organizations. Organization design dimensions are examined in more detail in later chapters to determine the appropriate level of each dimension needed to perform effectively in each organizational setting.

THE EVOLUTION OF ORGANIZATION THEORY AND DESIGN

Organization theory is not a collection of facts; it is a way of thinking about organizations. Organization theory is a way to see and analyze organizations more accurately and deeply than one otherwise could. The way to see and think about organizations is based on patterns and regularities in organizational design and behavior. Organization scholars search for these regularities, define them, measure them, and make them available to the rest of us. The facts from the research are not as important as the general patterns and insights into organizational functioning.

HISTORY

Organization design and management practices have varied over time in response to changes in the larger society.

You may recall from an earlier management course that the modern era of management theory began with the classical management perspective in the late

EXHIBIT 1.6   *Characteristics of Three Organizations*

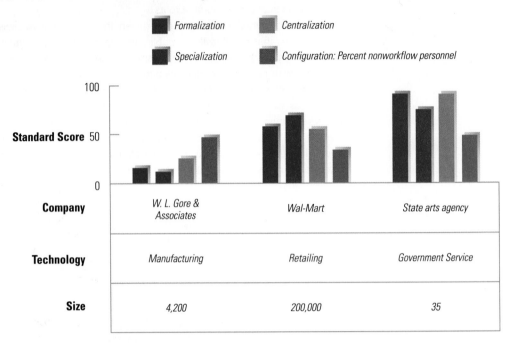

nineteenth and early twentieth century. The emergence of the factory system during the Industrial Revolution posed problems that earlier organizations had not encountered. As work was performed on a much larger scale by a larger number of workers, people began thinking about how to design and manage work in order to increase productivity and help organizations attain maximum efficiency. The classical perspective, which sought to make organizations run like efficient, well-oiled machines, is associated with the development of hierarchy and bureaucratic organizations and remains the basis of much of modern management theory and practice. Two subfields of the classical perspective are scientific management and administrative principles.

Scientific Management. Pioneered by Frederick Winslow Taylor, **scientific management** postulates that decisions about organizations and job design should be based on precise, scientific study of individual situations.[27] To use this approach, managers develop precise, standard procedures for doing each job, select workers with appropriate abilities, train workers in the standard procedures, carefully plan work, and provide wage incentives to increase output. Taylor's approach is illustrated by the unloading of iron from rail cars and reloading finished steel for the Bethlehem Steel plant in 1898. Taylor calculated that with correct movements, tools, and sequencing, each man was capable of loading 47.5 tons per day instead of the typical 12.5 tons. He also worked out an incentive system that paid each man $1.85 per day for meeting the new standard, an increase from the previous rate of $1.15. Productivity at Bethlehem Steel shot up overnight. These insights helped to establish organizational assumptions that the role of management is to maintain stability and efficiency, with top managers doing the thinking and workers doing what they are told.

Administrative Principles. Whereas scientific management focused primarily on the technical core—on work performed on the shop floor—**administrative principles** looked at the design and functioning of the organization as a whole. For example, Henri Fayol proposed fourteen principles of management, such as "each subordinate receives orders from only one superior" (unity of command) and "similar activities in an organization should be grouped together under one manager" (unity of direction). These principles formed the foundation for modern management practice and organization design. Fayol believed these principles could be applied in any organizational setting. The scientific management and administrative principles approaches were very powerful and gave organizations fundamental new ideas for establishing high productivity and increasing prosperity. Administrative principles in particular contributed to the development of **bureaucratic organizations**, which emphasized designing and managing organizations on an impersonal, rational basis through such elements as clearly defined authority and responsibility, formal recordkeeping, and uniform application of standard rules. Although the term *bureaucracy* has taken on negative connotations in today's organizations, bureaucratic characteristics worked extremely well for the needs of the Industrial Age. Following classical management theory, other academic approaches emerged to address issues such as the social context and workers' needs.

The Hawthorne Studies. Early work on industrial psychology and human relations received little attention because of the prominence of scientific management. However, a major breakthrough occurred with a series of experiments at a Chicago electric company, which came to be known as the **Hawthorne Studies**. Interpretations of these studies concluded that positive treatment of employees improved their motivation and productivity. The publication of these findings led to a revolution in worker treatment and laid the groundwork for subsequent work examining treatment of workers, leadership, motivation, and human resource management. These human relations and behavioral approaches added new and important contributions to the study of management and organizations.

However, the hierarchical system and bureaucratic approaches that developed during the Industrial Revolution remained the primary approach to organization design and functioning well into the 1970s and 1980s. In general, this approach has worked well for most organizations until the past few decades. However, during the 1980s, it began to lead to problems. Increased competition, especially on a global scale, changed the playing field. Many North American companies were saddled with bloated administrative ratios and professional staff ratios. International competition from Europe and Japan provided the rude awakening. For example, Xerox discovered it was using 1.3 overhead workers for every direct worker, while its Japanese affiliate needed only 0.6 overhead workers. By the 1980s North American companies had to find a better way. AT&T cut thirty thousand managers during the 1980s. The merger of Chevron and Gulf led to the dismissal of eighteen thousand employees, many of whom were managers. GE laid off fifty thousand salaried employees.[28]

The 1980s produced new corporate cultures that valued lean staff, flexibility, rapid response to the customer, motivated employees, caring for customers, and quality products. The world was changing fast because corporate boundaries were altered by waves of merger activity, much of it international, and increased international competition.

Today, the world—and thus the world of business—is undergoing a change more profound and far-reaching than any experienced since the dawn of the modern age and the scientific revolution. Just as civilization was altered irrevocably in the transition from the agrarian to the industrial age, emerging events are changing the ways in which we interact with one another in our personal and professional lives. Old organization forms and management methods are inadequate to cope with new problems in the emerging postmodern world.[29] The net effect of the evolving business environment and the evolving study of organization theory is the use of contingency theory to describe and convey organizational concepts, as well as a new, more flexible approach to management and organizational design.

Contingency Theory. Organizations are not all alike. Many problems occur when all organizations are treated as similar, which was the case with scientific management and administrative principles approaches that attempted to design all organizations alike. However, the structures and systems that work in the retail division of a conglomerate will not be appropriate for the manufacturing division. The organization charts and financial procedures that are best for a new entrepreneurial Internet firm like MaMaMedia will not work for a large food processing plant.

Contingency means that one thing depends on other things, and for organizations to be effective, there must be a "goodness of fit" between their structure and the conditions in their external environment.[30] What works in one setting may not work in another setting. There is not one best way. Contingency theory means "it depends." For example, some organizations may experience a certain environment, use a routine technology, and desire efficiency. In this situation, a management approach that uses bureaucratic control procedures, a functional structure, and formal communication would be appropriate. Likewise, free-flowing management processes work best in an uncertain environment with a nonroutine technology. The correct management approach is contingent on the organization's situation.

Today, almost all organizations operate in highly uncertain environments. Thus, we are involved in a significant period of transition, in which the dominant paradigm of organization theory and design is changing as dramatically as it was changed with the dawning of the Industrial Revolution.

THE CHANGING PARADIGM OF ORGANIZATION DESIGN

To a great extent, managers and organizations are still imprinted with the hierarchical, bureaucratic approach that arose more than a century ago. Yet the challenges presented by today's environment—global competitiveness, diversity, ethical concerns, rapid advances in technology, the rise of e-commerce, a shift to knowledge and information as organizations' most important form of capital, and the growing expectations of workers for meaningful work and opportunities for personal and professional growth—call for dramatically different responses from people and organizations. The perspectives of the past do not provide a road map for navigating the twenty-first century world of business. The managers of today and tomorrow will design and orchestrate new responses for a dramatically new world.

Today's organizations may be seen as shifting from a paradigm based on mechanical systems to one based on natural, biological systems. A **paradigm** is a shared mindset that represents a fundamental way of perceiving, conceptualizing, and understanding the world. Our beliefs and understandings direct our patterns of behavior.

Before the Industrial Revolution, most organizations were related to agriculture or craft work.[31] Communication was primarily face-to-face. Organizations were small, with simple structures and fuzzy boundaries, and were generally not interested in growing larger. In the modern, industrial age, however, a new organization paradigm emerged. Growth became a primary criterion for success. Organizations became large and complex, and boundaries between functional departments and between organizations were distinct. Environments were relatively stable, and technologies tended to be mass-production manufacturing processes. The primary forms of capital in the modern age were money, buildings, and machines. Internal structures became more complex, vertical, and bureaucratic. Leadership was based on solid management principles and tended to be autocratic; communication was primarily through formal memos, letters, and reports. Managers did all the planning and "thought work," while employees did the manual labor in exchange for wages and other compensation.

The environment for organizations today is anything *but* stable. With international competition, e-commerce, and other challenges, the environment for all organizations is unpredictable, characterized by complexity and surprise. Managers can't predict and control in traditional ways the drama unfolding inside or outside the organization. To cope, organizations need a shift to a newer paradigm, one based not on the mechanical assumptions of the industrial era but on concepts of a living, biological system. Many organizations are shifting to flexible, decentralized structures that emphasize horizontal collaboration. In addition, boundaries between organizations are becoming diffuse, as even competitors form partnerships to compete globally. The primary form of capital is not buildings or production machinery but *information* and *knowledge*. As a dramatic example, consider that the market value of companies whose product is information technology (for example, Excite, Yahoo, or iVillage) can often be one hundred to two hundred times greater than their fixed asset value, whereas in traditional companies, the market value and asset value are similar.

In this new environment, many managers are redesigning their companies toward something called the **learning organization**. The learning organization promotes communication and collaboration so that everyone is engaged in identifying and solving problems, enabling the organization to continuously experiment, improve, and increase its capability. The learning organization is based on equality, open information, little hierarchy, and a culture that encourages adaptability and participation, enabling ideas to bubble up from anywhere that can help the organization seize opportunities and handle crises. In a learning organization, the essential value is problem solving, as opposed to the traditional organization designed for efficient performance.

EFFICIENT PERFORMANCE VERSUS THE LEARNING ORGANIZATION

As managers struggle toward the learning organization, they are finding that specific dimensions of the organization have to change. Exhibit 1.7 compares organizations designed for efficient performance with those designed for continuous learning by looking at five elements of organization design: structure, tasks, systems, culture, and strategy.

EXHIBIT 1.7   *Two Organization Design Paradigms*

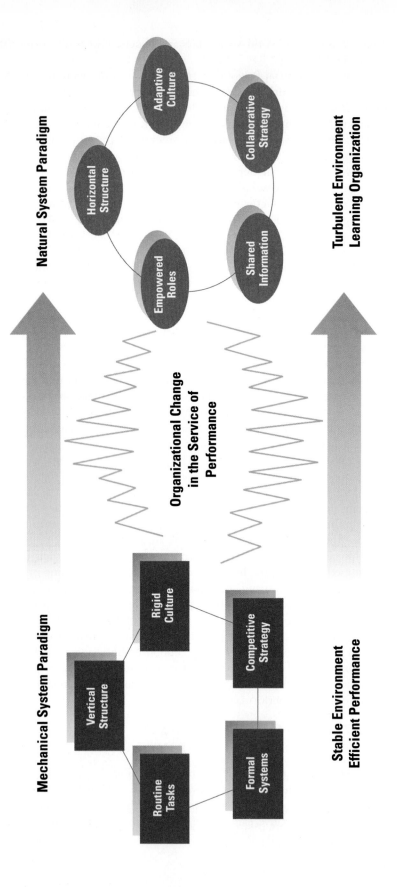

Mechanical System Paradigm

Vertical Structure

Rigid Culture

Routine Tasks

Formal Systems

Competitive Strategy

Stable Environment Efficient Performance

Organizational Change in the Service of Performance

Natural System Paradigm

Adaptive Culture

Horizontal Structure

Collaborative Strategy

Empowered Roles

Shared Information

Turbulent Environment Learning Organization

Source: Adapted from David K. Hurst, *Crisis and Renewal: Meeting the Challenge of Organizational Change* (Boston, Mass.: Harvard Business School Press, 1995).

From Vertical to Horizontal Structure. Traditionally, the most common organizational structure has been one in which activities are grouped together by common work from the bottom to the top of the organization. Generally little collaboration occurs across functional departments, and the whole organization is coordinated and controlled through the vertical hierarchy, with decision making authority residing with upper-level managers. This structure can be quite effective. It promotes efficient production and in-depth skill development, and the hierarchy of authority provides a sensible mechanism for supervision and control in large organizations. However, in a rapidly changing environment, the hierarchy becomes overloaded. Top executives are not able to respond rapidly enough to problems or opportunities.

In the learning organization, the vertical structure that creates distance between managers at the top of the organization and workers in the technical core is disbanded. Structure is created around horizontal workflows or processes rather than departmental functions. The vertical hierarchy is dramatically flattened, with perhaps only a few senior executives in traditional support functions such as finance or human resources. Self-directed teams are the fundamental work unit in the learning organization. Boundaries between functions are practically eliminated because teams include members from several functional areas. In some cases, organizations do away with departments altogether. For example, at Oticon Holding A/S, a Danish company that introduced the world's first digital hearing aid, there are no organization charts, no departments, no functions, and no titles. All vestiges of an organizational hierarchy have disappeared. All 150 employees are constantly forming and reforming into self-directed teams that work on specific projects.[32]

From Routine Tasks to Empowered Roles. Another shift in thinking relates to the degree of formal structure and control placed on employees in the performance of their work. Recall that scientific management advocated precisely defining each job and how it should be performed. A **task** is a narrowly defined piece of work assigned to a person. In traditional organizations, tasks are broken down into specialized, separate parts, as in a machine. Knowledge and control of tasks are centralized at the top of the organization, and employees are expected to do as they are told. A **role**, in contrast, is a part in a dynamic social system. A role has discretion and responsibility, allowing the person to use his or her discretion and ability to achieve an outcome or meet a goal. In learning organizations, employees play a role in the team or department and roles may be constantly redefined or adjusted. There are few rules or procedures, and knowledge and control of tasks are located with workers rather than with supervisors or top executives. Employees are encouraged to take care of problems by working with one another and with customers.

From Formal Control Systems to Shared Information. In young, small organizations, communication is generally informal and face-to-face. There are few formal control and information systems because the top leaders of the company usually work directly with employees in the day-to-day operation of the business. However, when organizations grow large and complex, the distance between top leaders and workers in the technical core increases. Formal systems are often implemented to manage the growing amount of complex information and to detect deviations from established standards and goals.[33]

In learning organizations, information serves a very different purpose. The widespread sharing of information keeps the organization functioning at an optimum level. The learning organization strives to return to the condition of a small, entrepreneurial firm in which all employees have complete information about the company so they can act quickly. Ideas and information are shared throughout the company. Rather than using information to control employees, a significant part of a manager's job is to find ways to open channels of communication so that ideas flow in all directions. In addition, learning organizations maintain open lines of communication with customers, suppliers, and even competitors to enhance learning capability. Information technology is one way to keep people in touch. For example, at Buckman Laboratories, a computerized knowledge network called K'Netix keeps 1,200 employees in 80 countries connected with one another and brings all of the organization's brainpower to bear in serving each customer.[34]

From Competitive to Collaborative Strategy. In traditional organizations designed for efficient performance, strategy is formulated by top managers and imposed on the organization. Top executives think about how the organization can best respond to competition, efficiently use resources, and cope with environmental changes. In the learning organization, in contrast, the accumulated actions of an informed and empowered workforce contribute to strategy development. Since all employees are in touch with customers, suppliers, and new technology, they help identify needs and solutions and participate in strategy making. In addition, strategy emerges from partnerships with suppliers, customers, and even competitors. Organizations become collaborators as well as competitors, experimenting to find the best way to learn and adapt. Johan Liedgren, the 34-year-old CEO of Honkworm International, an on-line entertainment agency, sits on the board of seven other Internet-commerce companies, some of whose CEOs, in turn, sit on his board of directors. They know one another's forecasts, marketing plans, and new product launches, and even share one another's financials.[35]

From Rigid to Adaptive Culture. For an organization to remain healthy, its culture should encourage adaptation to the external environment. However, a danger for many organizations is that the culture becomes fixed, as if set in concrete. Organizations that were highly successful in stable environments often became victims of their own success when the environment began to change dramatically. The cultural values, ideas, and practices that helped attain success were detrimental to effective performance in rapidly changing environments.

In a learning organization, the culture encourages openness, equality, continuous improvement, and change. People in the organization are aware of the whole system, how everything fits together, and how the various parts of the organization interact with one another and with the environment. This whole-system mindset minimizes boundaries within the organization and with other companies. In addition, activities and symbols that create status differences, such as executive dining rooms or reserved parking spaces, are discarded. Each person is a valued contributor and the organization becomes a place for creating a web of relationships that allows people to develop their full potential. The emphasis on treating everyone with care and respect creates a climate in which people have the freedom to experiment, take risks, and make mistakes, all of which encourages learning.

No company represents a perfect example of a learning organization, although many of today's most competitive organizations have shifted toward ideas and forms based on the concept of a living, dynamic system. Some of these organizations are spotlighted throughout this book in the Taking the Lead boxes. This chapter's Taking the Lead describes why Cisco Systems has sometimes been called "The Corporation of the Future."

As illustrated in Exhibit 1.7, today's managers are involved in a struggle as they attempt to change their companies into learning organizations. The challenge for managers is to maintain some level of stability as they actively promote change toward the new paradigm, to navigate between order and chaos.

Taking the Lead

Cisco Systems: Writing the Rules for the New World of Business

When he was working at IBM Corporation and Wang Laboratories, John Chambers, now CEO of Cisco Systems, got a firsthand look at how the reluctance to change can damage a company. He believes the new rules of business competition demand new organizational forms: ones based on change rather than stability, organized around networks rather than rigid hierarchies, and based on interdependencies with organizational partners.

Not surprisingly, Cisco—the leading maker of routers, switches, software, and other gear that keeps the Internet running—uses the Internet in virtually every aspect of its business, from sales and marketing to recruiting. Nearly 75 percent of all customer orders are handled via the Net, with the majority of those booked, credit checked, scheduled for manufacturing, and sent to the factory without human interference. In addition, the technology keeps more than 17,000 employees in 50 countries intimately connected and gives them access to whatever information they need. More than 1.7 million pages of information are available to Cisco employees on the network. The network also swiftly connects Cisco with its web of partners, making the constellation of suppliers, contract manufacturers, and assemblers look and act like one seamless company.

However, it isn't just technology that sets Cisco apart from the crowd. Just as important is the company's culture and mind-set. Chambers knows technology cannot replace human interaction, and he works hard to encourage open and direct communication among all employees and with Cisco's leaders. He holds quarterly meetings with employees and invites all employees in the month of their birthday to one of his "birthday breakfasts," where they can talk about anything they want. In addition, Chambers spends up to 55 percent of his time with customers. Customers,

not executives, drive the business at Cisco. Strategy is not something that is formulated in the executive suite; rather, it emerges from the network of employees, customers, and partners. One example of how customers help drive strategy comes from Boeing and Ford Motor Company. After both companies told Cisco employees that their future networking needs were unlikely to be met by Cisco, Cisco found out what the companies needed, then began searching for a company to acquire that would help solve the problem. That first acquisition, of local-area-network switchmaker Crescendo Communications, put Cisco into a new sector of the industry that now accounts for billions in annual revenue.

An egalitarian culture is central to the success of Cisco, because it builds teamwork and employee morale. "You never ask your team to do something you wouldn't do yourself," says Chambers, who always flies coach and has no reserved parking space at headquarters. In addition, Cisco's top managers work hard to include all employees, making them feel like true partners in the business. Broad-based stock option plans reward key employees. Leaders spend tremendous amounts of face-to-face time coaching, mentoring, and communicating with workers. The result is an energized, motivated work force that agrees with Chamber's conviction that his people and his organization are "in the sweet spot"—where technology and the future meet to transform business and everyday life.

Sources: John A. Byrne, "The Corporation of the Future," *Business Week,* August 31, 1998, 102-106; and "And the Winner Is . . . Cisco Systems," in "In Depth: Business 2.0 100," compiled by Walid Mougayar, project head; Michael Mattis, Kate McKinley, and Nissa Crawford, *Business 2.0,* May 1999, 58-94.

THE ROLE OF ORGANIZATION THEORY AND DESIGN

How can a study of organization theory help during this time of complexity and transition? For people who are or will be managers, organization theory provides significant insight and understanding to help them be better managers in a rapidly changing world. For example, one of the greatest threats to organizations today is the inability of management to adapt to the speed and chaos of technological change. Although companies have made massive investments in technology, they are only beginning to implement the organizational and management changes needed to make technology and the Internet competitive weapons. Understanding organization theory and design can help managers make those necessary changes by helping them see and understand how technology interacts with other elements of the organization and its environment. As in the case of IBM, many managers learn organization theory by trial and error. At IBM, managers did not initially understand the situation they were in or the contingencies to which they should respond.

In a very real sense, organization theory can make managers more competent and more influential by giving them an understanding of how organizations work. The study of organizations helps people see and understand things other people cannot see and understand. Organization theory provides ideas, concepts, and ways of thinking and interpreting that help managers guide organizations through the struggle to a new era. When the old approaches are no longer working, organization theory helps managers understand why and develop new approaches to meet changing conditions. At Cementos Mexicanos (Cemex), a team of managers used concepts based in organization theory to redesign their company to cope with the constant chaos of running a cement business in developing areas of the world.

In Practice 1.2

Cementos Mexicanos

To gain a competitive edge in the tough cement business, Cementos Mexicanos (Cemex) specializes in developing areas of the world—places where anything can, and usually does, go wrong. For example, even in its home country of Mexico, Cemex has to cope with unpredictable weather and traffic conditions, spontaneous labor disruptions, and arbitrary government inspections of construction sites that interfere with deliveries. In addition, more than half of all orders are changed or canceled by customers, usually at the last minute. Considering that a load of cement is never more than ninety minutes away from spoiling, that meant high costs, complex scheduling, and frustration for Cemex managers and employees, as well as for builders, who were lucky to get their cement delivered on the right day, let alone at the right hour.

Two internal consultants, Kenneth Massey and Homero Reséndez, analyzed the problem from all angles and concluded that customer chaos was inevitable, so they needed to find a way to solve the problem within that framework. The two formed a team to visit Federal Express in Memphis, Tennessee, and the Houston, Texas, 911 dispatch center to study how those organizations coped under extremely complex circumstances.. Based on their observations, the Cemex team developed a new approach to delivering cement, which they call "living with chaos." Rather than trying to change the customers, Cemex resolved to do business on the customers' own terms and design a system in which last-minute changes and unexpected problems are routine.

A core element of the new approach is a complex information technology system, including a global positioning satellite system and on-board computers in all delivery trucks, that is continuously fed with streams of day-to-day data on customer orders, production schedules, traffic problems, weather conditions, and so forth. Now Cemex trucks head out every morning to cruise the streets. When a customer order comes in, an employee checks the customer's credit status, locates a nearby truck, and relays directions for delivery. If the order is cancelled, computers automatically direct the plant to scale back production.

Cemex also made managerial and organizational changes to support the new approach. The company enrolled all its drivers, who had an average of six years of formal schooling, in weekly secondary-education classes and began training them in delivering not just cement but quality service. In addition, many strict and demanding work rules were abolished so that workers had more discretion and responsibility for solving problems, echoing the emergency-response expertise the team had witnessed at the 911 dispatch center. According to Francisco Perez, operations manager at Cemex in Guadalajara, "They used to think of themselves as drivers. But anyone can deliver concrete. Now our people know that they're delivering a service that the competition cannot deliver."

Same-day service and unlimited order changes are now standard operating procedure at Cemex. However, the most important outcome may be that Cemex thrives on constant change in a world of complexity.[36]

FRAMEWORK FOR THE BOOK

What topic areas are relevant to organization theory and design? How does a course in management or organizational behavior differ from a course in organization theory? The answer is related to the concept called level of analysis.

LEVELS OF ANALYSIS

In systems theory, each system is composed of subsystems. Systems are nested within systems, and one **level of analysis** has to be chosen as the primary focus. Four levels of analysis normally characterize organizations, as illustrated in Exhibit 1.8. The individual human being is the basic building block of organizations. The human being is to the organization what a cell is to a biological system. The next higher system level is the group or department. These are collections of individuals who work together to perform group tasks. The next level of analysis is the organization itself. An organization is a collection of groups or departments that combine into the total organization. Organizations themselves can be grouped together into the next higher level of analysis, which is the interorganizational set and community. The interorganizational set is the group of organizations with which a single organization interacts. Other organizations in the community also make up an important part of an organization's environment.

Organization theory focuses on the organizational level of analysis but with concern for groups and the environment. To explain the organization, one should look not only at its characteristics but also at the characteristics of the environment and of the departments and groups that make up the organization. The focus of this book is to help you understand organizations by examining their specific characteristics, the nature and relationships among groups and departments that make up the organization, and the collection of organizations that make up the environment.

EXHIBIT 1.8   *Levels of Analysis in Organizations*

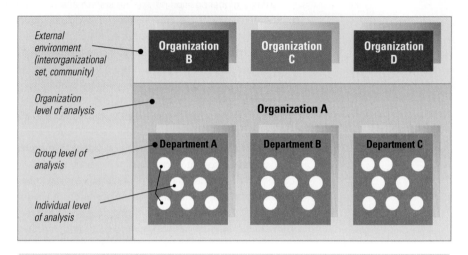

Source: Based on Andrew H. Van De Ven and Diane L. Ferry, *Measuring and Assessing Performance* (New York: Wiley, 1980), 8; and Richard L. Daft and Richard M. Steers, *Organizations: A Micro/Macro Approach* (Glenview, Ill.: Scott, Foresman, 1986), 8.

Are individuals included in organization theory? Organization theory does consider the behavior of individuals, but in the aggregate. People are important, but they are not the primary focus of analysis. Organization theory is distinct from organizational behavior. **Organizational behavior** is the micro approach to organizations because it focuses on the individuals within organizations as the relevant units of analysis. Organizational behavior examines concepts such as motivation, leadership style, and personality and is concerned with cognitive and emotional differences among people within organizations. **Organization theory** is a macro examination of organizations because it analyzes the whole organization as a unit. Organization theory is concerned with people aggregated into departments and organizations and with the differences in structure and behavior at the organization level of analysis. Organization theory is the sociology at organizations, while organizational behavior is the psychology of organizations.

A new approach to organization studies is called meso theory. Most organizational research and many management courses specialize in either organizational behavior or organization theory. **Meso theory** (*meso* means "in between") concerns the integration of both micro and macro levels of analysis. Individuals and groups affect the organization and the organization in return influences individuals and groups. To thrive in organizations, managers and employees need to understand multiple levels simultaneously. For example, research may show that employee diversity enhances innovation. To facilitate innovation, managers need to understand how structure and context (organization theory) are related to interactions among diverse employees (organizational behavior) to foster innovation, because both macro and micro variables account for innovations.[37]

For its part, organization theory is directly relevant to top- and middle-management concerns and partly relevant to lower management. Top managers are responsible for the entire organization and must set goals, develop strategy, interpret the external environment, and decide organization structure and design. Middle management is concerned with major departments, such as marketing or research, and must decide how the department relates to the rest of the organization. Middle managers must design their departments to fit work-unit technology and deal with issues of power and politics, intergroup conflict, and information and control systems, each of which is part of organization theory. Organization theory is only partly concerned with lower management because this level of supervision is concerned with employees who operate machines, type letters, teach classes, and sell goods. Organization theory is concerned with the big picture of the organization and its major departments.

PLAN OF THE BOOK

The topics within the field of organization theory are interrelated. Chapters are presented so that major ideas unfold in logical sequence. The framework that guides the organization of the book is shown in Exhibit 1.9. Part 1 introduces the basic idea of organizations as social systems and the nature of organization theory. This discussion provides the groundwork for Part 2, which is about strategic management, goals and effectiveness, and the fundamentals of organization structure. Organizations are open systems that exist for a purpose. This section examines how managers help the organization achieve its purpose, including the design of an appropriate structure, such as a functional, divisional, matrix, or horizontal structure. Part 3 looks at the various open system elements that influence organization structure and design, including the external environment, interorganizational relationships, and manufacturing and service technology. The section also includes a chapter that examines the significant impact of new information technology on how organizations are designed and managed.

Parts 4 and 5 look at processes inside the organization. Part 4 describes how organization design is related to such factors as size and control and organizational culture and ethical values. It also includes a chapter describing how structure can be designed to influence internal systems for innovation and change. Part 5 shifts to dynamic processes that exist within and between major organizational departments. The management of intergroup conflict, decision making, and power and politics are discussed. In addition, a final chapter explores contemporary issues related to organization design and management processes.

PLAN OF EACH CHAPTER

Each chapter begins with an organizational case to illustrate the topic to be covered. Theoretical concepts are introduced and explained in the body of the chapter. Several In Practice segments are included in each chapter to illustrate the concepts and show how they apply to real organizations. Book Marks are included in most chapters to present organizational issues managers face right now. These book reviews discuss current concepts and applications to deepen and enrich your understanding of organizations. The Taking the Lead examples illustrate the dramatic changes taking place in management thinking and practice. Each chapter closes with a Summary and Interpretation section and a Briefcase section. Summary and Interpretation reviews and interprets important theoretical concepts. The Briefcase section highlights key points for use in designing and managing organizations.

EXHIBIT 1.9   *Framework for the Book*

Part 1 Introduction to Organizations

CHAPTER 1
Organizations and Organization Theory

▼

Part 2 Organizational Purpose and Structural Design

CHAPTER 2
Strategy, Organization Design, and Effectiveness

CHAPTER 3
Fundamentals of Organization Structure

▼

Part 3 Open System Design Elements

CHAPTER 4
The External Environment

CHAPTER 5
Interorganizational Relationships

CHAPTER 6
Manufacturing and Service Technologies

CHAPTER 7
Information Technology and Knowledge Management

Part 4 Internal Design Elements

CHAPTER 8
Organization Size, Life Cycle, and Control

CHAPTER 9
Organizational Culture and Ethical Values

CHAPTER 10
Innovation and Change

▼

Part 5 Managing Dynamic Processes

CHAPTER 11
Decision-Making Processes

CHAPTER 12
Conflict, Power, and Politics

CHAPTER 13
Contemporary Trends in Organization Design

SUMMARY AND INTERPRETATION

One important idea in this chapter is that organizations are systems. In particular, they are open systems that must adapt to the environment to survive. Various parts of the organization are designed to perform the key subsystem functions of production, adaptation, maintenance, management, and boundary spanning. Five parts of the organization are the technical core, top management, middle management, technical support, and administrative support.

Turbulence has replaced stability as a defining trait for today's organizations. Some of the specific challenges managers and organizations face include competing globally, embracing change, competing through e-commerce, managing knowledge and information, supporting diversity, and maintaining high standards of ethics and social responsibility. These challenges are leading to changes in organization design and management practices. The trend is away from highly structured systems based on a mechanical model toward looser, more flexible systems based on a natural, biological model. Many managers are redesigning companies toward the learning organization, which is characterized by a horizontal structure, empowered employees, shared information, collaborative strategy, and an adaptive culture.

The focus of analysis for organization theory is not individual people but the organization itself. Relevant concepts include the dimensions of organization structure and context. The dimensions of formalization, specialization, hierarchy of authority, centralization, professionalism, personnel ratios, size, organizational technology, environment, goals and strategy, and culture provide labels for measuring and analyzing organizations. These dimensions vary widely from organization to organization. Subsequent chapters provide frameworks for analyzing organizations with these concepts.

Finally, most concepts pertain to the top- and middle-management levels of the organization. This book is concerned more with the topics of those levels than with the operational level topics of supervision and motivation of employees, which are discussed in courses on organizational behavior.

BRIEFCASE

As an organization manager, keep these guidelines in mind:

1. Do not ignore the external environment or protect the organization from it. Because the environment is unpredictable, do not expect to achieve complete order and rationality within the organization. Strive for a balance between order and flexibility.
2. Design the organization so that the five basic parts—technical core, technical support, administrative support, top management, and middle management—adequately perform the subsystem functions of production, maintenance, adaptation, management, and boundary spanning. Try to maintain a balance among the five parts so that they work together for organizational effectiveness.

3. Think of the organization as an entity distinct from the individuals who work in it. Describe the organization according to its size, formalization, decentralization, specialization, professionalism, personnel ratios, and the like. Use these characteristics to analyze the organization and to compare it with other organizations.

4. Be cautious when applying something that works in one situation to another situation. All organizational systems are not the same. Use organization theory to identify the correct structure, goals, strategy, and management systems for each organization.

5. When designing an organization for learning and adaptation in a turbulent environment, include elements such as horizontal structure, shared information, empowered roles, collaborative strategy, and adaptive culture. In stable environments, organizations can achieve efficient performance with a vertical structure, formal information and control systems, routine tasks, competitive strategy, and a rigid culture.

6. Make yourself a competent, influential manager by using the frameworks that organization theory provides to interpret and understand the organization around you.

KEY CONCEPTS

administrative principles
bureaucratic organizations
contextual dimensions
contingency
Hawthorne Studies
learning organization
level of analysis
meso theory
open system
organization theory

organizational behavior
organizations
paradigm
role
scientific management
structural dimensions
subsystems
system
task

DISCUSSION QUESTIONS

1. What is the definition of *organization*? Briefly explain each part of the definition.

2. What is the difference between an open system and a closed system? Can you give an example of a closed system?

3. Explain how Mintzberg's five basic parts of the organization perform the subsystem functions shown at the bottom of Exhibit 1.2. If an organization had to give up one of these five parts, which one could it survive the longest without? Discuss.

4. Why might human organizations be considered more complex than machine-type systems? What is the implication of this complexity for managers?

5. What is the difference between formalization and specialization? Do you think an organization high on one dimension would also be high on the other? Discuss.

6. What does *contingency* mean? What are the implications of contingency theories for managers?

7. What are the primary differences between an organization designed for efficient performance and one designed for learning and change? Which type of organization do you think would be easier to manage? Discuss.

8. Why is shared information so important in a learning organization as compared to an efficient performance organization? Discuss how an organization's approach to information-sharing might be related to other elements of organization design, such as structure, tasks, strategy, and culture.

9. What levels of analysis are typically studied in organization theory? How would these contrast with the level of analysis studied in a course in psychology? Sociology? Political science?

10. Early management theorists believed that organizations should strive to be logical and rational, with a place for everything and everything in its place. Discuss the pros and cons of this approach for today's organizations.

CHAPTER 1 WORKBOOK   *Measuring Dimensions of Organizations**

Analyze two organizations along the dimensions shown below. Indicate where you think each organization would fall on each of the scales. Use an "X" to indicate the first organization and an "★" to show the second.

You may choose any two organizations you are familiar with, such as your place of work, the university, a student organization, your church or synagogue, or your family.

Formalization

Many written rules   1 2 3 4 5 6 7 8 9 10   Few rules

Specialization

Separate tasks and roles   1 2 3 4 5 6 7 8 9 10   Overlapping tasks

Hierarchy

Tall hierarchy of authority   1 2 3 4 5 6 7 8 9 10   Flat hierarchy of authority

Technology

Product   1 2 3 4 5 6 7 8 9 10   Service

External Environment

Stable   1 2 3 4 5 6 7 8 9 10   Unstable

Culture

Clear norms and values   1 2 3 4 5 6 7 8 9 10   Ambiguous norms and values

Professionalism

High professional training   1 2 3 4 5 6 7 8 9 10   Low professional training

Goals

Well-defined goals   1 2 3 4 5 6 7 8 9 10   Goals not defined

Size

Small   1 2 3 4 5 6 7 8 9 10   Large

Organizational Paradigm

Mechanical system   1 2 3 4 5 6 7 8 9 10   Biological system

QUESTIONS

1. What are the main differences between the two organizations you evaluated?

2. Would you recommend that one or both of the organizations have different ratings on any of the scales? Why?

Case for Analysis *S-S Technologies Inc. (A)—Introduction** **IVEY**

In January 1994, Rick Brock and Keith Pritchard, owners of S-S Technologies Inc. (SST) were concerned with the rapid rate of growth facing their company. SST had revenues of $6.3 million in 1993 and employed 30 highly skilled workers. These numbers could double or triple in the next couple of years. To determine how well SST was structured to achieve its future goals, Brock hired a consultant he had worked with successfully in the past. The consultant's major role was to make recommendations as to the appropriate organizational design (culture, people, layers of management and administrative systems) in the event that SST grew from 30 to 60 or even 120 employees. As a by-product of his activities at SST, the consultant also questioned whether some marketing opportunities were being missed with the current operations. In addition, questions regarding employee compensation had begun to surface, and the owners wanted to address this issue as soon as possible. Finally, the consultant wondered if a more formalized measurement system, directly tied to the company's strategic objectives, was necessary for SST's growth and prosperity.

COMPANY INFORMATION

S-S Technologies Inc., incorporated in 1992, was a 100 percent Canadian-owned company which had focused on industrial software and hardware development. Previously, the same business had operated for 12 years as a division of Sutherland-Schultz Limited, a large integrated engineering and construction company. When Sutherland-Schultz changed ownership, the new owner sold the SST portion of the company to Brock. Ultimately, SST was owned by its CEO Rick Brock, former president of Sutherland-Schultz, and by Keith Pritchard, president of SST. A brief organization chart is provided as Exhibit 1.10

SST had unique expertise in the factory automation market. The company brought together engineers and technicians with different but synergistic expertise to focus on projects that other systems integrators were unable or unwilling to handle. Out of these efforts, several unique communication and simulation products evolved. The company recognized the opportunities these products represented, and expanded its capabilities to successfully bring these products to the global automation market. Over the last three years, SST had grown an average of 33 percent per year (the Products Group had grown an average of 64 percent and the Integrated Systems Group an average of 30 percent), as shown in Exhibit 1.11.

OPERATING GROUPS

As Exhibit 1.10 indicates, SST was divided into two distinct groups: the Products Group (PG), and the Integrated Systems Group (ISG), each with its own characteristics.

Products Group

PG was involved in the development and marketing of the company's unique hardware and software products. The products were sold around the world through licensed representatives, distributors and direct sales. There were two key types of products:

> **Direct-Link Interface Cards** were totally programmable interfaces designed to make it easier and quicker to exchange data between personal computers and industrial computers/programmable controllers. In layman's terms, the product allowed office computers to communicate with factory floor computers (commonly termed PLC's, or Programmable Logic Controllers). SST designed and manufactured the interfaces for both the factory floor computers and desktop computers, as well as complementary diagnostic software to ensure that computer networks were performing optimally. The Direct-Link cards received the *Canada Award for*

*Nancy Suttie prepared this case under the supervision of Al Mikalachki solely to provide material for class discussion. The authors do not intend to illustrate either effective or ineffective handling of a managerial situation. The authors may have disguised certain names and other identifying information may have been disguised to protect confidentiality. Ivey Management Services prohibits any form of reproduction, storage, or transmittal without its written permission. This material is not covered under authorization from CanCopy or any reproduction rights organization. To order copies or request permission to reproduce materials, contact Ivey Publishing, Ivey Management Services, c/o Richard Ivey School of Business, The University of Western Ontario, London, Ontario, Canada, N6A 3K7; phone 519-661-3208; fax 519-661-3882; e-mail cases@ivey.uwo.ca.

EXHIBIT 1.10   *SS-Technologies Organization Chart*

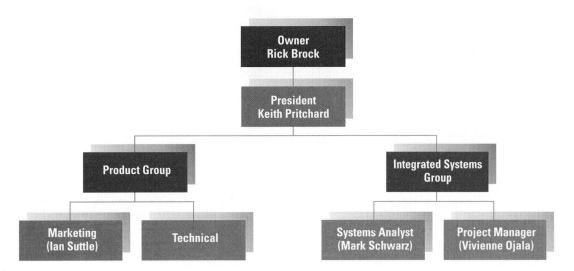

Business Excellence in Innovation from Industry, Science and Technology Canada in 1991.

PICS (Programmable Industrial Control Simulator) was a hardware and software package that allowed a personal computer (PC) to simulate, in real-time, an automated factory floor environment. To use PICS, a PC (running the PICS software) is connected directly to a PLC via a Direct-Link card. An experienced software developer then programs, under the PICS environment, a set of routines that send input to and receive output from the PLC, allowing the PC to act as if it were one or more automated factory machines. The PLC is, in essence, "tricked" into thinking it is actually running the automated factory floor, allowing the user to ensure that the PLC software is performing properly. The system can be used for debugging new industrial software, re-tooling, and employee training, all of which result in substantial time and cost savings for the user.

These products, developed by SST, were often the result of a solution to a technical problem no other company could solve. PG also had a number of other products and ideas under consideration for possible launch in 1994 or 1995.

PG's key success factors fell into two categories: products and marketing. Quality product performance was imperative. In case of faulty products, a replacement had to be provided quickly. In addition, new products were needed to maintain pace with a rapidly changing plant electronic environment. PG's growth also depended highly on marketing. Product awareness by systems integration engineers complemented by an efficient and effective distribution network was vital for PG's successful growth.

EXHIBIT 1.11   *SS-Technologies Revenues*

Year	Products	Integrated Systems	Total*
1990	$931,000	$1,100,000	$2,685,202
1991	$1,638,000	$1,200,000	$3,570,797
1992	$2,763,000	$1,300,000	$4,521,987
1993	$4,036,000	$2,270,000	$6,306,000
1994**	$5,200,000	$3,500,000	$8,700,000

*Includes other sources of income and expenses

**Projection

INTEGRATED SYSTEMS GROUP

ISG was involved in three distinct, yet often inter-related areas of services: consulting, system engineering, and customer support. ISG employed computer professionals and engineers who were dedicated to the development of software and hardware solutions for complex factory floor systems. Clients were provided with tested, reliable, and sophisticated solutions for data collection, custom control software, batching systems, diagnostic systems, and programmable controller simulation. ISG also implemented and commissioned packaged control software, and provided project management for large and technically complex projects. ISG customers included industrial manufacturers and institutional organizations.

ISG's key success factors were to complete projects on time, on budget, and of high quality. To date, ISG had received excellent feedback from clients. ISG's performance depended highly on the quality of its employees. Its goals were for manageable growth, focusing on projects within the company's scope and skills.

ENVIRONMENT

In early 1990, the North American economy was in a recession. Although recovery was widely predicted, some results of the recession were permanent. Companies sought to maintain margins during this recession through downsizing and reducing production costs. SST's Products Group benefited from this trend because PICS and Direct-Link cards offered ways of reducing the cost of automating a plant, a move that often reduced production costs. The market for PG grew despite the recession. The recession also meant that many companies eliminated or drastically reduced their in-house engineering capabilities and sought to subcontract this work, a trend that benefited ISG.

Case for Analysis   *S-S Technologies Inc. (D)—Organizational Design**

The task of designing an organization to support S-S Technologies Inc.'s (SST) growth was taken on by the company's CEO (Richard Brock), president (Keith Pritchard) and a consultant hired by Brock. They were to develop a structure and set of administrative systems (policies, performance appraisal, compensation and partnering program) that would achieve the company's key success factors (see S-S Technologies Inc. (A)—Introduction), maintain the existing culture, and attract the kind of people they wanted working for them.

SST'S TOP MANAGEMENT AND HUMAN RESOURCES

SST was directed by its two owners:

Richard R. Brock, P. Eng., was the CEO of SST. During his eight years as president of Sutherland-Schultz Limited, Brock recognized and nurtured the potential of the Products Group (PG) and Information Systems Group (ISG), which eventually formed S-S Technologies Inc. He continued to be involved in all aspects of the new company, and brought to it his extensive knowledge of business management and development.

Keith Pritchard was the president of SST. Pritchard had risen through the company ranks, starting as a systems analyst, becoming project manager, then group manager, and finally president in 1992. Pritchard also developed the PICS product which accounted for $500K of company sales. His unique set of skills in both management and technical areas made him an excellent leader for the company.

SST had a flat organizational structure that allowed it to respond quickly to technical and market changes. Anyone who had a door, left it open; employees felt free to take their concerns to whomever they believed could help. Decisions were often made using a consultative approach that empowered those involved and that led to "ownership" of problems and their solutions

Projects were assigned to individuals or teams, depending on the size. The individuals and teams were self-managed. Responsibility for project scheduling, budgeting and execution was left largely in

*Nancy Suttie prepared this case under the supervision of Al Mikalachki solely to provide material for class discussion. The authors do not intend to illustrate either effective or ineffective handling of a managerial situation. The authors may have disguised certain names and other identifying information to protect confidentiality. Ivey Management Services prohibits any form of reproduction, storage, or transmittal without its written permission. This material is not covered under authorization from CanCopy or any reproduction rights organization. To order copies or request permission to reproduce materials, contact Ivey Publishing, Ivey Management Services, c/o Richard Ivey School of Business, The University of Western Ontario, London, Ontario, Canada, N6A 3K7; phone 519-661-3208; fax 519-661-3882; e-mail cases@ivey.uwo.ca.

team members' hands. Such responsibility created commitment to the project for those who worked on it and led to the high motivation evident within the company.

Overhead resources, such as marketing and administration, were kept to a minimum. For example, there were only four people on the marketing team that managed more than $4 million in revenues. Administrative support was provided by two, or at times, three people. Even the controller (Doug Winger) shared his time with two other related organizations (SAF and Wilson Gas). SST was truly a lean organization.

Resources—PG

PG had highly competent, highly motivated technical teams. The technical people were leaders in their respective fields, with extensive and varied educations and backgrounds. They worked well together to meet R&D challenges, and to respond quickly and effectively to customers' inquiries. Many team members were involved in the original product development and expressed a personal commitment to PG's continued market success.

> Linda Oliver, B. Math., the lead programmer for the PICS product, had worked on the project as a designer and programmer since its inception.
>
> Bruce Andrews, Ph.D., was involved in the ongoing development of the PICS product, especially the communications tasks and testing; he also wrote the manuals.
>
> Lorne Diebel, C.E.T., developed a reputation as a communications guru. Lorne often traveled to far-off sites, on a moment's notice, to debug a customer's application problem.
>
> Jonathan Malton, B. Sc., a talented hardware designer, had been instrumental in advancing the Direct-Link cards from the old "through hole" format to the new "surface mount" technology.

Newer members were added to PG as the pace of R&D increased and customer support became more demanding. Newcomers brought their own areas of expertise, and worked alongside the more senior team members, whose enthusiasm for their work was infectious.

As a result of its progressive and applied R&D program, the technical team members were advanced on the learning curve. This allowed SST to keep ahead of the competition. As a result, large PLC vendors often came to SST to solve their communication and simulation problems, rather than investing in the learning curve themselves.

The marketing team had grown over the past few years as PG revenues grew. People from both a marketing and a technical background combined to create a well rounded, effective marketing department:

> Ian Suttie, P.Eng., the marketing manager, was involved in design review, marketing, distribution and sales of all products. His main function was to set up a network of distributors and representatives to reach all major markets in the United States, Europe, and beyond.
>
> Colleen Richmond had experience in marketing with other high-tech firms. She handled all the trade shows, promotional material, and advertising activities.
>
> Steve Blakely was the inside sales person, and came to SST with a technical background. He responded to inquiries for information, and was the first contact within SST for customers having technical difficulties.
>
> Colleen Dietrich was recently hired by SST to determine the extent to which leads generated through the various advertising media used by PG eventually resulted in sales.

The marketing team worked well together, buoyed by PG's success. However, they were stretched to the limit and team members admitted they were unable to do everything they wished to do because of personnel constraints. All known product complaints were acted upon; however, there was no formal audit of customer satisfaction.

Resources—ISG

ISG's most important resource was its people. The engineers and technicians were not only technically competent, but were highly motivated and loyal. The following is a brief summary of ISG people and the unique skills they brought to the company:

> Mark Schwarz, P.Eng., an accomplished systems analyst, wrote sales proposals, estimated projects, and did most of the marketing for ISG. He was very good at business development, seeking out large, extremely complicated projects, and often helping the customer define the scope and approach to the project. Convincing a customer that you could handle their large, technically complex job was tricky

business, but Schwarz exhibited a talent for it. Schwarz also had a talent for scheduling personnel and was interested in ensuring that everyone had something interesting to do.

Vivienne Ojala, P.Eng., an experienced and talented project manager, designer and programmer, was more than capable of handling all aspects of design and project management for the $2 million-plus projects ISG hoped to attract. She was excellent with customers who preferred her "straight" talk to the "techno-babble" others gave them. Ojala made the customer confident that the project was in good hands, which is very important when you have asked a manufacturer to give you a production system which could determine business success or failure. Ojala was also good at training those who worked on her projects, as well as developing people in general.

Peter Roeser, P.Eng., was a systems analyst with special skills in the area of communications and various operating systems.

Brian Thomson, P.Eng., was an expert in the area of real-time software development. He also managed projects.

Ted Hannah, P.Eng., was a project manager and systems analyst with extensive skills and experience.

Bruce Travers, who marketed ISG capabilities in Ontario and provided technical direction for projects, had over 20 years experience with industrial applications of information systems.

Due to the diverse skills of its people, ISG was able to tackle large, complex systems integration projects that most of the competitors could not. ISG had in-house expertise covering nearly every technology that would be applied to a project. Also, because ISG was not tied to a single supplier of PLC's or PC's (as many competitors were), it was able to be more flexible and innovative in the solutions that were presented to customers.

Another important ISG resource was its excellent reputation and relationship with a large Canadian manufacturer which had given ISG substantial repeat business. As well, ISG had completed many projects for several large North American companies and had never failed to deliver on its promises.

ISG was advanced on the learning curve. New customers benefited from the fact that ISG had faced many challenges before, and solved them successfully.

ISG's experience was more rounded, and hence more innovative and current than an in-house engineering department which had only worked in one type of factory.

CONSULTANT'S INTERVIEWS

The consultant interviewed all SST employees. Some of the observations that resulted from his interviews are grouped below by issues:

(i) Goals and Strategies

Other than Brock, Pritchard, Suttie, and Schwarz, few employees were aware of SST's goals and strategies or even those of their own Group. In addition, even within top management (Pritchard, Suttie and Schwarz), significant differences existed regarding SST's goals and strategy.

(ii) Hierarchical Structure

Pritchard viewed Suttie and Schwarz as PG and ISG managers respectively. However, PG members generally saw themselves as reporting to Pritchard and saw Suttie as performing the marketing function. When apprised of this situation by the consultant, Pritchard said it would take time for Suttie to establish his position.

The ISG situation also proved somewhat confusing. A number of ISG members saw Schwarz as the manager. However, there was some confusion as to his position vis-à-vis Ojala, who had recently returned to SST after leaving to work for a much larger technology company in Montreal. Ojala tells the story of Pritchard begging her to return to SST, a story that Pritchard confirms. Ojala saw herself as reporting to Pritchard (and so did Pritchard). Her "formal" relationship to Schwarz had to be worked out.

Before Ojala left SST (she was away for five months), both she and Schwarz reported to Pritchard directly. When Ojala left, many of her responsibilities, such as some of the proposal writing and personnel scheduling, were given to Schwarz. Now that Ojala was back, to everyone's relief, there was the question of how to structure her role, particularly in relation to Pritchard and Schwarz. Ojala would not report to Schwarz, and Schwarz would not report to Ojala.

(iii) Physical Space

SST had outgrown the location that it shared with two other companies, Wilson Gas and SAF. Brock owned SAF, which was part of SST holdings, and rented space out to Wilson Gas. Each company had about one-third of the building they shared. SST added a trailer to house additional personnel. Any expansion in the same building required evicting SAF, Wilson or both. Pritchard was adamant that all SST personnel be housed in one location and have easy access to one another.

(iv) Compensation

One of the most contentious issues that arose from the interviews dealt with bonuses and compensation. Historically, bonuses had been promised if the company succeeded. The amount and date of the bonus were at the discretion of Brock and Pritchard. To date, no bonuses had been paid. Given the company's growth and success, many employees were expecting a Christmas bonus. There was no policy regarding bonus or merit pay. Both Brock and Pritchard wondered what the policy should be and how that policy should be developed. Existing compensation tended to be at the low end of the spectrum for engineers. This was particularly true for the longer-term employees in ISG.

It became apparent during the interviews that it was important to formalize the bonus plan to end the speculation, uncertainty and disappointment caused by the present, seemingly random (to the employees at least) system. Historically, when SST was part of Sutherland-Schultz, the company had a few good years and generous bonuses were paid. However, when the recession hit, the construction side of Sutherland-Schultz slumped considerably and, although PG and ISG held their profitability, the company as a whole could not afford to pay bonuses. In fact, SST people were laid off and some of those who remained felt cheated. Now that SST was on its own, there was an opportunity to tie bonuses directly to the company's performance. Management wanted the bonus system to achieve the following goals:

* To develop a cooperative, team spirit
* To foster cooperation between ISG and PG, and limit interpersonal competition
* To provide extra reward for unique contributions
* To not reward weak performance

(v) Partnering

Given the experience of losing Ojala to another firm (albeit temporarily), Brock was anxious to develop a "partnering" system in which those crucial to the company's success could participate. He wanted to make people like Suttie, Schwarz and Ojala feel like owners or partners committed to the company, so they would not be lured away by the promise of greener pastures; after all, the job market for people of this calibre was extremely promising. This was true not only of those in management positions, but also of the best systems analysts and programmers: people like Linda Oliver and Lorne Diebel.

Brock wanted part of the partners' bonus to consist of stock in the company. The problem was that these people were all young, with growing families, and could not afford to have their money tied up in stock when they had mortgage payments and daycare costs to worry about. Generally, their immediate concern was cash flow, as they knew their long-term earning potential was excellent. Brock's concern was how to structure the partners' bonuses and compensation to keep key people on-side, while allowing room for more partners to be brought in as the company grew. The company had recently hired a half-dozen talented engineering and computer science students, all of whom had the potential to become the next Schwarz, Suttie, or Ojala. On top of all this, Brock still had his own return on equity to consider.

(vi) Commitment and Motivation

The consultant was overwhelmed by the high commitment to SST and the task motivation expressed by employees. The people loved the work environment, the lack of politics, the quick response to their technical needs (equipment and/or information), and the lack of talk-for-talk's-sake meetings. They were confident in their future and happy to come to work. For the consultant, this was a refreshing contrast to the downsizing gloom and doom that permeated many other companies he worked with in the 1990s.

The employees set their own working hours. They had to put in 40 hours per week, but could do this at any time. The flexible working hours allowed them to engage in other activities that occurred between 9 and 5, such as their children's school events. Employees kept track of their overtime and were paid either straight time or took the equivalent in extra holidays. Each employee recorded his/her overtime weekly and passed on the information to Pritchard. Previously, employees had noted the overtime information mentally. Pritchard had them write it out and report it weekly because he observed that their mental calculations erred on the side of the company (they remembered fewer hours than they worked overtime).

(vii) Personnel Function and Communications

New employees were generally assigned to a project manager who informally took on the induction and training role. In that way, new employees immediately tied into a task, and it was left to them to learn the culture and expectations of SST by osmosis. Should the employees not perform well, or fit into the culture, their employment was terminated.

Periodically, Pritchard would have a meeting of all employees to inform them of SST's progress, success and direction. Given these meetings, Pritchard was surprised to learn that only a few employees were aware of SST's goals and strategy.

One issue mentioned by a couple of employees dealt with performance appraisal and company benefits. Performance appraisal was conducted by Pritchard; however, he did not keep a record of the meeting and it was not done at regular intervals. Also, anyone interested in learning about benefits or salary ranges for various jobs did not know whom to contact. In contrast, all employees knew whom to contact for technical information. In fact, performance appraisal, compensation and benefits were managed in an ad hoc manner.

WHERE DO WE GO FROM HERE?

Brock, Pritchard, and the consultant wanted to design an organization that would contemplate an expansion to double or triple SST's existing size. They knew the existing SST culture attracted and nurtured highly motivated and committed employees who expanded the company successfully and rapidly (Exhibit 1.12). They also knew that they could not manage $50 million in revenue and 120 to 150 people as they managed $6 million in revenue and 30 people.

The trio's task was to design an organization that would allow SST to grow successfully. Given SST's culture and the kind of people it wanted to attract as shown in Exhibit 1.12, what were the best structure, performance appraisal, compensation/bonus plan, company policies, and partnering program that should be implemented?

EXHIBIT 1.12   *S-S Technologies' Desired Culture and People*

Culture	People
• Open communications at all levels	• Highly motivated
• Flexible working hours	• Highly skilled (tech)
• Few policies	• Entrepreneurial
• Profit sharing at all levels	• Team players
• Quick decision making	• High performers
• Initiative, not bureaucracy	

NOTES

1. Carol J. Loomis, "Dinosaurs?" *Fortune*, 3 May 1993, 36–42.

2. The analysis of IBM was based on Paul Carroll, *Big Blues: The Unmaking of IBM* (New York: Crown, 1993); Brent Schlender, "Big Blue Is Betting on Big Iron Again," *Fortune*, 29 April 1996, 102–112; Ira Sager, "The View from IBM," *Business Week*, 30 October 1995, 142–152; David Kirkpatrick, "First: With New PCs and a New Attitude, IBM Is Back," *Fortune*, 11 November 1996, 28–29; Judith H. Dobrzynski, "Rethinking IBM," *Business Week*, 4 October 1993, 86–97; Michael W. Miller and Laurence Hooper, "Akers Quits at IBM Under Heavy Pressure; Dividend Is Slashed," *The Wall Street Journal*, 27 January 1993, A1, A6; John W. Verity, "IBM: A Bull's-Eye and a Long Shot," *Business Week*, 13 December 1993, 88–89; G. Pascal Zachary and Stephen Kreider Yoder, "Computer Industry Divides into Camps of Winners and Losers," *The Wall Street Journal*, 27 January 1993, A1, A4; and David Kirkpatrick, "IBM: From Big Blue Dinosaur to E-Business Animal," *Fortune*, 26 April 1999, 116+; D. Quinn Mills, "The Decline and Rise of IBM," *Sloan Management Review*, Summer 1996, 78-82; and Sara Nathan, "IBM Stock Surges 9%," *USA Today*, 1B.

3. John A. Byrne, "Management Meccas," *Business Week*, 18 September 1995, 122–134; Catherine Arnst, "Now HP Stands for Hot Products," *Business Week*, 14 June 1993, 36; and Rachel Layne, "Xerox to Cut 9,000 Jobs," 7 April 1998, *http://www.naplesnews.com/today/business/d191799a.htm* accessed May 17, 1999; and "Competing through Constellations: The Case of Fuji Xerox," *Strategy & Business,* First Quarter, 1997*, http://www.strategy-business.com/casestudy/97108/page5.html* accessed on May 17, 1999.

4. Eileen Davis, "What's on American Managers' Minds?" *Management Review* (April 1995): 14–20.

5. Joseph B. White, "There Are No German or U.S. Companies, Only Successful Ones," *The Wall Street Journal*, 7 May 1998, A1.

6. Nilly Ostro-Landau and Hugh D. Menzies, "The New World Economic Order," in *International Business 97/98, Annual Editions*, Fred Maidment, ed. (Guilford, Conn.: Dushkin Publishing Group, 1997), 24–30; and Murray Weidenbaum, "American Isolationism Versus the Global Economy," in *International Business 97/98, Annual Editions,* 12-15.

7. Nicolas Imparato and Oren Harari, "When New Worlds Stir," *Management Review* (October 1994), 22-28.

8. Robert D. Hof with Gary McWilliams and Gabrielle Saveri, "The 'Click Here' Economy," *Business Week*, 22 June 1998, 122-128.

9. Bernard Wysocki Jr., "Corporate Caveat: Dell or Be Delled," *The Wall Street Journal*, 10 May 1999, A1.

10. Ibid.

11. Edward O. Welles, "Not Your Father's Industry," *Inc.*, January 1999, 25-28.

12. Thomas A. Stewart, "Is This Job Really Necessary?" *Fortune*, 12 January 1998, 154-155.

13. Justin Martin, "Are You as Good as You Think You Are?" *Fortune*, 30 September 1996, 142-52; and John A. Byrne, "Management Meccas," *Business Week*, 18 September 1995, 122-134.

14. Richard W. Judy and Carol D'Amico, *Workforce 2000: Work and Workers in the 21st Century* (Indianapolis, Ind.: Hudson Institute, 1997); and Gilbert W. Fairholm, *Leadership and the Culture of Trust* (Westport, Conn.: Praeger, 1994).

15. Douglas A. Blackmon, "A Factory in Alabama is the Merger in Microcosm," *The Wall Street Journal*, 8 May 1998, B1.

16. Joline Godfrey, "Been There, Doing That," *Inc.*, March 1996, 21–22; Paula Dwyer, Marsha Johnston, and Karen Lowry Miller, "Out of the Typing Pool, into Career Limbo," *Business Week*, 15 April 1996, 92–94.

17. Del Jones, "Doing the Wrong Thing," *USA Today*, 4 April 1997, 1A, 2A; William J. Morin, "Silent Sabotage: Mending the Crisis in Corporate Values," *Management Review* (July 1995) 10-14; and Michael J. Sniffen, "Price-Fixing Plot on Vitamins Nets Biggest Fine Ever," *Johnson City Press*, 21 May 1999, 1.

18. Jim Collins, "The Foundation for Doing Good," *Inc.,* December 1997, 41-42; and Jeffrey A. Tannenbaum, "Making Risky Hires into Valued Workers," *The Wall Street Journal*, 19 June 1997, B1, B2.

19. Howard Aldrich, *Organizations and Environments* (Englewood Cliffs, N.J.: Prentice-Hall, 1979), 3.

20. Robert N. Stern and Stephen R. Barley, "Organizations and Social Systems: Organization Theory's Neglected Mandate," *Administrative Science Quarterly* 41 (1996): 146-162.

21. Anne Stuart, "Kid Stuff," *CIO Web Business*, Section 2, 1 April 1999, 20-21.

22. Michael A. Hitt, R. Duane Ireland, and Robert E. Hoskisson, *Strategic Management: Competitiveness and Globalization* (St. Paul, Minn.: West, 1995), 238.

23. James D. Thompson, *Organizations in Action* (New York: McGraw-Hill, 1967), 4–13.

24. Henry Mintzberg, *The Structuring of Organizations* (Englewood Cliffs, N.J.: Prentice-Hall, 1979), 215-297; and Henry Mintzberg, "Organization Design: Fashion or Fit?" *Harvard Business Review* 59 (January-February 1981): 103-116.

25. The following discussion was heavily influenced by Richard H. Hall, *Organizations: Structures, Processes, and Outcomes* (Englewood Cliffs, N.J.: Prentice-Hall, 1991); D. S. Pugh, "The Measurement of Organization Structures: Does Context Determine Form?" *Organizational Dynamics* 1 (Spring 1973): 19–34; and D. S. Pugh, D. J. Hickson, C. R. Hinings, and C. Turner, "Dimensions of Organization Structure," *Administrative Science Quarterly* 13 (1968): 65–91.

26. Adapted from John Huey, "The New Post-Heroic Leadership," *Fortune*, 21 February 1994, 42–50; John Huey, "Wal-Mart: Will It Take Over the World?" *Fortune*, 30 January 1989, 52–61; and Howard Rudnitsky, "How Sam Walton Does It," *Forbes*, 16 August 1982, 42–44.

27. Robert Kanigel, *The One Best Way: Frederick Winslow Taylor and the Enigma of Efficiency* (New York: Viking, 1997); and Alan Farnham, "The Man Who Changed Work Forever," *Fortune*, July 21, 1997, 114. For a discussion of the impact of scientific management on American industry, government, and nonprofit organizations, also see Mauro F. Guillén, "Scientific Management's Lost Aesthetic: Architecture, Organization, and the Taylorized Beauty of the Mechanical," *Administrative Science Quarterly* 42 (1997) 682-715.

28. Amanda Bennett, *The Death of the Organization Man* (New York: William Morrow, 1990).

29. Ian I. Mitroff, Richard O. Mason, and Christine M. Pearson, "Radical Surgery: What Will Tomorrow's Organizations Look Like?" *Academy of Management Executive* 8, no. 2 (1994): 11–21; Nicholas Imparato and Oren Harari, "When New Worlds Stir," *Management Review* (October 1994): 22–28; William Bergquist, *The Postmodern Organization: Mastering the Art of Irreversible Change* (San Francisco: Jossey-Bass, 1993).

30. Johannes M. Pennings, "Structural Contingency Theory: A Reappraisal," *Research in Organizational Behavior* 14 (1992): 267–309.

31. This discussion is based in part on Bergquist, *The Postmodern Organization*.

32. Polly LaBarre, "This Organization is Disorganization," *Fast Company*, June-July 1996, 77+.

33. David K. Hurst, *Crisis and Renewal: Meeting the Challenge of Organizational Change* (Boston, Mass.: Harvard Business School Press, 1995), 32-52.

34. Glenn Rifkin, "Nothing But Net," *Fast Company*, June-July 1996, 118-127.

35. Edward C. Welles, "Not Your Father's Industry," *Inc.*, January, 1999, 25-28.

36. Thomas Petzinger Jr., "In Search of the New World (of Work), *Fast Company,* April 1999, 214-220+; and Peter Katel, "Bordering on Chaos," *Wired,* July 1997, 98-107.

37. Robert House, Denise M. Rousseau, and Melissa Thomas-Hunt, "The Meso Paradigm: A Framework for the Integration of Micro and Macro Organizational Behavior," *Research in Organizational Behavior* 17 (1995): 71–114.

Organizational Purpose and Structural Design

Strategy, Organization Design, and Effectiveness

CHAPTER 2

A LOOK INSIDE

Danone Group

*B*est known in the United States for Dannon yogurt and the premium-brand Evian mineral water, France's Danone Group has long been a giant of the food industry in Europe. But when Franck Riboud took over the chief executive's job from his father in 1996, profits were on a slide and investors doubted the young Riboud could match his father's impressive leadership. When his appointment as CEO was announced, Danone's shares fell sharply.

Despite the palpable skepticism, the younger Riboud set out to accomplish his vision of transforming Danone from a European champion into a global front-runner. Riboud had already been working toward that goal since 1992, when he took charge of international development. At that time, sales outside of Europe accounted for only 5 percent of Danone's total sales. As CEO, Riboud's specific goals for the company include:

- Refocus the company on its core products and sell off noncore assets to boost profitability.
- Reduce Danone's dependence on Europe; derive 33 percent of sales outside the Continent by 2000.
- Establish a high-profile presence in emerging markets of Asia and Latin America; boost marketing efforts to overcome dietary biases in these areas, where yogurt is not part of the traditional diet.
- Acquire local water companies around the world to compete in the lower-priced bottled water market.

So far, Riboud's strategy and performance have rivals on guard and investors cheering. Danone's profit slide has been reversed and share prices have nearly doubled. Riboud has sold off around $1.2 billion in noncore assets and made about the same amount's worth of acquisitions, primarily in Asia and Latin America. He has narrowed Danone's portfolio to three areas where the company can dominate in global markets: dairy products, bottled water, and cookies and crackers. Riboud recently snapped up water companies Aqua in Indonesia, Health in China, and Aquapenn in the United States.

Yet Riboud's battle has only begun. Danone faces bruising competition from giants such as Coca-Cola Corp. and PepsiCo Inc., which also have their eyes on the global market for bottled water. And in the fight for growth in emerging markets, food companies such as Nestlé and Unilever have a substantial lead over Danone. However, Riboud believes his goals and strategies are sound. Most analysts agree, predicting that Riboud will meet his target of boosting revenue outside of Europe to 33 percent of total sales and that the company's overall profits will jump by 12.7 percent in 2000.[1]

Top managers such as Franck Riboud are responsible for positioning their organizations for success by establishing goals and strategies that can help the company be competitive. An organizational goal is a desired state of affairs that the organization attempts to reach.[2] A goal represents a result or end point toward which organizational efforts are directed. The goals for Danone Group include increasing sales outside of Europe, pushing into emerging markets of Asia and Latin America, refocusing on core products, and boosting profitability. The choice of goals and strategy affects organization design, as we will discuss in this chapter.

PURPOSE OF THIS CHAPTER

Top managers give direction to organizations. They set goals and develop the strategies for their organization to attain those goals. The purpose of this chapter is to help you understand the types of goals organizations pursue and some of the competitive strategies managers develop to reach those goals. We will examine two significant frameworks for determining strategic action and look at how strategies affect organization design. The chapter also describes the most popular approaches to measuring the effectiveness of organizational efforts. To manage organizations well, managers need a clear sense of how to measure effectiveness.

TOP MANAGEMENT STRATEGIC DIRECTION

An organization is created and designed to achieve some end, which is decided by the chief executive officer and/or the top management team. Organization structure and design is an outcome of this purpose. Indeed, *the primary responsibility of top management is to determine an organization's goals, strategy, and design, therein adapting the organization to a changing environment.*[3] Middle managers do much the same thing for major departments within the guidelines provided by top management. The relationships through which top managers provide direction and then design are illustrated in Exhibit 2.1.

The direction-setting process typically begins with an assessment of the opportunities and threats in the external environment, including the amount of change, uncertainty, and resource availability, which we discuss in more detail in Chapter 4. Top management also assesses internal strengths and weaknesses to define the company's distinctive competence compared with other firms in the industry.[4] The assessment of internal environment often includes an evaluation of each department and is shaped by past performance and the leadership style of the CEO and top management team. The next step is to define overall mission and official goals based on the correct fit between external opportunities and internal strengths. Specific operational goals or strategies can then be formulated to define how the organization is to accomplish its overall mission.

In Exhibit 2.1, organization design reflects the way goals and strategies are implemented. Organization design is the administration and execution of the strategic plan. *This is the role of organization theory*. Organization direction is achieved through decisions about structural form, including whether the organization will be designed for a learning or an efficiency orientation, as discussed in Chapter 1, as well as choices about information and control systems, the type of production technology, human resource policies, culture, and linkages to other organizations. Changes in structure, technology, human resource policies, culture, and interorganization linkages will be discussed in subsequent chapters. Also note the arrow in Exhibit 2.1 running from organization design back to strategic management. This means that strategies are often made within the current structure of the organization, so that current design constrains or puts limits on goals and strategy. More often than not, however, the new goals and strategy are selected based on environmental needs, and then top management attempts to redesign the organization to achieve those ends.

Finally, Exhibit 2.1 illustrates how managers evaluate the effectiveness of organizational efforts—that is, the extent to which the organization realizes its

EXHIBIT 2.1   *Top Management Role in Organization Direction, Design, and Effectiveness*

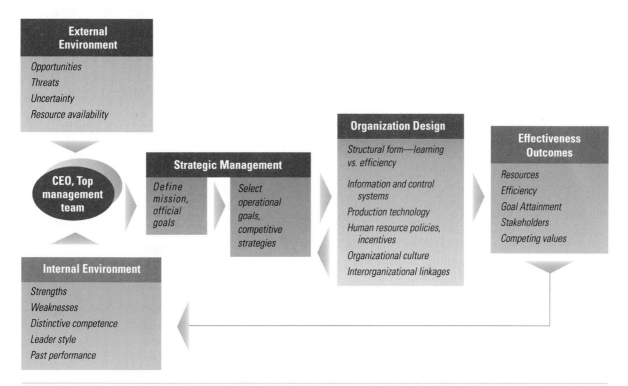

Source: Adapted from Arie Y. Lewin and Carroll U. Stephens, "Individual Properties of the CEO as Determinants of Organization Design," unpublished manuscript, Duke University, 1990; and Arie Y. Lewin and Carroll U. Stephens, "CEO Attributes as Determinants of Organization Design: An Integrated Model," *Organization Studies* 15, no. 2 (1994): 183–212.

goals. This chart reflects the most popular ways of measuring performance, each of which is discussed later in this chapter. It is important to note here that performance measurements feed back into the internal environment, so that past performance of the organization is assessed by top management in setting new goals and strategies for the future.

The role of top management is important because managers can interpret the environment differently and develop different goals. For example, as head of Sears Merchandise Group, Arthur Martinez (now CEO of Sears) turned a dinosaur into a cash cow by setting a goal to be the store of choice for today's "middle-American mom," rather than focusing on male-oriented businesses such as hardware, tools, and automotive, as the previous management had done. He also scrapped the revered Sears catalog, which previous leaders had considered the heart and soul of the retailer, redesigned stores and packed them with women's apparel and cosmetics, and began advertising "the softer side of Sears."[5] The choices top managers make about goals, strategies, and organization design have a tremendous impact on organizational effectiveness. This chapter's Book Mark discusses the need for managers to take a new approach to strategy in today's volatile environment.

Remember that goals and strategy are not fixed or taken for granted. Top managers and middle managers must select goals for their respective units, and the ability to make these choices largely determines firm success. Organization design is used to implement goals and strategy and also determines organization success. We will now discuss further the concept of organizational goals and strategy, and in the latter part of this chapter, we will discuss various ways to evaluate organizational effectiveness.

ORGANIZATIONAL PURPOSE

Organizations are created and continued in order to accomplish something. All organizations, including Sears, the American Red Cross, IBM, the Methodist Church, the U.S. Department of Agriculture, and the local video rental store, exist

$\mathcal{B}$ook $\mathcal{M}$ark 2.0

Have You Read This Book?

Competing on the Edge: Strategy as Structured Chaos

By Shona L. Brown and Kathleen M. Eisenhardt

In *Competing on the Edge*, Shona Brown and Kathleen Eisenhardt contend that today's companies must constantly reinvent themselves to prosper in a world of unstable markets, fierce global competition, and relentless change. Today's market leaders, the authors suggest, are those companies that find a balance between chaos and stability and allow strategy to emerge as the firm adapts to an unpredictable and rapidly changing business environment. They remain open and flexible in order to be innovative and creative, yet they maintain enough discipline and structure to successfully execute strategies and plans. As the authors explain: "The underlying insight behind competing on the edge is that strategy is the result of a firm's organizing to change constantly and letting a semicoherent strategic direction emerge from the organization. In other words, it is about combining the two parts of strategy by simultaneously addressing where you want to go and how you are going to get there."

RULES FOR COMPETING ON THE EDGE
Brown and Eisenhardt distill ten rules of strategy for competing on the edge. Some examples of these rules are:

- *Advantage is temporary.* To compete on the edge, managers should treat any strategy as temporary. Competitive advantage is fleeting, so company mangers focus on constantly generating new sources of advantage. They look for opportunities in the changes going on around them rather than looking for ways to defend themselves against change.
- *Strategy is diverse, emergent, and complicated.* In a high-velocity environment, strategy should be not a

single approach but a diverse collection of strategic moves. Managers allow strategy to emerge and then shape and articulate their plans around it. They take a variety of approaches, watch what happens, learn from it, and shift strategies and plans as necessary.

- *Drive strategy from the business level.* Strategy is not something that is formulated by top managers and imposed on the organization top-down. Too many factors are changing too rapidly and unpredictably to wait for strategy to trickle down through the hierarchy. Companies that complete on the edge allow strategy to be driven by the people closest to the action. Success comes not from carefully-planned ideas at the top, but from skilled, fast, and agile moves at the business level.

CONCLUSION
Although *Competing on the Edge* is inspired by scientific theories of complexity and chaos, it is firmly grounded in the practical realities facing business organizations. The authors present examples of organizations such as the Atlanta Braves, 3M, Nike, and Intel that remain market leaders in volatile industries by learning how to adapt and innovate in a business environment that is constantly in a state of flux. Through numerous detailed examples of successful and not-so-successful companies, tips on avoiding managerial traps, and explanations of new strategic concepts, Brown and Eisenhardt offer managers a valuable handbook for dealing with unpredictable change.

Competing on the Edge: Strategy as Structured Chaos, by Shona L. Brown and Kathleen Eisenhardt, is published by Harvard Business School Press.

for a purpose. This purpose may be referred to as the overall goal, or mission. Different parts of the organization establish their own goals and objectives to help meet the overall goal, mission, or purpose of the organization.

Many types of goals exist in an organization, and each type performs a different function. One major distinction is between the officially stated goals, or mission, of the organization and the operative goals the organization actually pursues.

MISSION

The overall goal for an organization is often called the **mission**—the organization's reason for existence. The mission describes the organization's vision, its shared values and beliefs, and its reason for being. It can have a powerful impact on an organization.[6] The mission is sometimes called the **official goals**, which are the formally stated definition of business scope and outcomes the organization is trying to achieve. Official goal statements typically define business operations and may focus on values, markets, and customers that distinguish the organization. Whether called a mission statement or official goals, the organization's general statement of its purpose and philosophy is often written down in a policy manual or the annual report. The mission statement for Hallmark is shown in Exhibit 2.2. Note how the overall mission, values, and goals are all defined.

OPERATIVE GOALS

Operative goals designate the ends sought through the actual operating procedures of the organization and explain what the organization is actually trying to do.[7] Operative goals describe specific measurable outcomes and are often concerned with the short run. Operative versus official goals represent actual versus stated goals. Operative goals typically pertain to the primary tasks an organization must perform, similar to the subsystem activities identified in Chapter 1.[8] These goals concern overall performance, boundary spanning, maintenance, adaptation, and production activities. Specific goals for each primary task provide direction for the day-to-day decisions and activities within departments.

Overall Performance. Profitability reflects the overall performance of for-profit organizations. Profitability may be expressed in terms of net income, earnings per share, or return on investment. Other overall goals are growth and output volume. Growth pertains to increases in sales or profits over time. Volume pertains to total sales or the amount of products or services delivered. Executives at Procter & Gamble have set a growth goal to double consumer-products sales to $70 billion by 2006.[9]

Not-for-profit organizations such as labor unions do not have goals of profitability, but they do have goals that attempt to specify the delivery of services to members within specified budget expense levels. Growth and volume goals also may be indicators of overall performance in not-for-profit organizations.

Resources. Resource goals pertain to the acquisition of needed material and financial resources from the environment. They may involve obtaining financing for the construction of new plants, finding less expensive sources for raw materials, or hiring top-quality college graduates. Many high-tech companies are having trouble hiring well-educated, computer-literate knowledge workers because of today's tight labor market. Companies such as Sun Microsystems are

EXHIBIT 2.2   *Hallmark's Mission Statement*

THIS IS HALLMARK

We believe:

That our *products and services* must enrich people's lives
and enhance their relationships.
That *creativity and quality*—in our concepts, products
and services—are essential to our success.
That the *people* of Hallmark are our company's
most valuable resource.
That distinguished *financial performance* is a must,
not as an end in itself, but as a means
to accomplish our broader mission.
That our *private ownership* must be preserved.

The values that guide us are:

Excellence in all we do.
Ethical and moral conduct at all times
and in all our relationships.
Innovation in all areas of our business as a means
of attaining and sustaining leadership.
Corporate social responsibility to Kansas City
and to each community in which we operate.

*These beliefs and values guide our business strategies,
our corporate behavior, and our relationships
with suppliers, customers, communities, and each other.*

Source: Hallmark, Cards, Inc. Used with permission.

investing heavily in online recruiting programs to help them meet their resource goals in this area.

Market. Market goals relate to the market share or market standing desired by the organization. Market goals are the responsibility of marketing, sales, and advertising departments. An example of a market goal is Cisco Systems' desire to be the leading maker of switches and other gear that keep the Internet running. Cisco has captured 80 percent of the market for Internet high-end routers. Cemex, described in the previous chapter, has 60 percent of the market for cement in Mexico and is the leading supplier in several emerging markets.[10] Both companies have an operative goal of having the largest market share in a specific industry.

Employee Development. Employee development pertains to the training, promotion, safety, and growth of employees. It includes both managers and workers. At Fetzer Vineyards, a primary goal is to contribute to the continuous growth and development of employees. The goal includes providing a comprehensive employee education program, with classes such as English as a second language, decision making, and communication. According to Barbara Wallace, Fetzer's director of human resources, ". . . our company feels that developing people's capabilities strengthens the organization. It's a way of creating loyalty."[11]

Innovation and Change. Innovation goals pertain to internal flexibility and readiness to adapt to unexpected changes in the environment. Innovation goals are often defined with respect to the development of specific new services, products, or production processes. For example, 3M has a goal of generating enough new products so that 30 percent of sales come from products introduced within the past four years.[12]

Productivity. Productivity goals concern the amount of output achieved from available resources. They typically describe the amount of resource inputs required to reach desired outputs and are thus stated in terms of "cost for a unit of production," "units produced per employee," or "resource cost per employee." For example, Rubbermaid set a productivity goal of increasing the number of units produced per worker per day. Total output increased from three hundred units per worker per day in 1952 to five hundred units in 1980 and 750 in 1988. Another productivity goal was to reduce the number of sales representatives and to increase the work force by only 50 percent while doubling sales. The resulting increases in productivity produced fresh profits for Rubbermaid.[13]

Successful organizations such as Rubbermaid and 3M use a carefully balanced set of operative goals. For example, although profitability is important, some of today's best companies recognize that a single-minded focus on bottom-line profits may not be the best way to achieve high performance. In a rapidly changing environment, innovation and change goals are increasingly important, even though they may initially cause a *decrease* in profits. Employee development goals are critical for helping to maintain a motivated, committed work force in a tight labor market.

THE IMPORTANCE OF GOALS

Both official goals and operative goals are important for the organization, but they serve very different purposes. Official goals provide legitimacy; operative goals provide employee direction, decision guidelines, and criteria of performance. These purposes are summarized in Exhibit 2.3.

Legitimacy. A mission statement (or official goals) communicates legitimacy to external and internal stakeholders. The mission describes the purpose of the organization so people know what it stands for and accept its existence. Moreover, employees join and become committed to an organization when they identify with the organization's stated goals.

Most top managers want their company to look good to other companies in their environment. Managers want customers, competitors, suppliers, and the local community to look on them in a favorable light. The dynamics of a company's interaction with the organizational environment often depend as much on cultural norms, symbols, and beliefs as on technological or material factors; and

EXHIBIT 2.3   *Goal Type and Purpose*

Type of Goals	Purpose of Goals
Official goals, mission:	Legitimacy
Operative goals:	Employee direction and motivation
	Decision guidelines
	Standard of performance

the concept of organizational legitimacy plays a critical role.[14] The mission statement is a powerful first step in communicating legitimacy to external and internal stakeholders and creating a positive impression.

Fortune magazine reflects the corporate concern for legitimacy with ratings of the reputations of corporations in a number of industries. In 1999, both Dell Computer Corp. and Wal-Mart entered the overall top ten, largely because of their strong commitment to customer service and obsession with operational efficiency. Companies such as Dell and Wal-Mart use mission and goal statements to help communicate their commitment to these core values. As another example, a national tabloid newspaper in Norway was severely criticized for offering sexually explicit dial-up message services. These lucrative services were canceled because managers determined that they were detrimental to the company's goal of serving as a respected national news medium.[15]

Employee Direction and Motivation. Goals give a sense of direction to organization participants. The stated end toward which an organization is striving and strategies for how to get there tell employees what they are working for. Goals help motivate participants, especially if participants help select the goals. For example, teams of workers at SOL Cleaning, described in Taking the Lead, set—and meet—goals that are much more ambitious than those top management would have set for them.

Decision Guidelines. The goals of an organization also act as guidelines for employee decision making. Organizational goals are a set of constraints on individual behavior and decisions.[16] They help define the correct decisions concerning organization structure, innovation, employee welfare, or growth. When Owens-Illinois, a glass container manufacturer, established the goal of reducing volume to improve profits, internal decisions were redirected. Owens-Illinois had been running marginal plants just to maintain volume. The new goal of increased profits provided decision guidelines that led to the closing of these marginal plants.

Criteria of Performance. Goals provide a standard for assessment. The level of organization performance, whether in terms of profits, units produced, or number of complaints, needs a basis for evaluation. Is a profit of 10 percent on sales good enough? The answer lies in goals. Goals reflect past experience and describe the desired state for the future. If the profit goal is 8 percent, then a 10 percent return is excellent. When Owens-Illinois shifted from volume to profit goals, profits increased by 30 percent. This increase occurred during the period when two competitors reported profit declines of 61 percent and 76 percent. Profit thus replaced production volume as the criterion of performance.[17]

SUMMARY

Official goals and mission statements describe a value system for the organization; operative goals represent the primary tasks of the organization. Official goals legitimize the organization; operative goals are more explicit and well defined. For example, to reach it's official goal of becoming "the world's most respected service brand," American Express Corp. established operative goals of superior value, customer service, distribution, and cost. These included developing products and services to meet the needs of smaller, more targeted customer segments; building long-lasting customer relationships; establishing partnerships to enhance distribution channels; and operating at a cost base "at or below our best competitors."[18] These operative goals provided direction for employees and helped them attain the overall company goal.

ORGANIZATIONAL STRATEGIES AND DESIGN

A **strategy** is a plan for interacting with the competitive environment to achieve organizational goals. Some managers think of goals and strategies as interchangeable, but for our purposes, goals define where the organization wants to go and

Taking the Lead

Shooting for the Stars

Liisa Joronen, chairman and owner of SOL Cleaning Service, one of northern Europe's most admired companies, believes that when workers set their own goals they'll shoot for the stars. Her conviction has proved to be right at SOL, where self-directed teams create their own budgets, do their own hiring, set their own performance objectives, and negotiate their own deals with customers. According to Joronen, "They set targets for themselves that are higher than what you would set for them. And because they set them, they hit them." SOL teams even have the chance to establish their own satellite offices across Finland if they recruit enough profitable business to cover rent, equipment, and training costs.

The ability of teams to set their own goals is only part of what makes SOL so successful. Even though SOL competes in one of the world's least glamorous businesses, industrial cleaning, the company is a high-energy, fast-paced, knowledge-driven organization. At headquarters, the walls are painted bright red, white, and yellow, and employees wander the halls talking on digital phones or gathering in "neighborhoods" with oddly shaped conference tables that can be put together like a jigsaw puzzle or meeting spaces designed like tree houses. There are no titles or secretaries, no individual offices, and no set working hours.

Teams, led by a supervisor, work when they want and how they want. SOL managers believe employees have to be happy to keep customers happy. Of course, the flip side of employee freedom is accountability, and SOL is fanatical about measuring performance. The most important measurements focus on customer satisfaction. Every time a team lands a contract, the salesperson, the team, and the customer sit down together and establish performance objectives. Every month, the customer rates the team's performance based on these benchmarks.

SOL's training program would be the envy of a high-tech firm. Employees get training in time management, budgeting, goal-setting, and people skills, enabling them to use their brains as well as their hands. Upgrading employee skills has enabled SOL to expand its business. In some large grocery stores, for example SOL teams now stock shelves as well as sweep the aisles. Some hospitals that use SOL cleaners are also using them for "night nurse" duties—helping patients to the bathroom or notifying doctors in an emergency. In Finland, and increasingly across northern Europe, SOL is an icon of what it takes to win in the new world of business.

Source: Gina Imperato. "Dirty Business. Bright Ideas." *Fast Company,* February—March 1997. 89—93.

strategies define how it will get there. For example, a goal may be to achieve 15 percent annual sales growth; strategies to reach that goal might include aggressive advertising to attract new customers, motivating salespeople to increase the average size of customer purchases, and acquiring other businesses that produce similar products. Strategies can include any number of techniques to achieve the goal. The essence of formulating strategies is choosing whether the organization will perform different activities than its competitors or will execute similar activities more efficiently than its competitors do.[19]

Two models for formulating strategies are the Porter model of competitive strategies and Miles and Snow's strategy typology. Each provides a framework for competitive action. After describing the two models, we will discuss how the choice of strategies affects organization design.

PORTER'S COMPETITIVE STRATEGIES

Michael E. Porter studied a number of businesses and introduced a framework describing three competitive strategies: low-cost leadership, differentiation, and focus.[20] The focus strategy, in which the organization concentrates on a specific market or buyer group, is further divided into *focused low cost* and *focused differentiation*. This yields four basic strategies, as illustrated in Exhibit 2.4. To use this model, managers evaluate two factors, competitive advantage and competitive scope. With respect to advantage, managers determine whether to compete through lower cost or through the ability to offer unique or distinctive products and services that can command a premium price. Managers then determine whether the organization will compete on a broad scope (competing in many customer segments) or a narrow scope (competing in a selected customer segment or group of segments). These choices determine the selection of strategies, as illustrated in Exhibit 2.4.

Differentiation. In a **differentiation** strategy, organizations attempt to distinguish their products or services from others in the industry. An organization may use advertising, distinctive product features, exceptional service, or new technology to achieve a product perceived as unique. This strategy usually targets customers who are not particularly concerned with price, so it can be quite profitable. Maytag appliances, Tommy Hilfiger clothing, and Intel Pentium chips are examples of products from companies using a differentiation strategy. Howard Schultz, chairman and CEO of Starbucks, used a differentiation strategy to create a premium brand from what was once only a commodity product.

In Practice 2.1

Starbucks Coffee Co.

You can get a cup of coffee at the diner on the corner for fifty cents. So why do nine million people a week clamor to pay two bucks for the same product at Starbucks? From its beginning in 1971 as a small, whole-bean store in Seattle, Starbucks has grown to more than 1,800 chic cafes where customers sip espressos, double skim lattes, and no-whip mochas. About 10 percent of Starbucks' customers come in twice a day.

One of the reasons is that customers are buying not just a great cup of coffee, but an experience. In a new store in Beijing, for instance, customers line up to have a barista dispense jolts of java from a "Mercury machine" strapped to his back. Starbucks recruits most of its "baristas," who prepare coffee drinks, from colleges and community groups and

EXHIBIT 2.4   *Porter's Competitive Strategies*

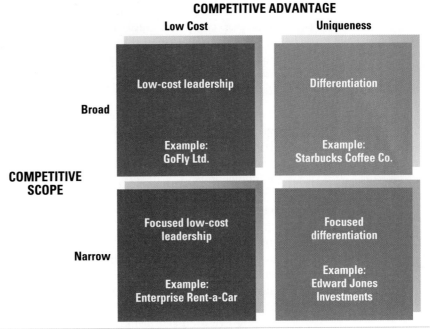

Source: Adapted from Michael E. Porter, *Competitive Advantage: Creating and Sustaining Superior Performance* (New York: The Free Press, 1985), 12. Used with permission.

provides them with extensive training in coffeemaking and lore. Employees' knowledge, as well as their ability to interact with customers, is key to the hip image and quality service that keeps customers coming back. Starbucks also emphasizes listening to customers and giving them what they want. In Atlanta, where business was slow at the company's first store in the region, employees noted that customers tended to come in later in the day and wanted to feel comfortable lingering for a while. So Starbucks began offering more appealing dessert options and opening bigger stores with amenities such as couches and outdoor tables so that people would feel comfortable just hanging out. The result was double-digit sales growth, making Atlanta—now home to thirty-three stores—one of the company's top markets. Starbucks is constantly innovating. "You might imagine that we came up with one idea and never looked back," says John Richards, head of Starbucks' North American retail division. "But . . . if we didn't change, we'd be at a real disadvantage."

Despite recent criticisms of Starbucks' rapid expansion plans and ventures into restaurants and supermarket sales, the company is as strong as ever. The cachet of Starbucks keeps loyal customers lining up all over the world. If you wonder why, listen to the answer of Starbucks' international president Howard Behar: "We're not in the business of filling bellies, we're in the business of filling souls."[21]

Starbucks' differentiation strategy is working. Companies that have tried to compete have found the going tough. Every company that has tried it is in trouble. Starbucks recently purchased one competitor, Pasqua Coffee, at a bargain price. Brothers Coffee, which got out of the retail coffee business several years ago to focus on the wholesale market, recently filed for bankruptcy. A differentiation strategy can reduce rivalry with competitors and fight off the threat of substitute products because customers are loyal to the company's brand. However, companies must remember that successful differentiation strategies require a number of costly activities, such as product research and design and extensive advertising. Companies that pursue a differentiation strategy need strong marketing abilities and creative employees who are given the time and resources to seek innovations.

Low-Cost Leadership. The **low-cost leadership** strategy tries to increase market share by emphasizing low cost compared to competitors. With a low-cost leadership strategy, the organization aggressively seeks efficient facilities, pursues cost reductions, and uses tight controls to produce products more efficiently than its competitors.

This strategy is concerned primarily with stability rather than taking risks or seeking new opportunities for innovation and growth. A low-cost position means the company can undercut competitors' prices and still offer comparable quality and earn a reasonable profit. GoFly Ltd., a startup airline based in London, England, is using a low-cost strategy to compete successfully against major carriers such as British Airways. CEO Barbara Cassani monitors costs closely so GoFly can keep prices low. For example, the company doesn't use travel agents, requiring that customers book flights directly by phone or on the Web. Rather than serving free food and drinks, GoFly offers travelers a choice of quality refreshments at a fair price.[22]

A low-cost strategy can help a company defend against current competitors because customers cannot find lower prices elsewhere. In addition, if substitute products or potential new competitors enter the picture, the low-cost producer is in a better position to prevent loss of market share.

Focus. With Porter's third strategy, the **focus strategy**, the organization concentrates on a specific regional market or buyer group. The company will try to achieve either a low-cost advantage or a differentiation advantage within a narrowly defined market. One example of focus strategy is Enterprise Rent-a-Car, which has made its mark by focusing on a market in which the major companies like Hertz and Avis don't even compete—the low-budget insurance replacement market. Customers whose cars have been wrecked or stolen have one less thing to worry about when Enterprise delivers a rental car right to their driveway. Enterprise has been able to grow rapidly by using a focused low-cost strategy. Edward Jones, a St. Louis-based brokerage house, succeeded by building its business in rural and small-town America and providing investors with conservative, long-term investments. Peter Drucker (the ultimate management guru, who has worked as a consultant to Edward Jones) points out that the firm's safety-first orientation means it delivers a product "that no Wall Street house has ever sold before: peace of mind." The company is expanding rapidly, aiming to become the "Wal-Mart of Wall Street," by using this focused differentiation strategy.[23]

MILES AND SNOW'S STRATEGY TYPOLOGY

Another business strategy typology was developed from the study of business strategies by Raymond Miles and Charles Snow.[24] The Miles and Snow typology is based on the idea that managers seek to formulate strategies that will be congruent with the external environment. Organizations strive for a fit among internal organization characteristics, strategy, and the external environment. The four strategies that can be developed are the prospector, the defender, the analyzer, and the reactor.

Prospector. The **prospector** strategy is to innovate, take risks, seek out new opportunities, and grow. This strategy is suited to a dynamic, growing environment, where creativity is more important than efficiency. Federal Express Corporation, which innovates in both services and production technology in the rapidly changing overnight mail industry, exemplifies the prospector strategy, as do today's leading high-tech companies, such as Microsoft or AOL.

Defender. The **defender** strategy is almost the opposite of the prospector. Rather than taking risks and seeking out new opportunities, the defender strategy is concerned with stability or even retrenchment. This strategy seeks to hold onto current customers, but it neither innovates nor seeks to grow. The defender is concerned primarily with internal efficiency and control to produce reliable, high-quality products for steady customers. This strategy can be successful when the organization exists in a declining industry or a stable environment. Philips Electronics used a defender strategy after a $2.2 billion loss nearly bankrupted the company. Philips managers began dramatic cost-cutting efforts, including eliminating thousands of jobs and selling off dozens of businesses.[25]

Analyzer. The **analyzer** tries to maintain a stable business while innovating on the periphery. It seems to lie midway between the prospector and the defender. Some products will be targeted toward stable environments in which an efficiency strategy designed to keep current customers is used. Others will be targeted toward new, more dynamic environments, where growth is possible. The analyzer attempts to balance efficient production for current product lines with the creative development of new product lines. Procter & Gamble has shifted to an analyzer strategy under new CEO Durk Jager. His strategy is to maintain a stable business for strong brands such as Tide, Crest, and Pampers, while also pushing the company to invent entirely new categories of products, such as a home dry cleaning product called Dryel.[26]

Reactor. The **reactor** strategy is not really a strategy at all. Rather, reactors respond to environmental threats and opportunities in an ad hoc fashion. In a reactor strategy, top management has not defined a long-range plan or given the organization an explicit mission or goal, so the organization takes whatever actions seem to meet immediate needs. Although the reactor strategy can sometimes be successful, it can also lead to failed companies. Some large, once highly successful companies, such as Kellogg and Kodak, are struggling because managers failed to adopt a strategy consistent with consumer trends.

HOW STRATEGIES AFFECT ORGANIZATION DESIGN

Choice of strategy affects internal organization characteristics. Organization design characteristics need to support the firm's competitive approach. For example, a company wanting to grow and invent new products looks and "feels" different from a company that is focused on maintaining market share for long-established products in a stable industry. Exhibit 2.5 summarizes organizational design characteristics associated with the Porter and Miles and Snow strategies.

EXHIBIT 2.5   *Organizational Design Outcomes of Strategy*

Porter's Competitive Strategies	Miles and Snow's Strategy Typology
Differentiation	**Prospector**
• Learning orientation; acts in a flexible, loosely-knit way, with strong horizontal coordination	• Learning orientation; flexible, fluid, decentralized structure
• Strong capability in research	• Strong capability in research
• Values and builds in mechanisms for customer intimacy	**Defender**
• Rewards employee creativity, risk-taking, and innovation	• Efficiency orientation; centralized authority and tight cost control
Low-Cost Leadership	• Emphasis on production efficiency; low overhead
• Efficiency orientation; strong central authority; tight cost control, with frequent, detail control reports	• Close supervision; little employee empowerment
• Standard operating procedures	**Analyzer**
• Highly efficient procurement and distribution systems	• Balances efficiency and learning; tight cost control with flexibility and adaptability
• Close supervision; routine tasks; limited employee empowerment	• Efficient production for stable product lines; emphasis on creativity, research, risk-taking for innovation
	Reactor
	• No clear organizational approach; design characteristics may shift abruptly depending on current needs

Source: Based on Michael E. Porter, *Competitive Strategy: Techniques for Analyzing Industries and Competitors* (New York: The Free Press, 1980); Michael Treacy and Fred Wiersema, "How Market Leaders Keep Their Edge," *Fortune,* 6 February 1995, 88-98; Michael Hitt, R. Duane Ireland, and Robert E. Hoskisson, *Strategic Management* (St. Paul, Minn.: West, 1995): 100-113; and Raymond E. Miles, Charles C. Snow, Alan D. Meyer, and Henry L. Coleman, Jr., "Organizational Strategy, Structure, and Process," *Academy of Management Review* 3 (1978): 546-562.

With a low-cost leadership strategy, managers take an efficiency approach to organization design, whereas a differentiation strategy calls for a learning approach. Recall from Chapter 1 that organizations designed for efficiency have different characteristics from those designed for learning. A low-cost leadership strategy (efficiency) is associated with strong, centralized authority and tight control, standard operating procedures, and emphasis on efficient procurement and distribution systems. Employees generally perform routine tasks under close supervision and control and are not empowered to make decisions or take action on their own. A differentiation strategy, on the other hand, requires that employees be constantly experimenting and learning. Structure is fluid and flexible, with strong horizontal coordination. Empowered employees work directly with customers and are rewarded for creativity and risk-taking. The organization values research, creativity, and innovativeness over efficiency and standard procedures.

The prospector strategy requires characteristics similar to a differentiation strategy, and the defender strategy takes an efficiency approach similar to low-cost leadership. Because the analyzer strategy attempts to balance efficiency for stable product lines with flexibility and learning for new products, it is associated with a mix of characteristics, as listed in Exhibit 2.5. With a reactor strategy, managers have left the organization with no direction and no clear approach to design.

OTHER FACTORS AFFECTING ORGANIZATION DESIGN

Strategy is one important factor that affects organization design. Ultimately, however, organization design is a result of numerous contingencies, which will be discussed throughout this book. The emphasis given to efficiency and control versus learning and flexibility is determined by the contingencies of strategy, environment, size and life cycle, technology, and organizational culture. The organization is designed to "fit" the contingency factors, as illustrated in Exhibit 2.6.

For example, in a stable environment, the organization can have a traditional structure that emphasizes vertical control, efficiency, specialization, standard procedures, and centralized decision making. However, a rapidly changing environment may call for a more flexible structure, with strong horizontal coordination and collaboration through teams or other mechanisms. Environment will be discussed in detail in Chapters 4 and 5. In terms of size and life cycle, young, small organizations are generally informal and have little division of labor, few rules and regulations, and ad hoc budgeting and performance systems. Large organizations such as IBM or Sears, on the other hand, have an extensive division of labor, numerous rules and regulations, and standard procedures and systems for budgeting, control, rewards, and innovation. Size and stages of the life cycle will be discussed in Chapter 8.

Design must also fit the workflow technology of the organization. For example, with mass production technology, such as a traditional automobile assembly line, the organization functions best by emphasizing efficiency, formalization, specialization, centralized decision making, and tight control. An e-business, on the other hand, may need to be very informal and flexible. Technology's impact on design will be discussed in detail in Chapters 6 and 7. A final contingency that affects organizational design is corporate culture. An organizational culture that values teamwork, collaboration, creativity, and open communication among all employees and managers, for example, would not function well with a tight, vertical structure and strict rules and regulations. The role of culture is discussed in Chapter 9.

EXHIBIT 2.6   *Contingency Factors Affecting Organization Design*

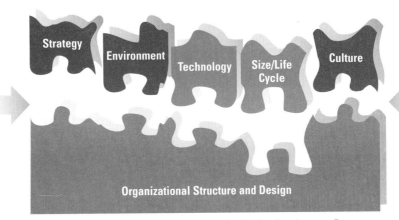

The Right Mix of Design Characteristics Fit the Contingency Factors

One responsibility of managers is to design organizations that fit the contingency factors of strategy, environment, size and life cycle, technology, and culture. Finding the right "fit" leads to organizational effectiveness, whereas a poor fit can lead to decline or even the demise of the organization.

ORGANIZATIONAL EFFECTIVENESS

Understanding organizational goals and strategies, as well as the concept of fitting design to various contingencies, is a first step toward understanding organizational effectiveness. Organizational goals represent the reason for an organization's existence and the outcomes it seeks to achieve. The next few sections of the chapter explore the topic of effectiveness and how effectiveness is measured in organizations.

Goals were defined earlier as the desired future state of the organization. Organizational **effectiveness** is the degree to which an organization realizes its goals.[27] Effectiveness is a broad concept. It implicitly takes into consideration a range of variables at both the organizational and departmental levels. Effectiveness evaluates the extent to which multiple goals—whether official or operative—are attained.

Efficiency is a more limited concept that pertains to the internal workings of the organization. Organizational efficiency is the amount of resources used to produce a unit of output.[28] It can be measured as the ratio of inputs to outputs. If one organization can achieve a given production level with fewer resources than another organization it would be described as more efficient.[29]

Sometimes efficiency leads to effectiveness. In other organizations, efficiency and effectiveness are not related. An organization may be highly efficient but fail to achieve its goals because it makes a product for which there is no demand. Likewise, an organization may achieve its profit goals but be inefficient.

Overall effectiveness is difficult to measure in organizations. Organizations are large, diverse, and fragmented. They perform many activities simultaneously. They pursue multiple goals. And they generate many outcomes, some intended and some unintended.[30] Managers determine what indicators to measure in order to gauge the effectiveness of their organizations. One study found that many managers have a difficult time with the concept of evaluating effectiveness based on characteristics that are not subject to hard, quantitative measurement.[31] However, top executives at some of today's leading companies are finding new ways to measure effectiveness, using indicators such as "customer delight" and employee satisfaction. A number of approaches to measuring effectiveness look at which measurements managers choose to track. These *contingency effectiveness approaches*, discussed in the next section, are based on looking at which part of the organization managers consider most important to measure. Later, we will examine *balanced effectiveness approaches*, which integrate concern for various parts of the organization.

CONTINGENCY EFFECTIVENESS APPROACHES

Contingency approaches to measuring effectiveness focus on different parts of the organization. Organizations bring resources in from the environment, and those resources are transformed into outputs delivered back into the environment, as shown in Exhibit 2.7. The **goal approach** to organizational effectiveness is

EXHIBIT 2.7   *Contingency Approaches to the Measurement of Organizational Effectiveness*

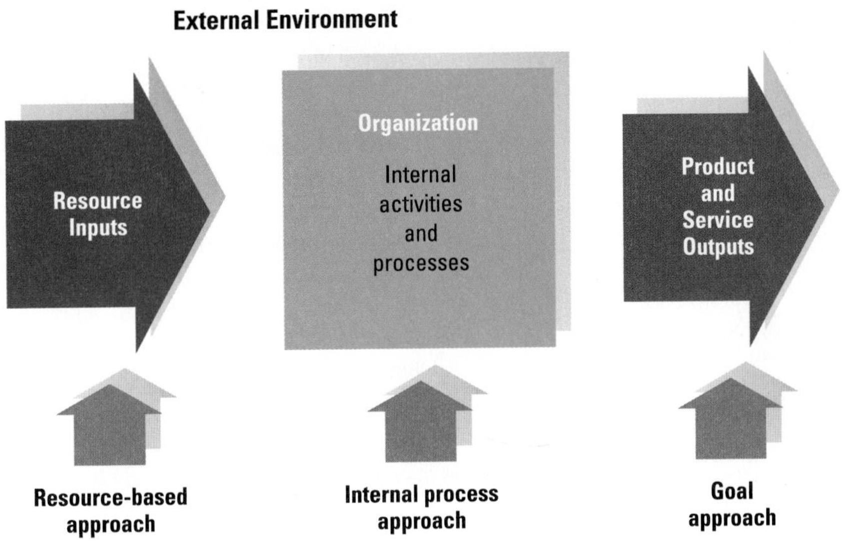

External Environment

Resource Inputs → **Organization** (Internal activities and processes) → **Product and Service Outputs**

Resource-based approach   **Internal process approach**   **Goal approach**

concerned with the output side and whether the organization achieves its goals in terms of desired levels of output.[32] The **resource-based approach** assesses effectiveness by observing the beginning of the process and evaluating whether the organization effectively obtains resources necessary for high performance. The **internal process approach** looks at internal activities and assesses effectiveness by indicators of internal health and efficiency.

This section first examines effectiveness as evaluated by the goal approach. Then it turns to the resource-based and internal process approaches to effectiveness. In the following section, we will examine approaches that attempt to balance and integrate these perspectives.

GOAL APPROACH

The goal approach to effectiveness consists of identifying an organization's output goals and assessing how well the organization has attained those goals.[33] This is a logical approach because organizations do try to attain certain levels of output, profit, or client satisfaction. The goal approach measures progress toward attainment of those goals. For example, an important measure for the Women's National Basketball Association is number of tickets sold per game. During the league's first season, President Val Ackerman set a goal of 4,000 to 5,000 tickets per game. The organization actually averaged nearly 9,700 tickets per game, indicating that the WNBA was highly effective in meeting its goal for attendance.[34]

Indicators. The important goals to consider are operative goals. Efforts to measure effectiveness have been more productive using operative goals than using official goals.[35] Official goals tend to be abstract and difficult to measure. Operative goals reflect activities the organization is actually performing.

One example of multiple goals is from a survey of U.S. business corporations.[36] Their reported goals are shown in Exhibit 2.8. Twelve goals were listed as being important to these companies. These twelve goals represent outcomes that

EXHIBIT 2.8   *Reported Goals of U.S. Corporations*

Goal	% Corporations
Profitability	89
Growth	82
Market share	66
Social responsibility	65
Employee welfare	62
Product quality and service	60
Research and development	54
Diversification	51
Efficiency	50
Financial stability	49
Resource conservation	39
Management development	35

Source: Adapted from Y. K. Shetty, "New Look at Corporate Goals," *California Management Review* 22, no. 2 (1979), 71–79.

cannot be achieved simultaneously. They illustrate the array of outcomes organizations attempt to achieve.

Usefulness. The goal approach is used in business organizations because output goals can be readily measured. Business firms typically evaluate performance in terms of profitability, growth, market share, and return on investment. However, identifying operative goals and measuring performance of an organization are not always easy. Two problems that must be resolved are the issues of multiple goals and subjective indicators of goal attainment.

Since organizations have multiple and conflicting goals, effectiveness often cannot be assessed by a single indicator. High achievement on one goal may mean low achievement on another. Moreover, there are department goals as well as overall performance goals. The full assessment of effectiveness should take into consideration several goals simultaneously. Many organizations, including Northern States Power Co., use a balanced approach to measuring goals. Northern States tracks measurements in four goal areas: financial performance, customer service and satisfaction, internal processes, and innovation and learning.[37]

The other issue to resolve with the goal approach is how to identify operative goals for an organization and how to measure goal attainment. For business organizations, there are often objective indicators for certain goals, such as profit or growth. However, subjective assessment is needed for other goals, such as employee welfare or social responsibility. Someone has to go into the organization and learn what the actual goals are by talking with the top management team. Once goals are identified, subjective perceptions of goal attainment have to be used when quantitative indicators are not available. Managers rely on information from customers, competitors, suppliers, and employees, as well as their own intuition, when considering these goals. Jerre Stead, Chairman and CEO of Ingram Micro Inc., the world's largest distributor of computer-technology products and services, communicates directly with hundreds of customers each week to measure the company's goal of achieving "customer delight." "These direct interactions don't provide hard numbers," he says, "but I sure do learn a lot."[38]

Although the goal approach seems to be the most logical way to assess organizational effectiveness, managers and evaluators should keep in mind that the actual measure of effectiveness is a complex process. The Office of National Drug Control Policy's attempt to set goals and measure results in the U.S. war against drugs illustrates how complex measuring effectiveness can be.

White House Office of National Drug Control Policy

The Office of National Drug Control Policy (ONDCP) is the coordinating authority in the national campaign to eliminate drug abuse. Recently, the ONDCP developed a ten-year plan that includes five major goals: educating youth to reject drugs, reducing drug-related crime, reducing the social and health costs of drug abuse, protecting U.S. borders, and breaking drug supply sources at home and abroad. Within these goals are 94 performance targets to be met by 2002 and 2007, including such things as "reduce drug use by 50 percent by 2007" and "reduce the availability of illicit drugs in the United States by 25 percent by 2002." Called the Performance Measure of Effectiveness, this ambitious plan links the efforts of 54 federal agencies; state, local, and foreign governments; and the private sector.

The task force faced an enormously complex task in setting goals and determining how to measure such things as attitudes toward drug use and people's propensity to use illegal drugs. Household survey methodology and forms are being revised to improve data and measure the changes in drug use and attitudes from year to year. An effort is also underway to more effectively estimate the current flow of illegal drugs and establish a baseline for measuring progress toward the goal of reducing availability. Officials acknowledge that developing the plan may turn out to be the easy part–measuring results could be even more complex. However, according to ONDCP's John Carnevale, organizations wanting to establish goal measurement systems shouldn't be constrained by the lack of data to measure results. "Think about what ought to be and then develop an agenda to go and get it," he says. The ONDCP and the more than 50 agencies participating in the Performance Measure of Effectiveness are trying to do just that.[39]

RESOURCE-BASED APPROACH

The resource-based approach looks at the input side of the transformation process shown in Exhibit 2.7. It assumes organizations must be successful in obtaining and managing valued resources in order to be effective. From a resource-based perspective, organizational effectiveness is defined as the ability of the organization, in either absolute or relative terms, to obtain scarce and valued resources and successfully integrate and manage them.[40]

Indicators. Obtaining and successfully managing resources is the criterion by which organizational effectiveness is assessed. In a broad sense, indicators of effectiveness according to the resource-based approach encompass the following dimensions:

- Bargaining position—the ability of the organization to obtain from its environment scarce and valued resources, including financial resources, raw materials, human resources, knowledge, and technology.
- The abilities of the organization's decision makers to perceive and correctly interpret the real properties of the external environment.
- The abilities of managers to use tangible (e.g., supplies, people) and intangible (e.g., knowledge, corporate culture) resources in day-to-day organizational activities to achieve superior performance.
- The ability of the organization to respond to changes in the environment.

Usefulness. The resource-based approach is valuable when other indicators of performance are difficult to obtain. In many not-for-profit and social welfare organizations, for example, it is hard to measure output goals or internal efficiency. Some for-profit organizations also use a resource-based approach. For example, Mathsoft, Inc., which provides a broad range of technical-calculation and analytical software for business and academia, evaluates its effectiveness partly by looking at how many top-rate Ph.D.s it can recruit. CEO Charles Digate believes Mathsoft has a higher ratio of Ph.D.s to total employees than any other software company, which directly affects product quality and the company's image.[41]

Although the resource-based approach is valuable when other measures of effectiveness are not available, it does have shortcomings. For one thing, the approach only vaguely considers the organization's link to the needs of customers in the external environment. A superior ability to acquire and use resources is important only if resources and capabilities are used to achieve something that meets a need in the environment. The resource-based approach is most valuable when measures of goal attainment cannot be readily obtained.

INTERNAL PROCESS APPROACH

In the internal process approach, effectiveness is measured as internal organizational health and efficiency. An effective organization has a smooth, well-oiled internal process. Employees are happy and satisfied. Departmental activities mesh with one another to ensure high productivity. This approach does not consider the external environment. The important element in effectiveness is what the organization does with the resources it has, as reflected in internal health and efficiency.

Indicators. One indicator of internal process effectiveness is the organization's economic efficiency. However, the best-known proponents of a process model are from the human relations approach to organizations. Such writers as Chris Argyris, Warren G. Bennis, Rensis Likert, and Richard Beckhard have all worked extensively with human resources in organizations and emphasize the connection between human resources and effectiveness.[42] Writers on corporate culture and organizational excellence have stressed the importance of internal processes. Results from a recent study of nearly two hundred secondary schools showed that both human resources and employee-oriented processes were important in explaining and promoting effectiveness in those organizations.[43]

There are seven indicators of an effective organization as seen from an internal process approach:

- Strong corporate culture and positive work climate
- Team spirit, group loyalty, and teamwork
- Confidence, trust, and communication between workers and management
- Decision making near sources of information, regardless of where those sources are on the organizational chart
- Undistorted horizontal and vertical communication; sharing of relevant facts and feelings
- Rewards to managers for performance, growth, and development of subordinates and for creating an effective working group
- Interaction between the organization and its parts, with conflict that occurs over projects resolved in the interest of the organization.[44]

Usefulness. The internal process approach is important because the efficient use of resources and harmonious internal functioning are ways to measure effectiveness.

Today, most managers believe that happy, committed, actively involved employees and a positive corporate culture are important measures of effectiveness. Gary White, CEO of The Gymboree Corp., for example, believes that keeping employees happy is the key to long-term success for his company, which runs parent-child play programs and operates more than 500 retail clothing stores.

The internal process approach also has shortcomings. Total output and the organization's relationship with the external environment are not evaluated. Also, evaluations of internal health and functioning are often subjective, because many aspects of inputs and internal processes are not quantifiable. Managers should be aware that this approach alone represents a limited view of organizational effectiveness.

BALANCED EFFECTIVENESS APPROACHES

The three approaches—goal, resource-based, internal process—to organizational effectiveness described earlier all have something to offer, but each one tells only part of the story. Some approaches try to balance a concern with various parts of the organization rather than focusing on one part. These integrative, balanced approaches to effectiveness acknowledge that organizations do many things and have many outcomes. These approaches combine several indicators of effectiveness into a single framework. They include the stakeholder and competing values approaches.

STAKEHOLDER APPROACH

One proposed approach integrates diverse organizational activities by focusing on organizational stakeholders. A **stakeholder** is any group within or outside an organization that has a stake in the organization's performance. Creditors, suppliers, employees, and owners are all stakeholders. In the **stakeholder approach** (also called the constituency approach), the satisfaction of such groups can be assessed as an indicator of the organization's performance.[45] Each stakeholder will have a different criterion of effectiveness because it has a different interest in the organization. Each stakeholder group has to be surveyed to learn whether the organization performs well from its viewpoint.

Indicators. The initial work on evaluating effectiveness on the basis of stakeholders included ninety-seven small businesses in Texas. Seven stakeholder groups relevant to those businesses were surveyed to determine the perception of effectiveness from each viewpoint.[46] The following table shows each stakeholder and its criterion of effectiveness.

Stakeholder	Effectiveness Criteria
1. Owners	Financial return
2. Employees	Worker satisfaction, pay, supervision
3. Customers	Quality of goods and services
4. Creditors	Creditworthiness
5. Community	Contribution to community affairs
6. Suppliers	Satisfactory transactions
7. Government	Obedience to laws, regulations

The survey of stakeholders showed that a small business found it difficult to simultaneously fulfill the demands of all groups. One business may have high employee satisfaction, but the satisfaction of other groups may be lower. Nevertheless, measuring all seven stakeholders provides a more accurate view of effectiveness than any single measure. Evaluating how organizations perform across each group offers an overall assessment of effectiveness.

Usefulness. The strength of the stakeholder approach is that it takes a broad view of effectiveness and examines factors in the environment as well as within the organization. The stakeholder approach includes the community's notion of social responsibility, which is not formally measured in the goal, resource-based, and internal process approaches. The stakeholder approach also handles several criteria simultaneously—inputs, internal processing, outputs—and acknowledges that there is no single measure of effectiveness. The well-being of employees is just as important as attaining the owner's financial goals.

The stakeholder approach is gaining in popularity, based on the view that effectiveness is a complex, multidimensional concept that has no single measure.[47] Recent research has shown that the assessment of multiple stakeholder groups is an accurate reflection of effectiveness, especially with respect to organizational adaptability.[48] Moreover, research shows that firms really do care about their reputational status and do attempt to shape stakeholders' assessments of their performance.[49] If an organization performs poorly according to several interest groups, it is probably not meeting its effectiveness goals. Top managers should be careful that in satisfying some stakeholders they do not alienate others, as Ronald Allen learned at Delta Airlines.

In Practice 2.3   Delta Air Lines

A few years ago, Delta Air Lines was in a financial tailspin. CEO Robert W. Allen began severe downsizing and other cost-cutting efforts that rescued the carrier and led to eight consecutive quarters of record profits, leaving shareholders cheering. However, other stakeholders, such as employees, customers, and the community, weren't so happy. After Allen said in an interview that if drastic cost-cutting had upset Delta employees, "so be it," workers began wearing "So Be It" buttons on their shirts as a sign of protest. In addition, Delta's long-time reputation for superb customer service was going down the tubes. Customer complaints about dirty planes and mishandled baggage dramatically increased. The relationship between Delta and its hometown of Atlanta was left in tatters, too. The local media began attacking the airline practically every chance it got. This loss of reputation in the carrier's hometown further damaged the morale of Atlanta workers, and the bad vibes rippled throughout the entire Delta system.

By 1997, Delta's board of directors declined to renew Allen's contract, "not because the company was going broke, but because its spirit was broken," as a *Wall Street Journal* article put it. Although Delta could be rated as effective based on financial performance, several stakeholder groups were seriously dissatisfied, leading the board to conclude that Delta was not meeting its effectiveness goals. Today, new CEO Leo Mullin is attempting to maintain the efficiencies instituted by Allen, yet also boost morale, bring back the company's reputation for Southern hospitality and quality service, and win back the affection of the community Delta has long called home.[50]

COMPETING VALUES APPROACH

Recall that organizational goals and performance criteria are defined by top and middle managers. The **competing values approach** to organizational effectiveness was developed by Robert Quinn and John Rohrbaugh to combine the diverse indicators of performance used by managers and researchers.[51] Using a comprehensive list of performance indicators, a panel of experts in organizational effectiveness rated the indicators for similarity. The analysis produced underlying dimensions of effectiveness criteria that represented competing management values in organizations.

Indicators. The first value dimension pertains to organizational **focus**, which is whether dominant values concern issues that are *internal* or *external* to the firm. Internal focus reflects a management concern for the well-being and efficiency of employees, and external focus represents an emphasis on the well-being of the organization itself with respect to the environment. The second value dimension pertains to organization **structure**, and whether *stability* versus *flexibility* is the dominant structural consideration. Stability reflects a management value for efficiency and top-down control, whereas flexibility represents a value for learning and change.

The value dimensions of structure and focus are illustrated in Exhibit 2.9. The combination of dimensions provides four models of organizational effectiveness, which, though seemingly different, are closely related. In real organizations, these competing values can and often do exist together. Each model reflects a different management emphasis with respect to structure and focus.[52]

EXHIBIT 2.9   *Four Models of Effectiveness Values*

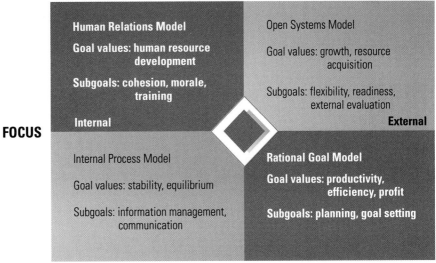

Source: Adapted from Robert E. Quinn and John Rohrbaugh, "A Spatial Model of Effectiveness Criteria: Toward a Competing Values Approach to Organizational Analysis," *Management Science* 29 (1983): 363–77; and Robert E. Quinn and Kim Cameron, "Organizational Life Cycles and Shifting Criteria of Effectiveness: Some Preliminary Evidence," *Management Science* 29 (1983): 33–51.

The **open systems model** reflects a combination of external focus and flexible structure. Management's primary goals are growth and resource acquisition. The organization accomplishes these goals through the subgoals of flexibility, readiness, and a positive external evaluation. The dominant value in this model is establishing a good relationship with the environment to acquire resources and grow. This model is similar in some ways to the system resource model described earlier.

The **rational goal model** represents management values of structural control and external focus. The primary goals are productivity, efficiency, and profit. The organization wants to achieve output goals in a controlled way. Subgoals that facilitate these outcomes are internal planning and goal setting, which are rational management tools. The rational goal model is similar to the goal approach described earlier.

The **internal process model** is in the lower-left section of Exhibit 2.9; it reflects the values of internal focus and structural control. The primary outcome is a stable organizational setting that maintains itself in an orderly way. Organizations that are well established in the environment and simply want to maintain their current position would fit this model. Subgoals for this model include mechanisms for efficient communication, information management, and decision making.

The **human relations model** incorporates the values of an internal focus and a flexible structure. Here, management concern is on the development of human resources. Employees are given opportunities for autonomy and development. Management works toward the subgoals of cohesion, morale, and training opportunities. Organizations adopting this model are more concerned with employees than with the environment.

The four models in Exhibit 2.9 represent opposing organizational values. Managers must decide which goal values will take priority in their organizations. The way two organizations are mapped onto the four models is shown in Exhibit 2.10.[53] Organization A is a young organization concerned with finding a niche and becoming established in the external environment. Primary emphasis is given to flexibility, innovation, the acquisition of resources from the environment, and the satisfaction of external constituencies. This organization gives moderate emphasis to human relations and even less emphasis to current productivity and profits. Satisfying and adapting to the environment are more important. The emphasis given to open systems values means that the internal process model is practically nonexistent. Stability and equilibrium receive little emphasis.

Organization B, in contrast, is an established business in which the dominant value is productivity and profits. This organization is characterized by planning and goal setting. Organization B is a large company that is well established in the environment and is primarily concerned with successful production and profits. Flexibility and human resources are not major concerns. This organization prefers stability and equilibrium to learning and innovation because it wants to take advantage of its established customers.

Usefulness. The competing values approach makes two contributions. First, it integrates diverse concepts of effectiveness into a single perspective. It incorporates the ideas of output goals, resource acquisition, and human resource development as goals the organization tries to accomplish. Second, the model calls attention to effectiveness criteria as management values and shows how opposing values exist at the same time. Managers must decide which values they wish to pursue and which

EXHIBIT 2.10   *Effectiveness Values for Two Organizations*

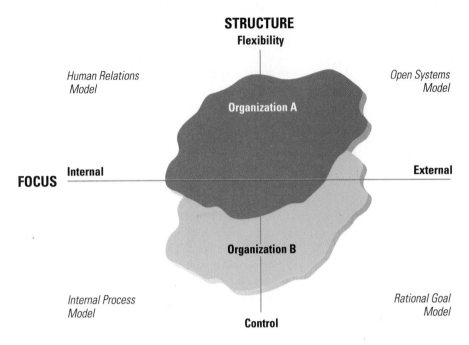

values will receive less emphasis. The four competing values exist simultaneously, but not all will receive equal priority. For example, a new, small organization that concentrates on establishing itself within a competitive environment will give less emphasis to developing employees than to the external environment.

The dominant values in an organization often change over time as organizations experience new environmental demands or new top leadership. For example, at Delta Air Lines, described in In Practice 2.3, Robert W. Allen emphasized values of efficiency, profit, and productivity, consistent with the rational model. New CEO Leo Mullin, on the other hand, is more concerned with developing employee morale and cohesion, shifting toward a human relations model. When traveling, Mullin spends several minutes talking with the pilots in the cockpit and takes an aisle seat so he can chat with flight attendants en route. He patrols Delta's airport facilities, talking with ramp and maintenance workers, and occasionally makes presentations to larger groups. Mullin also wants to improve training and development opportunities for Delta's employees. Values of human resource development (human relations model) have taken priority, although the organization is still concerned with efficiency and profit (rational model) and also gives some attention to establishing a good relationship with the external environment (open systems model).

SUMMARY AND INTERPRETATION

This chapter discussed organizational goals and the strategies top managers use to help organizations achieve those goals. Goals specify the mission or purpose of an organization and its desired future state; strategies define how the organization will reach its goals. The chapter also discussed the impact of strategy on organization design and how designing the organization to fit strategy and other contingencies can lead to organizational effectiveness. The chapter closed with an examination of the most popular approaches to measuring effectiveness, that is, how well the organization realizes its purpose and attains its desired future state.

Organizations exist for a purpose; top managers define a specific mission or task to be accomplished. The mission statement, or official goals, makes explicit the purpose and direction of an organization. Official and operative goals are a key element in organizations because they meet these needs—establishing legitimacy with external groups and setting standards of performance for participants.

Managers must develop strategies that describe the actions required to achieve goals. Strategies may include any number of techniques to achieve the stated goals. Two models for formulating strategies are Porter's competitive strategies and the Miles and Snow strategy typology. Organization design needs to fit the firm's competitive approach to contribute to organizational effectiveness.

Assessing organizational effectiveness is complex and reflects the complexity of organizations as a topic of study. No easy, simple, guaranteed measure will provide an unequivocal assessment of performance. Organizations must perform diverse activities well—from obtaining resource inputs to delivering outputs—to be successful. Contingency approaches use output goals, resource acquisition, or internal health and efficiency as the criteria of effectiveness. Balanced approaches consider multiple criteria simultaneously. Organizations can be assessed by surveying constituencies that have a stake in organizational performance or by evaluating competing values for effectiveness. No approach is suitable for every organization, but each offers some advantages that the others may lack.

From the point of view of managers, the goal approach to effectiveness and measures of internal efficiency are useful when measures are available. The attainment of output and profit goals reflects the purpose of the organization, and efficiency reflects the cost of attaining those goals. Other factors such as top-management preferences, the extent to which goals are measurable, and the scarcity of environmental resources may influence the use of effectiveness criteria. In not-for-profit organizations, where internal processes and output criteria are often not quantifiable, stakeholder satisfaction or resource acquisition may be the only available indicators of effectiveness.

From the point of view of people outside the organization, such as academic investigators or government researchers, the stakeholder and competing values approaches to organizational effectiveness may be preferable. The stakeholder approach evaluates the organization's contribution to various stakeholders, including owners, employees, customers, and the community. The competing values approach acknowledges different areas of focus (internal, external) and structure (flexibility, stability) and allows for managers to choose one value to emphasize.

BRIEFCASE

As an organization manager, keep these guidelines in mind:

1. Establish and communicate organizational mission and goals. Communicate official goals to provide a statement of the organization's mission to external constituents. Communicate operational goals to provide internal direction, guidelines, and standards of performance for employees.

2. After goals have been defined, select strategies for achieving those goals. Define specific strategies based on Porter's competitive strategies or Miles and Snow's strategy typology.

3. Design the organization to support the firm's competitive strategy. With a low-cost leadership or defender strategy, select design characteristics associated with an efficiency orientation. For a differentiation or prospector strategy, on the other hand, choose characteristics that encourage learning, innovation, and adaptation. Use a balanced mixture of characteristics for an analyzer strategy.

4. Assess the effectiveness of the organization. Use the goal approach, internal process approach, and resource-based approach to obtain specific pictures of effectiveness. Assess stakeholder satisfaction or competing values to obtain a broader, more balanced picture of effectiveness.

KEY CONCEPTS

analyzer	mission
competing values approach	official goals
defender	open systems model
differentiation	operative goals
efficiency	organizational goal
focus	prospector
focus strategy	rational goal model
goal approach	reactor
human relations model	resource-based approach
internal process approach	stakeholder approach
internal process model	strategy
low-cost leadership	structure

DISCUSSION QUESTIONS

1. Discuss the role of top management in setting organizational direction.

2. How might a company's goals for employee development be related to its goals for innovation and change? To goals for productivity? Can you discuss ways these types of goals might conflict in an organization?

3. What is a goal for the class for which you are reading this text? Who established this goal? Discuss how the goal affects your direction and motivation.

4. What is the difference between a goal and a strategy as defined in the text? Identify both a goal and a strategy for a campus or community organization with which you are involved.

5. Discuss the similarities and differences in the strategies described in Porter's competitive strategies and Miles and Snow's typology.

6. Do you believe mission statements and official goal statements provide an organization with genuine legitimacy in the external environment? Discuss.

7. Suppose you have been asked to evaluate the effectiveness of the police department in a medium-sized community. Where would you begin, and how would you proceed? What effectiveness approach would you prefer?

8. What are the advantages and disadvantages of the resource-based approach versus the goal approach for measuring organizational effectiveness?

9. What are the similarities and differences between assessing effectiveness on the basis of competing values versus stakeholders? Explain.

10. A noted organization theorist once said, "Organizational effectiveness can be whatever top management defines it to be." Discuss.

CHAPTER TWO WORKBOOK   *Identifying Company Goals and Strategies**

Choose three companies either in the same industry or in three different industries. Search the Internet for information on the companies, including annual reports. In each company look particularly at the goals expressed. Refer back to the goals in Exhibit 2.8 and also to Porter's competitive strategies in Exhibit 2.4.

	Goals from Exhibit 2.8 articulated	Strategies from Porter used
Company #1		
Company #2		
Company #3		

QUESTIONS

1. Which goals seem most important?

2. Look for differences in the goals and strategies of the three companies and develop an explanation for those differences.

3. Which of the goals or strategies should be changed? Why?

4. *Optional:* Compare your table with those of other students and look for common themes. Which companies seem to articulate and communicate their goals and strategies best?

Case for Analysis   *The University Art Museum**

Visitors to the campus were always shown the University Art Museum, of which the large and distinguished university was very proud. A photograph of the handsome neoclassical building that housed the museum had long been used by the university for the cover of its brochures and catalogues.

The building, together with a substantial endowment, was given to the university around 1912 by an alumnus, the son of the university's first president, who had become very wealthy as an investment banker. He also gave the university his own small, but high quality, collections—one of Etruscan figurines, and one, unique in America, of English pre-Raphaelite paintings. He then served as the museum's unpaid director until his death. During his tenure he brought a few additional collections to the museum, largely from other alumni of the university. Only rarely did the museum purchase anything. As a result, the museum housed several small collections of uneven quality. As long as the founder ran the museum, none of the collections was ever shown to anybody except a few members of the university's art history faculty, who were admitted as the founder's private guests.

After the founder's death, in the late 1920s, the university intended to bring in a professional museum director. Indeed, this had been part of the agreement under which the founder had given the museum. A search committee was to be appointed; but in the meantime a graduate student in art history, who had shown interest in the museum and who had spent a good many hours in it, took over temporarily. At first, she did not even have a title, let alone a salary. But she stayed on acting as the museum's director and over the next thirty years was promoted in stages to that title. But from the first day, whatever her title, she was in charge. She immediately set about changing the museum altogether. She catalogued the collections. She pursued new gifts, again primarily small collections from alumni and other friends of the university. She organized fund raising for the museum. But, above all, she began to integrate the museum into the work of the university. When a space problem arose in the years immediately following World War II, Miss Kirkoff offered the third floor of the museum to the art history faculty, which moved its offices there. She remodeled the building to include classrooms and a modern and well-appointed auditorium. She raised funds to build one of the best research and reference libraries in art history in the country. She also began to organize a series of special exhibitions built around one of the museum's own collections, complemented by loans from outside collections. For each of these exhibitions, she had a distinguished member of the university's art faculty write a catalogue. These catalogues speedily became the leading scholarly texts in the fields.

Miss Kirkoff ran the University Art Museum for almost half a century. But old age ultimately defeated her. At the age of 68, after suffering a severe stroke, she had to retire. In her letter of resignation she proudly pointed to the museum's growth and accomplishment under her stewardship. "Our endowment," she wrote, "now compares favorably with museums several times our size. We never have had to ask the university for any money other than our share of the university's insurance policies. Our collections in the areas of our strength, while small, are of first-rate quality and importance. Above all, we

are being used by more people than any museum of our size. Our lecture series, in which members of the university's art history faculty present a major subject to a university audience of students and faculty, attracts regularly three hundred to five hundred people; and if we had the seating capacity, we could easily have a larger audience. Our exhibitions are seen and studied by more visitors, most of them members of the university community, than all but the most highly publicized exhibitions in the very big museums ever draw. Above all, the courses and seminars offered in the museum have become one of the most popular and most rapidly growing educational features of the university. No other museum in this country or anywhere else," concluded Miss Kirkoff, "has so successfully integrated art into the life of a major university and a major university into the work of a museum."

Miss Kirkoff strongly recommended that the university bring in a professional museum director as her successor. "The museum is much too big and much too important to be entrusted to another amateur such as I was 45 years ago," she wrote. "And it needs careful thinking regarding its direction, its basis of support, and its future relationship with the university."

The university took Miss Kirkoff's advice. A search committee was duly appointed and, after one year's work, it produced a candidate whom everybody approved. The candidate was himself a graduate of the university who had then obtained his Ph.D. in art history and in museum work from the university. Both his teaching and his administrative record were sound, leading to his present museum directorship in a medium-sized city. There he converted an old, well-known, but rather sleepy museum to a lively, community-oriented museum whose exhibitions were well publicized and attracted large crowds.

The new museum director took over with great fanfare in September 1981. Less than three years later he left—with less fanfare, but still with considerable noise. Whether he resigned or was fired was not quite clear. But that there was bitterness on both sides was only too obvious.

The new director, upon his arrival, had announced that he looked upon the museum as a "major community resource" and intended to "make the tremendous artistic and scholarly resources of the museum fully available to the academic community as well as to the public." When he said these things in an interview with the college newspaper, everybody nodded in approval. It soon became clear that what he meant by "community resource" and what the faculty and students understood by these words were not the same. The museum had always been "open to the public" but, in practice, it was members of the college community who used the museum and attended its lectures, its exhibitions, and its frequent seminars.

The first thing the new director did, however, was to promote visits from the public schools in the area. He soon began to change the exhibition policy. Instead of organizing small shows, focused on a major collection of the museum and built around a scholarly catalogue, he began to organize "popular exhibitions" around "topics of general interest" such as "Women Artists through the Ages." He promoted these exhibitions vigorously in the newspapers, in radio and television interviews, and, above all, in the local schools. As a result, what had been a busy but quiet place was soon knee-deep with school children, taken to the museum in special buses that cluttered the access roads around the museum and throughout the campus. The faculty, which was not particularly happy with the resulting noise and confusion, became thoroughly upset when the scholarly old chairman of the art history department was mobbed by fourth-graders who sprayed him with their water pistols as he tried to push his way through the main hall to his office.

Increasingly, the new director did not design his own shows, but brought in traveling exhibitions from major museums, importing their catalogue as well rather than have his own faculty produce one.

The students too were apparently unenthusiastic after the first six or eight months, during which the new director had been somewhat of a campus hero. Attendance at the classes and seminars held at the art museum fell off sharply, as did attendance at the evening lectures. When the editor of the campus newspaper interviewed students for a story on the museum, he was told again and again that the museum had become too noisy and too "sensational" for students to enjoy the classes and to have a chance to learn.

What brought all this to a head was an Islamic art exhibit in late 1983. Since the museum had little Islamic art, nobody criticized the showing of a traveling exhibit, offered on very advantageous terms with generous financial assistance from some of the Arab governments. But then, instead of inviting one of the university's own faculty members to deliver

the customary talk at the opening of the exhibit, the director brought in a cultural attaché of one of the Arab embassies in Washington. The speaker, it was reported, used the occasion to deliver a violent attack on Israel and on the American policy of supporting Israel against the Arabs. A week later, the university senate decided to appoint an advisory committee, drawn mostly from members of the art history faculty, which, in the future, would have to approve all plans for exhibits and lectures. The director thereupon, in an interview with the campus newspaper, sharply attacked the faculty as "elitist" and "snobbish" and as believing that "art belongs to the rich." Six months later, in June 1984, his resignation was announced.

Under the bylaws of the university, the academic senate appoints a search committee. Normally, this is pure formality. The chairperson of the appropriate department submits the department's nominees for the committee who are approved and appointed, usually without debate. But when the academic senate early the following semester was asked to appoint the search committee, things were far from "normal." The dean who presided, sensing the tempers in the room, tried to smooth over things by saying, "Clearly, we picked the wrong person the last time. We will have to try very hard to find the right one this time."

He was immediately interrupted by an economist, known for his populism, who broke in and said, "I admit that the late director was probably not the right personality. But I strongly believe that his personality was not at the root of the problem. He tried to do what needs doing, and this got him in trouble with the faculty. He tried to make our museum a community resource, to bring in the community and to make art accessible to broad masses of people, to the blacks and the Puerto Ricans, to the kids from the ghetto schools and to a lay public. And this is what we really resented. Maybe his methods were not the most tactful ones—I admit I could have done without those interviews he gave. But what he tried to do was right. We had better commit ourselves to the policy he wanted to put into effect, or else we will have deserved his attacks on us as 'elitist' and 'snobbish.'"

"This is nonsense," cut in the usually silent and polite senate member from the art history faculty. "It makes absolutely no sense for our museum to become the kind of community resource our late director and my distinguished colleague want it to be. First, there is no need. The city has one of the world's finest and biggest museums, and it does exactly that and does it very well. Secondly, we have neither the artistic resources nor the financial resources to serve the community at large. We can do something different but equally important and indeed unique. Ours is the only museum in the country, and perhaps in the world, that is fully integrated with an academic community and truly a teaching institution. We are using it, or at least we used to until the last few unfortunate years, as a major educational resource for all our students. No other museum in the country, and as far as I know in the world, is bringing undergraduates into art the way we do. All of us, in addition to our scholarly and graduate work, teach undergraduate courses for people who are not going to be art majors or art historians. We work with the engineering students and show them what we do in our conservation and restoration work. We work with architecture students and show them the development of architecture through the ages. Above all, we work with liberal arts students, who often have had no exposure to art before they came here and who enjoy our courses all the more because they are scholarly and not just 'art appreciation.' This is unique and this is what our museum can do and should do."

"I doubt that this is really what we should be doing," commented the chairman of the mathematics department. "The museum, as far as I know, is part of the graduate faculty. It should concentrate on training art historians in its Ph.D. program, on its scholarly work, and on its research. I would strongly urge that the museum be considered an adjunct to graduate and especially to Ph.D. education, confine itself to this work, and stay out of all attempts to be

'popular,' both on campus and outside of it. The glory of the museum is the scholarly catalogues produced by our faculty, and our Ph.D. graduates who are sought after by art history faculties throughout the country. This is the museum's mission, which can only be impaired by the attempts to be 'popular,' whether with students or with the public."

"These are very interesting and important comments," said the dean, still trying to pacify. "But I think this can wait until we know who the new director is going to be. Then we should raise these questions with him."

"I beg to differ, Mr. Dean," said one of the elder statesmen of the faculty. "During the summer months, I discussed this question with an old friend and neighbor of mine in the country, the director of one of the nation's great museums. He said to me: 'You do not have a personality problem, you have a management problem. You have not, as a university, taken responsibility for the mission, the direction, and the objectives of your museum. Until you do this, no director can succeed. And this is your decision. In fact, you cannot hope to get a good man until you can tell him what your basic objectives are. If your late director is to blame—I know him and I know that he is abrasive—it is for being willing to take on a job when you, the university, had not faced up to the basic management decisions. There is no point talking about who should manage until it is clear what it is that has to be managed and for what.'"

At this point the dean realized that he had to adjourn the discussion unless he wanted the meeting to degenerate into a brawl. But he also realized that he had to identify the issues and possible decisions before the next faculty meeting a month later.

Case for Analysis   *Airstar, Inc.**

Airstar, Inc. manufactures, repairs, and overhauls pistons and jet engines for smaller, often previously owned aircraft. The company had a solid niche, and most managers had been with the founder for [more than] 20 years. With the founder's death five years ago, Roy Morgan took over as president at Airstar. Mr. Morgan has called you in as a consultant.

Your research indicates that this industry is changing rapidly. Airstar is feeling encroachment of huge conglomerates like General Electric and Pratt

&Whitney, and its backlog of orders is the lowest in several years. The company has always been known for its superior quality, safety, and customer service. However, it has never been under threat before, and senior managers are not sure which [strategic] direction to take. They have considered potential acquisitions, imports and exports, more research,

*Adapted from Bernard A. Deitzer and Karl A. Shilliff, *Contemporary Management Incidents* (Columbus, Ohio: Grid, Inc., 1977) 43-46. Reprinted by permission of John Wiley & Sons, Inc.

and additional repair lines. The organization is becoming more chaotic, which is frustrating Morgan and his vice presidents.

Before a meeting with his team, he confides to you, "Organizing is supposed to be easy. For maximum efficiency, work should be divided into simple, logical, routine tasks. These business tasks can be grouped by similar kinds of work characteristics and arranged within an organization under a particularly suited executive. So why are we having so many problems with our executives?"

Morgan met with several of his trusted corporate officers in the executive dining room to discuss what was happening to corporate leadership at Airstar. Morgan went on to explain that he was really becoming concerned with the situation. There have been outright conflicts between the vice president of marketing and controller over merger and acquisition opportunities. There have been many instances of duplication of work, with corporate officers trying to outmaneuver each other.

"Communications are atrocious," Morgan said to the others. "Why, I didn't even get a copy of the export finance report until my secretary made an effort to find one for me. My basis for evaluation and appraisal of corporate executive performance [and goal accomplishment] is fast becoming obsolete. Everyone has been working up their own job descriptions, and they all include overlapping responsibilities. Changes and decisions are being made on the basis of expediency and are perpetuating too many mistakes. We must take a good look at these organizational realities and correct the situation immediately."

Jim Robinson, vice president of manufacturing, pointed out to Morgan that Airstar is not really following the "principles of good organization." "For instance," explained Robinson, "let's review what we should be practicing as administrators." Some of the principles Robinson believed they should be following are:

1. Determine the [goals], policies, programs, plans [and strategies] that will best achieve the desired results for our company.
2. Determine the various business tasks to be done.
3. Divide the business tasks into a logical and understandable organizational structure.
4. Determine the suitable personnel to occupy positions within the organizational structure.
5. Define the responsibility and authority of each supervisor clearly in writing.
6. Keep the number and kinds of levels of authority at a minimum.

Robinson proposed that the group study the corporate organizational chart, as well as the various corporate business tasks. After reviewing the corporate organizational chart, Robinson, Morgan, and the others agreed that the number and kinds of formal corporate authority were logical and not much different from other corporations. The group then listed the various corporate business tasks that went on within Airstar.

Robinson continued. "How did we ever decide who should handle mergers or acquisitions?" Morgan answered, "I guess it just occurred over time that the vice president of marketing should have the responsibility." "But," Robinson queried, "where is it written down? How would the controller know it?" "Aha," Morgan exclaimed. "It looks like I'm part of the problem. There isn't anything in writing. Tasks were assigned superficially, as they became problems. This has all been rather informal. I'll establish a group to decide who should have responsibility for what so things can return to our previous level of efficiency."

CHAPTER TWO WORKSHOP   *Competing Values and Organizational Effectiveness**

1. Divide into groups of four to six members.
2. Select an organization to "study" for this exercise. It should be an organization one of you has worked at, or it could be the university.
3. Using the exhibit "Four Models of Effectiveness Values" (Exhibit 2.9), your group should list

eight potential measures that show a balanced view of performance. These should relate not only to work activities, but also to goal values for the company. Use the table on page 81.

Goal or subgoal		Performance gauge	How to measure	Source of data	What do you consider effective?
(Example) Equilibrium		Turnover rates	Compare percentages of workers who left	HRM files	25% reduction in first year
Open system	1.				
	2.				
Human relations	3.				
	4.				
Internal process	5.				
	6.				
Rational goal	7.				
	8.				

4. How will achieving these goal values help the organization to become more effective? Which values could be given more weight than others? Why?

5. Present your competing values chart to the rest of the class. Each group should explain why it chose those particular values and which are more important. Be prepared to defend your position to the other groups, which are encouraged to question your choices.

* Adapted by Dorothy Marcic from general ideas in Jennifer Howard and Larry Miller, *Team Management*, The Miller Consulting Group, 1994, p. 92.

NOTES

1. Gail Edmondson, "Danone Hits Its Stride," *Business Week*, 1 February 1999, 52–53.

2. Amitai Etzioni, *Modern Organizations* (Englewood Cliffs, N.J.: Prentice-Hall, 1964), 6.

3. John P. Kotter, "What Effective General Managers Really Do," *Harvard Business Review* (November-December 1982): 156–67; Henry Mintzberg, *The Nature of Managerial Work* (New York: Harper & Row, 1973).

4. Charles C. Snow and Lawrence G. Hrebiniak, "Strategy, Distinctive Competence, and Organizational Performance," *Administrative Science Quarterly* 25 (1980): 317–35.

5. Patricia Sellers, "The Turnaround is Ending, the Revolution's Begun," *Fortune*, 28 April 1997, 107–118.

6. David L. Calfee, "Get Your Mission Statement Working!" *Management Review* (January 1993) 54–57: John A. Pearce II and Fred David, "Corporate Mission Statements: The Bottom Line," *Academy of Management Executive* 1 (1987): 109–16; and Christopher K. Bart, "Sex, Lies, and Mission Statements," *Business Horizons*, November-December, 1997, 23–28.

7. Charles Perrow, "The Analysis of Goals in Complex Organizations," *American Sociological Review* 26 (1961): 854–66.

8. Johannes U. Stoelwinder and Martin P. Charns, "The Task Field Model of Organization Analysis and Design," *Human Relations* 34 (1981): 743–62; Anthony Raia, *Managing by Objectives* (Glenview, Ill.: Scott, Foresman, 1974).

9. Peter Galuszka and Ellen Neuborne with Wendy Zellner, "P&G's Hottest New Product: P&G," *Business Week*, 5 October 1998, 92, 96.

10. Walid Mougayar, Michael Mattis, Kate McKinley, and Nissa Crawford, "Business 2.0 100: And the Winner is ... Cisco Systems," *Business 2.0* (May

1999): 59–63; and Oren Harari, "The Concrete Intangibles," *Management Review,* May 1999, 30–33.

11. Miriam Schulman, "Winery with a Mission," *Issues in Ethics* (Spring 1996): 14–15.

12. Rahul Jacob, "Corporate Reputations," *Fortune,* 6 March 1995, 54–67.

13. Alex Taylor III, "Why the Bounce at Rubbermaid," *Fortune,* 13 April 1987, 77–78.

14. Mark C. Suchman, "Managing Legitimacy: Strategic and Institutional Approaches," *Academy of Management Review* 20, no. 3 (1995): 571–610.

15. Eryn Brown, "America's Most Admired Companies," *Fortune,* 1 March 1999, 68+; Ken Friedman, Norwegian School of Management, Oslo, Norway, personal communication.

16. James D. Thompson, *Organizations in Action* (New York: McGraw-Hill, 1967): 83–98.

17. "Owens-Illinois: Giving up Market Share to Improve Profits," *Business Week,* 11 May 1981, 81–82.

18. 1995 Annual Report, American Express Corp.

19. Michael E. Porter, "What is Strategy?" *Harvard Business Review* (November-December 1996,): 61–78.

20. Michael E. Porter, *Competitive Strategy: Techniques for Analyzing Industries and Competitors* (New York: Free Press, 1980).

21. Nelson D. Schwartz, "Still Perking After All These Years," *Fortune,* 24 May 1999; and Seanna Browder with Emily Thornton, "Reheating Starbucks" *Business Week,* 28 September 1998, 66, 68.

22. Lucy McCauley, ed., "Unit of One: Measure What Matters," *Fast Company,* May 1999, 97+.

23. Greg Burns, "It Only Hertz When Enterprise Laughs," *Business Week,* 12 December 1994, 44; Richard Teitelbaum, "The Wal-Mart of Wall Street," *Fortune,* 13 October 1997, 128-130.

24. Raymond E. Miles and Charles C. Snow, *Organizational Strategy, Structure, and Process,* (New York: McGraw-Hill, 1978).

25. Gail Edmondson, "Ultimatum at Philips," *Business Week,* 17 November 1997, 134-135.

26. Katrina Brooker, "Can Procter & Gamble Change Its Culture, Protect Its Market Share, and Find the Next Tide?" *Fortune,* 26 April 1999, 146-152.

27. Etzioni, *Modern Organizations,* 8.

28. Etzioni, *Modern Organizations,* 8; Gary D. Sandefur, "Efficiency in Social Service Organizations," *Administration and Society* 14 (1983): 449–68.

29. Richard M. Steers, *Organizational Effectiveness: A Behavioral View* (Santa Monica, Calif.: Goodyear, 1977), 51.

30. Karl E. Weick and Richard L. Daft, "The Effectiveness of Interpretation Systems," in Kim S. Cameron and David A. Whetten, eds., *Organizational Effectiveness: A Comparison of Multiple Models* (New York: Academic Press, 1982).

31. David L. Blenkhorn and Brian Gaber, "The Use of 'Warm Fuzzies' to Assess Organizational Effectiveness," *Journal of General Management,* 21, no. 2 (Winter 1995): 40–51.

32. Steven Strasser, J. D. Eveland, Gaylord Cummins, O. Lynn Deniston, and John H. Romani, "Conceptualizing the Goal and Systems Models of Organizational Effectiveness—Implications for Comparative Evaluation Research," *Journal of Management Studies* 18 (1981): 321–40.

33. James L. Price, "The Study of Organizational Effectiveness," *Sociological Quarterly* 13 (1972): 3–15.

34. McCauley, "Measure What Matters."

35. Richard H. Hall and John P. Clark, "An Ineffective Effectiveness Study and Some Suggestions for Future Research," *Sociological Quarterly* 21 (1980): 119–34; Price, "Study of Organizational Effectiveness;" Perrow, "Analysis of Goals."

36. George W. England, "Organizational Goals and Expected Behaviors in American Managers," *Academy of Management Journal* 10 (1967): 107–17.

37. Mark J. Fritsch, "Balanced Scorecard Helps Northern States Power's Quality Academy Achieve Extraordinary Performance," *Corporate University Review* (September-October 1997): 22.

38. McCauley, "Measure What Matters."

39. Katherine McIntire Peters, "High Stakes," *Government Executive* (July 1998), 16–24.

40. The discussion of the resource-based approach is based in part on Michael V. Russo and Paul A. Fouts, "A Resource-Based Perspective on Corporate Environmental Performance and Profitability," *Academy of Management Journal* 40, No. 3 (June 1997): 534-559; and Jay B. Barney, J. L. "Larry" Stempert, Loren T. Gustafson, and Yolanda Sarason, "Organizational Identity Within the Strategic Management Conversation: Contributions and Assumptions," in *Identity in Organizations: Building Theory through Conversations,* David A. Whetten and Paul C. Godfrey, eds.

(Thousand Oaks, CA: Sage Publications, 1998): 83-98.

41. Lucy McCauley, "Measure What Matters."

42. Chris Argyris, *Integrating the Individual and the Organization* (New York: Wiley, 1964); Warren G. Bennis, *Changing Organizations* (New York: McGraw-Hill, 1966); Rensis Likert, *The Human Organization* (New York: McGraw-Hill, 1967); Richard Beckhard, *Organization Development Strategies and Models* (Reading, Mass.: Addison-Wesley, 1969).

43. Cheri Ostroff and Neal Schmitt, "Configurations of Organizational Effectiveness and Efficiency," *Academy of Management Journal* 36 (1993): 1345–61; Peter J. Frost, Larry F. Moore, Meryl Reise Louis, Craig C. Lundburg, and Joanne Martin, *Organizational Culture* (Beverly Hills, Calif.: Sage, 1985).

44. J. Barton Cunningham, "Approaches to the Evaluation of Organizational Effectiveness," *Academy of Management Review* 2 (1977): 463–74; Beckhard, *Organization Development*.

45. Anne S. Tusi, "A Multiple-Constituency Model of Effectiveness: An Empirical Examination at the Human Resource Subunit Level," *Administrative Science Quarterly* 35 (1990): 458, 483; Charles Fombrun and Mark Shanley, "What's in a Name? Reputation Building and Corporate Strategy," *Academy of Management Journal* 33 (1990): 233–58; Terry Connolly, Edward J. Conlon, and Stuart Jay Deutsch, "Organizational Effectiveness: A Multiple-Constituency Approach," *Academy of Management Review* 5 (1980): 211–17.

46. Frank Friedlander and Hal Pickle, "Components of Effectiveness in Small Organizations," *Administrative Science Quarterly* 13 (1968): 289–304.

47. Kim S. Cameron, "The Effectiveness of Ineffectiveness," in Barry M. Staw and L. L. Cummings, eds., *Research in Organizational Behavior* (Greenwich, Conn.: JAI Press, 1984), 235–86; Rosabeth Moss Kanter and Derick Brinkerhoff, "Organizational Performance: Recent Developments in Measurement," *Annual Review of Sociology* 7 (1981): 321–49.

48. Tusi, "A Multiple-Constituency Model of Effectiveness."

49. Fombrun and Shanley, "What's in a Name?"

50. Martha Brannigan and Joseph B. White, "Why Delta Air Lines Decided It Was Time for CEO to Take Off," *The Wall Street Journal*, 30 May 1997, A1, A8; and Alex Taylor III, "Pulling Delta Out of Its Dive," *Fortune*, 7 December 1998, 156-164.

51. Robert E. Quinn and John Rohrbaugh, "A Spatial Model of Effectiveness Criteria: Toward a Competing Values Approach to Organizational Analysis," *Management Science* 29 (1983): 363–77.

52. Regina M. O'Neill and Robert E. Quinn, "Editor's Note: Applications of the Competing Values Framework," *Human Resource Management* 32 (Spring 1993): 1–7.

53. Robert E. Quinn and Kim Cameron, "Organizational Life Cycles and Shifting Criteria of Effectiveness: Some Preliminary Evidence," *Management Science* 29 (1983): 33–51.

Fundamentals of Organization Structure

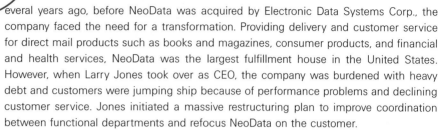

A LOOK INSIDE

NeoData

*S*everal years ago, before NeoData was acquired by Electronic Data Systems Corp., the company faced the need for a transformation. Providing delivery and customer service for direct mail products such as books and magazines, consumer products, and financial and health services, NeoData was the largest fulfillment house in the United States. However, when Larry Jones took over as CEO, the company was burdened with heavy debt and customers were jumping ship because of performance problems and declining customer service. Jones initiated a massive restructuring plan to improve coordination between functional departments and refocus NeoData on the customer.

The functional structure had previously worked well and allowed NeoData to grow to a 5,000-employee company with $240 million in revenues. But the company had become so large and departmentalized that an employee at the beginning of the fulfillment process had no idea what was going on at the other stages. The telemarketing operation, lettershop, warehouses, and distribution centers were physically and intellectually separated from one another, and clients felt that their business was lost in a gigantic shuffle. Jones's solution was to shift to a divisional structure and use cross-functional teams within each division. He restructured NeoData into three operating units, divided according to the type of industries they serve, and a separate international division. The Publishing Division focused on books and magazines, as well as online publishing; the Consumer Products Division dealt with consumer products companies such as Philip Morris; and the Services Division offered fulfillment for the telecommunications, financial services, and health care industries. The international division, based in Limerick, Ireland, handled all overseas clients. Within each division, Customer Service Center teams performed all of the services for one large client or several small clients. Employees became part of a team effort to provide a complete service rather than being committed only to lettershop or printing, for example.[1] Having teams focused on getting to know and understand the needs of customers helped NeoData transform its relationship with clients and improve its financial health, thus making it more attractive when EDS was looking for an acquisition to round out its Centrobe division, which provides integrated customer care solutions.

The problem Larry Jones encountered at NeoData was one of structural design. Coordination and communication among functional departments was poor and customers were dissatisfied with the level of service that resulted. Jones wanted to strengthen horizontal communication and get everyone focused on the customer.

Nearly every firm undergoes reorganization at some point, and today many companies are almost continuously changing and reorganizing to meet new challenges. Structural changes are needed to reflect new strategies or respond to changes in other contingency factors introduced in Chapter 2: environment, technology, size and life cycle, and culture. For example, at NeoData, a new structure was needed primarily because the company had reached the stage of its life cycle during which it grew so large and departmentalized that horizontal coordination began to suffer.

PURPOSE OF THIS CHAPTER

This chapter introduces basic concepts of organization structure and shows how to design structure as it appears on the organization chart. First we will define structure and provide an overview of structural design. Then, an information processing perspective explains how to design vertical and horizontal linkages to provide needed information flow. The chapter will next present basic design options, followed by strategies for grouping organizational activities into functional, divisional, matrix, horizontal, or hybrid structures. The final section will examine how the application of basic structures depends on the organization's situation and will outline the symptoms of structural misalignment.

ORGANIZATION STRUCTURE

The three key components in the definition of **organization structure** are:

1. Organization structure designates formal reporting relationships, including the number of levels in the hierarchy and the span of control of managers and supervisors.
2. Organization structure identifies the grouping together of individuals into departments and of departments into the total organization.
3. Organization structure includes the design of systems to ensure effective communication, coordination, and integration of effort across departments.[2]

These three elements of structure pertain to both vertical and horizontal aspects of organizing. For example, the first two elements are the structural *framework*, which is the vertical hierarchy.[3] The third element pertains to the pattern of *interactions* among organizational employees. An ideal structure encourages employees to provide horizontal information and coordination where and when it is needed.

Organization structure is reflected in the organization chart. It isn't possible to "see" the internal structure of an organization the way we might see its manufacturing tools, offices, or products. Although we might see employees going about their duties, performing different tasks, and working in different locations, the only way to actually see the structure underlying all this activity is through the organization chart. The organization chart is the visual representation of a whole set of underlying activities and processes in an organization. Exhibit 3.1 shows a sample organization chart. The organization chart can be quite useful in understanding how a company works. It shows the various parts of an organization, how they are interrelated, and how each position and department fits into the whole.

The concept of an organization chart, showing what positions exist, how they are grouped, and who reports to whom, has been around for centuries.[4] For example, diagrams outlining church hierarchy can be found in medieval churches in Spain. However, the use of the organization chart for business stems largely from the Industrial Revolution. As we discussed in Chapter 1, as work grew more complex and was performed by greater and greater numbers of workers, there was a pressing need to develop ways of managing and controlling organizations. The growth of the railroads provides an example. After the collision of two passenger trains in Massachusetts in 1841, the public demanded better control of the operation. As a result, the board of directors of the Western

EXHIBIT 3.1   *A Sample Organization Chart*

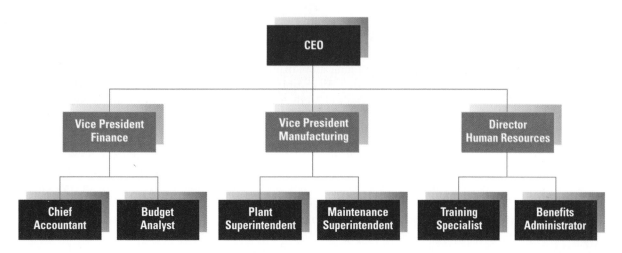

Railroad took steps to outline "definite responsibilities for each phase of the company's business, drawing solid lines of authority and command for the railroad's administration, maintenance, and operation."[5]

The type of organization structure that grew out of these efforts in the late nineteenth and early twentieth centuries was one in which the CEO was placed at the top and everyone else was arranged in layers down below, as illustrated in Exhibit 3.1. The thinking and decision making is done by those at the top, and the physical work is performed by employees who are organized into distinct, functional departments. This structure was quite effective and became entrenched in the business world for most of the twentieth century. However, this type of vertical structure is not always effective, particularly in rapidly changing environments. Over the years, organizations have developed other structural designs, many of them aimed at increasing horizontal coordination and communication and encouraging adaptation to external changes. This chapter will examine four basic structural designs and show how they are reflected in the organization chart.

INFORMATION-PROCESSING PERSPECTIVE ON STRUCTURE

The organization should be designed to provide both vertical and horizontal information flow as necessary to accomplish the organization's overall goals. If the structure doesn't fit the information requirements of the organization, people will have either too little information or will spend time processing information that is not vital to their tasks, thus reducing effectiveness.[6] However, there is an inherent tension between vertical and horizontal mechanisms in an organization. Whereas vertical linkages are designed primarily for control, horizontal linkages are designed for coordination and collaboration, which usually means reducing control.

Organizations can choose whether to orient toward a traditional organization designed for efficiency, which emphasizes vertical communication and control, or toward a contemporary learning organization, which emphasizes horizontal communication and coordination. Exhibit 3.2 compares organizations designed for efficiency with those designed for learning. An emphasis on efficiency and control is associated with specialized tasks, hierarchy of authority, rules and regulations, formal reporting systems, few teams or task forces, and centralized decision making. Emphasis on learning is associated with shared tasks, relaxed hierarchy and few rules, face-to-face communication, many teams and task forces, and informal, decentralized decision making. All organizations need a mix of vertical and horizontal linkages. Managers have to find the right balance to fit the organization's needs.

VERTICAL INFORMATION LINKAGES

Organization design should facilitate the communication among employees and departments that is necessary to accomplish the organization's overall task. *Linkage* is defined as the extent of communication and coordination among organizational elements. **Vertical linkages** are used to coordinate activities between the top and bottom of an organization and are designed primarily for control of the organization. Employees at lower levels should carry out activities consistent with top-level goals, and top executives must be informed of activities and accomplishments at the lower levels. Organizations may use any of a variety of structural devices to achieve vertical linkage, including hierarchical referral, rules, plans, and formal management information systems.[7]

Hierarchical Referral. The first vertical device is the hierarchy, or chain of command, which is illustrated by the vertical lines in Exhibit 3.1. If a problem arises that employees don't know how to solve, it can be referred up to the next level in the hierarchy. When the problem is solved, the answer is passed back down to lower levels. The lines of the organization chart act as communication channels.

Rules and Plans. The next linkage device is the use of rules and plans. To the extent that problems and decisions are repetitive, a rule or procedure can be established so employees know how to respond without communicating directly with their manager. Rules provide a standard information source enabling employees to be coordinated without actually communicating about every job. A plan also provides standing information for employees. The most widely used plan is the budget. With carefully designed budget plans, employees at lower levels can be left on their own to perform activities within their resource allotment.

EXHIBIT 3.2   *The Relationship of Organization Design to Efficiency vs. Learning Outcomes*

Vertical Information Systems. Vertical information systems are another strategy for increasing vertical information capacity. **Vertical information systems** include the periodic reports, written information, and computer-based communications distributed to managers. Information systems make communication up and down the hierarchy more efficient. Cisco Systems has turned vertical information systems into a competitive advantage by using the Internet in virtually every aspect of its operations. Larry Carter, Cisco's CFO, can call up the company's revenues, profit margins, and order information from the previous day with just a few mouse clicks. Financial data that once took weeks to gather are collected and organized automatically.[8]

Managers may use a variety of these mechanisms to provide vertical linkage and control. The other major issue in organizing is horizontal linkages for coordination and collaboration.

HORIZONTAL INFORMATION LINKAGES

Horizontal communication overcomes barriers between departments and provides opportunities for coordination among employees to achieve unity of effort and organizational objectives. **Horizontal linkage** refers to the amount of communication and coordination horizontally across organizational departments. Its importance was discovered by Lee Iacocca when he took over Chrysler Corporation.

> What I found at Chrysler were thirty-five vice presidents, each with his own turf. . . . I couldn't believe, for example, that the guy running engineering departments wasn't in constant touch with his counterpart in manufacturing. But that's how it was. Everybody worked independently. I took one look at that system and I almost threw up. That's when I knew I was in really deep trouble.
>
> . . . Nobody at Chrysler seemed to understand that interaction among the different functions in a company is absolutely critical. People in engineering and manufacturing almost have to be sleeping together. These guys weren't even flirting![9]

During his tenure at Chrysler (now DaimlerChrysler), Iacocca pushed horizontal coordination to a high level. Everyone working on a specific vehicle project—designers, engineers, and manufacturers, as well as representatives from marketing, finance, purchasing, and even outside suppliers—worked together on a single floor so they could constantly communicate. Ford and General Motors have also enhanced horizontal communication and coordination through mechanisms such as teams, task forces, and information systems.

Horizontal linkage mechanisms often are not drawn on the organization chart, but nevertheless are part of organization structure. The following devices are structural alternatives that can improve horizontal coordination and information flow.[10] Each device enables people to exchange information.

Information Systems. A significant method of providing horizontal linkage in today's organizations is the use of cross-functional information systems. Computerized information systems can enable managers or front-line workers throughout the organization to routinely exchange information about problems, opportunities, activities, or decisions. For example, at Ford, every car and truck model has its own internal Web site to track design, production, quality control, and delivery processes. Ford's product-development system is updated hourly, enabling engineers, designers, suppliers, and other employees around the world to work from the same data, keeping the process moving and saving time and money.[11]

Direct Contact. A higher level of horizontal linkage is direct contact between managers or employees affected by a problem. One way to promote direct contact is to create a special **liaison role**. A liaison person is located in one department but has the responsibility for communicating and achieving coordination with another department. Liaison roles often exist between engineering and manufacturing departments because engineering has to develop and test products to fit the limitations of manufacturing facilities. Monsanto Co. found another way to use direct contact. To get the R&D and commercial staffs working together, Monsanto pairs a scientist with a marketing or financial specialist as co-managers. For example, Frederick Perlak, a noted geneticist, and Kevin Holloway, with a background in marketing and human resources, oversee the global cotton team as co-directors. They work in adjoining cubicles, share a secretary, spend hours talking with one another, and together make all the key decisions about Monsanto's global cotton business. Monsanto hopes this unique mechanism, known internally as *two in the box*, will help transform the company from a chemical conglomerate into a life-sciences powerhouse.[12]

Task Forces. Direct contact and liaison roles usually link only two departments. When linkage involves several departments, a more complex device such as a task force is required. A **task force** is a temporary committee composed of representatives from each department affected by a problem.[13] Each member represents the interest of a department and can carry information from the meeting back to that department.

Task forces are an effective horizontal linkage device for temporary issues. They solve problems by direct horizontal coordination and reduce the information load on the vertical hierarchy. Typically, they are disbanded after their tasks are accomplished.

Commercial Casework, a $10 million woodworking and cabinetry shop in Fremont, California, used a task force to research and design the company's bonus plan. The U.S. Department of Defense set up a task force to reengineer its cumbersome travel system and make it cheaper, more efficient, and more customer friendly. The task force reduced the steps in the pretravel process from thirteen to only four. Another task force brought together employees from various functional departments to tackle the issue of how to simplify the Defense Department's travel regulations. Within three months, 230 pages of regulations had been reduced to a 16-page pamphlet.[14]

Full-time Integrator. A stronger horizontal linkage device is to create a full-time position or department solely for the purpose of coordination. A **full-time integrator** frequently has a title, such as product manager, project manager, program manager, or brand manager. Unlike the liaison person described earlier, the integrator does not report to one of the functional departments being coordinated. He or she is located outside the departments and has the responsibility for coordinating several departments.

The brand manager for Planters Peanuts, for example, coordinates the sales, distribution, and advertising for that product. General Motors set up brand managers who are responsible for marketing and sales strategies for each of GM's new models.[15]

The integrator can also be responsible for an innovation or change project, such as developing the design, financing, and marketing of a new product. An organization chart that illustrates the location of project managers for new product development is shown in Exhibit 3.3. The project managers are drawn to the side to indicate their separation from other departments. The arrows indicate project members assigned to the new product development. New Product A, for example, has a financial accountant assigned to keep track of costs and budgets. The engineering member provides design advice, and purchasing and manufacturing members represent their areas. The project manager is responsible for the entire project. He or she sees that the new product is completed on time, is introduced to the market, and achieves other project goals. The horizontal lines in Exhibit 3.3 indicate that project managers do not have formal authority over team members with respect to giving pay raises, hiring, or firing. Formal authority rests with the managers of the functional departments, who have formal authority over subordinates.

Integrators need excellent people skills. Integrators in most companies have a lot of responsibility but little authority. The integrator has to use expertise and persuasion to achieve coordination. He or she spans the boundary between departments and must be able to get people together, maintain their trust, confront problems, and resolve conflicts and disputes in the interest of the organization.[16] American Standard Companies dramatically improved the efficiency and effectiveness of its chinaware division, which makes toilets and bidets, with the use of full-time integrators.

EXHIBIT 3.3   *Project Manager Location in the Structure*

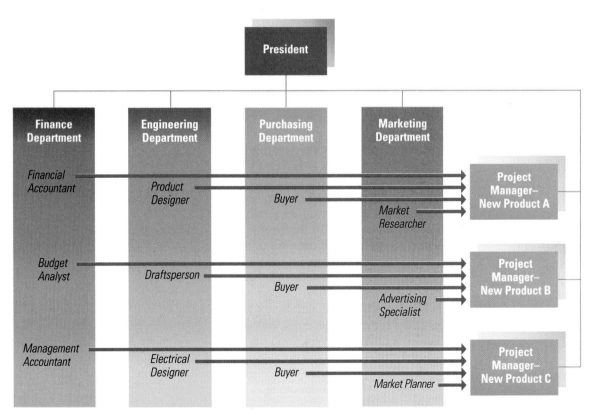

American Standard Companies

Hugh J. Hoffman began working at American Standard as a ceramic engineer in 1970. Today, he's a key player in the turnaround of American Standard's U.S. chinaware business. Hoffman, whose official title is Process Owner, Chinaware Order Fulfillment, works as a full-time integrator, coordinating all the activities that ensure that American Standard's factories fill customer orders and deliver them on time. Hoffman's job requires that he think about everything that happens between the time an order comes in until it gets paid for, including design, manufacturing, painting, sales, shipping and receiving, and numerous other tasks. He even becomes involved in demand forecasting and helping to ensure that factories crank up capacity in the appropriate ways. Integrators such as Hoffman have to act as if they are running their own business, setting goals and developing strategies for achieving them. It isn't always easy because Hoffman works outside the boundaries and authority structure of traditional departments. His years of expertise and good people skills help him motivate others and coordinate the work of many departments and geographically dispersed factories. "I move behind the scenes," Hoffman says. "I understand the workings of the company and know how to get things done."[17]

The primary goal of American Standard's integrators or process owners is to help the company do things faster, better, and cheaper than competitors. The approach is working—sales of American Standard's U.S. plumbing products surged to $465 million in 1998, thanks largely to faster and more reliable delivery of products. The use of integrators like Hoffman has helped the company achieve the highest customer order fill rates in the U.S. market. American Standard recently expanded its worldwide Process Organization training initiative, reflecting its commitment to the concept of using process owners to improve business operations. In addition, American Standard encourages managers to move around within the company in order to broaden their experience and develop the expertise and skills needed to become effective integrators.[18]

Teams. Project teams tend to be the strongest horizontal linkage mechanism. **Teams** are permanent task forces and are often used in conjunction with a full-time integrator. When activities among departments require strong coordination over a long period of time, a cross-functional team is often the solution. Special project teams may be used when organizations have a large-scale project, a major innovation, or a new product line.

Boeing used around 250 teams to design and manufacture the 777 aircraft. Some teams were created around sections of the plane, such as the wing, cockpit, or engines, while others were developed to serve specific customers, such as United Airlines or British Airways. Boeing's teams had to be tightly integrated and coordinated to accomplish this massive project. Even the U.S. Department of the Navy has discovered the power of cross-functional teams to improve horizontal coordination and increase productivity.[19]

The Rodney Hunt Company develops, manufactures, and markets heavy industrial equipment and uses teams to coordinate each product line across the manufacturing, engineering, and marketing departments. These teams are illustrated by the dashed lines and shaded areas in Exhibit 3.4. Members from each team meet the first thing each day as needed to resolve problems concerning customer needs, backlogs, engineering changes, scheduling conflicts, and any other problem with the product line.

EXHIBIT 3.4   *Teams Used for Horizontal Coordination at Rodney Hunt Company*

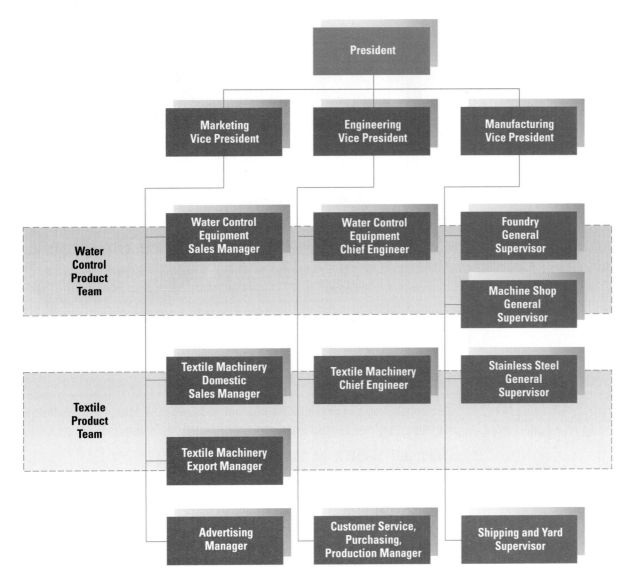

Exhibit 3.5 summarizes the mechanisms for achieving horizontal linkages. These devices represent alternatives that managers can select to increase horizontal coordination in any organization. The higher-level devices provide more horizontal information capacity, although the cost to the organization in terms of time and human resources is greater. If horizontal communication is insufficient, departments will find themselves out of synchronization and will not contribute to the overall goals of the organization. When the amount of horizontal coordination required is high, managers should select higher-level mechanisms.

EXHIBIT 3.5   *Ladder of Mechanisms for Horizontal Linkage and Coordination*

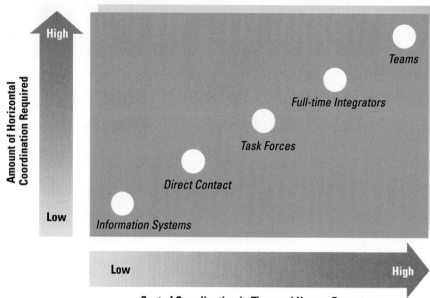

ORGANIZATION DESIGN ALTERNATIVES

The overall design of organization structure indicates three things—needed work activities, reporting relationships, and departmental groupings.

DEFINED WORK ACTIVITIES

Departments are created to perform tasks considered strategically important to the company. For example, when moving huge quantities of supplies in the Persian Gulf, the U.S. Army's logistics commander created a squad of fifteen soldiers called Ghostbusters who were charged with getting out among the troops, identifying logistics problems, and seeing that the problems got fixed. Richard H. Brown, CEO of Electronic Data Systems Corp. (EDS), has set a priority on reviving growth by helping companies launch e-commerce setups. Thus, Brown created an E-Business Solutions department to focus on the new business.[20] Defining a specific department is a way to accomplish tasks deemed valuable by the organization to accomplish its goals.

REPORTING RELATIONSHIPS

Reporting relationships, often called the chain of command, are represented by vertical lines on an organization chart. The chain of command should be an unbroken line of authority that links all persons in an organization and shows who reports to whom. In a large organization like EDS or Ford Motor Company, one hundred or more charts are required to identify reporting relationships among thousands of employees. The definition of departments and the drawing of reporting relationships defines how employees are to be grouped into departments.

DEPARTMENTAL GROUPING OPTIONS

Options for departmental grouping, including functional grouping, divisional grouping, multifocused grouping, and horizontal grouping, are illustrated in Exhibit 3.6. **Departmental grouping** affects employees because they share a common supervisor and common resources, are jointly responsible for performance, and

EXHIBIT 3.6   *Structural Design Options for Grouping Employees into Departments*

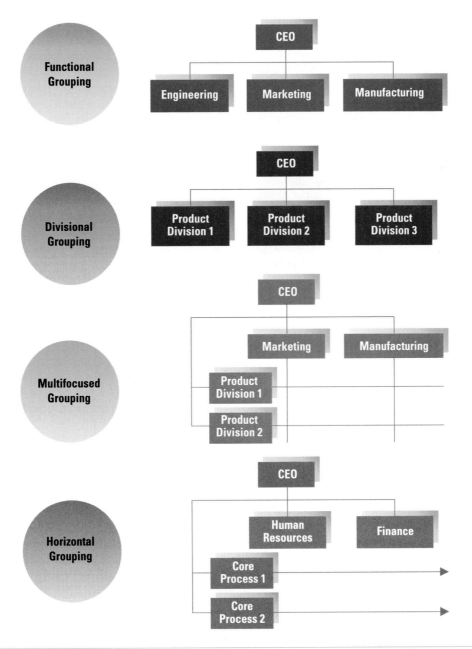

Source: Adapted from David Nadler and Michael Tushman, *Strategic Organization Design* (Glenview, Ill.: Scott Foresman, 1988), 68.

tend to identify and collaborate with one another.[21] For example, at Albany Ladder Company, the credit manager was shifted from the finance department to the marketing department. By being grouped with marketing, the credit manager started working with sales people to increase sales, thus becoming more liberal with credit than when he was located in the finance department.

Functional grouping places employees together who perform similar functions or work processes or who bring similar knowledge and skills to bear. For example, all marketing people would work together under the same supervisor, as would manufacturing and engineering people. All people associated with the assembly process for generators would be grouped together in one department. All chemists may be grouped in a department different from biologists because they represent different disciplines.

Divisional grouping means people are organized according to what the organization produces. All people required to produce toothpaste—including the marketing, manufacturing, and salespeople—are grouped together under one executive. In huge corporations such as EDS, some product or service lines may represent independent businesses, such as A. T. Kearney (management consulting), Centrobe (providing integrated customer care services), and Wendover Financial Services.

Multifocused grouping means an organization embraces two structural grouping alternatives simultaneously. These structural forms are often called *matrix* or *hybrid*. They will be discussed in more detail later in this chapter. An organization may need to group by function and product division simultaneously or perhaps by product division and geography.

Horizontal grouping means employees are organized around core work processes, the end-to-end work, information, and material flows that provide value directly to customers. All the people who work on a core process are brought together in a group rather than being separated into functional departments. For example, at field offices of the Occupational Safety and Health Administration, teams of workers representing various functions respond to complaints from American workers regarding health and safety issues, rather than having the work divided up among specialized workers.[22]

The organizational forms described in Exhibit 3.6 provide the overall options within which the organization chart is drawn and the detailed structure is designed. Each structural design alternative has significant strengths and weaknesses, to which we now turn.

FUNCTIONAL, DIVISIONAL, AND GEOGRAPHICAL DESIGNS

Functional grouping and divisional grouping are the two most common approaches to structural design.

FUNCTIONAL STRUCTURE

In a **functional structure**, activities are grouped together by common function from the bottom to the top of the organization. All engineers are located in the engineering department, and the vice president of engineering is responsible for all engineering activities. The same is true in marketing, research and development, and manufacturing. An example of the functional organization structure was shown in Exhibit 3.1 earlier in this chapter.

With a functional structure, all human knowledge and skills with respect to specific activities are consolidated, providing a valuable depth of knowledge for the organization. This structure is most effective when in-depth expertise is critical to meeting organizational goals, when the organization needs to be controlled and coordinated through the vertical hierarchy, and when efficiency is important. The structure can be quite effective is there is little need for horizontal coordination. Exhibit 3.7 summarizes the strengths and weaknesses of the functional structure.

One strength of the functional structure is that it promotes economy of scale within functions. Economy of scale means all employees are located in the same place and can share facilities. Producing all products in a single plant, for example, enables the plant to acquire the latest machinery. Constructing only one facility instead of separate facilities for each product line reduces duplication and waste. The functional structure also promotes in-depth skill development of employees. Employees are exposed to a range of functional activities within their own department.[23]

The main weakness of the functional structure is a slow response to environmental changes that require coordination across departments. The vertical hierarchy becomes overloaded. Decisions pile up, and top managers do not respond fast enough. Other disadvantages of the functional structure are that innovation is slow because of poor coordination, and each employee has a restricted view of overall goals.

Consider how the functional structure provides the coordination Blue Bell Creameries needs.

In Practice 3.2

Blue Bell Creameries, Inc.

Within seconds, the old-timer on the radio had taken listeners out of their bumper-to-bumper Houston world and placed them gently in Brenham, Texas, with its rolling hills and country air, in the era when the town got its first traffic light.

"You know," he said, "that's how Blue Bell Ice Cream is. Old-fashioned, uncomplicated, homemade good." He paused. "It's all made in that little creamery in Brenham."

EXHIBIT 3.7   *Strengths and Weaknesses of Functional Organization Structure*

Strengths
1. Allows economies of scale within functional departments
2. Enables in-depth knowledge and skill development
3. Enables organization to accomplish functional goals
4. Is best with only one or a few products

Weaknesses
1. Slow response time to environmental changes
2. May cause decisions to pile on top, hierarchy overload
3. Leads to poor horizontal coordination among departments
4. Results in less innovation
5. Involves restricted view of organizational goals

Source: Adapted from Robert Duncan, "What Is the Right Organization Structure? Decision Tree Analysis Provides the Answer," *Organizational Dynamics* (Winter 1979): 429.

That little creamery isn't little anymore, but the desire for first-quality homemade ice cream is stronger than when Blue Bell started in 1907. Today, Blue Bell has more than eight hundred employees and will sell over $160 million in ice cream. The company has an unbelievable 60 percent share of the ice cream market in Houston, Dallas, and San Antonio—Texas's three largest cities.

The company cannot meet the demand for Blue Bell Ice Cream. It doesn't even try. Top managers recently decided to expand slowly into Louisiana and Oklahoma. Management refuses to compromise quality by expanding into regions that cannot be adequately serviced or by growing so fast that it can't adequately train employees in the art of making ice cream.

Blue Bell's major departments are sales, quality control, production, maintenance, and distribution. There is also an accounting department and a small research and development group. Product changes are infrequent because the orientation is toward tried-and-true products. The environment is stable. The customer base is well established. The only change has been the increase in demand for Blue Bell Ice Cream.

Blue Bell's quality control department tests all incoming ingredients and ensures that only the best products go into its ice cream. Quality control also tests outgoing ice cream products. After years of experience, quality inspectors can taste the slightest deviation from expected quality. It's no wonder Blue Bell has successfully maintained the image of a small-town creamery making homemade ice cream.[24]

The functional structure is just right for Blue Bell Creameries. The organization has chosen to stay medium-sized and focus on making a single product—quality ice cream. However, as Blue Bell expands, it may have problems coordinating across departments, requiring stronger horizontal linkage mechanisms.

FUNCTIONAL STRUCTURE WITH HORIZONTAL LINKAGES

Today, there is a shift toward flatter, more horizontal structures because of the challenges introduced in Chapter 1. Very few of today's successful companies can maintain a strictly functional structure. Organizations compensate for the vertical functional hierarchy by installing horizontal linkages, as described earlier in this chapter. Managers improve horizontal coordination by using information systems, direct contact between departments, full-time integrators or project managers (illustrated in Exhibit 3.3), task forces, or teams (illustrated in 3.4). Not-for-profit organizations are also recognizing the importance of horizontal linkages. One interesting use of horizontal linkages occurred at Karolinska Hospital in Stockholm, Sweden, which had 47 functional departments. Even after top executives cut that down to eleven, coordination was still woefully inadequate. The team set about reorganizing workflow at the hospital around patient care. Instead of bouncing a patient from department to department, Karolinska now envisions the illness to recovery period as a process with pit stops in admissions, X-ray, surgery, and so forth. The most interesting aspect of the approach is the new position of nurse coordinator. Nurse coordinators serve as full-time integrators, looking for situations where the baton is dropped in the handoff within or between departments. The improved horizontal coordination dramatically improved productivity and patient care at Karolinska.[25] Karolinska is effectively using horizontal linkages to overcome some of the disadvantages of the functional structure.

DIVISIONAL STRUCTURE

The term **divisional structure** is used here as the generic term for what is sometimes called a *product structure* or *strategic business units*. With this structure, divisions can be organized according to individual products, services, product groups, major projects or programs, divisions, businesses, or profit centers. The distinctive feature of a divisional structure is that grouping is based on organizational outputs.

The difference between a divisional structure and a functional structure is illustrated in Exhibit 3.8. The functional structure can be redesigned into separate product groups, and each group contains the functional departments of R&D, manufacturing, accounting, and marketing. Coordination across functional departments within each product group is maximized. The divisional structure promotes flexibility and change because each unit is smaller and can adapt to the needs of its environment. Moreover, the divisional structure decentralizes decision making, because the lines of authority converge at a lower level in the hierarchy. The functional structure, by contrast, forces decisions all the way to the top before a problem affecting several functions can be resolved.

Strengths and weaknesses of the divisional structure are summarized in Exhibit 3.9. The divisional organization form of structure is excellent for achieving coordination across functional departments. It works well when organizations

EXHIBIT 3.8   *Reorganization from Functional Structure to Divisional Structure at Info-Tech*

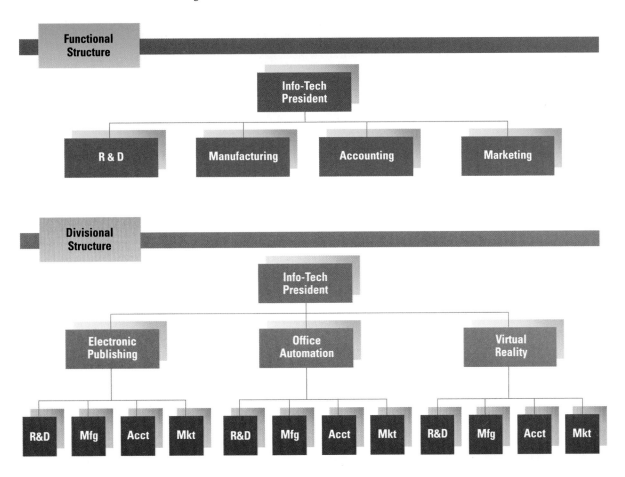

EXHIBIT 3.9   *Strengths and Weaknesses of Divisional Organization Structure*

Strengths
1. Suited to fast change in unstable environment
2. Leads to client satisfaction because product responsibility and contact points are clear
3. Involves high coordination across functions
4. Allows units to adapt to differences in products, regions, clients
5. Best in large organizations with several products
6. Decentralizes decision making

Weaknesses
1. Eliminates economies of scale in functional departments
2. Leads to poor coordination across product lines
3. Eliminates in-depth competence and technical specialization
4. Makes integration and standardization across product lines difficult

Source: Adapted from Robert Duncan, "What Is the Right Organization Structure? Decision Tree Analysis Provides the Answer," *Organization Dynamics* (Winter 1979): 431.

can no longer be adequately controlled through the traditional vertical hierarchy, and when goals are oriented toward adaptation and change. Giant, complex organizations such as General Electric, Nestlé, and Johnson & Johnson are subdivided into a series of smaller, self-contained organizations for better control and coordination. In these large companies, the units are sometimes called divisions, businesses, or strategic business units. The structure at Johnson & Johnson includes 180 separate operating units, including McNeil Consumer Products, makers of Tylenol; Ortho Pharmaceuticals, which makes Retin-A and birth control pills; and J & J Consumer Products, the company that brings us Johnson's Baby Shampoo and Band-Aids. Each division is a separately chartered, autonomous company operating under the guidance of Johnson & Johnson's corporate headquarters.[26]

At Microsoft, co-founder and chairman Bill Gates and CEO Steve Ballmer ripped apart the company's structure to create eight new divisions and give managers unprecedented authority to run things as they see fit.

In Practice 3.3

Microsoft Corp.

From the outside, Microsoft may seem to be moving at a lightning pace, but internally, complaints have been growing that things are just too darn slow. With 30,000 employees, more than 180 different products, and at least five layers of management, employees began complaining about the red tape and the snail's pace for decision making. The company has even lost a few important staffers because of the growing bureaucracy. In addition, Microsoft now faces new challenges with the U.S. Department of Justice ruling against the software giant and the merger of AOL and Time Warner, which could create a formidable Internet competitor.

So top executives are reinventing Microsoft. To be better able to respond to the rapid changes in the industry, they've created eight new divisions. The Business and Enterprise Division will focus on bringing software such as Windows 2000 to corporate customers, whereas the Home and Retail Division will handle games, home applications, children's software, and peripherals. A Business Productivity Group targets knowledge workers, developing applications like word processing, while the Sales and Support Group focuses on customer segments such as corporate accounts, Internet service providers, and small business. Other divisions include a Developer Group (creating tools used by corporate programmers), a Consumer and Commerce Group (linking merchants via the company's MSN Web portal), and a Consumer Windows Division, whose goal is to make the PC easier to use for consumers. The final division, Microsoft Research, conducts basic research on everything from speech recognition to advanced networking.

What really makes the new structure revolutionary for Microsoft is that the heads of the eight divisions are given the freedom and authority to run the businesses and spend their budgets as they see fit, provided they meet revenue and profit goals. Previously, Gates and Ballmer had been involved in every decision large and small—from deciding key features in Windows 2000 to reviewing response records for customer support lines. Managers of the divisions are charged up by the new authority and responsibility. One manager said he feels "like I am running my own little company."

"The Internet has changed everything," says Gates, so he recognizes that Microsoft must change as well. He's hoping the new structure is one step in the right direction.[27]

The divisional structure has several strengths that are of benefit to Microsoft.[28] This structure is suited to fast change in an unstable environment and provides high product visibility. Since each product is a separate division, clients are able to contact the correct division and achieve satisfaction. Coordination across functions is excellent. Each product can adapt to requirements of individual customers or regions. The divisional structure typically works best in organizations that have multiple products or services and enough personnel to staff separate functional units. At corporations like Johnson & Johnson, PepsiCo, and now Microsoft, decision making is pushed down to the lowest levels. Each division is small enough to be quick on its feet, responding rapidly to changes in the market.

One disadvantage of using divisional structuring is that the organization loses economies of scale. Instead of fifty research engineers sharing a common facility in a functional structure, ten engineers may be assigned to each of five product divisions. The critical mass required for in-depth research is lost, and physical facilities have to be duplicated for each product line. Another problem is that product lines become separate from each other, and coordination across product lines can be difficult. As one Johnson & Johnson executive said, "We have to keep reminding ourselves that we work for the same corporation."[29] There is some concern at Microsoft that the newly independent divisions might start offering products and services that conflict with one another.

Companies such as Hewlett-Packard and Xerox have a large number of divisions and have had real problems with horizontal coordination. The software division may produce programs that are incompatible with business computers sold by another division. Customers are frustrated when a sales representative from one division is unaware of developments in other divisions. Task forces and other linkage devices are needed to coordinate across divisions. A lack of technical specialization is also a problem in a divisional structure. Employees identify with the product line rather than with a functional specialty. R&D personnel, for example, tend to do applied research to benefit the product line rather than basic research to benefit the entire organization. Microsoft is avoiding this problem by creating a separate division to do basic research.

GEOGRAPHICAL STRUCTURE

Another basis for structural grouping is the organization's users or customers. The most common structure in this category is geography. Each region of the country may have distinct tastes and needs. Each geographic unit includes all functions required to produce and market products in that region. For multinational corporations, self-contained units are created for different countries and parts of the world.

Some years ago, Apple Computer reorganized from a functional to a geographical structure to facilitate manufacture and delivery of Apple computers to customers around the world. Exhibit 3.10 contains a partial organization structure illustrating the geographical thrust. Apple used this structure to focus managers and employees on specific geographical customers and sales targets. McDonald's divided its U.S. operations into five geographical divisions, each with its own president and staff functions such as human resources and legal.[30] The regional structure allows Apple and McDonald's to focus on the needs of customers in a geographical area.

The strengths and weaknesses of a geographic divisional structure are similar to the divisional organization characteristics listed in Exhibit 3.9. The organization can adapt to specific needs of its own region, and employees identify with regional goals rather than with national goals. Horizontal coordination within a region is emphasized rather than linkages across regions or to the national office.

MATRIX STRUCTURE

Sometimes, an organization's structure needs to be multifocused in that both product and function or product and geography are emphasized at the same time.

EXHIBIT 3.10 *Geographical Structure for Apple Computer*

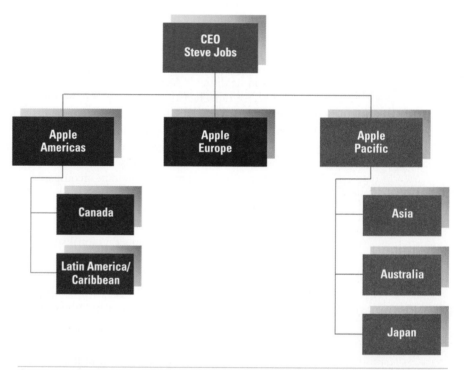

Source: Apple Computer, Inc. regions of the world. [Online] Available http://www.apple.com/find/areas.html, April 18, 2000.

One way to achieve this is through the **matrix structure**. The matrix can be used when both technical expertise and product innovation and change are important for meeting organizational goals. The matrix structure often is the answer when organizations find that neither the functional, divisional, nor geographical structures combined with horizontal linkage mechanisms will work.

The matrix is a strong form of horizontal linkage. The unique characteristic of the matrix organization is that both product division and functional structures (horizontal and vertical) are implemented simultaneously, as shown in Exhibit 3.11. The product managers and functional managers have equal authority within the organization, and employees report to both of them. The matrix structure is similar to the use of full-time integrators or product managers described earlier in this chapter (Exhibit 3.3), except that in the matrix structure the product managers (horizontal) are given formal authority equal to that of the functional managers (vertical).

CONDITIONS FOR THE MATRIX

A dual hierarchy may seem an unusual way to design an organization, but the matrix is the correct structure when the following conditions are met.[31]

EXHIBIT 3.11   *Dual-Authority Structure in a Matrix Organization*

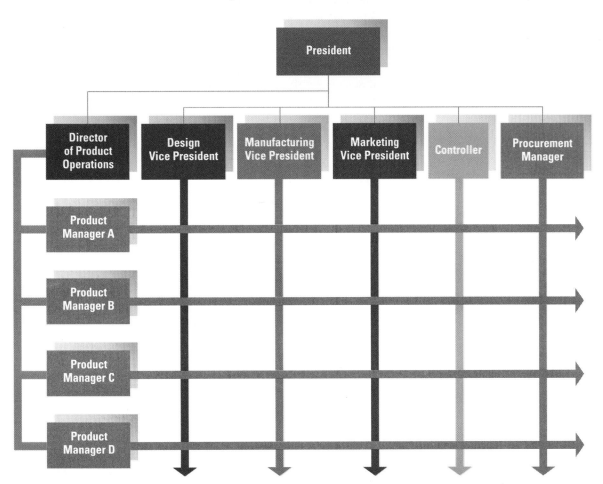

- *Condition 1.* Pressure exists to share scarce resources across product lines. The organization is typically medium-sized and has a moderate number of product lines. It feels pressure for the shared and flexible use of people and equipment across those products. For example, the organization is not large enough to assign engineers full-time to each product line, so engineers are assigned part-time to several products or projects.
- *Condition 2.* Environmental pressure exists for two or more critical outputs, such as for in-depth technical knowledge (functional structure) and frequent new products (divisional structure). This dual pressure means a balance of power is needed between the functional and product sides of the organization, and a dual-authority structure is needed to maintain that balance.
- *Condition 3.* The environmental domain of the organization is both complex and uncertain. Frequent external changes and high interdependence between departments require a large amount of coordination and information processing in both vertical and horizontal directions.

Under these three conditions, the vertical and horizontal lines of authority must be given equal recognition. A dual-authority structure is thereby created so the balance of power between them is equal.

Referring again to Exhibit 3.11, assume the matrix structure is for a clothing manufacturer. Product A is footwear, product B is outerwear, product C is sleepwear, and so on. Each product line serves a different market and customers. As a medium-size organization, the company must effectively use people from manufacturing, design, and marketing to work on each product line. There are not enough designers to warrant a separate design department for each product line, so the designers are shared across product lines. Moreover, by keeping the manufacturing, design, and marketing functions intact, employees can develop the in-depth expertise to serve all product lines efficiently.

The matrix formalizes horizontal teams along with the traditional vertical hierarchy and tries to give equal balance to both. However, the matrix may shift one way or the other. Many companies have found a balanced matrix hard to implement and maintain because one side of the authority structure often dominates. Recognizing this tendency, two variations of matrix structure have evolved—the **functional matrix** and the **product matrix**. In a functional matrix, the functional bosses have primary authority and the project or product managers simply coordinate product activities. In a product matrix, by contrast, the project or product managers have primary authority and functional managers simply assign technical personnel to projects and provide advisory expertise as needed. For many organizations, one of these approaches works better than the balanced matrix with dual lines of authority.[32]

All kinds of organizations have experimented with the matrix, including hospitals, consulting firms, banks, insurance companies, government agencies, and many types of industrial firms.[33] This structure has been used successfully by organizations such as IBM and Unilever, which fine-tuned the matrix to suit their own particular goals and culture.

STRENGTHS AND WEAKNESSES

The matrix structure is best when environmental change is high and when goals reflect a dual requirement, such as for both product and functional goals. The dual-authority structure facilitates communication and coordination to cope with rapid environmental change and enables an equal balance between product and functional bosses. The matrix facilitates discussion and adaptation to unexpected problems. It tends to work best in organizations of moderate size with a few product lines. The matrix is not needed for only a single product line, and too many product lines make it difficult to coordinate both directions at once. Exhibit 3.12 summarizes the strengths and weaknesses of the matrix structure based on what we know of organizations that use it.[34]

The strength of the matrix is that it enables an organization to meet dual demands from customers in the environment. Resources (people, equipment) can be flexibly allocated across different products, and the organization can adapt to changing external requirements.[35] This structure also provides an opportunity for employees to acquire either functional or general management skills, depending on their interests.

One disadvantage of the matrix is that some employees experience dual authority, which is frustrating and confusing. They need excellent interpersonal and conflict-resolution skills, which may require special training in human relations. The matrix also forces managers to spend a great deal of time in meetings.[36] If managers do not adapt to the information and power sharing required by the matrix, the system will not work. Managers must collaborate with one another rather than rely on vertical authority in decision making. The successful implementation of one matrix structure occurred at a steel company in Pittsburgh.

In Practice 3.4

Worldwide Steel

As far back as anyone could remember, the steel industry in the United States was stable and certain. If steel manufacturers could produce quality steel at a reasonable price, that steel would be sold. However, in the 1970s and 1980s, inflation, a national economic downturn, reduced consumption of autos, and competition from steelmakers in Germany and Japan forever changed the steel industry. Steelmakers shifted to specialized steel products. They had to market aggressively, make efficient use of internal resources, and adapt to rapid-fire changes.

Worldwide Steel employed 2,500 people, made 300,000 tons of steel a year, and was 170 years old. For 160 of those years, functional structure worked fine. As the environment became more turbulent and competitive, however, Worldwide Steel managers realized they were not keeping up. Fifty percent of Worldwide's orders were behind schedule. Profits were eroded by labor, material, and energy cost increases. Market share declined.

In consultation with outside experts, the president of Worldwide Steel saw that the company had to walk a tightrope. It had to specialize in a few high-value-added products tailored for separate markets, while maintaining economies of scale and sophisticated technology within functional departments. The dual pressure led to an unusual solution for a steel company: a matrix structure.

Worldwide Steel had four product lines: open-die forgings, ring-mill products, wheels and axles, and steelmaking. A business manager was given responsibility and authority of each line, which included preparing a business plan for each product line and developing targets for production costs, product inventory, shipping dates, and gross profit. They were given authority to meet those targets and to make their lines profitable. Functional vice presidents were responsible for technical decisions relating to their function. Functional managers were expected to stay abreast of the latest techniques in their areas and to keep personnel trained in new technologies that could apply to product lines. With twenty thousand recipes for specialty steels and several hundred new recipes ordered each month, functional personnel had to stay current. Two functional depart-ments—field sales and industrial relations—were not included in the matrix because they worked independently. The final design was a hybrid matrix structure with both matrix and functional relationships, as illustrated in Exhibit 3.13.

Implementation of the matrix was slow. Middle managers were confused. Meetings to coordinate across functional departments seemed to be held every day. After about a year of training by external consultants, Worldwide Steel was on track. Ninety percent of the orders were now delivered on time and market share recovered. Both productivity and profitability increased steadily. The managers thrived on matrix involvement. Meetings to coordinate product and functional decisions provided a growth experience. Middle managers began including younger managers in the matrix discussions as train-ing for future management responsibility.[37]

This example illustrates the correct use of a matrix structure. The dual pressure to maintain economies of scale and to market four product lines gave equal empha-sis to the functional and product hierarchies. Through continuous meetings for coordination, Worldwide Steel achieved both economies of scale and flexibility.

HORIZONTAL STRUCTURE

The most recent approach to organizing is the **horizontal structure**, which organizes employees around core processes. All the people who work on a par-ticular process are brought together so that they can easily communicate and coordinate their efforts and provide value directly to customers. The horizon-tal structure virtually eliminates both the vertical hierarchy and old depart-mental boundaries. Many of today's organizations are striving to reduce boundaries both within the organization and with other companies, as described in this chapter's Book Mark. The horizontal structure is largely a response to the profound changes that have occurred in the workplace and the

EXHIBIT 3.12   *Strengths and Weaknesses of Matrix Organization Structure*

Strengths
1. Achieves coordination necessary to meet dual demands from customers
2. Flexible sharing of human resources across products
3. Suited to complex decisions and frequent changes in unstable environment
4. Provides opportunity for both functional and product skill development
5. Best in medium-sized organizations with multiple products

Weaknesses
1. Causes participants to experience dual authority, which can be frustrating and confusing
2. Means participants need good interpersonal skills and extensive training
3. Is time-consuming; involves frequent meetings and conflict resolution sessions
4. Will not work unless participants understand it and adopt collegial rather than vertical-type relationships
5. Requires great effort to maintain power balance

Source: Adapted from Robert Duncan, "What Is the Right Organization Structure? Decision Tree Analysis Provides the Answer," *Organizational Dynamics* (Winter 1979): 429.

EXHIBIT 3.13   *Matrix Structure for Worldwide Steel*

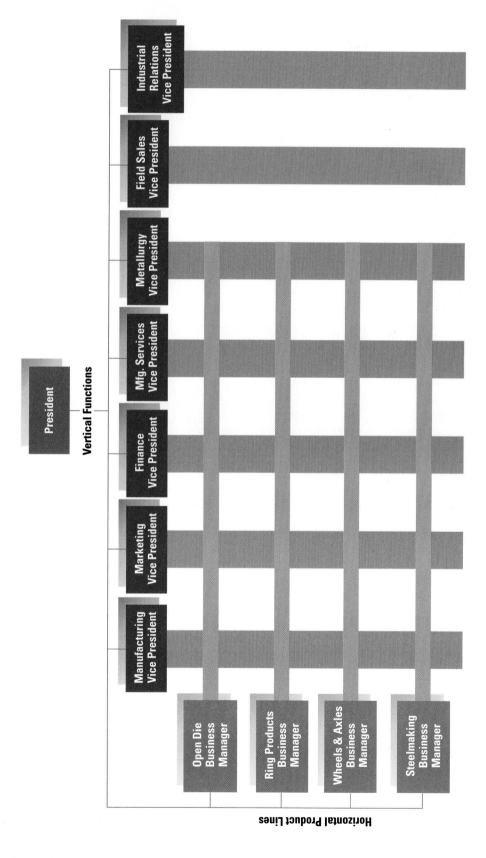

$\mathcal{B}$ook $\mathcal{M}$ark 3.0

The Boundaryless Organization: Breaking the Chains of Organizational Structure

By Ron Ashkenas, Dave Ulrich, Todd Jick, and Steve Kerr

The authors of this book argue that fluid boundaries both within and between organizations are necessary to achieve the speed, flexibility, integration, and innovation critical to company success. Managers must become "boundary-aware" and learn new leadership skills to find the right balance of permeability for their organizations. Two chapters on creating permeable boundaries between organizations are particularly useful because these boundaries are the least understood by most managers. *The Boundaryless Organization* uses case studies of well-known companies such as General Electric and SmithKline Beecham to illustrate the importance of creating boundaryless behavior in four essential areas.

FOUR BOUNDARIES THAT BLOCK SUCCESS

The authors describe four types of boundaries, examine the impact of each, and offer questionnaires, checklists, and mini-models that can help managers create cross-boundary linkages.

- *Vertical boundaries.* Four critical dimensions required to span vertical boundaries are information sharing, building competence, delegating authority, and distributing rewards.
- *Horizontal boundaries.* The best way to permeate horizontal boundaries is by focusing on the customer;

teams should be formed and re-formed as needed to serve customers.
- *External boundaries.* To create essential relationships with customers, suppliers, regulators, and other organizations, companies can determine where opportunities exist for collaboration and align and integrate systems, structure, and processes.
- *Geographic boundaries.* To attain globalization, companies must be committed to spanning geographic boundaries, identifying challenges and opportunities in the international marketplace, and recalibrating human resource practices and other organizational systems and processes.

CONCLUSION

The authors acknowledge that boundaries are necessary and will always exist, but they argue that traditional boundaries within and between organizations are dysfunctional in today's complex world. As the authors put it: "Boundaryless behavior is not about eliminating all administrative procedures and rules. ... it is about substituting permeable structures for concrete walls."

The Boundaryless Organization, by Ron Ashkenas, Dave Ulrich, Todd Jick, and Steve Kerr, is published by Jossey-Bass.

business environment over the past fifteen to twenty years. Technological progress emphasizes computer-based integration and coordination. Customers expect faster and better service, and employees want opportunities to use their minds, learn new skills, and assume greater responsibility. Organizations mired in a vertical mindset have a hard time meeting these challenges. Thus, numerous organizations have experimented with horizontal mechanisms such as cross-functional teams to achieve coordination across departments or task forces to accomplish temporary projects. Increasingly, organizations are shifting away from hierarchical, function-based structures to structures based on horizontal processes.

CHARACTERISTICS

A horizontal structure is illustrated in Exhibit 3.14 and has the following characteristics:[38]

- Structure is created around cross-functional core processes rather than tasks, functions, or geography. Thus, boundaries between departments are obliterated. Ford Motor Company's Customer Service Division, for example, has core process groups for business development, parts supply and logistics, vehicle service and programs, and technical support.
- Self-directed teams, not individuals, are the basis of organizational design and performance.
- Process owners have responsibility for each core process in its entirety. For Ford's parts supply and logistics process, for example, a number of teams may work on jobs such as parts analysis, purchasing, material flow, and distribution, but a process owner is responsible for coordinating the entire process.
- People on the team are given the skills, tools, motivation, and authority to make decisions central to the team's performance. Team members are cross-trained to perform one another's jobs, and the combined skills are sufficient to complete a major organizational task.
- Teams have the freedom to think creatively and respond flexibly to new challenges that arise.
- Customers drive the horizontal corporation. Effectiveness is measured by end-of-process performance objectives (based on the goal of bringing value

EXHIBIT 3.14   *A Horizontal Structure*

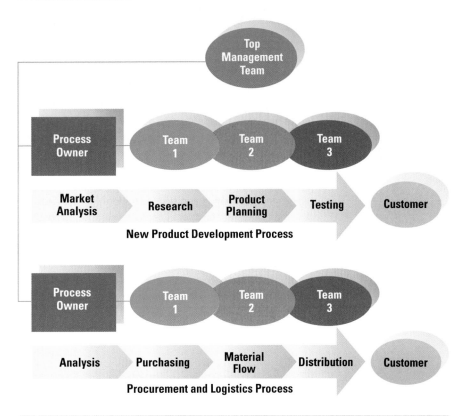

Source: Based on Frank Ostroff, *The Horizontal Organization* (New York: Oxford University Press, 1999); John A. Byrne, "The Horizontal Corporation," *Business Week,* 20 December 1993, 76–81; and Thomas A. Stewart, "The Search for the Organization of Tomorrow," *Fortune,* 18 May 1992, 92–98.

to the customer), as well as customer satisfaction, employee satisfaction, and financial contribution.
- The culture is one of openness, trust, and collaboration, focused on continuous improvement. The culture values employee empowerment, responsibility, and well being.

Experimentation with teams and horizontal organizing often begins at lower levels of the organization. Today, however, a few companies are structuring practically the entire organization horizontally, with perhaps only a few senior executives in traditional support functions such as human resources or finance. Xerox, for example, still maintains some elements of a vertical design, but below the level of executive vice president, the entire organization is structured horizontally.

In Practice 3.5

Xerox

When top executives at Xerox formulated the "Xerox 2005 Strategic Intent," they defined the company's specific goal as "a promise to provide unique value by offering leading-edge products using privileged technology that are of the highest quality and deliver total document solutions quickly and reliably." In addition, the company wanted to offer top-quality software, hardware, and service solutions backed by ongoing customer support and continuous business process improvements. Top managers believed that the only way Xerox could provide this total solution for customers was to reorganize the business into a number of horizontal, cross-functional groups based on work flows rather than functions. To restructure the company, they focused on the activities that would design and deliver value to customers.

Although the top managerial layers at Xerox remain vertical, responsibility for daily operations, marketing, customer relations, and other activities resides within horizontally aligned groups. For example, Business Groups such as Document Services, Office Document Products, Production Systems, Supplies, and Channels are "mini-businesses." Each group is made up of a number of linked multiskilled teams that focus on activities such as business planning, product design and development, manufacturing, marketing, sales, distribution, and customer support. Each set of teams is headed by a core process owner who has responsibility for the entire process. Teams are accountable for taking an idea through all the stages necessary to produce a marketable product—that is, each team has the information and skills to perform a major task that would once have been divided among separate functional departments. The Business Groups also work with horizontally aligned Customer Operations and Technology Management Groups.

The new structure at Xerox gives each group greater power to work directly with customers and suppliers, to reach out to new markets, and to become more profitable. The Business Group mini-businesses have been able to respond faster and more effectively to customer needs. For example, Xerox has launched more than 170 new products in only six years. More subtle, but just as important, are the increases in employee and customer satisfaction that Xerox has realized since implementing its new structure.[39]

STRENGTHS AND WEAKNESSES

Although Xerox has achieved impressive results with a horizontal structure, as with all structures, it has weaknesses as well as strengths. The strengths and weaknesses of the horizontal structure are listed in Exhibit 3.15.

The most significant strength of the horizontal structure is that it can dramatically increase the company's flexibility and response to changes in customer needs because of the enhanced coordination. The structure directs everyone's attention toward the customer, which leads to greater customer satisfaction as well as improvements in productivity, speed, and efficiency. In addition, because there are no boundaries between functional departments, employees take a broader view of organizational goals rather than being focused on the goals of a single department. The horizontal structure promotes an emphasis on teamwork and cooperation, such that team members share a commitment to meeting common objectives. Finally, the horizontal structure can improve the quality of life for employees by giving them opportunities to share responsibility, make decisions, and contribute significantly to the organization.

A weakness of the horizontal structure is that it can harm rather than help organizational performance unless managers carefully determine which core processes are critical for bringing value to customers. Simply defining the processes around which to organize can be difficult and time consuming. AT&T's Network Systems Division eventually counted 130 processes, then began working to pare them down to fewer than 15 core ones.[40] In addition, shifting to a horizontal structure is time consuming because it requires significant changes in culture, job design, management philosophy, and information and reward systems. Traditional managers may balk when they have to give up power and authority to serve instead as coaches and facilitators of teams. Employees have to be trained to work effectively in a team environment. Finally, because of the cross-functional nature of work, a horizontal structure can limit in-depth knowledge and skill development unless measures are taken to give employees opportunities to maintain and build technical expertise.

EXHIBIT 3.15   *Strengths and Weaknesses of Horizontal Structure*

Strengths
1. Promotes flexibility and rapid response to changes in customer needs
2. Directs the attention of everyone toward the production and delivery of value to the customer
3. Each employee has a broader view of organizational goals
4. Promotes a focus on teamwork and collaboration
5. Improves quality of life for employees by offering them the opportunity to share responsibility, make decisions, and be accountable for outcomes

Weaknesses
1. Determining core processes is difficult and time consuming
2. Requires changes in culture, job design, management philosophy, and information and reward systems
3. Traditional managers may balk when they have to give up power and authority
4. Requires significant training of employees to work effectively in a horizontal team environment
5. Can limit in-depth skill development

Sources: Based on Frank Ostroff, *The Horizontal Organization: What the Organization of the Future Looks Like and How It Delivers Value to Customers* (New York: Oxford University Press, 1999); and Richard L. Daft, *Organization Theory and Design*, 6th ed. (Cincinnati, Ohio: South-Western College Publishing, 1998), 253.

HYBRID STRUCTURE

As a practical matter, many structures in the real world do not exist in the pure forms we have outlined in this chapter. Particularly in today's complex business environment, organizations often use a **hybrid structure** that combines characteristics of various approaches tailored to specific strategic needs. Most companies combine characteristics of functional, divisional, geographical, or horizontal structures to take advantage of the strengths of various structures and to avoid some of the weaknesses. Hybrid structures tend to be used in rapidly changing environments because they offer the organization greater flexibility.

One type of hybrid that is often used is to combine characteristics of the functional and divisional structures. When a corporation grows large and has several products or markets, it typically is organized into self-contained divisions of some type. Functions that are important to each product or market are decentralized to the self-contained units. However, some functions that are relatively stable and require economies of scale and in-depth specialization are also centralized at headquarters. Sun Petroleum Products (SPPC) reorganized to a hybrid structure to be more responsive to changing markets. The new hybrid organization structure adopted by SPPC is illustrated in part 1 of Exhibit 3.16. Three major product divisions—fuels, lubricants, and chemicals—were created, each serving a different market and requiring a different strategy and management style. Each product line vice president is now in charge of all functions for that product, such as marketing, planning, supply and distribution, and manufacturing. However, activities such as human resources, legal, technology, and finance were centralized as functional departments at headquarters in order to achieve economies of scale. Each of these departments provides services for the entire organization.[41]

A second hybrid approach that is increasingly used today is to combine characteristics of functional and horizontal structures. Ford Motor Company's Customer Service Division, a global operation made up of 12,000 employees serving nearly 15,000 dealers, provides an example of this type of hybrid. Beginning in 1995, when Ford launched its "Ford 2000" initiative to become the world's leading automotive firm in the twenty-first century, top executives grew increasingly concerned about complaints regarding customer service. They decided that the horizontal model offered the best chance to gain a faster, more efficient, integrated approach to customer service. Part 2 of Exhibit 3.16 illustrates a portion of the Customer Service Division's hybrid structure. Several horizontally aligned groups, made up of multiskilled teams, focus on core processes such as parts supply and logistics (acquiring parts and getting them to dealers quickly and efficiently), vehicle service and programs (collecting and disseminating information about repair problems), and technical support (ensuring that every service department receives updated technical information). Each group has a process owner who is responsible for seeing that the teams meet overall objectives. Ford's Customer Service Division retained a functional structure for finance, strategy and communication, and human resources departments. Each of these departments provides services for the entire division.[42]

In a huge organization such as Ford, managers may use a variety of structural characteristics to meet the needs of the total organization. A hybrid structure is often preferred over the pure functional, divisional, or horizontal structure because it can provide some of the advantages of each and overcome some of the disadvantages.

EXHIBIT 3.16   *Two Hybrid Structures*

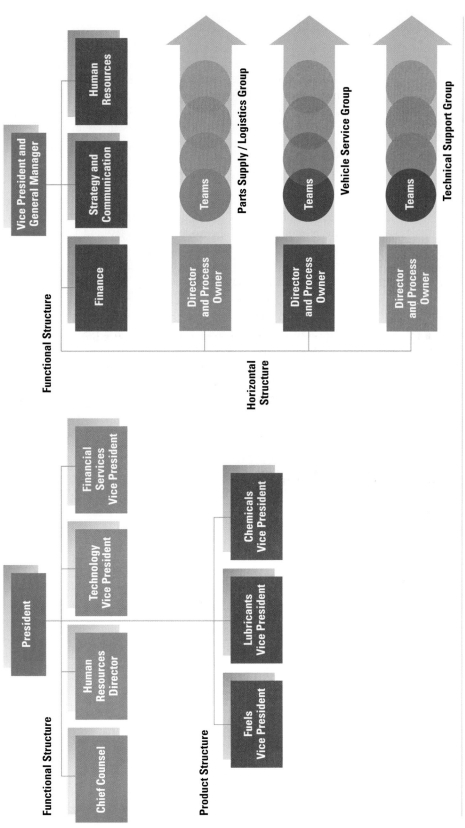

Part 1. Sun Petrochemical Products

Functional Structure

Part 2. Ford Customer Service Division

Functional Structure

Horizontal Structure

Product Structure

Sources: Based on Linda S. Ackerman, "Transition Management: An In-Depth Look at Managing Complex Change," *Organizational Dynamics* (Summer 1982): 46–66; and Frank Ostroff, *The Horizontal Organization* (New York: Oxford University Press, 1999), Fig 2.1, 34.

APPLICATIONS OF STRUCTURAL DESIGN

Each type of structure is applied in different situations and meets different needs. In describing the various structures, we touched briefly on conditions such as environmental stability or change and organizational size that are related to structure. Each form of structure—functional, divisional, matrix, horizontal, hybrid—represents a tool that can help managers make an organization more effective, depending on the demands of its situation.

STRUCTURAL CONTINGENCIES

Recall the idea of "contingencies" from Chapter 2 and that managers design the organization to fit the contingency factors. As illustrated in Exhibit 3.17, structure is influenced by environment, strategy and goals, culture, technology, and size. Of these contextual variables, the connection between competitive strategy and structure is of particular interest and has been widely studied. Structure typically reflects organizational strategy, and a change in product or market strategy

EXHIBIT 3.17   *Organization Contextual Variables that Influence Structure*

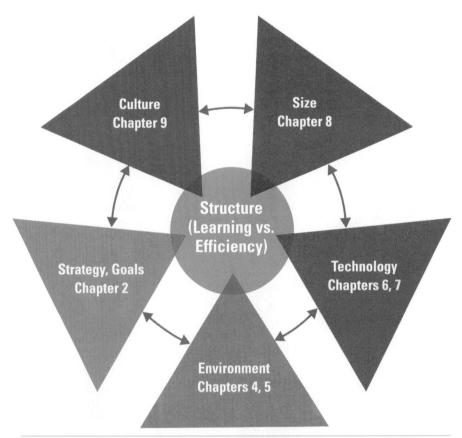

Sources: Adapted from Jay R. Galbraith, *Competing with Flexible Lateral Organizations*, 2nd ed. (Reading, Mass.: Addison-Wesley, 1994), ch. 1; Jay R. Galbraith, *Organization Design* (Reading, Mass.: Addison-Wesley, 1977), ch. 1.

frequently leads to a change in structure.[43] Strategy and goals were discussed in detail in Chapter 2. Once a company formulates a strategy by which it plans to achieve a competitive advantage in the marketplace, leaders design or redesign the structure to coordinate organizational activities to best achieve that advantage. As discussed earlier, Xerox shifted to a horizontal structure after CEO Paul Allaire and other top executives developed a new strategic direction that required flexibility and close horizontal coordination.

The remaining contingency factors—environment, culture, technology, and size—will be discussed in subsequent chapters. Each variable influences the appropriate structural design. Moreover, environment, culture, technology, goals, and size may also influence one another, as illustrated by the connecting lines among these contextual variables in Exhibit 3.17.

STRUCTURAL ALIGNMENT

Ultimately, the most important decision that managers make about structural design is to find the right balance between vertical control and horizontal coordination, depending on the needs of the organization. Vertical control is associated with goals of efficiency and stability, while horizontal coordination is associated with learning, innovation, and flexibility. Exhibit 3.18 shows a simplified continuum that illustrates how structural approaches are associated with vertical control versus horizontal coordination. The functional structure is appropriate when the organization needs to be coordinated through the vertical hierarchy and when efficiency is important for meeting organizational goals. The functional structure uses task specialization and a strict chain of command to gain efficient use of scarce resources, but it does not enable the organization to be flexible or innovative. At the opposite end of the scale, the horizontal structure is appropriate when the organization has a high need for coordination among functions to achieve innovation and promote learning. The horizontal structure enables organizations to differentiate themselves and respond quickly to changes, but at the expense of efficient resource use. Exhibit 3.18 also shows how other types of structure defined in this chapter—functional with horizontal linkages, divisional, and matrix—represent intermediate steps on the organization's path to efficiency or innovation and learning. The exhibit does not include all possible structures, but it illustrates how organizations attempt to balance the needs for efficiency and vertical control with innovation and horizontal coordination. In addition, as described in the chapter, many organizations use a hybrid structure to combine characteristics of these structural types.

SYMPTOMS OF STRUCTURAL DEFICIENCY

Top executives periodically evaluate organization structure to determine whether it is appropriate to changing organization needs. Many organizations try one organization structure, then reorganize to another structure in an effort to find the right fit between internal reporting relationships and the needs of the external environment. Compaq Computer Corporation, for example, switched from a functional structure to a divisional structure for about a year to develop new products and then switched back to a functional structure to reduce competition among its product lines.[44]

As a general rule, when organization structure is out of alignment with organization needs, one or more of the following **symptoms of structural deficiency** appear.[45]

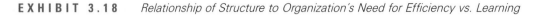

EXHIBIT 3.18   *Relationship of Structure to Organization's Need for Efficiency vs. Learning*

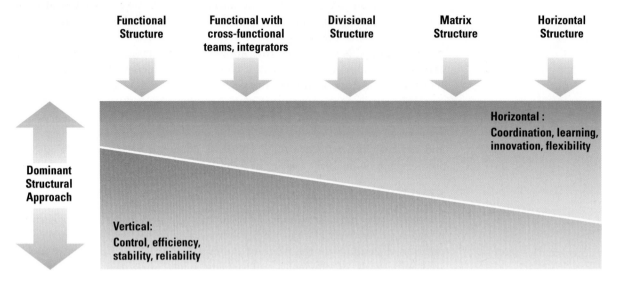

* *Decision making is delayed or lacking in quality.* Decision makers may be overloaded because the hierarchy funnels too many problems and decisions to them. Delegation to lower levels may be insufficient. Another cause of poor quality decisions is that information may not reach the correct people. Information linkages in either the vertical or horizontal direction may be inadequate to ensure decision quality.
* *The organization does not respond innovatively to a changing environment.* One reason for lack of innovation is that departments are not coordinated horizontally. The identification of customer needs by the marketing department and the identification of technological developments in the research department must be coordinated. Organization structure also has to specify departmental responsibilities that include environmental scanning and innovation.
* *Too much conflict is evident.* Organization structure should allow conflicting departmental goals to combine into a single set of goals for the entire organization. When departments act at cross purposes or are under pressure to achieve departmental goals at the expense of organizational goals, the structure is often at fault. Horizontal linkage mechanisms are not adequate.

SUMMARY AND INTERPRETATION

Organization structure must accomplish two things for the organization. It must provide a framework of responsibilities, reporting relationships, and groupings, and it must provide mechanisms for linking and coordinating organizational elements into a coherent whole. The structure is reflected on the organization chart. Linking the organization into a coherent whole requires the use of information systems and linkage devices in addition to the organization chart.

It is important to understand the information-processing perspective on structure. Organization structure can be designed to provide vertical and horizontal information linkages based on the information processing required to meet the organization's overall goal. Managers can choose whether to orient toward a traditional organization designed for efficiency, which emphasizes vertical linkages such as hierarchy, rules and plans, and formal information systems, or toward a contemporary learning organization, which emphasizes horizontal communication and coordination. Vertical linkages are not sufficient for most organizations today. Organizations provide horizontal linkages through cross-functional information systems, direct contact between managers across department lines, temporary task forces, full-time integrators, and teams.

Alternatives for grouping employees and departments into overall structural design include functional grouping, divisional grouping, multifocused grouping, and horizontal grouping. The choice among functional, divisional, and horizontal structures determines where coordination and integration will be greatest. With functional and divisional structures, managers also use horizontal linkage mechanisms to complement the vertical dimension and achieve integration of departments and levels into an organizational whole. With a horizontal structure, activities are organized horizontally around core work processes. The matrix structure attempts to achieve an equal balance between the vertical and horizontal dimensions of structure. Most organizations do not exist in these pure forms, using instead a hybrid structure that incorporates characteristics of two or more types of structure. Ultimately, managers attempt to find the correct balance between vertical control and horizontal coordination.

Finally, an organization chart is only so many lines and boxes on a piece of paper. A new organization structure will not necessarily solve an organization's problems. The organization chart simply reflects what people should do and what their responsibilities are. The purpose of the organization chart is to encourage and direct employees into activities and communications that enable the organization to achieve its goals. The organization chart provides the structure, but employees provide the behavior. The chart is a guideline to encourage people to work together, but management must implement the structure and carry it out.

BRIEFCASE

As an organization manager, keep these guidelines in mind:

1. Develop organization charts that describe task responsibilities, reporting relationships, and the grouping of individuals into departments. Provide sufficient documentation so that all people within the organization know to whom they report and how they fit into the total organization picture.
2. Provide vertical and horizontal information linkages to integrate diverse departments into a coherent whole. Achieve vertical linkage through hierarchy referral, rules and plans, and vertical information systems. Achieve horizontal linkage through cross-functional information systems, direct contact, task forces, full-time integrators, and teams.
3. When designing overall organization structure, choose a functional structure when efficiency is important, when in-depth knowledge and expertise are critical to meeting organizational goals, and when the organization needs to be controlled and coordinated through the vertical hierarchy. Use a divisional

structure in a large organization with multiple product lines and when you wish to give priority to product goals and coordination across functions.

4. Consider a matrix structure when the organization needs to give equal priority to both products and functions because of dual pressures from customers in the environment. Use either a functional matrix or a product matrix if the balanced matrix with dual lines of authority is not appropriate for your organization.

5. Consider a horizontal structure when customer needs and demands change rapidly and when learning and innovation are critical to organizational success. Carefully determine core processes and train managers and employees to work within the horizontal structure.

6. Implement hybrid structures, when needed, to combine characteristics of functional, divisional, and horizontal structures. Use a hybrid structure in complex environments to take advantage of the strengths of various structural characteristics and avoid some of the weaknesses.

7. Find the correct balance between vertical control and horizontal coordination to meet the needs of the organization. Consider a structural reorganization when symptoms of structural deficiency are observed.

KEY CONCEPTS

departmental grouping
divisional grouping
divisional structure
functional grouping
functional matrix
functional structure
horizontal grouping
horizontal linkage
horizontal structure
hybrid structure
integrator

liaison role
matrix structure
multifocused grouping
product matrix
structure
symptoms of structural deficiency
task force
teams
vertical information system
vertical linkages

DISCUSSION QUESTIONS

1. What is the definition of *organization structure*? Does organization structure appear on the organization chart? Explain.
2. How do rules and plans help an organization achieve vertical integration?
3. When is a functional structure preferable to a divisional structure?
4. Large corporations tend to use hybrid structures. Why?
5. What are the primary differences between a traditional organization designed for efficiency and a more contemporary organization designed for learning?
6. What is the difference between a task force and a team? Between liaison role and integrating role? Which of these provides the greatest amount of horizontal coordination?
7. What conditions usually have to be present before an organization should adopt a matrix structure?
8. The manager of a consumer products firm said, "We use the brand manager position to train future executives." Do you think the brand manager position is a good training ground? Discuss.

9. Why do companies using a horizontal structure have cultures that emphasize openness, employee empowerment, and responsibility? What do you think a manager's job would be like in a horizontally organized company?

10. How is structure related to the organization's need for efficiency versus its need for learning and innovation? How can managers tell if structure is out of alignment with the organization's needs?

CHAPTER 3 WORKBOOK   *You and Organization Structure**

To better understand the importance of organization structure in your life, do the following assignment.

Select one of the following situations to organize:

1. The registration process at your university or college
2. A new fast-food franchise
3. A sports rental in an ocean resort area, such as jet skis
4. A bakery

BACKGROUND

Organization is a way of gaining some power against an unreliable environment. The environment provides the organization with inputs, which include raw materials, human resources, and financial resources. There is a service or product to produce that involves technology. The output goes to clients, a group that must be nurtured. The complexities of the environment and the technology determine the complexity of the organization.

PLANNING YOUR ORGANIZATION

1. Write down the mission or purpose of the organization in a few sentences.

2. What are the specific things to be done to accomplish the mission?
3. Based on the specifics in No. 2, develop an organization chart. Each position in the chart will perform a specific task or is responsible for a certain outcome.
4. Add duties to each job position in the chart. These will be the job descriptions.
5. How can you make sure people in each position will work together?
6. What level of skill and abilities is required at each position and level in order to hire the right persons?
7. Make a list of the decisions that would have to be made as you developed your organization.
8. Who is responsible for customer satisfaction? How will you know if customers' needs are met?
9. How will information flow within the organization?

Adapted by Dorothy Marcic from "Organizing," in Donald D. White and H. William Vroman, *Action in Organizations*, 2nd ed. (Boston: Allyn and Bacon, 1982), 154.

Case for Analysis   *C & C Grocery Stores, Inc.**

The first C & C grocery store was started in 1947 by Doug Cummins and his brother Bob. Both were veterans who wanted to run their own business, so they used their savings to start the small grocery store in Charlotte, North Carolina. The store was immediately successful. The location was good, and Doug Cummins had a winning personality. Store employees adopted Doug's informal style and "serve the customer" attitude. C & C's increasing circle of customers enjoyed an abundance of good meats and produce.

By 1984, C & C had over 200 stores. A standard physical layout was used for new stores. Company

headquarters moved from Charlotte to Atlanta in 1975. The organization chart for C & C is shown in Exhibit 3.19. The central offices in Atlanta handled personnel, merchandising, financial, purchasing, real estate, and legal affairs for the entire chain. For management of individual stores, the organization was divided by regions. The southern, southeastern, and northeastern regions each had about seventy stores. Each region was divided into five districts of ten to fifteen stores each. A district director was responsible

---

*Prepared by Richard L. Daft, from Richard L. Daft and Richard Steers, *Organizations: a Micro/Macro Approach* (Glenview, Ill.: Scott, Foresman, 1986). Reprinted with permission.

for supervision and coordination of activities for the ten to fifteen district stores.

Each district was divided into four lines of authority based upon functional specialty. Three of these lines reached into the stores. The produce department manager within each store reported directly to the produce specialist for the division, and the same was true for the meat department manager, who reported directly to the district meat specialist. The meat and produce managers were responsible for all activities associated with the acquisition and sale of perishable products. The store manager's responsibility included the grocery line, front-end departments, and store operations. The store manager was responsible for appearance of personnel,

cleanliness, adequate check-out service, and price accuracy. A grocery manager reported to the store manger and maintained inventories and restocked shelves for grocery items. The district merchandising office was responsible for promotional campaigns, advertising circulars, district advertising, and for attracting customers into the stores. The grocery merchandisers were expected to coordinate their activities with each store in the district.

During the recession in 1980–81, business for the C & C chain dropped off in all regions and did not increase with the improved economic times in 1983–84. This caused concern among senior executives. They also were aware that other supermarket chains were adopting a trend toward one-stop

EXHIBIT 3.19   *Organization Structure for C & C Grocery Stores, Inc.*

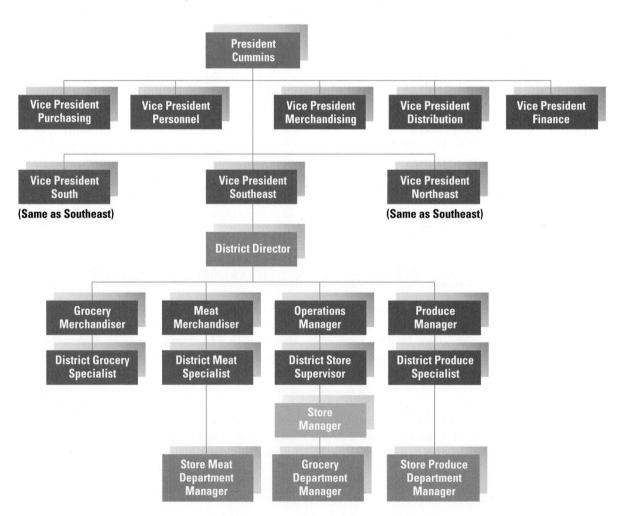

shopping, which meant the emergence of super stores that included a pharmacy, dry goods, and groceries—almost like a department store. Executives wondered whether C & C should move in this direction and how such changes could be assimilated into the current store organization. However, the most pressing problem was how to improve business with the grocery stores they now had. A consulting team from a major university was hired to investigate store structure and operations.

The consultants visited several stores in each region, talking to about fifty managers and employees. The consultants wrote a report that pinpointed four problem areas to be addressed by store executives.

1. The chain is slow to adapt to change. Store layout and structure were the same as had been designed fifteen years ago. Each store did things the same way, even though some stores were in low-income areas and other stores in suburban areas. A new grocery management system for ordering and stocking had been developed, but after two years was only partially implemented in the stores.

2. Roles of the district store supervisor and the store manager were causing dissatisfaction. The store managers wanted to learn general management skills for potential promotion into district or regional management positions. However, their jobs restricted them to operational activities and they learned little about merchandising, meat, and produce. Moreover, district store supervisors used store visits to inspect for cleanliness and adherence to operating standards rather than to train the store manager and help coordinate operations with perishable departments. Close supervision on the operational details had become the focus of operations management rather than development, training, and coordination.

3. Cooperation within stores was low and morale was poor. The informal, friendly atmosphere originally created by Doug Cummins was gone. One example of this problem occurred when the grocery merchandiser and store manager in a Louisiana store decided to promote Coke and Diet Coke as a loss leader. Thousands of cartons of Coke were brought in for the sale, but the stockroom was not prepared and did not have room. The store manager wanted to use floor area in the meat and produce sections to display Coke cartons, but those managers refused. The

produce department manager said that Diet Coke did not help his sales and it was okay with him if there was no promotion at all.

4. Long-term growth and development of the store chain would probably require reevaluation of long-term strategy. The percent of market share going to traditional grocery stores was declining nationwide due to competition from large super stores and convenience stores. In the future, C & C might need to introduce nonfood items into the stores for one-stop shopping, and add specialty sections within stores. Some stores could be limited to grocery items, but store location and marketing techniques should take advantage of the grocery emphasis.

To solve the first three problems, the consultants recommended reorganizing the district and the store structure as illustrated in Exhibit 3.20. Under this reorganization, the meat, grocery, and produce department managers would all report to the store manager. The store manager would have complete store control and would be responsible for coordination of all store activities. The district supervisor's role would be changed from supervision to training and development. The district supervisor would head a team that included himself and several meat, produce, and merchandise specialists who would visit area stores as a team to provide advice and help for the store managers and other employees. The team would act in a liaison capacity between district specialists and the stores.

The consultants were enthusiastic about the proposed structure. By removing one level of district operational supervision, store managers would have more freedom and responsibility. The district liaison team would establish a cooperative team approach to management that could be adopted within stores. The focus of store responsibility on a single manager would encourage coordination within stores, adaptation to local conditions, and provide a focus of responsibility for store-wide administrative changes.

The consultants also believed that the proposed structure could be expanded to accommodate non-grocery lines if enlarged stores were to be developed in the future. Within each store, a new department manager could be added for pharmacy, dry goods, or other major departments. The district team could be expanded to include specialists in these departments who would act as liaison for stores in the district.

EXHIBIT 3.20   *Proposed Reorganization of C & C Grocery Stores, Inc.*

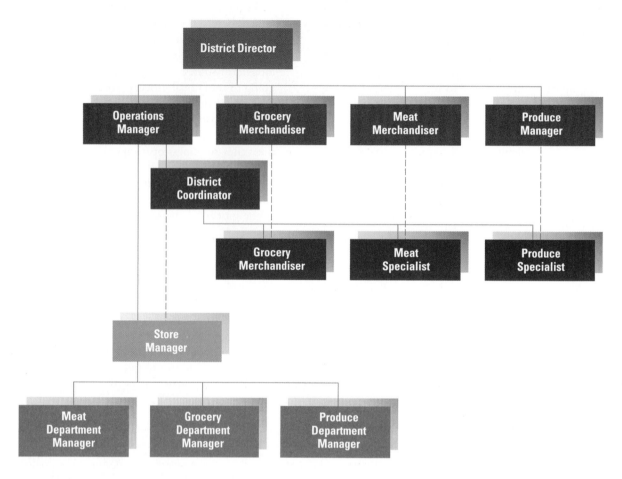

The Aquarius Advertising Agency is a middle-sized firm that offered two basic services to its clients: (1) customized plans for the content of an advertising campaign (for example, slogans, layouts) and (2) complete plans for media (such as radio, TV, newspapers, billboards, and magazines). Additional services included aid in marketing and distribution of products and marketing research to test advertising effectiveness.

Its activities were organized in a traditional manner. The formal organization is shown in Exhibit 3.21. Each department included similar functions.

Each client account was coordinated by an account executive who acted as a liaison between the client and the various specialists on the professional staff of the operations and marketing divisions. The number of direct communications and contacts

between clients and Aquarius specialists, clients and account executives, and Aquarius specialists and account executives, is indicated in Exhibit 3.22. These sociometric data were gathered by a consultant who conducted a study of the patterns of formal and informal communication. Each intersecting cell of Aquarius personnel and the clients contains an index of the direct contacts between them.

Although an account executive was designated to be the liaison between the client and specialists within the agency, communications frequently occurred directly between clients and specialists and bypassed the account executive. These direct contacts involved a wide range of interactions, such as

*Adapted from John F. Veiga and John N. Yanouzas, "Aquarius Advertising Agency," *The Dynamics of Organization Theory* (St. Paul, Minn.: West, 1984), 212–17, with permission.

EXHIBIT 3.21   *Aquarius Advertising Agency Organization Chart*

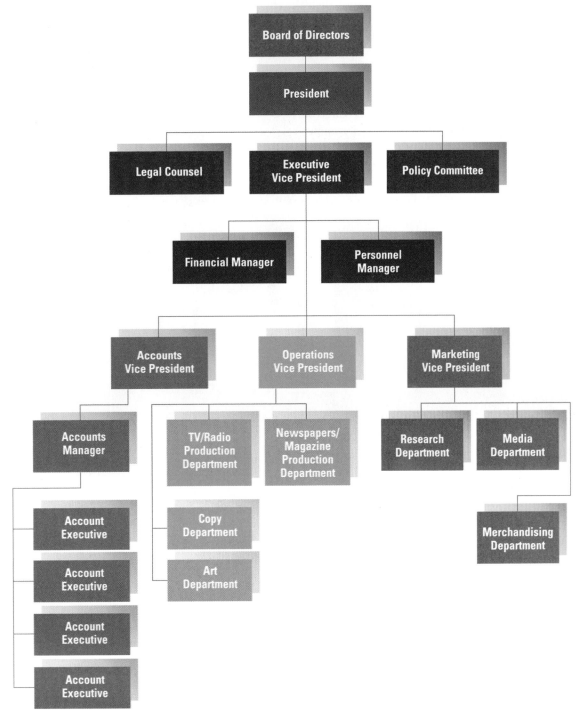

meetings, telephone calls, letters, and so on. A large number of direct communications occurred between agency specialists and their counterparts in the client organization. For example, an art specialist working as one member of a team on a particular client account would often be contacted directly by the client's in-house art specialist, and agency research personnel had direct communication with research people of the client firm. Also, some of the unstructured contacts often led to more formal meetings with clients in which agency personnel made presentations, interpreted and defended agency policy, and committed the agency to certain courses of action.

Both hierarchical and professional systems operated within the departments of the operations and marketing divisions. Each department was organized hierarchically with a director, an assistant director, and several levels of authority. Professional communications were widespread and mainly concerned with sharing knowledge and techniques, technical

evaluation of work, and development of professional interests. Control in each department was exercised mainly through control of promotions and supervision of work done by subordinates. Many account executives, however, felt the need for more influence, and one commented:

> Creativity and art. That's all I hear around here. It is hard as hell to effectively manage six or seven hotshots who claim they have to do their own thing. Each of them tries to sell his or her idea to the client, and most of the time I don't know what has happened until a week later. If I were a despot, I

EXHIBIT 3.22   *Sociometric Index of Contacts of Aquarius Personnel and Clients*

	Clients	Account Manager	Account Executives	TV/Radio Specialists	Newspaper/Magazine Specialists	Copy Specialists	Art Specialists	Merchandising Specialists	Media Specialists	Research Specialists
Clients	X	F	F	N	N	O	O	O	O	O
Account Manager		X	F	N	N	N	N	N	N	N
Account Executives			X	F	F	F	F	F	F	F
TV/Radio Specialists				X	N	O	O	N	N	O
Newspaper/Magazine Specialists					X	O	O	N	O	O
Copy Specialists						X	N	O	O	O
Art Specialists							X	O	O	O
Merchandising Specialists								X	F	F
Media Specialists									X	F
Research Specialists										X

F = Frequent—daily
O = Occasional—once or twice per project
N = None

would make all of them check with me first to get approval. Things would sure change around here.

The need for reorganization was made more acute by changes in the environment. Within a short period of time, there was a rapid turnover in the major accounts handled by the agency. It was typical for advertising agencies to gain or lose clients quickly, often with no advance warning as consumer behavior and life-style changes emerged and product innovations occurred.

An agency reorganization was one solution proposed by top management to increase flexibility in this unpredictable environment. The reorganization was aimed at reducing the agency's response time to environmental changes and at increasing cooperation and communication among specialists from different departments. The top managers are not sure what type of reorganization is appropriate. They would like your help analyzing their context and current structure and welcome your advice on proposing a new structure.

NOTES

1. Minda Zetlin, "From Fulfillment House to Strategic Partner," *Management Review* (October 1996): 33-37.
2. John Child, *Organization* (New York: Harper & Row, 1984).
3. Stuart Ranson, Bob Hinings, and Royston Greenwood, "The Structuring of Organizational Structures," *Administrative Science Quarterly* 25 (1980): 1–17; Hugh Willmott, "The Structuring of Organizational Structure: A Note," *Administrative Science Quarterly* 26 (1981): 470–74.
4. This section is based on Frank Ostroff, *The Horizontal Organization: What the Organization of the Future Looks Like and How It Delivers Value to Customers* (New York: Oxford University Press, 1999).
5. Stephen Salsbury, *The State, the Investor, and the Railroad: The Boston & Albany, 1825-1867* (Cambridge: Harvard University Press, 1967), 186-187.
6. David Nadler and Michael Tushman, *Strategic Organization Design* (Glenview, Ill.: Scott Foresman, 1988).
7. Based on Jay R. Galbraith, *Designing Complex Organizations* (Reading, Mass.: Addison-Wesley, 1973), and *Organization Design* (Reading, Mass.: Addison-Wesley, 1977), 81-127.
8. Eryn Brown, "9 Ways to Win on the Web," *Fortune*, 24 May 1999, 112-125.
9. Lee Iacocca with William Novak, *Iacocca: An Autobiography* (New York: Phantom Books, 1984), 152–53.
10. Based on Galbraith, *Designing Complex Organizations.*
11. Mary J. Cronin, "Intranets Reach the Factory Floor," *Fortune*, 18 August 1997, 208; and Brown, "9 Ways to Win on the Web."
12. Timothy D. Schellhardt, "Monsanto Bets on 'Box Buddies'," *The Wall Street Journal*, 23 February 1999, B1, B10.
13. Walter Kiechel III, "The Art of the Corporate Task Force," *Fortune*, 28 January 1991, 104–5; William J. Altier, "Task Forces: An Effective Management Tool," *Management Review* (February 1987): 52–57.
14. Richard Koonce, "Reengineering the Travel Game," *Government Executive* (May 1995): 28-34, 69-70.
15. Keith Naughton and Kathleen Kerwin, "At GM, Two Heads May Be Worse Than One," *Business Week*, 14 August 1995, 46.
16. Paul R. Lawrence and Jay W. Lorsch, "New Managerial Job: The Integrator," *Harvard Business Review* (November-December 1967): 142–51.
17. Jeffrey A. Tannenbaum, "Why Are Companies Paying Close Attention to This Toilet Maker?" (The Front Lines Column), *The Wall Street Journal*, 20 August 1999, B1.
18. Based on Tannenbaum, "Why Are Companies Paying Close Attention to This Toilet Maker?" and American Standard Companies 1998 Annual Report, *www.americanstandard.com/annual98/*, accessed on September 3, 1999.
19. Jay R. Galbraith, *Competing with Flexible Lateral Organizations*, 2nd ed. (Reading, Mass.: Addison-Wesley, 1994), 17–18; Laurie P. O'Leary, "Curing the Monday Blues: A U.S. Navy Guide for Structuring Cross-Functional Teams," *National Productivity Review* (Spring 1996): 43–51.
20. Wendy Zellner, "Can EDS Catch Up with the Net?" *Business Week*, 17 May 1999, 46.
21. Henry Mintzberg, *The Structuring of Organizations* (Englewood Cliffs, N.J.: Prentice-Hall, 1979).

22. Frank Ostroff, "Stovepipe Stomper," *Government Executive*, April 1999, 70

23. Based on Robert Duncan, "What Is the Right Organization Structure?" *Organizational Dynamics* (Winter 1979): 59–80; W. Alan Randolph and Gregory G. Dess, "The Congruence Perspective of Organization Design: A Conceptual Model and Multivariate Research Approach," *Academy of Management Review* 9 (1984): 114–27.

24. Toni Mack, "The Ice Cream Man Cometh," *Forbes*, 22 January 1990, 52–56; David Abdalla, J. Doehring, and Ann Windhager, "Blue Bell Creameries, Inc.: Case and Analysis" (Unpublished manuscript, Texas A&M University, 1981); Jorjanna Price, "Creamery Churns Its Ice Cream into Cool Millions," *Parade*, 21 February 1982, 18–22.

25. Rahul Jacob, "The Struggle to Create an Organization for the 21st Century," *Fortune*, 3 April 1995, 90–99.

26. Joseph Weber, "A Big Company That Works," *Business Week*, 4 May 1992, 124–132; and Elyse Tanouye, "Johnson & Johnson Stays Fit by Shuffling Its Mix of Businesses," *The Wall Street Journal*, 22 December 1992, A1, A4.

27. Michael Moeller, with Steve Hamm and Timothy J. Mullaney, "Remaking Microsoft," *Business Week*, 17 May 1999, 106–114.

28. Based on Duncan, "What Is the Right Organization Structure?"

29. Weber, "A Big Company That Works."

30. John Markoff, "John Sculley's Biggest Test," *New York Times*, 26 February 1989, sec. 3,1,26; and Shelly Branch, "What's Eating McDonald's?" *Fortune*, 13 October 1997, 122-125.

31. Stanley M. Davis and Paul R. Lawrence, *Matrix* (Reading, Mass.: Addison-Wesley, 1977): 11–24.

32. Eric W. Larson and David H. Gobeli, "Matrix Management: Contradictions and Insight," *California Management Review* 29 (Summer 1987): 126-138.

33. Davis and Lawrence, *Matrix*, 155-180.

34. Robert C. Ford and W. Alan Randolph, "Cross-Functional Structures: A Review and Integration of Matrix Organizations and Project Management," *Journal of Management* 18 (June 1992): 267–94; Duncan, "What Is the Right Organization Structure?"

35. Lawton R. Burns, "Matrix Management in Hospitals: Testing Theories of Matrix Structure and Development," *Administrative Science Quarterly* 34 (1989): 349–68.

36. Christopher A. Bartlett and Sumantra Ghoshal, "Matrix Management: Not a Structure, a Frame of Mind," *Harvard Business Review* (July-August 1990): 138–45.

37. This case was inspired by John E. Fogerty, "Integrative Management at Standard Steel" (Unpublished manuscript, Latrobe, Pennsylvania, 1980); Bill Saporito, "Allegheny Ludlum Has Steel Figured Out," *Fortune*, 25 June 1984, 40–44; "The Worldwide Steel Industry: Reshaping to Survive," *Business Week*, 20 August 1984, 150–54; Stephen Baker, "The Brutal Brawl Ahead in Steel," *Business Week*, 13 March 1995, 88–90, and "Why Steel Is Looking Sexy," *Business Week*, 4 April 1994, 106–8.

38. Based on Ostroff, *The Horizontal Organization*, and Richard L. Daft, *Organization Theory and Design*, 6th ed. (Cincinnati Ohio: South-Western College Publishing, 1998), 250-253.

39. Frank Ostroff, *The Horizontal Organization*, 130-143.

40. John A. Byrne, "The Horizontal Corporation," *Business Week*, 20 December 1993, 76-81.

41. Linda S. Ackerman, "Transition Management: An In-depth Look at Managing Complex Change," *Organizational Dynamics* (Summer 1982): 46–66.

42. Based on Ostroff, *The Horizontal Organization*, 29–44.

43. Jay R. Galbraith, *Competing with Flexible Lateral Organizations*, 2d ed. (Reading, Mass.: Addison-Wesley, 1994): ch. 2; Terry L. Amburgey and Tina Dacin, "As the Left Foot Follows the Right? The Dynamics of Strategic and Structural Change," *Academy of Management Journal* 37, No. 6 (1994): 427-452; and Raymond E. Miles and W. E. Douglas Creed, "Organizational Forms and Managerial Philosophies: A Descriptive and Analytical Review," *Research in Organizational Behavior* 17 (1995): 333-372.

44. Jo Ellen Davis, "Who's Afraid of IBM?" *Business Week*, 29 June 1987, 68–74.

45. Based on Child, *Organization*, ch. 1.

Open System Design Elements

PART

The External Environment

CHAPTER 4

A LOOK INSIDE

Barnes & Noble

*S*teve and Len Riggio started their bookselling business in the mid-1960s with a single store. Today they have more than a thousand outlets and have pushed many independent booksellers out of business with their book superstore concept. By the early 1990s, the Riggios were sitting at the top of the American publishing industry. However, they failed to notice the shifting landscape below them, or the tiny company that was about to change the bookselling business forever.

Amazon.com went against everything that had made Barnes & Noble a success. Barnes & Noble had succeeded by creating large, comfortable spaces that felt like college libraries or public squares, with sofas and coffee bars where customers could flip through books and make new friends. Amazon.com was ringing up online sales for more than a year before Barnes & Noble's managers even began investigating the Web. Even then, the Riggios believed the Internet would never be more than an innovative marketing tool. By the time Barnesandnoble.com actually started selling books over the Web, Amazon already owned the market. Accustomed to winning, Barnes & Noble's managers believed all they had to do was go online to crush the upstarts at Amazon. But, like a lot of established retailers, the Riggios discovered that their assumptions didn't hold up in the new world of e-commerce. Even though the company burned through $100 million in its effort to crush Amazon, Barnesandnoble.com was still selling only a pathetic 15 percent of books bought online, compared to Amazon.com's 75 percent.

Barnes & Noble's early efforts in e-commerce are marked by costly mistakes and missed opportunities. To recover, and to establish a significant e-commerce presence, the Riggios recently agreed to form Barnesandnoble.com as a separate company in a joint venture with Bertelsmann AG, the German corporation that has grown into the world's third largest media company through the acquisition of such American brand names as Doubleday, Bantam, and Random House. In addition, Steve Riggio stepped down as CEO to make way for Jonathan Bulkeley, an executive with substantial online marketing experience. Meanwhile, top executives are in the process of formulating new strategies to compete in the new world of bookselling.[1]

Barnes & Noble was surprised by the environment in the early 1990s, and now managers are working overtime to ensure that the same thing doesn't happen again. Executives are trying to define a strategy that markedly differentiates Barnesandnoble.com from its competition, primarily Amazon. It may have had a stroke of luck when Amazon.com began expanding to sell everything from flowers to pharmaceuticals. Barnesandnoble.com will concentrate on the evolution of books and bookselling. Managers want the company to be in first place when electronic distribution of books begins to replace conventional distribution. The company's CEO and other top managers know Barnesandnoble.com is operating in a highly competitive environment in which all the rules of business are new ones. Firms in numerous industries, from auto manufacturing to telecommunications to beverage companies, face similar uncertainty.

Perhaps the greatest tumult for today's companies has been created by the rapid expansion of the Internet, but many factors in the external environment cause turbulence and uncertainty for organizations. Anheuser-Busch's CEO, for example, admits that his company was "five years late in recognizing that microbreweries were going to take as much market share as they did and five years late in recognizing that we should have joined them."[2] Small retailers have long suffered threats from huge discount stores such as Wal-Mart and Home Depot. Now, with electronics superstore Best Buy selling CDs for about half what they cost in traditional music stores, some record-selling chains have been forced into bankruptcy. In Western Europe, privatization of formerly state-owned enterprises has caused tremendous uncertainty for companies such as Swisscom, which seems to be thriving in the new environment, and Telecom Italia, which is not. Several board members were ousted after arguments about the company's future direction, and Telecom Italia's strategy has been left in tatters as two successive alliances (with AT&T and Cable and Wireless) fell apart.[3] In the United States, the cattle industry has suffered declining prices because of increased imports of beef from Canada, Mexico, and Argentina. The list could go on and on. The external environment, including global competition, is the source of major threats facing today's organizations. The environment often imposes major constraints on the choices managers make for the organization.

PURPOSE OF THIS CHAPTER

The purpose of this chapter is to develop a framework for assessing environments and how organizations can respond to them. First, we will identify the organizational domain and the sectors that influence the organization. Then, we will explore two major environmental forces on the organization—the need for information and the need for resources. Organizations respond to these forces through structural design, planning systems, and attempts to change and control elements in the environment.

THE ENVIRONMENTAL DOMAIN

In a broad sense the environment is infinite and includes everything outside the organization. However, the analysis presented here considers only the aspects of the environment to which the organization is sensitive and must respond to survive. Thus, **organizational environment** is defined as all elements that exist outside the boundary of the organization and have the potential to affect all or part of the organization.

The environment of an organization can be understood by analyzing its domain within external sectors. An organization's **domain** is the chosen environmental field of action. It is the territory an organization stakes out for itself with respect to products, services, and markets served. Domain defines the organization's niche and defines those external sectors with which the organization will interact to accomplish its goals. Barnes & Noble ignored an important part of its domain when the bookselling environment changed. The company was slow to take advantage of new technology for e-commerce, allowing the competition to gain a huge advantage.

The environment comprises several **sectors** or subdivisions of the external environment that contain similar elements. Ten sectors can be analyzed for each organization: industry, raw materials, human resources, financial resources, market, technology, economic conditions, government, sociocultural, and international.

The sectors and a hypothetical organizational domain are illustrated in Exhibit 4.1. For most companies, the sectors in Exhibit 4.1 can be further subdivided into the task environment and general environment.

TASK ENVIRONMENT

The **task environment** includes sectors with which the organization interacts directly and that have a direct impact on the organization's ability to achieve its goals. The task environment typically includes the industry, raw materials, and market sectors, and perhaps the human resources and international sectors.

EXHIBIT 4.1   *An Organization's Environment*

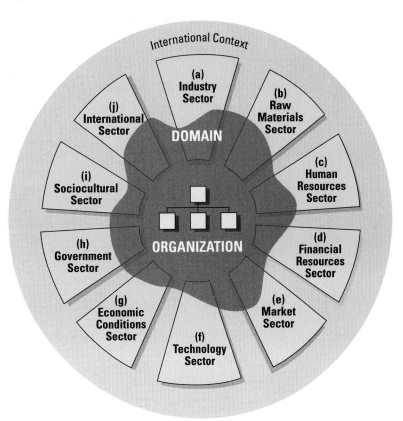

(a) Competitors, industry size and competitiveness, related industries
(b) Suppliers, manufacturers, real estate, services
(c) Labor market, employment agencies, universities, training schools, employees in other companies, unionization
(d) Stock markets, banks, savings and loans, private investors
(e) Customers, clients, potential users of products and services
(f) Techniques of production, science, computers, information technology, e-commerce

(g) Recession, unemployment rate, inflation rate, rate of investment, economics, growth
(h) City, state, federal laws and regulations, taxes, services, court system, political processes
(i) Age, values, beliefs, education, religion, work ethic, consumer and green movements
(j) Competition from and acquisition by foreign firms, entry into overseas markets, foreign customs, regulations, exchange rate

The following examples illustrate how each of these sectors can affect organizations:

- In the *industry sector*, cola rivals Coke and Pepsi are intensifying their competition in local markets. For example, in New York City, one of the few markets where Pepsi-Cola outsells Coca-Cola Classic, each Coca-Cola marketing rep visits up to 120 small stores a week to push snazzier displays, better placement, and more promotions. In Harlem, where five convenience stores now sport red and white awnings thanks to Coca-Cola, small-store sales of Coke have doubled.[4]

- An interesting example in the *raw materials sector* concerns the beverage can industry. Steelmakers owned the beverage can market until the mid-1960s, when Reynolds Aluminum Company launched a huge aluminum recycling program to gain a cheaper source of raw materials and make aluminum cans price-competitive with steel.[5]

- In the *market sector*, changes in toy-buying patterns, with parents wanting more educational toys and electronics, have stalled growth rates for companies such as Mattel and Hasbro. Even Barbie and GI Joe are suffering sales declines. Toys "R" Us, once the giant of toy retailers, is reevaluating strategies and marketing plans to respond to changing customer desires.[6]

- The *human resources sector* has become of significant concern to almost every business because of the tightest labor market in thirty years. Well-educated, computer-literate young workers, sometimes called *gold-collar workers*, can often demand high salaries and generous benefits because companies have great difficulty finding qualified workers.[7]

- For U.S. automobile manufacturers, the *international sector* is part of the task environment because these companies face tough foreign competition, including an increasing number of foreign-owned manufacturing plants built on U.S. soil. The international sector as part of the general environment is discussed in more detail later in this chapter.

GENERAL ENVIRONMENT

The **general environment** includes those sectors that may not have a direct impact on the daily operations of a firm but will indirectly influence it. The general environment often includes the government, sociocultural, economic conditions, technology, and financial resources sectors. These sectors affect all organizations eventually. Consider the following examples:

- In response to well-publicized problems with medical devices such as heart valves and breast implants, the FDA introduced more stringent regulations that significantly slowed the rate of reviewing and approving new products. ISS, a small company that manufactures surgical assistant systems that use 3-D computer imaging and robotic tools, could once bring a new product to market in two or three years; it is now lucky to make it in six because of these changes in the *government sector*.[8]

- In the *sociocultural sector*, changing demographics are impacting numerous companies. The huge baby-boom generation is aging and losing some of its interest in high-cost, brand-name goods. Meanwhile, the sons and daughters of baby boomers, sometimes called "Generation Y," disdain such once-favored brands as Nike and Levi Strauss. Companies are struggling to build loyalty among this new generation, which rivals the baby boom in size and will soon rival it in buying clout.[9]

- General *economic conditions* often affect the way a company does business. To remain competitive in an era of low inflation, furniture maker Ethan Allen needed to keep prices low. To make a profit without raising prices, the company turned to making simpler furniture designs and increasing its technological efficiency.[10]

- The most overwhelming change in the *technology sector* is the rapid expansion of the Internet as a place for doing business. The World Wide Web and other advances in information technology have changed the whole face of business. For example, new formats for storing and transmitting music over the Internet could alter the entire recording industry. Although Val Azzoli, co-CEO of $700-million-plus-a-year Atlantic Group, views the Web primarily as a marketing tool for Atlantic's artists, a privately owned Web site called MP3.com is already giving away digitized music over the Web.[11]

- All businesses have to be concerned with *financial resources*, but this sector is often first and foremost in the minds of entrepreneurs starting a new business. Scott Blum started Buy.com, which resells computers and other products at or below cost over the Internet, with money out of his own savings. A couple of years later, Blum raised $60 million from Japanese tech company Softbank in return for a 20 percent equity stake in the company.[12]

INTERNATIONAL CONTEXT

The international sector can directly affect many organizations, and it has become extremely important in the last few years. In addition, all domestic sectors can be affected by international events. Despite the significance of international events for today's organizations, many students fail to appreciate the importance of international events and still think domestically. Think again. Even if you stay in your hometown, your company may be purchased tomorrow by the English, Canadians, Japanese, or Germans. For example, General Shale Brick, with headquarters in a small community in East Tennessee, was recently bought by Wienerberger Baustoffindustrie AG, a Vienna, Austria, company that is the world's largest brickmaker. The Japanese alone own more than one thousand U.S. companies, including steel mills, rubber and tire factories, automobile assembly plants, and auto parts suppliers. Nationwide, more than 350,000 Americans work for Japanese companies. People employed by Pillsbury, Shell Oil, Firestone, and CBS Records are working for foreign bosses.[13]

The impact of the international sector has grown rapidly with advances in technology and communications. The distinctions between domestic and foreign companies have become increasingly irrelevant as advances in transportation and electronic technology have reduced the impact of distance and time, as well as the differences among political and monetary systems, tastes, and standards. Global trade has tripled in the past twenty-five years, and today it is relatively easy for a firm of any size to operate on a global scale.[14] One small company, Montague Corporation, designs unique folding mountain bikes in Cambridge, Massachusetts, makes them in Taiwan, and sells most of them in Europe. Design changes are sent back and forth across three continents, sometimes on a daily basis. U.S.-based Coca-Cola, Canada's Northern Telecom, Switzerland's Nestlé, and France's Carrefour, the retailer that invented the *hypermarket* concept, all get a large percentage of their sales from outside their home countries.[15] In this global environment, it is no surprise that foreign-born people with international experience have been appointed to run such U.S. companies as Coca-Cola, Ford, Gerber, NCR, and Heinz. Consider the following trends:[16]

- The North American Free Trade Agreement is spurring many U.S. companies, including small businesses, to move into Canada and Mexico, affecting the market and human resources sectors.
- The European Union (EU) and Association of Southeast Asian Nations (ASEAN) may spawn large, powerful companies that compete easily with U.S. firms. These companies could reshape the industry and market sectors as we now know them.
- Despite recent economic woes, some analysts believe that in the twenty-first century, most of the economic activity in the world will take place in Asia and the Pacific Basin, sharply affecting the economic conditions and financial resources sectors.
- Newly industrialized countries such as Korea, Taiwan, Singapore, and Spain produce huge volumes of low-cost, high-quality commodities that will have an impact on the competitiveness of many industries, markets, and raw materials in North America.
- Eastern Europe, Russia, and China are all shifting toward market economies that also will affect markets, raw materials, industry competition, and worldwide economic conditions.
- Hundreds of partnerships are taking place between North American firms and firms in all parts of the world, facilitating the exchange of technology and production capability, thereby redefining the technology, raw materials, and industry sectors.
- Many companies in the United States build twin plants—one in Texas and one in Mexico. The Mexican plants provide component assembly, and that helps combat Mexico's high unemployment. Called *maquiladoras*, these plants reshape the human resources and raw materials sectors.
- All of these international connections are spawning new state and federal regulations, thereby affecting the government sector; and beliefs and values are becoming shared worldwide, shaping the sociocultural sector.

The increasing global interconnections have both positive and negative results for organizations. The recent economic turmoil in Asia and Eastern Europe blindsided many companies, creating great uncertainty for organizations doing business there. In addition, as the economic malaise spread to Latin America, it had an even greater impact on some U. S. companies based in Florida, since Southern Florida's economy is closely integrated with that of Latin America. CHS Electronics, a Miami-based firm with extensive ties to Latin America, has seen more and more of its Latin customers paying with local currency, and is finding debts harder to collect.[17]

Global interconnections also mean that competitiveness has reached a new level, as companies are competing on a broader scale than ever before. Less-developed countries are challenging mature countries in a number of industries. For example, India is becoming a major player in software development, and consumer electronics manufacturing, which long ago left the United States for Japan, is now rapidly leaving Japan for other countries in Asia.

Yet there is also a positive side. Domestic markets are saturated for many companies and the primary potential for growth lies overseas. Kimberly-Clark and Procter & Gamble, which spent years slugging it out in the now-flat U.S. diaper market, are targeting new markets in China, India, Brazil, Israel, and Russia. The demand for steel in China, India, and Brazil together is expected to grow 10 percent annually in the coming years—three times the U.S. rate. Nucor, a U.S.-based steel company, is opening a minimill in Thailand and partnering with a Brazilian company for a $700 million steel mill in northeastern Brazil. Other steel companies, such as LTV Corp. and North Star Steel, are moving into Asia, Europe, and Australia.[18] And, despite the economic convulsions there, large Western companies such as Ford, Procter & Gamble, and Coca-Cola continue to view Southeast Asia as the big market of the future. When companies think globally, the whole world is their marketplace. But dealing with the international sector of the environment isn't always easy, even for a giant like Wal–Mart.

In Practice 4.1

Wal-Mart

Wal-Mart Stores Inc., based in Bentonville, Arkansas, has made its share of blunders in its quest for international expansion, including installing poorly translated store signs in Mexico, stocking footballs rather than soccer balls in Brazil, and selling 110-voltage appliances in Argentina, where 220 is the standard. In addition, Wal-Mart underestimated its global competitors, such as France's Carrefour and the Netherlands' SHV Makro, which already have a strong presence in foreign markets. Political and economic instability in foreign countries has produced other complications.

However, despite these problems, Wal-Mart's global expansion has grown from an initial investment in Mexico in 1991 to a division that now operates in eight countries with $12.5 billion in sales a year. The company has more than seven hundred international stores in China, Indonesia, Mexico, Canada, Puerto Rico, Brazil, and Argentina. Wal-Mart also recently launched its drive into Europe, purchasing the Westkauf chain of ninety-five supermarkets in Germany, and Britain's Asda Group PLC, the country's third-largest supermarket chain. Although Asda stores will continue operating under their own name, the purchase consolidates Wal-Mart's position in Europe. Wal-Mart is succeeding internationally because it rapidly learns from its mistakes and works hard to adapt its goods and layout to local needs, yet exports the information systems and efficiency that have made it the world's largest retailer. Because the company had few retail models to learn from, it studied international giants such as McDonald's and Ford Motor Company for ideas about running a global business, examining everything from their global structures to their supply chains to their profits. In some countries, Wal-Mart has moved quickly to find local partners—for example, CIFRA in Mexico, Lojas Americanas in Brazil, and the Lippo Group in Indonesia—who can help translate the business cross-culturally.

Just as Wal-Mart has faced uncertainty in global markets, it is also creating tremendous instability and uncertainty for other organizations, both at home and abroad. Foreign rivals have been forced to cut prices and improve service to remain competitive. In addition, many of Wal-Mart's domestic suppliers have little global experience and are ill-prepared to meet the giant retailer's needs in places such as China and Brazil. While foreign suppliers salivate at the chance to expand their sales through Wal-Mart, domestic vendors are struggling to adapt so they won't lose the company's business. One vendor, Pacific Connections, has invested so much in upgrading its systems that it won't turn a profit for several years. However, the CEO of Pacific is glad Wal-Mart forced the company to venture into the global arena. "If we don't go international, other people will," he says. "Americans have to wake up. We are not good international marketers, and Wal-Mart is giving us an opportunity."[19]

As Wal–Mart has discovered, the growing importance of the international sector means that the environment for all organizations has become extremely complex and extremely competitive. However, every organization faces uncertainty domestically as well as globally. One way in which Wal-Mart is coping with uncertainty is to establish partnerships in the foreign countries where it does business. In the following sections, we will discuss in greater detail how companies cope with and respond to environmental uncertainty and instability.

ENVIRONMENTAL UNCERTAINTY

How does the environment influence an organization? The patterns and events occurring across environmental sectors can be described along several dimensions, such as whether the environment is stable or unstable, homogeneous or heterogeneous, concentrated or dispersed, simple or complex; the extent of turbulence; and the amount of resources available to support the organization.[20] These dimensions boil down to two essential ways the environment influences organizations: (1) the need for information about the environment and (2) the need for resources from the environment. The environmental conditions of complexity and change create a greater need to gather information and to respond based on that information. The organization also is concerned with scarce material and financial resources and with the need to ensure availability of resources. Each sector can be analyzed relative to these three analytical categories. The remainder of this section will discuss the information perspective, which is concerned with the uncertainty that environmental complexity and change create for the organization. Later in the chapter, we will discuss how organizations control the environment to acquire needed resources.

Organizations must cope with and manage uncertainty to be effective. **Uncertainty** means that decision makers do not have sufficient information about environmental factors, and they have a difficult time predicting external changes. Uncertainty increases the risk of failure for organizational responses and makes it difficult to compute costs and probabilities associated with decision alternatives.[21] Characteristics of the environmental domain that influence uncertainty are the extent to which the external domain is simple or complex and the extent to which events are stable or unstable.[22]

SIMPLE-COMPLEX DIMENSION

The **simple-complex dimension** concerns environmental complexity, which refers to heterogeneity, or the number and dissimilarity of external elements relevant to an organization's operations. In a complex environment, many diverse external elements interact with and influence the organization. In a simple environment, as few as three or four similar external elements influence the organization.

Telecommunications firms such as AT&T and British Telecom have a complex environment, as do universities. Universities span a large number of technologies and are a focal point for cultural and value changes. Government regulatory and granting agencies interact with a university, and so do a variety of professional and scientific associations, alumni, parents, foundations, legislators, community residents, international agencies, donors, corporations, and athletic teams. A large number of external elements thus make up the organization's domain, creating a complex environment. On the other hand, a family-owned hardware store in a suburban community is in a simple environment. The only external elements of any real importance are a few competitors, suppliers, and customers. Government regulation is minimal, and cultural change has little impact. Human resources are not a problem because the store is run by family members or part-time help.

STABLE–UNSTABLE DIMENSION

The **stable–unstable dimension** refers to whether elements in the environment are dynamic. An environmental domain is stable if it remains the same over a period of months or years. Under unstable conditions, environmental elements shift abruptly. Instability may occur when competitors react with aggressive moves and countermoves regarding advertising and new products. For example, aggressive advertising and introduction of new products can create instability for companies, such as Coke's giving away 2 million Coca-Cola cards to build its teen market in New York City and the introduction of Surge to compete with Pepsi's Mountain Dew. Sometimes specific, unpredictable events–such as reports of syringes in cans of Pepsi or glass shards in Gerber's baby foods, the poisoning of Tylenol, or the Church of Scientology's attack on the antidepressant drug Prozac–create unstable conditions. Today, "hate sites" on the World Wide Web, such as Ihatemcdonalds.com and Walmartsucks.com, are an important source of instability for scores of companies, from Allstate Insurance to Toys "R" Us. Microsoft critics can visit more than twenty hate sites.[23]

Although environments are becoming more unstable for most organizations today, an example of a traditionally stable environment is a public utility.[24] In the rural Midwest, demand and supply factors for a public utility are stable. A gradual increase in demand may occur, which is easily predicted over time. Toy companies, by contrast, have an unstable environment. Hot new toys are difficult to predict, a problem compounded by the fact that toys are subject to fad buying. Coleco Industries, makers of the once-famous Cabbage Patch Kids, and Worlds of Wonder, creators of Teddy Ruxpin, went bankrupt because of the unstable nature of the toy environment, their once-winning creations replaced by Bandai's Mighty Morphin Power Rangers or Playmate Toys' Teenage Mutant Ninja Turtles.[25] Those toys, in turn, were replaced by fads such as Furby, Beanie Babies, Star Wars figures, and Pokémon.

FRAMEWORK

The simple-complex and stable-unstable dimensions are combined into a framework for assessing environmental uncertainty in Exhibit 4.2. In the *simple, stable* environment, uncertainty is low. There are only a few external elements to contend with, and they tend to remain stable. The *complex, stable* environment represents somewhat greater uncertainty. A large number of elements have to be scanned, analyzed, and acted upon for the organization to perform well. External elements do not change rapidly or unexpectedly in this environment.

Even greater uncertainty is felt in the *simple, unstable* environment.[26] Rapid change creates uncertainty for managers. Even though the organization has few external elements, those elements are hard to predict, and they react unexpectedly to organizational initiatives. The greatest uncertainty for an organization occurs in the *complex, unstable* environment. A large number of elements impinge upon the organization, and they shift frequently or react strongly to organizational initiatives. When several sectors change simultaneously, the environment becomes turbulent.[27]

EXHIBIT 4.2   *Framework for Assessing Environmental Uncertainty*

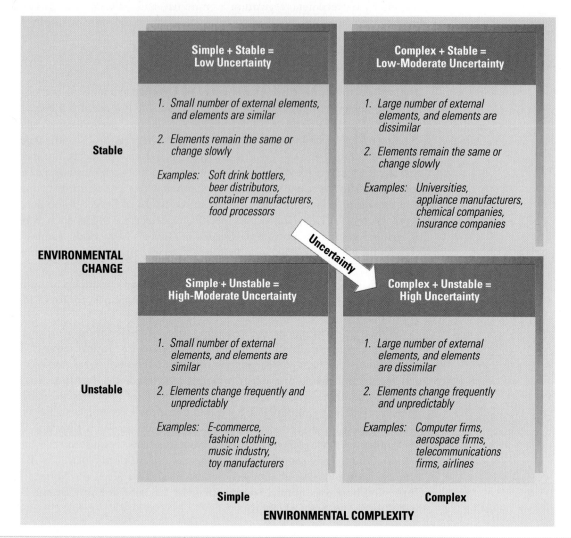

Source: Adapted and reprinted from "Characteristics of Perceived Environments and Perceived Environmental Uncertainty" by Robert B. Duncan, published in *Administrative Science Quarterly* 17 (1972): 313–27, by permission of *The Administrative Science Quarterly.* Copyright © 1972 by Cornell University.

A beer distributor functions in a simple, stable environment. Demand for beer changes only gradually. The distributor has an established delivery route, and supplies of beer arrive on schedule. State universities, appliance manufacturers, and insurance companies are in somewhat stable, complex environments. A large number of external elements are present, but although they change, changes are gradual and predictable.

Toy manufacturers are in simple, unstable environments. Organizations that design, make, and sell toys, as well as those that are involved in the clothing or music industry, face shifting supply and demand. Most e-commerce companies focus on a specific competitive niche and, hence, operate in simple but unstable environments. Although there may be few elements to contend with—e.g., technology, competitors—they are difficult to predict and change abruptly and unexpectedly.

The computer industry and the airline industry face complex, unstable environments. Many external sectors are changing simultaneously. In the case of airlines, in just a few years they were confronted with deregulation, the growth of regional airlines, surges in fuel costs, price cuts from competitors such as Southwest Airlines, shifting customer demand, an air-traffic controller shortage, overcrowded airports, and a reduction of scheduled flights.[28] A recent series of major air traffic disasters has further contributed to the complex, unstable environment for the industry.

In today's world of increased global competition, rapid technological breakthroughs, and shifting markets, companies in all industries are facing a greater level of complexity and change. Book Mark 4.0 discusses how organizations and managers can shift their ways of thinking and acting to remain competitive in this environment.

ADAPTING TO ENVIRONMENTAL UNCERTAINTY

Once you see how environments differ with respect to change and complexity, the next question is, "How do organizations adapt to each level of environmental uncertainty?" Environmental uncertainty represents an important contingency for organization structure and internal behaviors. Recall from Chapter 3 that organizations facing uncertainty generally have a more horizontal structure that encourages cross-functional communication and collaboration to help the company adapt to changes in the environment. In this section we will discuss in more detail how the environment affects organizations. An organization in a certain environment will be managed and controlled differently from an organization in an uncertain environment with respect to positions and departments, organizational differentiation and integration, control processes, and future planning and forecasting. Organizations need to have the right fit between internal structure and the external environment.

POSITIONS AND DEPARTMENTS

As the complexity in the external environment increases, so does the number of positions and departments within the organization, which in turn increases internal complexity. This relationship is part of being an open system. Each sector in the external environment requires an employee or department to deal with it. The human resources department deals with unemployed people who want to work for the company. The marketing department finds customers. Procurement employees obtain raw materials from hundreds of suppliers. The finance group deals with bankers. The legal department works with the courts and government agencies. Today, many companies are adding e-business departments to handle electronic commerce and information technology departments to deal with the increasing complexity of computerized information and knowledge management systems.

BUFFERING AND BOUNDARY SPANNING

The traditional approach to coping with environmental uncertainty was to establish buffer departments. The **buffering role** is to absorb uncertainty from the environment.[29] The technical core performs the primary production activity of an organization. Buffer departments surround the technical core and exchange materials, resources, and money between the environment and the organization.

ℬook ℳark 4.0

Have You Read This Book?

Open Boundaries: Creating Business Innovation Through Complexity

By Howard Sherman and Ron Schultz

The key argument of Howard Sherman and Ron Schultz's *Open Boundaries* is that, in today's turbulent environment, businesses that recognize themselves as open, complex, adaptive systems will be more successful than those that don't. For too long, they say, managers have failed to recognize that a company's business processes are often influenced by factors beyond anyone's control—the weather, for example, or unpredictable societal events. Their book is an attempt to change the way managers think about business in a complex environment.

NEW CONCEPTS FOR THE NEW WORLD OF BUSINESS

Managers are finding their traditional ideas and tools inadequate in a world of rapid change and complexity. According to the authors, managers need to rethink the way competition works in order to help their companies succeed in today's environment. Three concepts are key to their discussion of the direction business is going:

1. *Nonlinearity.* Sherman and Schultz argue that business today is not only faster but also fundamentally different. There is no continuity in the flow of competitive events, and competitive advantage is fleeting. Markets and technologies change so rapidly and dramatically that managers cannot predict which products or strategies will succeed.
2. *Self-Organization.* One implication of today's nonlinear business world is that traditional structures simply get in the way. The authors believe structures work best in a nonlinear world when they are self-organized. Rather

than imposing a structure on the organization, managers let the organization of people and resources evolve in response to changing demands from customers. The role of managers is to find and nurture the right people and provide them with the tools, information, and resources they need to work in self-organizing teams.

3. *Emergent Strategy.* Similarly, imposing strategy from above is of little value in a fast-changing environment. Because everything is evolving so rapidly and unpredictably, managers need to allow strategy to emerge out of current conditions. Managers do not have the time or knowledge to analyze market forces, develop strategic initiatives, or make sound financial projections. In a turbulent environment, such as that for many e-commerce organizations, managers' strategic responsibility is to create the right conditions for people throughout the organization to think, learn, and share knowledge.

CONCLUSION

The authors of *Open Boundaries* believe traditional management is too cumbersome for today's unpredictable environment. Their concepts of fluidity and self-organization give managers a new way to think about their businesses and about the role of managers. Particularly for today's Internet-based businesses, these ideas help managers create the right conditions to enable continuous learning and help the organization cope with changing markets and technologies.

Open Boundaries: Creating Business Innovation Through Complexity, by Howard Sherman and Ron Schultz, is published by Perseus Books.

They help the technical core function efficiently. The purchasing department buffers the technical core by stockpiling supplies and raw materials. The human resources department buffers the technical core by handling the uncertainty associated with finding, hiring, and training production employees.

A newer approach some organizations are trying is to drop the buffers and expose the technical core to the uncertain environment. These organizations no longer create buffers because they believe being well connected to customers and suppliers is more important than internal efficiency. For example, John Deere has assembly-line workers visiting local farms to determine and respond to customer concerns. Whirlpool pays hundreds of customers to test computer-simulated products and features.[30] Opening up the organization to the environment makes it more fluid and adaptable.

Boundary-spanning roles link and coordinate an organization with key elements in the external environment. Boundary spanning is primarily concerned with the exchange of information to (1) detect and bring into the organization information about changes in the environment and (2) send information into the environment that presents the organization in a favorable light.[31]

Organizations have to keep in touch with what is going on in the environment so that managers can respond to market changes and other developments. A survey of high-tech firms found that 97 percent of competitive failures resulted from lack of attention to market changes or the failure to act on vital information.[32] To detect and bring important information into the organization, boundary personnel scan the environment. For example, a market research department scans and monitors trends in consumer tastes. Boundary spanners in engineering and research and development (R&D) departments scan new technological developments, innovations, and raw materials. Boundary spanners prevent the organization from stagnating by keeping top managers informed about environmental changes. Often, the greater the uncertainty in the environment, the greater the importance of boundary spanners.[33]

One of the fastest growing areas of boundary spanning is competitive intelligence. Companies large and small are setting up competitive intelligence departments or hiring outside specialists to gather information on competitors. Competitive intelligence gives top executives a systematic way to collect and analyze public information about rivals and use it to make better decisions.[34] Using techniques that range from Internet surfing to digging through trash cans, intelligence professionals dig up information on competitors' new products, manufacturing costs, or training methods and share it with top leaders. For example, Nutrasweet's competitive intelligence department helped the company delay a costly advertising campaign when it learned that a rival sweetener was at least five years away from FDA approval.[35] In today's uncertain environment, competitive intelligence is a trend that is likely to increase. In addition, companies such as UtiliTech Inc. of Stratford, Connecticut, and WavePhore Inc. of Phoenix, Arizona, regularly monitor the Internet for large corporations to see what is being said about them on the Web. This provides important information to top executives about how the company is perceived in the environment.

The boundary task of sending information into the environment to represent the organization is used to influence other people's perception of the organization. In the marketing department, advertising and sales people represent the organization to customers. Purchasers may call on suppliers and describe purchasing needs. The legal department informs lobbyists and elected officials about the organization's needs or views on political matters. Many companies set up their own Web pages to present the organization in a favorable light. To counteract hate sites that criticize their labor practices in Third World countries, Nike and Unocal both created Web sites specifically to tell their side of the story.[36]

All organizations have to keep in touch with the environment. Here's how Tommy Hilfiger spans the boundary in the shifting environment of the fashion industry to stay ahead of the style curve.

Tommy Hilfiger

The No. 1 brand of jeans among young, hip consumers is no longer Levi's. According to a recent American Express Co. survey, Hilfiger jeans have taken the top spot among teenagers. That's largely because Hilfiger keeps in close touch with youth fashion trends.

The torrent of high-speed information available on the Internet means teen fashion changes faster than ever, and Tommy Hilfiger wants to stay ahead of the curve. So, when Hilfiger's distinctive logo-laden shirts and jackets first began showing up on urban rappers in the early 1990s, the company started sending researchers into music clubs all across America to see how this influential group of consumers was wearing the styles. This gave executives information they needed to keep shifting Hilfiger styles to keep up with the times. Hilfiger also used the information to bolster its traditional mass-media ads with unusual promotions such as giving free clothing to stars on MTV and VH1. Recognizing its customers' passion for computer games, the company sponsored a Nintendo competition and installed Nintendo terminals in its stores. So far, Hilfiger's efforts to stay close to young customers are working.

Compare Tommy Hilfiger's success with the decline of Levi Strauss. Levi jeans were an icon of baby boomer youth, but the company's market share has been slipping and the brand is losing popularity among teens. "We all got older," says David Spangler, director of market research for the company, "and as a consequence, we lost touch with teenagers." Levi Strauss is trying to correct the problem by revamping its Web site, redesigning its advertising, and setting up panels of teens to keep tabs on emerging trends in the ever-changing fashion world.[37]

DIFFERENTIATION AND INTEGRATION

Another response to environmental uncertainty is the amount of differentiation and integration among departments. Organization **differentiation** is "the differences in cognitive and emotional orientations among managers in different functional departments, and the difference in formal structure among these departments."[38] When the external environment is complex and rapidly changing, organizational departments become highly specialized to handle the uncertainty in their external sector. Success in each sector requires special expertise and behavior. Employees in a research and development department thus have unique attitudes, values, goals, and education that distinguish them from employees in manufacturing or sales departments.

A study by Paul Lawrence and Jay Lorsch examined three organizational departments—manufacturing, research, and sales—in ten corporations.[39] This study found that each department evolved toward a different orientation and structure to deal with specialized parts of the external environment. The market, scientific, and manufacturing subenvironments identified by Lawrence and Lorsch are illustrated in Exhibit 4.3. Each department interacted with different external groups. The differences that evolved among departments within the organizations are shown in Exhibit 4.4. To work effectively with the scientific subenvironment, R&D had a goal of quality work, a long time horizon (up to five years), an informal structure, and task-oriented employees. Sales was at the opposite extreme. It had a goal of customer satisfaction, was oriented toward the short term (two weeks or so), had a very formal structure, and was socially oriented.

One outcome of high differentiation is that coordination among departments becomes difficult. More time and resources must be devoted to achieving

EXHIBIT 4.3   *Organizational Departments Differentiate to Meet Needs of Subenvironments*

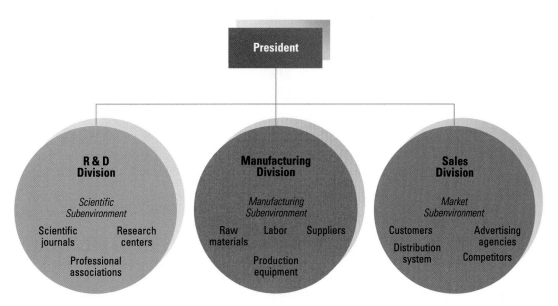

coordination when attitudes, goals, and work orientation differ so widely. **Integration** is the quality of collaboration among departments.[40] Formal integrators are often required to coordinate departments. When the environment is highly uncertain, frequent changes require more information processing to achieve horizontal coordination, so integrators become a necessary addition to the organization structure. Sometimes integrators are called liaison personnel, project managers, brand managers, or coordinators. As illustrated in Exhibit 4.5, organizations with highly uncertain environments and a highly differentiated structure assign about 22 percent of management personnel to integration activities, such as serving on committees, on task forces, or in liaison roles.[41] In organizations characterized by very simple, stable environments, almost no managers are assigned to integration roles. Exhibit 4.5 shows that, as environmental uncertainty increases, so does differentiation among departments; hence, the organization must assign a larger percentage of managers to coordinating roles.

Lawrence and Lorsch's research concluded that organizations perform better when the levels of differentiation and integration match the level of uncertainty in the environment. Organizations that performed well in uncertain environments

EXHIBIT 4.4   *Differences in Goals and Orientations Among Organizational Departments*

Characteristic	R & D Department	Manufacturing Department	Sales Department
Goals	New developments, quality	Efficient production	Customer satisfaction
Time horizon	Long	Short	Short
Interpersonal orientation	Mostly task	Task	Social
Formality of structure	Low	High	High

Source: Based on Paul R. Lawrence and Jay W. Lorsch, *Organization and Environment* (Homewood, Ill.: Irwin, 1969), 23–29.

EXHIBIT 4.5   *Environmental Uncertainty and Organizational Integrators*

	Plastics	Industry: Foods	Container
Environmental uncertainty	High	Moderate	Low
Departmental differentiation	High	Moderate	Low
Percent management in integrating roles	22%	17%	0%

Source: Based on Jay W. Lorsch and Paul R. Lawrence, "Environmental Factors and Organizational Integration," *Organizational Planning: Cases and Concepts* (Homewood, Ill.: Irwin and Dorsey, 1972), 45.

had high levels of both differentiation and integration, while those performing well in less uncertain environments had lower levels of differentiation and integration.

ORGANIC VERSUS MECHANISTIC MANAGEMENT PROCESSES

Another response to environmental uncertainty is the amount of formal structure and control imposed on employees. Tom Burns and G. M. Stalker observed twenty industrial firms in England and discovered that external environment was related to internal management structure.[42] When the external environment was stable, the internal organization was characterized by rules, procedures, and a clear hierarchy of authority. Organizations were formalized. They were also centralized, with most decisions made at the top. Burns and Stalker called this a **mechanistic** organization system.

In rapidly changing environments, the internal organization was much looser, free-flowing, and adaptive. Rules and regulations often were not written down or, if written down, were ignored. People had to find their own way through the system to figure out what to do. The hierarchy of authority was not clear. Decision-making authority was decentralized. Burns and Stalker used the term **organic** to characterize this type of management structure.

Exhibit 4.6 summarizes the differences in organic and mechanistic systems. As environmental uncertainty increases, organizations tend to become more organic, which means decentralizing authority and responsibility to lower levels, encouraging employees to take care of problems by working directly with one another, encouraging teamwork, and taking an informal approach to assigning

EXHIBIT 4.6   *Mechanistic and Organic Forms*

Mechanistic	Organic
1. Tasks are broken down into specialized separate parts.	1. Employees contribute to the common tasks of the department.
2. Tasks are rigidly defined.	2. Tasks are adjusted and redefined through employee teamwork.
3. There is a strict hierarchy of authority and control, and there are many rules.	3. There is less hierarchy of authority and control, and there are few rules.
4. Knowledge and control of tasks are centralized at the top of organization.	4. Knowledge and control of tasks are located anywhere in the organization.
5. Communication is vertical.	5. Communication is horizontal.

Source: Adapted from Gerald Zaltman, Robert Duncan, and Johnny Holbek, *Innovations and Organizations* (New York: Wiley, 1973), 131.

tasks and responsibility. Thus, the organization is more fluid and is able to adapt continually to changes in the external environment.[43]

The learning organization, described in Chapter 1, and the horizontal structure, described in Chapter 3, are organic organizational forms that are used by companies to compete in rapidly changing environments. One example of a company that shifted to a more organic system to cope with change and uncertainty is Rowe Furniture Company, described in the Taking the Lead box.

Taking the Lead

Rowe Furniture Company

Nestled in the foothills of the Appalachian mountains, the Rowe Furniture Company of Salem, Virginia, has been cranking out sofas, loveseats, and easy chairs for more than forty years. For most of that time, Rowe's workers punched their time cards, turned off their brains, and did exactly what the boss told them to do. When Charlene Pedrolie came to Rowe as the plant's new manufacturing chief, she found five hundred people working on a traditional assembly line, performing the same boring tasks over and over—one person cutting, another sewing, another gluing, and so forth. Rowe had been successful with this approach so far, but the marketplace was changing and top executives knew Rowe needed to change to keep pace.

Furniture shoppers used to be content to buy what was on the showroom floor or else wait months for a custom-made product. But not any longer—customers were demanding custom-designed pieces, but in today's fast-paced world, most wouldn't tolerate the long lead times, which could be up to six months. Rowe executives responded by installing a network of showroom computers, which allowed customers to select fabrics and furniture designs to their individual tastes, then promised delivery within a month. To meet that difficult challenge Rowe needed a hyper-efficient assembly process, and Pedrolie believed the solution resided in the collective minds of the people out on the shop floor. She eliminated most supervisory positions, cross trained employees to perform the different tasks required to build a piece of furniture, and then asked front line workers to form horizontal clusters, or *cells*, and design the new production system. Each group selected its own members from the various functional areas, then created the processes, schedules, and routines for a particular product line. The assembly line was a thing of the past. Five hundred workers who had been accustomed to standing in one place and having the furniture come to them were suddenly wandering from one partially assembled piece to another, performing a variety of tasks. For a while, it was sheer chaos, and some workers walked off the job and never came back. However, within a few weeks, the pieces fell into place. And when they did, productivity and quality shot through the roof. Before long, the factory was delivering custom-made pieces within thirty days. Only a few months later, that lead time had decreased to a mere ten days.

A key to Rowe's new system is open information. Every member of every team has instant access to current information about order flows, output, productivity, and quality. Data that were once closely guarded by management are now the common property of the shop floor. The sense of personal control and responsibility eventually led to a dramatic change in workers, who began holding impromptu meetings to discuss problems, check each other's progress, or talk about new ideas and better ways of doing things. One group came together as a "down-pillow task force" to invent a better stuffing process. Another came up with a way to increase the capacity of the drying kilns by feeding in sawdust as fuel; as the kilns became more and more efficient, they began selling the excess drying capacity to outside lumber treaters through their own marketing program, thereby creating an entirely new business for Rowe.

The shift to an organic system at Rowe was not easy, but managers believe the results were worth the effort, creating an environment in which workers are constantly learning, solving problems, and creating new and better ways of doing things.

Source: Thomas Petzinger, Jr., *The New Pioneers: The Men and Women Who Are Transforming the Workplace and Marketplace* (New York: Simon & Schuster, 1999), 27–32.

PLANNING AND FORECASTING

The final organizational response to uncertainty is to increase planning and environmental forecasting. When the environment is stable, the organization can concentrate on current operational problems and day-to-day efficiency. Long-range planning and forecasting are not needed because environmental demands in the future will be the same as they are today.

With increasing environmental uncertainty, planning and forecasting become necessary.[44] Planning can soften the adverse impact of external shifting. Organizations that have unstable environments often establish a separate planning department. In an unpredictable environment, planners scan environmental elements and analyze potential moves and countermoves by other organizations. Planning can be extensive and may forecast various scenarios for environmental contingencies. As time passes, plans are updated through replanning. However, planning does not substitute for other actions, such as boundary spanning. Indeed, under conditions of extraordinarily high uncertainty, formal planning may not be helpful because the future is so difficult to predict. Learning organizations keep everyone in constant touch with the environment so they can spot threats and opportunities, enabling the organization to respond immediately.

FRAMEWORK FOR ORGANIZATIONAL RESPONSES TO UNCERTAINTY

The ways environmental uncertainty influences organizational characteristics are summarized in Exhibit 4.7. The change and complexity dimensions are combined and illustrate four levels of uncertainty. The low uncertainty environment is simple and stable. Organizations in this environment have few departments and a mechanistic structure. In a low-moderate uncertainty environment, more departments are needed along with more integrating roles to coordinate the departments. Some planning may occur. Environments that are high-moderate uncertainty are unstable but simple. Organization structure is organic and decentralized. Planning is emphasized and managers are quick to make internal changes as needed. The high uncertainty environment is both complex and unstable and is the most difficult environment from a management perspective. Organizations are large and have many departments, but they are also organic. A large number of management personnel are assigned to coordination and integration, and the organization uses boundary spanning, planning, and forecasting.

RESOURCE DEPENDENCE

Thus far, this chapter has described several ways in which organizations adapt to the lack of information and to the uncertainty caused by environmental change and complexity. We turn now to the third characteristic of the organization-environment relationship that affects organizations, which is the need for material and financial resources. The environment is the source of scarce and valued resources essential to organizational survival. Research in this area is called the resource dependence perspective. **Resource dependence** means that organizations depend on the environment but strive to acquire control over resources to minimize their dependence.[45] Organizations are vulnerable if vital resources are controlled by other organizations, so they try to be as independent as possible. Organizations do not want to become too vulnerable to other organizations because of negative effects on performance. For example, several years ago the supplier for more than half of Mattress Warehouse's stock decided to open a factory-direct store in the same market. Mattress Warehouse had only a week's notice that the supplier relationship was terminated, leaving the company scrambling to find another bedding vendor. It was a wake-up call for Mattress Warehouse owner Kimberly Brown Knopf, who diversified her supplier base to prevent the loss of one supplier from jeopardizing her business in the future.[46]

When costs and risks are high, however, companies also team up to reduce resource dependence and the possibility of bankruptcy. In today's volatile environment, companies are collaborating as never before to share scarce resources and be more competitive on a global scale.

EXHIBIT 4.7   *Contingency Framework for Environmental Uncertainty and Organizational Responses*

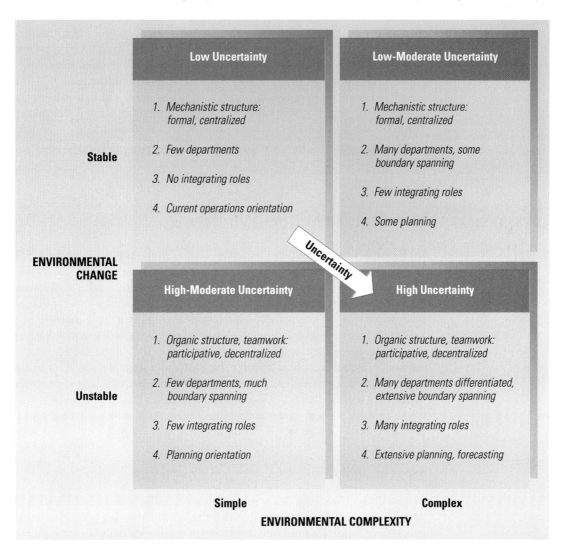

Formal relationships with other organizations, however, present a dilemma to managers. North American organizations seek to reduce vulnerability with respect to resources by developing links with other organizations, but they also like to maximize their own autonomy and independence. Organizational linkages require coordination,[47] and they reduce the freedom of each organization to make decisions without concern for the needs and goals of other organizations. Interorganizational relationships thus represent a tradeoff between resources and autonomy. To maintain autonomy, organizations that already have abundant resources will tend not to establish new linkages. Organizations that need resources will give up independence to acquire those resources.

Dependence on shared resources gives power to other organizations. Once an organization relies on others for valued resources, those other organizations can influence managerial decision making. When a large company like DuPont, Motorola, or Xerox forges a partnership with a supplier for parts, both sides benefit, but each loses a small amount of autonomy. For example, some of these large companies are now putting strong pressure on vendors to lower costs, and the vendors have few alternatives but to go along.[48] In much the same way, dependence on shared resources gives advertisers power over print and electronic media companies. For example, as newspapers face increasingly tough financial times, they are less likely to run stories that are critical of advertisers. Though newspapers insist advertisers don't get special treatment, some editors admit there is growing talk around the country of the need for "advertiser-friendly" newspapers.[49]

In another industry, Microsoft is so large and powerful that it has a virtual monopoly in personal computer operating systems, so its every technical change adversely affects producers of application software. Microsoft has been accused of abusing this power and of squashing small competitors that would like to link up with it.[50]

CONTROLLING ENVIRONMENTAL RESOURCES

In response to the need for resources, organizations try to maintain a balance between linkages with other organizations and their own independence. Organizations maintain this balance through attempts to modify, manipulate, or control other organizations.[51] To survive, the focal organization often tries to reach out and change or control elements in the environment. Two strategies can be adopted to manage resources in the external environment: (1) establish favorable linkages with key elements in the environment and (2) shape the environmental domain.[52] Techniques to accomplish each of these strategies are summarized in Exhibit 4.8. As a general rule, when organizations sense that valued resources are scarce, they will use the strategies in Exhibit 4.8 rather than go it alone. Notice how dissimilar these strategies are from the responses to environmental change and complexity described in Exhibit 4.7. The dissimilarity reflects the difference between responding to the need for information rather than to the need for resources.

ESTABLISHING INTERORGANIZATIONAL LINKAGES

Ownership. Companies use ownership to establish linkages when they buy a part of or a controlling interest in another company. This gives the company access to technology, products, or other resources it doesn't currently have. The

EXHIBIT 4.8   *Organizing Strategies for Controlling the External Environment*

Establishing Interorganizational Linkages	Controlling the Environmental Domain
1. Ownership	1. Change of domain
2. Contracts, joint ventures	2. Political activity, regulation
3. Cooptation, interlocking directorates	3. Trade associations
4. Executive recruitment	4. Illegitimate activities
5. Advertising, public relations	

communications and information technology industry has become particularly complex, and many companies have been teaming up worldwide.

A greater degree of ownership and control is obtained through acquisition or merger. An *acquisition* involves the purchase of one organization by another so that the buyer assumes control. A *merger* is the unification of two or more organizations into a single unit.[53] In the world of e-business, USWeb and CKS Group merged to create a company that pulls in more than a quarter of a billion dollars by helping companies set up and run Internet divisions. Its clients include the dot-com divisions of companies such as Apple, NBC, and Levi Strauss.[54] The creation of Pharmacia & Upjohn Inc. from the Upjohn Co. of Kalamazoo, Michigan, and Sweden's Pharmacia was a merger. Acquisition occurred when Hewlett-Packard bought VeriFone and when America Online purchased Netscape Communications. These forms of ownership reduce uncertainty in an area important to the acquiring company.

Formal Strategic Alliances. When there is a high level of complementarity between the business lines, geographical positions, or skills of two companies, the firms often go the route of a strategic alliance rather than ownership through merger or acquisition.[55] Such alliances are formed through contracts and joint ventures.

Contracts and joint ventures reduce uncertainty through a legal and binding relationship with another firm. Contracts come in the form of *license agreements* that involve the purchase of the right to use an asset (such as a new technology) for a specific time and *supplier arrangements* that contract for the sale of one firm's output to another. Contracts can provide long-term security by tying customers and suppliers to specific amounts and prices. For example, McDonald's contracts for an entire crop of russet potatoes to be certain of its supply of french fries. McDonald's also gains influence over suppliers through these contracts and has changed the way farmers grow potatoes and the profit margins they earn, which is consistent with the resource dependence perspective.[56] Large retailers such as Wal-Mart, Kmart, Toys 'R' Us, and Home Depot are gaining so much clout that they can almost dictate contracts telling manufacturers what to make, how to make it, and how much to charge for it. For example, CD companies edit songs and visual covers to cut out "offensive material" in order to get their products on the shelves of Wal-Mart, which sells more than 50 million CDs annually. As one manufacturing rep put it, "Most suppliers would do absolutely anything to sell Wal-Mart."[57] *Joint ventures* result in the creation of a new organization that is formally independent of the parents, although the parents will have some control.[58] In a joint venture, organizations share the risk and cost associated with large projects or innovations. As described in the opening case, Barnesandnoble.com is a joint venture between Barnes & Noble and Germany's Bertelsmann AG. Barnes & Noble and Bertelsmann have agreed to invest $100 million each and share the risks of the joint venture as it battles Amazon.com in the world of online bookselling.

Cooptation, Interlocking Directorates. Cooptation occurs when leaders from important sectors in the environment are made part of an organization. It takes place, for example, when influential customers or suppliers are appointed to the board of directors, such as when the senior executive of a bank sits on the board of a manufacturing company. As a board member, the banker may become psychologically coopted into the interests of the manufacturing firm. Community leaders also can be appointed to a company's board of directors or to other organizational committees or task forces. These influential people are thus introduced to the needs of the company and are more likely to include the company's interests in their decision making.

An **interlocking directorate** is a formal linkage that occurs when a member of the board of directors of one company sits on the board of directors of another company. The individual is a communications link between companies and can influence policies and decisions. Internet startups, such as the Seattle-based companies TechWave, AccountingNet, and Honkworm International, often use this strategy to share advice and resources.[59] When one individual is the link between two companies, this is typically referred to as a **direct interlock**. An **indirect interlock** occurs when a director of company A and a director of company B are both directors of company C. They have access to one another but do not have direct influence over their respective companies.[60] Recent research shows that, as a firm's financial fortunes decline, direct interlocks with financial institutions increase. Financial uncertainty facing an industry also has been associated with greater indirect interlocks between competing companies.[61]

Executive Recruitment. Transferring or exchanging executives also offers a method of establishing favorable linkages with external organizations. For example, each year the aerospace industry hires retired generals and executives from the Department of Defense. These generals have personal friends in the department, so the aerospace companies obtain better information about technical specifications, prices, and dates for new weapon systems. They can learn the needs of the defense department and are able to present their case for defense contracts in a more effective way. Companies without personal contacts find it nearly impossible to get a defense contract. Having channels of influence and communication between organizations serves to reduce financial uncertainty and dependence for an organization.

Advertising and Public Relations. A traditional way of establishing favorable relationships is through advertising. Organizations spend large amounts of money to influence the taste of consumers. Advertising is especially important in highly competitive consumer industries and in industries that experience variable demand. In the fashion industry, once-stodgy JCPenney turned its Arizona Jeans into one of the hottest brands around through hip advertising featuring rock music and Internet imagery. A recent ad campaign shows teens mocking ads that attempt to speak their language, ending with the tagline "Just show me the jeans."[62]

Public relations is similar to advertising, except that stories often are free and aimed at public opinion. Public relations people cast an organization in a favorable light in speeches, in press reports, and on television. Public relations attempts to shape the company's image in the minds of customers, suppliers, and government officials. For example, in an effort to survive in this antismoking era, tobacco companies have launched an aggressive public relations campaign touting smokers' rights and freedom of choice.

Summary. Organizations can use a variety of techniques to establish favorable linkages that ensure the availability of scarce resources. Linkages provide control over vulnerable environmental elements. Strategic alliances, interlocking directorates, and outright ownership provide mechanisms to reduce resource dependency on the environment. U.S. companies such as IBM, Apple, AT&T, and Motorola have been quick in recent years to turn rivalry into partnership. Perhaps surprisingly, Japan's electronics companies have been slower to become involved in joint ventures and other strategic alliances. Toshiba, however, has been living in the age of high-tech alliances for years and has the competitive edge to show for it.

In Practice 4.3

Toshiba

Strategic alliances have been a key element in Toshiba's corporate strategy since the early 1900s, when the company contracted to make light bulb filaments for General Electric. Since then, Toshiba has taken advantage of partnerships, licensing agreements, and joint ventures to become one of the world's leading manufacturers of electronic products. A joint venture with Motorola has made Toshiba the top maker of large-scale memory chips. Other partnerships aid the company in producing computers, fax machines, copiers, medical equipment, advanced semiconductors, home appliances, and nuclear and steam power-generating equipment, just for starters. Exhibit 4.9 shows some of the many linkages Toshiba has shared with other companies.

Toshiba is currently involved in more than two dozen major partnerships or joint ventures for two reasons. One is money: Toshiba, IBM, and Siemens shared the $1 billion cost of developing a new 64mb and 256mb memory chip facility in Nagoya that uses ultraviolet lithography to etch circuits less than one micron wide. The new technology was transferred back to an IBM facility in the United States as well. Toshiba and IBM also jointly make liquid-crystal display panels, even though the two companies use the LCDs in their fiercely competitive laptop computers. The second reason is speed: carefully chosen partners offer the best means of harnessing the resources needed to keep pace with rapid technological change and today's shifting global marketplace.[63]

Toshiba illustrates how linkages can be used to control resources and reduce dependency. The other major strategy companies can use to manage resource dependency is to control or redefine the external environmental domain.

CONTROLLING THE ENVIRONMENTAL DOMAIN

In addition to establishing favorable linkages to obtain resources, organizations often try to change the environment. There are four techniques for influencing or changing a firm's environmental domain.

Change of Domain. The ten sectors described earlier in this chapter are not fixed. The organization decides which business it is in, the market to enter, and the suppliers, banks, employees, and location to use, and this domain can be

EXHIBIT 4.9   *Interorganizational Linkages of Toshiba Corporation*

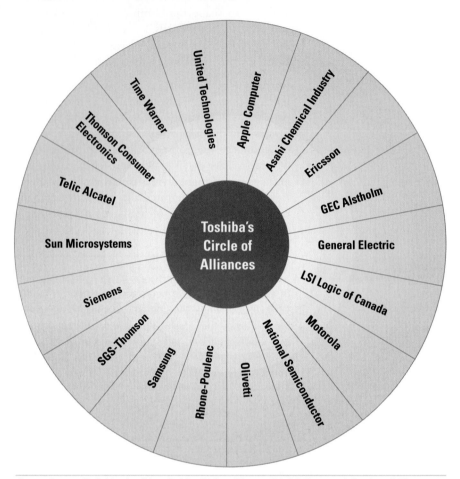

Source: Brenton R. Schlender, "How Toshiba Makes Alliances Work," *Fortune*, 4 October 1993, 116–120.

changed.[64] An organization can seek new environmental relationships and drop old ones. An organization may try to find a domain where there is little competition, no government regulation, abundant suppliers, affluent customers, and barriers to keep competitors out.

Acquisition and divestment are two techniques for altering the domain. Canada's Bombardier, maker of Ski-Doo snowmobiles, began a series of acquisitions to alter its domain when the energy crisis of the mid-1970s nearly wiped out the snowmobile industry. CEO Laurent Beaudoin gradually moved the company into the aerospace industry by negotiating deals to purchase Canadair, Boeing's deHaviland unit, business-jet pioneer Learjet, and Short Brothers of Northern Ireland. Deere & Co. felt vulnerable with the declining customer base for agricultural machinery, so Chairman and CEO Hans Becherer began reallocating resources into other lines of business, such as health care and financial services. Entering these new domains is helping Deere weather uncertain times and take some pressure off the machinery business.[65] An example of divestment is when Sears redefined its domain by selling off its financial services divisions, including Coldwell Banker, Allstate, and Dean Witter, to focus the company on retailing.

Political Activity, Regulation. Political activity includes techniques to influence government legislation and regulation. For example, General Motors used political activity to successfully settle a battle with the U.S. Transportation Department over the safety of some of its pickup trucks. The settlement requires that GM spend $51 million on safety programs over a five-year period but saved the company the cost of a $1 billion recall.[66]

In one technique, organizations pay lobbyists to express their views to members of federal and state legislatures. In the telecommunications industry, the Baby Bells hired powerful lobbyists to influence a sweeping new telecommunications bill giving local phone companies access to new markets.[67] Many CEOs, however, believe they should do their own lobbying. CEOs have easier access than lobbyists and can be especially effective when they do the politicking. Political activity is so important that "informal lobbyist" is an unwritten part of almost any CEO's job description.[68]

Political strategy can be used to erect regulatory barriers against new competitors or to squash unfavorable legislation. Corporations also try to influence the appointment to agencies of people who are sympathetic to their needs. The value of political activity is illustrated by the efforts of Sun Microsystems and Netscape to persuade the Justice Department to break up Microsoft, arguing that Microsoft had acted as a monopoly in controlling the software industry and now threatened to extend that power to Internet access. Some observers noted that if Microsoft had paid more attention to political lobbying earlier, it could have avoided Justice Department investigation.

Trade Associations. Much of the work to influence the external environment is accomplished jointly with other organizations that have similar interests. Most manufacturing companies are part of the National Association of Manufacturers and also belong to associations in their specific industry. By pooling resources, these organizations can pay people to carry out activities such as lobbying legislators, influencing new regulations, developing public relations campaigns, and making campaign contributions. For example, the National Tooling and Machining Association (NTMA) devotes a quarter of a million dollars each year to lobbying, mainly on issues that affect small business, such as taxes, health insurance, or government mandates. NTMA also gives its members statistics and information that help them become more competitive in the global marketplace.[69]

Illegitimate Activities. Illegitimate activities represent the final technique companies sometimes use to control their environmental domain. Certain conditions, such as low profits, pressure from senior managers, or scarce environmental resources, may lead managers to adopt behaviors not considered legitimate.[70] Many well-known companies have been found guilty of behavior considered unlawful. Example behaviors include payoffs to foreign governments, illegal political contributions, promotional gifts, and wiretapping. Intense competition among cement producers and in the oil business during a period of decline led to thefts and illegal kickbacks.[71] In the defense industry, the intense competition for declining contracts for major weapon systems led some companies to do almost anything to get an edge, including schemes to peddle inside information and to pay off officials.[72] One study found that companies in industries with low demand, shortages, and strikes were more likely to be convicted for illegal activities, implying that illegal acts are an attempt to cope with resource scarcity.[73] In another study, social movement organizations such as Earth First! and the AIDS Coalition to Unleash Power (ActUp) were found to have acted in ways considered illegitimate or even illegal to bolster their visibility and reputation.[74]

ORGANIZATION-ENVIRONMENT INTEGRATIVE FRAMEWORK

The relationships illustrated in Exhibit 4.10 summarize the two major themes about organization-environment relationships discussed in this chapter. One theme is that the amount of complexity and change in an organization's domain influences the need for information and hence the uncertainty felt within an organization. Greater information uncertainty is resolved through greater structural flexibility, and the assignment of additional departments and boundary roles. When uncertainty is low, management structures can be more mechanistic, and the number of departments and boundary roles can be fewer. The second theme pertains to the scarcity of material and financial resources. The more dependent an organization is on other organizations for those resources, the more important it is to either establish favorable linkages with those organizations or control entry into the domain. If dependence on external resources is

EXHIBIT 4.10   *Relationship Between Environmental Characteristics and Organizational Actions*

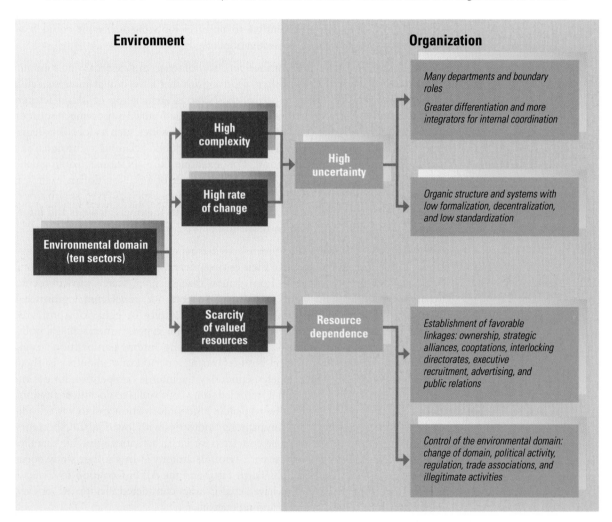

low, the organization can maintain autonomy and does not need to establish linkages or control the external domain.

SUMMARY AND INTERPRETATION

The external environment has an overwhelming impact on management uncertainty and organization functioning. Organizations are open social systems. Most are involved with hundreds of external elements. The change and complexity in environmental domains have major implications for organizational design and action. Most organizational decisions, activities, and outcomes can be traced to stimuli in the external environment.

Organizational environments differ in terms of uncertainty and resource dependence. Organizational uncertainty is the result of the stable-unstable and simple-complex dimensions of the environment. Resource dependence is the result of scarcity of the material and financial resources needed by the organization.

Organization design takes on a logical perspective when the environment is considered. Organizations try to survive and achieve efficiencies in a world characterized by uncertainty and scarcity. Specific departments and functions are created to deal with uncertainties. The organization can be conceptualized as a technical core and departments that buffer environmental uncertainty. Boundary-spanning roles provide information about the environment.

The concepts in this chapter provide specific frameworks for understanding how the environment influences the structure and functioning of an organization. Environmental complexity and change, for example, have specific impact on internal complexity and adaptability. Under great uncertainty, more resources are allocated to departments that will plan, deal with specific environmental elements, and integrate diverse internal activities. Moreover, when risk is great or resources are scarce, the organization can establish linkages through the acquisition of ownership and through strategic alliances, interlocking directorates, executive recruitment, or advertising and public relations that will minimize risk and maintain a supply of scarce resources. Other techniques for controlling the environment include a change of the domain in which the organization operates, political activity, participation in trade associations, and perhaps illegitimate activities.

Two important themes in this chapter are that organizations can learn and adapt to the environment and that organizations can change and control the environment. These strategies are especially true for large organizations that command many resources. Such organizations can adapt when necessary but can also neutralize or change problematic areas in the environment.

BRIEFCASE

As an organization manager, keep these guidelines in mind:

1. Organize elements in the external environment into ten sectors for analysis: industry, raw materials, human resources, financial resources, market, technology, economic, government, sociocultural, and international. Focus on sectors that may experience significant change at any time.

2. Scan the external environment for threats, changes, and opportunities. Use boundary-spanning roles, such as market research and competitive intelligence departments, to bring into the organization information about changes in the environment. Enhance boundary-spanning capabilities when the environment is uncertain.

3. Match internal organization structure to the external environment. If the external environment is complex, make the organization structure complex. Associate a stable environment with a mechanistic structure and an unstable environment with an organic structure. If the external environment is both complex and changing, make the organization highly differentiated and organic, and use mechanisms to achieve coordination across departments.

4. Reach out and control external sectors that threaten needed resources. Influence the domain by engaging in political activity, joining trade associations, and establishing favorable linkages. Establish linkages through ownership, strategic alliances, cooptation, interlocking directorates, executive recruitment, advertising, and public relations. Reduce the amount of change or threat from the external environment so the organization will not have to change internally.

KEY CONCEPTS

boundary-spanning roles	mechanistic
buffering roles	organic
cooptation	organizational environment
differentiation	resource dependence
direct interlock	sectors
domain	simple-complex dimension
general environment	stable-unstable dimension
indirect interlock	task environment
integration	uncertainty
interlocking directorate	

DISCUSSION QUESTIONS

1. Define *organizational environment*. Would the task environment for a new Internet-based company be the same as that of a government welfare agency? Discuss.

2. What are some forces that influence environmental uncertainty? Which typically has the greatest impact on uncertainty—environmental complexity or environmental change? Why?

3. Why does environmental complexity lead to organizational complexity? Explain.

4. Discuss the importance of the international sector for today's organizations, compared to domestic sectors. What are some ways in which the international sector affects organizations in your city or community?

5. Describe differentiation and integration. In what type of environmental uncertainty will differentiation and integration be greatest? Least?

6. Under what environmental conditions is organizational planning emphasized? Is planning an appropriate response to a turbulent environment?

7. What is an organic organization? A mechanistic organization? How does the environment influence organic and mechanistic structures?

8. Why do organizations become involved in interorganizational relationships? Do these relationships affect an organization's dependency? Performance?
9. Assume you have been asked to calculate the ratio of staff employees to production employees in two organizations—one in a simple, stable environment and one in a complex, shifting environment. How would you expect these ratios to differ? Why?
10. Is changing the organization's domain a feasible strategy for coping with a threatening environment? Explain.

C H A P T E R   4   W O R K B O O K   *Organizations You Rely On**

Below, list eight organizations you somehow rely on in your daily life. Examples might be a restaurant, a clothing or CD store, university, family, post office, telephone company, airline, pizza delivery, your place of work, and so on. In the first column, list those eight organizations. Then, in column 2, choose another organization you could use in case the ones in column 1 were not available. In column 3, evaluate your level of dependence on the organizations listed in column 1 as: Strong, Medium, or Weak. Finally, in column 4, rate the certainty of that organization being able to meet your needs as: High (certainty), Medium, or Low.

Column 1 Organization	Column 2 Backup	Column 3 Level of dependence	Column 4 Level of certainty
1.			
2.			
3.			
4.			
5.			
6.			
7.			
8.			

*Adapted by Dorothy Marcic from "Organizational Dependencies," in Ricky W. Griffin and Thomas C. Head, *Practicing Management*, 2nd ed. (Dallas: Houghton Mifflin), 2–3.

QUESTIONS

1. Do you have adequate backup organizations for those of high dependence? How might you create even more backups?
2. What would you do if an organization you rated high dependence and high certainty suddenly became high dependence and low certainty?

How would your behavior relate to the concept of resource dependence?

3. Have you ever used any behaviors similar to those in Exhibit 4.8 to manage your relationships with the organizations listed in column 1?

Case for Analysis   *The Paradoxical Twins: Acme and Omega Electronics**

PART I

In 1970, Technological Products of Erie, Pennsylvania, was bought out by a Cleveland manufacturer. The Cleveland firm had no interest in the electronics division of Technological Products and subsequently sold to different investors two plants that manufactured printed circuit boards. One of the plants, located in nearby Waterford, was renamed Acme Electronics; the other plant, within the city limits of Erie, was renamed Omega Electronics, Inc.

Acme retained its original management and upgraded its general manager to president. Omega hired a new president who had been a director of a large electronic research laboratory and upgraded several of the existing personnel within the plant. Acme and Omega often competed for the same contracts. As subcontractors, both firms benefited from the electronics boom of the 1970s, and both looked forward to future growth and expansion. Acme had annual sales of $100 million and employed 550 people. Omega had annual sales of $80 million and employed 480 people. Acme regularly achieved greater net profits, much to the chagrin of Omega's management.

Inside Acme

The president of Acme, John Tyler, was confident that, had the demand not been so great, Acme's competitor would not have survived. "In fact," he said, "we have been able to beat Omega regularly for the most profitable contracts, thereby increasing our profit." Tyler credited his firm's greater effectiveness to his managers' abilities to run a "tight ship." He explained that he had retained the basic structure developed by Technological Products because it was most efficient for the high-volume manufacture of printed circuits and their subsequent assembly. Acme had detailed organization charts and job descriptions. Tyler believed everyone should have clear responsibilities and narrowly defined jobs, which would lead to efficient performance and high company profits. People were generally satisfied with their work at Acme; however, some of the managers voiced the desire to have a little more latitude in their jobs.

Inside Omega

Omega's president, Jim Rawls, did not believe in organization charts. He felt his organization had departments similar to Acme's, but he thought Omega's plant was small enough that things such as organization charts just put artificial barriers between specialists who should be working together. Written memos were not allowed since, as Rawls expressed it, "the plant is small enough that if people want to communicate, they can just drop by and talk things over."

The head of the mechanical engineering department said, "Jim spends too much of his time and mine making sure everyone understands what we're doing and listening to suggestions." Rawls was concerned with employee satisfaction and wanted everyone to feel part of the organization. The top management team reflected Rawls's attitudes. They also believed that employees should be familiar with activities throughout the organization so that cooperation between departments would be increased. A newer member of the industrial engineering department said, "When I first got here, I wasn't sure what I was supposed to do. One day I worked with some mechanical engineers and the next day I helped the shipping department design some packing cartons. The first months on the job were hectic, but at least I got a real feel for what makes Omega tick."

*Adapted from John F. Veiga, "The Paradoxical Twins: Acme and Omega Electronics," in John F. Veiga and John N. Yanouzas, *The Dynamics of Organization Theory* (St. Paul: West, 1984), 132–38.

PART II

In 1981, integrated circuits began to cut deeply into the demand for printed circuit boards. The integrated circuits (ICs) or "chips" were the first step into microminiaturization in the electronics industry. Because the manufacturing process for ICs was a closely guarded secret, both Acme and Omega realized the potential threat to their futures, and both began to seek new customers aggressively.

In July 1981, a major photocopier manufacturer was looking for a subcontractor to assemble the memory unit of its new experimental copier. The projected contract for the job was estimated to be $5 to $7 million in annual sales.

Both Acme and Omega were geographically close to this manufacturer, and both submitted highly competitive bids for the production of one hundred prototypes. Acme's bid was slightly lower than Omega's; however, both firms were asked to produce one hundred units. The photocopier manufacturer told both firms speed was critical because its president had boasted to other manufacturers that the firm would have a finished copier available by Christmas. This boast, much to the designer's dismay, required pressure on all subcontractors to begin prototype production before the final design of the copier was complete. This meant Acme and Omega would have at most two weeks to produce the prototypes or delay the final copier production.

PART III

Inside Acme

As soon as John Tyler was given the blueprints (Monday, July 11, 1981), he sent a memo to the purchasing department asking to move forward on the purchase of all necessary materials. At the same time, he sent the blueprints to the drafting department and asked that it prepare manufacturing prints. The industrial engineering department was told to begin methods design work for use by the production department supervisors. Tyler also sent a memo to all department heads and executives indicating the critical time constraints of this job and how he expected that all employees would perform as efficiently as they had in the past.

The departments had little contact with one another for several days, and each seemed to work at its own speed. Each department also encountered problems. Purchasing could not acquire all the parts on time. Industrial engineering had difficulty arranging an efficient assembly sequence. Mechanical engineering did not take the deadline seriously and parceled its work to vendors so the engineers could work on other jobs scheduled previously. Tyler made it a point to stay in touch with the photocopier manufacturer to let it know things were progressing and to learn of any new developments. He traditionally worked to keep important clients happy. Tyler telephoned someone at the photocopier company at least twice a week and got to know the head designer quite well.

On July 15, Tyler learned that mechanical engineering was way behind in its development work, and he "hit the roof." To make matters worse, purchasing did not obtain all the parts, so the industrial engineers decided to assemble the product without one part, which would be inserted at the last minute. On Thursday, July 21, the final units were being assembled, although the process was delayed several times. On Friday, July 22, the last units were finished while Tyler paced around the plant. Late that afternoon, Tyler received a phone call from the head designer of the photocopier manufacturer, who told Tyler that he had received a call on Wednesday from Jim Rawls of Omega. He explained that Rawls's workers had found an error in the design of the connector cable and taken corrective action on their prototypes. He told Tyler that he had checked out the design error and that Omega was right. Tyler, a bit overwhelmed by this information, told the designer that he had all the memory units ready for shipment and that, as soon as they received the missing component on Monday or Tuesday, they would be able to deliver the final units. The designer explained that the design error would be rectified in a new blueprint he was sending over by messenger and that he would hold Acme to the Tuesday delivery date.

When the blueprint arrived, Tyler called in the production supervisor to assess the damage. The alterations in the design would call for total disassembly and the unsoldering of several connections. Tyler told the supervisor to put extra people on the alterations first thing Monday morning and to try to finish the job by Tuesday. Late Tuesday afternoon, the alterations were finished and the missing components were delivered. Wednesday morning, the production supervisor discovered that the units would have to be torn apart again to install the missing component. When John Tyler was told this, he again "hit the roof." He called industrial engineering and asked if it could help out. The production supervisor and the methods engineer couldn't agree on how to install the component. John Tyler settled the argument by ordering that all units be taken apart again and the missing component installed. He told shipping to prepare cartons for delivery on Friday afternoon.

On Friday, July 29, fifty prototypes were shipped from Acme without final inspection. John Tyler was concerned about his firm's reputation, so he waived the final inspection after he personally tested one unit and found it operational. On Tuesday, August 2, Acme shipped the last fifty units.

Inside Omega

On Friday, July 8, Jim Rawls called a meeting that included department heads to tell them about the potential contract they were to receive. He told them that as soon as he received the blueprints, work could begin. On Monday, July 11, the prints arrived and again the department heads met to discuss the project. At the end of the meeting, drafting had agreed to prepare manufacturing prints, while industrial engineering and production would begin methods design.

Two problems arose within Omega that were similar to those at Acme. Certain ordered parts could not be delivered on time, and the assembly sequence was difficult to engineer. The departments proposed ideas to help one another, however, and department heads and key employees had daily meetings to discuss progress. The head of electrical engineering knew of a Japanese source for the components that could not be purchased from normal suppliers. Most problems were solved by Saturday, July 16.

On Monday, July 18, a methods engineer and the production supervisor formulated the assembly plans,

and production was set to begin on Tuesday morning. On Monday afternoon, people from mechanical engineering, electrical engineering, production, and industrial engineering got together to produce a prototype just to ensure that there would be no snags in production. While they were building the unit, they discovered an error in the connector cable design. All the engineers agreed, after checking and rechecking the blueprints, that the cable was erroneously designed. People from mechanical engineering and electrical engineering spent Monday night redesigning the cable, and on Tuesday morning, the drafting department finalized the changes in the manufacturing prints. On Tuesday morning, Rawls was a bit apprehensive about the design changes and decided to get formal approval. Rawls received word on Wednesday from the head designer at the photocopier firm that they could proceed with the design changes as discussed on the phone. On Friday, July 22, the final units were inspected by quality control and were then shipped.

PART IV

Ten of Acme's final memory units were defective, while all of Omega's units passed the photocopier firm's tests. The photocopier firm was disappointed with Acme's delivery delay and incurred further delays in repairing the defective Acme units. However, rather than give the entire contract to one firm, the final contract was split between Acme and Omega with two directives added: (1) maintain zero defects and (2) reduce final cost. In 1982, through extensive cost-cutting efforts, Acme reduced its unit cost by 20 percent and was ultimately awarded the total contract.

NOTES

1. Warren St. John, "Barnes & Noble's Epiphany," *Wired* (June 1999): 132-144.
2. Gary Hamel, "Turning Your Business Upside Down," *Fortune,* 23 June 1997, 87-88.
3. Tim Carvell, "These Prices Really Are Insane," *Fortune,* 4 August 1997, 109-116; and Trevor Merriden, "Europe's Privatized Stars," *Management Review* June 1999, 16-23.
4. David Greising, "Cola Wars on the Mean Streets," *Business Week,* 3 August 1998, 78-79.
5. Dana Milbank, "Aluminum Producers, Aggressive and Agile, Outfight Steelmakers," *The Wall Street Journal,* 1 July 1992, A1.
6. Joseph Pereira and William M. Buckley, "Toy-Buying Patterns Are Changing and That Is Shaking the Industry," *The Wall Street Journal,* 16 June 1998, A1, A8.
7. Nina Munk, "The New Organization Man," *Fortune,* 16 March 1998, 63-74.
8. Bela L. Musits, "When Big Changes Happen to Small Companies," *Inc.* (August 1994): 27-28.
9. Michael Hickins, "Brand Names Losing Luster for Affluent Customers," *Management Review* (June 1999) 9; and Ellen Neuborne with Kathleen Kerwin, "Generation Y," *Business Week,* 15 February 1999, 80-88.

10. Lucinda Harper and Fred R. Bleakley, "An Era of Low Inflation Changes the Calculus for Buyers and Sellers," *The Wall Street Journal,* 14 January 1994, A1, A3.

11. Jodi Mardesich, "How the Internet Hits Big Music," *Fortune,* 10 May 1999, 96-102.

12. Eric Nee, "Meet Mister buy(everything).com," *Fortune,* 29 May 1999, 119-124.

13. Andrew Kupfer, "How American Industry Stacks Up," *Fortune,* 9 March 1992, 36–46.

14. Fred L. Steingraber, "How to Succeed in the Global Marketplace," *USA Today Magazine* (November 1997): 30-31.

15. Alan Farnham, "Global—or Just Globaloney?" *Fortune,* 27 June 1994, 97–100; William C. Symonds, Brian Bremner, Stewart Toy, and Karen Lowry Miller, "The Globetrotters Take Over," *Business Week,* 8 July 1996, 46–48; Carla Rapoport, "Nestlé's Brand Building Machine," *Fortune,* 19 September 1994, 147–156; "Execs with Global Vision," *USA Today,* International Edition, 9 February 1996, 12B.

16. Tom Peters, "Prometheus Barely Unbound," *Academy of Management Executive* 4 (1990): 70–84; and Clifford C. Hebard, "Managing Effectively in Asia," *Training & Development* (April 1996): 35–39.

17. Marlene Piturro, "What Are You Doing About the New Global Realities?" *Management Review* (March 1999): 16-22.

18. Raju Narisetti and Jonathan Friedland, "Diaper Wars of P&G and Kimberly-Clark Now Heat Up in Brazil," *The Wall Street Journal,* 4 June 1997; and Stephen Baker, "The Bridges That Steel is Building," *Business Week,* 2 June 1997, 39.

19. Jonathan Friedland and Louise Lee, "The Wal-Mart Way Sometimes Gets Lost in Translation Overseas," *The Wall Street Journal,* 8 October 1997, A1, A12; Wendy Zellner, Louisa Shepard, Ian Katz, and David Lindorff, "Wal-Mart Spoken Here," *Business Week,* 23 June 1997, 138+; and Sue Leeman, "Wal-Mart Buys British Retail Chain Asda," *Johnson City Press,* 15 June 1999, 12.

20. Allen C. Bluedorn, "Pilgrim's Progress: Trends and Convergence in Research on Organizational Size and Environment," *Journal of Management* 19 (1993): 163–91; Howard E. Aldrich, *Organizations and Environments* (Englewood, Cliffs, N.J.: Prentice-Hall, 1979); Fred E. Emery and Eric L. Trist, "The Casual Texture of Organizational Environments," *Human Relations* 18 (1965): 21–32.

21. Christine S. Koberg and Gerardo R. Ungson, "The Effects of Environmental Uncertainty and Dependence on Organizational Structure and Performance: A Comparative Study," *Journal of Management* 13 (1987): 725–37; Frances J. Milliken, "Three Types of Perceived Uncertainty About the Environment: State, Effect, and Response Uncertainty," *Academy of Management Review* 12 (1987): 133–43.

22. Robert B. Duncan, "Characteristics of Organizational Environment and Perceived Environmental Uncertainty," *Administrative Science Quarterly* 17 (1972): 313–27; Gregory G. Dess and Donald W. Beard, "Dimensions of Organizational Task Environments," *Administrative Science Quarterly* 29 (1984): 52–73; Ray Jurkovich, "A Core Typology of Organizational Environments," *Administrative Science Quarterly* 19 (1974): 380–94.

23. Greising, "Cola Wars on the Mean Streets"; and Mike France with Joann Muller, "A Site for Soreheads," *Business Week,* 12 April 1999, 86-90.

24. J. A. Litterer, *The Analysis of Organizations,* 2d ed. (New York: Wiley, 1973), 335.

25. Joseph Pereira, "Toy Industry Finds It Harder and Harder to Pick the Winners," *The Wall Street Journal,* 21 December 1993, A1, A5.

26. Rosalie L. Tung, "Dimensions of Organizational Environments: An Exploratory Study of Their Impact on Organizational Structure," *Academy of Management Journal* 22 (1979): 672–93.

27. Joseph E. McCann and John Selsky, "Hyper-turbulence and the Emergence of Type 5 Environments," *Academy of Management Review* 9 (1984): 460–70.

28. Judith Valente and Asra Q. Nomani, "Surge in Oil Price has Airlines Struggling, Some Just to Hang on," *The Wall Street Journal,* 10 August 1990, A1, A4.

29. James D. Thompson, *Organizations in Action* (New York: McGraw-Hill, 1967), 20–21.

30. Sally Solo, "Whirlpool: How to Listen to Consumers," *Fortune,* 11 January 1993, 77–79.

31. David B. Jemison, "The Importance of Boundary Spanning Roles in Strategic Decision-Making," *Journal of Management Studies* 21 (1984): 131–52; Mohamed Ibrahim Ahmad At-Twaijri and John R. Montanari, "The Impact of Context and Choice on the Boundary-Spanning Process: An Empirical Extension," *Human Relations* 40 (1987): 783–98.

32. Michelle Cook, "The Intelligentsia," *Business 2.0* (July 1999): 135-136.

33. Robert C. Schwab, Gerardo R. Ungson, and Warren B. Brown, "Redefining the Boundary-Spanning Environment Relationship," *Journal of Management* 11 (1985): 75–86.

34. Ken Western, "Ethical Spying," *Business Ethics* (September/October 1995): 22–23; Stan Crock, Geoffrey Smith, Joseph Weber, Richard A. Melcher, and Linda Himelstein, "They Snoop to Conquer," *Business Week,* 28 October 1996, 172–176; Kenneth A. Sawka, "Demystifying Business Intelligence," *Management Review* (October 1996): 47–51.

35. Crock, et. al, "They Snoop to Conquer."

36. France with Muller, "A Site for Soreheads."

37. Neuborne with Kerwin, "Generation Y."

38. Jay W. Lorsch, "Introduction to the Structural Design of Organizations," in Gene W. Dalton, Paul R. Lawrence, and Jay W. Lorsch, eds., *Organizational Structure and Design* (Homewood, Ill.: Irwin and Dorsey, 1970), 5.

39. Paul R. Lawrence and Jay W. Lorsch, *Organization and Environment* (Homewood, Ill.: Irwin, 1969).

40. Lorsch, "Introduction to the Structural Design of Organizations," 7.

41. Jay W. Lorsch and Paul R. Lawrence, "Environmental Factors and Organizational Integration," in J. W. Lorsch and Paul R. Lawrence, eds., *Organizational Planning: Cases and Concepts* (Homewood, Ill.: Irwin and Dorsey, 1972), 45.

42. Tom Burns and G. M. Stalker, *The Management of Innovation* (London: Tavistock, 1961).

43. John A. Courtright, Gail T. Fairhurst, and L. Edna Rogers, "Interaction Patterns in Organic and Mechanistic Systems," *Academy of Management Journal* 32 (1989): 773–802.

44. Thomas C. Powell, "Organizational Alignment as Competitive Advantage," *Strategic Management Journal* 13 (1992): 119–34. Mansour Javidan, "The Impact of Environmental Uncertainty on Long-Range Planning Practices of the U.S. Savings and Loan Industry," *Strategic Management Journal* 5 (1984): 381–92; Tung, "Dimensions of Organizational Environments," 672–93; Thompson, *Organizations in Action.*

45. David Ulrich and Jay B. Barney, "Perspectives in Organizations: Resource Dependence, Efficiency, and Population," *Academy of Management Review* 9 (1984): 471–81; Jeffrey Pfeffer and Gerald Salancik, *The External Control of Organizations: A Resource Dependent Perspective* (New York: Harper & Row, 1978).

46. Lana J. Chandler, "Something to Sleep On," *Nation's Business,* February 1998, 57–58.

47. Andrew H. Van de Ven and Gordon Walker, "The Dynamics of Interorganizational Coordination," *Administrative Science Quarterly* (1984): 598–621; Huseyin Leblebici and Gerald R. Salancik, "Stability in Interorganizational Exchanges: Rulemaking Processes of the Chicago Board of Trade," *Administrative Science Quarterly* 27 (1982): 227–42.

48. Kevin Kelly and Zachary Schiller with James B. Treece, "Cut Costs or Else: Companies Lay Down the Law to Suppliers," *Business Week,* 22 March 1993, 28–29.

49. G. Pascal Zachary, "Many Journalists See a Growing Reluctance to Criticize Advertisers," *The Wall Street Journal,* 6 February 1992, A1, A9.

50. Richard Brandt, "Microsoft Is Like an Elephant Rolling around, Squashing Ants," *Business Week,* 30 October 1989, 148–52.

51. Judith A. Babcock, *Organizational Responses to Resource Scarcity and Munificence: Adaptation and Modification in Colleges within a University* (Ph.D. diss., Pennsylvania State University, 1981).

52. Peter Smith Ring and Andrew H. Van de Ven, "Developmental Processes of Corporative Interorganizational Relationships," *Academy of Management Review* 19 (1994): 90–118; Jeffrey Pfeffer, "Beyond Management and the Worker: The Institutional Function of Management," *Academy of Management Review* 1 (April 1976): 36–46; John P. Kotter, "Managing External Dependence," *Academy of Management Review* 4 (1979): 87–92.

53. Bryan Borys and David B. Jemison, "Hybrid Arrangements as Strategic Alliances: Theoretical Issues in Organizational Combinations," *Academy of Management Review* 14 (1989): 234–49.

54. William R. Pape, "Little Giant," *Inc. Tech* (1999): No. 1, 27–28.

55. Julie Cohen Mason, "Strategic Alliances: Partnering for Success," *Management Review* (May 1993): 10–15.

56. John F. Love, *McDonald's: Behind the Arches* (New York: Bantam Books, 1986).

57. Zachary Schiller and Wendy Zellner with Ron Stodghill II and Mark Maremont, "Clout! More and More, Retail Giants Rule the Marketplace," *Business Week,* 21 December 1992, 66–73.

58. Borys and Jemison, "Hybrid Arrangements as Strategic Alliances."

59. Edward O. Welles, "Not Your Father's Industry," *Inc.* (January 1999): 25-28.

60. Donald Palmer, "Broken Ties: Interlocking Directorates and Intercorporate Coordination," *Administrative Science Quarterly* 28 (1983): 40–55; F. David Shoorman, Max H. Bazerman, and Robert S. Atkin, "Interlocking Directorates: A Strategy for Reducing Environmental Uncertainty," *Academy of Management Review* 6 (1981): 243–51; Ronald S. Burt, *Toward a Structural Theory of Action* (New York: Academic Press, 1982).

61. James R. Lang and Daniel E. Lockhart, "Increased Environmental Uncertainty and Changes in Board Linkage Patterns," *Academy of Management Journal* 33 (1990): 106–28; Mark S. Mizruchi and Linda Brewster Stearns, "A Longitudinal Study of the Formation of Interlocking Directorates," *Administrative Science Quarterly* 33 (1988): 194–210.

62. Neuborne with Kerwin, "Generation Y."

63. Brian Bremmer with Zachary Schiller, Tim Smart, and William J. Holstein, "*Keiretsu* Connections," *Business Week,* 22 July 1996, 52-54; and Brenton R. Schlender, "How Toshiba Makes Alliances Work," *Fortune,* 4 October 1993, 116-120.

64. Kotter, "Managing External Dependence."

65. William C. Symonds, with Farah Nayeri, Geri Smith, and Ted Plafker, "Bombardier's Blitz," *Business Week,* 6 February 1995, 62-66; Joseph Weber, with Wendy Zellner and Geri Smith, "Loud Noises at Bombardier," *Business Week,* 26 January 1998, 94-95; and Anita Lienert, "Plowing Ahead in Uncertain Times," *Management Review,* December 1998, 16–21.

66. Daniel Pearl and Gabriella Stern, "How GM Managed to Wring Pickup Pact and Keep on Truckin'," *The Wall Street Journal,* 5 December 1994, A1.

67. Rick Wartzman and John Harwood, "For the Baby Bells, Government Lobbying Is Hardly Child's Play," *The Wall Street Journal,* 15 March 1994, A1.

68. David B. Yoffie, "How an Industry Builds Political Advantage," *Harvard Business Review* (May-June 1988): 82–89; Jeffrey H. Birnbaum, "Chief Executives Head to Washington to Ply the Lobbyist's Trade," *The Wall Street Journal,* 19 March 1990, A1, A16.

69. David Whitford, "Built By Association," *Inc.* (July 1994): 71–75.

70. Anthony J. Daboub, Abdul M. A. Rasheed, Richard L. Priem, and David A. Gray, "Top Management Team Characteristics and Corporate Illegal Activity," *Academy of Management Review* 20, no. 1 (1995): 138–70.

71. Bryan Burrough, "Oil-Field Investigators Say Fraud Flourishes from Wells to Offices," *The Wall Street Journal,* 15 January 1985, 1, 20; Irwin Ross, "How Lawless Are Big Companies?" *Fortune,* 1 December 1980, 57–64.

72. Stewart Toy, "The Defense Scandal," *Business Week,* 4 July 1988, 28–30.

73. Barry M. Staw and Eugene Szwajkowski, "The Scarcity-Munificence Component of Organizational Environments and the Commission of Illegal Acts," *Administrative Science Quarterly* 20 (1975): 345–54.

74. Kimberly D. Elsbach and Robert I. Sutton, "Acquiring Organizational Legitimacy through Illegitimate Actions: A Marriage of Institutional and Impression Management Theories," *Academy of Management Journal* 35 (1992): 699–738.

Interorganizational Relationships

A LOOK INSIDE

Cisco Systems

isco Systems, the pioneer of "Internetworking," is one of the fastest-growing companies in Silicon Valley, and one of the hottest stocks of the decade. But managers at Cisco are among the first to admit that they didn't get there on their own. Cisco has achieved its status primarily through strategic relationships with other organizations.

Cisco Systems was founded in the mid-1980s by a husband-and-wife team who devised a means to connect incompatible computer networks at Stanford University. A series of mergers and acquisitions with startup companies such as Crescendo Communications, a maker of hubs, and StrataCom, a maker of relay devices and switches, turned Cisco into a full-service provider of networking equipment and garnered the technological know-how to keep the company on the cutting edge. Just as important are the numerous partnerships Cisco has with other high-tech companies. For example, Cisco partners with Hewlett-Packard to develop and sell Internet-based corporate computing systems built with each other's products. A strategic alliance with MCI means Cisco will deliver premium Internet services via MCI's data-networking infrastructure. Microsoft and Intel—the two giants of computing—have joined with Cisco in a project called the Networked Multimedia Lab, which explores how the Internet can deliver voice, video, and interactive multimedia with the clarity and reliability of conventional telephone and cable TV networks.

Cisco's CEO John T. Chambers considers picking the right partners to be critical to the company's success. He hopes the partnership with Microsoft and Intel signals that the three will form a triumvirate that will plot the course of the digital revolution. "We've always known networking is too complex for any one company to tackle—even for MCI, HP, Microsoft, or Intel," Chambers says. "They know it now too. It's better to partner than to compete because . . . it grows the pie bigger for everybody faster."[1]

Organizations have been rethinking every aspect of how they do business. A recent trend is to reduce boundaries and increase collaboration between companies—even competitors—to survive in today's chaotic environment. High-tech companies such as Cisco Systems depend on strategic partnerships with other organizations. However, the trend toward interorganizational collaboration is affecting companies of all sizes in all industries. Global competition and rapid advances in technology, communications, and transportation have created amazing new opportunities for organizations, but they have also raised the cost of doing business and made it increasingly difficult for any company to take advantage of those opportunities on its own. In this new economy, webs of organizations are emerging. A large company like Wal-Mart develops a special relationship with a supplier such as Procter & Gamble that eliminates middlemen by sharing complete information and reducing the costs of salespersons and distributors. Several small companies may join together to produce and market noncompeting products. You can see the results of interorganizational collaboration when movies such as *Star Wars: Episode I—The Phantom Menace*, *Tarzan*, or *Wild Wild West* are launched. Prior to seeing the movie, you may read a cover story in *People* or *Entertainment Weekly*, see a preview clip or chat live with the stars at an online site such as Entertainment Asylum, find action toys being given away at a fast food franchise, and notice retail stores loaded with movie-related merchandise. For a movie like *The Lion King*, coordinated action among companies yielded $200 million in addition to box-office and video profits. In the new economy, organizations think of themselves as teams that create value jointly rather than as autonomous companies that are in competition with all others.

PURPOSE OF THIS CHAPTER

This chapter explores the most recent trend in organizing, which is the increasingly dense web of relationships among organizations. Companies have always been dependent on other organizations for supplies, materials, and information. The question is how these relationships are managed. At one time it was a matter of a large, powerful company like General Motors tightening the screws on small suppliers. Today a company can choose to develop positive, trusting relationships. Or a large company like General Motors may find it difficult to adapt to the environment and create a new organizational form, such as Saturn, to operate with a different structure and culture. The notion of horizontal relationships described in Chapter 3, and the understanding of environmental uncertainty in Chapter 4, are leading to the next stage of organizational evolution, which is horizontal relationships *across* organizations. Organizations can choose to build relationships in many ways, such as appointing preferred suppliers, establishing agreements, business partnering, joint ventures, or even mergers and acquisitions.

Interorganizational research has yielded perspectives such as resource dependence, networks, population ecology, and institutionalism. The sum total of these ideas can be daunting, because it means managers no longer can rest in the safety of managing a single organization. They have to figure out how to manage a whole set of interorganizational relationships, which is a great deal more challenging and complex.

ORGANIZATIONAL ECOSYSTEMS

Interorganizational relationships are the relatively enduring resource transactions, flows, and linkages that occur among two or more organizations.[2] Traditionally, these transactions and relationships have been seen as a necessary evil to obtain what an organization needs. The presumption has been that the world is composed of distinct businesses that thrive on autonomy and compete for supremacy. A company may be forced into interorganizational relationships depending on its needs and the stability of the environment.

A new view described by James Moore argues that organizations are now evolving into business ecosystems. An **organizational ecosystem** is a system formed by the interaction of a community of organizations and their environment. An ecosystem cuts across traditional industry lines. A company can create its own ecosystem. Microsoft travels in four major industries: consumer electronics, information, communications, and personal computers. Its ecosystem also includes hundreds of suppliers, including Hewlett-Packard and Intel, and millions of customers across many markets.[3] Traditional boundaries are dissolving. Circuit City uses its expertise gained from selling televisions and stereos to sell used cars. Shell Oil is the largest seller of packaged sausages in the Scandinavian countries.

Wal-Mart created an ecosystem based on well-known brands and low prices in rural and small-town markets. Today, Wal-Mart cannot be categorized simply as a retailer. It is also a wholesaler, a logistics company, and an information services company. Wal-Mart, like other business ecosystems, develops relationships with hundreds of organizations cutting across traditional business boundaries.

IS COMPETITION DEAD?

No company can go it alone under a constant onslaught of international competitors, changing technology, and new regulations. Thus competition, which assumes a distinct company competing for survival and supremacy with other stand-alone businesses, no longer exists. In that sense competition is dead. However, most managers recognize that the competitive stakes are higher than ever in a world where market share can crumble overnight and no industry is immune from almost instant obsolescence.[4] In today's world, a new form of competition is in fact intensifying.[5]

For one thing, companies now need to coevolve with others in the ecosystem so that everyone gets stronger. Consider the wolf and the caribou. Wolves cull weaker caribou, which strengthens the herd. A strong herd means that wolves must become stronger themselves. With coevolution, the whole system becomes stronger. In the same way, companies coevolve through discussion with each other, shared visions, alliances, and managing complex relationships, as we saw with Cisco Systems and its partners in the opening case. Exhibit 5.1 illustrates the complexity of an organizational ecosystem and the myriad overlapping relationships in which today's high-tech companies are involved. The words of British biologist Brian Goodwin apply to today's businesses as well as to nature: "Competition has no special status . . . . What is important is the pattern of relationships and interactions that exist and how they contribute to the system as an integrated whole."[6] This chapter's Book Mark describes how an increasing emphasis on relationships and alliances is altering the competitive landscape.

Conflict and cooperation often exist at the same time. In New York City, Time Warner refused to carry Fox's twenty-four-hour news channel on its New York City cable systems. The two companies engaged in all-out war that included court lawsuits and front-page headlines. This all-out conflict, however, masked a simple fact: the two companies can't live without each other. Fox and Time Warner are wedded to one another in separate business deals around the world. They will never let the local competition in New York upset their larger interdependence on a global scale. Mutual dependencies and partnerships have become a fact of life in business ecosystems. Companies no longer operate autonomously or with a single voice. A senior executive at DreamWorks sued Disney, but that hasn't stopped Disney's ABC network from acquiring television shows from DreamWorks. Companies today may use their strength to win conflicts and negotiations, but ultimately cooperation carries the day.[7]

THE CHANGING ROLE OF MANAGEMENT

Within business ecosystems managers learn to move beyond traditional responsibilities of corporate strategy and designing hierarchical structures and control systems. If a top manager looks down to enforce order and uniformity, the company is missing opportunities for new and evolving external relationships.[8] In this new world, managers think about horizontal processes rather than vertical structures. Important initiatives are not just top down, they cut across the

EXHIBIT 5.1   *An Organizational Ecosystem*

The largest companies (those with more than 10,000 employees) are, not surprisingly, the hubs of the digital universe: they tend to have the most strategic partnerships (black lines) and investments (red lines).*

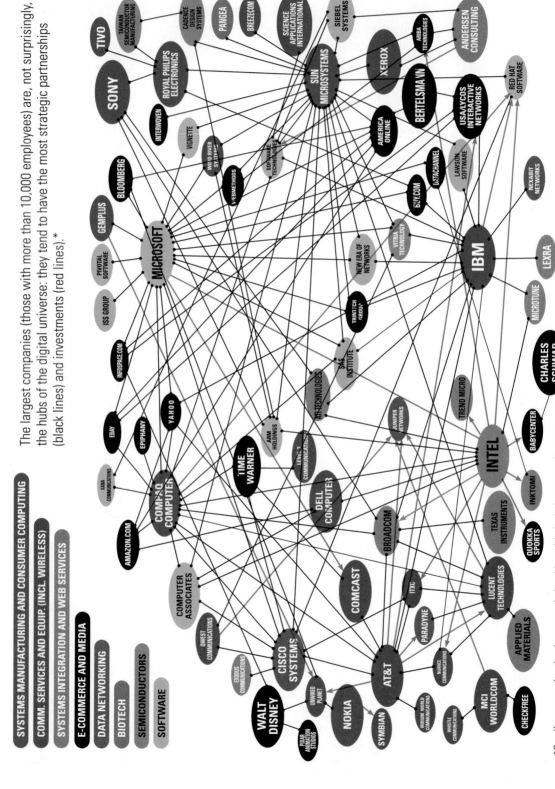

SYSTEMS MANUFACTURING AND CONSUMER COMPUTING

COMM. SERVICES AND EQUIP. (INCL. WIRELESS)

SYSTEMS INTEGRATION AND WEB SERVICES

E-COMMERCE AND MEDIA

DATA NETWORKING

BIOTECH

SEMICONDUCTORS

SOFTWARE

*Smaller companies that have no relationships with the hubs are not featured.

$\mathcal{B}$ook $\mathcal{M}$ark 5.0

The Trillion-Dollar Enterprise: How the Alliance Revolution Will Transform Global Business

By Cyrus F. Freidheim, Jr.

During the last few years of the twentieth century, mergers and acquisitions created global corporations of unprecedented scale. However, in his book *The Trillion-Dollar Enterprise*, Cyrus Freidheim suggests that these megamergers are only a tiny part of the story of globalization. He argues that there is a "silent revolution" taking place that will forever transform the competitive landscape. Freidheim believes a new form of global business is emerging—one that is made up of networks of independent companies that share financial risks and management skills and provide access to one another's technologies and markets. Head-to-head competition among firms is giving way to competition among networks of alliances. The author, who is chairman of management consultancy Booz, Allen & Hamilton, Inc., believes such alliances, or "relationship enterprises," will eventually control two-thirds of the global market in their respective industries.

THE EMERGING TRILLION-DOLLAR ENTERPRISE

As these alliances mature over the next decade or so, Freidheim says we will see the emergence of the trillion-dollar enterprise, networks that will generate more than $1 trillion in revenues. Through case studies and examples from numerous industries, the author provides evidence that the trend is taking firm hold.

- During the 1970s, the number of strategic alliances taking place each year was in the hundreds. By 1990, the annual rate hit 2,000; by 1995 it was 10,000; and it reached 20,000 by 2000. More than 20 percent of all revenue earned by *Fortune* 1000 companies is derived from alliance activities. In addition, alliances are becoming central to the partner firms' strategies, rather than being short-term projects that have a single, limited purpose.
- The aerospace industry is controlled by two networks—those of Boeing and Airbus, each of which consists of more than one hundred partners. In telecommunications, the Global One joint venture led by Sprint, Deutsche Telekom, and France Telecom serves sixty-five countries and functions as one company to serve the telecom needs of global corporations. Global One will face competition from a handful of other networks, such as the alliance that includes AT&T, British Telecom, Microsoft, and Qualcom.
- On average, alliances are more profitable than the regular operations of single firms. Three studies by Booz, Allen & Hamilton found that from 1988 to 1998, alliances showed better returns than the average for single corporations. In addition, the return on investment rises significantly as companies gain more experience. Companies with nine or more alliance experiences earn twice the return on investment on their alliances as inexperienced firms.

THE MANAGER'S CHALLENGE

What does the emerging relationship enterprise mean for twenty-first-century managers? Creating successful alliances is not a natural skill for most corporations and managers. However, today's executives need to focus less on their traditional role of managing the firm's finances and more on building relationships and negotiating among partners.

Freidheim believes that to succeed in a relationship enterprise, executives must move toward a participative and collegial style of management. To gain the cooperation of alliance partners and motivate people without the traditional tools of command and authority requires new relationship skills. Managers who will thrive in the new environment will be multicultural, multilingual, politically sensitive, and diplomatically skilled. Business schools, corporations, and individuals, Freidheim says, must work fast to retool managers for success in the emerging world of the relationship enterprise.

The Trillion-Dollar Enterprise, by Cyrus F. Freidheim, Jr., is published by Perseus Books.

boundaries separating organizational units. Moreover, horizontal relationships, as described in Chapter 3, now include linkages with suppliers and customers, who become part of the team. Business leaders can learn to lead economic coevolution. Managers learn to see and appreciate the rich environment of opportunities that grow from cooperative relationships with other contributors to the ecosystem. Rather than trying to force suppliers into low prices or customers into high prices, managers strive to strengthen the larger system evolving around them, finding ways to understand this big picture and how to contribute.

This is a broader leadership role than ever before. For example, Harry Brown, president of EBC Industries (formerly Erie Bolt Corp.), formed a network with about fifty of his company's competitors to jointly market their skills and capabilities and acquire business that none of the companies could possibly get alone. They share information about quality systems, consult one another before investing in machinery, use one another's sales reps, and even pass on customers to one another. Although members of the network still compete in some areas, cooperation often increases revenues, reduces costs, and improves quality. For example, Brown works with a machine shop in Buffalo to produce metal studs because the combined expertise of the two companies results in larger profit margins for both companies and a higher-quality product for the customer. However, the two companies bid competitively on other jobs for which each has the ability to produce a quality product efficiently.[9]

INTERORGANIZATIONAL FRAMEWORK

Understanding this larger organizational ecosystem is one of the most exciting areas of organization theory. The models and perspectives for understanding interorganizational relationships ultimately help managers change their role from top-down management to horizontal management across organizations. A framework for analyzing the different views of interorganizational relationships is in Exhibit 5.2. Relationships among organizations can be characterized by whether the organizations are dissimilar or similar, and whether relationships are competitive or

E X H I B I T   5 . 2   *A Framework of Interorganizational Relationships**

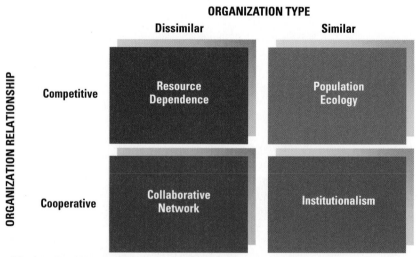

*Thanks to Anand Narasimhan for suggesting this framework.

cooperative. By understanding these perspectives, managers can assess their environment and adopt strategies to suit their needs. The first perspective is called resource dependence theory, which was briefly described in Chapter 4. It describes rational ways organizations deal with each other to reduce dependence on the environment. The second perspective is about collaborative networks, wherein organizations allow themselves to become dependent on other organizations to increase value and productivity for both. The third perspective is population ecology, which examines how new organizations fill niches left open by established organizations, and how a rich variety of new organizational forms benefit society. The final approach is called institutionalism and explains why and how organizations legitimate themselves in the larger environment and design structures by borrowing ideas from each other. These four approaches to the study of interorganizational relationships will be described in the remainder of this chapter.

RESOURCE DEPENDENCE

Resource dependence represents the traditional view of relationships among organizations. As described in Chapter 4, **resource dependence** theory argues that organizations try to minimize their dependence on other organizations for the supply of important resources and try to influence the environment to make resources available.[10] Organizations succeed by striving for independence and autonomy. When threatened by greater dependence, organizations will assert control over external resources to minimize that dependence. Resource dependence theory argues that organizations do not want to become vulnerable to other organizations because of negative effects on performance.

The amount of dependence on a resource is based on two factors. First is the importance of the resource to the firm, and second is how much discretion or monopoly power those who control a resource have over its allocation and use.[11] For example, a Wisconsin manufacturer made scientific instruments with internal electronics. It acquired parts from a supplier that provided adequate quality at the lowest price. The supplier was not involved in the manufacturer's product design but was able to provide industry-standard capacitors at fifty cents each. As industry standards changed, other suppliers of the capacitor switched to other products, and in one year the cost of the capacitor increased to $2 each. The Wisconsin firm had no choice but to pay the higher price. Within eighteen months, the price of the capacitor increased to $10 each, and then the supplier discontinued production altogether. Without capacitors, production came to a halt for six months. The scientific instruments manufacturer allowed itself to become dependent on a single supplier and made no plans for redesign to use substitute capacitors or to develop new suppliers. A single supplier had sufficient power to increase prices beyond reason and to almost put the Wisconsin firm out of business.[12]

Organizations aware of resource dependence tend to develop strategies to reduce their dependence on the environment and learn how to use their power differences.

RESOURCE STRATEGIES

When organizations feel resource or supply constraints, the resource dependence perspective says they maneuver to maintain their autonomy through a variety of strategies, several of which were described in Chapter 4. One strategy is to adapt to or alter the interdependent relationships. This could mean purchasing ownership in suppliers, developing long-term contracts or joint ventures to lock in necessary resources, or building relationships in other ways. For example, interlocking directorships occur when boards of directors include members of the boards of supplier companies. Organizations may join trade associations to coordinate their needs, sign trade agreements, or merge with another firm to guarantee resource and material supplies. Some organizations may take political action, such as lobbying for new regulations or deregulation, favorable taxation, tariffs, or subsidies, or push for new standards that make resource acquisition easier. Organizations operating under the resource dependence philosophy will do whatever is needed to avoid excessive dependence on the environment to maintain control of resources and hence reduce uncertainty.

POWER STRATEGIES

In resource dependence theory, large, independent companies have power over small suppliers.[13] For example, power in consumer products has shifted from vendors such as Rubbermaid and Procter & Gamble to the big discount retail chains such as Wal-Mart and Kmart. In manufacturing, behemoths like General Electric and Ford can account for 10 to 50 percent of many suppliers' revenue, giving the large company enormous power. For example, General Electric called in three hundred suppliers to its appliance division and told them they must slash costs by 10 percent. Similarly, health maintenance organizations have growing power to dictate terms to pharmaceutical companies because they may account for 40 percent or more of a drugmaker's U.S. sales. Group Health Cooperative of Puget Sound ordered its doctors to stop prescribing all but an essential handful of drugs from Merck and Pfizer because the two drugmakers refused to discount their prices. The Seattle-based HMO instead began using equivalent drugs from rival suppliers who were willing to cut prices 10 to 20 percent. The loss in revenues prompted Merck's president to personally visit Group Health and begin offering discounts.[14] When one company has power over another, it can ask suppliers to absorb more costs, ship more efficiently, and provide more services than ever before, often without a price increase. Huge automakers like General Motors expect their suppliers to provide a broad range of services in one-stop shopping fashion while also meeting specific quality standards, such as ISO 9000 specifications.[15] Often the suppliers have no choice but to go along, and those who fail to do so may go out of business.

COLLABORATIVE NETWORKS

North American companies typically have worked alone, competing with each other and believing in the tradition of individualism and self-reliance. Today, however, thanks to an uncertain international environment, a realignment in corporate relationships is taking place. The collaborative network perspective is an emerging alternative to resource dependence theory. Companies join together to become more competitive and to share scarce resources. As a new wave of technology based on digital communications builds, for example, computer manufacturers, local phone companies, cable television operators, cellular phone companies, and even water and gas utilities have been teaming up. Biotechnology companies collaborate to share resources and knowledge and spur innovation. Consulting firms, investment companies, and accounting firms may join in an alliance to meet customer demands for expanded services.[16] As companies move into their own uncharted territory, they are also racing into alliances as a way to share risks and cash in on rewards. In many cases companies are learning to work closely together. Consider the following examples:

- As can be seen in Exhibit 5.1 earlier in the chapter, AT&T is reaching out everywhere these days, dropping its traditional do-it–from-scratch approach to team up with such major, established companies as Comcast Communications and Cisco Systems, as well as small pioneering companies, ensconcing itself in almost every corner of the rapidly changing communications industry.
- Large computer and software companies such as IBM, Sun Microsystems, and Microsoft are joining forces with small e-commerce companies. The large firms get access to innovative new technologies and markets, while the emerging companies gain the benefit of the larger firm's financing and marketing capabilities.
- With corporate research budgets under pressure and technologies increasingly complex, the hottest R&D trend is collaboration. Companies are figuring out how to fruitfully connect with outside experts in other companies, consortiums, universities, and government labs. GE Aircraft Engines teamed up with archrival Pratt & Whitney to share the $1 billion cost of designing a new jet engine. Texas Instruments and Hitachi joined their semiconductor businesses to share the best design and engineering abilities of both companies.[17]
- Small companies are banding together to compete against much larger firms. A group of seven wireless-telephone companies in the United States and Canada are jointly marketing digital wireless phone service to challenge such telecommunications giants as AT&T and Sprint Communications.[18] Forty local microbreweries formed the Oregon Brewers Guild to gain the resources needed to compete against craft brews from Miller and Anheuser-Busch.[19]

INTERNATIONAL ORIGINS

Why all this interest in interorganizational collaboration? Major reasons are sharing risks when entering new markets, mounting expensive new programs and reducing costs, and enhancing organizational profile in selected industries or technologies. Cooperation is a prerequisite for greater innovation, problem solving, and performance.[20] In addition, partnerships are a major avenue for entering global markets, with both large and small firms developing partnerships overseas and in North America.

North Americans have learned from their international experience just how effective interorganizational relationships can be. Both Japan and Korea have long traditions of corporate clans or industrial groups that collaborate and assist each other. In Japan this grouping is called *keiretsu*. A *keiretsu* is a collection of companies that share holdings in one another, have interlocking boards of directors, and undertake joint ventures in long-term business relationships. A *keiretsu* has long-term historical linkages through educational backgrounds of executives that literally create a family of companies.[21] North Americans typically have considered interdependence a bad thing, believing it would reduce competition. In a *keiretsu*, no single company dominates, and competition is fierce. It's as if the brothers and sisters of a single family went into separate businesses and want to outdo one another, but they still love one another and will help each other when needed.

Companies in a *keiretsu* enjoy a safety net that encourages long-term investment and risk-taking for entering new markets and trying new technologies. The following story from Toyota illustrates how powerful and beneficial the *keiretsu* can be to Japanese companies.

Toyota Motor Corporation

When fire roared through Aisin Seiki Co.'s Factory No. 1 in Kariya, Japan, early one February morning, it not only leveled the huge auto parts plant but also shut down twenty Toyota factories. The plant was the main source of a crucial brake valve that Toyota uses in most of its cars. Because of Aisin's high quality and low cost, Toyota had come to rely on the company for all but 1 percent of its "P-valves," which control pressure on rear brakes and help prevent skidding. Aisin shipped parts to Toyota's plants under a just-in-time inventory system: several times a day, shipping just enough valves for a few hours of production. Many people thought Toyota would be crippled for weeks, if not longer. But what happened next illustrates one reason Toyota is among the world's most admired and respected manufacturers.

Toyota's family of parts suppliers and other local companies rushed to the rescue, much like an old-fashioned barn-raising. Within hours, they were taking blueprints for the valve, improvising tooling systems, and setting up makeshift production lines. Parts makers rapidly assembled tools, dies, drills, and other fixtures for machining systems that would normally take several months to perfect. One sewing machine company that had never before made auto parts spent about 500 worker-hours refitting a milling machine just to provide an additional 40 valves per day. Within a few days, 36 suppliers, aided by more than 150 other subcontractors, had nearly 50 separate lines producing brake valves for Toyota. Only five days after the fire, Toyota's factories were once again in operation.

The secret to Toyota's quick recovery, said Yoshio Yunokawa, general manager of Toyota Machine Works Ltd., "is attributable to the power of the group, which handled it without thinking about money or business contracts." The approach, common in Japan's *keiretsu*, has perhaps never been more vividly illustrated. Suppliers and other members of the group never asked Toyota or Aisin what they would be paid for rushing out the valves. As one member put it, "We trusted them." Even though Aisin and Toyota paid for everything, the most important reward may have been the promise from Toyota's president that the automaker will never forget the "family members" who pitched in during its crisis.[22]

Although North American companies may never cooperate to the extent that members of Toyota's *keiretsu* do, interorganizational linkages can help firms achieve higher levels of innovation and performance, especially as they learn to shift from an adversarial to a partnership mind-set.[23]

FROM ADVERSARIES TO PARTNERS

Fresh flowers are blooming on the battle-scarred landscape where once-bitter rivalries among suppliers, customers, and competitors took place. In North America, collaboration among organizations initially occurred in not-for-profit social service and mental health organizations where public interest was involved. Community organizations collaborated to achieve greater effectiveness for each party and better utilize scarce resources.[24] With the push from international competitors and international examples, hard-nosed American managers are shifting to a new partnership paradigm on which to base their relationships.

Consider the example of Eastman Kodak Co. and Sun Chemical Corp. The two companies have competed vigorously for years, selling film and offset-printing supplies to the same set of customers. However, they forged a partnership to develop and market graphic-arts products in order to compete worldwide against Agfa-Gevart Group, the world's largest supplier of graphic-arts materials. As a Kodak spokesman put it, "We at Eastman Kodak came to the conclusion that it is better to join forces with another competitor than to continue competing, with Agfa staring us in the face."[25]

A summary of this change in mindset is in Exhibit 5.3. More companies are changing from a traditional adversarial mindset to a partnership orientation. More and more evidence from studies of General Electric, Corning, Amoco, and Whirlpool indicate that partnering allows reduced cost and increased value for both parties in a predatory world economy.[26] The new model is based on trust and the ability of partners to develop equitable solutions to conflicts that inevitably arise. In the new orientation, people try to add value to both sides and believe in high commitment rather than suspicion and competition. Companies work toward equitable profits for both sides rather than just for their own benefit. The new model is characterized by lots of shared information, including electronic linkages for automatic ordering and face-to-face discussions to provide corrective feedback and solve problems. Sometimes people from other companies are on site to enable very close coordination. Partners are involved in each other's product design and production and invest for the long term. It's not unusual for business partners to help each other outside whatever is specified in the contract.[27]

For example, AMP, a manufacturer of electronic and electrical connectors, was contacted by a customer about a broken connector that posed serious problems. It wasn't even AMP's connector, but the vice president and his sales manager went to a warehouse on a weekend and found replacement parts to get the customer back on line. They provided the service with no charge as a way to enhance the relationship. Indeed, this kind of teamwork treats partner companies almost like departments of one's own company.[28]

E X H I B I T   5 . 3   *Changing Characteristics of Interorganizational Relationships*

Traditional Orientation: Adversarial	New Orientation Partnership
Suspicion, competition, arm's length	Trust, addition of value to both sides, high commitment
Price, efficiency, own profits	Equity, fair dealing, all profit
Limited information and feedback	Electronic linkages to share key information, problem feedback, and discussion
Legal resolution of conflict	Mechanisms for close coordination, people on site
Minimal involvement and up-front investment	Involvement in partner's product design and production
Short-term contracts	Long-term contracts
Contract limiting the relationship	Business assistance beyond the contract

Source: Based on Jeffrey H. Dyer, "How Chrysler Created an American *Keiretsu,*" *Harvard Business Review* (July–August 1996): 42–56; Myron Magnet, "The New Golden Rule of Business," *Fortune,* 21 February 1994, 60–64; and Peter Grittner, "Four Elements of Successful Sourcing Strategies," *Management Review* (October 1995): 41–45.

Companies like Whirlpool Corporation use suppliers to design new products. The design work for the gas burner system for a new Whirlpool gas range was done by supplier Eaton Corporation. In this new view of partnerships, dependence on another company is seen to reduce rather than increase risks. Greater value can be achieved by both parties. By being imbedded in a system of interorganizational relationships, similar to a Japanese *keiretsu*, everyone does better by helping each other. This is a far cry from the belief that organizations do best by being autonomous and independent. Sales representatives may have a desk on the customer's factory floor, and they have access to information systems and the research lab.[29] Coordination is so intimate that it's hard to tell one organization from another. An example of how partnership can boost both parties is Empire Equipment.

In Practice 5.2

Empire Equipment Company

"[Empire Equipment], a New York equipment manufacturer, decided to introduce a more analytical approach to its supply-chain management, with the goal of reducing procurement costs of filters, an important but expensive component. The New York firm was happy with the quality of its supplier's product, but felt it was paying too much for the part.

A team of experts and managers was put together, visited the supplier and explained the study goal: to better understand the functions, activities and demands that added cost to the filter they built, and to explore potential avenues for reducing those costs. Based on a commitment from the manufacturer that the supplier would be a partner in the strategy and would share in any cost-saving measures that emerged, the supplier agreed to cooperate.

The team toured the supplier's operation, tracking each step of the production process: raw materials cost, direct labor, equipment usage, set-up time, order processing, production planning, and overhead costs. It became obvious that the direct-manufacturing costs were a fraction of the total product costs—about 30 percent. The other 70 percent was buried in the contribution margin supporting the indirect functions of marketing, developing, engineering, testing, packaging and shipping [Empire's] filter. But which indirect functions added the most cost, and why?

To answer that question, the team met with engineering staff, production managers, quality inspectors, and other personnel—including top management—involved in servicing the New York company. They learned that much of the indirect costs were attributable to two factors: erratic and inefficient ordering patterns, and excessive and redundant post-production specifications for quality measurement and testing.

By making long-term volume commitments, improving forecasting, coordinating order size and altering quality specifications that were inefficient or overlapping, the team was able to reduce total product costs from $7,300 to $4,000, a 46 percent savings."[30]

By becoming intimately involved in the supplier's production with the attitude of fair dealing and adding value to both sides, Empire Equipment achieved savings for itself and additional value for its supplier. In the next generation of collaborative networks, suppliers may build products from components that arrive at one point to be assembled into a final product. Germany's Volkswagen is attempting to achieve this new form of organization in the automobile industry, as described in the Taking the Lead box.

POPULATION ECOLOGY

This section introduces a different perspective on relationships among organizations. The **population ecology** perspective differs from the other perspectives because it focuses on organizational diversity and adaptation within a population of organizations.[31] A **population** is a set of organizations engaged in similar activities with similar patterns of resource utilization and outcomes. Organizations within a population compete for similar resources or similar customers, such as financial institutions in the Seattle area.

Within a population, the question asked by ecology researchers is about the large number and variation of organizations in society. Why are new organizational forms constantly appearing that create such diversity? Their answer is that

Taking the Lead

Volkswagen

Volkswagen executives have started a new industrial revolution (initiated by José López, formerly of General Motors) in a Volkswagen plant in the Brazilian hinterland. U.S. automakers have created closer partnerships with key suppliers. Volkswagen, Europe's biggest automaker, has moved to another level; the company collaborates with twelve international suppliers who make their own components and then fasten them together into finished trucks and buses. This approach is becoming a model for other new automotive factories in Brazil. Although no other company has stretched the supplier relationship as far as VW, nine new plants in Brazil, including DaimlerChrysler, General Motors, and Ford, are all closely integrating suppliers into the production process.

The problems in achieving this vision were immense. In this system, hundreds of suppliers were reduced to twelve final assemblers that work in the Brazilian factory. Each has second-and third-tier suppliers, which must be coordinated for on-time delivery and must provide top-notch quality. Some of Volkswagen's assemblers are:

Engine and transmission	Motoren-Werke Mannheim (Germany)
	Cummins (United States)
Chassis	Iochpe-Maxion (Brazil)
Cab	Tamet (Brazil)
Steering and instruments	VDO Kienzle (Germany)
Axles, brakes, suspension	Rockwell (United States)
Wheels and tires	Iochpe-Maxion (Brazil)
	Bridgestone (Japan)
	Borlen (Brazil)
Painting	Eisenmann (Germany)

Each assembler has a marked-off area on the plant floor. For example, VDO Kienzle's workers install everything from seats to instrument panels in the steel shell of a truck cab. The cab moves down the assembly line to other suppliers' spaces. In a factory of around fourteen hundred workers, only two hundred are VW employees; the rest are provided by the suppliers. It seems to many observers that an international collection of suppliers could never assemble a defect-free vehicle. The solution is to shift from the traditional plant hierarchy to partnership and teamwork. The plant manager holds a daily round-table discussion with suppliers; and he sees himself as just a partner at the table, not the owner. Working as partners requires the breakdown of competitive mindsets, which is essential to the success of this concept.

Called coproduction and a modular consortium, the new approach is appealing because VW's capital investment drops because suppliers provide needed equipment and inventory. The number of hours it takes to build each vehicle also decreases.

Other automakers are trying variations of the modular consortium approach because it offers so many advantages.

Source: Based on David Woodruff with Ian Katz and Keith Naughton, "VW's Factory of the Future," *Business Week*, 7 October 1996, 52-56; Diana Jean Schemo, "Is VW's New Plant Lean, or Just Mean?" *New York Times*, 19 November 1996, D1; and Philip Siekman, "Building 'Em Better in Brazil," *Fortune*, September 6, 1999, 246(c)-246(v).

individual organizational adaptation is severely limited compared to the changes demanded by the environment. Innovation and change in a population of organizations take place through the birth of new forms and kinds of organizations more so than by the reform and change of existing organizations. Indeed, organizational forms are considered relatively stable, and the good of a whole society is served by the development of new forms of organization through entrepreneurial initiatives. New organizations meet the new needs of society more so than established organizations that are slow to change.[32]

What does this theory mean in practical terms? It means that large established organizations often become dinosaurs. Established companies such as Toys "R" Us and Barnes & Noble, for example, have had tremendous difficulty adapting to a rapidly changing environment. Hence, new organizational forms that fit the current environment will emerge, such as eToys and Amazon.com, that fill a new niche and over time take away business from established companies. Large, established companies are finding it nearly impossible to make the shift to an Internet-based business model.

Why do established organizations have such a hard time adapting to a rapidly changing environment? Michael Hannan and John Freeman, originators of the population ecology model of organization, argue that there are many limitations on the ability of organizations to change. The limitations come from heavy investment in plant, equipment, and specialized personnel, limited information, established viewpoints of decision makers, the organization's own successful history that justifies current procedures, and the difficulty of changing corporate culture. True transformation is a rare and unlikely event in the face of all these barriers.[33]

At this very moment, new organizational forms are emerging. Consider the changing gas station. Two decades ago, gas stations sold gas and maybe offered auto repair. Today, most gas pumps are located in front of convenience stores where customers can pick up a six-pack or buy a loaf of bread and a gallon of milk. Some stores are quite large, often including a deli or doughnut shop. Now, a new organizational form is emerging that includes multiple stores on one site—for example, a gas station, a fast-food restaurant, and a dry cleaner. In today's fast-paced world, customers want convenience on a level not even considered in the 1970s.[34] In the travel industry, which was once dominated by a few large carriers, low-fare airlines such as Southwest Airlines in the United States, WestJet in Canada, GoFly Ltd. in Britain, and Ryanair in Ireland are taking business away from the giants. Another recent change is the development of corporate universities within large companies like Motorola and Fedex. There are more than one thousand corporate universities, compared to just two hundred a few years ago. One reason they've developed so fast is that companies can't get desired services from established universities, which are too stuck in traditional ways of thinking and teaching.[35]

According to the population ecology view, when looking at an organizational population as a whole, the changing environment determines which organizations survive or fail. The assumption is that individual organizations suffer from structural inertia and find it difficult to adapt to environmental changes. Thus, when rapid change occurs, old organizations are likely to decline or fail, and new organizations emerge that are better suited to the needs of the environment.

Currently, huge AT&T is working hard to renew itself in the rapidly changing telecommunications world. A part of this strategy was the appointment of a new chief executive, Michael Armstrong, to replace long-time CEO Robert Allen. Based on the history of telephone companies, population ecology researchers would say that successful change is unlikely.[36] For example, in the early 1900s when the telephone industry was new, over four hundred telephone companies existed in Pennsylvania alone. Most used magneto technology, which means each telephone carried its own battery. A major innovation was a common battery—a power source located within the central office used for voice transmission among all telephones connected there. This was a powerful innovation, but most phone companies failed to adapt. Thus as the common battery became more popular, the magneto-based companies went out of business.[37] Over the years consolidation occurred until only a few phone companies are left, and now AT&T, the dominant long-distance carrier, may be in the twilight of its dominance.

The population ecology model is developed from theories of natural selection in biology, and the terms *evolution* and *selection* are used to refer to the underlying behavioral processes. Theories of biological evolution try to explain why certain life forms appear and survive whereas others perish. Some theories suggest the forms that survive are typically best fitted to the immediate environment.

In 1987, *Forbes* magazine reported a study of American businesses over seventy years, from 1917 to 1987. Do you recall Baldwin Locomotive, Studebaker, or Lehigh Coal & Navigation? These companies were among 78 percent of the top one hundred in 1917 that did not see 1987. Of the twenty-two that remained in the top one hundred, only eleven did so under their original names. The environment of the 1940s and 1950s was suitable to Woolworth, but new organizational forms like Wal-Mart and Kmart became dominant in the 1980s. In 1917, most of the top one hundred companies were huge steel and mining industrial organizations, which were replaced by high-technology companies such as IBM and Merck.[38] Two companies that seemed to prosper over a long period were Ford and General Motors, but they are now being threatened by world changes in the automobile industry. No company is immune to the processes of social change. From just 1979 to 1989, 187 of the companies on the *Fortune* 500 list ceased to exist as independent companies. Some were acquired, some merged, and some were liquidated.[39] Meanwhile, technology was changing the environment again. Cellular phone technology made Qualcomm a major player in the 1990s. And the Internet explosion made millionaires out of many who bought America Online stock at $0.36 a share when it went public in 1992. In just a few years, AOL went from being just a good idea to being a *Fortune* 500 powerhouse.[40]

ORGANIZATIONAL FORM AND NICHE

The population ecology model is concerned with organizational forms. **Organizational form** is an organization's specific technology, structure, products, goals, and personnel, which can be selected or rejected by the environment. Each new organization tries to find a **niche** (a domain of unique environmental resources and needs) sufficient to support it. The niche is usually small in the early stages of an organization but may increase in size over time if the organization is successful. If a niche is not available, the organization will decline and may perish.

From the viewpoint of a single firm, luck, chance, and randomness play important parts in survival. New products and ideas are continually being proposed by both entrepreneurs and large organizations. Whether these ideas and organizational forms survive or fail is often a matter of chance—whether external circumstances happen to support them. A woman who started a small electrical contracting business in a rapidly growing Florida community would have an excellent chance of success. If the same woman were to start the same business in a declining community elsewhere in the United States, the chance of success would be far less. Success or failure of a single firm thus is predicted by the characteristics of the environment as much as by the skills or strategies used by the organization.

PROCESS OF ECOLOGICAL CHANGE

The population ecology model assumes that new organizations are always appearing in the population. Thus, organization populations are continually undergoing change. The process of change in the population is defined by three principles that occur in stages: **variation**, **selection**, and **retention**. These stages are summarized in Exhibit 5.4.

- *Variation.* New organizational forms continually appear in a population of organizations. They are initiated by entrepreneurs, established with venture capital by large corporations, or set up by a government seeking to provide new services. Some forms may be conceived to cope with a perceived need in the external environment. In your own neighborhood, for example, a new restaurant may be started to meet a perceived need. In recent years, a large number of new firms have been initiated to develop computer software, to provide consulting and other services to large corporations, and to develop products and technologies for Internet commerce. Other new organizations produce a traditional product such as steel, but do it using minimal technology and new management techniques that make the new steel companies such as Nucor far more able to survive. Organizational variations are analogous to mutations in biology, and they add to the scope and complexity of organizational forms in the environment.

- *Selection.* Some variations will suit the external environment better than others. Some prove beneficial and thus are able to find a niche and acquire the resources from the environment necessary to survive. Other variations fail to meet the needs of the environment and perish. When there is insufficient demand for a firm's product and when insufficient resources are available to the organization, that organization will be "selected out." Only a few variations are "selected in" by the environment and survive over the long term.

- *Retention.* Retention is the preservation and institutionalization of selected organizational forms. Certain technologies, products, and services are highly valued by the environment. The retained organizational form may become a dominant part of the environment. Many forms of organizations have been institutionalized, such as government, schools, churches, and automobile manufacturers. McDonald's, which owns a huge share of the fast-food market and provides the first job for many teenagers, has become institutionalized in American life.

E X H I B I T   5 . 4   *Elements in the Population Ecology Model of Organizations*

Institutionalized organizations like McDonald's seem to be relatively permanent features in the population of organizations, but they are not permanent in the long run. The environment is always changing, and, if the dominant organizational forms do not adapt to external change, they will gradually diminish and be replaced by other organizations. Taco Bell captured some of McDonald's customers because the Mexican fast-food chain kept lowering prices while McDonald's consistently raised them. Unless it adapts, McDonald's might no longer be price-competitive in the fast-food market.[41]

From the population ecology perspective, the environment is the important determinant of organizational success or failure. The organization must meet an environmental need, or it will be selected out. The process of variation, selection, and retention leads to the establishment of new organizational forms in a population of organizations.

STRATEGIES FOR SURVIVAL

Another principle that underlies the population ecology model is the **struggle for existence**, or competition. Organizations and populations of organizations are engaged in a competitive struggle over resources, and each organizational form is fighting to survive. The struggle is most intense among new organizations, and both the birth and survival frequencies of new organizations are related to factors in the larger environment. Factors such as size of urban area, percentage of immigrants, political turbulence, industry growth rate, and environmental variability have influenced the launching and survival of newspapers, telecommunication firms, railroads, government agencies, labor unions, and even voluntary organizations.[42]

In the population ecology perspective, **generalist** and **specialist** strategies distinguish organizational forms in the struggle for survival. Organizations with a wide niche or domain, that is, those that offer a broad range of products or services or that serve a broad market, are generalists. Organizations that provide a narrower range of goods or services or that serve a narrower market are specialists.

In the natural environment, a specialist form of flora and fauna would evolve in protective isolation in a place like Hawaii, where the nearest body of land is two thousand miles away. The flora and fauna are heavily protected. In contrast, a place like Costa Rica, which experienced wave after wave of external influences, developed a generalist set of flora and fauna that has better resilience and flexibility for adapting to a broad range of circumstances. In the business world, Amazon.com started with a specialist strategy, selling books over the Internet, but evolved to a generalist strategy with the addition of music, video, greeting cards, and other products, plus links to sites selling drugstore goods, pet supplies, and flowers. A company such as Olmec Corporation, which sells African American and Hispanic dolls, would be considered a specialist, whereas Mattel is a generalist, marketing a broad range of toys for boys and girls of all ages.[43]

Specialists are generally more competitive than generalists in the narrow area in which their domains overlap. However, the breadth of the generalist's domain serves to protect it somewhat from environmental changes. Though demand may decrease for some of the generalist's products or services, it usually increases for others at the same time. In addition, because of the diversity of products, services, and customers, generalists are able to reallocate resources internally to adapt to a changing environment, whereas specialists are not. However, because specialists are often smaller companies, they can sometimes move faster and be more flexible in adapting to a changing environment.[44]

Managerial impact on company success often comes from selecting a strategy that steers a company into an open niche in the environment. Charles Schwab Corp. was established and became successful by creating a new niche for discount brokerage houses. More recently, Schwab managers spotted an open niche based on on-line securities trading, helping the company grab the lion's share in a new market.

In Practice 5.3

Charles Schwab Corp.

How did Charles Schwab Corp., a traditional discount brokerage firm, become the player to beat in on-line financial services? Managers spotted a niche and moved early and quickly to set up an e-commerce unit, while those at companies such as Merrill Lynch held out, believing their customer service and marketing savvy would help them fight off online rivals.

Founder Charles R. Schwab and other top managers recognized the Web's potential as early as 1995, the first year more personal computers were sold in the United States than televisions. A key to successfully launching the online business was that Schwab established it as a separate unit, so workers would have an entrepreneurial spirit. Schwab recognized that the new unit needed to be totally focused, have the freedom to innovate, and have the ability to push aside worries about cannibalizing Schwab's traditional business. The founder's interest and support was crucial in the early days, as the fledgling unit had to fight Schwab's expanding international division and others for corporate investment dollars. Originally, Schwab's full-service customers were paying $65 to trade on the Net, while Schwab.com users paid only $29.95. Faced with growing complaints, top leaders took the risks and priced all Internet trades at the lower level. The decision cut $150 million from expected revenue and sent the company's shares tumbling. But it paid off big when volume and profits from the online service soared. Today, Charles Schwab has moved the core of its business online, gets 76 million hits a day, and has captured more than 40 percent of the assets invested in online trading accounts.[45]

INSTITUTIONALISM

The institutional perspective provides yet another view of interorganizational relationships.[46] Organizations are highly interconnected. Just as companies need efficient production to survive, the institutional view argues that organizations need legitimacy from their stakeholders. Companies perform well when they are perceived by the larger environment to have a legitimate right to exist. Thus, the **institutional perspective** describes how organizations survive and succeed through congruence between an organization and the expectations from its environment. The **institutional environment** is composed of norms and values from stakeholders (customers, investors, associations, boards, government, collaborating organizations). Thus the institutional view believes that organizations adopt structures and processes to please outsiders, and these activities come to take on rulelike status in organizations. The institutional environment reflects what the greater society views as correct ways of organizing and behaving.[47]

Legitimacy is defined as the general perspective that an organization's actions are desirable, proper, and appropriate within the environment's system of norms, values, and beliefs.[48] Institutional theory thus is concerned with the set of intangible norms and values that shape behavior, as opposed to the tangible elements of technology and structure. Organizations must fit within the cognitive and emotional expectations of their audience. For example, people will not deposit money in a bank unless it sends signals of safety and compliance with norms of wise financial management.

Another example is the widespread interest among business firms in the annual *Fortune* magazine survey that ranks corporations based on their reputation. Consider also your local government and whether it could raise property taxes for increased school funding if community residents did not approve of the school district's policies and activities. The Soviet Union collapsed and communism quickly disappeared because communism held little legitimacy in the minds of citizens in Russia and Eastern Europe. Just as important, when Westerners tried to construct a market-based economy in Russia, those efforts failed because citizens did not have a mental framework that saw competitive organizations as legitimate. Gradually institutions will grow and flourish in Russia consistent with the values held in the larger culture.

The notion of legitimacy answers an important question for institutional theorists. Why is there so much homogeneity in the forms and practices of established organizations? For example, visit banks, high schools, hospitals, government departments, or business firms in a similar industry, in any part of the country, and they will look strikingly similar. When an organizational field is just getting started, such as in e-commerce, then diversity is the norm. New organizations fill emerging niches. However, once an industry becomes established, there is an invisible push toward similarity. *Isomorphism* is the term used to describe this move toward similarity.

The institutional view also sees organizations as having two essential dimensions—technical and institutional. The technical dimension is the day-to-day work technology and operating requirements. The institutional structure is that part of the organization most visible to the outside public. Moreover, the technical dimension is governed by norms of rationality and efficiency, but the institutional dimension is governed by expectations from the external environment. As a result of pressure to do things in a proper and correct way, the formal structures of many organizations reflect the expectations and values of the environment rather than the demand of work activities. This means that an organization may incorporate positions or activities (equal employment officer, e-commerce division) perceived as important by the larger society and thus increase its legitimacy and survival prospects, even though these elements may decrease efficiency. Compaq Computer Corp.'s board ousted CEO Eckhard Pfeiffer because he was unwilling to cut out the company's distributors and sell computers direct online. Having a dot-com division is perceived as essential by the larger society today. The formal structure and design of an organization may not be rational with respect to work flow and products or services, but it will assure survival in the larger environment.

Organizations adapt to the environment by signaling their congruence with the demands and expectations stemming from cultural norms, standards set by professional bodies, funding agencies, and customers. Structure is something of a facade disconnected from technical work through which the organization obtains approval, legitimacy, and continuing support. The adoption of structures thus may not be linked to actual production needs, and may occur regardless of whether specific internal problems are solved. Formal structure is separated from technical action in this view.[49]

INSTITUTIONAL SIMILARITY

Organizations have a strong need to appear legitimate. In so doing, many aspects of structure and behavior may be targeted toward environmental acceptance rather than toward internal technical efficiency. Interorganizational relationships thus are characterized by forces that cause organizations in a similar population to look like one another. Institutional similarity, called *institutional isomorphism* in the academic literature, is the emergence of a common structure and approach among organizations in the same field. Isomorphism is the process that causes one unit in a population to resemble other units that face the same set of environmental conditions.[50]

Exactly how does increasing similarity occur? How are these forces realized? A summary of three mechanisms for institutional adaptation are summarized in Exhibit 5.5. There are three core mechanisms: mimetic forces, which result from responses to uncertainty, normative forces, which result from common training and professionalism, and coercive forces, which stem from political influence.[51]

Mimetic Forces. Most organizations, especially business organizations, face great uncertainty. It is not clear to senior executives exactly what products, services, or technologies will achieve desired goals, and sometimes the goals themselves are not clear. In the face of this uncertainty, **mimetic forces** occur, which is the pressure to copy or model other organizations.

Executives see an innovation in a firm generally regarded as successful, so the management practice is quickly copied. This modeling is done without any clear proof that performance will be improved. Mimetic processes explain why fads and fashions occur in the business world. Once a new idea starts, many organizations grab onto it, only to learn that the application is difficult and may cause more problems than it solves. This was the case with the recent frenzy around reengineering and the merger wave that swept many industries. Of course there were successes reported in both instances but also a large number of failures. Techniques such as job enrichment, total quality management, and the balanced scorecard have all been adopted without clear evidence for efficiency or effectiveness. The one certain benefit is that management's feelings of uncertainty will be reduced, and the company's image will be enhanced because the firm is seen as using the latest management techniques.

EXHIBIT 5.5   *Three Mechanisms for Institutional Adaptation*

	Mimetic	**Coercive**	**Normative**
Reason to become similar:	Uncertainty	Dependence	Duty, obligation
Events:	Innovation visibility	Political law, rules, sanctions	Professionalism— certification, accreditation
Social basis:	Culturally supported	Legal	Moral
Example:	Reengineering, benchmarking	Pollution controls, school regulations	Accounting standards, consultant training

Source: Adapted from W. Richard Scott, *Institutions and Organizations* (Thousand Oaks, Calif.: Sage, 1995).

Perhaps the clearest example of official copying is the technique of benchmarking that occurs as part of the total quality movement. *Benchmarking* means identifying who's best at something in an industry and then duplicating the technique for creating excellence, perhaps even improving it in the process. Rank Xerox, the subsidiary of Xerox that sells copiers in Europe, uses benchmarking to find out what competitors are doing and then copies the best techniques.[52]

The mimetic process works because organizations face continuous high uncertainty, they are aware of innovations occurring in the environment, and the innovations are culturally supported, thereby giving legitimacy to adopters. This is a strong mechanism by which a group of banks, or high schools, or manufacturing firms begin to look and act like one another.

Coercive Forces. All organizations are subject to pressure, both formal and informal, from government, regulatory agencies, and other important organizations in the environment, especially those on which a company is dependent. **Coercive forces** are the external pressures exerted on organizations to adopt structures, techniques, or behaviors similar to other organizations. Some pressures may have the force of law, such as government mandates to adopt new pollution control equipment. Health and safety regulations may demand that a safety officer be appointed. Due to increasing political pressure at the local, state, and national level, more than twenty gun manufacturers recently adopted a policy of installing child safety locks on handguns. As with other changes, those brought about because of coercive forces may not make the organization more effective, but it will "look" more effective and will be accepted as legitimate in the environment.

Coercive pressures often occur between organizations where there is a power difference, as described in the resource dependence section earlier in this chapter. It is not unusual for a large retailer like Wal-Mart or a manufacturer like General Motors to insist on certain policies, procedures, and techniques used by its suppliers. When Honda picked Donnelly Corporation to make all the mirrors for its U.S.-manufactured cars, Honda insisted that Donnelly empower its workers. Because Donnelly had already taken major steps in this direction, it won the contract. Unless an organization knows how to foster collaborative relationships internally, Honda believes the company won't be good at making a partnership work between the two companies.

Organizational changes that result from coercive forces occur when an organization is dependent on another, when there are political factors such as rules, laws, and sanctions involved, or when some other contractual or legal basis defines the relationship. Organizations operating under those constraints will adopt changes and relate to one another in a way that increases homogeneity and limits diversity.

Normative Forces. The third reason organizations change according to the institutional view is normative. **Normative forces** mean that organizations are expected to change to achieve standards of professionalism, and to adopt techniques that are considered by the professional community to be up to date and effective. Changes may be in any area, such as information technology, accounting requirements, or marketing techniques. Professionals share a body of formal education based on university degrees and professional networks through which ideas are exchanged by consultants and professional leaders. Universities, consulting firms, and professional training institutions develop norms among professional managers. People are exposed to similar training and standards, and adopt shared values, which are implemented in organizations with which they work. Business schools teach finance, marketing, and human resource majors that certain techniques are better than others, so using those techniques becomes a standard in the field. In one study, for example, a radio station changed from a functional to a multidivisional structure because a consultant recommended it as a "higher standard" of doing business. There was no proof that this structure was better, but the radio station wanted legitimacy and to be perceived as fully professional and up to date in its management techniques. As another example, studies show great homogeneity among superintendents in the U.S. public school system and among board members of *Fortune* 500 companies. Through education and experience, people are subjected to considerable pressure to gain legitimacy by acting exactly the same way as people already in those positions.

Companies accept normative pressure to become like one another through a sense of obligation or duty to high standards of performance based on professional norms shared by managers and specialists in their respective organizations. These norms are conveyed through professional education and certification and have almost a moral or ethical requirement based on the highest standards accepted by the profession at that time.

A company may use any or all of the mechanisms of mimetic, coercive, or normative forces to change itself for greater legitimacy in the institutional environment. Firms tend to use these mechanisms when they are acting under conditions of dependence, uncertainty, ambiguous goals, and reliance on professional credentials. The outcome of these processes is that organizations become far more homogeneous than would be expected from the natural diversity among managers and environments.

SUMMARY AND INTERPRETATION

This chapter has been about the important evolution in interorganizational relationships. At one time organizations considered themselves autonomous and separate, trying to outdo other companies. Today more organizations see themselves as part of an ecosystem. The organization may span several industries and will be anchored in a dense web of relationships with other companies. In this ecosystem, collaboration is as important as competition. Indeed, organizations may compete and collaborate at the same time depending on the location and issue. In this business ecosystem, the role of management is changing to include the development of horizontal relationships with other organizations.

Four perspectives have been developed to explain relationships among organizations. The resource dependence perspective is the most traditional, arguing that organizations try to avoid excessive dependence on other organizations. In this view, organizations devote considerable effort to controlling the environment to assure ample resources while maintaining independence. Moreover, powerful organizations will exploit the dependence of small companies. The collaborative network perspective is an emerging alternative. Organizations welcome collaboration and interdependence with other organizations to enhance value for both. The success of collaboration has been revealed in not-for-profit organizations and in international industrial groups such as the Japanese *keiretsu*. Many executives are changing mindsets away from autonomy toward collaboration, often with previous corporate enemies. The new mindset emphasizes trust, fair dealing, and achieving profits for all parties in a relationship.

The population ecology perspective explains why organizational diversity continuously increases with the appearance of new organizations filling niches left open by established companies. This perspective says that large companies usually cannot adapt to meet a changing environment, hence new companies emerge with the appropriate form and skills to serve new needs. Through the process of variation, selection, and retention, some organizations will survive and grow while others perish. Companies may adopt a generalist or specialist strategy to survive in the population of organizations.

The institutional perspective argues that interorganizational relationships are shaped as much by a company's need for legitimacy as by the need for providing products and services. The need for legitimacy means that the organization will adopt structures and activities that are perceived as valid, proper, and up to date by external stakeholders. In this way, established organizations copy techniques from one another and begin to look very similar. The emerging common structures and approaches in the same field is called institutional similarity or institutional isomorphism. There are three core mechanisms that explain increasing organizational homogeneity: mimetic forces, which result from responses to uncertainty; normative forces, which result from common training and professionalism; and coercive forces, which stem from power differences and political influences.

Each of these four perspectives is valid. They represent different lenses through which the world of interorganizational relationships can be viewed: organizations experience a competitive struggle for autonomy; they can thrive through collaborative relationships with others; the slowness to adapt provides openings for new organizations to flourish; and organizations seek legitimacy as well as profits from the external environment. The important thing is for managers to be aware of interorganizational relationships and to consciously manage them.

BRIEFCASE

As an organization manager, keep these guidelines in mind:

1. Look for and develop relationships with other organizations. Don't limit your thinking to a single industry or business type. Build an ecosystem of which your organization is a part.

2. Reach out and control external sectors that threaten needed resources. Adopt strategies to control resources especially when your organization is dependent and has little power. Assert your company's influence when you have power and control over resources.

3. Seek collaborative partnerships that enable mutual dependence and enhance value and gain for both sides. Get deeply involved in your partner's business, and vice versa, to benefit both.

4. Adapt your organization to new variations being selected and retained in the external environment. If you are starting a new organization, find a niche that contains a strong environmental need for your product or service, and be prepared for a competitive struggle over scarce resources.

5. Pursue legitimacy with your organization's major stakeholders in the external environment. Adopt strategies, structures, and new management techniques that meet the expectations of significant parties, thereby assuring their cooperation and resources. Enhance legitimacy by borrowing good ideas from other firms, complying with laws and regulations, and following procedures considered best for your company.

KEY CONCEPTS

<table>
<tr><td>coercive forces</td><td>organizational ecosystem</td></tr>
<tr><td>collaborative network</td><td>organizational form</td></tr>
<tr><td>generalist</td><td>population</td></tr>
<tr><td>institutional environment</td><td>population ecology</td></tr>
<tr><td>institutional perspective</td><td>resource dependence</td></tr>
<tr><td>institutional similarity</td><td>retention</td></tr>
<tr><td>interorganization relationships</td><td>selection</td></tr>
<tr><td>legitimacy</td><td>specialist</td></tr>
<tr><td>mimetic forces</td><td>struggle for existence</td></tr>
<tr><td>niche</td><td>variation</td></tr>
<tr><td>normative forces</td><td></td></tr>
</table>

DISCUSSION QUESTIONS

1. The concept of business ecosystems implies that organizations are more interdependent than ever before. From personal experience do you agree? Explain.

2. How do you feel about the prospect of becoming a manager and having to manage a set of relationships with other companies rather than just managing your own company? Discuss.

3. Assume you are the manager of a small firm that is dependent on a large computer manufacturing customer that uses the resource dependence perspective. Put yourself in the position of the small firm, and describe what actions you would take to survive and succeed. What actions would you take from the perspective of the large firm?

4. Many managers today were trained under assumptions of adversarial relationships with other companies. Do you think operating as adversaries is easier or more difficult than operating as partners with other companies? Discuss.

5. Discuss how the adversarial versus partnership orientations work among students in class. Is there a sense of competition for grades? Is it possible to develop true partnerships in which your work depends on others?

6. The population ecology perspective argues that it is healthy for society to have new organizations emerging and old organizations dying as the environment changes. Do you agree? Why would European countries pass laws to sustain traditional organizations and inhibit the emergence of new ones?

7. Explain how the process of variation, selection, and retention might explain innovations that take place within an organization.

8. Do you believe that legitimacy really motivates organizations? Is acceptance by other people a motivation for individuals? Explain.

9. How does the desire for legitimacy result in organizations becoming more similar over time?

10. How do mimetic forces differ from normative forces? Give an example of each.

CHAPTER 5 WORKBOOK   *Management Fads*[*]

Look up one or two articles on current trends or fads in management. Then, find one or two articles on a management fad from several years ago. Finally, surf the Internet for information on both the current and previous fads.

1. How were these fads used in organizations? Use real examples from your readings.
2. Why do you think the fads were adopted? To what extent were the fads adopted to truly improve productivity and morale versus the company's desire to appear current in its management techniques compared to the competition?
3. Give an example in which a fad did not work as expected. Explain the reason it did not work.

Case for Analysis   *Hugh Russel Inc.*[*]

The following story is a personal recollection by David Hurst of the experience of a group of managers in a mature organization undergoing profound change.... The precipitating event in this change was a serious business crisis....

When I joined Hugh Russel Inc. in 1979, it was a medium-sized Canadian distributor of steel and industrial products. With sales of CDN$535 million and three thousand employees, the business was controlled by the chairman, Archie Russel, who owned 16 percent of the common shares. The business consisted of four groups—the core steel distribution activities (called "Russelsteel"), industrial bearings and valves distribution, a chain of wholesalers of hardware and sporting goods, and a small manufacturing business....

The company was structured for performance.... The management was professional, with each of the divisional hierarchies headed by a group president reporting to Peter Foster in his capacity as president of the corporation. Jobs were described in job descriptions, and their mode of execution was specified in detailed standard operating procedures. Three volumes of the corporate manual spelled out policy on everything from accounting to vacation pay. Extensive accounting and data-processing systems allowed managers to track the progress of individual operations against budgets and plans. Compensation was performance-based, with return on net assets (RONA) as the primary measure and large bonuses (up to 100 percent of base) for managers who made their targets.

At the senior management level, the culture was polite but formal. The board of directors consisted of Archie's friends and associates together with management insiders. Archie and Peter ran the organization as if they were majority owners. Their interaction with management outside of the head office was restricted to the occasional field trip....

CRISIS

Nine months after I joined the company as a financial planner, we were put "in play" by a raider and, after a fierce bidding war, were acquired in a hostile takeover. Our acquirer was a private company controlled by the eldest son of an entrepreneur of legendary wealth and ability, so we had no inkling at the time of the roller-coaster ride that lay ahead of us. We were unaware that not only did the son not have the support of his father in this venture but he had also neglected to consult his two brothers, who were joint owners of the acquiring company! As he had taken on $300 million of debt to do the deal, this left each of the brothers on the hook for a personal guarantee of $100 million. They were not amused, and it showed!

Within days of the deal, we were inundated by waves of consultants, lawyers, and accountants: each shareholder seemed to have his or her own panel of advisers. After six weeks of intensive analysis, it was clear that far too much had been paid for us and that the transaction was vastly overleveraged. At the start of the deal, the acquirer had approached our bankers and asked them if they wanted a piece of the "action." Concerned at the possible loss of our banking business and eager to be associated with such a prominent family, our bankers had agreed to provide the initial financing on a handshake. Now, as they saw the detailed numbers for the first time and became aware

[*]David K. Hurst, *Crisis and Renewal: Meeting the Challenge of Organizational Change* (Boston: Harvard Business School Press, 1995).

of the dissent among the shareholders, they withdrew their support and demanded their money back. We needed to refinance $300 million of debt—fast. . . .

CHANGE

The takeover and the subsequent merger of our new owner's moribund steel-fabricating operations into Hugh Russel changed our agenda completely. We had new shareholders (who fought with each other constantly), new bankers, and new businesses in an environment of soaring interest rates and plummeting demand for our products and services. Almost overnight, the corporation went from a growth-oriented, acquisitive, earnings-driven operation to a cash-starved cripple, desperate to survive. Closures, layoffs, downsizing, delayering, asset sales, and "rationalization" became our new priorities. . . . At the head office, the clarity of jobs vanished. For example, I had been hired to do financial forecasting and raise capital in the equity markets, but with the company a financial basket case, this clearly could not be done. For all of us, the future looked dangerous and frightening as bankruptcy, both personal and corporate, loomed ahead.

And so it was in an atmosphere of crisis that Wayne Mang, the new president (Archie Russel and Peter Foster left the organization soon after the deal), gathered the first group of managers together to discuss the situation. Wayne Mang had been in the steel business for many years and was trusted and respected by the Hugh Russel people. An accountant by training, he used to call himself the "personnel manager" to underscore his belief in both the ability of people to make the difference in the organization and the responsibility of line management to make this happen. The hastily called first meeting consisted of people whom Wayne respected and trusted from all over the organization. They had been selected without regard for their position in the old hierarchy.

The content and style of that first meeting were a revelation to many! Few of them had ever been summoned to the head office for anything but a haranguing over their budgets. Now they were being told the complete gory details of the company's situation and, for the first time, being treated as if they had something to contribute. Wayne asked for their help.

During that first meeting, we counted nineteen major issues confronting the corporation. None of them fell under a single functional area. We arranged ourselves into task forces to deal with them. I say "arranged ourselves" because that was the way it seemed to happen. Individuals volunteered without coercion to work on issues in which they were interested or for which their skills were relevant. They also "volunteered" others who were not at the meeting but, it was thought, could help. There was some guidance—each task force had one person from the head office whose function it was to report what was happening back to the "center"—and some members found themselves on too many task forces, which required that substitutes be found. But that was the extent of the conscious management of the process.

The meeting broke up at 2:00 a.m., when we all went home to tell our incredulous spouses what had happened. . . .

The cross-functional project team rapidly became our preferred method of organizing new initiatives, and at the head office, the old formal structure virtually disappeared. The teams could be formed at a moment's notice to handle a fast-breaking issue and dissolved just as quickly. We found, for example, that even when we weren't having formal meetings, we seemed to spend most of our time talking to each other informally. Two people would start a conversation in someone's office, and almost before you knew it, others had wandered in and a small group session was going. Later on, we called these events "bubbles"; they became our equivalent of the Bushmen's campfire meetings. . . .

Later, when I became executive vice president, Wayne and I deliberately shared an office so we could each hear what the other was doing in real time and create an environment in which "bubbles" might form spontaneously. As people wandered past our open door, we would wave them in to talk; others would wander in after them. The content of these sessions always had to do with our predicament, both corporate and personal. It was serious stuff, but the atmosphere was light and open. Our fate was potentially a bad one, but at least it would be shared. All of us who were involved then cannot remember ever having laughed so much. We laughed at ourselves and at the desperate situation. We laughed at the foolishness of the bankers in having financed such a mess, and we laughed at the antics of the feuding shareholders, whose outrageous manners and language we learned to mimic to perfection.

I think it was the atmosphere from these informal sessions that gradually permeated all our interactions—with employees, bankers, suppliers, everyone with whom we came into contact. Certainly, we often had tough meetings, filled with tension and threat, but we were always able to "bootstrap" ourselves back up emotionally at the informal debriefings afterward. . . .

Perhaps the best example of both the change in structure and the blurring of the boundaries of the organization was our changing relationships with our bankers. In the beginning, at least for the brief time that the loan was in good standing, the association was polite and at arm's length. Communication was formal. As the bank realized the full horror of what it had financed (a process that took about eighteen months), the relationship steadily grew more hostile. Senior executives of the bank became threatening, spelling out what actions they might take if we did not solve our problem. This hostility culminated in an investigation by the bank for possible fraud (a standard procedure in many banks when faced with a significant loss).

Throughout this period, we had seen a succession of different bankers, each of whom had been assigned to our account for a few months. As a result of our efforts to brief every new face that appeared, we had built a significant network of contacts within the bank with whom we had openly shared a good deal of information and opinion. When no fraud was found, the bank polled its own people on what to do. Our views presented so coherently by our people (because everyone knew what was going on), and shared so widely with so many bankers, had an enormous influence on the outcome of this process. The result was the formation of a joint company-bank team to address a shared problem that together we could solve. The boundary between the corporation and the bank was now blurred: to an outside observer, it would have been unclear where the corporation ended and the bank began. . . .

Our corporation had extensive formal reporting systems to allow the monitoring of operations on a regular basis. After the takeover, these systems required substantial modifications. For example, . . . we had to report our results to the public every quarter at a time when we were losing nearly two million dollars a week! We knew that unless we got to our suppliers ahead of time, they could easily panic and refuse us credit. Hasty moves on their part could have had fatal consequences for the business.

In addition, our closure plans for plants all over Canada and the United States brought us into contact with unions and governments in an entirely different way. We realized that we had no option but to deal with these audiences in advance of events.

I have already described how our relationship with the bankers changed as a result of our open communication. We found exactly the same effect with these new audiences. Initially, our major suppliers could not understand why we had told them we were in trouble before we had to. We succeeded, however, in framing the situation in a way that enlisted their cooperation in our survival, and by the time the "war story" was news, we had their full support. Similarly, most government and union organizations were so pleased to be involved in the process before announcements were made that they bent over backward to be of assistance. Just as had been the case with the bank, we set up joint task forces with these "outside" agencies to resolve what had become shared problems. A significant contributor to our ability to pull this off was the high quality of our internal communication. Everyone on the teams knew the complete, up-to-date picture of what was happening. An outside agency could talk to anyone on a team and get the same story. In this way, we constructed a formidable network of contacts, many of whom had special skills and experience in areas that would turn out to be of great help to us in the future.

The addition of multiple networks to our information systems enhanced our ability both to gather and to disseminate information. The informality and openness of the networks, together with the high volume of face-to-face dialogues, gave us an early warning system with which to detect hurt feelings and possible hostile moves on the part of shareholders, suppliers, nervous bankers, and even customers. This information helped us head off trouble before it happened. The networks also acted as a broadcast system through which we could test plans and actions before announcing them formally. In this way, we not only got excellent suggestions for improvement, but everyone felt that he or she had been consulted before action was taken. . . .

We had a similar experience with a group of people outside the company during the hectic last six months of 1983, when we were trying to finalize a deal for the shareholders and bankers to sell the steel distribution business to new owners. The group of people in question comprised the secretaries of the numerous lawyers and accountants involved in the deal. . . .

We made these secretaries part of the network, briefing them in advance on the situation, explaining why things were needed, and keeping them updated on the progress of the deal. We were astounded at the cooperation we received: our calls were put through, our messages received prompt responses, drafts and opinions were produced on time. In the final event, a complex deal that should have taken nine months to complete was done in three. All of this was accomplished by ordinary people going far beyond what might have been expected of them. . . .

We had been thrust into crisis without warning, and our initial activities were almost entirely reactions to issues that imposed themselves upon us. But as we muddled along in the task forces, we began to find that we had unexpected sources of influence over what was happening. The changing relationship with the bank illustrates this neatly. Although we had no formal power in that situation, we found that by framing a confusing predicament in a coherent way, we could, via our network, influence the outcomes of the bank's decisions. The same applied to suppliers: by briefing them ahead of time and presenting a reasonable scenario for the recovery of their advances, we could influence the decisions they would make.

Slowly we began to realize that, although we were powerless in a formal sense, our networks, together with our own internal coherence, gave us an ability to get things done invisibly. As we discussed the situation with all the parties involved, a strategy began to emerge. A complicated financial/tax structure would allow the bank to "manage" its loss and give it an incentive not to call on the shareholders' personal guarantees. The core steel distribution business could be refinanced in the process and sold to new owners. The wrangle between the shareholders could be resolved, and each could go his or her own way. All that had to be done was to bring all the parties together, including a buyer for the steel business, and have them agree that this was the best course to follow. Using our newfound skills, we managed to pull it off.

It was not without excitement: at the last minute, the shareholders raised further objections to the deal. Only the bank could make them sell, and they were reluctant to do so, fearful that they might attract a lawsuit. Discreet calls to the major suppliers, several of whose executives were on the board of the bank, did the trick. "This business needs to be sold and recapitalized," the suppliers were told. "If the deal does not go through, you should probably reduce your credit exposure." The deal went through. By the end of 1983, we had new owners, just in time to benefit from the general business recovery. The ordeal was over. . . .

CHAPTER 5 WORKSHOP *Ugli Orange Case**

1. Form groups of three members. One person will be Dr. Roland, one person will be Dr. Jones, and the third person will be an observer.
2. Roland and Jones will read only their own roles, but the observer will read both.
3. Role play: Instructor announces "I am Mr./Ms. Cardoza, the owner of the remaining Ugli oranges. My fruit export firm is based in South America. My country does not have diplomatic relations with your country, although we do have strong trade relations."

   The groups will spend about ten minutes meeting with the other firm's representative and will decide on a course of action. Be prepared to answer the following questions:
   a. What do you plan to do?
   b. If you want to buy the oranges, what price will you offer?
   c. To whom and how will the oranges be delivered?
4. The observers will report the solutions reached. The groups will describe the decision-making process used.

5. The instructor will lead a discussion on the exercise addressing the following questions:
   a. Which groups had the most trust? How did that influence behavior?
   b. Which groups shared more information? Why?
   c. How are trust and disclosure important in negotiations?

ROLE OF "DR. JONES"

You are Dr. John W. Jones, a biological research scientist employed by a pharmaceutical firm. You have recently developed a synthetic chemical useful for curing and preventing Rudosen. Rudosen is a disease contracted by pregnant women. If not caught in the first four weeks of pregnancy, the disease causes serious brain, eye, and ear damage to the unborn child. Recently there has been an outbreak of Rudosen in your state, and several thousand women have contracted the disease. You have found, with volunteer patients, that your recently developed synthetic

---

*By Dr. Robert House, University of Toronto. Used with permission.

serum cures Rudosen in its early stages. Unfortunately, the serum is made from the juice of the Ugli orange, which is a very rare fruit. Only a small quantity (approximately four thousand) of these oranges were produced last season. No additional Ugli oranges will be available until next season, which will be too late to cure the present Rudosen victims.

You've demonstrated that your synthetic serum is in no way harmful to pregnant women. Consequently, there are no side effects. The Food and Drug Administration has approved production and distribution of the serum as a cure for Rudosen. Unfortunately, the present outbreak was unexpected, and your firm had not planned on having the compound serum available for six months. Your firm holds the patent on the synthetic serum, and it is expected to be a highly profitable product when it is generally available to the public.

You have recently been informed on good evidence that Mr. R.H. Cardoza, a South American fruit exporter, is in possession of three thousand Ugli oranges in good condition. If you could obtain the juice of all three thousand you would be able to both cure present victims and provide sufficient inoculation for the remaining pregnant women in the state. No other state currently has a Rudosen threat.

You have recently been informed that Dr. P. W. Roland is also urgently seeking Ugli oranges and is also aware of Mr. Cardoza's possession of the three thousand available. Dr. Roland is employed by a competing pharmaceutical firm. He has been working on biological warfare research for the past several years. There is a great deal of industrial espionage in the pharmaceutical industry. Over the past several years, Dr. Roland's firm and yours have sued each other for infringement of patent rights and espionage law violations several times.

You've been authorized by your firm to approach Mr. Cardoza to purchase the three thousand Ugli oranges. You have been told he will sell them to the highest bidder. Your firm has authorized you to bid as high as $250,000 to obtain the juice of the three thousand available oranges.

ROLE OF "DR. ROLAND"

You are Dr. P. W. Roland. You work as a research biologist for a pharmaceutical firm. The firm is under contract with the government to do research on methods to combat enemy uses of biological warfare.

Recently several World War II experimental nerve gas bombs were moved from the United States to a small island just off the U.S. coast in the Pacific. In the process of transporting them, two of the bombs developed a leak. The leak is currently controlled by government scientists, who believe that the gas will permeate the bomb chambers within two weeks. They know of no method of preventing the gas from getting into the atmosphere and spreading to other islands and very likely to the West Coast as well. If this occurs, it is likely that several thousand people will incur serious brain damage or die.

You've developed a synthetic vapor that will neutralize the nerve gas if it is injected into the bomb chamber before the gas leaks out. The vapor is made with a chemical taken from the rind of the Ugli orange, a very rare fruit. Unfortunately, only four thousand of these oranges were produced this season.

You've been informed on good evidence, that a Mr. R. H. Cardoza, a fruit exporter in South America, is in possession of three thousand Ugli oranges. The chemicals from the rinds of all three thousand oranges would be sufficient to neutralize the gas if the serum is developed and injected efficiently. You have also been informed that the rinds of these oranges are in good condition.

You have also been informed that Dr. J. W. Jones is also urgently seeking purchase of Ugli oranges, and he is aware of Mr. Cardoza's possession of the three thousand available. Dr. Jones works for a firm with which your firm is highly competitive. There is a great deal of industrial espionage in the pharmaceutical industry. Over the years, your firm and Dr. Jones's have sued each other for violations of industrial espionage laws and infringement of patent rights several times. Litigation on two suits is still in process.

The federal government has asked your firm for assistance. You've been authorized by your firm to approach Mr. Cardoza to purchase three thousand Ugli oranges. You have been told he will sell them to the highest bidder. Your firm has authorized you to bid as high as $250,000 to obtain the rind of the oranges.

Before approaching Mr. Cardoza, you have decided to talk to Dr. Jones to influence him so that he will not prevent you from purchasing the oranges.

NOTES

1. Brent Schlender, "Computing's Next Superpower," *Fortune,* 12 May 1997, 88-101.

2. Christine Oliver, "Determinants of Interorganizational Relationships: Integration and Future Directions," *Academy of Management Review* 15 (1990): 241–65.

3. James Moore, *The Death of Competition: Leadership and Strategy in the Age of Business Ecosystems* (New York: HarperCollins, 1996).

4. Thomas Petzinger, Jr., *The New Pioneers: The Men and Women Who Are Transforming the Workplace and Marketplace* (New York: Simon & Schuster, 1999): 53-54.

5. James Moore, "The Death of Competition," *Fortune,* 15 April 1996, 142–44.

6. Brian Goodwin, *How the Leopard Changed Its Spots: The Evolution of Complexity*, (New York: Touchstone, 1994), 181, quoted in Petzinger, *The New Pioneers*, 53.

7. Elizabeth Jensen and Eben Shapiro, "Time Warner's Fight with News Corp. Belies Mutual Dependence," *The Wall Street Journal,* 28 October 1996, A1, A6.

8. Sumantra Ghoshal and Christopher A. Bartlett, "Changing the Role of Top Management: Beyond Structure and Process," *Harvard Business Review* (January-February 1995): 86–96.

9. Donna Fenn, "Sleeping with the Enemy," *Inc.,* November 1997, 78-88.

10. J. Pfeffer and G. R. Salancik, *The External Control of Organizations: A Resource Dependence Perspective* (New York: Harper & Row, 1978).

11. Derek S. Pugh and David J. Hickson, *Writers on Organizations,* 5th ed. (Thousand Oaks, Calif.: Sage, 1996).

12. Peter Grittner, "Four Elements of Successful Sourcing Strategies," *Management Review* (October 1996): 41–45.

13. This discussion is based on Matthew Schifrin, "The Big Squeeze," *Forbes,* 11 March 1996, 45–46; Wendy Zellner with Marti Benedetti, "CLOUT!" *Business Week,* 21 December 1992, 62–73; Kevin Kelly and Zachary Schiller with James B. Treece, "Cut Costs or Else," *Business Week,* 22 March 1993, 28–29; Lee Berton, "Push From Above," *The Wall Street Journal,* 23 May 1996, R24.

14. Joseph Weber with Sunita Wadekar Bhargava, "Drugmakers Get a Taste of Their Own Medicine," Business Week, 26 April 1993, 104.

15. Fenn, "Sleeping with the Enemy."

16. Mitchell P. Koza and Arie Y. Lewin, "The Co-Evolution of Network Alliances: A Longitudinal Analysis of an International Professional Service Network," Center for Research on New Organizational Forms, Working Paper 98-09-02; Kathy Rebello with Richard Brandt, Peter Coy, and Mark Lewyn, "Your Digital Future," *Business Week,* 7 September 1992, 56–64.

17. Lee Berton, "Shall We Dance?" *CFO* (January 1998) 28-35.

18. Berton, "Shall We Dance?"

19. Fenn, "Sleeping with the Enemy."

20. Christine Oliver, "Determinants of Interorganizational Relationships: Integration and Future Directions," *Academy of Management Review,* 15 (1990): 241–65; Ken G. Smith, Stephen J. Carroll, and Susan Ashford, "Intra- and Interorganizational Cooperation: Toward a Research Agenda," *Academy of Management Journal,* 38 (1995): 7–23; Timothy M. Stearns, Alan N. Hoffman, and Jan B. Heide, "Performance of Commercial Television Stations as an Outcome of Interorganizational Linkages and Environmental Conditions," *Academy of Management Journal* 30 (1987): 71–90; Keith G. Provan, "Technology and Interorganizational Activity as Predictors of Client Referrals," *Academy of Management Journal* 27 (1984): 811–29; David A. Whetten and Thomas K. Kueng, "The Instrumental Value of Interorganizational Relations: Antecedents and Consequences of Linkage Formation," *Academy of Management Journal* 22 (1979): 325–44.

21. Michael L. Gerlach, "The Japanese Corporate Network: A Blockmodel Analysis," *Administrative Science Quarterly* 37 (1992): 105–39.

22. Valerie Reitman, "Toyota's Fast Rebound After Fire at Supplier Shows Why It Is Tough," *The Wall Street Journal,* 8 May 1997, A1, A16.

23. Smith et al., "Intra- and Interorganizational Cooperation: Toward a Research Agenda."

24. Keith G. Provan and H. Brinton Milward, "A Preliminary Theory of Interorganizational Network Effectiveness: A Comparative of Four Community Mental Health Systems," *Administrative Science Quarterly* 40 (1995): 1–33.

25. Berton, "Shall We Dance?"

26. Myron Magnet, "The New Golden Rule of Business," *Fortune,* 21 February 1994, 60–64;

Grittner, "Four Elements of Successful Sourcing Strategies."

27. Peter Smith Ring and Andrew H. Van de Ven, "Developmental Processes of Corporate Interorganizational Relationships," *Academy of Management Review* 19 (1994): 90–118; Dyer, "How Chrysler Created an American Keiretsu"; Magnet, "The New Golden Rule of Business"; Grittner, "Four Elements of Successful Sourcing Strategies."

28. Magnet, "The New Golden Rule of Business"; Grittner, "Four Elements of Successful Sourcing Strategies."

29. Fred R. Blekley, "Some Companies Let Suppliers Work on Site and Even Place Orders," *The Wall Street Journal,* 13 January 1995, A1, A6.

30. Peter Grittner, "Four Elements of Successful Sourcing Strategies," *Management Review* (October 1996): 42. Used with permission.

31. This section draws from Joel A. C. Baum, "Organizational Ecology," in Steward R. Clegg, Cynthia Hardy, and Walter R. Nord, eds, *Handbook of Organization Studies* (Thousand Oaks, Calif.: Sage, 1996); Jitendra V. Singh, *Organizational Evolution: New Directions* (Newbury Park, Calif.: Sage, 1990); Howard Aldrich, Bill McKelvey, and Dave Ulrich, "Design Strategy from the Population Perspective," *Journal of Management* 10 (1984): 67–86; Aldrich, *Organizations and Environments;* Michael Hannan and John Freeman, "The Population Ecology of Organizations," *American Journal of Sociology* 82 (1977): 929–64; Dave Ulrich, "The Population Perspective: Review, Critique, and Relevance," *Human Relations* 40 (1987): 137–52; Jitendra V. Singh and Charles J. Lumsden, "Theory and Research in Organizational Ecology," *Annual Review of Sociology* 16 (1990): 161–95; Howard E. Aldrich, "Understanding, Not Integration: Vital Signs from Three Perspectives on Organizations," in Michael Reed and Michael D. Hughes, eds., *Rethinking Organizations: New Directories in Organizational Theory and Analysis* (London: Sage: forthcoming); Jitendra V. Singh, David J. Tucker, and Robert J. House, "Organizational Legitimacy and the Liability of Newness," *Administrative Science Quarterly* 31 (1986): 171–93; Douglas R. Wholey and Jack W. Brittain, "Organizational Ecology: Findings and Implications," *Academy of Management Review* 11 (1986): 513–33.

32. Derek S. Pugh and David J. Hickson, *Writers on Organizations;* Lex Donaldson, *American Anti-Management Theories of Organization* (New York: Cambridge University Press, 1995).

33. Michael T. Hannan and John Freeman, "The Population Ecology of Organizations."

34. Sallie L. Gaines, "Stations Fill Up With Other Business," *Chicago Tribune,* 22 September 1997, Section 4, 4.

35. Thomas Moore, "The Corporate University: Transforming Management Education" (Presentation in August, 1996. Thomas Moore is the Dean of the Arthur D. Little University).

36. John J. Keller, "A Telecom Novice Is Handed Challenge of Remaking AT&T," *The Wall Street Journal,* 24 October 1996, A1, A6.

37. William P. Barnett, "The Organizational Ecology of a Technology System," *Administrative Science Quarterly,* 35 (1990): 31–60.

38. Peter Newcomb, "No One is Safe," *Forbes,* 13 July 1987, 121; "It's Tough Up There," *Forbes,* 13 July 1987, 145–60.

39. Stewart Feldman, "Here One Decade, Gone the Next," *Management Review* (November 1990): 5–6.

40. *Value Line Investment Survey* (New York: Value Line Publishing, 1998), 778, 2233.

41. Patricia Sellers, "Pepsi Keeps on Going after No. 1." *Fortune,* 11 March 1991, 61–70.

42. David J. Tucker, Jitendra V. Singh, and Agnes G. Meinhard, "Organizational Form, Population Dynamics, and Institutional Change: The Founding Patterns of Voluntary Organizations," *Academy of Management Journal* 33 (1990): 151–78; Glenn R. Carroll and Michael T. Hannan, "Density Delay in the Evolution of Organizational Populations: A Model and Five Empirical Tests," *Administrative Science Quarterly* 34 (1989): 411–30; Jacques Delacroix and Glenn R. Carroll, "Organizational Foundings: An Ecological Study of the Newspaper Industries of Argentina and Ireland," *Administrative Science Quarterly* 28 (1983): 274–91; Johannes M. Pennings, "Organizational Birth Frequencies: An Empirical Investigation," *Administrative Science Quarterly* 27 (1982): 120–44; David Marple, "Technological Innovation and Organizational Survival: A Population Ecology Study of Nineteenth-Century American Railroads," *Sociological*

Quarterly 23 (1982): 107–16; Thomas G. Rundall and John O. McClain, "Environmental Selection and Physician Supply," *American Journal of Sociology* 87 (1982): 1090–1112.

43. Robert D. Hof and Linda Himelstein, "eBay vs. Amazon.com," *Business Week,* 31 May 1999, 128-132; and Maria Mallory with Stephanie Anderson Forest, "Waking Up to a Major Market," *Business Week,* 23 March 1992, 70-73.

44. Arthur G. Bedeian and Raymond F. Zammuto, *Organizations: Theory and Design* (Orlando, Fla.: Dryden Press, 1991); Richard L. Hall, *Organizations: Structure, Process and Outcomes* (Englewood Cliffs, N.J.: Prentice-Hall, 1991).

45. Nanette Byrnes and Paul C. Judge, "Internet Anxiety," *Business Week,* 28 June 1999, 79-88.

46. Thanks to Tina Dacin for her material and suggestions for this section of the chapter.

47. J. Meyer and B. Rowan, "Institutionalized Organizations: Formal Structure as Myth and Ceremony," *American Journal of Sociology* 83 (1990): 340–63.

48. Mark C. Suchman, "Managing Legitimacy: Strategic and Institutional Approaches," *Academy of Management Review* 20 (1995): 571–610.

49. Pamela S. Tolbert and Lynne G. Zucker, "The Institutionalization of Institutional Theory," in Stewart R. Clegg, Cynthia Hardy, and Walter R. Nord, eds., *Handbook of Organization Studies* (Thousand Oaks, Calif.: Sage, 1996).

50. Pugh and Hickson, *Writers on Organizations;* Paul J. DiMaggio and Walter W. Powell, "The Iron Cage Revisited: Institutional Isomorphism and Collective Rationality in Organizational Fields," *American Sociological Review* 48 (1983): 147–60.

51. This section is based largely on DiMaggio and Powell, "The Iron Cage Revisited"; Pugh and Hickson, *Writers on Organizations;* and W. Richard Scott, *Institutions and Organizations* (Thousand Oaks, Calif.: Sage, 1995).

52. Thomas A. Stewart, "Beat the Budget and Astound Your CFO," *Fortune,* 28 October 1996, 187–89.

CHAPTER 6

Manufacturing and Service Technologies

A LOOK INSIDE

French Rags

In 1978, Brenda French started a scarf-making company in a spare bedroom of her home. Ten years later, leading department stores like Neiman Marcus, Bonwit Teller, and Bloomingdale's were showcasing her line of custom-made knitwear. French Rags seemed, to outsiders, like a booming success, but Brenda French knew better. Her business was beset by a multitude of problems and had difficulty competing against mass manufacturers with greater resources selling at lower prices. French Rags could offer customers the variety they wanted but production output was limited and costs were high.

Faced with closing the business, French began looking into new technology that offered a dazzling possibility: mass customization. She invested in a German-made Stoll knitting machine that combines new technology and timeless craft by using thousands of precisely angled needles to make clothes one stitch at a time. In addition, the company now uses computer-aided design and manufacturing technology, enabling French Rags to produce custom-made garments at virtually the same speed—and the same cost—as the cookie-cutter offerings of mass producers. Custom software produces knit-by-numbers templates that enable fast and easy switching from one garment to another. About one hundred employees at French Rags' Los Angeles factory augment the automated knitting line with the necessary human touch. The next step French took was to create a sales force of her most affluent customers, who sell French Rags out of their homes. After customers make their selections and pick out preferred color combinations, individual measurements are taken, the order is faxed or sent by modem to the French Rags factory, and the garment is custom made and shipped directly to the customer's home. Inventory costs and problems have been virtually eliminated.

Combining new technology with new ways of thinking turned Brenda French's small company into a $5 million full-line clothing manufacturer and put French Rags on the cutting edge of a revolution in manufacturing.[1]

French Rags is among the growing number of small companies that are combining craftsmanship with advanced manufacturing technology. These companies, sometimes called *craftories*, produce individualized products and respond quickly to the specific needs of retailers and customers. Overall, manufacturing has been on the decline in the United States and other developed countries, with services becoming an increasingly greater part of the economy. However, small companies such as French Rags have led the way in gaining a new competitive edge in manufacturing.

This chapter explores both service and manufacturing technologies and how technology is related to organizational structure. **Technology** refers to the tools, techniques, machines, and actions used to transform organizational inputs (materials, information, ideas) into outputs (products and services).[2] Technology is an organization's production process and includes work procedures as well as machinery.

Organization technology begins with raw materials of some type (for example, unfinished steel castings in a valve manufacturing plant). Employees take action on the raw material to make a change in it (they machine steel castings), which transforms the raw material into the output of the organization (control valves ready for shipment to oil refineries). For a service organization like Federal

Express, the production technology includes the equipment and procedures for delivering overnight mail.

Exhibit 6.1 features an example of production technology for a manufacturing plant. Note how the technology consists of raw material inputs, a transformation process that changes and adds value to these items, and the ultimate product or service output that is sold to consumers in the environment. In today's large, complex organizations, it can be hard to pinpoint technology. Technology can be partly assessed by examining the raw materials flowing into the organization,[3] the variability of work activities,[4] the degree to which the production process is mechanized,[5] the extent to which one task depends upon another in the work flow,[6] or the number of new product or service outputs.[7]

Recall from Chapter 1 that organizations have a technical core that reflects the organization's primary purpose. The technical core contains the transformation process that represents the organization's technology. As today's organizations try to become more flexible in a changing environment, new technology may influence organizational structure, but decisions about organizational structure may also shape or limit technology. Thus, the interaction between core technology and structure leads to a patterned relationship in many organizations.[8]

Organizations are made up of many departments, each of which may use a different technology to produce its outputs and meet departmental goals. Thus, research and development transforms ideas into new product proposals, and marketing transforms inventory into sales, each using a different technology. Moreover, the administrative technology used by managers to run the organization represents yet another technology. New information technology, which will be discussed in Chapter 7, has a tremendous impact on the administrative arena.

PURPOSE OF THIS CHAPTER

In this chapter, we will explore the nature of organizational technologies and the relationship between technology and organization structure. Chapters 4 and 5 described how the environment influences organization design. The question addressed in this chapter is, "How should the organization structure be designed

EXHIBIT 6.1   *Transformation Process for a Manufacturing Company*

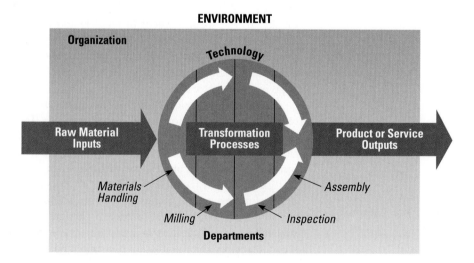

to accommodate and facilitate the production process?" Form usually follows function, so the form of the organization's structure should be tailored to fit the needs of the production technology.

The remainder of the chapter will unfold as follows. First, we will examine how the technology for the organization as a whole influences organization structure and design. This discussion will include both manufacturing and service technologies. Next, we will examine differences in departmental technologies and how the technologies influence the design and management of organizational subunits. Third, we will explore how interdependence—flow of materials and information—among departments affects structure.

ORGANIZATION-LEVEL MANUFACTURING TECHNOLOGY

Manufacturing technologies include traditional manufacturing processes and new computer-based manufacturing systems.

MANUFACTURING FIRMS

Woodward's Study. The first and most influential study of manufacturing technology was conducted by Joan Woodward, a British industrial sociologist. Her research began as a field study of management principles in south Essex. The prevailing management wisdom at the time (1950s) was contained in what was known as universal principles of management. These principles were "one best way" prescriptions that effective organizations were expected to adopt. Woodward surveyed one hundred manufacturing firms firsthand to learn how they were organized.[9] She and her research team visited each firm, interviewed managers, examined company records, and observed the manufacturing operations. Her data included a wide range of structural characteristics (span of control, levels of management) and dimensions of management style (written versus verbal communications, use of rewards) and the type of manufacturing process. Data were also obtained that reflected commercial success of the firms.

Woodward developed a scale and organized the firms according to technical complexity of the manufacturing process. **Technical complexity** represents the extent of mechanization of the manufacturing process. High technical complexity means most of the work is performed by machines. Low technical complexity means workers play a larger role in the production process. Woodward's scale of technical complexity originally had ten categories, as summarized in Exhibit 6.2. These categories were further consolidated into three basic technology groups:

- *Group I: Small-batch and unit production.* These firms tend to be job shop operations that manufacture and assemble small orders to meet specific needs of customers. Custom work is the norm. **Small-batch production** relies heavily on the human operator; it is thus not highly mechanized. Steinway & Sons is an example of small-batch production. Although computerized machines are now used to cut wood more precisely than human hands, much of the work of building a Steinway piano is done by craftsmen in much the same way it was done a century ago. Compared to competitors, who turn out hundreds of thousands of pianos annually, Steinway's artisans build only 2,500 in the United States and 2,000 in Germany each year.[10]

EXHIBIT 6.2   *Woodward's Classification of One Hundred British Firms According to Their Systems of Production*

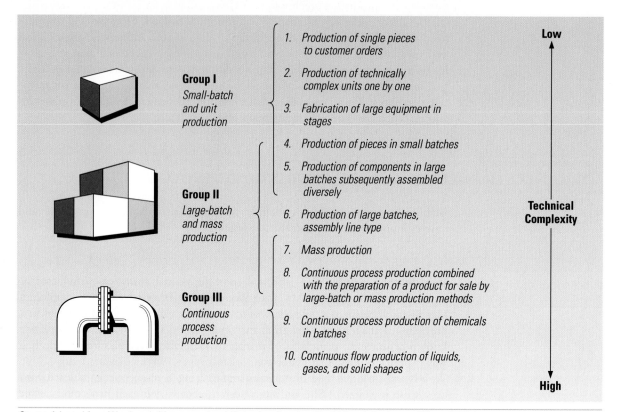

1. Production of single pieces to customer orders

2. Production of technically complex units one by one

Group I
Small-batch and unit production

3. Fabrication of large equipment in stages

4. Production of pieces in small batches

5. Production of components in large batches subsequently assembled diversely

Group II
Large-batch and mass production

6. Production of large batches, assembly line type

7. Mass production

8. Continuous process production combined with the preparation of a product for sale by large-batch or mass production methods

Group III
Continuous process production

9. Continuous process production of chemicals in batches

10. Continuous flow production of liquids, gases, and solid shapes

Low

Technical Complexity

High

Source: Adapted from Woodward, *Management and Technology* (London: Her Majesty's Stationery Office, 1958). Used with permission of Her Britannic Majesty's Stationery Office.

- *Group II: Large-batch and mass production.* **Large-batch production** is a manufacturing process characterized by long production runs of standardized parts. Output often goes into inventory from which orders are filled, because customers do not have special needs. Examples include most assembly lines, such as for automobiles or trailer homes.

- *Group III: Continuous process production.* In **continuous process production** the entire process is mechanized. There is no starting and stopping. This represents mechanization and standardization one step beyond those in an assembly line. Automated machines control the continuous process, and outcomes are highly predictable. Examples would include chemical plants, oil refineries, liquor producers, and nuclear power plants.

Using this classification of technology, Woodward's data made sense. A few of her key findings are given in Exhibit 6.3. The number of management levels and the manager/total personnel ratio, for example, show definite increases as technical complexity increases from unit production to continuous process. This indicates that greater management intensity is needed to manage complex technology. Direct/indirect labor ratio decreases with technical complexity because more indirect workers are required to support and maintain complex machinery. Other characteristics, such as span of control, formalized procedures,

E X H I B I T   6 . 3   *Relationship Between Technical Complexity and Structural Characteristics*

Structural Characteristic	Technology		
	Unit Production	Mass Production	Continuous Process
Number of management levels	3	4	6
Supervisor span of control	23	48	15
Direct/indirect labor ratio	9:1	4:1	1:1
Manager/total personnel ratio	Low	Medium	High
Workers' skill level	High	Low	High
Formalized procedures	Low	High	Low
Centralization	Low	High	Low
Amount of verbal communication	High	Low	High
Amount of written communication	Low	High	Low
Overall structure	Organic	Mechanistic	Organic

Source: Joan Woodward, *Industrial Organization: Theory and Practice* (London: Oxford University Press, 1965). Used with permission.

and centralization, are high for mass production technology but low for other technologies because the work is standardized. Unit production and continuous process technologies require highly skilled workers to run the machines and verbal communication to adapt to changing conditions. Mass production is standardized and routinized, so few exceptions occur, little verbal communication is needed, and employees are less skilled.

Overall, the management systems in both unit production and continuous process technology are characterized as organic, as defined in Chapter 4. They are more free-flowing and adaptive, with fewer procedures and less standardization. Mass production, however, is mechanistic, with standardized jobs and formalized procedures. Woodward's discovery about technology thus provided substantial new insight into the causes of organization structure. In Joan Woodward's own words, "Different technologies impose different kinds of demands on individuals and organizations, and those demands had to be met through an appropriate structure."[11]

Strategy, Technology, and Performance. Another portion of Woodward's study examined the success of the firms along dimensions such as profitability, market share, stock price, and reputation. As indicated in Chapter 2, the measurement of effectiveness is not simple or precise, but Woodward was able to rank firms on a scale of commercial success according to whether they displayed above-average, average, or below-average performance on strategic objectives.

Woodward compared the structure-technology relationship against commercial success and discovered that successful firms tended to be those that had complementary structures and technologies. Many of the organizational characteristics of the successful firms were near the average of their technology category, as shown in Exhibit 6.3. Below-average firms tended to depart from the structural characteristics for their technology type. Another conclusion was that structural characteristics could be interpreted as clustering into organic and mechanistic management systems. Successful small-batch and continuous process organizations had organic structures, and successful mass production organizations had mechanistic structures. Subsequent research has replicated her findings.[12]

What this illustrates for today's companies is that strategy, structure, and technology need to be aligned, especially when competitive conditions change.[13] Some insurance companies in the United States are currently realigning strategy, structure, and technology because of increased competition in the insurance business. Companies such as Geico and USAA are growing rapidly through the use of direct mail and phone solicitation, avoiding the costs associated with doing business through independent insurance agents. Agency-based companies like State Farm and Allstate have had to put new emphasis on a low-cost strategy and are adopting efficiency-oriented information technology to cut costs and more effectively serve customers. Another example is the Madame Alexander doll factory in Harlem, where a new production system led to a restructuring of employees into teams. Now, instead of individually producing parts such as wigs, shoes, and all the other tiny bits that go into a doll, employees work in teams that each produce about three hundred complete doll or wardrobe assemblies a day.[14]

Failing to adopt appropriate new technologies to support strategy, or adopting a new technology and failing to realign strategy to match it, can lead to poor performance. Today's increased global competition means more volatile markets, shorter product life cycles, and more sophisticated and knowledgeable consumers; and flexibility to meet these new demands has become a strategic imperative for many companies.[15] Manufacturing companies can adopt new technologies to support the strategy of flexibility. However, organization structures and management processes must also be realigned, as a highly mechanistic structure hampers flexibility and prevents the company from reaping the benefits of the new technology.[16] The need for new ways of thinking in today's manufacturing firms is discussed in Book Mark 6.0.

For utility companies, once the strategy and technology for providing electricity are chosen, the structure and management approach must also be aligned to achieve strategic objectives, as illustrated in the following example of nuclear power plants.

In Practice 6.1

Northeast Utilities and Boston Edison Company

Northeast Utilities' Millstone 1 nuclear plant, located in Waterford, Connecticut, is considered by the Nuclear Regulatory Commission (NRC) to be one of the best-managed plants in the industry. Northeast Utilities' management long ago realized that managing a nuclear power plant is different from managing a fossil fuel plant. Nuclear plants are bigger and more complex, and their complex technical systems and safety features require extensive maintenance. For these reasons, a large number of skilled workers are on the payroll, and each worker spends one week of every six in training classes. Northeast Utilities also assigns its best people to manage Millstone. The superintendent stays personally involved with employees by visiting the control room each day and chatting face to face with the staff.

Boston Edison Company's Pilgrim nuclear power plant, located just eight miles to the north of Millstone, is comparable in size, design, and vintage, but is considered by the NRC to be one of the worst-managed nuclear plants in the United States. Pilgrim hasn't had a major accident, but it was criticized by the NRC and has been shut down. Boston Edison didn't seem to realize that the complexity of nuclear technology required special management, that a nuclear plant is not just another boiler. At Pilgrim, operators rarely saw the superintendent face to face in the control room. A backlog of twelve thousand maintenance items indicated the need for more maintenance people. Moreover, Boston Edison traditionally did not assign its best managers to the nuclear plant. Edison is now trying to overcome its shortcomings by hiring a new plant manager, recruiting highly skilled operators, and doubling the maintenance staff.

The problem of managing nuclear plants was illustrated by the chairman of Georgia Power Company, who emphasized that "the world of a utility executive that has a nuclear power plant is different from one who doesn't, and if he doesn't understand that, he's in trouble."[17]

The nuclear power plant is a continuous process technology. Its automated equipment is highly complex and requires skilled employees along with a high number of maintenance personnel. Greater management skills and intensity are required to ensure close supervision and to provide backup expertise in a crisis. The failure of Boston Edison's management to diagnose the special management needs of nuclear technology cost the company and its ratepayers dearly. When the Pilgrim plant was closed for upgrading, Boston Edison spent $200,000 a day to buy electricity to replace what Pilgrim would have generated.[18]

COMPUTER-INTEGRATED MANUFACTURING

In the years since Woodward's research, new developments have occurred in manufacturing technology. New manufacturing technologies include robots, numerically controlled machine tools, and computerized software for product design, engineering analysis, and remote control of machinery. The ultimate technology is called **computer-integrated manufacturing** (CIM).[19] Also called *advanced manufacturing technology, agile manufacturing,* the *factory of the future, smart factories,* or *flexible manufacturing systems,* CIM links together manufacturing components that previously stood alone. Thus, robots, machines, product design, and engineering analysis are coordinated by a single computer.

The result has already revolutionized the shop floor, enabling large factories to deliver a wide range of custom-made products at low mass production costs.[20] As illustrated by the chapter opening case, computer-integrated manufacturing also enables small companies to go toe-to-toe with large factories and low-cost foreign competitors. Techknits, Inc., a small manufacturer located in New York City, competes successfully against low-cost sweater-makers in the Far East by using $8 million worth of computerized looms and other machinery. The work of designing sweaters, which once took two days, can now be accomplished in two hours. Looms operate round-the-clock and crank out 60,000 sweaters a week, enabling Techknits to fill customer orders faster than foreign competitors.[21]

Computer-integrated manufacturing is typically the result of three subcomponents.

- *Computer-aided design (CAD).* Computers are used to assist in the drafting, design, and engineering of new parts. Designers guide their computers to draw specified configurations on the screen, including dimensions and component details. Hundreds of design alternatives can be explored, as can scaled-up or scaled-down versions of the original.[22]
- *Computer-aided manufacturing (CAM).* Computer-controlled machines in materials handling, fabrication, production, and assembly greatly increase the speed at which items can be manufactured. CAM also permits a production line to shift rapidly from producing one product to any variety of other products by changing the instruction tapes or software in the computer.

CAM enables the production line to quickly honor customer requests for changes in product design and product mix.[23]

- *Integrated Information Network.* A computerized system links all aspects of the firm—including accounting, purchasing, marketing, inventory control, design, production, and so forth. This system, based on a common data and information base, enables managers to make decisions and direct the manufacturing process in a truly integrated fashion.

The combination of CAD, CAM, and integrated information systems represents the highest level of computer–integrated manufacturing. A new product can be designed on the computer, and a prototype can be produced untouched by human hands. The ideal factory can switch quickly from one product to another,

*B*ook *M*ark *6.0*

Have You Read This Book?

Lean Thinking: Banish Waste and Create Wealth in Your Corporation

By James P. Womack and Daniel T. Jones

Even after North America has restructured and reengineered its companies, firms are still trying to pinpoint the best path to continuous growth and prosperity. The authors of *Lean Thinking* posit that, by relying on their current structures and old definitions for value, companies have created *muda*—a Japanese term meaning waste: a resource-using human activity that creates no value. Through an exploration of fifty mostly manufacturing firms, James Womack and Daniel Jones show that companies can banish this waste by employing lean thinking, which searches for ways to cut out the fat in the production process, extending from the design to the sale of a customer-desired product. Lean thinking can revitalize productivity, revenue, and employee satisfaction.

FIVE PRINCIPLES OF LEAN THINKING
Womack and Jones offer five sequential principles to realize an organization characterized by lean thinking:

1. *Specify value.* Accurately define product value based on a dialogue with customers.
2. *Identify value stream.* Map out all the manufacturing activities entailed in bringing a specific product from design to the customer, eliminating wasteful steps.
3. *Flow.* Take the value-creating activities and make them move fluidly, continuously.
4. *Pull.* Allow the customer to demand a product as needed from the manufacturer. Don't push your products on customers.
5. *Perfection.* Strive for perfection with the first four principles working in a "virtuous circle"; this makes

value flow quicker and reveals hidden *muda* to be removed from the value stream.

ACTION PLAN FOR TRANSFORMATION
The authors provide a step-by-step action plan to achieve a lean-thinking organization:

- *Get started.* Find a change agent, get lean knowledge, find a lever, map value streams, expand your scope.
- *Create a new organization.* Reorganize by product family, create a lean function, devise a policy for excess people, devise a growth strategy, remove anchor-draggers, instill a "perfection" mind-set.
- *Instill business systems.* Introduce lean accounting, relate pay to firm performance, implement transparency, initiate policy deployment, introduce lean learning, find right-sized tools.
- *Complete the transformation.* Apply these steps to your suppliers/customers, develop global strategy, transition from top-down to bottom-up environment.

THE LEAN ENTERPRISE
The authors close the book with a discussion of the lean enterprise, which is a combination of the best attributes of American, German, and Japanese industrial traditions. This collection of features can be used in every economic activity to produce lean-thinking companies—a new way of "thinking, being, and doing."

Lean Thinking: Banish Waste and Create Wealth in Your Corporation, by James P. Womack and Daniel T. Jones, is published by Simon and Schuster.

working fast and with precision, without paperwork or recordkeeping to bog down the system.[24]

A company can adopt CAD in its engineering design department and/or CAM in its production area and make substantial improvements in efficiency and quality. However, when all three components are brought together in a truly advanced plant, the results are breathtaking. Companies such as Xerox, Texas Instruments, Hewlett-Packard, and Boeing are leading the way. Boeing's 777, the largest twin-engine plane ever built, has been called the first "paperless" jetliner. The company designed the plane with eight IBM mainframe computers supporting 2,200 workstations that eventually handled 3,500 billion bits of information. The digital design system reduced the possibility of human error and cut engineering changes and reworking of ill-fitting components by more than 50 percent over previous plane projects.[25]

This ultra-advanced system is not achieved piecemeal. CIM reaches its ultimate level to improve quality, customer service, and cost-cutting when all parts are used interdependently. The integration of CIM and flexible work processes is changing the face of manufacturing. The wave of the manufacturing future is **mass customization**, whereby factories are able to mass-produce products designed to exact customer specification. Today, you can buy a computer assembled to your exact specifications, jeans customized for your body, glasses molded to precisely fit and flatter your face, CDs with music tracks that you select, and pills with the exact blend of vitamins and minerals you want. Acumin, for example, is an Internet-based company that blends vitamins, herbs, and minerals according to each customer's instructions, compressing up to ninety-five ingredients into three to five pills. At Custom Foot stores, customers mix and match design components such as style, color, and material. A high-tech electronic scanner measures the customer's foot, then the complete order is sent by modem to the company's headquarters in Florence, Italy. Shoes are generally ready in about three weeks and often cost less than many premium brands sold off the shelf.[26] Ross Controls, a seventy-year-old manufacturer of pneumatic valves, invested $8 million in computerized design and manufacturing technology to be able to tailor products to exact customer needs.[27] Even automobiles are moving toward mass customization, and 60 percent of the cars BMW sells in Europe are built to order.[28] Although so far, most U.S. customers have not been willing to wait the several months it takes for a custom-ordered vehicle, some business leaders envision a time in the near future when cars can be custom made in as little as three days.[29]

Performance. The awesome advantage of CIM is that products of different sizes, types, and customer requirements freely intermingle on the assembly line. Bar codes imprinted on a part enable machines to make instantaneous changes—such as putting a larger screw in a different location—without slowing the production line. A manufacturer can turn out an infinite variety of products in unlimited batch sizes, as illustrated in Exhibit 6.4. In traditional manufacturing systems studied by Woodward, choices were limited to the diagonal. Small batch allowed for high product flexibility and custom orders, but because of the "craftsmanship" involved in custom-making products, batch size was necessarily small. Mass production could have large-batch size, but offered limited product flexibility. Continuous process could produce a single standard product in unlimited quantities. Computer-integrated manufacturing allows plants to break free of this diagonal and to increase both batch size and product flexibility at the same time. When taken to its ultimate level, CIM allows for mass customization, with each

E X H I B I T   6 . 4   *Relationship of Computer-Integrated Manufacturing Technology to Traditional Technologies*

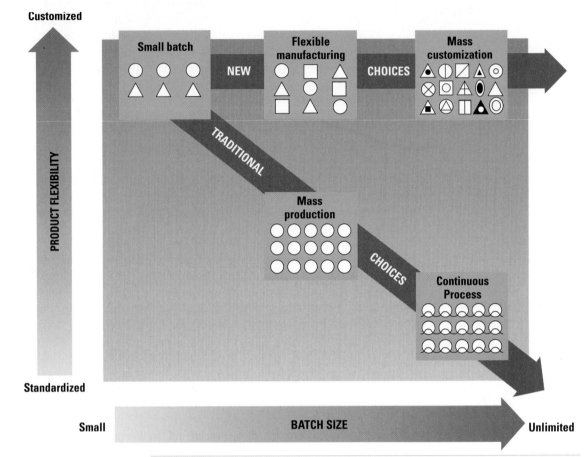

Source: Based on Jack Meredith, "The Strategic Advantages of New Manufacturing Technologies for Small Firms," *Strategic Management Journal* 8 (1987): 249–58; Paul Adler, "Managing Flexible Automation," *California Management Review* (Spring 1988): 34–56; and Otis Port, "Custom-made Direct from the Plant," *Business Week/21st Century Capitalism,* 18 November 1994, 158–59.

specific product tailored to customer specification. This high-level use of CIM has been referred to as *computer-aided craftsmanship* because computers tailor each product to meet a customer's exact needs.[30] The Internet plays an important role in the trend toward mass customization because it enables companies to keep in close touch with each individual customer in addition to making it easier and faster to coordinate customer orders with factory tooling and supply requirements.

Studies suggest that with CIM, machine utilization is more efficient, labor productivity increases, scrap rates decrease, and product variety and customer satisfaction increase.[31] Many U.S. manufacturing companies are reinventing the factory using CIM and associated management systems to increase productivity.

Structural Implications. Research into the relationship between CIM and organizational characteristics is beginning to emerge, and the patterns are summarized in Exhibit 6.5. Compared with traditional mass production technologies, CIM has a narrow span of control, few hierarchical levels, adaptive tasks, low specialization, decentralization, and the overall environment is characterized

EXHIBIT 6.5 *Comparison of Organizational Characteristics Associated with Mass Production and Computer Integrated Manufacturing*

Characteristic	Mass Production	CIM
Structure		
Span of control	Wide	Narrow
Hierarchical levels	Many	Few
Tasks	Routine, repetitive	Adaptive, craftlike
Specialization	High	Low
Decision making	Centralized	Decentralized
Overall	Bureaucratic, mechanistic	Self-regulating, organic
Human Resources		
Interactions	Stand alone	Teamwork
Training	Narrow, one time	Broad, frequent
Expertise	Manual, technical	Cognitive, social Solve problems
Interorganizational		
Customer demand	Stable	Changing
Suppliers	Many, arm's length	Few, close relations

Source: Based on Patricia L. Nemetz and Louis W. Fry, "Flexible Manufacturing Organizations: Implications for Strategy Formulation and Organization Design," *Academy of Management Review* 13 (1988): 627–38; Paul S. Adler, "Managing Flexible Automation," *California Management Review* (Spring 1988): 34–56; and Jeremy Main, "Manufacturing the Right Way," *Fortune,* 21 May 1990, 54–64.

as organic and self-regulative. Employees need the skills to participate in teams, training is broad (so workers are not overly specialized) and frequent (so workers are up to date). Expertise tends to be cognitive so workers can process abstract ideas and solve problems. Interorganizational relationships in CIM firms are characterized by changing demand from customers—which is easily handled with the new technology—and close relationships with a few suppliers that provide top-quality raw materials.[32]

Technology alone cannot give organizations the benefits of flexibility, quality, increased production, and greater customer satisfaction. Research suggests that CIM can become a competitive burden rather than a competitive advantage unless organizational structures and management processes are redesigned to take advantage of the new technology.[33] However, when top managers make a commitment to implement new structures and processes that empower workers and support a learning and knowledge-creating environment, CIM can help companies be more competitive.[34] The Taking the Lead box describes how managers at Deere & Co. are combining advanced manufacturing technology with new approaches to management as they reinvent one of the oldest businesses in the United States.

ORGANIZATION-LEVEL SERVICE TECHNOLOGY

One of the biggest changes occurring in the technology of organizations is the growing service sector. The percentage of the work force employed in manufacturing continues to decline, not only in the United States, but in Canada, France, Germany, the United Kingdom, and Sweden as well. In the United States, services now generate 74 percent of the gross domestic product and account for 79 percent of all jobs.[35] Service technologies are different from manufacturing technologies and, in turn, require a specific organization structure.

SERVICE FIRMS

Definition. Whereas manufacturing organizations achieve their primary purpose through the production of products, service organizations accomplish their primary purpose through the production and provision of services, such as education, health care, transportation, banking, and hospitality. Studies of service organizations have focused on the unique dimensions of service technologies. The characteristics of **service technology** are compared to those of manufacturing technology in Exhibit 6.6.

The most obvious difference is that service technology produces an *intangible output*, rather than a tangible product, such as a refrigerator produced by a manufacturing firm. A service is abstract and often consists of knowledge and ideas rather than a physical product. Thus, whereas manufacturers' products can be inventoried for later sale, services are characterized by *simultaneous production and consumption*. A client meets with a doctor or attorney, for example, and students and teachers come together in the classroom. A service is an intangible product that does not exist until it is requested by the customer. It cannot be stored, inventoried, or viewed as a finished good. If a service is not consumed immediately upon production, it disappears.[36] This typically means that service firms are *labor and knowledge intensive*, with many employees needed to meet the needs of customers,

EXHIBIT   6.6   *Differences Between Manufacturing and Service Technologies*

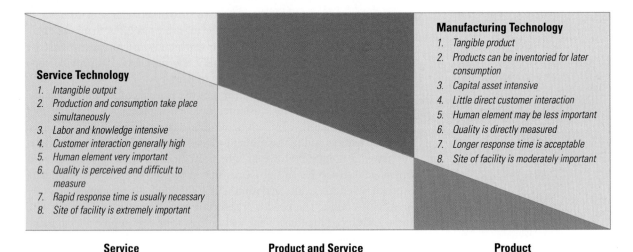

Service Technology
1. Intangible output
2. Production and consumption take place simultaneously
3. Labor and knowledge intensive
4. Customer interaction generally high
5. Human element very important
6. Quality is perceived and difficult to measure
7. Rapid response time is usually necessary
8. Site of facility is extremely important

Manufacturing Technology
1. Tangible product
2. Products can be inventoried for later consumption
3. Capital asset intensive
4. Little direct customer interaction
5. Human element may be less important
6. Quality is directly measured
7. Longer response time is acceptable
8. Site of facility is moderately important

Service	**Product and Service**	**Product**
Airlines	Fast-food outlets	Soft drink companies
Hotels	Cosmetics	Steel companies
Consultants	Real estate	Automobile manufacturers
Health care	Stockbrokers	Mining corporations
Law firms	Retail stores	Food processing plants

Sources: Based on F. F. Reichheld and W. E. Sasser, Jr., "Zero Defections: Quality Comes to Services," *Harvard Business Review* 68 (September–October 1990): 105–11; and David E. Bowen, Caren Siehl, and Benjamin Schneider, "A Framework for Analyzing Customer Service Orientations in Manufacturing," *Academy of Management Review* 14 (1989): 75–95.

whereas manufacturing firms tend to be capital intensive, relying on mass production, continuous process, and advanced manufacturing technologies.[37]

Direct interaction between customer and employee is generally very high with services, while there is little direct interaction between customers and employees in the technical core of a manufacturing firm. This direct interaction means that the *human element* (employees) becomes extremely important in service firms. Whereas most people never meet the workers who manufactured their cars, they interact directly with the salesperson who sold them their Subaru or Pontiac Grand Am. The treatment received from the salesperson—or by a doctor, lawyer, or hairstylist—affects the perception of the service received and the customer's level of satisfaction. The *quality of a service is perceived* and cannot be directly measured and compared in the same way that the quality of a product can. Another characteristic that affects customer satisfaction and perception of quality service is *rapid response time*. A service must be provided when the customer wants and needs it. When you take a friend to dinner, you want to be seated and served in a timely manner; you would not be very satisfied if the hostess or manager told you to come back tomorrow when there would be more tables or servers available to accommodate you.

Taking the Lead

Deere & Co.

Storm clouds seem to always be looming on the horizon for equipment manufacturers like Deere and Co. The 161-year-old company was the only agricultural machinery manufacturer in the world that survived the farm crisis of the 1980s with its corporate structure intact. After Deere took another pounding in the early 1990s, with a sales slump of 11 percent and a loss of $20 million, top executives began thinking about the need to shed outmoded attitudes and embrace change.

One of the new concepts that is helping Deere compete in an era of declining demand and increasing competition is mass customization. In the past, Deere sold farmers half-million-dollar pieces of equipment and then left it to small mom-and-pop shops to profit from helping farmers customize the equipment to their individual needs. Now, Deere salespeople ask each customer a series of questions such as how many rows must be planted and how closely spaced they will be. The salesperson electronically sends an order to a Deere factory, and in less than a day a team of Deere workers—in essence working as a small, custom shop inside the factory—creates a one-of-a-kind piece of machinery designed specifically for the customer. Deere offers more than six million possible configurations. Farmers who at one time bought Deere equipment only every six to ten years are now regularly buying custom attachments.

New computerized machinery and revised work processes for mass customization are only part of the huge wave of change that is sweeping the company. The new technology also required that workers be trained to work in teams rather than on mass-production assembly lines. Chairman and CEO Hans Becherer wants change and risk-taking to become entrenched in the company's culture and a driving force for everything Deere does. He has created highly autonomous divisions and pushed authority and responsibility to lower levels. In addition, Deere's Business Process Excellence Initiative was created to give workers the freedom and power to reinvent operations. The initiative, which currently has more than two hundred cross-functional teams working on about eight hundred different projects, makes everybody in the company a change agent.

Change is never easy, and some mid-level managers literally broke down and wept as the company began tearing down long-entrenched vertical hierarchies. But top managers recognize that a willingness to take risks is the key to keeping Deere & Co. healthy as it heads toward its third century of doing business.

Source: Anita Lienert, "Plowing Ahead in Uncertain Times," *Management Review* (December 1998) 16-21.

The final defining characteristic of service technology is that *site selection is often much more important* than with manufacturing. Because services are intangible, they have to be located where the customer wants to be served. Services are dispersed and located geographically close to customers. For example, fast-food franchises usually disperse their facilities into local stores. Most towns of even moderate size today have two or more McDonald's restaurants rather than one huge one in order to provide service where customers want it.

In reality, it is difficult to find organizations that reflect 100 percent service or 100 percent manufacturing characteristics. Some service firms take on characteristics of manufacturers, and vice versa. Many manufacturing firms are placing a greater emphasis on customer service to differentiate themselves and be more competitive, which is one reason for the increased use of computer-integrated manufacturing. In addition, manufacturing organizations have departments such as purchasing, human resources, and marketing that are based on service technology. On the other hand, organizations such as gas stations, stockbrokers, retail stores, and fast-food restaurants may belong to the service sector, even though the provision of a product is a significant part of the transaction. The vast majority of organizations involve some combination of products and services. The important point is that all organizations can be classified along a continuum that includes both manufacturing and service characteristics, as illustrated in Exhibit 6.6.

New Directions in Services. Service firms have always tended toward providing *customized output*—that is, providing exactly the service each customer wants and needs. For example, when you visit a hairstylist, you don't automatically get the same cut the stylist gave the three previous clients. The stylist cuts your hair the way you request it. However, the trend toward mass customization that is revolutionizing manufacturing has had a significant impact on the service sector as well. Customer expectations of what constitutes good service are rising.[38] Service companies such as the Ritz-Carlton Hotels, USAA, an insurance and financial services company, and Wells Fargo Bank are using new technology to keep customers coming back. All Ritz-Carlton hotels are linked to a database filled with the preferences of half-a-million guests, allowing any desk clerk or bellhop to find out what your favorite wine is, whether you're allergic to feather pillows, and how many extra towels you want in your room. At Wells Fargo, customers can apply over the Internet and get a three-second decision on a loan structured specifically for them.[39] Vincent Oliva, Paul Sanchez, and Joel Myers based their new company, Capital Protection Insurance Services, on the mass customization concept after they grew frustrated with the inflexibility of many insurance companies.

In Practice 6.2

Capital Protection Insurance Services

With more than sixty years of insurance experience among them, Vincent Oliva, Paul Sanchez, and Joel Myers had seen a lot of potential customers alienated and too many others not covered appropriately because of the inflexibility of traditional insurance companies. So they set up Capital Protection Insurance (CPI) Services to sell businesses tailor-made strategies for managing risk.

Traditionally, businesses seeking insurance had two options: a standard policy that left them overinsured and paying too much, or a policy that left them underinsured and at risk. CPI Services has no standard approach and no standard policy. The partners consider each customer's situation individually and draw up a tailor-made risk management plan. To make the system work, the trio is investing in customized actuarial and statistical-modeling software that will start with a standard plan and deviate from it based on each customer's individual traits, such as its historical losses. The new software gives the company a consistent foundation so that underwriters don't have to use nonobjective factors to evaluate clients.

Because CPI Services is a new company, there is no evidence of whether the strategy will succeed, but Oliva, Sanchez, and Myers are optimistic about the mass customization of the insurance industry. "We formed our company on the premise that we would be demand driven," says Oliva. "We wanted to close the gap between what customers need and what insurance companies have offered."[40]

DESIGNING THE SERVICE ORGANIZATION

The feature of service technologies with a distinct influence on organizational structure and control systems is the need for technical core employees to be close to the customer.[41] The differences between service and product organizations necessitated by customer contact are summarized in Exhibit 6.7.

The impact of customer contact on organization structure is reflected in the use of boundary roles and structural disaggregation.[42] Boundary roles are used extensively in manufacturing firms to handle customers and to reduce disruptions for the technical core. They are used less in service firms because a service is intangible and cannot be passed along by boundary spanners, so service customers must interact directly with technical employees, such as doctors or brokers.

A service firm deals in information and intangible outputs and does not need to be large. Its greatest economies are achieved through disaggregation into small units that can be located close to customers. Stockbrokers, doctors' clinics, consulting firms, and banks disperse their facilities into regional and local offices. Some fast-food chains, such as Taco Bell, are taking this a step further, selling chicken tacos and bean burritos anywhere people gather—airports, supermarkets, college campuses, or street corners. Manufacturing firms, on the other hand, tend to aggregate operations in a single area that has raw materials and an available work force. A large manufacturing firm can take advantage of economies derived from expensive machinery and long production runs.

Service technology also influences internal organization characteristics used to direct and control the organization. For one thing, the skills of technical core employees need to be higher. These employees need enough knowledge and

EXHIBIT 6.7   *Configuration and Structural Characteristics of Service Organizations Versus Product Organizations*

Structure	Service	Product
1. Separate boundary roles	Few	Many
2. Geographical dispersion	Much	Little
3. Decision making	Decentralized	Centralized
4. Formalization	Lower	Higher
Human Resources		
1. Employee skill level	Higher	Lower
2. Skill emphasis	Interpersonal	Technical

awareness to handle customer problems rather than just enough to perform a single, mechanical task. Some service organizations give their employees the knowledge and freedom to make decisions and do whatever is needed to satisfy customers, whereas others, such as McDonald's, have set rules and procedures for customer service. Yet in all cases, service employees need social and interpersonal skills as well as technical skills.[43] Because of higher skills and structural dispersion, decision making often tends to be decentralized in service firms, and formalization tends to be low. Many Taco Bell outlets operate with no manager on the premises. Self-directed teams manage inventory, schedule work, order supplies, and train new employees.

Understanding the nature of service technology helps managers align strategy, structure, and management processes that may be quite different from those for a product-based or traditional manufacturing technology. In addition, as mentioned earlier, manufacturing organizations are placing greater emphasis on service, and managers can use these concepts and ideas to strengthen their company's service orientation.

Now let's turn to another perspective on technology, that of production activities within specific organizational departments. Departments often have characteristics similar to those of service technology, providing services to other departments within the organization.

DEPARTMENTAL TECHNOLOGY

This section shifts to the department level of analysis for departments not necessarily within the technical core. Each department in an organization has a production process that consists of a distinct technology. General Motors has departments for engineering, R&D, human resources, advertising, quality control, finance, and dozens of other functions. This section analyzes the nature of departmental technology and its relationship with departmental structure.

The framework that has had the greatest impact on the understanding of departmental technologies was developed by Charles Perrow.[44] Perrow's model has been useful for a broad range of technologies, which made it ideal for research into departmental activities.

VARIETY

Perrow specified two dimensions of departmental activities that were relevant to organization structure and process. The first is the number of exceptions in the work. This refers to task **variety**, which is the frequency of unexpected and novel events that occur in the conversion process. When individuals encounter a large number of unexpected situations, with frequent problems, variety is considered high. When there are few problems, and when day-to-day job requirements are repetitious, technology contains little variety. Variety in departments can range from repeating a single act, such as on an assembly line, to working on a series of unrelated problems or projects.

ANALYZABILITY

The second dimension of technology concerns the **analyzability** of work activities. When the conversion process is analyzable, the work can be reduced to mechanical steps and participants can follow an objective, computational procedure to solve problems. Problem solution may involve the use of standard procedures, such as instructions and manuals, or technical knowledge, such as that in a textbook or handbook. On the other hand, some work is not analyzable. When problems arise, it is difficult to identify the correct solution. There is no store of techniques or procedures to tell a person exactly what to do. The cause of or solution to a problem is not clear, so employees rely on accumulated experience, intuition, and judgment. The final solution to a problem is often the result of wisdom and experience and not the result of standard procedures. Philippos Poulos, a tone regulator at Steinway & Sons, has an unanalyzable technology. Tone regulators carefully check each piano's hammers to be sure they produce the proper Steinway sound.[45] These quality control tasks require years of experience and practice. Standard procedures will not tell a person how to do such tasks.

FRAMEWORK

The two dimensions of technology and examples of departmental activities on Perrow's framework are shown in Exhibit 6.8. The dimensions of variety and analyzability form the basis for four major categories of technology: routine, craft, engineering, and nonroutine.

EXHIBIT 6.8   *Framework for Department Technologies*

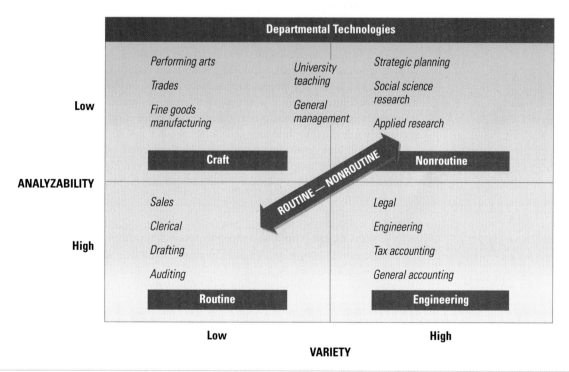

Source: Adapted with permission from Richard Daft and Norman Macintosh, "A New Approach to Design and Use of Management Information," *California Management Review* 21 (1978): 82–92. Copyright © 1978 by the Regents of the University of California. Reprinted by permission of the Regents.

Routine technologies are characterized by little task variety and the use of objective, computational procedures. The tasks are formalized and standardized. Examples include an automobile assembly line and a bank teller department.

Craft technologies are characterized by a fairly stable stream of activities, but the conversion process is not analyzable or well understood. Tasks require extensive training and experience because employees respond to intangible factors on the basis of wisdom, intuition, and experience. Although advances in machine technologies seem to have reduced the number of craft technologies in organizations, a few craft technologies remain. For example, steel furnace engineers continue to mix steel based on intuition and experience, pattern makers at apparel firms still convert rough designers' sketches into salable garments, and gas and oil explorationists use their internal divining rod to determine where millions will be spent on drilling operations.

Engineering technologies tend to be complex because there is substantial variety in the tasks performed. However, the various activities are usually handled on the basis of established formulas, procedures, and techniques. Employees normally refer to a well-developed body of knowledge to handle problems. Engineering and accounting tasks usually fall in this category.

Nonroutine technologies have high task variety, and the conversion process is not analyzable or well understood. In nonroutine technology, a great deal of effort is devoted to analyzing problems and activities. Several equally acceptable options typically can be found. Experience and technical knowledge are used to solve problems and perform the work. Basic research, strategic planning, and other work that involves new projects and unexpected problems are nonroutine.

Routine Versus Nonroutine. Exhibit 6.8 also illustrates that variety and analyzability can be combined into a single dimension of technology. This dimension is called routine versus nonroutine technology, and it is the diagonal line in Exhibit 6.8. The analyzability and variety dimensions are often correlated in departments, meaning that technologies high in variety tend to be low in analyzability, and technologies low in variety tend to be analyzable. Departments can be evaluated along a single dimension of routine versus nonroutine that combines both analyzability and variety, which is a useful shorthand measure for analyzing departmental technology.

The following questions show how departmental technology can be analyzed for determining its placement on Perrow's technology framework in Exhibit 6.8.[46] Employees normally circle a number from one to seven in response to each question.

Variety
1. To what extent would you say your work is routine?
2. Does most everyone in this unit do about the same job in the same way most of the time?
3. Are unit members performing repetitive activities in doing their jobs?

Analyzability
1. To what extent is there a clearly known way to do the major types of work you normally encounter?
2. To what extent is there an understandable sequence of steps that can be followed in doing your work?
3. To do your work, to what extent can you actually rely on established procedures and practices?

If answers to the above questions indicate high scores for analyzability and low scores for variety, the department would have a routine technology. If the opposite occurs, the technology would be nonroutine. Low variety and low analyzability indicate a craft technology, and high variety and high analyzability indicate an engineering technology. As a practical matter, most departments fit somewhere along the diagonal and can be most easily characterized as routine or nonroutine.

DEPARTMENT DESIGN

Once the nature of a department's technology has been identified, then the appropriate structure can be determined. Department technology tends to be associated with a cluster of departmental characteristics, such as the skill level of employees, formalization, and pattern of communication. Definite patterns do exist in the relationship between work unit technology and structural characteristics, which are associated with departmental performance.[47] Key relationships between technology and other dimensions of departments are described in this section and are summarized in Exhibit 6.9.

The overall structure of departments may be characterized as either organic or mechanistic. Routine technologies are associated with a mechanistic structure and processes, with formal rules and rigid management processes. Nonroutine technologies are associated with an organic structure, and department management is more flexible and free-flowing. The specific design characteristics of formalization, centralization, worker skill level, span of control, and communication and coordination vary, depending on work unit technology.

1. *Formalization.* Routine technology is characterized by standardization and division of labor into small tasks that are governed by formal rules and procedures. For nonroutine tasks, the structure is less formal and less standardized. When variety is high, as in a research department, fewer activities are covered by formal procedures.[48]

2. *Decentralization.* In routine technologies, most decision making about task activities is centralized to management.[49] In engineering technologies, employees with technical training tend to acquire moderate decision authority because technical knowledge is important to task accomplishment. Production employees who have long experience obtain decision authority in craft technologies because they know how to respond to problems. Decentralization to employees is greatest in nonroutine settings, where many decisions are made by employees.

3. *Worker skill level.* Work staff in routine technologies typically require little education or experience, which is congruent with repetitious work activities. In work units with greater variety, staff are more skilled and often have formal training in technical schools or universities. Training for craft activities, which are less analyzable, is more likely to be through job experience. Nonroutine activities require both formal education and job experience.[50]

4. *Span of control.* Span of control is the number of employees who report to a single manager or supervisor. This characteristic is normally influenced by departmental technology. The more complex and nonroutine the task, the more problems arise in which the supervisor becomes involved. Although the span of control may be influenced by other factors, such as skill level of

EXHIBIT 6.9   *Relationship of Department Technology to Structural and Management Characteristics*

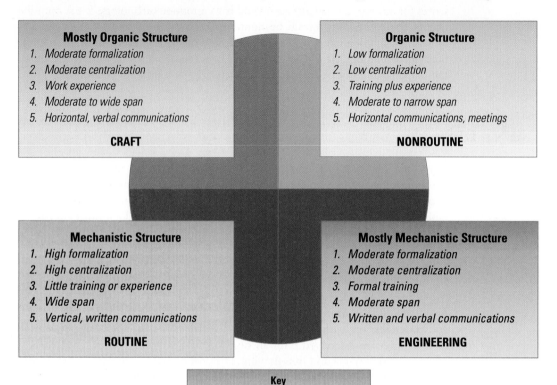

Mostly Organic Structure
1. *Moderate formalization*
2. *Moderate centralization*
3. *Work experience*
4. *Moderate to wide span*
5. *Horizontal, verbal communications*

CRAFT

Organic Structure
1. *Low formalization*
2. *Low centralization*
3. *Training plus experience*
4. *Moderate to narrow span*
5. *Horizontal communications, meetings*

NONROUTINE

Mechanistic Structure
1. *High formalization*
2. *High centralization*
3. *Little training or experience*
4. *Wide span*
5. *Vertical, written communications*

ROUTINE

Mostly Mechanistic Structure
1. *Moderate formalization*
2. *Moderate centralization*
3. *Formal training*
4. *Moderate span*
5. *Written and verbal communications*

ENGINEERING

Key
1. *Formalization*
2. *Centralization*
3. *Staff qualifications*
4. *Span of control*
5. *Communication and coordination*

employees, it typically should be smaller for complex tasks because on such tasks the supervisor and subordinate must interact frequently.[51]

5. *Communication and coordination.* Communication activity and frequency increase as task variety increases.[52] Frequent problems require more information sharing to solve problems and ensure proper completion of activities. The direction of communication is typically horizontal in nonroutine work units and vertical in routine work units.[53] The form of communication varies by task analyzability.[54] When tasks are highly analyzable, statistical and written forms of communication (memos, reports, rules, and procedures) are frequent. When tasks are less analyzable, information typically is conveyed face-to-face, over the telephone, or in group meetings.

Two important points are reflected in Exhibit 6.9. First, departments do differ from one another and can be categorized according to their workflow technology.[55] Second, structural and management processes differ based on departmental technology. Managers should design their departments so that requirements based on technology can be met. Design problems are most visible when the design is clearly inconsistent with technology. Studies have found that when structure and communication characteristics did not reflect technology, departments tended to be less effective.[56] Employees could not communicate with the frequency needed to solve problems. Sometimes employees have to deviate from misplaced rules to behave as needed to fit the technology, as in the following case.

In Practice 6.3

"M*A*S*H" Versus "E.R."

The *M*A*S*H* television series illustrated how well-intentioned army managers who imposed a tight, mechanistic structure on nonroutine hospital units worked against the requirements of the unit's technology. The humor in the *M*A*S*H* programs resulted from the efforts of Hawkeye, Potter, and O'Reilly to get their work done despite the army's bureaucracy, which was designed for routine infantry activities. Colonel Potter's ability to let the MASH unit run in free-flowing, organic fashion enabled the unit to be far more effective than would be the case if all rules and procedures were followed.[57]

The dramatic series *E.R.*, on the other hand, attempts to reveal the nature of the modern emergency room, where highly skilled employees have the authority to respond on their own initiative and discretion based on problems that arise. Following strict procedures would inhibit emergency room personnel from responding correctly to unexpected problems. Strict rules are appropriate, however, for routine hospital activities. Some of the dramatic tension in *E.R.* comes from the efforts of emergency room employees to maintain autonomy within a system that by necessity relies on rules and procedures.

WORKFLOW INTERDEPENDENCE AMONG DEPARTMENTS

So far this chapter has explored how organization and department technologies influence structural design. The final characteristic of technology that influences structure is called interdependence. **Interdependence** means the extent to which departments depend on each other for resources or materials to accomplish their tasks. Low interdependence means that departments can do their work independently of each other and have little need for interaction, consultation, or exchange of materials. High interdependence means departments must constantly exchange resources.

TYPES

James Thompson defined three types of interdependence that influence organization structure.[58] These interdependencies are illustrated in Exhibit 6.10 and are discussed in the following sections.

Pooled. Pooled interdependence is the lowest form of interdependence among departments. In this form, work does not flow between units. Each department is part of the organization and contributes to the common good of the organization, but works independently. McDonald's restaurants or branch banks are examples of pooled interdependence. An outlet in Chicago need not interact with an outlet in Urbana. Pooled interdependence may be associated with the relationships within a *divisional structure*, defined in Chapter 3. Divisions or branches share financial resources from a common pool, and the success of each division contributes to the success of the overall organization.

Thompson proposed that pooled interdependence would exist in firms with what he called a mediating technology. A **mediating technology** provides

EXHIBIT 6.10 *Thompson's Classification of Interdependence and Management Implications*

Form of Interdependence	Demands on Horizontal Communication, Decision Making	Type of Coordination Required	Priority for Locating Units Close Together
Pooled (bank) 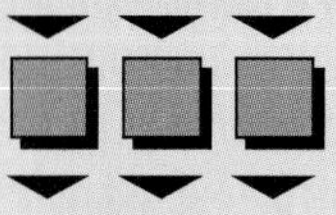 Clients	Low communication	Standardization, rules, procedures Divisional Structure	Low
Sequential (assembly line) 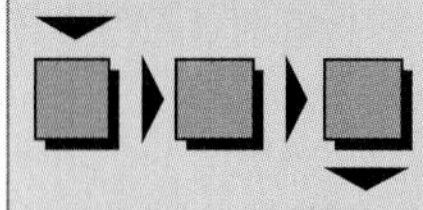 Client	Medium communication	Plans, schedules, feedback Task forces	Medium
Reciprocal (hospital) 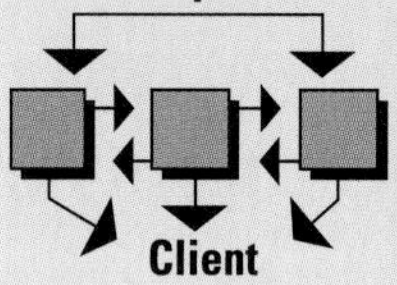 Client	High communication	Mutual adjustment, cross-departmental meetings, teamwork Horizontal structure	High

products or services that mediate or link clients from the external environment and, in so doing, allows each department to work independently. Banks, brokerage firms, and real estate offices all mediate between buyers and sellers, but the offices work independently within the organization.

The management implications associated with pooled interdependence are quite simple. Thompson argued that managers should use rules and procedures to standardize activities across departments. Each department should use the same procedures and financial statements so the outcomes of all departments can be measured and pooled. Very little day-to-day coordination is required among units.

Sequential. When interdependence is of serial form, with parts produced in one department becoming inputs to another department, then it is called **sequential interdependence**. The first department must perform correctly for the second department to perform correctly. This is a higher level of interdependence than pooled, because departments exchange resources and depend upon others to perform well. Sequential interdependence creates a greater need for horizontal mechanisms such as integrators or task forces.

Sequential interdependence occurs in what Thompson called **long-linked technology**, which "refers to the combination in one organization of successive stages of production; each stage of production uses as its inputs the production of the preceding stage and produces inputs for the following stage."[59] Large organizations that use assembly line production, such as in the automobile industry, use long-linked technologies and are characterized by sequential interdependence. between plants or departments. For example, a United Auto Workers' strike at two General Motors parts plants in the summer of 1998 eventually halted production at all but one of GM's assembly plants in North America. Assembly plants were unable to continue work because they could not get the parts they needed.

The management requirements for sequential interdependence are more demanding than for pooled interdependence. Coordination among the linked plants or departments is required. Since the interdependence implies a one-way flow of materials, extensive planning and scheduling are generally needed. Plant B needs to know what to expect from Plant A so both can perform effectively. Some day-to-day communication among plants is also needed to handle unexpected problems and exceptions that arise.

Reciprocal. The highest level of interdependence is **reciprocal interdependence**. This exists when the output of operation A is the input to operation B, and the output of operation B is the input back again to operation A. The outputs of departments influence those departments in reciprocal fashion.

Reciprocal interdependence tends to occur in organizations with what Thompson called **intensive technologies**, which provide a variety of products or services in combination to a client. Hospitals are an excellent example because they provide coordinated services to patients. A patient may move back and forth between X ray, surgery, and physical therapy as needed to be cured. A firm developing new products is another example. Intense coordination is needed between design, engineering, manufacturing, and marketing to combine all their resources to suit the customer's product need.

Management requirements are greatest in the case of reciprocal interdependence. Because reciprocal interdependence requires that departments work together intimately and be closely coordinated, a horizontal structure may be appropriate. The structure must allow for frequent horizontal communication and adjustment. Extensive planning is required in hospitals, for example, but plans will not anticipate or solve all problems. Daily interaction and mutual adjustment among departments are required. Managers from several departments are jointly involved in face-to-face coordination, teamwork, and decision making. Reciprocal interdependence is the most complex interdependence for organizations to handle.

STRUCTURAL PRIORITY

As indicated in Exhibit 6.10, since decision making, communication, and coordination problems are greatest for reciprocal interdependence, reciprocal interdependence should receive first priority in organization structure. New product development is one area of reciprocal interdependence that is of growing concern to managers as companies face increasing pressure to get new products to market fast. Many firms are revamping the design-manufacturing relationship by closely integrating computer-aided design (CAD) and computer-aided manufacturing (CAM) technologies discussed earlier in this chapter.[60] Activities that are reciprocally interdependent should be grouped close together in the organization so managers have easy access to one another for mutual adjustment. These units should report to the same person on the organization chart and should be physically close so the time and effort for coordination can be minimized. A horizontal structure, with linked sets of teams working on core processes, can provide the close coordination needed to support reciprocal interdependence. Poor coordination will result in poor performance for the organization. If reciprocally interdependent units are not located close together, the organization should design mechanisms for coordination, such as daily meetings between departments or an intranet to facilitate communication. The next priority is given to sequential interdependencies, and finally to pooled interdependencies.

This strategy of organizing keeps the communication channels short where coordination is most critical to organizational success. For example, Boise Cascade Corporation experienced poor service to customers because customer service reps located in New York City were not coordinating with production planners in Oregon plants. Customers couldn't get delivery as needed. Boise was reorganized, and the two groups were consolidated under one roof, reporting to the same supervisor at division headquarters. Now customer needs are met because customer service reps work with production planning to schedule customer orders.

STRUCTURAL IMPLICATIONS

Most organizations experience various levels of interdependence, and structure can be designed to fit these needs, as illustrated in Exhibit 6.11.[61] In a manufacturing firm, new product development entails reciprocal interdependence among the design, engineering, purchasing, manufacturing, and sales departments. Perhaps a horizontal structure or cross-functional teams could be used to handle the back-and-forth flow of information and resources. Once a product is designed, its actual manufacture would be sequential interdependence, with a flow of goods from one department to another, such as among purchasing, inventory, production control, manufacturing, and assembly. The actual ordering and delivery of products is pooled interdependence, with warehouses working independently. Customers

EXHIBIT 6.11   *Primary Means to Achieve Coordination for Different Levels of Task Interdependence in a Manufacturing Firm*

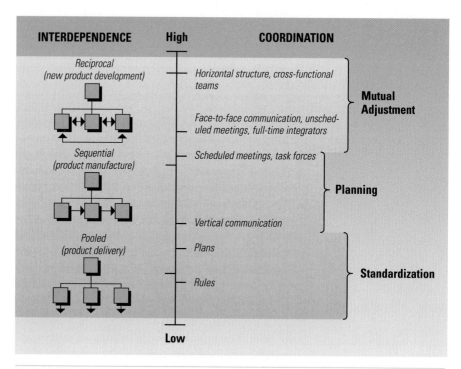

Source: Adapted from Andrew H. Van de Ven, Andre Delbecq, and Richard Koenig, "Determinants of Communication Modes Within Organizations," *American Sociological Review* 41 (1976): 330.

could place an order with the nearest facility, which would not require coordination among warehouses, except in unusual cases such as a stock outage.

When consultants analyzed NCR to learn why the development of new products was so slow, they followed the path from initial idea to implementation. The problem was that the development, production, and marketing of products took place in separate divisions, and communication across the three interdependent groups was difficult. NCR broke up its traditional organization structure and created several stand-alone units of about five hundred people, each with its own development, production, and marketing people. The new structure enabled new products to be introduced in record time.

The three levels of interdependence are illustrated by a study of athletic teams that examined interdependency among players and how it influences other aspects of baseball, football, and basketball teams.

In Practice 6.4

Athletic Teams

A major difference among baseball, football, and basketball is the interdependence among players. Baseball is low in interdependence, football is medium, and basketball represents the highest player interdependence. The relationships among interdependence and other characteristics of team play are illustrated in Exhibit 6.12.

Pete Rose said, "Baseball is a team game, but nine men who reach their individual goals make a nice team." In baseball, interdependence among team players is low and can be defined as pooled. Each member acts independently, taking a turn at bat and playing his or her own position. When interaction does occur, it is between only two or three players, as in a double play. Players are physically dispersed, and the rules of the game are the primary means of coordinating players. Players practice and develop their skills individually, such as by taking batting practice and undergoing physical conditioning. Management's job is to select good players. If each player is successful as an individual, the team should win.

In football, interdependence among players is higher and tends to be sequential. The line first blocks the opponents to enable the backs to run or pass. Plays are performed sequentially from first down to fourth down. Physical dispersion is medium, which allows players to operate as a coordinated unit. The primary mechanism for coordinating players is developing a game plan along with rules that govern the behavior of team members. Each player has an assignment that fits with other assignments, and management designs the game plan to achieve victory.

EXHIBIT 6.12   *Relationships Among Interdependence and Other Characteristics of Team Play*

	Baseball	**Football**	**Basketball**
Interdependence	Pooled	Sequential	Reciprocal
Physical dispersion of players	High	Medium	Low
Coordination	Rules that govern the sport	Game plan and position roles	Mutual adjustment and shared responsibility
Key management job	Select players and develop their skills	Prepare and execute game	Influence flow of game

Source: Based on William Passmore, Carol E. Francis, and Jeffrey Haldeman, "Sociotechnical Systems: A North American Reflection on the Empirical Studies of the 70s," *Human Relations* 35 (1982): 1179–1204.

In basketball, interdependence tends to be reciprocal. The game is free-flowing, and the division of labor is less precise than in other sports. Each player is involved in both offense and defense, handles the ball, and attempts to score. The ball flows back and forth among players. Team members interact in a dynamic flow to achieve victory. Management skills involve the ability to influence this dynamic process, either by substituting players or by working the ball into certain areas. Players must learn to adapt to the flow of the game and to one another as events unfold.

Interdependence among players is a primary factor explaining the difference among the three sports. Baseball is organized around an autonomous individual, football around groups that are sequentially interdependent, and basketball around the free flow of reciprocal players.[62]

IMPACT OF TECHNOLOGY ON JOB DESIGN

So far, this chapter has described models for analyzing how manufacturing, service, and department technologies influence structure and management processes. The relation between a new technology and organization seems to follow a pattern, beginning with immediate effects on the content of jobs followed (after a longer period) by impact on design of the organization. The ultimate impact of technology on employees can be partially understood through the concepts of job design and sociotechnical systems.

JOB DESIGN

Job design includes the assignment of goals and tasks to be accomplished by employees. Managers may consciously change job design to improve productivity or worker motivation. For example, when workers are involved in performing boring, repetitive tasks, managers may introduce **job rotation**, which means moving employees from job to job to give them a greater variety of tasks. However, managers may also unconsciously influence job design through the introduction of new technologies, which can change how jobs are done and the very nature of jobs.[63] Managers should understand how the introduction of a new technology may affect employees' jobs. The common theme of new technologies in the workplace is that they in some way substitute machinery for human labor in transforming inputs into outputs. Automated teller machines (ATMs) have replaced thousands of human bank tellers, for example. IBM has even built a plant in Austin, Texas, that can produce laptop computers without the help of a single worker.[64]

In addition to actually replacing human workers, technology may have several different effects on the human jobs that remain. Research has indicated that mass production technologies tend to produce **job simplification**, which means that the variety and difficulty of tasks performed by a single person is reduced. The consequence is boring, repetitive jobs that generally provide little satisfaction. More advanced technology, on the other hand, tends to cause **job enrichment**, meaning that the job provides greater responsibility, recognition, and opportunities for growth and development. These technologies create a greater need for employee training and education because workers need higher-level skills and greater competence to master their tasks. For example, ATMs took most the routine tasks (deposits and withdrawals) away from bank tellers and left them with the more complex tasks that require higher-level skills. Studies of computer-integrated manufacturing found that it produces three noticeable results for employees: more opportunities for intellectual mastery and enhanced cognitive skills for workers; more worker responsibility for results; and greater interdependence among workers, enabling more social interaction and the development of teamwork and coordination skills.[65] Advanced manufacturing technology may also contribute to **job enlargement**, which is an expansion of the number of different tasks performed by an employee. Because fewer workers are needed with the new technology, each employee has to be able to perform a greater number and variety of tasks.

With advanced technology, workers have to keep learning new skills because technology is changing so rapidly. Advances in *information technology*, to be discussed in detail in the next chapter, are having a significant effect on jobs in the service industry, including doctors' offices and medical clinics, law firms, financial planners, and libraries. Workers may find that their jobs change almost daily because of new software programs, increased use of the Internet, and other advances in information technology.

Advanced technology does not always have a positive effect on employees, but research findings in general are encouraging, suggesting that jobs for workers are enriched rather than simplified, engaging their higher mental capacities, offering opportunities for learning and growth, and providing greater job satisfaction.

SOCIOTECHNICAL SYSTEMS

The **sociotechnical systems approach** recognizes the interaction of technical and human needs in effective job design, combining the needs of people with the organization's need for technical efficiency. The *socio* portion of the approach refers to the people and groups who work in organizations and how work is organized and coordinated. The *technical* portion refers to the materials, tools, machines, and processes used to transform organizational inputs into outputs.

Exhibit 6.13 illustrates the three primary components of the sociotechnical systems model.[66] The *social system* includes all human elements—such as individual and team behaviors, organizational culture, management practices, and degree

EXHIBIT 6.13   *Sociotechnical Systems Model*

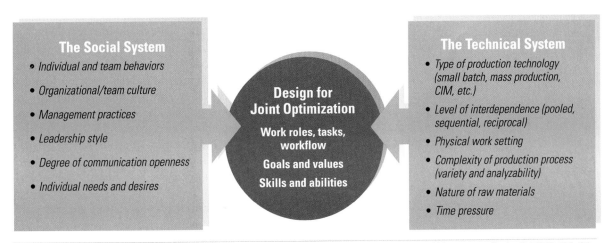

Sources: Based on T. Cummings, "Self-Regulating Work Groups: A Socio-Technical Synthesis," *Academy of Management Review* 3 (1978): 625–34; Don Hellriegel, John W. Slocum, and Richard W. Woodman, *Organizational Behavior,* 8th ed. (Cincinnati, Ohio: South-Western College Publishing, 1998), 492; and Gregory B. Northcraft and Margaret A. Neale, *Organizational Behavior: A Management Challenge,* 2nd ed. (Fort Worth, Tex.: The Dryden Press, 1994), 551.

of communication openness—that can influence the performance of work. The *technical system* refers to the type of production technology, the level of interdependence, the complexity of tasks, and so forth. The goal of the sociotechnical systems approach is to design the organization for **joint optimization**, which means that an organization functions best only when the social and technical systems are designed to fit the needs of one another. Designing the organization to meet human needs while ignoring the technical systems, or changing technology to improve efficiency while ignoring human needs, may inadvertently cause performance problems. The sociotechnical systems approach attempts to find a balance between what workers want and need and the technical requirements of the organization's production system.[67]

One example come from a museum that installed a closed-circuit TV system. Rather than having several guards patrolling the museum and grounds, the television could easily be monitored by a single guard. Although the technology saved money because only one guard was needed per shift, it led to unexpected performance problems. Guards had previously enjoyed the social interaction provided by patrolling; monitoring a closed-circuit television led to alienation and boredom. When a federal agency did an eighteen-month test of the system, only 5 percent of several thousand experimental covert intrusions were detected by the guard.[68] The system was inadequate because human needs were not taken into account.

Sociotechnical principles evolved from the work of the Tavistock Institute, a research organization in England, during the 1950s and 1960s.[69] Examples of organizational change using sociotechnical systems principles have occurred in numerous organizations, including General Motors, Volvo, the Tennessee Valley Authority (TVA), and Procter & Gamble.[70] Although there have been failures, in many of these applications, the joint optimization of changes in technology and structure to meet the needs of people as well as efficiency improved performance, safety, quality, absenteeism, and turnover. In some cases, work design was not the most efficient based on technical and scientific principles, but worker involvement and commitment more than made up for the difference. Thus, once again research shows that new technologies need not have a negative impact on workers, because the technology often requires higher-level mental and social skills and can be organized to encourage the involvement and commitment of employees, thereby benefiting both the employee and the organization.

The sociotechnical systems principle that people should be viewed as resources and provided with appropriate skills, meaningful work, and suitable rewards becomes even more important in today's world of growing technological complexity.[71] One study of paper manufacturers found that organizations that put too much faith in machines and technology and pay little attention to the appropriate management of people do not achieve advances in productivity and flexibility. Today's most successful companies strive to find the right mix of machines, computer systems, and people and the most effective way to coordinate them.[72] Systems based on maximum technical efficiency, tight top-down control, and assumptions that workers are irresponsible and mindless are increasingly ineffective.

Although many principles of sociotechnical systems theory are still valid, current scholars and researchers are also arguing for an expansion of the approach to capture the dynamic nature of today's organizations, the chaotic environment, and the shift from routine to nonroutine jobs brought about by advances in technology.[73]

SUMMARY AND INTERPRETATION

This chapter reviewed several frameworks and key research findings on the topic of organizational technology. The potential importance of technology as a factor in organizational structure was discovered during the 1960s. During the 1970s and 1980s, a flurry of research activity was undertaken to understand more precisely the relationship of technology to other characteristics of organizations.

Five ideas in the technology literature stand out. The first is Woodward's research into manufacturing technology. Woodward went into organizations and collected practical data on technology characteristics, organization structure, and management systems. She found clear relationships between technology and structure in high-performing organizations. Her findings are so clear that managers can analyze their own organizations on the same dimensions of technology and structure. In addition, technology and structure can be coaligned with organizational strategy to meet changing needs and provide new competitive advantages.

The second important idea is that service technologies differ in a systematic way from manufacturing technologies. Service technologies are characterized by intangible outcomes and direct client involvement in the production process. Service firms do not have the fixed, machine-based technologies that appear in manufacturing organizations; hence, organization design often differs also.

The third significant idea is Perrow's framework applied to department technologies. Understanding the variety and analyzability of a technology tells one about the management style, structure, and process that should characterize that department. Routine technologies are characterized by mechanistic structure and nonroutine technologies by organic structure. Applying the wrong management system to a department will result in dissatisfaction and reduced efficiency.

The fourth important idea is interdependence among departments. The extent to which departments depend on each other for materials, information, or other resources determines the amount of coordination required between them. As interdependence increases, demands on the organization for coordination increase. Organization design must allow for the correct amount of communication and coordination to handle interdependence across departments.

The fifth important idea is that new computer-integrated manufacturing technologies are being adopted by organizations and having impact on organization design. For the most part, the impact is positive, with shifts toward more organic structures both on the shop floor and in the management hierarchy. These technologies replace routine jobs, give employees more autonomy, produce more challenging jobs, encourage teamwork, and let the organization be more flexible and responsive. The new technologies are enriching jobs to the point where organizations are happier places to work.

Several principles of sociotechnical systems theory, which attempts to design the technical and human aspects of an organization to fit one another, are increasingly important as advances in technology alter the nature of jobs and social interaction in today's companies.

BRIEFCASE

As an organization manager, keep these guidelines in mind:

1. Relate organization structure to technology. Use the two dimensions of variety and analyzability to discover whether the work in a department is routine or nonroutine. If the work in a department is routine, use a mechanistic structure and process. If the work in a department is nonroutine, use an organic management process. Exhibit 6.9 illustrates this relationship between department technology and organization structure.

2. Use the categories developed by Woodward to diagnose whether the production technology in a manufacturing firm is small batch, mass production, or continuous process. Use a more organic structure with small batch or continuous process technologies, and with new computer-integrated manufacturing systems. Use a mechanistic structure with mass production technologies. When adopting a new technology, realign strategy, structure, and management processes to achieve top performance.

3. Use the concept of service technology to evaluate the production process in nonmanufacturing firms. Service technologies are intangible and must be located close to the customer. Hence, service organizations may have an organization structure with fewer boundary roles, greater geographical dispersion, decentralization, highly skilled employees in the technical core, and generally less control than in manufacturing organizations.

4. Evaluate the interdependencies among organizational departments. Use the general rule that, as interdependencies increase, mechanisms for coordination must also increase. Consider a divisional structure for pooled interdependence. For sequential interdependence, use task forces and integrators for greater horizontal coordination. At the highest level of interdependence (reciprocal interdependence), a horizontal structure may be appropriate.

5. Be aware that the introduction of a new technology has significant impact on job design. Consider using the sociotechnical systems approach to balance the needs of workers with the requirements of the new technological system.

KEY CONCEPTS

analyzability
computer-integrated manufacturing
continuous process production
craft technologies
engineering technologies
intensive technologies
interdependence
job design
job enlargement
job enrichment
job rotation
job simplification
joint optimization
large-batch production

long-linked technology
mass customization
mediating technology
nonroutine technologies
pooled interdependence
reciprocal interdependence
routine technologies
sequential interdependence
service technology
small-batch production
sociotechnical systems approach
technical complexity
technology
variety

DISCUSSION QUESTIONS

1. Where would your university or college department be located on Perrow's technology framework? Look for the underlying variety and analyzability characteristics when making your assessment. Would a department devoted exclusively to teaching be put in a different quadrant from a department devoted exclusively to research?

2. Explain Thompson's levels of interdependence. Identify an example of each level of interdependence in the university or college setting. What kinds of coordination mechanisms should an administration develop to handle each level of interdependence?

3. Describe Woodward's classification of organizational technologies. Explain why each of the three technology groups is related differently to organization structure and management processes.

4. What relationships did Woodward discover between supervisor span of control and technological complexity?

5. How does computer-integrated manufacturing differ from other manufacturing technologies? What is the primary advantage of CIM?

6. What is a service technology? Are different types of service technologies likely to be associated with different structures? Explain.

7. Mass customization of products has become a common approach in manufacturing organizations. Discuss ways in which mass customization can be applied to service firms as well.

8. In what primary ways does the design of service firms typically differ from that of product firms? Why?

9. A top executive claimed that top-level management is a craft technology because the work contains intangibles, such as handling personnel, interpreting the environment, and coping with unusual situations that have to be learned through experience. If this is true, is it appropriate to teach management in a business school? Does teaching management from a textbook assume that the manager's job is analyzable, and hence that formal training rather than experience is most important?

10. In which quadrant of Perrow's framework would a mass production technology be placed? Where would small batch and continuous process technologies be placed? Why? Would Perrow's framework lead to the same recommendation about organic versus mechanistic structures that Woodward made?

11. To what extent does the development of new technologies simplify and routinize the jobs of employees? How can new technology lead to job enlargement? Discuss.

12. Describe the sociotechnical systems model. Why might some managers oppose a sociotechnical systems approach?

CHAPTER 6 WORKBOOK   *Bistro Technology**

You will be analyzing the technology used in three different restaurants—McDonald's, Burger King, and a typical family restaurant. Your instructor will tell you whether to do this assignment as individuals or in a group.

*Adapted loosely by Dorothy Marcic from "Hamburger Technology," in Douglas T. Hall, et al., *Experiences in Management and Organizational Behavior*, 2nd ed. (New York: Wiley, 1982) 244–47, as well as "Behavior, Technology, and Work Design" in A. B. Shani and James B. Lau, *Behavior in Organizations* (Chicago: Irwin, 1996), M16–23 to M16–26.

You must visit all three restaurants and infer how the work is done, according to the following criteria. You are not allowed to "interview" any employees, but instead you will be an observer. Take lots of notes when you are there.

	McDonald's	Burger King	Family Restaurant
Organization goals: Speed, service, atmosphere, etc.			
Authority structure			
Type of technology using Woodward's model			
Organization structure: Mechanistic or organic?			
Team versus individual: Do people work together or alone?			
Interdependence: How do employees depend on each other?			
Tasks: Routine versus nonroutine			
Specialization of tasks by employees			
Standardization: How varied are tasks and products?			
Expertise required: Technical versus social			
Decision making: Centralized versus decentralized			

QUESTIONS

1. Is the technology used the best one for each restaurant, considering its goals and environment?
2. From the preceding data, determine if the structure and other characteristics fit the technology.
3. If you were part of a consulting team assigned to improve the operations of each organization, what recommendations would you make?

Case for Analysis   *Acetate Department*

The Acetate Department's product consisted of about twenty different kinds of viscous liquid acetate used by another department to manufacture transparent film to be left clear, or coated with photographic emulsion or iron oxide.

Before the change: The Department was located in an old four-story building as in Exhibit 6.14. The work flow was as follows:

1. Twenty kinds of powder arrived daily in 50-pound paper bags. In addition, storage tanks of liquid would be filled weekly from tank trucks.
2. Two or three Acetate Helpers would jointly unload pallets of bags into the storage area using a lift truck.
3. Several times a shift, the Helpers would bring the bagged material up the elevator to the third floor where it would be temporarily stored along the walls.
4. Mixing batches was under the direction of the Group Leader and was rather like baking a cake. Following a prescribed formula, the Group Leader, Mixers, and Helpers operated valves to feed in the proper solvent and manually dump in the proper weight and mixture of solid material. The glob would be mixed by giant egg beaters and heated according to the recipe.

5. When the batch was completed, it was pumped to a finished product storage tank.
6. After completing each batch, the crew would thoroughly clean the work area of dust and empty bags because cleanliness was extremely important to the finished product.

To accomplish this work, the Department was structured as in Exhibit 6.15.

The Helpers were usually young men 18-25 years of age, the Mixers 25 to 40, and the Group Leaders and Foremen 40 to 60. Foremen were on salary, Group Leaders, Mixers and Helpers on hourly pay.

To produce 20,000,000 pounds of product per year, the Department operated 24 hours a day, 7 days a week. Four crews rotated shifts: for example, Shift Foreman A and his two Group Leaders and crews would work two weeks on the day shift 8:00 a.m. to 4:00 p.m., then two weeks on the evening shift 4:00

*From "Redesigning the Acetate Department," by David L. Hampton, Charles E. Summer, and Ross A. Webber, *Organizational Behavior and the Practice of Management* (Glenview, IL: Scott, Foresman and Company, 1982), 751–55. Used with permission.

EXHIBIT 6.14   *Elevation View of Acetate Department Before Change*

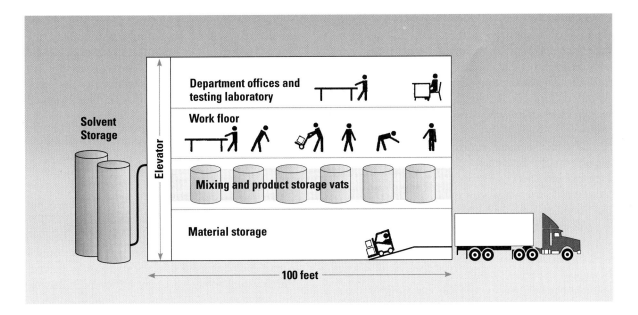

EXHIBIT 6.15   *Organizational Chart of Acetate Department Before Change*

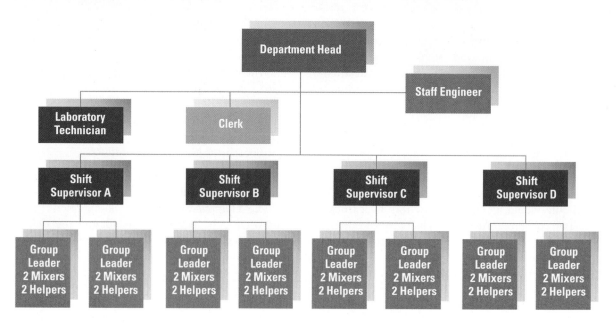

p.m. to midnight, then two weeks on the night shift midnight to 8:00 a.m. There were two days off between shift changes.

During a typical shift, a Group Leader and his crew would complete two or three batches. A batch would frequently be started on one shift and completed by the next shift crew. There was slightly less work on the evening and night shifts because no deliveries were made, but these crews engaged in a little more cleaning. The Shift Foreman would give instructions to the two Group Leaders at the beginning of each shift as to the status of batches in process, batches to be mixed, what deliveries were expected and what cleaning was to be done. Periodically throughout the shift, the Foreman would collect samples in small bottles, which he would leave at the laboratory technicians' desk for testing.

The management and office staff (Department Head, Staff Engineer, Lab Technician, and Department Clerk) only worked on the day shift, although if an emergency arose on the other shifts, the Foreman might call.

All in all, the Department was a pleasant place in which to work. The work floor was a little warm, but well-lighted, quiet, and clean. Substantial banter and horseplay occurred when the crew wasn't actually loading batches, particularly on the nonday shifts.

The men had a dartboard in the work area and competition was fierce and loud. Frequently a crew would go bowling right after work, even at 1:00 a.m., for the community's alleys were open 24 hours a day. Department turnover and absenteeism were low. Most employees spent their entire career with the Company, many in one department. The corporation was large, paternalistic, well-paying, and offered attractive fringe benefits including large, virtually automatic bonuses for all. Then came the change. . . .

The new system: To improve productivity, the Acetate Department was completely redesigned; the technology changed from batches to continuous processing. The basic building was retained, but substantially modified as in Exhibit 6.16. The modified work flow is as follows:

1. Most solid raw materials are delivered via trucks in large aluminum bins holding 500 pounds.
2. One Handler (formerly Helper) is on duty at all times in the first floor to receive raw materials and to dump the bins into the semi-automatic screw feeder.
3. The Head Operator (former Group Leader) directs the mixing operations from his control panel on the fourth floor located along one wall across from the Department Offices. The mixing

EXHIBIT 6.16   *Elevation View of Acetate Department After Change*

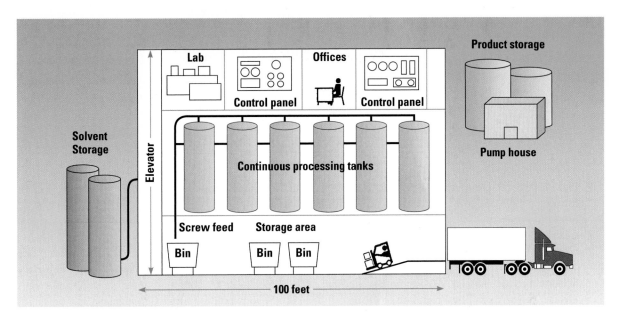

is virtually an automatic operation once the solid material has been sent up the screw feed; a tape program opens and closes the necessary valves to add solvent, heat, mixing, etc. Sitting at a table before his panel, the Head Operator monitors the process to see that everything is operating within specified temperatures and pressures.

This technical change allowed the Department to greatly reduce its manpower. The new structure is illustrated in Exhibit 6.17. One new position was created, that of a pump operator who is located in a small separate shack about 300 feet from the main building. He operates pumps and valves that move the finished product among various storage tanks.

EXHIBIT 6.17   *Organizational Chart of Acetate Department After Change*

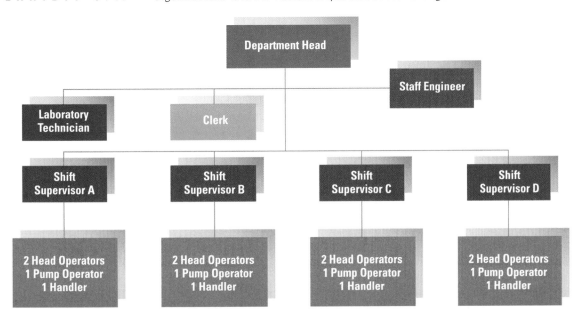

Under the new system, production capacity was increased to 25,000,000 pounds per year. All remaining employees received a 15 percent increase in pay. Former personnel not retained in the Dope Department were transferred to other departments in the company. No one was dismissed.

Unfortunately, actual output has lagged well below capacity in the several months since the

construction work and technical training was completed. Actual production is virtually identical with that under the old technology. Absenteeism has increased markedly, and several judgmental errors by operators have resulted in substantial losses.

NOTES

1. Hal Plotkin, "Riches From Rags," *Inc. Technology* (Summer 1995): 62–67; and Joel Kotkin, "Tailor-Made in America," *Inc.*, August 1996, 25-26.
2. Charles Perrow, "A Framework for the Comparative Analysis of Organizations," *American Sociological Review* 32 (1967): 194–208; R. J. Schonberger, *World Class Manufacturing: The Next Decade,* (New York: The Free Press, 1996).
3. Linda Argote, "Input Uncertainty and Organizational Coordination in Hospital Emergency Units," *Administrative Science Quarterly* 27 (1982): 420–34; Charles Perrow, *Organizational Analysis: A Sociological Approach* (Belmont, Calif.: Wadsworth, 1970); William Rushing, "Hardness of Material as Related to the Division of Labor in Manufacturing Industries," *Administrative Science Quarterly* 13 (1968): 229–45.
4. Lawrence B. Mohr, "Organizational Technology and Organization Structure," *Administrative Science Quarterly* 16 (1971): 444–59; David Hickson, Derek Pugh, and Diana Pheysey, "Operations Technology and Organization Structure: An Empirical Reappraisal," *Administrative Science Quarterly* 14 (1969): 378–97.
5. Joan Woodward, *Industrial Organization: Theory and Practice* (London: Oxford University Press, 1965); Joan Woodward, *Management and Technology* (London: Her Majesty's Stationery Office, 1958).
6. Hickson, Pugh, and Pheysey, "Operations Technology and Organization Structure"; James D. Thompson, *Organizations in Action* (New York: McGraw-Hill, 1967).
7. Edward Harvey, "Technology and the Structure of Organizations," *American Sociological Review* 33 (1968): 241–59.
8. Wanda J. Orlikowski, "The Duality of Technology: Rethinking the Concept of Technology in Organizations," *Organization Science* 3 (1992): 398–427.
9. Based on Woodward, *Industrial Organization and Management and Technology.*
10. Jim Morrison, "Grand Tour. Making Music: The Craft of the Steinway Piano," *Spirit,* February 1997, 42-49, 100.
11. Woodward, *Industrial Organization,* vi.
12. William L. Zwerman, *New Perspectives on Organizational Theory* (Westport, Conn.: Greenwood, 1970); Harvey, "Technology and the Structure of Organizations," 241–59.
13. Dean M. Schroeder, Steven W. Congden, and C. Gopinath, "Linking Competitive Strategy and Manufacturing Process Technology," *Journal of Management Studies* 32, no. 2 (March 1995): 163–89.
14. Alex Taylor III, "It Worked for Toyota. Can It Work for Toys?" *Fortune,* 11 January 1999, 36.
15. Fernando F. Suarez, Michael A. Cusumano, and Charles H. Fine, "An Empirical Study of Flexibility in Manufacturing," *Sloan Management Review* (Fall 1995): 25–32.
16. Raymond F. Zammuto and Edward J. O'Connor, "Gaining Advanced Manufacturing Technologies' Benefits: The Roles of Organization Design and Culture," *Academy of Management Review* 17, no. 4 (1992): 701–28; Dean Schroeder, Steven W. Congdon, and C. Gopinath, "Linking Competitive Strategy and Manufacturing Process Technology."
17. David Wessel, "Pilgrim and Millstone, Two Nuclear Plants, Have Disparate Fates," *The Wall Street Journal,* 28 July 1987, 1, 18; Arlen J. Large, "Federal Agency Prods Nuclear-Plant Official to Raise Performance," *The Wall Street Journal,* 10 May 1984, 1, 22.
18. Wessel, "Pilgrim and Millstone."

19. Jack R. Meredith, "The Strategic Advantages of the Factory of the Future," *California Management Review* 29 (Spring 1987): 27–41; Jack Meredith, "The Strategic Advantages of the New Manufacturing Technologies for Small Firms," *Strategic Management Journal* 8 (1987): 249–58; Althea Jones and Terry Webb, "Introducing Computer Integrated Manufacturing," *Journal of General Management* 12 (Summer 1987): 60–74.

20. Raymond F. Zammuto and Edward J. O'Connor, "Gaining Advanced Manufacturing Technologies' Benefits: The Roles of Organization Design and Culture," *Academy of Management Review* 17 (1992): 701–28.

21. John S. DeMott, "Small Factories' Big Lessons," *Nation's Business* (April 1995): 29–30.

22. Paul S. Adler, "Managing Flexible Automation," *California Management Review* (Spring 1988): 34–56.

23. Bela Gold, "Computerization in Domestic and International Manufacturing," *California Management Review* (Winter 1989): 129–43.

24. Graham Dudley and John Hassard, "Design Issues in the Development of Computer Integrated Manufacturing (CIM)," *Journal of General Management* 16 (1990): 43–53.

25. John Holusha, "Can Boeing's New Baby Fly Financially?" *New York Times,* 27 March 1994, Section 3, 1, 6.

26. Joel D. Goldhar and David Lei, "Variety is Free: Manufacturing In the Twenty-First Century," *Academy of Management Executive* 9, no. 4 (1995): 73–86; and Justin Martin, "Give 'Em *Exactly* What They Want," *Fortune,* 10 October 1997, 283-285.

27. Sarah Schafer, "Have It Your Way," *Inc. Tech* no. 4 (1997): 56-64.

28. Erick Schonfeld, "The Customized, Digitized, Have-It-Your-Way Economy," *Fortune,* 28 September 1998, 115-124.

29. Len Estrin, "The Dawn of Manufacturing," *Enterprise* (April 1994): 31–35; Otis Port, "The Responsive Factory," *Business Week/Enterprise* (1993): 48–52.

30. Goldhar and Lei, "Variety is Free: Manufacturing In the Twenty-First Century."

31. Meredith, "Strategic Advantages of the Factory of the Future."

32. Patricia L. Nemetz and Louis W. Fry, "Flexible Manufacturing Organizations: Implementations for Strategy Formulation and Organization Design," *Academy of Management Review* 13 (1988): 627–38; Paul S. Adler, "Managing Flexible Automation," *California Management Review* (Spring 1988): 34–56; Jeremy Main, "Manufacturing the Right Way," *Fortune,* 21 May 1990, 54–64; Frank M. Hull and Paul D. Collins, "High-Technology Batch Production Systems: Woodward's Missing Type," *Academy of Management Journal* 30 (1987): 786–97.

33. Goldhar and Lei, "Variety Is Free: Manufacturing In The Twenty-First Century"; P. Robert Duimering, Frank Safayeni, and Lyn Purdy, "Integrated Manufacturing: Redesign the Organization before Implementing Flexible Technology," *Sloan Management Review* (Summer 1993): 47–56; Zammuto and O'Connor, "Gaining Advanced Manufacturing Technologies' Benefits."

34. Goldhar and Lei, "Variety is Free: Manufacturing In the Twenty-First Century."

35. "Manufacturing's Decline," *Johnson City Press,* 17 July 1999, 9; Ronald Henkoff, "Service Is Everybody's Business," *Fortune,* 27 June 1994, 48–60; Ronald Henkoff, "Finding, Training, and Keeping the Best Service Workers," *Fortune,* 3 October 1994, 110–22.

36. Byron J. Finch and Richard L. Luebbe, *Operations Management: Competing in a Changing Environment* (Fort Worth, Tex.: The Dryden Press, 1995), 51.

37. David E. Bowen, Caren Siehl, and Benjamin Schneider, "A Framework for Analyzing Customer Service Orientations in Manufacturing," *Academy of Management Review* 14 (1989): 79–95; Peter K. Mills and Newton Margulies, "Toward a Core Typology of Service Organizations," *Academy of Management Review* 5 (1980): 255–65; Peter K. Mills and Dennis J. Moberg, "Perspectives on the Technology of Service Operations," *Academy of Management Review* 7 (1982): 467–78; G. Lynn Shostack, "Breaking Free from Product Marketing," *Journal of Marketing* (April 1977): 73–80.

38. Ron Zemke, "The Service Revolution: Who Won?" *Management Review* (March 1997): 10-15; and Wayne Wilhelm and Bill Rossello, "The Care and Feeding of Customers," *Management Review* (March 1997): 19-23.

39. Schonfeld, "The Customized, Digitized, Have-It-Your-Way Economy."

40. Schafer, "Have It Your Way."

41. Richard B. Chase and David A. Tansik, "The Customer Contact Model for Organization Design," *Management Science* 29 (1983): 1037–50.

42. Ibid.

43. David E. Bowen and Edward E. Lawler III, "The Empowerment of Service Workers: What, Why, How, and When," *Sloan Management Review* (Spring 1992): 31–39: Gregory B. Northcraft and Richard B. Chase, "Managing Service Demand at the Point of Delivery," *Academy of Management Review* 10 (1985): 66–75; Roger W. Schmenner, "How Can Service Businesses Survive and Prosper?" *Sloan Management Review* 27 (Spring 1986): 21–32.

44. Perrow, "Framework for Comparative Analysis" and *Organizational Analysis.*

45. Morrison, "Grand Tour."

46. Michael Withey, Richard L. Daft, and William C. Cooper, "Measures of Perrow's Work Unit Technology: An Empirical Assessment and a New Scale," *Academy of Management Journal* 25 (1983): 45–63.

47. Christopher Gresov, "Exploring Fit and Misfit with Multiple Contingencies," *Administrative Science Quarterly* 34 (1989): 431–53; Dale L. Goodhue and Ronald L. Thompson, "Task-Technology Fit and Individual Performance," *MIS Quarterly* (June 1995): 213–36.

48. Gresov, "Exploring Fit and Misfit with Multiple Contingencies"; Charles A. Glisson, "Dependence of Technological Routinization on Structural Variables in Human Service Organizations," *Administrative Science Quarterly* 23 (1978): 383–95; Jerald Hage and Michael Aiken, "Routine Technology, Social Structure and Organizational Goals," *Administrative Science Quarterly* 14 (1969): 368–79.

49. Gresov, "Exploring Fit and Misfit with Multiple Contingencies"; A. J. Grimes and S. M. Kline, "The Technological Imperative: The Relative Impact of Task Unit, Modal Technology, and Hierarchy on Structure," *Academy of Management Journal* 16 (1973): 583–97; Lawrence G. Hrebiniak, "Job Technologies, Supervision and Work Group Structure," *Administrative Science Quarterly* 19 (1974): 395–410; Jeffrey Pfeffer, *Organizational Design* (Arlington Heights, Ill.: AHM, 1978), ch. 1.

50. Patrick E. Connor, *Organizations: Theory and Design* (Chicago: Science Research Associates, 1980); Richard L. Daft and Norman B. Macintosh, "A Tentative Exploration into Amount and Equivocality of Information Processing in Organizational Work Units," *Administrative Science Quarterly* 26 (1981): 207–24.

51. Paul D. Collins and Frank Hull, "Technology and Span of Control: Woodward Revisited," *Journal of Management Studies* 23 (1986): 143–64; Gerald D. Bell, "The Influence of Technological Components of Work upon Management Control," *Academy of Management Journal* 8 (1965): 127–32; Peter M. Blau and Richard A. Schoenherr, *The Structure of Organizations* (New York: Basic Books, 1971).

52. W. Alan Randolph, "Matching Technology and the Design of Organization Units," *California Management Review* 22–23 (1980–81): 39–48; Daft and Macintosh, "Tentative Exploration into Amount and Equivocality of Information Processing"; Michael L. Tushman, "Work Characteristics and Subunit Communication Structure: A Contingency Analysis," *Administrative Science Quarterly* 24 (1979): 82–98.

53. Andrew H. Van de Ven and Diane L. Ferry, *Measuring and Assessing Organizations* (New York: Wiley, 1980); Randolph, "Matching Technology and the Design of Organization Units."

54. Richard L. Daft and Robert H. Lengel, "Information Richness: A New Approach to Managerial Behavior and Organization Design," in Barry Staw and Larry L. Cummings, eds., *Research in Organizational Behavior,* vol. 6 (Greenwich, Conn.: JAI Press, 1984), 191–233; Richard L. Daft and Norman B. Macintosh, "A New Approach into Design and Use of Management Information," *California Management Review* 21 (1978): 82–92; Daft and Macintosh, "Tentative Exploration in Amount and Equivocality of Information Processing"; W. Alan Randolph, "Organizational Technology and the Media and Purpose Dimensions of Organizational Communication," *Journal of Business Research* 6 (1978): 237–59; Linda Argote, "Input Uncertainty and Organizational Coordination in Hospital Emergency Units," *Administrative Science Quarterly* 27 (1982): 420–34; Andrew H. Van de Ven and Andre Delbecq, "A Task Contingent Model of Work Unit Structure," *Administrative Science Quarterly* 19 (1974): 183–97.

55. Peggy Leatt and Rodney Schneck, "Criteria for Grouping Nursing Subunits in Hospitals,"

Academy of Management Journal 27 (1984): 150–65; Robert T. Keller, "Technology-Information Processing," *Academy of Management Journal* 37, no. 1 (1994): 167–79.

56. Gresov, "Exploring Fit and Misfit with Multiple Contingencies"; Michael L. Tushman, "Technological Communication in R&D Laboratories: The Impact of Project Work Characteristics," *Academy of Management Journal* 21 (1978): 624–45; Robert T. Keller, "Technology-Information Processing Fit and the Performance of R&D Project Groups: A Test of Contingency Theory," *Academy of Management Journal* 37, no. 1 (1994): 167–79.

57. Thanks to Gail Russ for suggesting this example of a technology-structure mismatch.

58. James Thompson, *Organizations in Action* (New York: McGraw-Hill, 1967).

59. *Ibid.*, 40.

60. Paul S. Adler, "Interdepartmental Interdependence and Coordination: The Case of the Design/Manufacturing Interface," *Organization Science* 6, no. 2 (March–April 1995): 147–67.

61. Christopher Gresov, "Effects of Dependence and Tasks on Unit Design and Efficiency," *Organization Studies* 11 (1990): 503–29; Andrew H. Van de Ven, Andre Delbecq, and Richard Koenig, "Determinants of Coordination Modes within Organizations," *American Sociological Review* 41 (1976): 322–38; Linda Argote, "Input Uncertainty and Organizational Coordination in Hospital Emergency Units"; Jack K. Ito and Richard B. Peterson, "Effects of Task Difficulty and Interdependence on Information Processing Systems," *Academy of Management Journal* 29 (1986): 139–49; Joseph L. C. Cheng, "Interdependence and Coordination in Organizations: A Role-System Analysis," *Academy of Management Journal* 26 (1983): 156–62.

62. Robert W. Keidel, "Team Sports Models as a Generic Organizational Framework," *Human Relations* 40 (1987): 591–612; Robert W. Keidel, "Baseball, Football, and Basketball: Models for Business," *Organizational Dynamics* (Winter 1984): 5–18; Richard L. Daft and Richard M. Steers, *Organizations: A Micro-Macro Approach* (Glenview, Ill.: Scott, Foresman, 1986).

63. Michele Liu, Héléné Denis, Harvey Kolodny, and Benjt Stymne, "Organization Design for Technological Change," *Human Relations* 43 (January 1990): 7–22.

64. Stephen P. Robbins, *Organizational Behavior,* (Upper Saddle River, N.J.: Prentice-Hall, 1998), 521.

65. Gerald I. Susman and Richard B. Chase, "A Sociotechnical Analysis of the Integrated Factory," *Journal of Applied Behavioral Science* 22 (1986): 257–70; Paul Adler, "New Technologies, New Skills," *California Management Review* 29 (Fall 1986): 9–28.

66. Based on Don Hellriegel, John W. Slocum, Jr., and Richard W. Woodman, *Organizational Behavior,* 8th ed. (Cincinnati, Ohio: South-Western College Publishing, 1998), 491-495; and Gregory B. Northcraft and Margaret A. Neale, *Organizational Behavior: A Management Challenge,* 2nd ed., (Fort Worth, Tex.: The Dryden Press, 1994), 550-553.

67. F. Emery, "Characteristics of Sociotechnical Systems," Tavistock Institute of Human Relations, document 527, 1959; Passmore, Francis, and Haldeman, "Sociotechnical Systems"; and William M. Fox, "Sociotechnical System Principles and Guidelines: Past and Present," *Journal of Applied Behavioral Science* 31, no. 1 (March 1995): 91–105.

68. W. S. Cascio, *Managing Human Resources* (New York: McGraw-Hill, 1986), 19.

69. Eric Trist and Hugh Murray, eds., *The Social Engagement of Social Science: A Tavistock Anthology,* Vol. 11, (Philadelphia: University of Pennsylvania Press, 1993); and William A. Pasmore, "Social Science Transformed: The Socio-Technical Perspective," *Human Relations* 48, No. 1 (1995) 1-21.

70. R. E. Walton, "From Control to Commitment in the Workplace," *Harvard Business Review* 63, No. 2 (1985), 76-84; E. W. Lawler, III, *High Involvement Management* (London: Jossey-Bass, 1986), 84; and Hellriegel, Slocum, and Woodman, *Organizational Behavior,* 491.

71. William A. Pasmore, "Social Science Transformed: The Socio-Technical Perspective," *Human Relations* 48, no. 1 (1995) 1–21.

72. David M. Upton, "What Really Makes Factories Flexible?" *Harvard Business Review* (July–August 1995): 74–84.

73. Pasmore, "Social Science Transformed: The Socio-Technical Perspective"; and H. Scarbrough, "Review Article: *The Social Engagement of Social Science: A Tavistock Anthology,* Vol. II," *Human Relations* 48, no. 1 (1995): 23–33.

Information Technology and Knowledge Management

A LOOK INSIDE

Weyerhaeuser Company

n the mid-1990s, Weyerhaeuser Co.'s door factory in Marshfield, Wisconsin, was on its last legs—plagued by soaring costs, sagging sales, and a demoralized work force that prompted Weyerhaeuser Vice President Jerry Mannigel to comment, "You had to practically beat people with a stick to get them to come back to work every morning."[1] Executives decided to see if an in-house information network could revive the plant by helping people work faster and smarter. Top managers wanted to link people from different departments and provide them with information from within the company as well as tap into the power of the burgeoning Internet.

Equipped with software to do such jobs as track inventory, calculate prices based on cost of manufacturing, schedule production, and automate order-taking, the new system, called DoorBuilder, helped Weyerhaeuser cut both manufacturing costs and production time. Production nearly doubled to 800,000 doors annually, on-time deliveries increased from 40 percent to 70 percent, and the company's return on assets grew from –2 percent in 1993 to 27 percent five years later. Now, the company is taking DoorBuilder to the next level by linking with key suppliers and distributors, helping to speed up the ordering process while also eliminating costly errors and waste. The system helps Weyerhaeuser offer faster turnaround and, in some cases, lower prices than competitors. Since phase-in of DoorBuilder began, the company's share of the U.S. commercial door market has grown from 12 percent to 26 percent. Revenues are growing at an annual 10–15 percent rate.

The dramatic changes DoorBuilder has brought to Weyerhaeuser are illustrated by the order-taking process. Since each door is custom-built, with literally millions of design and pricing options, as well as varied building-code requirements, order taking used to be a painstaking job that could take weeks or even months to complete, with sales reps, distributors, and builders haggling over options and pricing. Now, DoorBuilder can sort through all the data and calculate the math in seconds. In addition, customers who are linked into Weyerhaeuser's network can assemble their own custom door packages and zap them electronically directly to the factory floor. The result of this sophisticated system is that orders that once took weeks are now completed in only minutes, errors are reduced because there are no paper slips to get lost or damaged during production, and prices are based on precise information about manufacturing costs rather than hunches or favoritism.[2]

The example of Weyerhaeuser illustrates a fact of life for today's organizations—the Internet and the information revolution are changing practically everything about doing business. Effectively using information technology in knowledge-based firms such as consulting firm KPMG Peat Marwick, Reuters Group PLC, which provides financial information, and Business Wire, a provider of business and corporate information, has long been fundamental to the business. Today, information technology and knowledge management have become crucial weapons helping companies in all industries maintain a competitive edge in the face of growing global competition and rising customer demands for speed, convenience, quality, and value. The rapidly growing use of the **Internet** over the past several years has provided both new avenues for commercial activity, as well as new ways to gather and disseminate information across a global network. It is estimated that by 2002, U.S. businesses alone will exchange more than $300 billion in goods and services over the Net. More than 90 million people routinely exchange information over the Internet, and the number continues to grow.[3] This presents new challenges for managers. For one thing, the balance of power has shifted to the customer. With the unlimited access to information provided by the Internet, customers are much better informed and much more demanding, making customer loyalty harder to build.[4] In addition, the concept of electronically linking suppliers, partners, and customers is forcing companies to rethink their strategies, organization design, and business processes. The pace of business is moving at "warp speed."[5] Planning horizons have become shorter, expectations of customers change rapidly, and new competitors spring up almost overnight. All this means managers, as well as employees throughout the organization, need quality information at their fingertips.

Highly successful organizations today are typically those that most effectively collect, store, distribute, and use information. More than facilities, equipment, or even products, it is the information a company has and how it uses it that defines organization success—some would say even organization survival.[6] Information technology can increase the power and motivation of employees by giving them complete information they need to do their jobs well, enabling them to share ideas with colleagues, and offering them opportunities to propose new ways of doing things. It can also increase the brainpower of an organization and enable the company to move to a higher level of competitiveness. Top managers look for ways to manage, leverage, and protect what is rapidly becoming the most valuable asset of any organization: information and knowledge.

PURPOSE OF THIS CHAPTER

Information technology and knowledge management are essential components of successful organizations. Managers spend at least 80 percent of their time actively exchanging information. They need this information to hold the organization together. For example, the vertical and horizontal information linkages described in Chapter 3 are designed to provide managers with relevant information for decision making and evaluation. This chapter examines the evolution of information technology, discusses how it can provide a strategic advantage, and examines the ways it affects organization design and interorganizational relationships. The final sections of the chapter discuss the recent concept of knowledge management, a new approach to organizing, sharing, and using information to leverage professional knowledge.

INFORMATION TECHNOLOGY EVOLUTION

The evolution of information technology is illustrated in Exhibit 7.1. First-line management is typically concerned with well-defined problems about operational issues and past events. Top management, by contrast, deals mostly with uncertain, ambiguous issues, such as strategy and planning. As the complexity of computer-based information technology systems has increased, applications have grown to support effective top management decision making about complex and uncertain problems.

EXHIBIT 7.1   *Evolution of Organizational Applications of Information Technology*

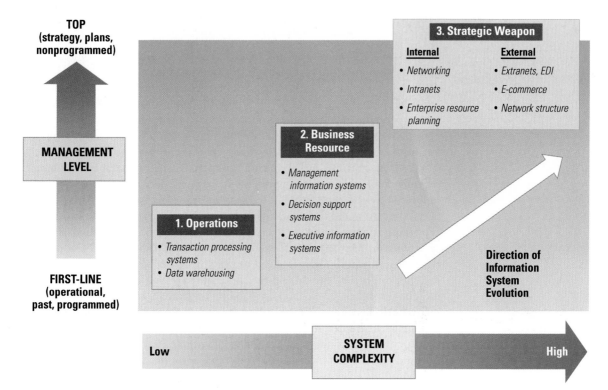

OPERATIONS AND BUSINESS RESOURCE APPLICATIONS

The initial applications were based on the notion of machine room efficiency—that is, current operations could be performed more efficiently with the use of computer technology. The goal was to reduce labor cost by having computers take over some tasks. These systems became known as **transaction processing systems** (TPS), which automate the organization's routine, day-to-day business transactions. A TPS collects data from transactions such as sales, purchases from suppliers, and inventory changes and stores them in a database. For example, Starbucks Coffee uses a transaction processing system to keep track of sales in all its stores worldwide. As data from transactions accumulate, they may be stored in various company databases.

In recent years, the concept of data warehousing and data mining has expanded the usefulness of these accumulated data. **Data warehousing** is the use of huge databases that combine all of a company's data and allow users to access the data directly, create reports, and obtain responses to what-if questions. Building a database at a large corporation is a huge undertaking that includes defining hundreds of gigabytes of data from many existing systems, providing a means of continually updating the data, making it all compatible, and linking it to other software that makes it possible for users to search and analyze the data and produce helpful reports. Software for **data mining** helps users make sense of all this data. Data mining tools use sophisticated decision-making processes to search raw data for patterns and relationships that may be significant. Catalog retailer Fingerhut Corporation has a seven-trillion-byte database and can analyze individual customers in terms of up to 2,000 variables. Data mining helped managers learn that when customers move to a new home, they buy three times as much over the next three months, particularly in categories such as furniture, telecommunications equipment, and home decorations. This enabled the company to create a special catalog and target it to movers.[7] Data warehousing and data mining can thus become a business resource by supporting management decision making.

Using information technology as a business resource is the next stage of evolution illustrated in Exhibit 7.1. Through the application of management information systems and decision support systems, managers had tools to improve performance of departments and the organization as a whole. These applications use computer technology to help managers make important decisions.

A **management information system** is a computer-based system that provides information and support for managerial decision making. The MIS is supported by the organization's transaction processing systems and by organizational databases (and frequently databases of external data as well). **Information reporting systems**, the most common form of MIS, provide mid-level managers with reports that summarize data and support day-to-day decision making. For example, when managers need to make decisions about production scheduling, they can review the data on the anticipated number of orders within the next month, inventory levels, and availability of human resources. An **executive information system** (EIS) is a higher-level application that facilitates decision making at the highest levels of management. These systems are typically based on software that can convert large amounts of complex data into pertinent information and provide that information to top managers in a timely fashion. For example, Motorola's Semiconductor Products Sector, based in Austin, Texas, had massive amounts of stored data but users couldn't easily find what they needed. The company implemented an EIS using online analytical processing software so that more than a thousand senior executives, as well as managers and project analysts in finance, marketing, sales, and accounting departments around the world, could quickly and easily get information about customer buying trends, manufacturing, and so forth, right from their desktop computers, without having to learn complex and arcane search commands.[8]

A **decision support system** (DSS) provides specific benefits to managers at all levels of the organization. These interactive, computer-based systems rely on decision models and integrated databases. Using decision support software, users can pose a series of "what if" questions to test possible alternatives. Based on assumptions used in the software or specified by the user, managers can explore various alternatives and receive information to help them choose the alternative that will likely have the best outcome.

Wal-Mart uses EIS and DSS that rely on a massive database to make decisions about what to stock, how to price and promote it, and when to reorder. Department managers at each store can keep track of which items are top sellers in their department and make sure those items are in stock. Handheld scanners enable managers to keep close tabs on inventory. Back at headquarters, top managers use executive information systems to analyze buying patterns and other information, enabling them to spot problems or opportunities. For example, executives discovered that particular items are frequently purchased together, so they spotted an opportunity to cross-promote those items and increase sales.[9] Companies such as Wal-Mart and Motorola use information technology so well that it has become a strategic weapon.

INFORMATION TECHNOLOGY AS A STRATEGIC WEAPON

Using information technology as a strategic weapon is the highest level of application (Exhibit 7.1). Information technology can help build and enhance strategy by providing better data and information within the organization (internal application) as well as help the organization redefine and support relationships with customers, suppliers, and other organizations (external application). Internal applications include networking, intranets, and enterprise resource planning (ERP) systems. Extranets, e-commerce, and network structures are external applications.

Networking, which links people and departments within a particular building or even across corporate offices, enabling them to share information and cooperate on projects, has become an important strategic weapon for many companies. Networks may take many forms, but the fastest-growing form of corporate networking is the **intranet**, a private companywide information system that uses the communications protocols and standards of the Internet and the World Wide Web but is accessible only to people within the company. To view files and information, users simply navigate the site with a standard Web browser, clicking on links.[10] Although the intranet looks and acts like a Web site, it is cordoned off from the public with the use of software programs known as *firewalls*. Because intranets are Web-based, they can be accessed from any type of computer or workstation. A single company may have many types of computers and software. With a traditional network, organizations face a challenge of how to enable them all to communicate with one another. One solution is a category of software known as *middleware*, which mediates among myriad types of hardware and software and enables these varied components to communicate on a network.

Today, most companies with intranets have moved their management information systems, executive information systems, and so forth over to the intranet so they can easily be accessed by anyone who needs them. In addition, having these systems as part of the intranet means new features and applications can easily be added and accessed through a standard browser. Motorola's Semiconductor Products Sector (SPS) described earlier moved its existing executive information system over to a global intranet. Intranets can improve internal communications and unlock hidden information. They enable employees to keep in touch with what's going on around the organization, quickly and easily find information they need, share ideas, and work on projects collaboratively. The most advanced intranets, such as those at SPS, Ford Motor Company, Nike, and Weyerhaeuser, described in the opening case, are linked into the proprietary systems that govern a company's business functions. Ford's global intranet connects more than 100,000 workstations to thousands of sites offering proprietary information such as market research, analyses of competitor's components, and product development.[11]

Another recent approach to information management helps pull together various types of information to see how decisions and actions in one part of the organization affect other parts of the firm. A growing number of companies are setting up broad-scale information systems that take a comprehensive view of the organization's activities. These **enterprise resource planning** (ERP) systems collect, process, and provide information about a company's entire enterprise, including order processing, product design, purchasing, inventory, manufacturing, distribution, human resources, receipt of payments, and forecasting of future demand. An ERP can serve as the backbone for an entire organization by integrating key business and management processes. It has been estimated that 70 percent of the 1,000 largest U.S. corporations use enterprise resource planning.[12] An ERP system can provide the kind of information provided by transaction processing systems, as well as that provided by decision support systems or executive information systems. The key is that ERP weaves all these systems together so that managers can see the big picture and act quickly, based on the information.[13] In addition, ERP gives everyone from the CEO to workers on the shop floor instant access to critical information that can help the company be smarter and more competitive.

Companies frequently modify the basic ERP software to match their strategic goals. Owens Corning, for example, incorporated individualized distribution costs, a key capability the company considered a competitive advantage.[14] For Kaye Instruments, which makes thermal-measuring equipment used in producing drugs, ERP was central to meeting the high quality standards and product consistency needed to earn ISO 9001 certification, putting the company in a much stronger position to compete globally. ERP helped Kaye closely integrate engineering and manufacturing by enabling workers to instantly call up specifications for products and the latest engineering revisions.[15]

To keep in touch with customers and other organizations, organizations extend the intranet's function with an **extranet**, which gives access to key partners, suppliers, or customers. Extranets can improve communications and enhance the interorganizational relationships described in Chapter 5. An extranet helped McKesson Corp., the large San Francisco-based pharmaceutical supply business, cut costs and improve customer service. The company ships to more than 30,000 hospitals, pharmacies, and retail stores, but most belong to huge chains that pay bills from a central office. McKeeson used to fax hundreds of billing statements to its customers' central accounting offices, but now uses an invoice inquiry system on the extranet. Customers can see bills from all their varied locations in one place, dramatically reducing communications and labor costs.[16]

The concept of linking with other organizations is spreading throughout all industries. Companies as diverse as herbal soap manufacturer Woodspirits and computer giant IBM are farming out activities to contractors who are linked electronically to the company. Cisco Systems Inc., which outsources nearly 70 percent of its products, electronically shares sensitive product and sales data with contract manufacturers, enabling the company to ship routers and other products anywhere in the world in less than two days.[17] The concept of electronically linking with outside contractors finds its ultimate expression in the network organization structure, which means that a firm subcontracts most of its major functions to separate companies and coordinates their activities from a small headquarters organization.[18] The network organization and the concept of networking with other organizations and customers will be discussed in further detail later in this chapter.

E-commerce, which essentially augments or replaces the swapping of products or money with the exchange of information between computer systems, is a significant way companies use technology as a strategic weapon.[19] E-commerce can be carried out between businesses or between a business and consumers. Business-to-business purchasing online continues to grow. General Electric buys around $5 billion of supplies online. And business-to-customer commerce has zoomed. Goods and services sold to consumers over the Internet in North America topped $8 million in 1998, and the number of households using the Net for shopping continues to grow.[20] E-commerce will also be discussed in detail later in this chapter.

Studies have shown that the appropriate use of information technology, such as executive information systems, intranets and extranets, and enterprise resource planning systems, can improve the efficiency and effectiveness of the strategic decision–making process. Information technology enhances the ability of top executives to identify problems as well as the speed at which they generate solutions.[21] Consider how Turner Industries has used information technology to gain a competitive edge in a tough industry.

In Practice 7.1

Turner Industries Ltd.

In a business where competition is cutthroat, profit margins are slim, and missing deadlines means losing big money, Turner Industries has achieved record-setting growth, profit margins well above the industry average, and a string of "Excellence in Construction" awards from Associated Builders and Contractors Inc. Recently named as one of *Forbes'* "500 Top Private Companies," Turner has developed such good relationships with customers that many of them don't even ask for bids—they just give the job to Turner. The company's success is largely due to super-sophisticated information technology systems that helped Turner set new standards in efficiency, accuracy, and customer satisfaction.

Turner Industries, based in Baton Rouge, Louisiana, specializes in some of the most complicated jobs around, providing all the services needed to complete huge industrial projects, such as large-scale construction and scheduled maintenance projects for refineries and petrochemical businesses. Even a routine maintenance project can involve more than 40,000 tasks and thousands of contract laborers. Turner manages these complex jobs with a homemade software application, called Interplan, that integrates proprietary estimating and project control systems with off-the-shelf ERP and scheduling software.

When Turner's estimators receive blueprints and a list of materials for a job, they enter specifications into the database, and a software program automatically calculates the specific tasks that will need to be performed, the number of hours the project will take, and all associated costs for materials and labor. The estimating program alone has saved hundreds of thousands of dollars because estimators work twice as fast as before. It also saves money for customers, because Turner can accurately estimate a project's time and costs down to the last nail. When a customer approves the estimate, costing data are automatically sent to the ERP software, which will track costs from the job site every day, eliminating unplanned expenditures and nasty surprises for the customer at the end of the project. Scheduling data are automatically sent to another program that gives managers an up-to-date idea of when each job will end. Finally, data concerning labor and required tasks are sent to Turner's project control program, called WinPCS, which generates a punch list of each and every task, right down to "tightening a bolt" or "welding a section of pipe." Project foremen on the job site estimate how much of each task is completed at the end of each day and transmit the data electronically to managers back at headquarters.

Turner's information technology is so powerful that the company often finishes jobs ahead of schedule. One job for Exxon Corp. was completed ten weeks early, translating into a savings of $8 million for Exxon. Exxon and other large corporations prefer Turner Industries because the company is efficient and accurate, which means higher revenues and profits for Turner.[22]

STRATEGIC USE OF INFORMATION TECHNOLOGY

Managers are increasingly considering the role of information management in their constant search for the right combination of strategy, motivation, technology, and business design to maintain a competitive edge.[23]

Recall from Chapter 2 that two of the competitive strategies firms can adopt are *low-cost leadership* and *differentiation*. The low-cost leader incurs low production costs and can price its product or service offerings low enough so it makes a profit while rival firms are sustaining losses. Differentiation means a firm offers a unique product or service based on product features, superb service, or rapid delivery. Top managers look for ways to use information technology to achieve low-cost leadership or differentiation. Information technology might be used to create closer relationships with customers, barriers to entry for new firms, or efficient relationships with suppliers that can alter competitive balance with respect to cost leadership or differentiation.[24] Kansas City Power and Light's Web site has evolved into a competitive weapon by helping to differentiate the company in the recently deregulated, increasingly competitive utilities business. KCPL started the site as a way to keep in touch with customers and let them know what was going on in the changing industry, but it has now become a place where customers can monitor their own power consumption as well as pay their bills and learn how to keep costs down. KCPL invested in a wireless automatic meter-reading system that can check the meters of 400,000 homes and businesses at any time. By linking it into the Web site, the utility can give customers with Internet access the ability to monitor their own power usage minute by minute, any time of the day or night. Some KCPL customers track the information diligently to keep control of their power costs. This value-added service differentiates Kansas City Power and Light from other utility companies. The automated meter-reading system has also increased KCPL's efficiency. Repair units can simply check the Web site to see if a problem is inside the customer's home or in the wiring leading to the house, which has saved an average of 105,000 field service trips per year.[25]

Other organizations find other ways of using information technology for strategic advantage. Wal-Mart's pioneering use of computer networks to conduct business electronically squeezed time and costs out of unwieldy supply chains and made the company the largest retailer in the world. Wal-Mart uses technology to convert information into action almost immediately, keeping it a step ahead of the competition.[26]

Exhibit 7.2 lists a few ways information technology can be used to give companies a strategic edge over competitors.

LOW-COST LEADERSHIP

Perhaps the most obvious way information technology can lower cost is through *operational efficiency*; but this means more than simply doing the same work faster. One recent advance in operational efficiency has been the use of ERP systems. These integrated systems can not only automatically control operations ranging from the procurement of supplies to shop floor manufacturing, but also facilitate the highest levels of strategic decision making, helping senior managers diagnose

EXHIBIT 7.2   *Strategic Advantages from Information Technology*

Low-Cost Leadership	Differentiation
Operational efficiency	Lock in customers
Interdepartmental coordination	Customer service
Rapid resupply	Product development, market niches

problems and develop solutions. Executives at Hershey Foods Corporation use an ERP system to study business practices in each of the corporation's divisions and adopt best practices for key strategic activities.[27]

Intranets, extranets, and use of the World Wide Web can also improve operational efficiency. When Motorola needed to ramp up production quickly on new high-speed cable modems, it turned to an intranet to speed the process. Assembling these complex projects would have taken extensive documentation, including drawings of each component. Instead, Motorola used a digital camera to photograph each part and posted them on the intranet along with instructions for assembly, testing, packaging, and shipping.[28]

Advances in information technology are also leading to greater *interdepartmental coordination* as well as growing linkages between organizations. Thanks to networks and intranets, boundaries between departments within organizations as well as between organizations seem to dissolve, making a division or company across the world seem as close as one down the hall. Networks allow computers to talk to one another about all aspects of business, such as customer orders, parts requirements, invoices, manufacturing dates, and market share slippage.[29] At Ford Motor Company, every car and truck model has its own internal Web site on the intranet to track design, procurement, production, delivery processes, and so forth. Manufacturing, for example, can immediately see if a new dashboard design will slow assembly and alert engineering of the problem.[30]

Many organizations have long used one specific type of interorganizational linkage, called **electronic data interchange** (EDI), which ties businesses with suppliers. EDI, which links a computer at one company to a computer at another for the transmission of business data, such as sales statistics, without human interference, can enable businesses to achieve low-cost leadership through *rapid resupply*. Companies can save millions of dollars by using EDI to coordinate materials movement. Exhibit 7.3 shows how EDI can electronically connect several organizations to facilitate trade on both domestic and international levels.

Some large organizations with a low-cost strategy once had difficulty working with small suppliers because the smaller organizations didn't have the financial resources to become EDI-capable. "The guy who supplies our wood pallets has five employees," said Ray Hill of Pitney Bowes. "He's not going to go out and buy a mainframe just to do EDI with us."[31] However, recent advances using the Internet have allowed many small companies to remain viable by giving them EDI capability they otherwise might not be able to afford. Pitney Bowes uses a Web product called VendorSite, which allows suppliers to see how many of its products Pitney has on hand and how many it will need. Eventually, Pitney wants suppliers to be able to deliver products just as they are needed.

The Automotive Network Exchange (ANX) is a virtual private network that allows companies in the automotive industry to transmit EDI data over the Web. Taylor Steel's data communications charges dropped by 70 percent after the company started using ANX. Industry analysts predict that use of ANX could slash $1 billion in auto industry costs per year.[32]

DIFFERENTIATION

A way to differentiate a company is to *lock in customers* with information technology. The innovator of this strategy was American Hospital Supply Corporation. Senior executives decided more than 15 years ago to give computer terminals free to hospitals around the country, linking hospital purchasers directly with AHS,

EXHIBIT 7.3 *Electronic Data Interchange for International Transactions*

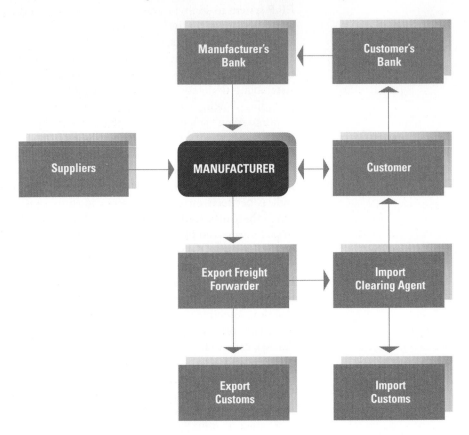

enabling customers to directly place orders for any of more than 100,000 products. AHS immediately gained sales and market share at competitors' expense.[33]

Today's industry leaders in pharmaceutical drug wholesaling, including McKesson Corp., Cardinal Health, and Bergen Brunswig, differentiate themselves by providing sophisticated reporting services to their large, national customers. In addition, large drug wholesalers have further locked in customers by developing proprietary automated dispensing and reporting systems, along with consulting services. Value-added information services are increasingly used as customer lock-in methods.[34]

Improving customer service can also differentiate a company from competitors. For example, automating the sales force can dramatically reduce the time it takes to close an order as well as increase the rate of successful closes. Deere Power Systems, a division of John Deere that makes diesel engines and other heavy equipment, found that its salespeople might spend a full day logging into various databases and calling different departments for information before going on a call. In the meantime, competitors would step in and beat Deere to the deal. With new information technology, departments that once kept information to themselves are sharing it on a network, and a salesperson is generally able to get all the information needed for a call in half a day or less.[35]

As another example, Jiffy Lube improved customer service by using an information technology system called Automate to automatically remind customers when routine service is due, suggest auto maintenance based on each manufacturer's recommendations, and store individual customer preferences. If a particular customer never wants the tires filled, the Jiffy Lube associate will know that automatically without the customer having to explain each time he or she comes in for service.[36]

A third dimension of differentiation is new *product development* or product development for specialized *market niches*. Companies from General Electric to Manpower Inc. are using the Internet to track market trends and spot new niches.[37] Nike uses an intranet to improve global collaboration for new product development.

| In Practice 7.2 | Nike Inc. |

The cycle that turns a designer's dream into a shoe on a store shelf takes approximately eighteen months, during which employees are juggling different schedules for three seasons and hundreds of new products. In 1995, Nike began redesigning its footwear process in an effort called Future Vision, with a goal of improving decision making and product development. A significant aspect of the Future Vision project was an intranet aimed at providing a seamless flow of information around the world throughout the footwear development process.

The system, called Global Product Information Network (GPIN), gives each Nike product a Web-based home page. Content is grouped by category areas rather than by function—that way, designers working on running shoes deal only with running and tennis marketers deal only with tennis. GPIN is designed to offer rich product information online, from the earliest stages of design and planning. For example, marketing managers enter their original forecasts, which flow to a corporate forecasting application. Designers scan their sketches and design boards so that anyone on the system can keep in touch with the design process. Merchandisers can sort product lines by color, price, and target audience. Top executives can view confidential reports on the top sellers in each category for each season. Because much of GPIN's product information is highly confidential, managers are searching for ways to limit confidential information early in the development process and then make it available to more and more employees. For example, the sketch for the hottest shoe design for 2001 should be seen by only a handful of people in January 2000, but more and more employees must be brought into the loop as development progresses. By the time the line launches, complete information will be available to salespeople, customer service representatives, and retailers.

GPIN gives managers and product directors better information for making faster decisions. For example, Ellen Devlin, product creation director for Nike's branded athletic wear, can quickly show designs and ideas to her European and Asian counterparts, giving them a chance to offer suggestions online. Face-to-face meetings have become less frequent but more productive. Development time and costs are also reduced because oversees employees can view designs and changes online rather than needing physical shoe samples. Nike believes that, by speeding information around the globe, GPIN has helped improve collaboration, reduce cycle time, and cut costs.[38]

E-COMMERCE

A primary way many companies are using information technology as a strategic weapon is through electronic commerce, or e-commerce. One only needs to think of Amazon.com, which created huge headaches for bookstores such as Barnes & Noble and Borders—and which has a market value higher than all the bricks-and-mortar bookstores in the world combined—in order to understand the significance of e-commerce in today's business world.[39] E-commerce can be useful for either a low-cost leadership or a differentiation strategy.

E-commerce is a very broad term, which basically means any commercial activity that takes place by digital processes over a computer network. E-commerce replaces or enhances the exchange of money and products with the exchange of information from one computer to another. As such, applications such as EDI, extranets, and so forth are all aspects of e-commerce. Today, most e-commerce takes place on the Internet. Two aspects of e-commerce are business-to-business transactions and business-to-consumer transactions. Market researchers at International Data Corporation predict that the amount of overall e-commerce will top $1 trillion by 2003.

One company that has integrated e-commerce into its entire business strategy is Dell Computer Corp., which now offers Internet transaction capabilities in thirty-six countries and eighteen languages.[40] Dell uses end-to-end digital networks to keep in touch with customers, take orders, pull together components as needed from suppliers, and assemble and ship customized products directly to the purchaser. The system enables Dell to compete with both cost advantages and speed. For example, by connecting directly with suppliers, Dell can eliminate costly inventory, but the company can frequently obtain needed parts and supplies in a matter of minutes. A customer order placed with Dell at 9 A.M. on Monday can be on a delivery truck by 9 P.M. Tuesday.[41] Similarly, Cisco Systems is electronically connected not only to customers and employees but also to suppliers, contract manufacturers, assemblers, and other business partners. High-tech companies like Dell and Cisco Systems are leaders in business-to-business commerce, but even low-tech companies are getting into the game. U.S. Office Products, a leading supplier of business products and services to companies of all sizes, offers online ordering, checking of order status and tracking, online payment options, and online reporting/usage information. A new feature is a procurement management system that enables USOP to give its customers a way to streamline and control their purchasing process, reduce costs, and improve efficiency. This service differentiates USOP in the highly competitive office products market.[42]

Although business-to-business commerce over the Internet is growing rapidly, perhaps the most visible expression of e-commerce is selling products and services directly to consumers over the Internet. Until very recently, the Internet has been used much more intensively by consumers than by business executives.[43] For example, eToys offers more than 6,000 items from almost 500 manufacturers. Customers choose what they want from the Web site, type in their credit card numbers, and receive shipments of toys within a few days. The company can do business much less expensively than a company like Toys "R" Us that has to maintain buildings, store inventory, and so forth. Other Internet companies, such as iVillage, which has become the No. 1 women's site on the Web, offer services such as chats with doctors about children's health problems or discussion groups about women's business opportunities.[44]

Web sites that offer a place to participate in an online community are increasingly popular. Other rapidly growing areas of e-commerce include finance and insurance, travel, online auctions, and computer sales. Marriott International put together its first online reservation system in 1996 and did $1 billion in business the first year. Today, Marriott's interactive Web site is linked to numerous other travel-related sites. The site is personalized for each visitor, averages 15,000 hits a day, and generates more than $2 million in Internet-related revenues a month. Marriott executives believe its value-added approach differentiates the chain from other hotels and helps to build customer loyalty.[45]

Most established organizations are recognizing that they will have to get into the business of e-commerce or be slaughtered by start-up companies. Companies such as Southwest Airlines, Office Depot, Fingerhut, and even the U.S. Postal Service have established successful e-commerce units. Even such old-line companies as Sears and Whirlpool are jumping on the e-commerce bandwagon.[46] An important consideration for such companies is whether to incorporate a new e-commerce division within the traditional organization or to create a spin-off company. Sears CEO Arthur Martinez once considered the Internet "the domain of fanatics," but is now investing heavily in a new e-commerce division aimed at making Sears the "definitive online source for the home." Although the division is a part of the larger organization, executives are striving to give employees the right combination of freedom and incentives they need to be creative and take the necessary risks. Martinez doesn't believe a spinoff is the only way to give an e-commerce unit the autonomy it needs to succeed. Whirlpool, on the other hand, created a start-up company called Brandwise.com to help build its Internet-related business. Because the Brandwise site is designed to help consumers find the best products and value, it could potentially *lose* business for Whirlpool, but the company believes the risks are worth the potential rewards. Whirlpool hopes to gain access to valuable information about its business and customers. In addition, top executives believe the start-up provides a valuable breeding ground for the organization's next generation of leaders, who will need a deep understanding of e-commerce and be skilled at working in "Internet-time."[47]

Although companies in the United States and Canada are the leading participants in e-commerce, the revolution is beginning to affect the way the rest of the world does business as well. European e-commerce, for example, is expected to grow from $5 billion in 1997 to $197 billion in 2002. Scandinavian-based Internet start-ups are competing head-to-head with U.S.-based Web giants in Britain as well as the largely untapped cybermarkets of Germany, France, and Italy.[48]

NEW OPTIONS FOR ORGANIZATION DESIGN

E-commerce and other advances in electronic technology are having a significant impact on organization design. New technologies enable the electronic communication of richer, more complex information and remove the barriers of time and distance that have traditionally defined organizational structures. Virtual teams, for example, made up of members from divisions around the world, can collaborate on projects via intranets or networks. Whirlpool Corp.'s North American Appliance Group used a virtual team made up of members from the United States, Brazil, and Italy to develop the company's chlorofluorocarbon-free refrigerator. A company may also use virtual teams in partnership with suppliers or even competitors to pull together the best minds to complete a project or speed a new product to market.[49] An organization structure that takes the virtual approach a step further is the dynamic network structure.

DYNAMIC NETWORK STRUCTURE

A growing trend is for companies to limit themselves to only a few activities that they do extremely well and let outside specialists handle the rest. With a **network organization structure**, a company subcontracts most of its major functions to separate companies and coordinates their activities from a small headquarters organization.[50] In Chapter 3, we discussed a number of fundamental organization structures, including the functional, divisional, matrix, and horizontal structure. The network may also be considered a type of horizontal structure, but it represents a totally different approach to structuring the organization. The network may be viewed as a central hub surrounded by a network of outside specialists, as illustrated in Exhibit 7.4. Rather than being housed under one roof, or located within one organization, services such as accounting, design, manufacturing, and distribution are outsourced to separate organizations that are connected electronically to the central hub. For example, Monorail Inc., based in Marietta, Georgia, has no factories, no warehouses, no credit department, and no help desks or call centers.

In Practice 7.3

Monorail

Monorail's founders believe there are only two things you can't outsource: world-class management expertise and a knack for establishing the right partnerships. Monorail has managed to grow rapidly by using a network structure. The company's core group of employees concentrates on product design and marketing and outsources everything else to other organizations. Founders Doug Johns, David Hocker, and Nicholas Forlenza (all former Compaq Corp. managers) emphasize that relationships with subcontractors are the glue that holds the company together.

Here's how it works: When a retailer such as CompUSA orders a computer from Monorail, the order is transmitted electronically through FedEx Logistics Services to one of Monorail's many contract manufacturers, which assembles the PC and ships it directly to the retailer. Meanwhile, FedEx wires an invoice to Sun Trust Bank in Atlanta, whose factoring department handles billing and credit approvals for Monorail. Monorail gets its payment directly from Sun Trust, which assumes the risk of collecting funds from CompUSA. Whenever Monorail customers need technical help, they call a service center that is run by Sykes Enterprises Inc., a call center outsourcing company based in Tampa, Florida. Monorail's success depends on seamless integration with its business partners—particularly FedEx and Sun Trust, which play a central role in operations. For example, Monorail designed its PCs to fit into a standard FedEx box.

By using the network approach, Monorail has managed to be one of the leanest companies in the computer industry, enabling the organization to keep costs low and grow rapidly. Doug Johns points out that when he left Compaq he was managing 6 million square feet of warehouse and office space. Now, at Monorail, he and his fifty employees work on a single leased floor of an office building near Atlanta. "We've got the shortest supply lines in the world," he says.[51]

The network incorporates a free-market style to replace the traditional vertical hierarchy. Subcontractors flow into and out of the system as needed to meet changing needs. The speed and ease of electronic communication today make networking a viable option for companies looking to keep costs low but expand activities or market visibility. For example, Rhoda Makoff started R&D

EXHIBIT 7.4   *The Dynamic Network Organization Structure*

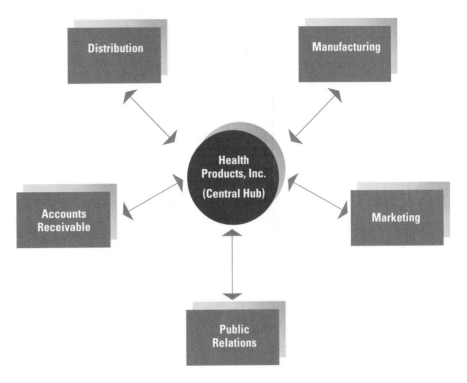

Laboratories Inc. to develop specialized vitamin and mineral supplements for dialysis patients. The products are manufactured and packaged by subcontracted pharmaceutical companies, and two hundred wholesalers handle warehousing and distribution. Using the network approach enabled quantum leaps in growth for R&D Labs. As soon as the small company has a promising new product, Makoff can ramp up production just by making a few phone calls.[52]

A major strategic advantage for network structures is that the organization, no matter how small, can be truly global, drawing on resources worldwide to achieve the best quality and price and then selling products or services worldwide just as easily through subcontractors. In addition, the network structure can allow companies to develop new products and get them to market rapidly without huge investments. The ability to arrange and rearrange resources to meet changing needs and best serve customers gives the network organization greater flexibility and rapid response. Managerial and technical talent can be focused on key activities that provide competitive advantage, as at Monorail, while other functions are outsourced.[53]

INTERORGANIZATIONAL RELATIONSHIPS

Even organizations that do not use a network structure are rapidly evolving from self-contained, vertical organizations to firms that rely on business partners to fulfill major parts of their company's activities and purpose, helping them cut costs and be more responsive to customers.[54] As we described in Chapter 5, many companies today depend on strategic partnerships to remain competitive, and electronic connections are a critical aspect of this trend.

Many computer and other high-tech firms are electronically connected to varied manufacturing subcontractors. For example, when a customer places an order for a low-end router on Cisco System's Web site, the order goes directly to Flextronics Ltd., a contract manufacturer in San Jose, California. Cisco relies so heavily on outside manufacturers and distributors that it can ship products anywhere in the world within a couple of days without ever touching the product. Nortel Networks has announced that by 2002, it will close or sell seventeen of its twenty-four factories—the company has calculated that it can save $300 million a year by outsourcing.[55]

Another significant trend is developing electronic relationships with suppliers and customers. Exhibit 7.5 shows differences between traditional interorganizational relationship characteristics and emerging relationship characteristics. Traditionally, organizations had an arm's-length relationship with suppliers. However, as we discussed in Chapter 5, suppliers are becoming closer partners, tied electronically to the organization for orders, invoices, and payments. In addition, relationships with customers are changing dramatically. New information technology has increased the power of consumers by giving them electronic access to a wealth of information from thousands of companies just by clicking a mouse. Already, 16 percent of new car buyers check dealer prices online before visiting a dealership to shop for a new car.

In addition, by giving consumers direct access to manufacturers, the Internet has radically altered customer expectations about convenience, speed, and service. For example, N2K.com is giving music lovers a chance to custom-build their own CDs, track by track, by downloading music off the Internet and storing it in a home audiovideo server.[56] Continually evolving information technology both responds to and expands the trend toward connectivity and cooperation among organizations and with consumers. Companies that want to thrive in the new

EXHIBIT 7.5   *Key Characteristics of Traditional vs. Emerging Interorganizational Relationships*

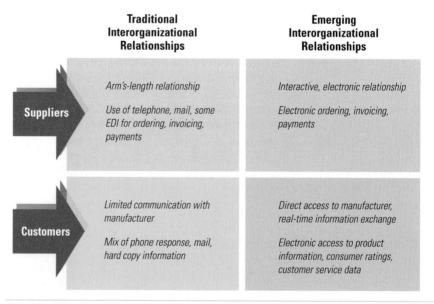

Source: Based on Charles V. Callahan and Bruce A. Pasternack, "Corporate Strategy in the Digital Age," *Strategy & Business,* Issue 15 (Second Quarter 1999): 10–14.

"networked" economy have to learn and adapt quickly. As described in this chapter's Book Mark, managers can take steps to ensure that their organizations use new information technology for learning and adaptation. Further in this chapter, we will discuss the concept of knowledge management, which is helping organizations stay ahead in this highly volatile and competitive environment.

IT IMPACT ON ORGANIZATION DESIGN

Advances in information technology are having a tremendous impact on all organizations in every industry. Some of the implications of these advances for organization design are:

1. *Smaller organizations.* Information technology enables organizations to outsource many functions and thus use fewer in-house resources. The hub of a network organization, for example, may be made up of only a few people. In addition, some Internet-based businesses exist almost entirely in cyberspace; there is no formal "organization" in terms of a building with offices, desks, and so forth. One or a few people may maintain the site from their homes or a rented work space. Information technology may also enable traditional organizations to do the same amount of work with fewer people, which also contributes to a decline in organization size. For example, Allstate Corp. recently announced the closing of four regional offices and a field support center as the company begins to do more business through electronic commerce and over the Internet. The closings will eliminate at least four thousand jobs.[57]

2. *Decentralized organization structures.* Advanced information technology has enabled organizations to reduce layers of management and decentralize decision making. Information that may have previously been available only to top managers at headquarters can be quickly and easily shared throughout the organization, even across great geographical distances. Managers in varied business divisions or offices have the information they need to make important decisions quickly rather than waiting for decisions from headquarters. Technologies that enable people to meet and coordinate online can facilitate communication and decision making among distributed, autonomous groups of workers. In addition, technology allows for telecommuting, whereby individual workers can perform work that was once done in the office from their computers at home or other remote locations. People and groups no longer have to be located under one roof to collaborate and share information. An organization may be made up of numerous small teams or even individuals who work autonomously but coordinate electronically. Although management philosophy and corporate culture have a substantial impact on whether information technology is used to decentralize information and authority or to reinforce a centralized authority structure,[58] most organizations today use technology to further decentralization.

3. *Improved internal and external coordination.* Perhaps one of the greatest outcomes of advanced information technology is its potential to improve coordination and communication both within the firm and with other organizations. Intranets, extranets, and other networks can connect people even when their offices, factories, or stores are scattered around the world. For example, General Motors' intranet, dubbed Socrates on the basis that the Greek philosopher would be recognizable worldwide, connects some 100,000 staff members around the globe. Managers use the intranet to communicate with one another

and to stay aware of organizational activities and outcomes.[59] Electronic technology also enables the network organization and other forms of organizational interdependence. Recent studies have shown that interorganizational information networks tend to heighten integration, blur organizational boundaries, and create shared strategic contingencies among firms.[60] Organizations can cooperate and collaborate with other companies no matter where they are geographically located.

4. *Additional professional staff and departments.* The implementation of sophisticated information technology systems means that organizations need more

Book Mark 7.0

Have You Read This Book?

Business @ the Speed of Thought: Using a Digital Nervous System

By Bill Gates with Collins Hemingway

In his second book, *Business @ the Speed of Thought*, Bill Gates offers advice for leaders who want to use information technology to create "digital nervous systems" and facilitate a new way of working based on information sharing and collaboration. Throughout the book, Gates, co-founder and chairman of Microsoft, relates anecdotes about his own company's ups and downs in using the Internet and describes the experiences of some of Microsoft's biggest customers. He points out how the Internet is transforming consumers' lifestyles and altering their expectations of business.

GUIDELINES FOR E-BUSINESS

Gates describes twelve key steps that can help organizations make the flow of digital information an integral part of the company. Some of these steps are as follows:

*   *Insist that communication flow through e-mail.* The use of e-mail can flatten the hierarchy, empower employees to speak up, and encourage managers to listen and act on information that flows upward through the organization. That's why Gates lists it as the first thing an organization can do to get more value out of their information systems and encourage collaboration. In addition, the company should value and reward the sharing rather than hoarding of knowledge and information.
*   *Use digital tools to create virtual teams.* A collaborative culture, combined with digital information flow, enables people throughout the company to stay connected. "When you get a critical mass of high-IQ people working in concert, the energy level shoots way

up. Knowledge management is a fancy term for a simple idea." Digital tools can be used to enhance the way people work together, communicate, share ideas and insights, and then act together for a common purpose.

*   *Use digital tools to eliminate single-task jobs.* The industrial age approach was to break jobs into small, discrete tasks and assign each task to one employee who would perform it over and over. In the new world of work, however, employees should focus on whole processes rather than single tasks. This gives people more interesting, challenging work and allows the organization to gain the advantage of their intelligence, experience, and creativity. Boring, repetitive work should be taken over by machines, so that people are free to think and build the organization's knowledge.

CONCLUSION

Internet technology, Gates contends, is primarily about empowering the individual. Organizations that give employees responsibility and authority without giving them the information they need set people up for failure. Information technology can spread power throughout the organization. The result is happier employees, more satisfied customers, and a stronger organization. "Investments in technology should provide better information to every worker who might possibly use it. Knowledge workers are the brains of the company. If they're disconnected from the company's important data, how can they function, how can they be empowered? You can give people responsibility and authority, but without information, they are helpless."

Business @ The Speed of Thought, by Bill Gates with Collins Hemingway, is published by Warner Books.

people with professional skills and knowledge to use and maintain the systems. As we discussed in the previous chapter, as organizational technology grows more complex, the complexity of the organization increases as well. Many firms are adding chief information officers, and some create whole new departments to help the organization manage and keep pace with rapidly changing information technology. In addition, when companies become involved in e-commerce, the need for professional staff greatly increases. The only way a company can successfully implement an e-commerce strategy is to create a separate professional department or division devoted specifically to electronic commerce. Land's End, for example, created a new department headed by a vice-president of e-commerce to manage its Internet business. Sears has more than fifty professionals setting up its new e-commerce division, discussed earlier in this chapter.

5. *Greater employee participation.* With today's technology, workers on the front lines can have instant access to pertinent information about their jobs, allowing greater participation and autonomy. For example, at the Chesebrough-Ponds Inc. plant in Jefferson City, Missouri, line workers routinely tap into the company's computer network to track shipments, schedule their own workloads, order production increases, and perform other functions that used to be the province of management.[61] Particularly in learning organizations, everyone throughout the company is wired into the computer network and has complete information about all aspects of the business, enabling them to fully participate in solving problems, making decisions, and moving the organization forward.

Increasingly sophisticated information technology will continue to have a significant impact on organization design. Although a few organizations have used technology to reinforce rigid hierarchies, centralize decision making, and routinize work, the trend in general is toward greater decentralization, improved coordination and information sharing, more challenging work, and greater opportunities for participation.

KNOWLEDGE MANAGEMENT

One primary goal for information technology systems today is to support efforts to manage and leverage organizational knowledge. Having greater access to information is useless unless that information is put to use to further the goals and success of the organization. In today's economy, the basic economic resource is no longer capital, or labor, or natural resources, but *knowledge*. Peter Drucker coined the term *knowledge work* in the early 1960s[62] but only in recent years have managers begun to recognize knowledge as an important resource that should be managed, just as they manage cash flow, human resources, or raw materials. Particularly for companies that are striving to be learning organizations, knowledge management is a critical job for organization executives. Learning organizations effectively acquire, create, and transfer knowledge across the company and modify their activities to reflect new knowledge and insights.[63]

Knowledge management is a new way to think about organizing and sharing an organization's intellectual and creative resources. It refers to the efforts to systematically find, organize, and make available a company's intellectual capital and to foster a culture of continuous learning and knowledge sharing so that organizational activities build on what is already known.[64] The company's intellectual capital is the sum of its information, experience, understanding, relationships, processes, innovations, and discoveries. Although information technology plays an important role by enabling the storage and dissemination of data and information across the organization, technology is only one part of a larger puzzle.[65] A complete knowledge management system includes not only processes for capturing and storing knowledge and organizing it for easy access, but also ways to generate new knowledge through learning and to share knowledge throughout the organization. Information technology alone is not enough to handle this complex problem.

WHAT IS KNOWLEDGE?

Knowledge is not the same thing as data or information, although it uses both. **Data** are simple, absolute facts and figures that, in and of themselves, may be of little use. A company might have data that show 30 percent of a particular product is sold to customers in Florida. To be useful to the organization, the data are processed into finished *information* by connecting them with other data—for example, nine out of ten of the products sold in Florida are bought by people over the age of sixty. **Information** is data that have been linked with other data and converted into a useful context for specific use. **Knowledge** goes a step further; it is a conclusion drawn from the information after it is linked to other information and compared to what is already known. Knowledge, as opposed to information and data, always has a human factor. Books can contain information, but the information becomes knowledge only when a person absorbs it and puts it to use.[66] Knowledge is based on prior information, hands-on experience, intuition, and understanding—it involves recognizing how to take action on the information to accomplish the organization's goals. For example, a manager might recognize that targeting people over the age of sixty in Florida will double sales, but targeting the same age group in Maine or Minnesota will do nothing but increase marketing costs. Knowledge is something that is in employees' collective brains, not something stored in a database or printed out by an executive information system.

Organizations deal with both explicit knowledge and implicit, or *tacit*, knowledge.[67] **Explicit knowledge** is formal, systematic knowledge that can be codified, written down, and passed on to others in documents or general instructions. Tacit knowledge, on the other hand, is often very difficult to put into words. **Tacit knowledge** is based on personal experience, rules of thumb, intuition, and judgment. It includes professional know-how and expertise, individual insight and experience, and creative solutions that are often difficult to communicate and pass on to others. Explicit knowledge may be equated with *knowing about*; whereas tacit knowledge is equated with *knowing how*.[68] For example, recent graduates of an agricultural college may *know about* the best times and locations for planting soybeans, the best soils and fertilizers to help ensure a healthy crop, and the appropriate time to harvest the crop. They can test soil samples, track weather conditions, calculate the growing period, and plan for harvesting. A third-generation soybean farmer may not know about any of those things. However, the seasoned farmer *knows how* to grow a successful soybean crop, based on years of experience. Such farmers know which fields are best for growing soybeans, when to plant, and how to tend the crop, and they use their judgment to know when crops are ready to harvest, which may or may not be the date the first farmers would have calculated.

If asked to explain how to grow soybeans, the ag-school graduate could write a detailed, scientific report. The third-generation farmer might be unable to provide a set of clear, precise instructions, even though he or she knows how to grow a superb crop. The farmer's expert knowledge is not easily codified. Similarly, in organizations, there are many people who know *how* to do certain things that they might not be able to put into clear, precise instructions for others. For learning organizations, finding ways to transfer both explicit and tacit knowledge—the knowing about and the knowing how—across the organization is critical. Although explicit knowledge can easily be captured and shared in documents and through information technology systems, as much as 80 percent of an organization's valuable knowledge may be tacit knowledge that is not easily captured and transferred.[69]

APPROACHES TO KNOWLEDGE MANAGEMENT

Knowledge management is not new, but only recently have organization executives begun thinking about deliberate, systematic ways to create, capture, organize, and transfer knowledge. There are three driving forces behind the surge of interest in knowledge management. First, a large part of the momentum comes from the rapid advances in information technology that make it possible to share explicit knowledge more quickly and easily as well as to connect people in networks for the sharing of tacit knowledge. Second, as the economic basis of organizations shifts from natural resources to intellectual capital, top executives have found it imperative to appraise their organizations' knowledge resources and how to leverage them. Finally, the growing interest in knowledge management is closely related to companies' efforts to become *learning organizations,* in which managers strive to create a culture and a system for creating new knowledge and for capturing both explicit and tacit knowledge and getting it to the right place at the right time.[70] A survey of CEOs attending the World Economic Forum's 1999 annual meeting found that 97 percent of senior executives see knowledge management as a critical issue for their organizations.[71]

Two distinct approaches to knowledge management are outlined in Exhibit 7.6. Critical to both approaches is a cultural mindset that encourages collaboration and knowledge sharing. Since knowledge gives people power within the organization, there is a strong impulse to hoard rather than share it. Thus, knowledge management often requires major culture change. For example, Jorma Ollila, CEO of Nokia Telecommunications, introduced a new cultural direction with the statement, "Knowledge in Nokia is power only when it is shared." Texas Instruments awards the "Not-Invented-Here-But-I-Did-It-Anyway" prize to encourage people to share knowledge.[72]

The first approach to knowledge management deals primarily with the collection and sharing of explicit knowledge, largely through the use of sophisticated information technology systems.[73] Explicit knowledge may include intellectual properties such as patents and licenses, work processes such as policies and procedures, specific information on customers, markets, suppliers or competitors, competitive intelligence reports, benchmark data, and so forth. When an organization uses this approach, the focus is on collecting and codifying knowledge and storing it in databases where it can easily be accessed and reused by anyone in the organization. Knowledge is gathered from the individuals who possess it and is organized into documents that others can access and reuse. This "people-to-documents" approach is used by some consulting firms. For example, Ernst & Young collects knowledge such as interview tips, work schedules, benchmark data, and market segmentation analyses and stores them in an electronic database for reuse.

EXHIBIT 7.6   *Two Approaches to Knowledge Management*

Explicit	Knowledge Management Strategy	**Tacit**
Provide high-quality, reliable, and fast information systems for access of codified, reusable knowledge		Channel individual expertise to provide creative advice on strategic problems
People-to-documents approach		**Person-to-person approach**
Develop an electronic document system that codifies, stores, disseminates, and allows reuse of knowledge	Knowledge Management Strategy	*Develop networks for linking people so that tacit knowledge can be shared*
Invest heavily in information technology, with a goal of connecting people with resusable, codified knowledge	Technology	*Invest moderately in information technology, with a goal of facilitating conversations and the exchange of tacit knowledge*
Data warehousing and data mining *Knowledge mapping* *Electronic libraries*	Mechanisms	*Dialogue* *Learning histories and storytelling* *Communities of practice*

Source: Based on Morten T. Hansen, Nitin Nohria, and Thomas Tierney, "What's Your Strategy for Managing Knowledge?" *Harvard Business Review* (March–April 1999): 106–16.

The second approach focuses on leveraging individual expertise and know-how—tacit knowledge—by connecting people face-to-face or through interactive media. Tacit knowledge includes professional know-how, individual insights and creativity, and personal experience and intuition. With this approach, managers concentrate on developing personal networks that link people together for the sharing of tacit knowledge. Although information technology is used, it primarily supports and facilitates conversations and person-to-person sharing of tacit knowledge. Consider how DPR Construction Inc., one of the fastest-growing and most successful general contracting businesses in the United States, creates and transfers both explicit and tacit knowledge.

In Practice 7.4

DPR Construction Inc.

Doug Woods, Peter Nosler, and Ronald Davidowski didn't set out to reinvent the construction industry. They just wanted to build a great company that worked in an industry where many companies don't work very well. They succeeded—DPR worked so well that it grew from 12 people to 2,000 and from annual revenues of less than $1 million to more than $1.3 billion in only eight years. The company, whose motto is "DPR Exists to Build Great Things," specializes in building for six industries—biotechnology, pharmaceuticals, microelectronics, entertainment, health care, and corporate-office development. Part of the reason DPR has become so successful is that it absorbed many of the ideas that drive its fast-moving clients—companies such as Novell, Charles Schwab, Sun Microsystems, and Genentech. One of those ideas is managing and transferring knowledge.

At the start of any project, DPR uses in-house facilitators to align the interests of the project's numerous constituencies, including architects, contractors, subcontractors, clients, and suppliers. This emphasis on team-building makes sure everyone has an opportunity to have input from the beginning—and DPR has a rich mechanism for acquiring new knowledge. When DPR contracted to build lab facilities for Stanford University, it brought students into the process to learn from them how the facilities could better meet their needs. The process was so successful that DPR now tries to learn everything it can from the intended users on all its projects. This kind of learning and tacit knowledge sharing is evident throughout DPR. Regular team meetings focus on solving specific problems. Regional and national meetings involve employees in deep conversations about how to improve performance in seven critical areas that DPR has identified as essential to organizational success.

However, DPR also uses computer-based information technology to give employees broad access to explicit knowledge. On almost every project, the company sets up a communications trailer, complete with servers, routers, and cellular connections. Every new hire gets a state-of-the-art laptop with core applications for estimating and project management as well as for communicating with colleagues. To harness organizational brainpower, DPR encourages employees—or anyone on a job site—to submit OFI (opportunity for improvement) forms. These may be suggestions for how to do a task more quickly, how to solve a specific problem, or how to complete a segment of a project more efficiently, for example. The OFIs get logged into a database so that any employee can search through every project and find where others did things better, more efficiently, faster, or safer. The database can be searched by keyword, by cost, or by one of DPR's seven critical success factors. "It's just one hell of a resource," says Jim Webb, superintendent for a renovation project at Summit Medical Center in Oakland, California. "No one at this company has done everything. But a lot of us have specialties. So when you find a problem that's beyond your expertise, you get on the computer and draw on other resources."[74]

DPR successfully uses mechanisms for both explicit and tacit knowledge management. In the following sections, we will examine specific mechanisms in detail.

MECHANISMS FOR EXPLICIT KNOWLEDGE MANAGEMENT

Organizations can use a number of mechanisms to support the collection and sharing of knowledge resources. Some mechanisms that are particularly useful for explicit knowledge management are data warehousing, knowledge mapping, and electronic libraries. In addition, intranets or other networks for connecting people throughout the organization are important for sharing both explicit and tacit knowledge. These mechanisms are listed in Exhibit 7.6 and described in detail here.

1. *Data warehousing and data mining.* As described earlier in the chapter, data warehousing allows companies to combine all their data into huge databases for easy access, and data mining helps users make sense of the data by searching for patterns that can help solve organizational problems or take advantage of new opportunities. Data warehousing and data mining can be particularly useful for building customer relationships or entering new markets. Kimberly-Clark Corp. has expanded its customer base by using its data warehouse in the business-to-business sector to identify individuals that its distributors sell to and then targeting them with promotional mailings about

Kimberly-Clark products. At Ernst & Young, each of the more than forty practice areas has a staff member who helps to codify employee's explicit knowledge and store it in databases, which are linked through a network. An E&Y team preparing a bid to install an ERP system for a large industrial manufacturer used the database to search out previously developed solutions. By reusing the material, the team saved Ernst & Young, as well as the client, more than a year of work.[75]

2. *Knowledge mapping.* Some companies are undertaking **knowledge mapping** projects that identify where knowledge is located in the organization and how to access it. Although there are varied approaches, the purpose of knowledge mapping is to guide people to knowledge resources within the company. Hughes Space & Communications is building a knowledge expressway using Lotus Notes, videoconferencing, employee home pages, and numerous other technologies. The map is used to transfer new management practices, track licenses and patents, gather competitive intelligence, and so forth. For example, the engineering group might tap into a "lessons learned" database using hypertext links to directories, abstracts, and other documents. Hughes also hopes to use knowledge mapping to support tacit knowledge sharing by guiding people to pockets of expertise and fostering communication and storytelling.[76]

3. *Electronic libraries.* **Electronic libraries**, databases of specific types of information for specific uses, provide another way to store knowledge and make it available throughout the organization. Users may be able to "check out" and reuse specific pieces of knowledge. For example, Sun Microsystems has created a shared-code library, a central communication hub from which programmers can check out whole pieces of software code without having to recreate them every time.[77] Sequent Computers Inc. has used an indexed library called Sequent Electronic Corporate Library (SECL) since 1995 to hold sales presentations, technical papers, and so forth.[78] In the United Kingdom, Anglian Water Services is developing an "encyclopedia of water" as part of its efforts to become a learning organization. The electronic encyclopedia contains knowledge about all aspects of water, such as treatment technologies or services management, that has previously been stored in separate books, documents, articles, and process descriptions.[79]

Intranets and other networks are critical tools to give people throughout the organization access to explicit knowledge that is stored in databases, electronic libraries, and so forth. San Jose-based Cadence Design Systems Inc. uses an in-house Web site for new sales representatives that provides a step-by-step guide through the sales process, product specifications, and profiles of customers and leads. The system has helped Cadence get sales reps out into the field two to four months faster, which saves the company millions of dollars.[80] Some companies, including US West, Paradyne Co., and Metropolitan Life Insurance, use intranets for gathering competitive intelligence. Salespeople, marketing staff, technicians, and others, in addition to competitive intelligence professionals, post information and views on technologies, customers, products, and industry developments.[81]

MECHANISMS FOR TACIT KNOWLEDGE MANAGEMENT

Although tacit knowledge management systems also use information technology, the emphasis is more on human interaction. For tacit knowledge management, effective mechanisms include dialogue, learning histories and storytelling, and communities of practice, also listed in Exhibit 7.6. Intranets and networks can also support the sharing of tacit knowledge, particularly in global organizations. For example, Xerox once tried to codify the knowledge of its service technicians and embed it in an expert decision system that was installed in the copiers. The idea was that technicians could be guided by the system and complete repairs more quickly, sometimes even off-site. However, the project failed because it did not take into account the tacit knowledge—the nuances and details—that could not be codified. After an eighteen-month study by anthropologists, behavioral scientists, and engineers found that service techs shared their knowledge primarily by telling "war stories," Xerox developed a system called "Eureka" to link 25,000 field service representatives. Eureka, which enables technicians to electronically share war stories and tips for repairing copiers, has cut average repair time by 50 percent.[82]

1. *Dialogue.* The primary mechanism for tacit knowledge sharing is to connect people in a dialogue—getting people talking face-to-face, or at least through videoconferencing or other interactive media. The goal of **dialogue** is to create a collective intelligence—people together arrive at a shared understanding of a problem and a collective solution that blends the ideas of many people. One way to understand dialogue is to compare it with debate. In a debate, people state and advocate their solutions to a problem with the intent to convince others to adopt those solutions. A dialogue, on the other hand, assumes that many people have different pieces of the answer to a problem and that together they can craft a solution.[83] Dialogue focuses on exploring assumptions and discovering common ground and shared issues. Participants in a dialogue do not presume to have a "right" answer because the answer emerges from the collective intelligence of the group. As new and deeper solutions are developed, a trusting relationship is built among the participants, which can transform communication patterns within the organization.

Some organizations set up forums on an intranet where people can get together and engage in dialogue about specific problems. Novartis, a $24 billion life sciences company, holds knowledge fairs about four times a year to give scientists and other employees a chance to engage in dialogue face-to-face. Then, when they go back to their respective divisions, they pick up the dialogue in Virtual Forums, as described in the Taking the Lead box.

Organizations that excel at tacit knowledge management find ways to encourage and facilitate continuous dialogue among employees. For example, one Japanese pharmaceutical company has a tea room where researchers sit and drink tea, and discuss their projects with fellow scientists; in this informal, relaxed setting, knowledge that can't be easily written down in documents or stored in a database is exchanged among professionals. To help encourage dialogue at Datafusion Inc., an information technology products and consulting services firm in San Francisco, Bipin Junnarkar, president and chief operating officer, has employees take pictures at the business conferences they attend and then share them with others as a way to recount what they learned at the conference, much like a family uses vacation slide shows or videotapes to recount their experiences to others.[84]

2. *Learning histories and storytelling.* Another approach to tacit knowledge management is to get people to share **learning histories**, which are designed to get at the story of how critical decisions were made and problems were solved (or not solved) so that knowledge is transferred to others. This technique is based on the ancient tradition of storytelling—in hunting and gathering societies, for

example, young men become successful hunters partly by sharing the story of a big hunt, where each person tells his version of what happened and a shaman comments on the narrative and guides the group to understand the story's significance and why the hunt succeeded or failed.[85] In organizations, a learning history is a written narrative of a specific major event or project, based on the recollections and insights of everyone who participated—managers, line workers, secretaries, even customers and suppliers. Each person is quoted directly, and the reminiscences are woven into a compelling story. In addition, a team of learning consultants and organizational employees identifies recurring

Taking the Lead

Creating Knowledge at Novartis

Novartis, a $24 billion life sciences corporation, produces diverse items such as pharmaceuticals, genetically engineered seeds, baby food, contact lenses, and animal health products. Created from the merger of Sandoz and Ciba-Geigy, Novartis has created some of the world's best-selling drugs and chemicals. Yet, with such a breadth of products and technologies, Novartis faces a tremendous challenge in terms of how to collect, manage, and transfer its sophisticated and diverse knowledge and, even more significantly, create new knowledge. Since the company depends on innovation to survive, executives knew they had to find a way.

Novartis prefers the term *knowledge networking* to knowledge management because it reflects top executives' emphasis on connecting people for the exchange of tacit knowledge and implies that it is the network of employees rather than a management hierarchy that makes the difference for the company's future. Novartis focuses primarily on engaging scientists, managers, and other professionals in ongoing dialogue, believing that the creation and transfer of tacit knowledge will determine the company's future competitiveness. About four times a year, Novartis sponsors knowledge fairs to provide people in this global corporation a rare opportunity to talk face to face. For example, at a recent fair, a scientist from the generic drugs unit in Vienna began talking about protein engineering, a technology that might enable a molecule to taste sweeter. During the dialogue, a manager from Ciba-Geigy's contact lens company in Aschaffenburg, Germany, began to wonder if the technology could be used to make contact lenses biocompatible. Ideas and insights such as this fly back and forth during the knowledge fairs, but unfortunately, participants ultimately have

to go back to their respective business units—some to Germany, some to the United States, other to Switzerland or Columbia. Once they get there, however, Novartis executives hope they will continue to participate in dialogues through the company's Virtual Forum, which provides electronic meeting rooms that are intended, in part, to continue the sharing of knowledge that people begin at the fairs. The ultimate goal is to have some of the knowledge tossed about at fairs and online bubble up into new technologies for use inside the company or be translated into new products and components, the lifeblood of Novartis. One idea that grew out of a knowledge fair is for using artificial neural networks—computer programs that learn by recognizing patterns of data—to improve financial forecasting for the management of Novartis's $14 billion investment portfolio.

The greatest challenge is sustaining the momentum when people move to dialogue online rather than face to face. One group decided to open each dialogue online with a provocative question to keep people energized. In addition, Novartis's officer of the science boards, Joerg Staeheli, who performs the function of senior officer of knowledge management, will frequently send a round of e-mails and online messages to prod people into further dialogue. To keep the energy flowing, he says, "you have to continuously feed the furnace, challenging people to come back." Staeheli particularly encourages people who might be reluctant to participate because they think they "don't know enough." He believes it is that kind of reaching out that opens up space for the creation of new knowledge.

Source: Based on Gary Abramson, "Wiring the Corporate Brain," *CIO Enterprise,* Section 2, 15 March 1999: 30–36.

themes, poses questions about the story's assumptions and implications, and raises "undiscussable" issues that don't come through in the narrative.

The completed learning history is used as the basis for discussion groups. The people who were involved reexperience the event and collectively learn its significance. For employees facing similar projects, the learning history provides a way to plan their own activities. A similar approach is the *after-action review*, developed by the U.S. Army, which means that participants in a project or activity take fifteen minutes or so to talk about what was supposed to happen, what actually happened, why there is a discrepancy between the two, and what can be learned from the experience.[86] These and other varieties of *corporate storytelling* are increasingly being used to transfer tacit knowledge. When people share their understanding and expertise in stories, it establishes a context for important pieces of knowledge and key decisions that others in the organization may share. Stories work because they allow people to subtly raise issues that they might be afraid to openly discuss in a more formal way, leading to greater opportunities for learning and sharing knowledge.

3. *Communities of Practice.* Communities of practice form spontaneously in organizations as people gravitate toward others who share their interests and face similar problems. **Communities of practice** are made up of individuals who are informally bound to one another through exposure to a similar set of problems and a common pursuit of solutions.[87] For example, a community of practice might be copier technicians at Xerox who share tips around the water cooler, freelance writers who have coffee once a week and talk about their current projects and problems, a district sales office that has a goal of being the top district office in the country, or people located in various departments of a manufacturing organization who share an interest in computer games. Communities of practice are similar to professional societies—people join them and stay in them *by choice*, because they think they have something to learn and something to contribute. Organizations cannot manage communities of practice in the traditional sense, but they can encourage and support them to help speed learning and the transfer of knowledge.

Even though true communities of practice cannot be formalized, some organizations use the idea to amass and concentrate knowledge and intellectual energy related to specific critical issues. James Euchner, a vice-president in Nynex's research and development department, hired an anthropologist to find out why some groups were so slow to set up data services for customers. She found that the different departments involved never communicated informally so they didn't understand one another's roles and needs. Euchner put the workers together in the same room and allowed people to form themselves into informal groups around various tasks and the problem was solved.[88] Similarly, when George Fisher first became CEO of Kodak, he found task forces all over the company trying to find ways to use digital imaging in Kodak's product line. The problem was, the small groups were all separated by functional and divisional boundaries, so they were unable to share their knowledge and expertise. At one time, for example, there were twenty-three separate groups working to develop digital scanners. Fisher dismantled the separate task forces and brought everyone working on digital imaging together, and the company quickly began to see results of their collective knowledge.[89]

LEVERAGING PROFESSIONAL KNOWLEDGE AND EXPERTISE

What's the ultimate purpose of all these mechanisms? Why do organization managers encourage and support activities such as dialogue and storytelling? A significant goal of knowledge management systems, whether we are talking about electronic libraries or communities of practice, is to leverage professional knowledge and expertise. Rather than having separate pockets of expertise scattered about the organization, knowledge management systems aim to bring knowledge together and spread it throughout the company. People can use the knowledge that already exists and build on it to create new knowledge. Consulting firms often set up databases of best practices that include detailed descriptions of projects so that consultants around the world can draw on one another's expertise. Other organizations create electronic libraries so workers can "check out" and reuse previously developed components or solutions. Xerox has estimated that sharing best practices through knowledge management has enabled the company to reduce costs by as much as $1 billion.[90]

Mechanisms such as databases, knowledge mapping, and electronic libraries are excellent tools for the management and transfer of explicit knowledge that can be codified and written down. However, in order to leverage tacit knowledge—professional insights and understanding that cannot be stored in a database—organizations use mechanisms such as dialogue, storytelling, and communities of practice. When people talk openly about their projects and problems, ideas and solutions often emerge from the collective brain of the group. Technology alone cannot achieve the ambitious goal of leveraging professional knowledge. For example, one large consumer products firm asked all professional staff to document their key work processes in a database. Most employees felt that their jobs were too varied and complex to capture in a set of written procedures, but at the insistence of top management, the task was completed. However, the resulting database was of little use—it simply did not capture the nuances, details, and insights that people needed to improve their work.[91] Although computer technology can be highly useful for leveraging knowledge, managers should understand its limitations. In addition, managers should recognize that the ultimate key to leveraging knowledge is changing organizational culture and management practices to encourage and support knowledge sharing. Culture will be discussed in detail in Chapter 9, and Chapter 10 will include approaches for changing organizational cultures toward greater learning and knowledge sharing.

SUMMARY AND INTERPRETATION

This chapter covered a number of important topics related to information technology and knowledge management. The information revolution has had a tremendous impact on organizations in all industries. Highly successful organizations today are generally those that most effectively collect, store, distribute, and use information. Information technology systems have evolved to a variety of applications to meet organizations' information needs. Operations applications are applied to well-defined tasks at lower organization levels and help to improve efficiency. These include transaction processing systems, data warehousing, and data mining. Management information systems, executive information systems, and decision support systems are used as business resources at middle- and upper-management levels. Today, all of these various systems have begun to merge into an overall information technology system that can be used as a strategic weapon. Using information technology as a strategic weapon is the highest level of application. Networking, intranets, and enterprise resource planning systems are used primarily to support greater internal coordination and flexibility. Applications such as extranets, e-commerce, and network structures redefine and support relationships with customers, suppliers, and other organizations.

Information technology plays an important role in helping organizations achieve a competitive advantage through low-cost leadership or differentiation. Technology can increase operational efficiency, coordination, and the speed of resupply, and can lock in customers, improve customer service, and enhance product development. E-commerce, which can support either a low-cost or a differentiation strategy, is a primary way companies are using new technology for strategic advantage. Two aspects of e-commerce are business-to-business transactions and business-to-consumer transactions. Most e-commerce takes place over the Internet.

E-commerce and other advances in electronic technology are having a significant impact on organization design. Technology has enabled creation of the network organization structure, in which a company subcontracts most of its major functions to separate companies that are connected electronically to the headquarters organization. The structure allows an organization to arrange resources to meet changing needs and best serve customers. Even organizations that do not use a network structure are rapidly evolving toward greater interorganizational collaboration. Specific implications of advances in technology for organization design include smaller organizations, decentralized organization structures, improved internal and external coordination, additional professional staff, and greater employee participation.

Information technology is a driving force behind the recent trend toward knowledge management. Organizations look for ways to leverage both explicit knowledge and tacit knowledge. Mechanisms such as data warehousing and data mining, knowledge mapping, and electronic libraries are useful for explicit knowledge management. For tacit knowledge management, organizations use mechanisms such as dialogue, learning histories and storytelling, and communities of practice. Intranets are important for supporting the sharing of both explicit and tacit knowledge. The key to leveraging knowledge is changing organizational culture to encourage people to share rather than hoard knowledge.

BRIEFCASE

As an organization manager, keep these guidelines in mind:

1. Use information technology as a strategic weapon. Improve internal coordination, integration, and information sharing with intranets, networks, and enterprise resource planning systems. Strengthen relationships with suppliers, customers, and other organizations with the use of extranets, interorganizational linkages, and e-commerce.
2. Use technology to achieve differentiation or low-cost leadership by becoming more efficient, locking in customers and suppliers, or developing new products. Become involved in e-commerce and use the power of the Internet to support a low-cost or differentiation strategy.

3. Consider a network organization structure to give the organization greater flexibility and rapid response in a volatile environment. Use electronic technology to strengthen coordination and collaboration with other organizations and with customers.

4. With greater use of information technology, allow for decentralized structures, improved coordination, more professional staff, and greater employee participation.

5. Leverage professional knowledge and expertise by developing mechanisms for both explicit and tacit knowledge management. Use mechanisms such as data warehousing and data mining, knowledge mapping, and electronic libraries for explicit knowledge management. Use dialogue, learning histories and story-telling, and communities of practice to support tacit knowledge management.

KEY CONCEPTS

communities of practice	extranet
data	information
data mining	information reporting system
data warehousing	Internet
decision support system	intranet
dialogue	knowledge
e-commerce	learning histories
electronic data interchange	management information system
electronic libraries	networking
enterprise resource planning	network organization structure
executive information system	tacit knowledge
explicit knowledge	transaction processing

DISCUSSION QUESTIONS

1. Do you think technology will eventually enable top managers to do their job with little face-to-face communication? Discuss.

2. Why might a company consider using an intranet rather than traditional management and executive information systems?

3. How might an enterprise resource planning system be used to improve strategic management of a manufacturing organization?

4. Discuss some ways in which a video rental store might use information technology to support a differentiation strategy.

5. Have you made a purchase via the Internet? What forms of business-to-consumer transactions do you think will be replaced by e-commerce? Discuss.

6. How does the network organization structure enable an organization to respond rapidly in a volatile environment? What might be some disadvantages to this type of structure?

7. How might the adoption of information technology affect how an organization is designed?

8. Describe your use of explicit knowledge when you research and write a term paper. Do you also use tacit knowledge regarding this activity? Discuss.

9. Why is knowledge management particularly important to a company that wants to become a learning organization?

10. Do you think the idea of developing communities of practice is realistic for most organizations? In what type of organization do you think it would be most applicable? Least applicable? Discuss.

DOES YOUR BUSINESS HAVE WHAT IT TAKES TO MOVE AT INTERNET SPEED?

What is an Internet year? It's the time in which an e-company needs to accomplish the kind of business goals that once took a year. Conventional wisdom puts an Internet year anywhere from 60 to 90 days. Regardless, few will argue that companies need to move faster now than ever imagined.

Can you afford the luxury of in-depth analysis, full due diligence, building consensus, test marketing—all the cornerstones of responsible corporate management? Does their value change when you weigh it against the cost to your company's scarcest commodity—time? Kelsey Biggers, executive vice president of Micro Modeling Associates (MMA), offers the following scenarios to help determine whether you are capable of operating at Internet speed. Choose the best course of action from the choices given (answers below):

1. You have met a company that can be a potential strategic partner for marketing your service to a new industry online. The vibes are good, and you want to map out the potential relationship, but to do so you need to share client and billing information. A nondisclosure agreement is necessary, and the company hands you its standard agreement. What do you do?

   a. Get a copy of your company's standard nondisclosure agreement and submit it to your potential partner as an alternative to their NDA.

   b. Fax the agreement to your lawyer and ask her to get back to you ASAP with any amendments so you can continue the conversation.

   c. Look over the agreement and sign it right away.

2. You're looking for a creative director for your Web site, and you know the position will be critical to your whole look and feel online. You hope to have three or four excellent candidates to choose from and have considered doing a retained search for the position. Out of nowhere your old college roommate, whom you respect enormously, refers you to an associate for the position. You meet the candidate for breakfast and you are blown away by the person's credentials and personality. You have three choices:

   a. Offer the candidate the job before the check arrives.

   b. Give the candidate a strong "warm and fuzzy" about the job while you initiate a quick search for a couple of alternate candidates.

   c. Schedule a round of interviews with your senior colleagues back in the office to confirm your positive instincts, while also identifying one or two alternative candidates for comparison.

3. Your online strategy calls for targeting two vertical markets for your service in the next nine months. Your service can be tailored to meet the buying needs of companies in several industries, so it's a matter of picking the right industries to target. High-growth, dynamic industries are obviously preferred. Which approach would you select?

   a. Hire an MBA with finance and marketing to create high-level screening criteria for target industries and identify the five best fits for your services.

   b. Hire your neighbor, who happens to be a doctor and knows the healthcare industry and can make several introductions into HMOs and pharmaceutical companies.

   c. Ask an intern to research publicly available information from Gartner Group, Forrester Research, and other industry analyst organizations for online spending habits in different industries and make recommendations.

4. Your company has been looking to merge with a strategic partner for some time. You have identified three companies that would be good fits, but each has its advantages and disadvantages. Which would you choose:

   a. Company A offers a service that is perfectly complementary to your own, and the price is right. However, the company has indicated that it doesn't think it has enough scale to do a merger now and would rather wait nine months until after the holiday selling season to complete the transaction.

   b. Company B is smaller and dynamic, but has grown too fast and has a bad balance sheet.

They could be picked up immediately, but your company would have to assume some unwanted debt along with the merger.

c. Company C has a great off-line presence in its space, but has not yet executed its e-commerce plan. The two companies might be a great fit once Company C had established its online presence by midsummer.

5. Your e-commerce strategy requires a real-time fulfillment system that can process orders straight through and provide data on client-buying patterns. You have looked outside your firm for technology support to help bring this capability online and have been presented with three alternatives:

a. A senior programmer from your prior firm is now a freelance consultant. He can get started immediately and hire a dozen coders who promise to get a capability up and running in sixty days and grow out the functionality.

b. Your internal technology group can staff a team of a dozen people to build out the system in a year and will then have the ability to support and grow the service when it goes live.

c. An e-solutions consultancy can project manage and build the entire system, but would want to take sixty days to design the technical architecture before starting development. They insist this time is necessary to ensure a scalable service.

ANSWERS: (Each correct answer is worth one point)

Question 1
c. The objective is to make a decision quickly and to move the process forward without a great deal of red tape and delay. The legal process can oftentimes slow decision-making—whether by three

weeks or three months—and time is of the essence in the online world. Moreover, when was the last time an NDA about client information materially affected your business? Better to spend your time building trust than protecting against an unlikely downside.

Question 2
a. Give the candidate a job while waiting for the check. If he has been vouched for by someone you trust and you love his work, grab him while he's available and put him to work. If you think he's a great hire, chances are so will your competitors.

Question 3
b. Hire your neighbor. Any list of dynamic industries you put together is bound to include health care, and your biggest challenge is to find a credible person with industry know-how and contacts who can take you into the industry. Your neighbor can do that. Now start looking for the other industries you want to focus on.

Question 4
b. Buy Company B. Company B has proven itself fast moving and dynamic, and their balance sheet issues make them open to a favorable price. Companies A and C are both tying their success to future events—a strong holiday selling season or a successful online launch—either of which may not happen and are in the distant Internet future.

Question 5
c. The one area a company cannot afford to get wrong is its technical architecture. It must scale and be reliable, or your whole business will be at risk. Programmers without a blueprint cannot ensure a successful online environment, and staffing internally is time consuming and uncertain. Better to outsource the project immediately while building an internal team to take it over after its launch.

Case for Analysis   *Century Medical* *

Sam Nolan clicked the mouse for one more round of solitaire on the computer in his den. He'd been at it for more than an hour, and his wife had long ago given up trying to persuade him to join her for a movie or a rare Saturday night on the town. The mind-numbing game seemed to be all that calmed

Sam down enough to stop thinking about work and how his job seemed to get worse every day.

* Based on Carol Hildebrand, "New Boss Blues," *CIO Enterprise*, Section 2 (15 November 1998): 53–58; and Megan Santosus, "Advanced Micro Devices' Web-Based Purchasing System," *CIO*, Section 1 (15 May 1998): 84.

Nolan was chief information officer at Century Medical, a large medical products company based in Connecticut. He had joined the company four years ago, and since that time Century had made great progress integrating technology into its systems and processes. Nolan had already led projects to design and build two highly successful systems for Century. One was a benefits-administration system for the company's human resources department. The other was a complex Web-based purchasing system that streamlined the process of purchasing supplies and capital goods. Although the system had been up and running for only a few months, modest projections were that it would save Century nearly $2 million annually. Previously, Century's purchasing managers were bogged down with shuffling and processing paper. The purchasing process would begin when an employee filled out a materials request form. Then the form would travel through various offices for approval and signatures before eventually being converted into a purchase order. The new Web-based system allowed employees to fill out electronic request forms that were automatically e-mailed to everyone whose approval was needed. The time for processing request forms was cut from weeks to days or even hours. When authorization was complete, the system would automatically launch a purchase order to the appropriate supplier. In addition, because the new system had dramatically cut the time purchasing managers spent shuffling paper, they now had more time to work collaboratively with key stakeholders to identify and select the best suppliers and negotiate better deals.

Nolan thought wearily of all the hours he had put in developing trust with people throughout the company and showing them how technology could not only save time and money but also support team-based work and give people more control over their own jobs. He smiled briefly as he recalled one long-term HR employee, 61-year-old Ethel Moore. She had been terrified when Nolan first began showing her the company's intranet, but she was now one of his biggest supporters. In fact, it had been Ethel who had first approached him with an idea about a Web-based job posting system. The two had pulled together a team and developed an idea for linking Century managers, internal recruiters, and job applicants using artificial intelligence software on top of an integrated Web-based system. When Nolan had presented the idea to his boss, executive vice-president Sandra Ivey, she had enthusiastically endorsed it, and within a few weeks the team had authorization to proceed with the project.

But everything began to change when Ivey resigned her position six months later to take a plum job in New York. Ivey's successor, Tom Carr, seemed to have little interest in the project. During their first meeting, Carr had openly referred to the project as a waste of time and money. He immediately disapproved several new features suggested by the company's internal recruiters, even though the project team argued that the features could double internal hiring and save millions in training costs. "Just stick to the original plan and get it done. All this stuff needs to be handled on a personal basis anyway," Carr countered. "You can't learn more from a computer than you can talking to real people—and as for internal recruiting, it shouldn't be so hard to talk to people if they're already working right here in the company." Carr seemed to have no understanding of how and why technology was being used. He became irritated when Ethel Moore referred to the system as "Web-based." He boasted that he had never visited Century's intranet site and suggested that "this Internet fad" would blow over in a year or so anyway. Even Ethel's enthusiasm couldn't get through to him. She tried to show him some of the HR resources available on the intranet and explain how it had benefited the department and the company, but he waved her away. "Technology is for those people in the IS department. My job is people, and yours should be too." Ethel was crushed, and Nolan realized it would be like beating his head against a brick wall to try to persuade Carr to the team's point of view. Near the end of the meeting, Carr even jokingly suggested that the project team should just buy a couple of filing cabinets and save everyone some time and money.

Just when the team thought things couldn't get any worse, Carr dropped the other bomb. They would no longer be allowed to gather input from users of the new system. Nolan feared that without the input of potential users, the system wouldn't meet their needs, or even that users would boycott the system because they hadn't been allowed to participate. No doubt that would put a great big "I told you so" smile right on Carr's face.

Nolan sighed and leaned back in his chair. The project had begun to feel like a joke. The vibrant and innovative human resources department his team had imagined now seemed like nothing more than a pipe dream. But despite his frustration, a new thought entered Nolan's mind: "Is Carr just stubborn and narrow-minded or does he have a point that HR is a people business that doesn't need a high-tech job posting system?"

Case for Analysis   *Product X* *

Several years ago the top management of a multibillion-dollar corporation decided that Product X was a failure and should be disbanded. The losses involved exceeded $100 million. At least five people knew that Product X was a failure six years before the decision was taken to stop producing it. Three of those people were plant managers who lived daily with the production problems. The other two were marketing officials who realized that the manufacturing problems were not solvable without expenditures that would raise the price of the product to the point where it would no longer be competitive in the market.

There are several reasons why this information did not get to the top sooner. At first, the subordinates believed that with exceptionally hard work they might turn the errors into successes. But the more they struggled, the more they realized the massiveness of the original error. The next task was to communicate the bad news upward so that it would be heard. They knew that in their company bad news would not be well received at the upper levels if it was not accompanied with suggestions for positive action. They also knew that the top management was enthusiastically describing Product X as a new leader in its field. Therefore, they spent much time composing memos that would communicate the realities without shocking top management.

Middle management read the memos and found them too open and forthright. Since they had done the production and marketing studies that resulted in the decision to produce X, the memos from the lower-level management questioned the validity of their analysis. They wanted time to really check these gloomy predictions and, if they were accurate, to design alternative corrective strategies. If the pessimistic information was to be sent upward, middle management wanted it accompanied with optimistic action alternatives. Hence further delay.

Once middle management was convinced that the gloomy predictions were valid, they began to release some of the bad news to the top—but in carefully measured doses. They managed the releases carefully to make certain they were covered if top management became upset. The tactic they used was to cut the memos drastically and summarize the findings. They argued that the cuts were necessary because top management was always complaining about receiving long memos; indeed, some top executives had let it be known that good memos were memos of one page or less. The result was that top management received fragmented information underplaying the intensity of the problem (not the problem itself) and overplaying the degree to which middle management and the technicians were in control of the problem.

Top management therefore continued to speak glowingly about the product, partially to assure that it would get the financial backing it needed from within the company. Lower-level management became confused and eventually depressed because they could not understand this continued top management support, nor why studies were ordered to evaluate the production and marketing difficulties that they had already identified. Their reaction was to reduce the frequency of their memos and the intensity of their alarm, while simultaneously turning over the responsibility for dealing with the problem to middle-management people. When local plant managers, in turn, were asked by their foremen and employees what was happening, the only response they gave was that the company was studying the situation and continuing its support. This information bewildered the foremen and led them to reduce their own concern.

* Excerpted from C. Argyris and D. Schon, *Organizational Learning: A Theory of Action Perspective.* Argyris/Schon, *Organizational Learning,* © 1978, Addison-Wesley Publishing Co., Inc., Reading, Massachusetts. Pages 1–2. Reprinted with permission. Case appeared in Gareth Morgan, *Creative Organization Theory* (1989), Sage Publications.

NOTES

1. Marcia Stepanek, "How an Intranet Opened Up the Door to Profits," *Business Week E.Biz,* 26 July 26, 1999, EB32–EB38.
2. Stepanek, "How an Intranet Opened Up the Door to Profits." Case based on Stepanek, "How an Intranet Opened," and Bill Richards, "A Total Overhaul," *The Wall Street Journal,* 7 December 1998, R30.
3. Robert D. Hof with Gary McWilliams and Gabrielle Saveri, "The 'Click Here' Economy," *Business Week,* 22 June 1998, 122–28.

4. Charles V. Callahan and Bruce R. Pasternack, "Corporate Strategy in the Digital Age," *Strategy & Business*, Issue 15 (Second Quarter 1999): 10–14.

5. Ibid.

6. Richards, "A Total Overhaul."

7. David Pearson, "Marketing for Survival," *CIO* (15 April 1998): 44–48.

8. Megan Santosus, "Motorola's Semiconductor Products Sector's EIS," (Working Smart column), *CIO*, Section 1, (15 November 1998): 84.

9. Christopher Palmeri, "Believe in Yourself, Believe in the Merchandise," *Continental,* (December 1997): 49–51.

10. Wayne Kawamoto, "Click Here for Efficiency," *Business Week Enterprise,* 7 December 1998, Ent. 12–Ent 14.

11. Mary J. Cronin, "Ford's Intranet Success," *Fortune,* 30 March 1998, 158; and Eryn Brown, "9 Ways to Win on the Web," *Fortune,* 24 May 1999, 112-25.

12. Derek Slater, "What is ERP?" *CIO Enterprise,* Section 2, (15 May 1999): 86; and Jeffrey Zygmont, "The Ties That Bind," *Inc. Tech* (1998): No. 3, 70–84.

13. Nancy Ferris, "ERP: Sizzling or Stumbling?" *Government Executive,* (July 1999) 99–102.

14. Scott Buckhout, Edward Frey, and Joseph Nemec Jr., "Making ERP Succeed: Turning Fear into Promise," *Strategy & Business,* Issue 15 (Second Quarter 1999): 60–72.

15. Zygmont, "The Ties That Bind."

16. Andy Raskin, "The ROIght Stuff," *CIO Web Business,* Section 2 (1 February 1999): 49–54.

17. Peter Burrows, "Job Shops Take Center Stage," *Business Week,* 21 June 1999, 124–28.

18. Raymond E. Miles and Charles C. Snow, "Organizations: New Concepts for New Forms," *California Management Review* 28 (Spring 1986): 62–73; Gianni Lorenzoni and Charles Baden-Fuller, "Creating a Strategic Center to Manage a Web of Partners," *California Management Review* 37, No. 3 (Spring 1995): 146–63; and Gregory G. Dess, Abdul M. A. Rasheed, Kevin J. McLaughlin, and Richard L. Priem, "The New Corporate Architecture," *Academy of Management Executive* 9, No. 3 (1995): 7–20.

19. Derek Slater, "What Is E-Commerce?" *CIO Enterprise,* Section 2, (15 June 1999): 82.

20. Todd Datz, "How to Speak Geek," *CIO Enterprise,* Section 2, (15 April 1999): 46–52.

21. Steve Molloy and Charles R. Schwenk, "The Effects of Information Technology on Strategic Decision Making," *Journal of Management Studies* 32:3 (May 1995): 283–311; Dorothy E. Leidner and Joyce J. Elam, "The Impact of Executive Information Systems on Organizational Design, Intelligence, and Decision Making," *Organization Science* 6, no. 6 (November–December 1995): 645–64.

22. Matt Villano, "A Lead-Pipe Cinch," *CIO,* Section 1, (15 March 1999): 51–59.

23. Renae Broderick and John W. Boudreau, "Human Resource Management, Information Technology and the Competitive Edge," *Academy of Management Executive* 6, no. 2 (1992): 7–17.

24. Mark C. S. Lee and Dennis A. Adams, "A Manager's Guide to the Strategic Potential of Information Systems," *Information and Management* (1990): 169–82; David W. L. Wightman, "Competitive Advantage through Information Technology," *Journal of General Management* 12 (Summer 1987): 36–45.

25. Art Jahnke, "Power Play," *CIO Web Business,* Section 2, (1 July 1998): 23–42.

26. Bill Saporito, "What Sam Walton Taught America," *Fortune,* 4 May 1992, 104–05.

27. Michael H. Martin, "Smart Managing: Best Practices, Careers, and Ideas," *Fortune,* 2 February 1998, 149–51.

28. Mary J. Cronin, "Intranets Reach the Factory Floor," *Fortune,* 18 August 1997, 208.

29. Myron Magnet, "Who's Winning the Information Revolution," *Fortune,* 30 November 1992, 110–17; Jeremy Main, "Computers of the World, Unite!" *Fortune,* 24 September 1990, 114–22.

30. Eryn Brown, "9 Ways to Win on the Web."

31. Ibid.

32. Peter Fabris, "Save $71 on Your Next New Car," *CIO Web Business,* Section 2 (1 December 1998): 18.

33. Robert I. Benjamin, John F. Rockart, Michael S. Scott Morton, and John Wyman, "Information Technology: A Strategic Opportunity," *Sloan Management Review* 25 (Spring 1984): 3–10.

34. Carl Shapiro and Hal R. Varian, "Lock 'Em Up," *CIO,* Section 1 (15 December 1998): 72–76.

35. John W. Verity, "Taking a Laptop on a Call," *Business Week*, 25 October 1993, 124–25.

36. Lauren Gibbons Paul, "Pretty Slick," *CIO Enterprise,* Section 2 (15 May 1999): 72–77.

37. Gary McWilliams, "Taming the Info Monster," *Business Week,* 22 June 1998, 170–72.
38. Sari Kalin, "Sneaker Net," *CIO Web Business,* Section 2 (1 August 1999): 29–35.
39. George Donnelly, "New Attitude," *CFO* (June 1999): 42–54.
40. Bill Gates with Collins Hemingway, *Business @ the Speed of Thought; Using a Digital Nervous System* (New York: Warner Books, 1999): 100.
41. Gary McWilliams, "Whirlwind on the Web," *Business Week,* 7 April 1997, 132–36; and David Kirkpatrick, "Now Everybody in PCs Wants to Be Like Mike," *Fortune,* 8 September 1997, 91–92.
42. "E-commerce: You're Closer Than You Think," special informational advertisement by Microsoft Corporation, *Fortune,* 8 November 1999.
43. Gates with Hemingway, *Business @ the Speed of Thought.*
44. Sari Kalin, "Whoever Sells the Most Toys Wins," *CIO Web Business,* Section 2 (1 December 1998): 41–46; Eryn Brown, "9 Ways to Win on the Web," *Fortune,* 24 May 1999, 112–25; Heather Green, "A Site of One's Own," *Business Week,* 20 July 1998, 62.
45. Gates with Hemingway, *Business @ the Speed of Thought,* 92, 102-06.
46. "10 Companies That Get It," *Fortune,* 8 November 1999, 115–17.
47. Eryn Brown, "Big Business Meets the e-World," *Fortune,* 8 November 1999, 88–98.
48. Stephen Baker, "Invasion of the E-Vikings," *Business Week E-Biz,* 26 July 1999, 52–57.
49. Beverly Geber, "Virtual Teams," *Training* (April 1995): 36–40.
50. Raymond E. Miles and Charles C. Snow, "The New Network Firm: A Spherical Structure Built on a Human Investment Philosophy," *Organizational Dynamics* (Spring 1995): 5–18; and Raymond E. Miles, Charles C. Snow, John A. Matthews, Grant Miles, and Henry J. Coleman, Jr., "Organizing in the Knowledge Age: Anticipating the Cellular Form," *Academy of Management Executive* 11, No. 4 (1997): 7–24.
51. Heath Row, "This 'Virtual' Company is for Real," *Fast Company* (December-January 1998): 48–50; and Evan Ramstad, "A PC Maker's Low-Tech Formula: Start with the Box," *The Wall Street Journal,* 29 December 1997, B1, B8.
52. John Case, "The Age of the Specialist," *Inc.,* August 1995, 15–16.
53. Miles and Snow, "The New Network Firm," and Gregory G. Dess, Abdul M. A. Rasheed, Kevin J. McLaughlin, and Richard L. Priem, "The New Corporate Architecture," *Academy of Management Executive* 9, No. 2 (1995): 7–20.
54. Dale Kutnick, "The Externalization Imperative," *CIO,* 15 December 1998–1 January 1999, 120-24.
55. Burrows, "Job Shops Take Center Stage."
56. Gary Hamel and Jeff Sampler, "The e-Corporation," *Fortune,* 7 December 1998, 80–92.
57. Herbert G. McCann, "Allstate Announced Plan to Cut 4,000 Jobs," *Johnson City Press,* 11 November 1999, 8.
58. Siobhan O'Mahony and Stephen R. Barley, "Do Digital Telecommunications Affect Work and Organization? The State of Our Knowledge," *Research in Organizational Behavior* 21 (1999): 125–61.
59. Sari Kalin, "Overdrive," *CIO Web Business,* Section 2, 1 July 1999, 36–40.
60. O'Mahoney and Barley, "Do Digital Telecommunications Affect Work and Organization?"
61. James B. Treece, "Breaking the Chains of Command," *Business Week/The Information Revolution,* 112-114.
62. See Peter Drucker, *Post-Capitalist Society,* (Oxford: Butterworth Heinemann, 1993), 5.
63. David A. Garvin, "Building a Learning Organization," in *Harvard Business Review on Knowledge Management* (Boston, Mass.: President and Fellows of Harvard College, 1998), 47–80.
64. Based on Andrew Mayo, "Memory Bankers," *People Management* (22 January 22, 1998): 34–38; William Miller, "Building the Ultimate Resource," *Management Review* (January 1999): 42–45; and Todd Datz, "How to Speak Geek," *CIO Enterprise,* Section 2, (15 April 1999): 46–52.
65. Louisa Wah, "Behind the Buzz," *Management Review* (April 1999): 17–26.
66. Richard McDermott, "Why Information Technology Inspired But Cannot Deliver Knowledge Management," *California Management Review* 41, No. 4 (Summer 1999): 103–17.
67. Based on Ikujiro Nonaka and Hirotaka Takeuchi, *The Knowledge-Creating Company: How Japanese Companies Create the Dynamics of Innovation* (New York: Oxford University Press, 1995): 8-9; and Robert M. Grant, "Toward a Knowledge-Based Theory of the Firm," *Strategic Management Journal* 17 (Winter 1996): 109–22.

68. Grant, "Toward a Knowledge-Based Theory of the Firm."

69. C. Jackson Grayson Jr. and Carla S. O'Dell, "Mining Your Hidden Resources," *Across the Board* (April 1998): 23–28.

70. Morten T. Hansen, Nitin Nohria, and Thomas Tierney, "What's Your Strategy for Managing Knowledge?" *Harvard Business Review* (March-April 1999): 106–16.

71. Andrew Mayo, "Memory Bankers," *People Management* (22 January 1998): 34–38; and Gary Abramson, "On the KM Midway," *CIO Enterprise,* Section 2 (15 May 1999): 63–70.

72. Mayo, "Memory Bankers."

73. Based on Morten T. Hansen, Nitin Nohria, and Thomas Tierney, "What's Your Strategy for Managing Knowledge?" *Harvard Business Review* (March–April 1999): 106–16.

74. Eric Ransdell, "Building the New Economy," *Fast Company* (December 1998): 222–36.

75. Jennifer Bresnahan, "Improving the Odds," *CIO Enterprise,* Section 2, 15 November 1998, 36-48; Hansen, Nohria, and Tierney, "What's Your Strategy for Knowledge Management?"

76. Verna Allee, *The Knowledge Evolution* (Oxford: Butterworth-Heinemann, 1997), 216–17.

77. Louisa Wah, "Making Knowledge Stick."

78. Jenny C. McCune, "Thirst for Knowledge," *Management Review* (April 1999): 10–12.

79. Andrew Mayo, "Memory Bankers."

80. Gary McWilliams with Marcia Stepanek, "Taming the Info Monster," *Business Week,* 22 June 1998, 170–72.

81. Gary Abramson, "All Along the Watchtower," *CIO Enterprise,* Section 2, 15 July 1999, 24–34.

82. Hansen, Nohria, and Tierney, "What's Your Strategy for Managing Knowledge?"; Louisa Wah, "Behind the Buzz," *Management Review* (April 1999): 17–26; and Jenny C. McCune, "Thirst for Knowledge," *Management Review,* (April 1999): 10–12.

83. The discussion of dialogue is based on Edgar Schein, "On Dialogue, Culture, and Organization Learning," *Organizational Dynamics* (Autumn 1993): 46; and Glenna Gerard and Linda Teurfs, "Dialogue and Organizational Transformation," in *Community Building: Renewing Spirit and Learning in Business,* Kazimierz Gozdz, ed., (New Leaders Press, 1995).

84. Louisa Wah, "Behind the Buzz"; and Louisa Wah, "Making Knowledge Stick."

85. The discussion of learning histories is based on Art Kleiner and George Roth, "How to Make Experience Your Company's Best Teacher," in *Harvard Business Review on Knowledge Management,* (Boston, Mass.: President and Fellows of Harvard College, 1998), 137–51.

86. Thomas A. Stewart, "Telling Tales at BP Amoco, *Fortune,* 7 June 1999, 220–22.

87. Verna Allee, *The Knowledge Evolution,* 218–19; and Thomas A. Stewart, *Intellectual Capital* (New York: Bantam Books, 1998), 96–100.

88. Stewart, *Intellectual Capital,* 97.

89. Thomas A. Stewart, "Brain Power: Who Owns It . . . How They Profit From It," *Fortune,* 17 March 1997, 105–10.

90. Grayson and O'Dell, "Mining Your Hidden Resources."

91. Richard McDermott, "Why Information Technology Inspired But Cannot Deliver Knowledge Management," *California Management Review* 41, No. 4 (Summer 1999): 103–17.

Internal Design Elements

Organization Size, Life Cycle, and Control

CHAPTER 8

hen Stephen Wiggins founded Oxford Health Plans Inc., he inspired his employees with the vision that Oxford was reinventing health care. The new HMO rapidly became an industry pacesetter by offering top-notch doctors, renowned hospitals, and reasonable rates. Within a few years, Oxford began to move beyond its core clientele of high-end customers into new markets, such as primary care clinics in poor neighborhoods, state Medicaid programs, and a network of alternative medicine practitioners. In addition, the company pushed aggressively to sign up Medicare recipients.

The strategies for growth worked: Within a five-year period, Oxford's membership grew almost tenfold, to 2.1 million people, pushing revenues to more than $4 billion and the company's payroll to over 7,000 employees. However, as Oxford grew larger and revenues and share prices soared, trouble was brewing beneath the surface. By the fall of 1998, New York state regulators were describing Oxford as a company spiraling out of control: its financial reports were untrustworthy, its reserves against future claims were inadequate, and internal financial controls were seriously deficient. Oxford's stock plunged more than 62 percent in one day. But the worst was yet to come, and Oxford reported a fourth-quarter loss of almost $285 million—wiping out all the earnings it had ever reported in seven years as a public company.

Although Oxford was very successful and grew rapidly, managers had failed to implement the controls necessary to keep the company on track and financially sound as it grew larger and more complex. Staff members negotiated contracts with doctors and employers on the fly, according to one manager, making things up as they went along. On the one hand, this flexibility was a strength—Oxford essentially customized rates and benefits for dozens of different clients and providers. However, it also made it much more difficult for managers to keep track of medical costs and premiums. In addition, the company's computer system, designed in-house, was woefully inadequate. The system for paying claims broke down, leading to a slew of late-payment complaints from doctors and hospitals. At the same time, due to computer glitches, monthly bills weren't sent to thousands of accounts. Costs in some programs were out of control. For example, while Oxford's Medicare revenue per person rose 4.3 percent one year, the company's cost of actually caring for those clients increased 21 percent, yet no one at Oxford even knew it.

As Oxford's membership and revenues steadily declined, the organization was ripe for takeover by a more stable managed care company.[1]

Most entrepreneurs, like Stephen Wiggins, want their organizations to grow. However, as a company grows larger and more complex, managers have to develop systems and procedures that can help them guide and control the organization. Today's organizations—large and small—are looking for ways to be flexible and responsive in a rapidly changing marketplace. Yet, as in the case of Oxford Health Plans, flexibility without adequate control can lead to disaster. One reason Wiggins failed to set up proper controls was that he feared the company would become "bureaucratic," which he associated with red tape, inefficiency, and inflexibility.

Although bureaucracy has been accused of many sins, including inefficiency, rigidity, and demeaning, routinized work that alienates both employees and customers, bureaucratic characteristics also bring many positive effects. Over the past thirty years, bureaucracy has been a major topic of study in organization theory.[2] Today, most large organizations have bureaucratic characteristics. These organizations provide us with abundant goods and services and surprise us with astonishing feats that are testimony to their effectiveness.

PURPOSE OF THIS CHAPTER

In this chapter, we will explore the question of large versus small organization and how size is related to structure and control. Organization size is a contextual variable that influences organizational design and functioning just as do the contextual variables—technology, environment, goals—discussed in previous chapters. In the first section, we will look at the advantages of large versus small size. Then, we will examine the historical need for bureaucracy as a means to control large organizations and how managers today attack bureaucracy in some large organizations. Next, we will explore what is called an organization's life cycle and the structural characteristics at each stage. Finally, we will examine mechanisms for organizational control and how managers determine the best means for controlling the organization. By the end of this chapter, you should understand the nature of bureaucracy and its strengths and weaknesses. You should be able to recognize when bureaucratic control can make an organization effective, as well as when other types of control are more appropriate. The chapter will also introduce the balanced scorecard approach, which managers use to integrate various control approaches.

ORGANIZATION SIZE: IS BIGGER BETTER?

The question of big versus small begins with the notion of growth and the reasons so many organizations feel the need to grow large.

PRESSURES FOR GROWTH

In the early 1990s, America's management guru, Peter Drucker, declared that "the *Fortune* 500 is over"; yet the dream of practically every businessperson is still to have his or her company become a member of the *Fortune* 500 list—to grow fast and to grow large.[3] Sometimes this goal is more urgent than to make the best products or show the greatest profits. Some observers believe the United States is entering a new era of "bigness," as companies strive to acquire the size and resources to compete on a global scale, to invest in new technology and to control distribution channels and guarantee access to markets. For example, more than $1.6 trillion in mergers took place worldwide in 1997 alone, with over half of that activity in the United States.[4]

There are other pressures for organizations to grow. Many executives have found that firms must grow to stay economically healthy. To stop growing is to stagnate. To be stable means that customers may not have their demands met fully or that competitors will increase market share at the expense of your company. Scale is crucial to economic health in marketing-intensive companies such as Coca-Cola and Anheuser-Busch. Greater size gives these companies power in the marketplace and thus increased revenues.[5] In addition, growing organizations are vibrant, exciting places to work, which enables these companies to attract and keep quality employees. When the number of employees is expanding, the company can offer many challenges and opportunities for advancement.

LARGE VERSUS SMALL

Organizations feel compelled to grow, but how much and how large? What size organization is better poised to compete in a global environment? The arguments are summarized in Exhibit 8.1.

Large. Huge resources and economies of scale are needed for many organizations to compete globally. Only large organizations can build a massive pipeline in Alaska. Only a large corporation like Boeing can afford to build a 747, and only a large American Airlines can buy it. Only a large Johnson & Johnson can invest hundreds of millions in new products such as bifocal contact lenses and a birth control patch that delivers contraceptives through the skin.

Large companies also are standardized, often mechanistically run, and complex. The complexity offers hundreds of functional specialties within the organization to perform complex tasks and to produce complex products. Moreover, large organizations, once established, can be a presence that stabilizes a market for years. Managers can join the company and expect a career reminiscent of the "organization men" of the 1950s and 1960s. The organization can provide longevity, raises, and promotions.

Small. The competing argument says small is beautiful because the crucial requirements for success in a global economy are responsiveness and flexibility in fast-changing markets. While the U.S. economy contains many large organizations, research shows that as global trade has accelerated, smaller organizations

EXHIBIT 8.1   *Differences Between Large and Small Organizations*

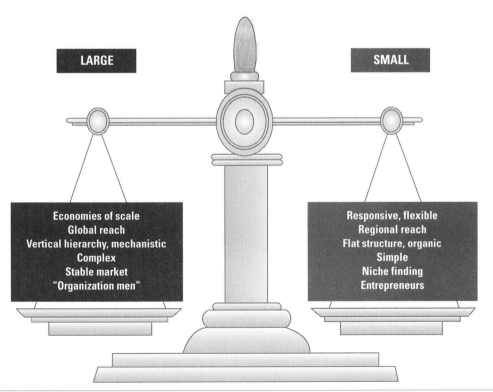

LARGE	SMALL
Economies of scale	Responsive, flexible
Global reach	Regional reach
Vertical hierarchy, mechanistic	Flat structure, organic
Complex	Simple
Stable market	Niche finding
"Organization men"	Entrepreneurs

Source: Based on John A. Byrne, "Is Your Company Too Big?" *Business Week*, 27 March 1989, 84–94.

have become the norm. Since the mid-1960s, most of the then-existing large businesses have lost market share worldwide.[6] Today, fully 96 percent of exporters are small businesses.[7] The economic vitality of the United States, as well as most of the rest of the developed world, is tied to small and mid-sized businesses. Although many large companies have become even larger through merger, they are also less numerous as a result. Countless small businesses have sprung up to fill specialized niches and serve targeted markets.[8] The development of the Internet has provided fertile ground for the growth of small firms. In addition, the rapidly growing service sector, as discussed in Chapter 6, also contributes to a decrease in average organization size, since most service companies remain small to be more responsive to customers.[9]

The percentage of employees working in large organizations continues to decrease. Whereas numerous jobs were wiped out through downsizing at large corporations in the 1980s and 1990s, jobs were springing up in small firms to replace them. Exhibit 8.2 reflects the decrease in the average number of employees per firm for the United States, Germany, and Britain. Small organizations have a flat structure and an organic, free-flowing management style that encourages entrepreneurship and innovation. Today's leading biotechnological drugs, for

EXHIBIT 8.2   *Average Size of Industrial Firms in Three Countries*

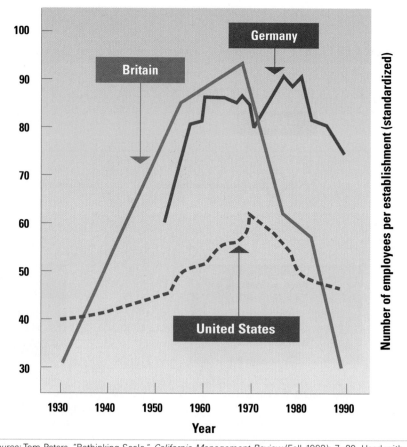

Source: Tom Peters, "Rethinking Scale," *California Management Review* (Fall 1992): 7–29. Used with permission.

example, were all discovered by small firms, such as Chiron, which developed the hepatitis B vaccines, rather than by huge pharmaceutical companies, such as Merck.[10] Moreover, the personal involvement of employees in small firms encourages motivation and commitment because employees personally identify with the company's mission.

Big-Company/Small-Company Hybrid. The paradox is that the advantages of small companies enable them to succeed and, hence, grow large. *Fortune* magazine reported that the fastest growing companies in America are small firms characterized by an emphasis on putting the customer first and being fast and flexible in responding to the environment.[11] Small companies, however, can become victims of their own success as they grow large, shifting to a mechanistic structure emphasizing vertical hierarchies and spawning "organization men" rather than entrepreneurs.

The solution is what Jack Welch, chairman of General Electric, calls the "big-company/small-company hybrid" that combines a large corporation's resources and reach with a small company's simplicity and flexibility. The divisional structure, described in Chapter 3, is one way organizations such as General Electric and Johnson & Johnson attain this. By reorganizing into groups of small companies, these huge corporations capture the mind-set and advantages of smallness. Johnson & Johnson is actually a group of 180 separate companies. When a new product is created in one of J&J's fifty-six labs, a new company is created along with it.[12] When he was CEO of power equipment giant Asea Brown Boveri Ltd. (ABB), Percy Barnevik blasted a 200,000-employee global enterprise into 5,000 units, averaging just forty people each.[13]

Another approach to creating a big company/small company hybrid is called the front/back approach. Rather than dividing the company into separate businesses, each with its own products and customers, the company is divided into units with different *roles*. The "back" part of the organization focuses on creating and producing products and services, while the "front" focuses on integrating and delivering products and services to customers. This approach is becoming increasingly popular among financial services companies such as Merrill Lynch and Fidelity, as well as multiple-product technology firms such as Sun Microsystems.[14]

Full-service, global firms need a strong resource base and sufficient complexity and hierarchy to serve clients around the world. The development of new organization forms, with an emphasis on decentralizing authority and cutting out layers of the hierarchy, combined with the increasing use of information technology described in the previous chapter, is making it easier than ever for companies to be simultaneously large and small, thus capturing the advantages of each. Retail giants Home Depot and Wal-Mart, for example, use the advantage of size in areas such as advertising, purchasing, and raising capital; however, they also give each individual store the autonomy needed to serve customers as if it were a small, hometown shop.[15] Small companies that are growing can also use these ideas to help their organizations retain the flexibility and customer focus that fueled their growth. Howard Schultz, chairman and CEO of Starbucks, refers to achieving "a fragile balance." Starbucks, which grew in a decade from 100 employees to almost 30,000, still allows local managers to experiment without permission from the top. One experimental coffee drink, Frappuccino, was eventually marketed nationwide and generated $100 million in revenue during its first year.[16]

ORGANIZATIONAL LIFE CYCLE

A useful way to think about organizational growth and change is the concept of an organizational **life cycle**,[17] which suggests that organizations are born, grow older, and eventually die. Organization structure, leadership style, and administrative systems follow a fairly predictable pattern through stages in the life cycle. Stages are sequential in nature and follow a natural progression.

STAGES OF LIFE CYCLE DEVELOPMENT

Recent work on organizational life cycle suggests that four major stages characterize organizational development.[18] These stages are illustrated in Exhibit 8.3 along with the problems associated with transition to each stage. Growth is not easy. This chapter's Book Mark offers some advice for how managers can keep their organizations strong and growing through all stages of the life cycle. Each time an organization enters a new stage in the life cycle, it enters a whole new ballgame with a new set of rules for how the organization functions internally and how it relates to the external environment.[19]

EXHIBIT 8.3   *Organizational Life Cycle*

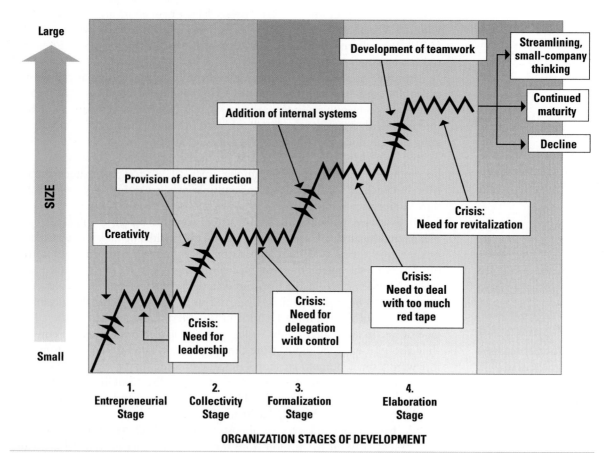

Source: Adapted from Robert E. Quinn and Kim Cameron, "Organizational Life Cycles and Shifting Criteria of Effectiveness: Some Preliminary Evidence," *Management Science* 29 (1983): 33–51; and Larry E. Greiner, "Evolution and Revolution as Organizations Grow," *Harvard Business Review* 50 (July–August 1972): 37–46.

1.   *Entrepreneurial Stage.* When an organization is born, the emphasis is on creating a product and surviving in the marketplace. The founders are entrepreneurs, and they devote their full energies to the technical activities of production and marketing. The organization is informal and nonbureaucratic. The hours of work are long. Control is based on the owners' personal supervision. Growth is from a creative new product or service. Apple Computer was in the **entrepreneurial stage** when it was created by Steve

ℬook ℳark 8.0

Have You Read This Book?

The Alchemy of Growth: Practical Insights for Building the Enduring Enterprise

By Mehrdad Baghai, Stephen Coley, and David White

The authors of *The Alchemy of Growth* have carefully studied the elements that contribute to sustainable corporate growth and present a framework for understanding what works and why. Using well-known examples such as Johnson & Johnson, Frito-Lay, and Gillette as well as lesser-known firms such as CRC of Ireland, Village Roadshow of Australia, and Kyocera of Japan, they begin with the premise that double-digit growth over decades in mature industries can be achieved. Based on extensive research and case studies, they present practical and straightforward advice for how managers can keep their organizations healthy and growing over the long term. The authors, who are all consultants with McKinsey & Co., consider a company's growth potential to be related to three phases, or "horizons."

THE HORIZONS OF GROWTH

Every company, large or small, no matter what industry or stage of the life cycle, needs to simultaneously consider three horizons of growth.

- *Maximizing current business.* Horizon 1 consists of the core businesses of the organization, which often account for the greatest part of revenues and profits. For a company like Gillette, for example, this would be razors such as the Sensor and Mach3. Intel Corp.'s Horizon 1 consists of Pentium microprocessors.
- *Building emerging ideas.* Horizon 2 businesses are emerging growth opportunities. These are in the entrepreneurial phase—budding ventures that are poised for rapid growth but may not be making money when Horizon 1 businesses reach maturity. These businesses need attention and investment to build them up into producing sustained revenue

when Horizon 1 sales flatten. For Intel, this might consist of next-generation multimedia processors.
- *Planting seeds for tomorrow.* Horizon 3 businesses are the most risky and speculative—these ideas may not develop into solid performers for half a decade or even longer. These projects are just now working their way through the R & D lab. For example, at Intel, a $50 million project aimed at the home network market is being developed at the company's Beaverton, Oregon, research center. Many companies become involved in alliances and joint ventures to minimize their risks regarding Horizon 3 businesses.

CAPITALIZING ON OPPORTUNITIES

Companies should work to improve performance across all three horizons in order to achieve sustainable growth. The authors suggest methodical step-wise improvements rather than dramatic and risky leaps. For example, the book describes how Johnson & Johnson built its "skill staircase" in contact lenses by first acquiring a small lens manufacturer (Frontier) in 1981, next acquiring advanced molding technology through a license agreement in 1982, and then outsourcing precision-injection-molding to cut costs tenfold in 1983. Only at that point did the company make a huge dollar investment and finally launched disposable lenses in 1988—seven years after the acquisition of Frontier. By following a growth staircase, the authors say, companies can manage current businesses and keep profits strong while nurturing horizon 2 and 3 businesses for the future.

The Alchemy of Growth, by Mehrdad Baghai, Stephen Coley, and David White, is published by Perseus Books.

Jobs and Stephen Wozniak in Wozniak's parents' garage. Small Internet-based companies such as HomeRuns, Peapod, and ShopLink, which sell groceries online, are currently in the entrepreneurial stage.

Crisis: Need for Leadership. As the organization starts to grow, the larger number of employees causes problems. The creative and technically oriented owners are confronted with management issues, but they may prefer to focus their energies on making and selling the product or inventing new products and services. At this time of crisis, entrepreneurs must either adjust the structure of the organization to accommodate continued growth or else bring in strong managers who can do so. When Apple began a period of rapid growth, A. C. Markkula was brought in as a leader because neither Jobs nor Wozniak was qualified or cared to manage the expanding company.

2. *Collectivity Stage.* If the leadership crisis is resolved, strong leadership is obtained and the organization begins to develop clear goals and direction. Departments are established along with a hierarchy of authority, job assignments, and a beginning division of labor. Employees identify with the mission of the organization and spend long hours helping the organization succeed. Members feel part of a collective, and communication and control are mostly informal although a few formal systems begin to appear. Apple Computer was in the **collectivity stage** during the rapid growth years from 1978 to 1981. Employees threw themselves into the business as the major product line was established and more than two thousand dealers signed on.

Crisis: Need for Delegation. If the new management has been successful, lower-level employees gradually find themselves restricted by the strong top-down leadership. Lower-level managers begin to acquire confidence in their own functional areas and want more discretion. An autonomy crisis occurs when top managers, who were successful because of their strong leadership and vision, do not want to give up responsibility. Top managers want to make sure that all parts of the organization are coordinated and pulling together. The organization needs to find mechanisms to control and coordinate departments without direct supervision from the top.

3. *Formalization Stage.* The **formalization stage** involves the installation and use of rules, procedures, and control systems. Communication is less frequent and more formal. Engineers, human resource specialists, and other staff may be added. Top management becomes concerned with issues such as strategy and planning, and leaves the operations of the firm to middle management. Product groups or other decentralized units may be formed to improve coordination. Incentive systems based on profits may be implemented to ensure that managers work toward what is best for the overall company. When effective, the new coordination and control systems enable the organization to continue growing by establishing linkage mechanisms between top management and field units. Apple Computer was in the formalization stage in the mid-1980s.

Crisis: Too Much Red Tape. At this point in the organization's development, the proliferation of systems and programs may begin to strangle middle-level executives. The organization seems bureaucratized. Middle management may resent the intrusion of staff people. Innovation may be restricted. The organization seems too large and complex to be managed through formal programs. It was at this stage of Apple's growth that Jobs resigned from the company and CEO John Sculley took full control to face his own management challenges.

4. *Elaboration Stage.* The solution to the red tape crisis is a new sense of collaboration and teamwork. Throughout the organization, managers develop skills for confronting problems and working together. Bureaucracy may have reached its limit. Social control and self-discipline reduce the need for additional formal controls. Managers learn to work within the bureaucracy without adding to it. Formal systems may be simplified and replaced by manager teams and task forces. To achieve collaboration, teams are often formed across functions or divisions of the company. The organization may also be split into multiple divisions to maintain a small-company philosophy. Apple Computer is currently in the **elaboration stage** of the life cycle, as are such large companies as Caterpillar and Motorola.

> Crisis: Need for Revitalization. After the organization reaches maturity, it may enter periods of temporary decline.[20] A need for renewal may occur every ten to twenty years. The organization shifts out of alignment with the environment or perhaps becomes slow moving and overbureaucratized and must go through a stage of streamlining and innovation. Top managers are often replaced during this period. At Apple, the top spot has changed hands a number of times as the company struggles to revitalize. CEOs John Sculley, Michael Spindler, and Gilbert Amelio were each ousted by the board as Apple's problems deepened. Now, Stephen Jobs—who had returned to the company as a special advisor to Amelio—is serving as CEO of the company he founded almost 25 years ago. Many believe Jobs has gained the management skills needed to help Apple weather the crisis at this stage and move forward into a new era. He has reorganized the company, weeded out inefficiencies, and refocused Apple on the consumer market. The sleek, jelly-bean colored iMac, one of the hottest computer launches ever, has Apple's sales growing faster than the industry average for the first time in years.[21] However, although Jobs has brought life back to Apple, he also must be able to sustain it. If mature organizations do not go through periodic revitalizations, they will decline, as shown in the last stage of Exhibit 8.3.

Summary. Eighty-four percent of businesses that make it past the first year still fail within five years because they can't make the transition from the entrepreneurial stage.[22] The transitions become even more difficult as organizations progress through future stages of the life cycle. Organizations that do not successfully resolve the problems associated with these transitions are restricted in their growth and may even fail. From within an organization, the life cycle crises are very real, as illustrated by the case of Biogen, a small biotechnology company.

In Practice 8.1   Biogen Inc.

Founded in 1978 by a group of scientists that included two Nobel laureates, Biogen had a vision of remaking and dominating both medicine and industrial chemistry. In the early 1980s, the company raised and consumed vast amounts of capital to conduct cutting-edge scientific research. However, Biogen still had no real products. Its only income was royalties derived from some early discoveries in immune-system proteins called interferons, which had been licensed to Schering Plough Corporation. By 1985, the company was teetering on the edge of disaster, with growing losses and no way to raise more money. Many thought the company's only option was to sell the scientific assets to a larger company.

That's when James L. Vincent was recruited as president and chief executive, to provide clear direction for the organization and help turn brilliant science into products—and profits. Although the founders had hired great scientists, they hadn't paid much attention to the need for good managers. Vincent set about building a strong senior management team and focusing the company on research projects that offered the greatest potential for producing new products. New managers also set up systems and procedures to keep the company on track. Although the transition was difficult for Biogen employees, the strong leadership eventually led to a stronger sense of commitment and community. It also led to Biogen's first drug. Within seven months of its introduction, Avonex, which slows the progression of multiple sclerosis, captured more than 50 percent of its target market and made Biogen the second-largest independent biotech company. Vincent and his management team have helped take Biogen to the formalization stage of the life cycle. Employees are still enjoying their success, but the proliferation of systems and procedures that helped the organization grow to this stage will eventually lead to a new crisis.[23]

ORGANIZATIONAL CHARACTERISTICS DURING THE LIFE CYCLE

As organizations evolve through the four stages of the life cycle, changes take place in structure, control systems, innovation, and goals. The organizational characteristics associated with each stage are summarized in Exhibit 8.4.

Entrepreneurial. Initially, the organization is small, nonbureaucratic, and a one-person show. The top manager provides the structure and control system. Organizational energy is devoted to survival and the production of a single product or service.

EXHIBIT 8.4   *Organization Characteristics During Four Stages of Life Cycle*

Characteristic	1. Entrepreneurial Nonbureaucratic	2. Collectivity Prebureaucratic	3. Formalization Bureaucratic	4. Elaboration Very Bureaucratic
Structure	Informal, one-person show	Mostly informal, some procedures	Formal procedures, division of labor, new specialties added	Teamwork within bureaucracy, small-company thinking
Products or services	Single product or service	Major product or service, with variations	Line of products or services	Multiple product or service lines
Reward and control systems	Personal, paternalistic	Personal, contribution to success	Impersonal, formalized systems	Extensive, tailored to product and department
Innovation	By owner-manager	By employees and managers	By separate innovation group	By institutionalized R & D department
Goal	Survival	Growth	Internal stability, market expansion	Reputation, complete organization
Top management style	Individualistic, entrepreneurial	Charismatic, direction-giving	Delegation with control	Team approach, attack bureaucracy

Source: Adapted from Larry E. Greiner, "Evolution and Revolution as Organizations Grow," *Harvard Business Review* 50 (July–August 1972): 37–46; G. L. Lippitt and W. H. Schmidt, "Crises in a Developing Organization," *Harvard Business Review* 45 (November–December 1967): 102–12; B. R. Scott, "The Industrial State: Old Myths and New Realities," *Harvard Business Review* 51 (March–April 1973): 133–48; Robert E. Quinn and Kim Cameron, "Organizational Life Cycles and Shifting Criteria of Effectiveness," *Management Science* 29 (1983): 33–51.

Collectivity. This is the organization's youth. Growth is rapid, and employees are excited and committed to the organization's mission. The structure is still mostly informal, although some procedures are emerging. Strong charismatic leaders like Scott McNealy of Sun Microsystems or Steve Jobs of Apple provide direction and goals for the organization. Continued growth is a major goal.

Formalization. At this point, the organization is entering midlife. Bureaucratic characteristics emerge. The organization adds staff support groups, formalizes procedures, and establishes a clear hierarchy and division of labor. Innovation may be achieved by establishing a separate research and development department. Major goals are internal stability and market expansion. Top management has to delegate, but it also implements formal control systems.

At Dell Computer, for example, entrepreneurial whiz-kid Michael Dell has hired a cadre of experienced managers to help him develop and implement formal planning, management, and budgeting systems. According to vice chairman Kevin B. Rollins, "Michael realized that he needed professionals to run this company, so that he could continue to be a visionary."[24] At the formalization stage, organizations may also develop complementary products to offer a complete product line.

Elaboration. The mature organization is large and bureaucratic, with extensive control systems, rules, and procedures. Organization managers attempt to develop a team orientation within the bureaucracy to prevent further bureaucratization. Top managers are concerned with establishing a complete organization. Organizational stature and reputation are important. Innovation is institutionalized through an R&D department. Management may attack the bureaucracy and streamline it.

Summary. Growing organizations move through stages of a life cycle, and each stage is associated with specific characteristics of structure, control systems, goals, and innovation. The life cycle phenomenon is a powerful concept used for understanding problems facing organizations and how managers can respond in a positive way to move an organization to the next stage.

ORGANIZATIONAL BUREAUCRACY AND CONTROL

As organizations progress through the life cycle, they usually take on bureaucratic characteristics as they grow larger and more complex. The systematic study of bureaucracy was launched by Max Weber, a sociologist who studied government organizations in Europe and developed a framework of administrative characteristics that would make large organizations rational and efficient.[25] Weber wanted to understand how organizations could be designed to play a positive role in the larger society.

WHAT IS BUREAUCRACY?

Although Weber perceived **bureaucracy** as a threat to basic personal liberties, he also recognized it as the most efficient possible system of organizing. He predicted the triumph of bureaucracy because of its ability to ensure more efficient functioning of organizations in both business and government settings. Weber identified a set of organizational characteristics, listed in Exhibit 8.5, that could be found in successful bureaucratic organizations.

Rules and standard procedures enabled organizational activities to be performed in a predictable, routine manner. Specialized duties meant that each

EXHIBIT 8.5   *Weber's Dimensions of Bureaucracy and Bases of Organizational Authority*

Bureaucracy	Legitimate Bases of Authority
1. Rules and procedures	1. Rational-legal
2. Specialization and division of labor	2. Traditional
3. Hierarchy of authority	3. Charismatic
4. Technically qualified personnel	
5. Separate position and incumbent	
6. Written communications and records	

employee had a clear task to perform. Hierarchy of authority provided a sensible mechanism for supervision and control. Technical competence was the basis by which people were hired rather than friendship, family ties, and favoritism that dramatically reduced work performance. The separation of the position from the position holder meant that individuals did not own or have an inherent right to the job, thus promoting efficiency. Written records provided an organizational memory and continuity over time.

Although bureaucratic characteristics carried to an extreme are widely criticized today, the rational control introduced by Weber was a significant idea and a new form of organization. Bureaucracy provided many advantages over organization forms based upon favoritism, social status, family connections, or graft, which are often unfair. For example, in Mexico, a retired American lawyer had to pay a $500 bribe to purchase a telephone, then discovered that a government official had sold his telephone number to another family. In China, the tradition of giving government posts to relatives is widespread even under communism. China's emerging class of educated people doesn't like seeing the best jobs going to children and relatives of officials.[26] By comparison, the logical and rational form of organization described by Weber allows work to be conducted efficiently and according to established rules.

SIZE AND STRUCTURAL CONTROL

In the field of organization theory, organization size has been described as an important variable that influences structural design and methods of control. Should an organization become more bureaucratic as it grows larger? In what size organizations are bureaucratic characteristics most appropriate? More than one hundred studies have attempted to answer these questions.[27] Most of these studies indicate that large organizations are different from small organizations along several dimensions of bureaucratic structure, including formalization, centralization, and personnel ratios.

Formalization and Centralization. **Formalization**, as described in Chapter 1, refers to rules, procedures, and written documentation, such as policy manuals and job descriptions, that prescribe the rights and duties of employees.[28] The evidence supports the conclusion that large organizations are more formalized. The reason is that large organizations rely on rules, procedures, and paperwork to achieve standardization and control across their large numbers of employees and departments, whereas top managers can use personal observation to control a small organization.[29]

Centralization refers to the level of hierarchy with authority to make decisions. In centralized organizations, decisions tend to be made at the top. In decentralized organizations, similar decisions would be made at a lower level.

Decentralization represents a paradox because, in the perfect bureaucracy, all decisions would be made by the top administrator, who would have perfect control. However, as an organization grows larger and has more people and departments, decisions cannot be passed to the top, or senior managers would be overloaded. Thus, the research on organization size indicates that larger organizations permit greater decentrailization.[30] Hewlett-Packard decentralizes almost every aspect of its business to speed up decision making. In small startup organizations, on the other hand, the founder or top executive is often involved in every decision, large and small.

Personnel Ratios. Another characteristic of bureaucracy is **personnel ratios** for administrative, clerical, and professional support staff. The most frequently studied ratio is the administrative ratio.[31] Two patterns have emerged. The first is that the ratio of top administration to total employees is actually smaller in large organizations,[32] indicating that organizations experience administrative economies as they grow larger. The second pattern concerns clerical and professional support staff ratios.[33] These groups tend to *increase* in proportion to organization size. The clerical ratio increases because of the greater communication and reporting requirements needed as organizations grow larger. The professional staff ratio increases because of the greater need for specialized skills in larger, complex organizations.

Exhibit 8.6 illustrates administrative and support ratios for small and large organizations. As organizations increase in size, the administrative ratio declines and the ratios for other support groups increase.[34] The net effect for direct workers is that they decline as a percentage of total employees. In summary, while top administrators do not make up a disproportionate number of employees in large organizations, the idea that proportionately greater overhead is required in large organizations is supported. Although large organizations reduced overhead during the difficult economic years of the 1980s, recent studies indicate that overhead costs for many American corporations began creeping back up again as revenues soared during the late 1990s.[35] Keeping costs for administrative, clerical, and professional support staff low represents an ongoing challenge for today's large organizations.[36]

BUREAUCRACY IN A CHANGING WORLD

Weber's prediction of the triumph of bureaucracy proved accurate. Bureaucratic characteristics have many advantages and have worked extremely well for many of the needs of the industrial age.[37] By establishing a hierarchy of authority and specific rules and procedures, bureaucracy provided an effective way to bring order to large groups of people and prevent abuses of power. Impersonal relationships based on roles rather than people reduced the favoritism and nepotism characteristic of many preindustrial organizations. Bureaucracy also provided for systematic and rational ways to organize and manage tasks too complex to be understood and handled by a few individuals, thus greatly improving the efficiency and effectiveness of large organizations.

The world is rapidly changing, however, and the machinelike bureaucratic system of the industrial age no longer works so well as organizations face new challenges. With global competition and uncertain environments, many organizations

EXHIBIT 8.6   *Percentage of Personnel Allocated to Administrative and Support Activities*

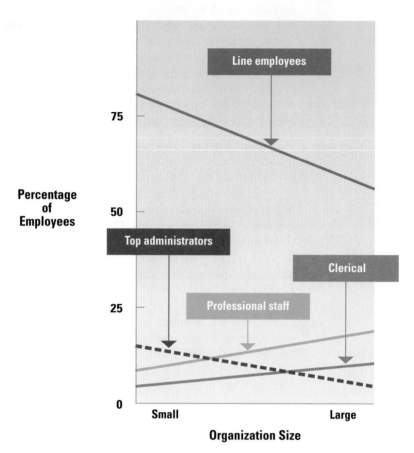

are fighting against increasing formalization and professional staff ratios. The problems caused by large bureaucracies have perhaps nowhere been more evident than in the U.S. government. From the bureaucratic obstacles to providing emergency relief following Hurricane Andrew to the bungling by the U.S. Marshal's Service that put a convicted drug kingpin back on the streets, such actions by federal government agencies show how excessive bureaucracy can impede the effectiveness and productivity of organizations.[38]

Today, large organizations are cutting layers of the hierarchy, keeping headquarters staff small, and giving lower-level workers greater freedom to make decisions rather than burdening them with excessive rules and regulations. At Nucor Corp., headquarters is staffed by only twenty-three people. Nucor's plant managers handle everything from marketing to personnel to production. Centex Corporation, which has annual revenues of about $3.8 billion, is run from a modest headquarters in Dallas by a staff of fewer than one hundred. Centex decentralizes authority and responsibility to the operating divisions.[39] The point is to not overload headquarters with lawyers, accountants, and financial analysts who will inhibit the flexibility and autonomy of divisions. Of course, many companies must be large to have sufficient resources and complexity to produce products for a global environment; but companies such as Johnson & Johnson, Wal-Mart, 3M, Coca-Cola, Emerson Electric, and Heinz are striving toward greater decentralization and leanness. They are giving front-line workers more authority and responsibility to define and direct their own jobs, often by creating self-directed teams that find ways to coordinate work, improve productivity, and better serve customers.

Another attack on bureaucracy is from the increasing professionalism of employees. Professionalism is defined as the length of formal training and experience of employees. More employees need college degrees, MBAs, and other professional degrees to work as attorneys, researchers, or doctors at General Motors, Kmart, and Bristol-Myers Squibb Company. In addition, Internet-based companies, a rapidly growing segment of the economy, are generally staffed entirely by well-educated knowledge workers. Studies of professionals show that formalization is not needed because professional training regularizes a high standard of behavior for employees that acts as a substitute for bureaucracy.[40] Companies also enhance this trend when they provide ongoing training for *all* employees, from the front office to the shop floor, in a push for continuous individual and organizational learning. Increased training substitutes for bureaucratic rules and procedures that can constrain the creativity of employees to solve problems and increase organizational capability.

A form of organization called the *professional partnership* has emerged that is made up completely of professionals.[41] These organizations include medical practices, law firms, and consulting firms, such as McKinsey & Co. and PricewaterhouseCoopers. The general finding concerning professional partnerships is that branches have substantial autonomy and decentralized authority to make necessary decisions. They work with a consensus orientation rather than top-down direction typical of traditional business and government organizations. Thus, the trend of increasing professionalism combined with rapidly changing environments is leading to less bureaucracy in corporate North America.

DYNAMIC CONTROL SYSTEMS

Even though many organizations are trying to decrease bureaucracy and reduce rules and procedures that constrain employees, every organization needs systems for guiding and controlling the organization. Employees may have more freedom in today's companies, but control is still a major responsibility of management.

Managers at the top and middle levels of an organization can choose among three overall approaches for control. These approaches come from a framework for organizational control proposed by William Ouchi of the University of California at Los Angeles. Ouchi suggested three control strategies that organizations could adopt—bureaucratic, market and clan.[42] Each form of control uses different types of information. However, all three types may appear simultaneously in an organization. The requirements for each control strategy are given in Exhibit 8.7.

BUREAUCRATIC CONTROL

Bureaucratic control is the use of rules, policies, hierarchy of authority, written documentation, standardization, and other bureaucratic mechanisms to standardize behavior and assess performance. Bureaucratic control uses the bureaucratic characteristics defined by Weber. The primary purpose of bureaucratic rules and procedures is to standardize and control employee behavior.

EXHIBIT 8.7   *Three Organizational Control Strategies*

Type	Requirements
Bureaucracy	Rules, standards, hierarchy, legitimate authority
Market	Prices, competition, exchange relationship
Clan	Tradition, shared values and beliefs, trust

Source: Based upon William G. Ouchi, "A Conceptual Framework for the Design of Organizational Control Mechanisms," *Management Science* 25 (1979): 833–48.

Recall that as organizations progress through the life cycle and grow larger, they become more formalized and standardized. Within a large organization, thousands of work behaviors and information exchanges take place both vertically and horizontally. Rules and policies evolve through a process of trial and error to regulate these behaviors. Some degree of bureaucratic control is used in virtually every organization. Rules, regulations, and directives contain information about a range of behaviors.

Bases of Control. To make bureaucratic control work, managers must have the authority to maintain control over the organization. Weber argued that legitimate, rational authority granted to managers was preferred over other types of control (for example, favoritism or payoffs) as the basis for organizational decisions and activities. Within the larger society, however, Weber identified three types of authority that could explain the creation and control of a large organization.[43]

Rational–legal authority is based on employees' belief in the legality of rules and the right of those elevated to positions of authority to issue commands. Rational–legal authority is the basis for both creation and control of most government organizations and is the most common base of control in organizations worldwide. Enterprise resource planning and other complex information systems discussed in the previous chapter can increase the rational–legal authority of managers. **Traditional authority** is the belief in traditions and in the legitimacy of the status of people exercising authority through those traditions. Traditional authority is the basis for control for monarchies and churches and for some organizations in Latin America and the Persian Gulf. **Charismatic authority** is based on devotion to the exemplary character or to the heroism of an individual person and the order defined by him or her. Revolutionary military organizations are often based on the leader's charisma, as are North American organizations led by charismatic individuals such as Jack Welch or Herb Kelleher.

More than one type of authority—such as long tradition and the leader's special charisma—may exist in today's organizations, but rational–legal authority is the most widely used form to govern internal work activities and decision making, particularly in large organizations.

Management Control Systems. The basic idea of using information technology for organizational control was introduced in the previous chapter. The information and control systems discussed in that chapter are critical tools to help managers control organizational operations.

Management control systems are broadly defined as the formalized routines, reports, and procedures that use information to maintain or alter patterns in organizational activity.[44] Control systems include the formalized information-based activities for planning, budgeting, performance evaluation, resource allocation, and employee rewards. These systems operate as feedback systems, with the targets set in advance, outcomes compared with targets, and variance reported to managers for remedial actions.[45] These systems are valuable tools to help managers monitor and control the organization. However, as discussed in the Taking the Lead box, conventional tools of measurement and control are being replaced by new methods of measurement in today's e-commerce companies.

For traditional organizations, the four control system elements listed in Exhibit 8.8 are often considered the core of management control systems. These four elements include the budget, periodic nonfinancial statistical reports, reward systems, and standard operating procedures.[46] The management control system elements enable middle and upper management to both monitor and influence major departments.

The operating budget is used to set financial targets for the year and then report costs on a monthly or quarterly basis. Periodic statistical reports are used to evaluate and monitor nonfinancial performance. These reports typically are computer-based and may be available daily, weekly, or monthly.

Reward systems offer incentives for managers and employees to improve performance and meet departmental goals. Managers and superiors may sit down and evaluate how well previous goals were met, set new goals for the year, and establish rewards for meeting the new targets. Operating procedures are traditional rules and regulations. Managers use all of these systems to correct variances and bring activities back into line.

One finding from research into management control systems is that each of the four control systems focuses on a different aspect of the production process. These four systems thus form an overall management control system that provides middle managers with control information about resource inputs, process efficiency, and output.[47] Moreover, the use of and reliance on control systems depend on the strategic targets set by top management.

The budget is used primarily to allocate resource inputs. Managers use the budget for planning the future and reducing uncertainty about the availability of human and material resources needed to perform department tasks. Computer-based statistical reports are used to control outputs. These reports contain data about output volume and quality and other indicators that provide feedback to middle management about departmental results. The reward system and the policies and procedures are directed at the production process. Operating procedures give explicit guidelines about appropriate behaviors. Reward systems provide incentives to meet goals and can help guide and correct employee

EXHIBIT 8.8   *Management Control Systems Used as Part of Bureaucratic Control*

Subsystem	Content and Frequency
Budget	Financial, resource expenditures, monthly
Statistical reports	Nonfinancial outputs, weekly or monthly, often computer-based
Reward systems	Annual evaluation of managers based on department goals and performance
Operating procedures	Rules and regulations, policies that prescribe correct behavior, continuous

Source: Based on Richard L. Daft and Norman B. Macintosh, "The Nature and Use of Formal Control Systems for Management Control and Strategy Implementation," *Journal of Management* 10 (1984): 43–66.

activities. Managers also use direct supervision to keep departmental work activities within desired limits.

Advances in computer technology have dramatically improved the efficiency and effectiveness of management control systems. The British express delivery and logistics company TNT UK uses computerized management control systems to measure and control every aspect of the company's performance, helping TNT UK win the prestigious 1998 European Quality Award.

In Practice 8.2

TNT UK

TNT UK's management control systems track performance so regularly and in such detail that every manager is constantly aware of existing problems and every employee has the information to help correct them. When most delivery companies measure customer satisfaction, they look at whether packages are delivered on time, assuming that customers are happy when this standard is met. Not TNT—it tracks every aspect of the service it provides. One biannual customer satisfaction survey asks 4,000 randomly selected customers to rank key delivery attributes—such as reliability, price, staff professionalism, range of services, and so forth—in order of importance and then to score the company's performance on each attribute. Targets are set each year to exceed the company's previous best performance. TNT managers develop tight definitions of what quality service means for every aspect of the business, providing employees with clear guidelines that spell out how to make improvements.

Far from feeling constrained by the tight measurements and procedures, employees are energized and motivated to meet service targets. For example, the company's thirty-three depots, which submit their results to top management each week, have an intense rivalry. Each wants to top the ranking charts. As a result, the proportion of perfect transactions—meaning the package is delivered on time and intact, the delivery documentation is completed on a clean invoice, and payment is received by TNT by the due date—increased from 57 percent in 1995 to 87 percent three years later. Managers are careful not to let number-crunching get in the way of meeting the needs and goals of staff members. Alan Jones, managing director of TNT UK, motivates van drivers with personal telephone calls or notes congratulating them on particular achievements. And low scores, rather than leading to a reprimand, bring a note encouraging the team to keep their chins up. As Jones points out, without the data provided by computerized management control systems, he wouldn't be able to provide that level of continuous feedback to his employees.[48]

MARKET CONTROL

Market control occurs when price competition is used to evaluate the output and productivity of an organization. The idea of market control originated in economics.[49] A dollar price is an efficient form of control because managers can compare prices and profits to evaluate the efficiency of their corporation. Top managers nearly always use the price mechanism to evaluate performance in corporations. Corporate sales and costs are summarized in a profit-and-loss statement that can be compared against performance in previous years or with that of other corporations.

The use of market control requires that outputs be sufficiently explicit for a price to be assigned and that competition exist. Without competition, the price will not accurately reflect internal efficiency. Even some government and traditionally not-for-profit organizations are turning to market control. For example, the U.S. Federal Aviation Administration took bids to operate its payroll computers (the Department of Agriculture beat out IBM and two other private companies to win the bid). Seventy-three percent of local governments now use private janitorial services and 54 percent use private garbage collectors.[50] The city of Indianapolis requires all its departments to bid against private companies. When the transportation department was underbid by a private company on a contract to fill potholes, the city's union workers made a counterproposal that involved eliminating most of the department's middle managers and reengineering union jobs to save money. Eighteen supervisors were laid off, costs were cut by 25 percent, and the department won the bid.[51]

Market control was once used primarily at the level of the entire organization, but it is increasingly used in product divisions. Profit centers are self-contained product divisions, such as those described in Chapter 3. Each division contains resource inputs needed to produce a product. Each division can be evaluated on the basis of profit or loss compared with other divisions. Asea Brown Boveri (ABB), a multinational electrical contractor and manufacturer of electrical equipment, includes three different types of profit centers, all operating according to their own bottom line and all interacting through buying and selling with one another and with outside customers.[52]

Some firms require that individual departments interact with one another at market prices—buying and selling products or services among themselves at

Taking the Lead

E-Commerce Metrics

Managers at Amazon.com don't worry about meeting annual financial targets. Even though the company's market capitalization is more than $27 billion, Amazon lost $124 million on revenues of $610 million in 1998 and shows no promise of delivering profits in the near future. But for now, the metric that matters most to Amazon, eBay, Lycos, Theglobe.com, and other Internet-based companies is *eyeballs*—people who are habitual visitors to a company's site. Although e-commerce companies use novel metrics to evaluate their performance, some standard measurements are emerging. One important Internet metric is *unique users*, unduplicated computer users who visit a company's site. Other measures include *average time spent per month* on a company's site, *page views per day*, and something called *reach*, which is an estimated percentage of Internet users who visit a particular site.

All this doesn't mean the usual measures have been completely tossed out. For now the emphasis is on *growth rates*, but these companies hope to eventually reap huge profits. *Gross profit margins* are of concern to Internet companies because they represent potential profit before marketing costs and acquisitions eat it up. Onsale, an Internet

auctioneer of closed-out computer equipment, carefully tracks *sales per employee*. Managers of Internet companies are also increasingly looking at measurements such as *cost per addition* (or how cost-effectively the firm finds new customers) and *churn rates* (how successfully they retain those customers). Other kinds of measurements for supporting the company's internal needs, such as supporting traffic growth, haven't even been developed yet. For example, there's no precise way to determine how much it costs to support a certain number of page views.

Tools are gradually being developed that can help managers of e-commerce companies better measure, guide, and control their organizations. However, the world of e-commerce is constantly—and rapidly—evolving. Managers have to embrace risk and rapid change, often making decisions with limited information. "If you don't adapt in this environment," says James Condon, president and COO of CyberCash, "you will not survive."

Source: George Donnelly, "New @ttitude," *CFO* (June 1999): 42–54; and Steven Vonder Haar, "Web Metrics: Go Figure," *Business 2.0* (June 1999): 46–47.

prices equivalent to those quoted outside the firm. To make the market control system work, internal units also have the option to buy and sell with outside companies. Imperial Oil Limited of Canada (formerly Esso), transformed its R & D department into a semiautonomous profit center several years ago.

Imperial Oil Limited

In the early 1990s, Imperial Oil's R & D was a monopoly service provider allocated an annual budget of about $45 million. Imperial felt that this method of operating gave the two hundred scientists and staff little incentive to control costs or advance quality. Today, R & D receives a much smaller budget and essentially supports itself through applied research and lab-services contracts negotiated with internal and external customers. Contracts spell out the costs of each program, analysis, or other service, and cost-conscious Imperial managers can shop for lower prices among external labs.

R & D has even introduced competition within its own small unit. For example, research teams are free to buy some lab services outside the company if they feel their own laboratories are overpriced or inefficient. However, quality and efficiency have dramatically improved at Imperial R & D, and the unit's high-quality, low-cost services are attracting a great deal of business from outside the company. Canadian companies routinely send samples of used motor oil to the R & D labs for analysis. Manufacturers use R & D to autopsy equipment failures. Vehicle makers like GM and Ford test new engines at Imperial R & D's chassis dynamometer lab. According to John Charlton, Imperial's corporate strategic planning manager, applying market control to R & D has led to an increase in the amount of work the unit does, as well as a 12 percent reduction in internal costs.[53]

Market control can only be used when the output of a company, division, or department can be assigned a dollar price and when there is competition. Companies are finding that they can apply the market control concept to internal departments such as accounting, data processing, legal departments, and information services.

CLAN CONTROL

Clan control is the use of social characteristics, such as corporate culture, shared values, commitment, traditions, and beliefs, to control behavior. Organizations that use clan control require shared values and trust among employees.[54] Clan control is important when ambiguity and uncertainty are high. High uncertainty means the organization cannot put a price on its services, and things change so fast that rules and regulations are not able to specify every correct behavior. Under clan control, people may be hired because they are committed to the organization's purpose, such as in a religious organization. New employees may be subjected to a long period of socialization to gain acceptance by colleagues. Clan control is most often used in small, informal organizations or in organizations with a strong culture, because of personal involvement in and commitment to the organization's purpose. For example, St. Luke's Communications Ltd., a London advertising firm committed to equal employee ownership, is especially careful to bring in only new employees who believe in the agency's philosophy and mission. The company even turned down a $90 million contract because it would mean rapidly recruiting new employees who might not fit with St. Luke's distinctive culture. Chairman Andy Law says that kind of decision isn't tough to make if you put a belief in human capital and human interaction. Clan control works for St. Luke's; the agency is highly respected and its revenues continue to grow, increasing by 75 percent last year.[55]

The growing use of computer networks and the Internet, which often leads to a democratic spread of information throughout the organization, may force many companies to depend less on bureaucratic control and more on shared values that guide individual actions for the corporate good.[56]

Traditional control mechanisms based on strict rules and close supervision are ineffective for controlling behavior in conditions of high uncertainty and rapid change.[57] Today's companies that are trying to become learning organizations often use clan control or *self-control* rather than relying on rules and regulations. Self-control is similar to clan control, but whereas clan control is a function of being socialized into a group, self-control stems from individual values, goals, and standards. The organization attempts to induce a change such that individual employees' own internal values and work preferences are brought in line with the organization's values and goals.[58] With self-control, employees generally set their own goals and monitor their own performance, yet companies relying on self-control need strong leaders who can clarify boundaries within which employees exercise their own knowledge and discretion.

Clan or self-control may also be used in certain departments, such as strategic planning, where uncertainty is high and performance is difficult to measure. Managers of departments that rely on these informal control mechanisms must not assume that the absence of written, bureaucratic control means no control is present. Clan control is invisible yet very powerful. One recent study found that the actions of employees were controlled even more powerfully and completely with clan control than with a bureaucratic hierarchy.[59] When clan control works, bureaucratic control is not needed, as in the following case.

In Practice 8.4

Columbus Mills

Martha Thomas was proud of being the first woman to work her way up through the manufacturing ranks at Columbus Mills, a large producer of fabrics, carpets, and specialty rugs. She was accustomed to using lengthy budgets and statistical reports, in which almost every manufacturing activity was counted and evaluated weekly. When Thomas was promoted to executive vice-president of Columbus, one of the first things she wanted to do was get the research and development department "under control." She had noticed that the department was run very loosely and people had the freedom to do as they pleased, even working at night instead of during regular business hours if they preferred.

Thomas's first step was to install a detailed budget system. A budget was established for each research project. Even minor expenditures had to be budgeted. The research and development director was expected to keep each expense category on target. Statistical reports were implemented to keep track of all nonfinancial items, such as how employees spent their time and the productivity level for each project. The amount of computer time used, travel, and use of equipment were all measured and monitored.

As the detail and intensity of the bureaucratic control system increased, satisfaction and productivity within the department decreased. At least once a week the executive vice president and the R & D director battled over differences between actual expenditures and budget or over the interpretation of activity reports. After about a year, the director resigned. This was followed by the resignations of several key researchers.

The board of directors asked that a management consultant examine the problems in the department. She found that the control procedures were not appropriate in an R & D department characterized by a long time horizon, frequent change, and uncertainty. Precise, detailed reports may work for a stable manufacturing department, but they do not capture the uncertain nature of R & D activities. Minor deviations from budget are the rule rather than the exception. A less precise control system used just to plan future projects and keep output consistent with company goals would be more effective. The consultant recommended that the bureaucratic control be reduced so that the shared values and commitment of professional employees regulate behavior.

Martha Thomas had spent many years successfully using bureaucratic control mechanisms in the manufacturing unit of Columbus, and she failed to recognize and understand the strong system of clan control that was operating in the R & D department. Employees were socialized into professional norms and practices and shared a strong departmental culture. Most researchers worked extra hours at night to finish projects because they were deeply committed and liked the chance to talk informally among themselves about ideas they were exploring. The lack of bureaucratic control mechanisms did not mean lack of control.

THE BALANCED SCORECARD

Organizations may use a combination of bureaucratic, market, and clan control to best meet the needs of various departments and the total organization. The most recent innovation is to try to integrate the various dimensions of control, combining internal financial measurements and statistical reports with a concern for markets and customers as well as employees. Whereas many managers once focused primarily on measuring and controlling financial performance, they are increasingly recognizing the need to assess other aspects of performance.

One fresh approach, called the balanced scorecard, integrates the various dimensions of control so that managers have a fuller picture of organizational performance. The **balanced scorecard** is a comprehensive management control system that balances traditional financial measures with operational measures relating to a company's critical success factors.[60] A balanced scorecard contains four major perspectives, as illustrated in Exhibit 8.9: financial performance, customer service, internal business processes, and the organization's capacity for learning and growth.[61] Within these four areas, managers identify key performance indicators the organization will track, generally limiting the number of measures to five per area for a total of twenty control metrics. The *financial perspective* reflects a concern that the organization's activities contribute to improving short- and long-term financial performance. It includes traditional measures such as net income and return on investment. *Customer service indicators* measure such things as how customers view the organization, as well as customer retention and satisfaction. *Business process indicators* focus on production and operating statistics, such as order fulfillment or cost per order. The final component looks at the organization's *potential for learning and growth*, focusing on how well resources and human capital are being managed for the company's future. Measurements include such things as employee retention, business process improvements, and the introduction of new products. The

EXHIBIT 8.9   *Major Perspectives of the Balanced Scorecard*

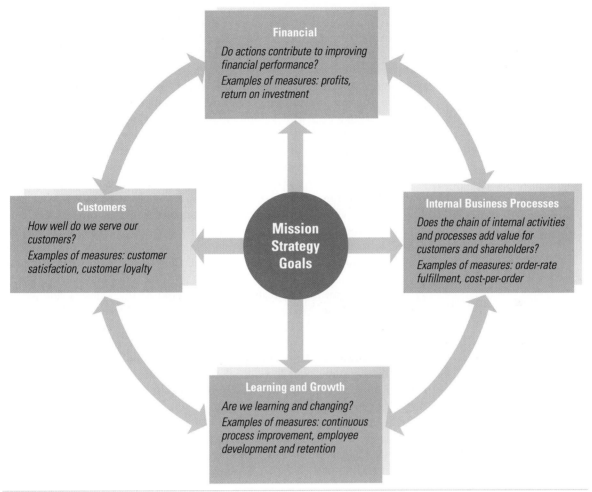

Source: Based on Robert S. Kaplan and David P. Norton, "Using the Balanced Scorecard as a Strategic Management System," *Harvard Business Review,* January–February 1996, 75–85; Chee W. Chow, Kamal M,. Haddad, and James E. Williamson, "Applying the Balanced Scorecard to Small Companies," *Management Accounting* 79, No. 2 (August 1997), 21–27; and Cathy Lazere, "All Together Now," *CFO,* February 1998, 28–36.

components of the scorecard are designed in an integrative manner so that they reinforce one another and link short-term actions with long-term strategic goals, as illustrated in Exhibit 8.9.

The balanced scorecard helps managers focus on the key strategic measures that define the success of a particular organization over time and communicate them clearly throughout the organization. The scorecard has become the core management system for many organizations today, including Tenneco, Allstate, KPMG Peat Marwick, Nationwide Financial Services, Amoco Corp., and Bell Emergis (a division of Bell Canada). Managers can use the scorecard to set goals, allocate resources, plan budgets, and determine rewards.[62]

The primary advantage of the balanced scorecard is that it can bring together different approaches described in this chapter into a comprehensive control system. The four components of the scorecard embrace elements of bureaucratic, market, and clan control in one overall control system.

SUMMARY AND INTERPRETATION

The material covered in this chapter contains several important ideas about organizations. Organizations evolve through distinct life cycle stages as they grow and mature. Organization structure, internal systems, and management issues are different for each stage of development. Growth creates crises and revolutions along the way toward large size. A major task of managers is to guide the organization through the entrepreneurial, collectivity, formalization, and elaboration stages of development. As organizations progress through the life cycle and grow larger and more complex, they generally take on bureaucratic characteristics, such as rules, division of labor, written records, hierarchy of authority, and impersonal procedures. Bureaucracy is a logical form of organizing that lets firms use resources efficiently. However, in many large corporate and government organizations, bureaucracy has come under attack with attempts to decentralize authority, flatten organization structure, reduce rules and written records, and create a small-company mind-set. These companies are willing to trade economies of scale for responsive, adaptive organizations. Many companies are subdividing into small divisions to gain small-company advantages.

In large organizations, greater support is required from clerical and professional staff specialists. This is a logical outcome of employee specialization and the division of labor. By dividing an organization's tasks and having specialists perform each part, the organization can become more efficient.

All organizations, large and small, need systems for control. Managers can choose among three overall approaches to control: market, bureaucratic, and clan. Bureaucratic control relies on standard rules and the rational-legal authority of managers, as well as on the four internal management control systems of budgets, statistical reports, operating procedures, and reward systems. Market control is used where product or service outputs can be priced and competition exists. Clan control, and more recently self-control, are associated with uncertain and rapidly changing organization processes. They rely on commitment, tradition, and shared values for control. Managers may use a combination of control approaches to meet the organization's needs. A new approach to control, the balanced scorecard, attempts to integrate various control dimensions and balance a concern for traditional financial measures with a concern for the operational measures of customer service, internal business processes, and organizational learning capability.

In the final analysis, large organization size and accompanying bureaucracy have many advantages, but they also have shortcomings. Large size and bureaucratic characteristics are important but can impede an organization that must act as if it is small, is a professional partnership, or needs to survive in a rapidly changing environment.

BRIEFCASE

As an organization manager, keep these guidelines in mind:

1. Decide whether your organization should act like a large or small company. To the extent that economies of scale, global reach, and complexity are important, introduce greater bureaucratization as the organization increases in size. As it becomes necessary, add rules and regulations, written documentation, job specialization, technical competence in hiring and promotion, and decentralization.

2. If responsiveness, flexibility, simplicity, and niche finding are important, subdivide the organization into simple, autonomous divisions that have freedom and a small-company approach.

3. Grow when possible. With growth, you can provide opportunities for employee advancement and greater profitability and effectiveness. Apply new management systems and structural configurations at each stage of an organization's development. Interpret the needs of the growing organization and respond with the management and internal systems that will carry the organization through to the next stage of development.

4. Implement one of the three basic choices—bureaucratic, clan, market—as the primary means of organizational control. Use bureaucratic control when organizations are large, have a stable environment, and use routine technology. Use clan control in small, uncertain departments. Use market control when outputs can be priced and when competitive bidding is available.

5. Use a balanced scorecard to integrate various control dimensions and gain a more complete picture of organizational performance. Select key indicators in the areas of financial performance, customer service, internal business processes, and learning and growth. Design the scorecard so that these four components reinforce one another and link organizational activities to mission, strategy, and goals.

KEY CONCEPTS

balanced scorecard	formalization
bureaucracy	formalization stage
bureaucratic control	life cycle
centralization	management control systems
charismatic authority	market control
clan control	personnel ratios
collectivity stage	rational–legal authority
elaboration stage	reasons organizations grow
entrepreneurial stage	traditional authority

DISCUSSION QUESTIONS

1. Discuss the key differences between large and small organizations. Which kinds of organizations would be better off acting as large organizations, and which are best trying to act as big-company/small-company hybrids?

2. Why do large organizations tend to be more formalized?

3. If you were managing a department of college professors, how might you structure the department differently than if you were managing a department of bookkeepers? Why?

4. Apply the concept of life cycle to an organization with which you are familiar, such as a university or a local business. What stage is the organization in now? How did the organization handle or pass through its life cycle crises?

5. Describe the three bases of authority identified by Weber. Is it possible for each of these types of authority to function at the same time within an organization?

6. In writing about types of control, William Ouchi said, "The Market is like the trout and the Clan like the salmon, each a beautiful highly specialized species which requires uncommon conditions for its survival. In comparison, the bureaucratic method of control is the catfish—clumsy, ugly, but able to live in the widest range of environments and ultimately, the dominant species." Discuss what Ouchi meant with that analogy.

7. Government organizations often seem more bureaucratic than for-profit organizations. Could this partly be the result of the type of control used in government organizations? Explain.

8. Discuss advantages and disadvantages of rules and regulations.

9. Discuss the following statements: "Things under tight control are better than things under loose control." "The more data managers have, the better decisions they make."

10. Discuss how the four perspectives of the balanced scorecard could embrace some of the elements of each major control approach–bureaucratic, market, and clan.

CHAPTER 8 WORKBOOK *Control Mechanisms**

Think of two situations in your life: your work and your school experiences. How is control exerted? Fill out the tables.

ON THE JOB

Your job responsibilities	How your boss controls	Positives of this control	Negatives of this control	How you would improve control
1.				
2.				
3.				
4.				

AT THE UNIVERSITY

Items	How professor A (small class) controls	How professor B (large class) controls	How these controls influence you	What you think is a better control
1. Exams				
2. Assignments/ papers				
3. Class participation				
4. Attendance				
5. Other				

QUESTIONS

1. What are advantages and disadvantages of the various controls?

2. What happens when there is too much control? Too little?

3. Does the type of control depend on the situation and the number of people involved?

4. *Optional:* How do the control mechanisms in your tables compare to those of other students?

Case for Analysis   *Sunflower Incorporated**

Sunflower Incorporated is a large distribution company with more than five thousand employees and gross sales of more than $550 million (1992). The company purchases salty snack foods and liquor and distributes them to independent retail stores throughout the United States and Canada. Salty snack foods include corn chips, potato chips, cheese curls, tortilla chips, and peanuts. The United States and Canada are divided into twenty-two regions, each with its own central warehouse, sales people, finance department, and purchasing department. The company distributes national as well as local brands, and packages some items under private labels. Competition in this industry is intense. The demand for liquor has been declining, and competitors like Procter & Gamble and Frito-Lay develop new snack foods to gain market share from smaller companies like Sunflower. The head office encourages each region to be autonomous because of local tastes and practices. In the northeast United States, for example,

people consume a greater percentage of Canadian whisky and American bourbon, while in the West, they consume more light liquors, such as vodka, gin, and rum. Snack foods in the Southwest are often seasoned to reflect Mexican tastes.

Early in 1988, Sunflower began using a financial reporting system that compared sales, costs, and profits across company regions. Each region was a profit center, and top management was surprised to learn that profits varied widely. By 1990, the differences were so great that management decided some standardization was necessary. Managers believed highly profitable regions were sometimes using lower-quality items, even seconds, to boost profit margins. This practice could hurt Sunflower's image. Most regions were

*This case was inspired by "Frito-Lay May Find Itself in a Competition Crunch," *Business Week*, 19 July 1982, 186; "Dashman Company," in Paul R. Lawrence and John A. Seiler, *Organizational Behavior and Administration: Cases, Concepts, and Research Findings* (Homewood, Ill: Irwin and Dorsey, 1965), 16–17; and Laurie M. Grossman, "Price Wars Bring Flavor to Once Quiet Snack Market," *The Wall Street Journal*, 23 May 1991, B1, B3.

facing cutthroat price competition to hold market share. Triggered by price cuts by Anheuser-Busch Company's Eagle Snacks division, national distributors, such as Frito-Lay, Borden, Nabisco, Procter & Gamble (Pringles), and Standard Brands (Planters Peanuts), were pushing to hold or increase market share by cutting prices and launching new products.

As these problems accumulated, Joe Steelman, president of Sunflower, decided to create a new position to monitor pricing and purchasing practices. Loretta Williams was hired from the finance department of a competing organization. Her new title was director of pricing and purchasing, and she reported to the vice president of finance, Peter Langly. Langly gave Williams great latitude in organizing her job and encouraged her to establish whatever rules and procedures were necessary. She was also encouraged to gather information from each region. Each region was notified of her appointment by an official memo sent to the twenty-two regional directors. A copy of the memo was posted on each warehouse bulletin board. The announcement was also made in the company newspaper.

After three weeks on the job, Williams decided two problems needed her attention. Over the long term, Sunflower should make better use of information technology. Williams believed information technology could provide more information to headquarters for decision making. Top managers in the divisions were connected to headquarters by an electronic messaging system, but lower employees and sales people were not connected. Only a few senior managers in about half the divisions used the system regularly.

In the short term, Williams decided fragmented pricing and purchasing decisions were a problem and these decisions should be standardized across regions. This should be undertaken immediately. As a first step, she wanted the financial executive in each region to notify her of any change in local prices of more than 3 percent. She also decided that all new contracts for local purchases of more than $5,000 should be cleared through her office. (Approximately 60 percent of items distributed in the regions were purchased in large quantities and supplied from the home office. The other 40 percent were purchased and distributed within the region.) Williams believed the only way to standardize operations was for each region to notify the home office in advance of any change in prices or purchases. She

discussed the proposed policy with Langly. He agreed, so they submitted a formal proposal to the president and board of directors, who approved the plan. The changes represented a complicated shift in policy procedures, and Sunflower was moving into peak holiday season, so Williams wanted to implement the new procedures right away. She decided to send an e-mail message followed by a fax to the financial and purchasing executives in each region notifying them of the new procedures. The change would be inserted in all policy and procedure manuals throughout Sunflower within four months.

Williams showed a draft of the message to Langly and invited his comments. Langly said the message was a good idea but wondered if it was sufficient. The regions handled hundreds of items and were used to decentralized decision making. Langly suggested that Williams ought to visit the regions and discuss purchasing and pricing policies with the executives. Williams refused, saying that such trips would be expensive and time-consuming. She had so many things to do at headquarters that trips were impossible. Langly also suggested waiting to implement the procedures until after the annual company meeting in three months, when Williams could meet the regional directors personally. Williams said this would take too long, because the procedures would then not take effect until after the peak sales season. She believed the procedures were needed now. The messages went out the next day.

During the next few days, e-mail replies came in from seven regions. The managers said they were in agreement and said they would be happy to cooperate.

Eight weeks later, Williams had not received notices from any regions about local price or purchase changes. Other executives who had visited regional warehouses indicated to her that the regions were busy as usual. Regional executives seemed to be following usual procedures for that time of year. She telephoned one of the regional managers and discovered that he did not know who she was and had never heard of the position called director of pricing and purchasing. Besides, he said, "we have enough to worry about reaching profit goals without additional procedures from headquarters." Williams was chagrined that her position and her suggested changes in procedure had no impact. She wondered whether field managers were disobedient or whether she should have used another communication strategy.

CHAPTER 8 WORKSHOP *Windsock, Inc.**

1. *Introduction.* Class is divided into four groups: Central Office, Product Design, Marketing/Sales, and Production. Central Office is a slightly smaller group. If groups are large enough, assign observers to each one. Central Office is given 500 straws and 750 pins. Each person reads *only* the role description relevant to that group. (*Materials needed:* Plastic milk straws (500) and a box (750) of straight pins.)
2. *Perform task.* Depending on length of class, step 2 may take 30 to 60 minutes. Groups perform functions and prepare for a two-minute report for "stockholders."
3. *Group reports.* Each group gives a two-minute presentation to "stockholders."
4. *Observers' reports (optional).* Observers share insights with subgroups.
5. *Class discussion.*
   a. What helped or blocked intergroup cooperation and coordination?
   b. To what extent was there open versus closed communication? What impact did that have?
   c. What styles of leadership were exhibited?
   d. What types of team interdependencies emerged?

ROLES

Central Office

Your team is the central management and administration of WINDSOCK, INC. You are the heart and pulse of the organization, because without your coordination and resource allocation, the organization would go under. Your task is to manage the operations of the organization, not an easy responsibility because you have to coordinate the activities of three distinct groups of personnel: the Marketing/Sales group, the Production group, and the Product Design group. In addition, you have to manage resources including materials (pins and straws), time deadlines, communications, and product requirements.

In this exercise, you are to do whatever is necessary to accomplish the mission and to keep the organization operating in a harmonious and efficient manner.

WINDSOCK, INC. has a total of 30 minutes (more if instructor assigns) to design an advertising campaign and ad copy, to design the windmill, and to produce the first windmill prototypes for delivery. Good luck to you all.

Product Design

Your team is the research and product design group of WINDSOCK, INC. You are the brain and creative aspect of the operation, because without an innovative and successfully designed product, the organization would go under. Your duties are to design products that will compete favorably in the marketplace, keeping in mind function, aesthetics, cost, ease of production, and available materials.

In this exercise, you are to come up with a workable plan for a product that will be built by your production team. Your windmill must be light, portable, easy to assemble, and aesthetically pleasing. Central Office controls the budget and allocates material for your division.

WINDSOCK, INC. as an organization has a total of 30 minutes (more if instructor assigns) to design an advertising campaign, to design the windmill (your group's task), and to produce the first windmill prototypes for delivery. Good luck to you all.

Marketing/Sales

Your team is the marketing/sales group of WINDSOCK, INC. You are the backbone of the operation, because without customers and sales the organization would go under. Your task is to determine the market, develop an advertising campaign to promote your company's unique product, produce ad copy, and develop a sales force and sales procedures for both potential customers and the public at large.

For the purpose of this exercise, you may assume that a market analysis has been completed. Your team is now in a position to produce an advertising campaign and ad copy for the product. To be effective, you have to become very familiar with the characteristics of the product and how it is different from those products already on the market. The Central Office controls your budget and allocates materials for use by your division.

WINDSOCK, INC. has a total of 30 minutes (more if instructor assigns) to design an advertising campaign and ad (your group's task), to design the windmill, and to produce the first windmill prototypes for delivery. Good luck to you all.

*Adapted by Dorothy Marcic from Christopher Taylor and Saundra Taylor in "Teaching Organizational Team-Building Through Simulations," *Organizational Behavior Teaching Review,* XI(3): 86–87.

Production

Your team is the production group of WINDSOCK, INC. You are the heart of the operation, because without a group to produce the product, the organization would go under. You have the responsibility to coordinate and produce the product for delivery. The product involves an innovative "windmill" design that is cheaper, lighter, more portable, more flexible, and more aesthetically pleasing than other designs currently available in the marketplace. Your task is to build windmills within cost guidelines, according to specifications, within a prescribed time period, using predetermined materials.

For the purpose of this exercise, you are to organize your team, set production schedules, and build the windmills. Central Office has control over your budget and materials, as well as the specifications.

WINDSOCK, INC. has a total of thirty minutes (more if instructor assigns) to design an advertising campaign, to design the windmill, and to produce the first windmill prototypes (your group's task) for delivery. Good luck to you all.

NOTES

1. Ron Winslow and Scot J. Paltrow, "Oxford Health Plans Grew with Scant Heed to Financial Controls," *The Wall Street Journal*, 29 April 1998, A1, A14.
2. James Q. Wilson, *Bureaucracy* (Basic Books: 1989); and Charles Perrow, *Complex Organizations: A Critical Essay* (Glenview, Ill.: Scott, Foresman, 1979), 4.
3. Tom Peters, "Rethinking Scale," *California Management Review* (Fall 1992): 7–29.
4. David Friedman, "Is Big Back? Or Is Small Still Beautiful?" *Inc.* (April 1998): 23–28.
5. James B. Treece, "Sometimes, You've Still Gotta Have Size," *Business Week/Enterprise,* 1993, 200–01.
6. Friedman, "Is Big Back?
7. Peter F. Drucker, "Toward the New Organization," *Executive Excellence* (February 1997): 7.
8. Thomas Petzinger, Jr., *The New Pioneers: The Men and Women Who Are Transforming the Workplace and Marketplace* (New York: Simon & Schuster, 1999), 21.
9. Glenn R. Carroll, "Organizations . . . The Smaller They Get," *California Management Review* 37, no. 1 (Fall 1994): 28–41.
10. Alan Deutschman, "America's Fastest Risers," *Fortune,* 7 October 1991, 46–57.
11. Ibid.
12. Richard A. Melcher, "How Goliaths Can Act Like Davids," *Business Week/Enterprise*, 1993, 192-201.
13. Tom Peters, *The Pursuit of WOW! Every Person's Guide to Topsy-Turvy Times* (New York: Vintage, 1994), 31.
14. Edward E. Lawler III, "Rethinking Organization Size," *Organizational Dynamics* (Autumn 1997): 24–35.
15. Ibid.
16. Anna Muoio, ed., "Growing Smart," *Fast Company* (August 1998): 73-83.
17. John R. Kimberly, Robert H. Miles, and Associates, *The Organizational Life Cycle* (San Francisco: Jossey-Bass, 1980); Ichak Adices, "Organizational Passages—Diagnosing and Treating Lifecycle Problems of Organizations," *Organizational Dynamics* (Summer 1979): 3–25; Danny Miller and Peter H. Friesen, "A Longitudinal Study of the Corporate Life Cycle," *Management Science* 30 (October 1984): 1161–83; Neil C. Churchill and Virginia L. Lewis, "The Five Stages of Small Business Growth," *Harvard Business Review* 61 (May–June 1983): 30–50.
18. Larry E. Greiner, "Evolution and Revolution as Organizations Grow," *Harvard Business Review* 50 (July–August 1972): 37–46; Robert E. Quinn and Kim Cameron, "Organizational Life Cycles and Shifting Criteria of Effectiveness: Some Preliminary Evidence," *Management Science* 29 (1983): 33–51.
19. George Land and Beth Jarman, "Moving beyond Breakpoint," in Michael Ray and Alan Rinzler, eds., *The New Paradigm* (New York: Jeremy P. Tarcher/Perigee Books, 1993), 250–66; Michael L. Tushman, William H. Newman, and Elaine Romanelli, "Convergence and Upheaval: Managing the Unsteady Pace of Organizational Evolution," *California Management Review* 29 (1987): 1–16.

20. David A. Whetten, "Sources, Responses, and Effects of Organizational Decline," in John R. Kimberly, Robert H. Miles, and Associates, *The Organizational Life Cycle* (San Francisco: Jossey-Bass, 1980), 342–74.

21. David Kirkpatrick, "The Second Coming of Apple," *Fortune*, 9 November 1998, 86–92; Ira Sager and Peter Burrows with Andy Reinhardt, *Business Week*, 25 May 1998, 56–60; and Peter Burrows, "A Peek at Steve Jobs' Plan," *Business Week*, 17 November 1997, 144–46.

22. Land and Jarman, "Moving Beyond Breakpoint."

23. Lawrence M. Fisher, "The Rocky Road from Startup to Big-Time Player: Biogen's Triumph Against the Odds," *Strategy & Business*, Issue 8, 1997, 55–63.

24. Richard Murphy, "Michael Dell," *Success*, January 1999, 50–53.

25. Max Weber, *The Theory of Social and Economic Organizations*, translated by A. M. Henderson and T. Parsons (New York: Free Press, 1947).

26. John Crewdson, "Corruption Viewed as a Way of Life," *Bryan-College Station Eagle*, 28 November 1982, 13A; Barry Kramer, "Chinese Officials Still Give Preference to Kin, Despite Peking Policies," *The Wall Street Journal*, 29 October 1985, 1, 21.

27. Allen C. Bluedorn, "Pilgrim's Progress: Trends and Convergence in Research on Organizational Size and Environment," *Journal of Management Studies* 19 (Summer 1993): 163–91; John R. Kimberly, "Organizational Size and the Structuralist Perspective: A Review, Critique, and Proposal," *Administrative Science Quarterly* (1976): 571–97; Richard L. Daft and Selwyn W. Becker, "Managerial, Institutional, and Technical Influences on Administration: A Longitudinal Analysis," *Social Forces* 59 (1980): 392–413.

28. James P. Walsh and Robert D. Dewar, "Formalization and the Organizational Life Cycle," *Journal of Management Studies* 24 (May 1987): 215–31.

29. Nancy M. Carter and Thomas L. Keon, "Specialization as a Multidimensional Construct," *Journal of Management Studies* 26 (1989): 11–28; Cheng-Kuang Hsu, Robert M. March, and Hiroshi Mannari, "An Examination of the Determinants of Organizational Structure," *American Journal of Sociology* 88 (1983): 975–96; Guy Geeraerts, "The Effect of Ownership on the Organization Structure in Small Firms," *Administrative Science Quarterly* 29 (1984): 232–37; Bernard Reimann, "On the Dimensions of Bureaucratic Structure: An Empirical Reappraisal," *Administrative Science Quarterly* 18 (1973): 462–76; Richard H. Hall, "The Concept of Bureaucracy: An Empirical Assessment," *American Journal of Sociology* 69 (1963): 32–40; William A. Rushing, "Organizational Rules and Surveillance: A Proposition in Comparative Organizational Analysis," *Administrative Science Quarterly* 10 (1966): 423–43.

30. Jerald Hage and Michael Aiken, "Relationship of Centralization to Other Structural Properties," *Administrative Science Quarterly* 12 (1967): 72–91.

31. Peter Brimelow, "How Do You Cure Injelitance?" *Forbes*, 7 August 1989, 42–44; and Jeffrey D. Ford and John W. Slocum, Jr., "Size, Technology, Environment and the Structure of Organizations," *Academy of Management Review* 2 (1977): 561–75; John D. Kasarda, "The Structural Implications of Social System Size: A Three-Level Analysis," *American Sociological Review* 39 (1974): 19–28.

32. Graham Astley, "Organizational Size and Bureaucratic Structure," *Organization Studies* 6 (1985): 201–28; Spyros K. Lioukas and Demitris A. Xerokostas, "Size and Administrative Intensity in Organizational Divisions," *Management Science* 28 (1982): 854–68; Peter M. Blau, "Interdependence and Hierarchy in Organizations," *Social Science Research* 1 (1972): 1–24; Peter M. Blau and R. A. Schoenherr, *The Structure of Organizations* (New York: Basic Books, 1971); A. Hawley, W. Boland, and M. Boland, "Population Size and Administration in Institutions of Higher Education," *American Sociological Review* 30 (1965): 252–55; Richard L. Daft, "System Influence on Organization Decision-Making: The Case of Resource Allocation," *Academy of Management Journal* 21 (1978): 6–22; B. P. Indik, "The Relationship between Organization Size and the Supervisory Ratio," *Administrative Science Quarterly* 9 (1964): 301–12.

33. T. F. James, "The Administrative Component in Complex Organizations," *Sociological Quarterly* 13 (1972): 533–39; Daft, "System Influence on Organization Decision-Making"; E. A. Holdaway and E. A. Blowers, "Administrative Ratios and Organization Size: A Longitudinal Examination,"

American Sociological Review 36 (1971): 278–86; John Child, "Parkinson's Progress: Accounting for the Number of Specialists in Organizations," *Administrative Science Quarterly* 18 (1973): 328–48.

34. Richard L. Daft and Selwyn Becker, "School District Size and the Development of Personnel Resources," *Alberta Journal of Educational Research* 24 (1978): 173–87.

35. Thomas A. Stewart, "Yikes! Deadwood is Creeping Back," *Fortune,* 18 August 1997, 221–222.

36. Cathy Lazere, "Resisting Temptation: The Fourth Annual SG&A Survey," *CFO* (December 1997): 64–70.

37. Based on Gifford and Elizabeth Pinchot, *The End of Bureaucracy and the Rise of the Intelligent Organization* (San Francisco: Berrett-Koehler Publishers, 1993), 21–29.

38. Bob Davis, "Federal Relief Agency Is Slowed by Infighting, Patronage, Regulations," *The Wall Street Journal,* 31 August 1992, A1, A12; Paul M. Barrett, "Bureaucratic Bungling Helps Fugitives Evade Capture by Feds," *The Wall Street Journal,* 7 August 1991, A1, A6.

39. Lazere, "Resisting Temptation."

40. Philip M. Padsakoff, Larry J. Williams, and William D. Todor, "Effects of Organizational Formalization on Alienation among Professionals and Nonprofessionals," *Academy of Management Journal* 29 (1986): 820–31.

41. Royston Greenwood, C. R. Hinings, and John Brown, "'P2-Form' Strategic Management: Corporate Practices in Professional Partnerships," *Academy of Management Journal* 33 (1990): 725–55; Royston Greenwood and C. R. Hinings, "Understanding Strategic Change: The Contribution of Archtypes," *Academy of Management Journal* 36 (1993): 1052–81.

42. William G. Ouchi, "Markets, Bureaucracies, and Clans," *Administrative Science Quarterly* 25 (1980): 129–41;—idem, "A Conceptual Framework for the Design of Organizational Control Mechanisms," *Management Science* 25 (1979): 833–48.

43. Weber, *Theory of Social and Economic Organizations,* 328–340.

44. Robert Simons, "Strategic Organizations and Top Management Attention to Control Systems," *Strategic Management Journal* 12 (1991): 491-62.

45. Stephen G. Green and M. Ann Welsh, "Cybernetics and Dependents: Reframing the Control Concept," *Academy of Management Review* 13 (1988): 287–301.

46. Richard L. Daft and Norman B. Macintosh, "The Nature and Use of Formal Control Systems for Management Control and Strategy Implementation," *Journal of Management* 10 (1984): 43–66.

47. Ibid.; Scott S. Cowen and J. Kendall Middaugh II, "Matching an Organization's Planning and Control System to Its Environment," *Journal of General Management* 16 (1990): 69–84.

48. Trevor Merriden, "Measured for Success," *Management Review* (April 1999): 27–32.

49. Oliver A. Williamson, *Markets and Hierarchies: Analyses and Antitrust Implications* (New York: Free Press, 1975).

50. David Wessel and John Harwood, "Capitalism is Giddy with Triumph: Is It Possible to Overdo It?" *The Wall Street Journal,* 14 May 1998, A1, A10.

51. Anita Micossi, "Creating Internal Markets," *Enterprise* (April 1994): 43–44.

52. Raymond E. Miles, Henry J. Coleman, Jr., and W. E. Douglas Creed, "Keys to Success in Corporate Redesign," *California Management Review* 37, no. 3 (Spring 1995): 128–45.

53. Micossi, "Creating Internal Markets."

54. Ouchi, "Markets, Bureaucracies, and Clans."

55. Muoio, ed., "Growing Smart."

56. Stratford Sherman, "The New Computer Revolution," *Fortune,* 14 June 1993, 56–80.

57. Richard Leifer and Peter K. Mills, "An Information Processing Approach for Deciding Upon Control Strategies and Reducing Control Loss in Emerging Organizations," *Journal of Management* 22, no. 1 (1996): 113–37.

58. Leifer and Mills, "An Information Processing Approach for Deciding Upon Control Strategies"; Laurie J. Kirsch, "The Management of Complex Tasks in Organizations: Controlling the Systems Development Process," *Organization Science* 7, no. 1 (January-February 1996): 1–21.

59. James R. Barker, "Tightening the Iron Cage: Concertive Control in Self-Managing Teams," *Administrative Science Quarterly* 38 (1993): 408–37.

60. Chee W. Chow, Kamal M. Haddad, and James E. Williamson, "Applying the Balanced Scorecard to Small Companies," *Management Accounting* 79,

No. 2 (August 1997): 21–27; and Robert Kaplan and David Norton, "The Balanced Scorecard: Measures That Drive Performance," *Harvard Business Review,* (January–February 1992): 71–79.

61. Based on Kaplan and Norton, "The Balanced Scorecard"; Chow, Haddad, and Williamson, "Applying the Balanced Scorecard"; and Cathy Lazere, "All Together Now," *CFO,* (February 1998): 28–36.

62. Debby Young, "Score It a Hit," *CIO Enterprise,* Section 2, 15 November 1998, 27+.

Organizational Culture and Ethical Values

CHAPTER

A LOOK INSIDE

SAS Institute

*E*mployees in most high-tech companies have a great deal of freedom, but they often pay for it with long hours working under intense pressure. Not at SAS Institute, which seems like an oasis of calm in a world of frantic competition. SAS, which stands for *statistical analysis software*, writes software that makes it possible to gather and understand data, producing products that set the industry standard in the world of knowledge management. It's a competitive field with high stakes, but the atmosphere at SAS headquarters in Cary, North Carolina, is relaxed, almost serene. One employee took a 10 percent pay cut to work at SAS. Others routinely turn down offers from other companies trying to lure them with higher salaries and stock options. As one said, "It's better to be happy than to have a little more money."

Jim Goodnight, president and cofounder of SAS, has created a culture of sanity in a company where employees are respected and "treated like adults." SAS's culture places a high value on people and human relationships. Managers at the company trust employees to do their jobs to the best of their ability—and then they expect them to go home and enjoy their friends and families. At SAS, employees are encouraged to lead a balanced life rather than to work long hours and express a hard-charging competitive spirit. Salaries are average, but the benefits are amazing. The company offers two Montessori day-care centers, a 36,000 square-foot fitness center, unlimited sick days, an on-site health clinic, elder-care advice and referrals, and live piano music in the cafeteria, where employees can eat with their families if they like. The company has even adopted a seven-hour workday so employees have more personal time. The company's free snacks are the stuff of local legend—on Mondays, fresh fruit baskets are available. Employees enjoy muffins and bagels on Fridays. And every Wednesday afternoon, hundreds of pounds of M&Ms are distributed throughout the building. Another key value at SAS is equality. Goodnight still spends a large part of his day banging out code just like his employees do. He drives a modest station wagon, refuses to have a reserved parking space at work, and has lunch with employees in the cafeteria.

Although the atmosphere at SAS is informal and people never have someone looking over their shoulder to make sure they get their jobs done, employees are highly productive. As one worker puts it, "Because you're treated well, you treat the company well. When you walk down the halls here, it's rare that you hear people talking about anything but work."[1]

SAS Institute has definite values that make it unique. SAS has created a culture that engages employees' hearts and minds as well as their bodies. Annual employee turnover is around 4 percent, compared to an industry average of 15 percent. People are so eager to work at SAS, the saying goes, that even those on the landscaping crew have graduate degrees.[2]

Organizational success or failure is often attributed to culture. In *Fortune* magazine's survey of the most admired companies, the single best predictor of overall excellence was the ability to attract, motivate, and retain talented people, and CEOs say organizational culture is their most important mechanism for enhancing this capability.[3] Southwest Airlines, Johnson & Johnson, and 3M have been praised for their innovative cultures. Culture has also been implicated in problems faced by companies such as Kodak and Kellogg, where changing the culture is considered a key to ultimate success.

PURPOSE OF THIS CHAPTER

This chapter explores ideas about corporate culture and associated ethical values and how these are influenced by organizations. The first section will describe the nature of corporate culture, its origins and purpose, and how to identify and interpret culture through ceremonies, stories, and symbols. We will then examine how culture reinforces the strategy and structural design the organization needs to be effective in its environment and discuss the important role of culture in creating a learning organization. Next, the chapter turns to ethical values in organizations and how managers implement the structures and systems that will influence employee behavior. We will also discuss how leaders shape culture and ethical values in a direction suitable for strategy and performance outcomes. The chapter closes with a brief overview of the complex cultural issues managers face in an international environment.

ORGANIZATIONAL CULTURE

The popularity of the organizational culture topic raises a number of questions. Can we identify cultures? Can culture be aligned with strategy? How can cultures be managed or changed? The best place to start is by defining culture and explaining how it can be identified in organizations.

WHAT IS CULTURE?

Culture is the set of values, guiding beliefs, understandings, and ways of thinking that is shared by members of an organization and taught to new members as correct.[4] It represents the unwritten, feeling part of the organization. Everyone participates in culture, but culture generally goes unnoticed. It is only when organizations try to implement new strategies or programs that go against basic culture norms and values that they come face to face with the power of culture.

Organizational culture exists at two levels, as illustrated in Exhibit 9.1. On the surface are visible artifacts and observable behaviors—the ways people dress and act and the symbols, stories, and ceremonies organization members share. The visible elements of culture, however, reflect deeper values in the minds of organization members. These underlying values, assumptions, beliefs, and thought processes are the true culture.[5] For example, at Southwest Airlines, red "LUV" hearts emblazon the company's training manuals and other materials. The hearts are a visible symbol; the underlying value is that "we are one family of people who truly care about each other." The attributes of culture display themselves in many ways but typically evolve into a patterned set of activities carried out through social interactions.[6] Those patterns can be used to interpret culture.

EMERGENCE AND PURPOSE OF CULTURE

Culture provides members with a sense of organizational identity and generates a commitment to beliefs and values that are larger than themselves. Though ideas that become part of culture can come from anywhere within the organization, an organization's culture generally begins with a founder or early leader who articulates and implements particular ideas and values as a vision, philosophy, or business strategy. When these ideas and values lead to success, they

EXHIBIT 9.1   *Levels of Corporate Culture*

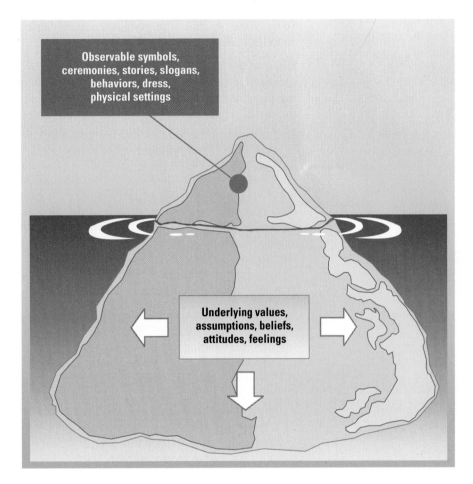

become institutionalized, and an organizational culture emerges that reflects the vision and strategy of the founder or leader, as it did at SAS Institute.[7]

Cultures serve two critical functions in organizations: (1) to integrate members so that they know how to relate to one another, and (2) to help the organization adapt to the external environment. **Internal integration** means that members develop a collective identity and know how to work together effectively. It is culture that guides day-to-day working relationships and determines how people communicate within the organization, what behavior is acceptable or not acceptable, and how power and status are allocated. **External adaptation** refers to how the organization meets goals and deals with outsiders. Culture helps guide the daily activities of workers to meet certain goals. It can help the organization respond rapidly to customer needs or the moves of a competitor. We will discuss culture and adaptation in more detail later in the chapter.

INTERPRETING CULTURE

To identify and interpret the content of culture requires that people make inferences based on observable artifacts. Artifacts can be studied but are hard to decipher accurately. An award ceremony in one company may have a different meaning than in another company. To decipher what is really going on in an organization requires detective work and probably some experience as an insider. Some of the typical and important observable aspects of culture are rites and ceremonies, stories, symbols, and language.

Rites and Ceremonies. Important artifacts for culture are **rites and ceremonies**, the elaborate, planned activities that make up a special event and are often conducted for the benefit of an audience. Managers can hold rites and ceremonies to provide dramatic examples of what a company values. These are special occasions that reinforce specific values, create a bond among people for sharing an important understanding, and anoint and celebrate heroes and heroines who symbolize important beliefs and activities.[8]

Four types of rites that appear in organizations are summarized in Exhibit 9.2. *Rites of passage* facilitate the transition of employees into new social roles. *Rites of enhancement* create stronger social identities and increase the status of employees. *Rites of renewal* reflect training and development activities that improve organization functioning. *Rites of integration* create common bonds and good feelings among employees and increase commitment to the organization. The following examples illustrate how these rites and ceremonies are used by top managers to reinforce important cultural values.

- In a major bank, election as an officer was seen as the key event in a successful career. A series of activities accompanied every promotion to bank officer, including a special method of notification, taking the new officer to the officers' dining room for the first time, and the new officer buying drinks on Friday after his or her notification.[9] This is a rite of passage.
- Mary Kay Cosmetics Company holds elaborate awards ceremonies, presenting gold and diamond pins, furs, and pink Cadillacs to high-achieving sales consultants. The most successful consultants are introduced by film clips, such as the kind used to introduce award nominees in the entertainment industry. This is a rite of enhancement.
- An important annual event at McDonald's is the nationwide contest to determine the best hamburger cooking team in the country. The contest encourages all stores to reexamine the details of how they cook hamburgers.

EXHIBIT 9.2   *A Typology of Organizational Rites and Their Social Consequences*

Type of Rite	Example	Social Consequences
Passage	Induction and basic training, U.S. Army	Facilitate transition of persons into social roles and statuses that are new for them
Enhancement	Annual awards night	Enhance social identities and increase status of employees
Renewal	Organizational development activities	Refurbish social structures and improve organization functioning
Integration	Office Christmas party	Encourage and revive common feelings that bind members together and commit them to the organization

Source: Adapted from Harrison M. Trice and Janice M. Beyer, "Studying Organizational Cultures through Rites and Ceremonials," *Academy of Management Review* 9 (1984): 653–59. Used with permission.

The ceremony is highly visible and communicates to all employees the McDonald's value of hamburger quality.[10] This is a rite of renewal.

- Whenever a Wal-Mart executive visits one of the stores, he or she leads employees in the Wal-Mart cheer: "Give me a W! Give me an A! Give me an L! Give me a squiggly! (all do a version of the twist) Give me an M! Give me an A! Give me an R! Give me a T! What's that spell? Wal-Mart! What's that spell? Wal-Mart! Who's No. 1? THE CUSTOMER!" The cheer strengthens bonds among employees and reinforces their commitment to common goals.[11] This is a rite of integration.

Stories. Stories are narratives based on true events that are frequently shared among organizational employees and told to new employees to inform them about an organization. Many stories are about company **heroes** who serve as models or ideals for serving cultural norms and values. Some stories are considered **legends** because the events are historic and may have been embellished with fictional details. Other stories are **myths**, which are consistent with the values and beliefs of the organization but are not supported by facts.[12] Stories keep alive the primary values of the organization and provide a shared understanding among all employees. Examples of how stories shape culture are as follows:

- At 3M Corp., the story is told of a vice-president who was fired early in his career for persisting with a new product even after his boss had told him to stop because he thought it was a stupid idea. After the worker was fired, he stayed in an unused office, working without a salary on the new product idea. Eventually he was rehired, the product was a success, and he was promoted to vice-president. The story symbolizes the 3M value of persisting in what you believe in.[13]
- One FedEx story concerns a delivery person who had misplaced the key to a FedEx drop box. Rather than allow the packages to be late, the employee uprooted the box, put it in his delivery truck, and rushed it back to the sorting station, where they were able to pry it open and get the contents to their destination the following day.[14] By telling this story, FedEx workers communicate the importance of putting the customer first.

Symbols. Another tool for interpreting culture is the symbol. A symbol is something that represents another thing. In one sense, ceremonies, stories, slogans, and rites are all symbols. They symbolize deeper values of an organization. Another symbol is a physical artifact of the organization. Physical symbols are powerful because they focus attention on a specific item. Examples of physical symbols are as follows:

- Nordstrom department store symbolizes the importance of supporting lower-level employees with the organization chart in Exhibit 9.3. Nordstrom's is known for its extraordinary customer service, and the organization chart symbolizes that managers are to support the employees who give the service rather than be managers who control them.[15]
- At St. Luke's, a London advertising agency, the office layout symbolizes the company's commitment to values of openness, equality, flexibility, and creativity. There are no individual desks and personal work spaces: teams gather in large, client-specific brand rooms to generate ideas for new accounts and store work in progress.[16]

EXHIBIT 9.3   *Organization Chart for Nordstrom, Inc.*

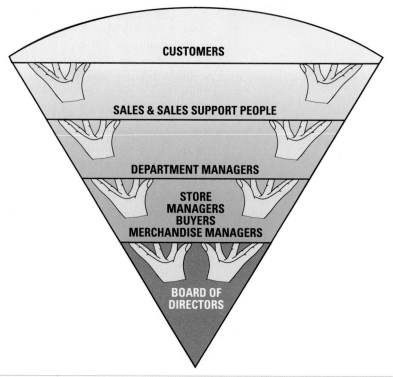

Source: Used with permission of Nordstrom, Inc.

Language. The final technique for influencing culture is **language**. Many companies use a specific saying, slogan, metaphor, or other form of language to convey special meaning to employees. Slogans can be readily picked up and repeated by employees as well as customers of the company. Bank One promotes its emphasis on customer service through the slogan, "Whatever it takes." Bank One's culture encourages employees to do whatever it takes to exceed customer expectations. Other significant uses of language to shape culture are as follows:

- At PeopleSoft Inc., which sells enterprise resource planning (ERP) software, employees call themselves PeoplePeople, shop at the company PeopleStore, and munch on company-funded PeopleSnacks. The use of this special lingo reinforces PeopleSoft's close-knit "family" culture.[17]
- T. J. Watson, Jr., son of the founder of International Business Machines, used the metaphor "wild ducks" to describe the type of employees needed by IBM. His point was, "You can make wild ducks tame, but you can never make tame ducks wild again."[18] Wild ducks symbolized the freedom and opportunity that must be available to keep from taming creative employees at IBM.

Recall that culture exists at two levels—the underlying values and assumptions and the visible artifacts and observable behaviors. The slogans, symbols, and ceremonies just described are artifacts that reflect underlying company values. These visible artifacts and behaviors can be used by managers to shape company values and to strengthen organizational culture.

ORGANIZATIONAL DESIGN AND CULTURE

Corporate culture should reinforce the strategy and structural design that the organization needs to be effective within its environment. For example, if the external environment requires flexibility and responsiveness, such as the environment for emerging Internet-based companies, the culture should encourage adaptability. The correct relationship among cultural values, organizational strategy and structure, and the environment can enhance organizational performance.

Studies of culture and effectiveness propose that the fit among culture, strategy and structure, and the environment is associated with four categories of culture, which are illustrated in Exhibit 9.4.[19] These categories are based on two factors: (1) the extent to which the competitive environment requires flexibility or stability, and (2) the extent to which the strategic focus and strength is internal or external. The four categories associated with these differences are adaptability/entrepreneurial, mission, clan, and bureaucratic. Each of the four cultures can be successful, depending on the needs of the external environment and the organization's strategic focus.

THE ADAPTABILITY/ENTREPRENEURIAL CULTURE

The **adaptability/entrepreneurial culture** is characterized by strategic focus on the external environment through flexibility and change to meet customer

EXHIBIT 9.4   *Relationship of Environment and Strategy to Corporate Culture*

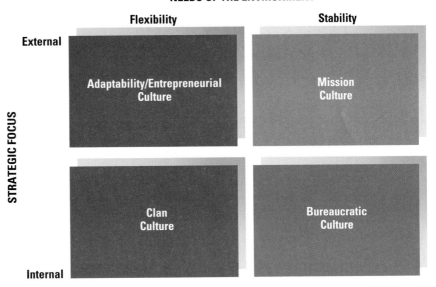

Source: Based on Daniel R. Denison and Aneil K. Mishra, "Toward a Theory of Organizational Culture and Effectiveness," *Organization Science* 6, no. 2 (March–April 1995): 204–23; R. Hooijberg and F. Petrock, "On Cultural Change: Using the Competing Values Framework to Help Leaders Execute a Transformational Strategy," *Human Resource Management* 32 (1993): 29–50; and R. E. Quinn, *Beyond Rational Management: Mastering the Paradoxes and Competing Demands of High Performance* (San Francisco: Jossey-Bass, 1988).

needs. The culture encourages norms and beliefs that support the capacity of the organization to detect, interpret, and translate signals from the environment into new behavior responses. This type of company, however, doesn't just react quickly to environmental changes—it actively creates change. Innovation, creativity, and risk-taking are valued and rewarded.

An example of the adaptability/entrepreneurial culture is 3M, a company whose values promote individual initiative and entrepreneurship. All new employees attend a class on risk-taking, where they are told to pursue their ideas even if it means defying their supervisors. Acxiom Corp., based in Conway, Arkansas, began changing to an adaptability/entrepreneurial culture in the early 1990s. After years of rapid growth and an explosion of interest in data management products and services, managers discovered that the company's culture, which emphasized internal efficiency, consistency in following established rules and procedures, and top-down decision making, was no longer suitable to meet the demands of the rapidly changing environment. Acxiom shifted to an external focus emphasizing the importance of employee empowerment, flexibility, and initiative.[20] Most e-commerce companies, such as eBay, Drugstore.com and Buy.com, as well as companies in the marketing, electronics, and cosmetics industries, use this type of culture because they must move quickly to satisfy customers.

THE MISSION CULTURE

An organization concerned with serving specific customers in the external environment, but without the need for rapid change, is suited to the mission culture. The **mission culture** is characterized by emphasis on a clear vision of the organization's purpose and on the achievement of goals, such as sales growth, profitability, or market share, to help achieve the purpose. Individual employees may be responsible for a specified level of performance, and the organization promises specified rewards in return. Managers shape behavior by envisioning and communicating a desired future state for the organization. Because the environment is stable, they can translate the vision into measurable goals and evaluate employee performance for meeting them. In some cases, mission cultures reflect a high level of competitiveness and a profit-making orientation.

One example is PepsiCo, where former CEO Wayne Calloway set a vision to be the best consumer products company in the world. Managers who met the high performance standards were generously rewarded—first class air travel, fully loaded company cars, stock options, bonuses, and rapid promotion. Annual performance reviews focus specifically on meeting performance goals, such as sales targets or marketing goals.[21] Another example of a mission culture is Nucor Corp., a steel company with headquarters in Charlotte, North Carolina. Nucor keeps employees focused on bottom-line profits and long-term survival. It asks its managers to produce more steel for less money and rewards them well for doing so.[22]

THE CLAN CULTURE

The **clan culture** has a primary focus on the involvement and participation of the organization's members and on rapidly changing expectations from the external environment. This culture is similar to the clan form of control described in Chapter 8. More than any other, this culture focuses on the needs of employees as the route to high performance. Involvement and participation create a sense of responsibility and ownership and, hence, greater commitment to the organization.

SAS Institute, described at the beginning of this chapter, is an example of a clan culture. The most important value is taking care of employees and making sure they have whatever they need to help them be satisfied as well as productive. By taking care of employees, SAS is able to adapt to competition and changing markets. The creativity of employees is highly valued at SAS, where more than 30 percent of revenues are plowed back into research and development. Companies in the fashion and retail industries also use this culture because it releases the creativity of employees to respond to rapidly changing tastes.

THE BUREAUCRATIC CULTURE

The **bureaucratic culture** has an internal focus and a consistency orientation for a stable environment. This organization has a culture that supports a methodical approach to doing business. Symbols, heroes, and ceremonies support cooperation, tradition, and following established policies and practices as a way to achieve goals. Personal involvement is somewhat lower here, but that is outweighed by a high level of consistency, conformity, and collaboration among members. This organization succeeds by being highly integrated and efficient.

One example of a bureaucratic culture is Safeco Insurance Company, considered by some to be stuffy and regimented. Employees take their coffee breaks at an assigned time, and the dress codes specify white shirts and suits for men and no beards. However, employees like this culture. Reliability counts. Extra work is not required. The culture is appropriate for the insurance company, which succeeds because it can be trusted to deliver on insurance policies as agreed.[23]

CULTURE STRENGTH AND ORGANIZATIONAL SUBCULTURES

A strong organizational culture can have a powerful impact on company performance. **Culture strength** refers to the degree of agreement among members of an organization about the importance of specific values. If widespread consensus exists about the importance of those values, the culture is cohesive and strong; if little agreement exists, the culture is weak.[24]

A strong culture is typically associated with the frequent use of ceremonies, symbols, stories, heroes, and slogans. These elements increase employee commitment to the values and strategy of a company. In addition, managers who want to create and maintain strong corporate cultures often give emphasis to the selection and socialization of employees. For example, at Southwest Airlines, prospective employees are subjected to rigorous interviewing, sometimes even by Southwest's regular customers, so that only those who fit the culture are hired. At Trilogy Software, Inc., one of today's fastest-growing software companies, selection and socialization of new employees is a companywide mission, as described in the Taking the Lead box.

However, culture is not always uniform throughout the organization. Even in organizations that have strong cultures, there may be several sets of subcultures, particularly within large organizations. **Subcultures** develop to reflect the common problems, goals, and experiences that members of a team, department, or other unit share. An office, branch, or unit of a company that is physically separated from the company's main operations may also take on a distinctive subculture.

For example, although the dominant culture of an organization may be a mission culture, various departments may also reflect characteristics of adaptability/entrepreneurial, clan, or bureaucratic cultures. The manufacturing department of a large organization may thrive in an environment that emphasizes order, efficiency, and obedience to rules, whereas the research and development department may be characterized by employee empowerment, flexibility, and customer focus. This is similar to the concept of differentiation described in Chapter 4, where employees in manufacturing, sales, and research departments studied by Paul Lawrence and Jay Lorsch[25] developed different values with respect to time horizon, interpersonal relationships, and formality in order to perform the job of each particular department most effectively. The credit division of Pitney Bowes, a huge corporation that manufactures postage meters, copiers, and other office equipment, developed a distinctive subculture to encourage innovation and risk-taking.

| **In Practice 9.1** | Pitney Bowes Credit Corporation |

Pitney Bowes, a maker of postage meters and other office equipment, has long thrived in an environment of order and predictability. Its headquarters reflects a typical corporate environment and an orderly culture with its blank walls and bland carpeting. But step onto the third floor of the Pitney Bowes building in Shelton, Connecticut, and you might think you're at a different company. The domain of Pitney Bowes Credit Corporation (PBCC) looks more like an indoor theme park, featuring cobblestone-patterned carpets, faux gas lamps, and an ornate town-square-style clock. It also has a French-style café, a 1950s style diner, and the "Cranial Kitchen," where employees sit in cozy booths to surf the Internet or watch training videos. The friendly hallways encourage impromptu conversations, where employees can exchange information and share ideas they wouldn't otherwise share.

PBCC traditionally helped customers finance their business with the parent company. However, Matthew Kisner, PBCC's president and CEO, has worked with other managers to redefine the division as a *creator* of services rather than just a provider of services. Rather than just financing sales and leasing of existing products, PBCC now creates new services for customers to buy. For example, Purchase Power is a revolving line of credit that helps companies finance their postage costs. It was profitable within nine months and now has more than 400,000 customers. When PBCC redefined its job, it began redefining its subculture to match, by emphasizing values of teamwork, risk-taking, and creativity. "We wanted a fun space that would embody our culture," Kissner says. "No straight lines, no linear thinking. Because we're a financial services company, our biggest advantage is the quality of our ideas." So far, PBCC's new approach is working. In one recent year, the division, whose 600 employees make up less than 2 percent of Pitney Bowes' total work force, generated 36 percent of the company's net profits.[26]

Subcultures typically include the basic values of the dominant organizational culture plus additional values unique to members of the subculture. However, subcultural differences can sometimes lead to conflicts between departments, especially in organizations that do not have strong overall corporate cultures. When subcultural values become too strong and outweigh the corporate cultural values, organizational performance may suffer. Conflict will be discussed in detail in Chapter 12.

CULTURE AND THE LEARNING ORGANIZATION

One of the primary characteristics of a learning organization is a strong organizational culture. In addition, the culture of a learning organization encourages change and adaptation. A danger for many successful organizations is that the culture becomes set and the company fails to adapt as the environment changes. When organizations are successful, the values, ideas, and practices that helped attain success become institutionalized. As the environment changes, these values may become detrimental to future performance. Many organizations become victims of their own success, clinging to outmoded and even destructive values and behaviors. Durk Jager, the new CEO of Procter & Gamble, is struggling to change a rigid culture that insists on "the P&G way of doing things." P&G is a great American company, but it has stopped growing. Whereas many competitors take only months to move new products from idea to the market, P&G typically takes five years. Jager wants to create a culture that encourages speed, innovation, and initiative. In one training video, he admonishes employees to trash their *Current Best Approaches* manuals—long a mainstay at P&G—and think for themselves.[27]

Thus, the impact of a strong organizational culture may not always be positive. Some organizations have cultures that encourage a healthy adaptation to the external environment while others have cultures that encourage rigidity and stability. Learning organizations have strong, adaptive cultures that incorporate the following values:

Taking the Lead

Trilogy Software Inc.

Trilogy Software has been called everything from "the cult on the hill" to "the software sweatshop." None of it bothers founder, president, and CEO Joe Liemandt—or his corps of young, hardworking, hard-playing employees. The average age at the company is twenty six (Liemandt himself is only thirty) and almost every one of Trilogy's seven hundred employees is an overachiever dedicated to accomplishing Liemandt's vision to be the world's next great software company. Those who aren't don't last long. A "just-do-it-now" spirit is instilled throughout the company's culture.

Liemandt has built Trilogy's distinctive culture through one of the most rigorous selection and socialization processes in the business world. Trilogy aggressively pursues young, talented overachievers at college campuses across the country. The selection process is designed to find people who are "a good technical and cultural fit." Some of Trilogy's top software developers conduct the first-round interviews. Next, Trilogy flies the top candidates, along with their boyfriends, girlfriends, or spouses, to headquarters in Austin, where they are joined by a dozen or more "Trilogians" for a night on the town. A morning of grueling, highly technical interviews the next day might be followed by an afternoon of mountain biking or roller blading. The process is time consuming and expensive—around $13,000 per hire—but Trilogy believes it's worth every minute and every penny.

After employees are hired, they spend three exhausting, exhilarating months at Trilogy University (TU), where they bond with one another and learn about the company and the software industry. They work on projects to improve Trilogy's existing products and create entirely new ones. They also get a crash course in Trilogy culture—"how we operate, how we talk, how we party, how we work." Recruits learn quickly that at Trilogy, you work hard, play hard, practice teamwork, and take risks. A small sign lists TU's business hours as 8 A.M. to midnight, Monday through Saturday, and noon to 8 P.M. on Sunday. Liemandt makes it clear to his new employees that he will push them to the limit, give them really hard work and lots of responsibility, and then reward them accordingly. For example, three weeks into one recent TU, Liemandt flew the entire group to Las Vegas for a weekend because class members had delivered so much so quickly.

Trilogy's culture has helped it emerge as a flagship company of the new economy. The company is racing to keep up with demand for its "front office" products that optimize and streamline complicated sales and marketing processes for big companies like IBM, Whirlpool, and Goodyear Tire & Rubber, which spend millions of dollars on Trilogy technology. Liemandt knows Trilogy's hard-charging culture isn't for everyone. "But," he says, "it's definitely an environment where people who are passionate about what they do can thrive."

Source: Chuck Salter, "Insanity Inc.," *Fast Company* (January 1999): 100–108.

1. *The whole is more important than the part and boundaries between parts are mini-mized.*[28] In learning organizations, people are aware of the whole system, how everything fits together, and the relationships among various organizational parts. Everyone considers how their actions affect other parts and the total organization. This emphasis on the whole reduces boundaries both within the organization and with other companies. Although subcultures may form, everyone's primary attitudes and behaviors reflect the organization's dominant culture. The free flow of people, ideas, and information allows coordinated action and continuous learning. At the Mayo Clinic, founded more than a century ago in Rochester, Minnesota, teamwork permeates the clinic's organizational culture. Doctors are expected to consult with doctors in other departments, with the patient, and with anyone else inside or outside the clinic who might help in dealing with any aspect of a patient's problem. Collaboration and sharing of ideas and information is incorporated into everything Mayo does, from diagnosis and surgery to policy making, strategic planning, and leadership.[29]

2. *Equality is a primary value.* The culture of a learning organization creates a sense of community and caring for one another. The organization is a place for creating a web of relationships that allows people to take risks and develop to their full potential. Activities such as assigned parking spaces and executive dining rooms that create status differences are discarded. At Fastenal Co. in Winona, Minnesota, CEO Bob Kierlin has no reserved parking space and often sorts the mail himself. Kierlin treats all his employees the same, whether you're a janitor or a vice-president. The sense of equality and fairness is a core element of Fastenal's culture.[30] The emphasis on treating everyone with care and respect creates a climate of safety and trust that allows experimentation, frequent mistakes, and learning.

3. *The culture encourages risk taking, change, and improvement.* A basic value of a learning organization is to question the status quo. Constant questioning of assumptions opens the gates to creativity and improvement. The culture rewards and celebrates the creators of new ideas, products, and work processes. To symbolize the importance of taking risks, a learning organization culture may also reward those who fail in order to learn and grow.

The culture of a learning organization encourages openness, boundarylessness, equality, continuous improvement, and risk-taking. Even though the internal culture is strong, the cultural values encourage a healthy adaptation to a changing external environment. As illustrated in Exhibit 9.5, adaptive corporate cultures have different values and behavior patterns than unadaptive cultures.[31] In adaptive cultures, managers are concerned with customers and employees as well as the internal processes and procedures that bring about useful change. Behavior is flexible and managers initiate change when needed, even if it involves risk. In unadaptive cultures, managers are more concerned about themselves or their own special projects, and their values discourage risk-taking and change. Thus, strong healthy cultures, such as those in learning companies, help organizations adapt to the external environment, whereas strong unhealthy cultures can encourage an organization to march resolutely in the wrong direction. As discussed in Book Mark 9.0, a strong adaptive culture is a key determining factor in the success of companies such as Wal-Mart, Johnson & Johnson, and Hewlett-Packard. Netscape Communications, recently acquired by America Online, reflects the values of a strong, adaptive organizational culture.

EXHIBIT 9.5   *Adaptive Versus Nonadaptive Corporate Cultures*

	Adaptive Corporate Cultures	**Unadaptive Corporate Cultures**
Core Values	Managers care deeply about customers, stockholders, and employees. They also strongly value people and processes that can create useful change (for example, leadership initiatives up and down the management hierarchy).	Managers care mainly about themselves, their immediate work group, or some product (or technology) associated with that work group. They value the orderly and risk-reducing management process much more highly than leadership initiatives.
Common Behavior	Managers pay close attention to all their constituencies, especially customers, and initiate change when needed to serve their legitimate interests, even if it entails taking some risks.	Managers tend to be somewhat isolated, political, and bureaucratic. As a result, they do not change their strategies quickly to adjust to or take advantage of changes in their business environments.

Source: Adapted and reprinted with the permission of The Free Press, an imprint of Simon & Schuster, from *Corporate Culture and Performance* by John P. Kotter and James L. Heskett. Copyright © 1992 by Kotter Associates, Inc. and James L. Heskett.

In Practice 9.2

Netscape Communications Corp.

Netscape Communications is viewed by many as one of today's companies that is defining the workplace of the future: it's fast, nimble, exciting, and continuously changing. "I'm constantly surprised over the years how at times I thought we were doomed but then things panned out," says Mike McCool, a software engineer who's been with the company almost since the beginning.

    The secret to Netscape's survival is its adaptive corporate culture, which encourages creativity, sharing of ideas, change, and learning. Employees are free to come and go as they please and even work at home if they like. Independence, responsibility, and accountability are cultural hallmarks. However, Netscape also rewards teamwork and the sharing of information and ideas, and most employees thrive in the fast-paced environment at Netscape. Even at 1 A.M. there's usually someone at the company to bounce ideas around and discuss problems or new projects. To keep employees tuned in to what's going on in other departments, Netscape holds quarterly "all hands" meetings where top managers talk about what's going on in the entire company. Product development groups also hold open weekly meetings to share the status of products or new technologies. These efforts help foster a sense of community so that employees feel involved with the whole company, not just their team or department.

    All employees at Netscape are encouraged to participate and have a voice, and equality is a primary value. Everyone, including President and CEO Jim Barksdale, works in an open cubicle. People can see across the dividers and call out to colleagues. Learning is also highly valued. Although the company offers a full range of training programs, what employees value most is the opportunity to learn and expand their skills on the job. Managers encourage employees to try new things, experiment, take risks, and make mistakes. Employees are never punished for failures—Netscape's managers realize that some experiments fail, and mistakes are keys to learning. Netscape's adaptive culture has helped the company weather a number of crises and is playing a significant role as the company once again shifts gears after the acquisition by AOL.[32]

ETHICAL VALUES IN ORGANIZATIONS

Of the values that make up an organization's culture, ethical values are now considered among the most important. Ethical standards are becoming part of the formal policies and informal cultures of many organizations, and courses in ethics are taught in many business schools. **Ethics** is the code of moral principles and values that governs the behaviors of a person or group with respect to what is right or wrong. Ethical values set standards as to what is good or bad in conduct and decision making.[33]

Ethics is distinct from behaviors governed by law. The **rule of law** arises from a set of codified principles and regulations that describe how people are required to act, are generally accepted in society, and are enforceable in the courts.[34]

The relationship between ethical standards and legal requirements is illustrated in Exhibit 9.6. Ethical standards for the most part apply to behavior not

Book Mark 9.0

Have You Read This Book?

Built to Last: Successful Habits of Visionary Companies

By James C. Collins and Jerry I. Porras

In a six-year study comparing eighteen companies that have experienced long-term success with eighteen similar companies that have not performed as well, James Collins and Jerry Porras found a key determining factor in the successful companies to be a culture in which employees share such a strong vision that they know in their hearts what is right for the company. *Built to Last* describes how companies such as 3M, Boeing, Wal-Mart, Merck, Nordstrom, Hewlett-Packard, and others have successfully adapted to a changing world without losing sight of the core values that guide the organization. Collins and Porras found that the successful companies were guided by a "core ideology"—values and a sense of purpose that go beyond just making money and that provide a guide for employee behavior.

TIMELESS FUNDAMENTALS

The book offers four key concepts that show how managers can contribute to building successful companies.

- *Be a clock builder, not a time teller.* Products and market opportunities are vehicles for building a great organization, not the other way around. Visionary leaders concentrate on building adaptive cultures and systems that remain strong despite changes in products, services, or markets.

- *Embrace the "Genius of the AND."* Successful organizations simultaneously embrace two extremes, such as continuity and change, stability and revolution, predictability and chaos.

- *Preserve the core/Stimulate progress.* The core ideology is balanced with a relentless drive for progress. Successful companies set ambitious goals and create an atmosphere that encourages experimentation and learning.

- *Seek consistent alignment.* Strive to make all aspects of the company work in unison with the core ideology. At Disneyland, employees are "cast members" and customers are "guests." Hewlett-Packard's policies reinforce its commitment to respect for each individual.

CONCLUSION

Built to Last offers important lessons on how managers can build organizations that stand the test of time. By concentrating on the timeless fundamentals, organizations can adapt and thrive in a changing world.

Built to Last: Successful Habits of Visionary Companies, by James C. Collins and Jerry I. Porras, is published by HarperCollins.

EXHIBIT 9.6   *Relationship Between the Rule of Law and Ethical Standards*

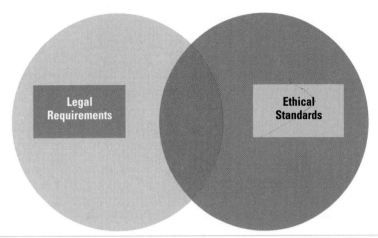

Source: LaRue Tone Hosmer, *The Ethics of Management,* 2d ed. (Homewood, Ill.: Irwin, 1991).

covered by the law, and the rule of law covers behaviors not necessarily covered by ethical standards. Current laws often reflect combined moral judgments, but not all moral judgments are codified into law. The morality of aiding a drowning person, for example, is not specified by law, and driving on the righthand side of the road has no moral basis; but in areas such as robbery or murder, rules and moral standards overlap.

Unethical conduct in organizations is surprisingly widespread. More than 54 percent of human resource professionals polled by the Society for Human Resource Management and the Ethics Resource Center reported observing employees lying to supervisors or coworkers, falsifying reports or records, or abusing drugs or alcohol while on the job.[35] Many people believe that if you are not breaking the law, then you are behaving in an ethical manner, but ethics often go far beyond the law.[36] Many behaviors have not been codified, and managers must be sensitive to emerging norms and values about those issues. **Managerial ethics** are principles that guide the decisions and behaviors of managers with regard to whether they are right or wrong in a moral sense. The notion of **social responsibility** is an extension of this idea and refers to management's obligation to make choices and take action so that the organization contributes to the welfare and interest of society as well as to itself.[37]

Examples of the need for managerial ethics are as follows:[38]

- The supervisor of a travel agency was aware that her agents and she could receive large bonuses for booking one hundred or more clients each month with an auto rental firm, although clients typically wanted the rental agency selected on the basis of lowest cost.
- The executive in charge of a parts distribution facility told employees to tell phone customers that inventory was in stock even if it was not. Replenishing the item only took one to two days, no one was hurt by the delay, and the business was kept from competitors.
- The project manager for a consulting project wondered whether some facts should be left out of a report because the marketing executives paying for the report would look bad if the facts were reported.

- A North American manufacturer operating abroad was asked to make cash payments (a bribe) to government officials and was told it was consistent with local customs, despite being illegal in North America.

These issues are exceedingly difficult to resolve and often represent dilemmas. An **ethical dilemma** arises when each alternative choice or behavior seems undesirable because of a potentially negative ethical consequence. Right or wrong cannot be clearly identified. These choices can be aided by establishing ethical values within the organization as part of corporate culture. Corporate culture can embrace the ethical values needed for business success.

SOURCES OF ETHICAL VALUES IN ORGANIZATIONS

The standards for ethical or socially responsible conduct are embodied within each employee as well as within the organization itself. In addition, external stakeholders can influence standards of what is ethical and socially responsible. The immediate forces that impinge on ethical decisions are summarized in Exhibit 9.7. Individual beliefs and values, a person's ethical decision framework, and moral development influence personal ethics. Organization culture, as we have already discussed, shapes the overall framework of values within the organization. Moreover, formal organization systems influence values and behaviors according to the organization's policy framework and reward systems.

EXHIBIT 9.7   *Forces That Shape Managerial Ethics*

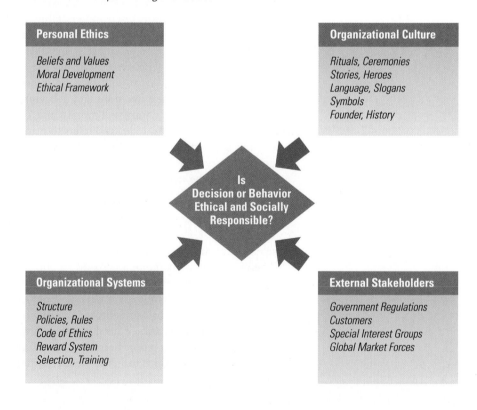

Personal Ethics

Beliefs and Values
Moral Development
Ethical Framework

Organizational Culture

Rituals, Ceremonies
Stories, Heroes
Language, Slogans
Symbols
Founder, History

Is Decision or Behavior Ethical and Socially Responsible?

Organizational Systems

Structure
Policies, Rules
Code of Ethics
Reward System
Selection, Training

External Stakeholders

Government Regulations
Customers
Special Interest Groups
Global Market Forces

Companies also respond to numerous stakeholders in determining what is right. They consider how their actions may be viewed by customers, government agencies, shareholders, and the general community, as well as the impact each alternative course of action may have on various stakeholders. All of these factors can be explored to understand ethical decisions in organizations.[39]

PERSONAL ETHICS

Every individual brings a set of personal beliefs and values into the workplace. Personal values and the moral reasoning that translates these values into behavior are an important aspect of ethical decision making in organizations.[40]

The family backgrounds and spiritual values of managers provide principles by which they carry out business. In addition, people go through stages of moral development that affect their ability to translate values into behavior. For example, children have a low level of moral development, making decisions and behaving to obtain rewards and avoid physical punishment. At an intermediate level of development, people learn to conform to expectations of good behavior as defined by colleagues and society. Most managers are at this level, willingly upholding the law and responding to societal expectations. At the highest level of moral development are people who develop an internal set of standards. These are self-chosen ethical principles that are more important to decisions than external expectations. Only a few people reach this high level, which can mean breaking laws if necessary to sustain higher moral principles.[41]

The other personal factor is whether managers have developed an *ethical framework* that guides their decisions. *Utilitarian theory*, for example, argues that ethical decisions should be made to generate the greatest benefits for the largest number of people. This framework is often consistent with business decisions because costs and benefits can be calculated in dollars. The *personal liberty* framework argues that decisions should be made to ensure the greatest possible freedom of choice and liberty for individuals. Liberties include freedom to act on one's conscience, free speech, due process, and the right to privacy. The *distributive justice* framework holds that moral decisions are those that promote equity, fairness, and impartiality with respect to the distribution of rewards and the administration of rules, which are essential for social cooperation.[42]

ORGANIZATIONAL CULTURE

Rarely can ethical or unethical business practices be attributed entirely to the personal ethics of a single individual. Because business practices reflect the values, attitudes, and behavior patterns of an organization's culture, ethics is as much an organizational issue as a personal one. To promote ethical behavior in the workplace, companies should make ethics an integral part of the organization's culture. At Certified Transmission Rebuilders, a small company based in Omaha, Nebraska, the culture is built on putting the customers' interests first. Employees receive ongoing in-house training to develop "honest communication" skills. Owner Peter Fink doesn't pay diagnosticians on commission because he doesn't want that to influence their decisions. Customers who have had their transmission repaired at Certified are asked to bring the car back in fifteen days for a free re-check to make sure everything is working right, even though the process is expensive and time-consuming. If Certified has to redo any work, it provides the customer with a rental car, plus the additional work, at no charge. Fink has built a highly successful business by giving customers the assurance that they're not paying for repairs they don't really need.[43]

One large company in which ethical standards are embedded in the organizational culture is Johnson & Johnson. Although the company's handling of the Tylenol poisoning incident has sometimes been attributed to the ethical standards of then-CEO James Burke, Burke himself has pointed out that the decisions in connection with that crisis reflected a set of values and principles that has been deeply ingrained throughout the company since its early days.[44]

ORGANIZATIONAL SYSTEMS

The third category of influences that shape managerial ethics is formal organizational systems. This includes the basic architecture of the organization, such as whether ethical values are incorporated in policies and rules; whether an explicit code of ethics is available and issued to members; whether organizational rewards, including praise, attention, and promotions, are linked to ethical behavior; and whether ethics is a consideration in the selection and training of employees. These formal efforts can reinforce ethical values that exist in the informal culture.

Today, more and more companies are establishing formal ethics programs. For example, after being maligned by the national press and pursued by federal officials for questionable billing practices and fraud, Columbia/HCA Healthcare Corp., an $18.8 billion hospital chain based in Nashville, Tennessee, brought in a new management team to clean up the mess and make sure similar ethical and legal problems never happen again. When he was hired as senior vice-president of ethics, compliance, and corporate responsibility, Alan R. Yuspeh found only a rudimentary compliance program and a set of perfunctory ethical guidelines that no one could understand. Yuspeh drafted a clear and concise code of conduct that emphasized the values of compassion, honesty, fairness, loyalty, respect, and kindness, then posted it on the intranet for comment from the company's entire work force. The final version was distributed to all 285,000 Columbia/HCA employees. In addition, Yuspeh developed a massive ethics program that includes comprehensive training for all employees and an ethics hotline that answers about 1,200 employee calls annually.[45]

EXTERNAL STAKEHOLDERS

Managerial ethics and social responsibility are also influenced by a variety of external stakeholders, groups outside the organization that have a stake in the organization's performance. Ethical and socially responsible decision making recognizes that the organization is part of a larger community and considers the impact of a decision or action on all stakeholders.[46] Important external stakeholders are government agencies, customers, special interest groups such as those concerned with the natural environment, and global market forces.

Companies must operate within the limits of certain government regulations, such as safety laws, environmental protection requirements, and many other laws and regulations. At Columbia/HCA, part of the training program is designed to make sure all employees are familiar with health care laws and regulations. Customers are concerned about the quality, safety, and availability of goods and services. For example, even though Dow Corning has an ambitious ethics program, the company's reputation as an ethical company was seriously damaged by the failure to keep customers satisfied with the safety of its silicone breast implants.[47]

Special interest groups continue to be one of the largest stakeholder concerns that companies face. Today, those concerned with corporate responsibility to the natural environment are particularly vocal. Thus, environmentalism is becoming an integral part of organizational planning and decision making for leading companies. The concept of *sustainable development*, a dual concern for economic growth and environmental sustainability, has been gaining ground among many business leaders. The public is no longer comfortable with organizations focusing solely on profit at the expense of the natural environment. Environmental sustainability—meaning that what is taken out of the environmental system for food, shelter, clothing, energy, and other human uses is restored to the system in waste that can be reused—is a part of strategy for companies like Monsanto, Interface, IKEA, Electrolux, Scandic Hotels, and MacMillan-Bloedel. Interface, the $1-billion leader in the floor covering industry, is instituting changes that will allow the company to manufacture without pollution, waste, or fossil fuels. CEO Ray Anderson is so committed to the concept of environmental sustainability that he had the following credo set in bronze at his newest factory: "If we are successful, then we will spend the rest of our days harvesting yesteryear's carpet and other petrochemically derived products, recycling them into new materials, converting sunlight into energy—with zero scrap going into the landfill and zero emissions going into the ecosystem. And we'll be doing well—very well—by doing good."[48]

Another growing pressure on organizations is related to the rapidly changing global market. Companies operating globally face difficult ethical issues. Thousands of U.S. workers have lost jobs or earning power because companies can get the same work done overseas for lower costs. For example, Yakima Products, located in Arcata, California, transferred all production of its cartop carrying systems for bikes, skis and other sporting gear to Mexico. Although the decision was financially sound and clearly served the interests of shareholders, employees and the local community felt angry and betrayed.[49] Levi Strauss contracted for low-cost labor in Burma and China but later felt ethically compelled to pull out of those contracts because of human rights violations in those countries. As the business world becomes increasingly global, issues of ethics and social responsibility will likely become even more difficult.[50]

HOW LEADERS SHAPE CULTURE AND ETHICS

A report issued by the Business Roundtable—an association of chief executives from 250 large corporations—discussed ethics, policy, and practice in one hundred member companies, including GTE, Xerox, Johnson & Johnson, Boeing, and Hewlett-Packard.[51] In the experience of the surveyed companies, the single most important factor in ethical decision making was the role of top management in providing commitment, leadership, and example for ethical values. The CEO and other top managers must be committed to specific values and must give constant leadership in tending and renewing those values. Values can be communicated in a number of ways—speeches, company publications, policy statements, and, especially, personal actions. Top leaders are responsible for creating and sustaining a culture that emphasizes the importance of ethical behavior for all employees every day. When the CEO engages in unethical practices or fails to take firm and decisive action in response to the unethical practices of others, this attitude filters down through the organization. Formal ethics codes and training programs are worthless if leaders do not set and live up to high standards of ethical conduct.[52]

The following sections examine how managers signal and implement values through leadership as well as through the formal systems of the organization.

VALUES-BASED LEADERSHIP

The underlying value system of an organization cannot be managed in the traditional way. Issuing an authoritative directive, for example, has little or no impact on an organization's value system. Organizational values are developed and strengthened primarily through **values-based leadership**, a relationship between a leader and followers that is based on shared, strongly internalized values that are advocated and acted upon by the leader.[53] Leaders influence cultural and ethical values by clearly articulating a vision for organizational values that employees can believe in, communicating the vision throughout the organization, and institutionalizing the vision through everyday behavior, rituals, ceremonies, and symbols, as well as through organizational systems and policies.

Leaders must remember that every statement and action has impact on culture and values, perhaps without their realizing it. For example, a survey of readers of *The Secretary* magazine found that employees are acutely aware of their bosses' ethical lapses. Something as simple as having a secretary notarize a document without witnessing the signature may seem insignificant, but it communicates that the manager doesn't value honesty.[54] Employees learn about values, beliefs, and goals from watching managers, just as students learn which topics are important for an exam, what professors like, and how to get a good grade from watching professors. To be effective values-based leaders, executives often use symbols, ceremonies, speeches, and slogans that match the values. Most important, actions speak louder than words, so values-based leaders "walk their talk."[55] At Eastman Kodak, for example, CEO George Fisher emphasized the organization's commitment to social responsibility by linking a portion of his own pay to social factors.[56]

Values-based leaders engender a high level of trust and respect from employees, based not only on their stated values but also on the courage, determination, and self-sacrifice they demonstrate in upholding those values. Leaders can use this respect and trust to motivate employees toward high performance and a sense of purpose in achieving the organizational vision. When leaders are willing to make personal sacrifices for the sake of values, employees also become more willing to do so. This element of self-sacrifice puts a somewhat spiritual connotation on the process of leadership. Indeed, one writer in organization theory, Karl Weick, has said that, "Managerial work can be viewed as managing myth, symbols, and labels. . . . ; because managers traffic so often in images, the appropriate role for the manager may be evangelist rather than accountant."[57]

An excellent example of a values-based leader is Max De Pree, retired CEO of Herman Miller, whose books, *Leadership Is an Art* and *Leadership Jazz,* offer insights into his success as a leader.

In Practice 9.3

Herman Miller

Herman Miller, a manufacturer of office furniture, was founded on the strong values of D. J. De Pree, who believed in employee participation and the importance of treating each individual with respect. The company adopted a plan as early as 1950 to provide workers extra pay when their unit's goals were met. Another noteworthy characteristic was limiting the CEO's salary to twenty times the amount made by the average factory worker, far less than the 117 times that a typical *Fortune* 500 CEO earns.

D. J. De Pree's son, Max, served in a number of capacities at the company, eventually becoming CEO. Max De Pree built on the values of worker participation espoused by his father in his "covenant" model of leadership. He defines a *covenant* as an emotional bond creating mutual trust built on shared goals and values. De Pree believes effective leadership can occur only when there is a "sacred" relationship between leaders and followers. For De Pree, leadership and ethics intersect at these primary points:

1. Ethical leadership withers without justice. There should be a fair distribution of profits, and leaders should recognize their indebtedness to those who follow.
2. Leaders assume stewardship of limited resources and exercise personal restraint so that meaningful relationships in the lives of followers are honored.
3. Leaders subsume their needs to those of their followers and learn how to make a commitment to the common good.
4. Leaders know how to bear, not inflict, pain.

Max De Pree was a hero to his workers. He symbolized hard work, integrity, and a constant awareness of how his decisions affected those who followed his leadership. He believed that leadership should "[liberate] people to do what is required of them in the most effective and humane way possible." De Pree worked to create and sustain an environment in which each employee wanted to do his or her best, helping the company gain recognition by *Fortune* magazine as one of the ten best-managed, most innovative companies in America.[58]

FORMAL STRUCTURE AND SYSTEMS

Another set of tools leaders can use to shape cultural and ethical values is the formal structure and systems of the organization. These systems have been especially effective in recent years for influencing managerial ethics.

Structure. Managers can assign responsibility for ethical values to a specific position. This not only allocates organization time and energy to the problem but symbolizes to everyone the importance of ethics. One example is an **ethics committee**, which is a group of executives appointed to oversee company ethics. The committee provides rulings on questionable ethical issues and assumes responsibility for disciplining wrongdoers.

Many companies are setting up ethics offices that go beyond a "police" mentality to act more as counseling centers. Alfred C. Martinez, chairman and CEO of Sears, set up an ethics and business practices office as part of his efforts to revive the company. Martinez recognized that Sears's image had been severely damaged by an early-1990s scandal in the auto centers, where employees allegedly misled customers and charged them for unnecessary repairs in order to make larger commissions. The new ethics department promotes the values in Sears's code of conduct and deals with day-to-day ethical dilemmas, questions, and appeals for advice, focusing more on helping employees make the right choices than on punishing wrongdoers.[59]

Another example is an **ethics ombudsperson**, who is a single manager, perhaps with a staff, who serves as the corporate conscience. As work forces become more diverse and organizations continue to emphasize greater employee involvement, it is likely that more and more companies will assign ombudspersons to listen to grievances, investigate ethical complaints, and point out employee concerns and possible ethical abuses to top management. For the system to work, it is necessary for the person in this position to have direct access to the chairman or CEO, as does the corporate ombudsperson for Pitney Bowes.[60]

Disclosure Mechanisms. The ethics office, committee, or ombudsperson provides mechanisms for employees to voice concerns about ethical practices. One important function is to establish supportive policies and procedures about whistle-blowing. **Whistle-blowing** is employee disclosure of illegal, immoral, or illegitimate practices on the part of the organization.[61] One value of corporate policy is to protect whistle-blowers so they will not be transferred to lower-level positions or fired because of their ethical concerns. A policy can also encourage whistle-blowers to stay within the organization—for instance, to quietly blow the whistle to responsible managers.[62] Whistle-blowers have the option to stop organizational activities by going to newspaper or television reporters, but as a last resort.

Although whistle-blowing has become widespread in recent years, it is still risky for employees, who can lose their jobs or be ostracized by co-workers. Sometimes managers believe a whistle-blower is out of line and think they are acting correctly to fire or sabotage that employee. As ethical problems in the corporate world increase, many companies are looking for ways to protect whistle-blowers. In addition, calls are increasing for legal protection for those who report illegal or unethical business activities.[63]

When there are no protective measures, whistle-blowers suffer, and the company may continue its unethical or illegal practices. When Curtis Overall reported nearly two hundred broken screws at the bottom of a massive ice condenser system at TVA's Watts Bar nuclear plant, he thought he was just doing his job, making sure the primary safety system would work properly once the reactor was fired up. However, Overall lost his job and security clearance and endured an escalating series of threats, which eventually caused him to seek treatment for stress and depression. Although he eventually won his job back, he left again after a fake bomb was planted in his pickup truck. The Nuclear Regulatory Commission is still investigating the situation at Watts Bar.[64]

Although many whistle-blowers are prepared to suffer financial loss to maintain ethical standards, many companies have created a climate in which employees feel free to point out problems. A growing number of corporations, including Texas Instruments, Raytheon, Pacific Bell, and Northern Telecom, are setting up ethics hot lines that give employees a confidential way to report misconduct. These hot lines also serve as help lines. According to Gary Edwards, president of the Ethics Resource Center, about 65 to 85 percent of calls to hot lines in the organizations he advises are calls for counsel on ethical issues rather than calls to blow the whistle on wrongdoers. Northrup Grumman's "Openline" fields about 1,400 calls a year, of which only one-fourth are reports of misdeeds.[65]

Code of Ethics. A study by the Center for Business Ethics found that 90 percent of *Fortune* 500 companies and almost half of all other companies have developed a corporate code of ethics.[66] The code clarifies company expectations of employee conduct and makes clear that the company expects its personnel to recognize the ethical dimensions of corporate behavior.

Some companies use broader values statements within which ethics is a part. These statements define ethical values as well as corporate culture and contain language about company responsibility, quality of product, and treatment of employees. A formal statement of values can serve as a fundamental organizational document that defines what the organization stands for and legitimizes value choices for employees.[67] United Technologies Corporation, GTE, and Liz Claiborne, Inc. have all established statements of cultural and ethical values. Northern Telecom's *Code of Business Conduct,* which is provided to all employees in booklet form and is also available on the Internet, is a set of standards and guidelines that illustrates how the company's core values and mission translate into ethical business practices.

A code of ethics states the values or behaviors that are expected as well as those that will not be tolerated or backed up by management's action. A code of ethics or larger values statement is an important tool in the management of organizational values.

Training Programs. To ensure that ethical issues are considered in daily decision making, companies can supplement a written code of ethics with employee training programs.[68] A recent survey showed that 45 percent of responding companies were including ethics training in employee seminars. At Sears, all managers receive literature on ethics, attend ethics training courses at Sears University, and annually re-sign a contract signifying their commitment to the company's code of conduct. Texas Instruments employees go through an eight-hour ethics training course, which includes case examples that give participants a chance to wrestle with ethical dilemmas. In addition, TI incorporates an ethics component into every training course it offers.[69]

In an important step, ethics programs also include frameworks for ethical decision making, such as the utilitarian approach described earlier in this chapter. Learning these frameworks helps managers act autonomously and still think their way through a difficult decision. In a few companies, managers are also taught about the stages of moral development, which helps to bring them to a high stage of ethical decision making. This training has been an important catalyst for establishing ethical behavior and integrity as critical components of strategic competitiveness.[70]

These formal systems and structures can be highly effective. However, they alone are not sufficient to build and sustain an ethical company. Leaders should integrate ethics into the organizational culture and support and renew ethical values through their words and actions. The Holt Companies, with headquarters in San Antonio, Texas, has very little formal structure for dealing with ethics, but the company provides a model of ethical business management.

In Practice 9.4

Holt Companies

The Holt Companies has no formal ethics office and no separate ethics officer or committee. The company's executive committee serves as its ethics committee, and the designated ethics officer is the vice-president of human resources. Every meeting opens with "Values in Action" stories that highlight recent values-relevant events, how they were handled, and how the company can learn from them. Most importantly, everyone in the firm, especially the CEO, Peter Holt, is expected to be responsible for ethics. Ethical values are woven into the organizational culture, and Holt continually works to renew the values and signal his total commitment to them.

Holt began developing his approach to ethics in the mid-1980s after joining the company founded by his great-grandfather a century ago. The Holt Companies have more than 1,200 employees in fourteen Texas and Ohio locations. To develop his Values-Based Leadership (VBL) process, Holt first involved the entire work force in determining a set of core values that would guide everything the company did. The final list puts ethical values, including being honest, showing integrity, being consistent, and providing fair treatment, at the top, followed in order by values of attaining success through meeting goals, achieving continuous improvement, commitment to the long-term health of the company, and pursuing new strategic opportunities through creativity and change.

All new employees attend a two-day training program, where they learn about the values and discuss values-related cases and dilemmas. In addition, the Holt Companies presents a two-day ethics awareness course for all managers and supervisors. Peter Holt visits each of the firm's locations twice a year to conduct two-hour meetings with employees, where he discloses financial information, answers questions, and talks about the importance of each employee upholding Holt's core values every day in every action. The close involvement of the CEO and other top leaders has contributed to an environment of candor and respect between management and workers. Holt's evaluation and reward systems are also tied to the values-based leadership process. Because ethical values are entrenched in the organizational culture, Holt has not found a need for more formal systems.[71]

By integrating ethics throughout the organization, companies like Holt make personal and organizational integrity a part of day-to-day business. Holt's system was not an overnight success. It took several years to develop the level of trust needed to make it work. Only when employees are convinced that ethical values play a key role in all management decisions and actions can they become committed to making them a part of their everyday behavior.

CORPORATE CULTURE IN A GLOBAL ENVIRONMENT

A Hudson Institute report, *Workforce 2020*, states, "The rest of the world matters to a degree that it never did in the past."[72] Managers are finding this to be true not only in terms of economics or human resources issues, but also in terms of cultural and ethical values. How do managers translate the ideas for developing strong corporate cultures to a complex global environment? As business increasingly crosses geographical and cultural boundaries, the need to be aware of and sensitive to other cultures, as well as to understand the impact of national culture on the organization, becomes paramount. About 75 percent of companies believe they have had alliances that failed because of an incompatibility between the national and the corporate culture.[73] Corporate culture and national culture are often intertwined, and the global diversity of many of today's companies presents a challenge to managers trying to build a strong organizational culture. Employees who come from different countries often have varied attitudes and beliefs that make it difficult to establish a sense of community and cohesiveness based on the corporate culture. In fact, research has indicated that national culture has a greater impact on employees than does corporate culture.[74]

However, in this multicultural environment some companies are developing a broad global perspective that permeates the entire organizational culture. For example, Omron, a global company with headquarters in Kyoto, Japan, has offices on each continent. However, until a few years ago, Omron had always assigned Japanese managers to head them. Today, it relies on local expertise in each geographical area and blends the insights and perspectives of local managers into a global whole. Global planning meetings are held in offices around the world. In addition, Omron established a global database and standardized its software to ensure a smooth exchange of information among its offices worldwide. It takes time to develop a broad cultural mind-set and spread it throughout the company, but firms such as Omron manage to bring a multicultural approach to every business issue.

Vijay Govindarajan, a professor of international business and director of the "Global Leadership 2020" management program at Dartmouth College, offers some guidance for managers trying to build a global culture. His research indicates that, even though organizational cultures may vary widely, there are specific components that characterize a global culture. These include an emphasis on multicultural rather than national values, basing status on merit rather than nationality, being open to new ideas from other cultures, showing excitement rather than trepidation when entering new cultural environments, and being sensitive to cultural differences without being limited by them.[75] In the twenty-first century, organizations will continue to evolve in their ability to work with varied cultures, blend them into a cohesive whole, and cope with the conflicts that may arise when working in a multicultural environment.

SUMMARY AND INTERPRETATION

This chapter covered a range of material on corporate culture, the importance of cultural and ethical values, and techniques managers can use to influence these values. Culture is the set of key values, beliefs, and understandings shared by members of an organization. Organizational cultures serve two critically important functions—to integrate members so that they know how to relate to one another and to help the organization adapt to the external environment. Culture can be observed and interpreted through rites and ceremonies, stories and heroes, symbols, and language.

Organizational culture should reinforce the strategy and structure that the organization needs to be successful in its environment. Four types of culture that may exist in organizations are adaptability/entrepreneurial culture, mission culture, clan culture, and bureaucratic culture. When widespread consensus exists about the importance of specific values, the organizational culture is strong and cohesive. However, even in organizations with strong cultures, several sets of subcultures may emerge, particularly in large organizations. Strong cultures can be either adaptive or unadaptive. One of the characteristics of a learning organization is a strong adaptive organizational culture that encourages openness, boundarylessness, equality, continuous change, and risk taking. Adaptive cultures have different values and different behavior patterns than unadaptive cultures. Strong but unhealthy cultures can be detrimental to a company's chances for success.

An important aspect of organizational values is management ethics, which is the set of values governing behavior with respect to what is right or wrong. Ethical decision making in organizations is shaped by many factors: personal characteristics, which include personal beliefs, moral development, and the adoption of ethical frameworks for decision making; organizational culture, which is the extent to which values, heroes, traditions, and symbols reinforce ethical decision making; organizational systems, which pertain to the formal structure, policies, codes of ethics, and reward systems that reinforce ethical or unethical choices; and the interests and concerns of external stakeholders, which include government agencies, customers, special interest groups, and global market forces.

The chapter discussed how leaders can shape culture and ethics. One important idea is values-based leadership, which means leaders define a vision of proper values, communicate it throughout the organization, and institutionalize it through everyday behavior, rituals, ceremonies, and symbols. We also discussed formal systems that are important for shaping ethical values. Formal systems include an ethics committee, an ethics ombudsperson, disclosure mechanisms for whistle-blowing, ethics training programs, and a code of ethics or values statement that specifies ethical values. As business increasingly crosses geographical and cultural boundaries, leaders face difficult challenges in establishing strong cultural values with which all employees can identify and agree. Companies that develop global cultures emphasize multicultural values, base status on merit rather than nationality, are excited about new cultural environments, remain open to ideas from other cultures, and are sensitive to different cultural values without being limited by them.

BRIEFCASE

As an organization manager, keep these guidelines in mind:

1. Pay attention to corporate culture. Understand the underlying values, assumptions, and beliefs on which culture is based as well as its observable manifestations. Evaluate corporate culture based on rites and ceremonies, stories and heroes, symbols, and language.
2. Make sure corporate culture is consistent with strategy and environment. Culture can be shaped to fit the needs of both. Four types of culture are adaptability/entrepreneurial culture, mission culture, clan culture, and bureaucratic culture.
3. Take control of ethical values in the organization. Ethics is not the same as following the law. Ethical decisions are influenced by management's personal background, by organizational culture, and by organizational systems.
4. Act as a leader for the internal culture and ethical values that are important to the organization. Influence the value system through values-based leadership, including the use of ceremonies, slogans, symbols, and stories. Communicate important values to employees to enhance organizational effectiveness, and remember that actions speak louder than words.
5. Use the formal systems of the organization to implement desired cultural and ethical values. These systems include an ethics committee, ethics ombudsperson, disclosure mechanisms, a code of ethics, a mission statement, and training in ethical decision-making frameworks.

KEY CONCEPTS

adaptability/entrepreneurial culture	legends
bureaucratic culture	managerial ethics
clan culture	mission culture
culture	myths
culture strength	rites and ceremonies
ethical dilemma	rule of law
ethics	social responsibility
ethics committee	stories
ethics ombudsperson	subcultures
external adaptation	symbol
heroes	values-based leadership
internal integration	whistle-blowing
language	

DISCUSSION QUESTIONS

1. Describe observable symbols, ceremonies, dress, or other aspects of culture and the underlying values they represent for an organization where you have worked.
2. What might be some of the advantages of having several subcultures within an organization? The disadvantages?
3. Do you think a bureaucratic culture would be less employee-oriented than a clan culture? Discuss.
4. Discuss the differences among rites of enhancement, renewal, and integration.
5. Why is values-based leadership so important to the influence of culture? Does a symbolic act communicate more about company values than an explicit statement? Discuss.
6. Are you aware of a situation where either you or someone you know was confronted by an ethical dilemma, such as being encouraged to inflate an expense account? Do you think the person's decision was affected by individual moral development or by the accepted values within the company? Explain.
7. Why is "equality" an important value in the culture of a learning organization? Discuss.
8. What importance would you attribute to leadership statements and actions for influencing ethical values and decision making in an organization?
9. How do external stakeholders influence ethical decision making in an organization? Discuss why globalization has contributed to more complex ethical issues for today's organizations.
10. Codes of ethics have been criticized for transferring responsibility for ethical behavior from the organization to the individual employee. Do you agree? Do you think a code of ethics is valuable for an organization?

CHAPTER 9 WORKBOOK *Shop 'til You Drop: Corporate Culture in the Retail World**

To understand more about corporate culture, visit two retail stores and compare them according to various factors. Go to one discount/low-end store, such as Kmart or Wal-Mart, and to one high-end store, such as Saks Fifth Avenue, Dayton/Hudson's, Goldwater's, or Dillard's. Do not interview any employees, but instead be an observer or a shopper. After your visits, fill out the following table for each store. Spend at least two hours in each store on a busy day and be very observant.

Culture Item	Discount Store	High-End Department Store
1. Mission of store: What is it, and is it clear to employees?		
2. Individual initiative: Is it encouraged?		

Culture Item	Discount Store	High-End Department Store
3. Reward System: What are employees rewarded for?		
4. Teamwork: Do people within one department or across departments work together or talk with each other?		
5. Company loyalty: Is there evidence of loyalty or of enthusiasm to be working there?		
6. Dress: Are there uniforms? Is there a dress code? How strong is it? How do you rate employees' personal appearance in general?		
7. Diversity or commonality of employees: Is there diversity or commonality in age, education, race, personality, and so on?		
8. Service orientation: Is the customer valued or tolerated?		
9. Human resource development: Is there opportunity for growth and advancement?		

QUESTIONS

1. How does the culture seem to influence employee behavior in each store?
2. What effect does employees' behavior have on customers?
3. Which store was more pleasant to be in? How does that relate to the mission of the store?

Case for Analysis   *Implementing Change at National Industrial Products**

Curtis Simpson sat staring out the window of his office. What would he say to Tom Lawrence when they met this afternoon? Tom had clearly met the challenge Simpson set for him when he hired him as president of National Industrial Products a little more than a year ago, but the company seemed to be coming apart at the seams. As chairman and CEO of Simpson Industries, which had bought National several years ago, Simpson was faced with the task of understanding the problem and clearly communicating his ideas and beliefs to Lawrence.

National Industrial Products is a medium-sized producer of mechanical seals, pumps, and other flow-control products. When Simpson Industries acquired the company, it was under the leadership of Jim Carpenter, who had been CEO for almost three decades and was very well-liked by employees at National. Carpenter had always treated his employees like "family." He knew most of them by name, often visited them in their homes if they were ill, and spent part of each day just chatting with workers on the factory floor. National sponsored an annual holiday party for its workers, as well as company picnics or other social events several times a year, and Carpenter was always in attendance. He considered these activities to be just as important as his visits with customers or negotiations with suppliers. Carpenter believed it was important to treat people right so they would have a sense of loyalty to the company. If business was slow, he would find something else for workers to do, even if it was just sweeping the parking lot, rather than lay people off. He figured the company couldn't afford to lose skilled workers who were so difficult to replace. "If you treat people right," he said, "they'll do a good job for you without you having to push them."

Carpenter had never set performance objectives and standards for the various departments, and he trusted his managers to run their departments as they saw fit. He offered training programs in communications and human relations for managers and team leaders several times each year. Carpenter's approach had seemed to work quite well for much of National's history. Employees were very loyal to Carpenter and the company, and there were many instances in which workers had gone above and beyond the call of duty. For example, when two National pumps that supplied water to a U. S. Navy ship failed on a Saturday night just before the ship's scheduled departure, two employees had worked throughout the night to make new seals and deliver them for installation before the ship left port. Most of National's managers and employees had been with the company for many years, and National boasted the lowest turnover in the industry.

However, as the industry began to change in recent years, National's competitiveness began to decline. Four of National's major rivals had recently merged into two large companies that were better able to meet customer needs, which was one factor that led to National being acquired by Simpson Industries. Following the acquisition, National's sales and profits had continued to decline, while costs kept going up. In addition, Simpson's top executives were concerned about low productivity at National. Although they had been happy to have Carpenter stay on through the transition, within a year they had gently pressured him into early retirement. Some of the top managers believed Carpenter tolerated poor performance and low productivity in order to maintain a friendly atmosphere. "In today's world, you just can't do that," one had said. "We've got to bring in someone who can implement change and turn this company around in a hurry, or National's going to go bankrupt." That's when Tom Lawrence was brought on board, with a mandate to cut costs and improve productivity and profits.

Lawrence had a growing reputation as a young, dynamic manager who could get things done fast. He quickly began making changes at National. First, he cut costs by discontinuing the company-sponsored social activities, and he even refused to allow the impromptu birthday celebrations that had once been a regular part of life at National. He cut the training programs in communications and human relations, arguing that they were a waste of time and money. "We're not here to make people feel good," he told his managers. "If people don't want to work, get rid of them and find someone else who does." He often referred to workers who complained about the changes at National as "crybabies."

*Based on Gary Yukl, "Consolidated Products," in *Leadership in Organizations,* 4th ed. (Englewood Cliffs, N.J.: Prentice-Hall, 1998): 66–67; John M. Champion and John H. James, "Implementing Strategic Change," in *Critical Incidents in Management: Decision and Policy Issues,* 6th ed. (Homewood, Ill.: Irwin, 1989): 138–140; and William C. Symonds "Where Paternalism Equals Good Business," *Business Week,* 20 July 1998, 16E4, 16E6.

Lawrence established strict performance standards for his vice presidents and department managers and ordered them to do the same for their employees. He held weekly meetings with each manager to review department performance and discuss problems. All employees were now subject to regular performance reviews. Any worker who had substandard performance was to be given one warning and then fired if performance did not improve within two weeks. And, whereas managers and sales representatives had once been paid on a straight salary basis, with seniority being the sole criterion for advancement, Lawrence implemented a revised system that rewarded them for meeting productivity, sales, and profit goals. For those who met the standards, rewards were generous, including large bonuses and perks such as company cars and first-class air travel to industry meetings. Those who fell behind were often chided in front of their colleagues to set an example, and if they didn't shape up soon, Lawrence didn't hesitate to fire them.

By the end of Lawrence's first year as president of National, production costs had been reduced by nearly 20 percent, while output was up 10 percent and sales increased by nearly 10 percent as well. However, three experienced and well-respected National managers had left the company for jobs with competitors, and turnover among production workers had increased alarmingly. In today's tight labor market, replacements were not easily found. Most disturbing to Simpson were the results of a survey he had commissioned by an outside consultant. The survey indicated that morale at National was in the pits. Workers viewed their supervisors with antagonism and a touch of fear. They expressed the belief that managers are obsessed with profits and quotas and care nothing about workers' needs and feelings. They also noted that the collegial, friendly atmosphere that made National a great place to work has been replaced by an environment of aggressive internal competition and distrust.

Simpson is pleased that Lawrence has brought National's profits and productivity up to the standards Simpson Industries expects. However, he is concerned that the low morale and high turnover will seriously damage the company in the long run. Is Lawrence correct that many of the employees at National are just being "crybabies"? Are they so accustomed to being coddled by Carpenter that they aren't willing to make the changes that are necessary to keep the company competitive in today's environment? Finally, Simpson wonders if a spirit of competition can exist in an atmosphere of collegiality and cooperativeness such as that fostered by Carpenter.

Case for Analysis   *Does This Milkshake Taste Funny?**

George Stein, a college student working for Eastern Dairy during the summer, was suddenly faced with an ethical dilemma. George had very little time to think about his choices, less than a minute. On the one hand, he could do what Paul told him to do, and his shift could go home on time. However, he found it tough to shake the gross mental image of all those innocent kids drinking milkshakes contaminated with pulverized maggots. If he chose instead to go against Paul, what would the guys say? He could almost hear their derisive comments already: "wimp . . ., college kid. . . ."

BACKGROUND
George Stein had lived his entire life in various suburbs of a major city on the east coast. His father's salary as a manager provided the family with a solid middle-class lifestyle. His mother was a homemaker. George's major interests in life were the local teenage gathering place—a drive-in restaurant—hot rod cars, and his girlfriend, Cathy. He had not really wanted to attend college, but relentless pressure by his parents convinced him to try it for a year. He chose mechanical engineering as his major, hoping there might be some similarity between being a

*This case was prepared by Roland B. Cousins, LaGrange College, and Linda E. Benitz, InterCel, Inc., as a basis for class discussion and not to illustrate either effective or ineffective handling of an administrative situation. The names of the firm, individuals, and the location involved have been disguised to preserve anonymity. The situation reported is factual. The authors thank Anne T. Lawrence for her assistance in the development of this case.

mechanical engineer and being a mechanic. After one year of engineering school, however, he has not seen any similarity yet. Once again this summer, his parents had to prod and cajole him to agree to return to school in the fall. They only succeeded by promising to give their blessing to his marriage to Cathy following his sophomore year.

George worked at menial jobs each of the last four summers to satisfy his immediate need for dating and car money. He did manage to put away a bit to be used for spending money during the school year. He had saved very little for the day that he and Cathy would start their life together, but they planned for Cathy to support them with her earnings as secretary until George either finished or quit school.

The day after George returned home this summer, he heard that Eastern Dairy might hire summer help. He applied at the local plant the next day. Eastern Dairy was unionized, and the wages paid were over twice the minimum wage George had been paid on previous jobs, so he was quite interested in a position.

Eastern Dairy manufactured milkshake and ice cream mix for a number of customers in the metropolitan area. It sold the ice cream mix in five- and ten-gallon containers to other firms, which then added the flavoring ingredients (e.g., strawberries or blueberries), packaged and froze the mix, and sold the ice cream under their own brand names. Eastern Dairy sold the milkshake mix in five-gallon cardboard cartons, which contained a plastic liner. These packages were delivered to many restaurants in the area. The packaging was designed to fit into automatic milkshake machines used in many types of restaurants, including most fast-food restaurants and drive-ins.

George was elated when he received the call asking him to come to the plant on June 8. After a brief visit with the human resources director, at which time George filled out the necessary employment forms, he was instructed to report for work at 11:00 P.M. that night. He was assigned to the night shift, working from 11:00 P.M. until 7:00 A.M. six nights per week—Sunday through Friday. With the regular wages paid at Eastern Dairy, supplemented by time and one-half for eight hours of guaranteed overtime each week, George thought he could save a tidy sum before he had to return to school at the end of the first week in September.

When George reported to work, he discovered that there were no managers assigned to the night

shift. The entire plant was operated by a six-person crew of operators. One member of this crew, a young man named Paul Burnham, received each night's production orders from the day shift superintendent as the superintendent left for the day. Although Paul's status was no different from that of his five colleagues, the other crew members looked to him for direction. Paul passed the production orders to the mixer (who was the first stage of the production process) and kept the production records for the shift.

The production process was really quite simple. Mixes moved between various pieces of equipment (including mixing vats, pasteurizers, coolers, homogenizers, and filling machines) through stainless steel pipes suspended from the ceiling. All of the pipes had to be disassembled, thoroughly cleaned, and reinstalled by the conclusion of the night shift. This process took approximately one hour, so all the mix had to be run by 6:00 A.M. in order to complete the cleanup by the 7:00 A.M. quitting time. Paul and one other worker, Fred (the mixer), cleaned the giant mixing vats while the other four on the shift, including George, cleaned and reinstalled the pipes and filters.

George soon learned that Paul felt a sense of responsibility for completing all of the assigned work before the end of the shift. However, as long as that objective was achieved, he did not seem to care about what else went on during the shift. A great deal of story-telling and horseplay was the norm, but the work was always completed by quitting time. George was soon enjoying the easy camaraderie of the work group, the outrageous pranks they pulled on one another, and even the work itself.

George's position required that he station himself beside the conveyor in a large freezer room. He removed containers of mix as they came down the line and stacked them in the appropriate places. Periodically, Paul would decide that they had all worked hard enough and would shut down the line for a while so that they could engage in some nonwork activity like joke telling, hiding each other's lunch boxes, or "balloon" fights. The balloons were actually the five-gallon, flexible liners for the cardboard boxes in which the mix was sold.

While George did not relish being hit by an exploding bag containing five gallons of heavy mix, he found it great fun to lob one at one of his coworkers. The loss of 10 to 40 gallons of mix on a shift did not seem to concern anyone, and these fights were never curtailed.

George quickly learned that management had only two expectations of the night shift. First, the shift was expected to complete the production orders each night. Second, management expected the equipment, including the pipes, to be spotlessly clean at the conclusion of the shift. Paul told George that inspectors from the county health department would occasionally drop by unannounced at the end of the shift to inspect the vats and pipes after they had been disassembled and scrubbed. Paul also told George that management would be very upset if the inspectors registered any complaints about cleanliness.

George did join the union but saw very little evidence of their involvement in the day-to-day operations of the plant. Labor relations seemed quite amicable, and George only thought of the union when he looked at a pay stub and noticed that union dues had been deducted from his gross pay. The difference George noticed in working for Eastern Dairy compared to his previous employers was not the presence of the union but the absence of management.

THE CURRENT SITUATION

Things seemed to be going quite well for George on the job—until a few minutes ago. The problem first surfaced when the milkshake mix that was being run started spewing out of one of the joints in the overhead pipe network. The pumps were shut down while George disassembled the joint to see what the problem was. George removed the filter screen from the pipe at the leaking joint and saw that it was completely packed with solid matter. Closer inspection revealed that maggots were the culprits. George hurriedly took the filter to Paul to show him the blockage. Paul did not seem too concerned and told George to clean the filter and reassemble the joint. When George asked how this could have happened, Paul said maggots occasionally got into the bags of certain ingredients that were stored in a warehouse at the back of the lot. "But you do not have to worry," said Paul. "The filters will catch any solid matter."

Feeling somewhat reassured, George cleaned the filter and reassembled the pipe. But still, the image of maggots floating in a milkshake was hard to shake. And, unfortunately for George, this was not the end of it.

Shortly after the pumps were re-started, the mix began to flow out of another joint. Once again, a filter plugged with maggots was found to be the cause.

For the second time, George cleaned the filter and reassembled the connection. This time Paul had seemed a bit more concerned as he noted that they barely had enough time to run the last 500 gallons remaining in the vats before they needed to clean up in preparation for the end of the shift.

Moments after the equipment was again restarted, another joint started to spew. When maggots were found to be clogging this filter, too, Paul called George over and told him to remove all five filters from the line so the last 500 gallons could be run without any filters. Paul laughed when he saw the shocked look on George's face.

"George," he said, "don't forget that all of this stuff goes through the homogenizer, so any solid matter will be completely pulverized. And when it's heated in the pasteurization process, any bacteria will be killed. No one will ever know about this, the company can save a lot of mix—that's money—and, most important, we can run this through and go home on time."

George knew that they would never get this lot packaged if they had to shut down every minute to clean filters, and there was no reason to believe it would not be this way for the rest of the run. The product had been thoroughly mixed in the mixing vats at the beginning of the process, which meant that contaminants would be distributed uniformly throughout the 500 gallons. George also knew that the 500 gallons of milkshake was very expensive. He did not think management would just want it dumped down the drain. Finally, Paul was definitely right about one thing, removing all of the filters, a ten-minute job at most, would assure that they could get everything cleaned up and be out on time.

As George walked to the first filter joint, he felt a knot forming in his stomach as he thought of kids drinking all of the milkshakes they were about to produce. He had already decided he would not have another milkshake for at least a month, in order to be absolutely sure that this batch was no longer being served at restaurants. After all, he did not know exactly which restaurants would receive this mix. As he picked up his wrench and approached the first pipe joint that contained a filter, he still could not help wondering if he should not do or say something more.

Note: This case appeared in Paul F. Buller and Randall S. Schuler, *Managing Organizations and People,* South-Western College Publishing © 2000.

CHAPTER 9 WORKSHOP *The Power of Ethics**

This exercise will help you to better understand the concept of ethics and what it means to you.

1. Spend about five minutes individually answering the questions below.
2. Divide into groups of four to six members.
3. Have each group try to achieve consensus with answers to each of the four questions. For question 3, choose one scenario to highlight. You will have twenty to forty minutes for this exercise, depending on the instructor.
4. Have groups share their answers with the whole class, after which the instructor will lead a discussion on ethics and its power in business.

QUESTIONS

1. In your own words, define the concept of ethics in one or two sentences.

2. If you were a manager, how would you motivate your employees to follow ethical behavior? Use no more than two sentences.
3. Describe a situation in which you were faced with an ethical dilemma. What was your decision and behavior? How did you decide to do that? Can you relate your decision to any concept in the chapter?
4. What do you think is a powerful ethical message for others? Where did you get it from? How will it influence your behavior in the future?

---

*Adapted by Dorothy Marcic from Allayne Barrilleaux Pizzolatto's "Ethical Management: An Exercise in Understanding Its Power," *Journal of Management Education* 17 no. 1 (February 1993): 107–9.

NOTES

1. Charles Fishman, "Sanity Inc.," *Fast Company* (January 1999): 85–96; and Sharon Overton, "And to All a Goodnight," *Sky* (October 1996): 37-40.
2. Overton, "And to All a Goodnight."
3. Jeremy Kahn, "What Makes a Company Great?" *Fortune*, 26 October 1998, 218.
4. W. Jack Duncan, "Organizational Culture: 'Getting a Fix' on an Elusive Concept," *Academy of Management Executive* 3 (1989): 229–36; Linda Smircich, "Concepts of Culture and Organizational Analysis," *Administrative Science Quarterly* 28 (1983): 339–58; Andrew D. Brown and Ken Starkey, "The Effect of Organizational Culture on Communication and Information," *Journal of Management Studies* 31 no. 6 (November 1994): 807–28.
5. Edgar H. Schein, "Organizational Culture," *American Psychologist* 45 (February 1990): 109–19.
6. Harrison M. Trice and Janice M. Beyer, "Studying Organizational Cultures through Rites and Ceremonials," *Academy of Management Review* 9 (1984): 653–69; Janice M. Beyer and Harrison M. Trice, "How an Organization's Rites Reveal Its Culture," *Organizational Dynamics* 15 (Spring 1987): 5–24; Steven P. Feldman, "Management in Context: An Essay on the Relevance of Culture to the Understanding of Organizational Change," *Journal of Management Studies* 23 (1986): 589–607; Mary Jo Hatch, "The Dynamics of Organizational Culture," *Academy of Management Review* 18 (1993): 657–93.
7. This discussion is based on Edgar H. Schein, *Organizational Culture and Leadership,* 2d ed. (Homewood, Ill.: Richard D. Irwin, 1992); John P. Kotter and James L. Heskett, *Corporate Culture and Performance* (New York: Free Press, 1992).
8. Charlotte B. Sutton, "Richness Hierarchy of the Cultural Network: The Communication of Corporate Values" (Unpublished manuscript, Texas A & M University, 1985); Terrence E. Deal and Allan A. Kennedy, "Culture: A New Look through Old Lenses," *Journal of Applied Behavioral Science* 19 (1983): 498–505.
9. Thomas C. Dandridge, "Symbols at Work" (Working paper, School of Business, State University of New York at Albany, 1978), 1.
10. Thomas J. Peters and Robert H. Waterman, Jr., *In Search of Excellence* (New York: Harper & Row, 1982).

11. Don Hellriegel and John W. Slocum, Jr., *Management,* 7th ed. (Cincinnati, Ohio: South-Western, 1996), 537.

12. Trice and Beyer, "Studying Organizational Cultures through Rites and Ceremonials."

13. Sutton, "Richness Hierarchy of the Cultural Network"; Deal and Kennedy, *Corporate Cultures.*

14. Matt Siegel, "The Perils of Culture Conflict," *Fortune,* 9 November 1998, 257-262; and *Blueprints for Service Quality: The Federal Express Approach, AMA Management Briefing* (New York: American Management Association Membership Publications Division, 1991), 29-30.

15. "FYI," *Inc.,* April 1991, 14.

16. Stevan Alburty, "The Ad Agency to End All Ad Agencies," *Fast Company* (December–January 1997); 116–24.

17. Quentin Hardy, "A Software Star Sees Its 'Family' Culture Turn Dysfunctional," *The Wall Street Journal,* 5 May 1999, A1, A12; and Paul Roberts, "We Are One Company, No Matter Where We Are," *Fast Company* (April–May 1998): 122–28.

18. Richard Ott, "Are Wild Ducks Really Wild: Symbolism and Behavior in the Corporate Environment" (Paper presented at the Northeastern Anthropological Association, March 1979).

19. Based on Daniel R. Denison, *Corporate Culture and Organizational Effectiveness* (New York: Wiley, 1990), 11–15; Daniel R. Denison and Aneil K. Mishra, "Toward a Theory of Organizational Culture and Effectiveness," *Organization Science* 6, no. 2 (March-April 1995): 204–23; R. Hooijberg and F. Petrock, "On Cultural Change: Using the Competing Values Framework to Help Leaders Execute a Transformational Strategy," *Human Resource Management* 32 (1993), 29–50; R. E. Quinn, *Beyond Rational Management: Mastering the Paradoxes and Competing Demands of High Performance* (San Francisco: Jossey-Bass, 1988).

20. Daintry Duffy, "Cultural Evolution," *CIO Enterprise,* Section 2, 15 January 1999, 44–50.

21. Brian Dumaine, "Those High Flying PepsiCo Managers," *Fortune,* 10 April 1989; L. Zinn, J. Berry, and G. Burns, "Will the Pepsi Brass Be Drinking Hemlock?" *Business Week,* 25 July 1994, 31; S. Lubove, "We Have a Big Pond to Play In," *Forbes,* 12 September 1993, 216–24; J. Wolfe, "PepsiCo and the Fast Food Industry," in M. A. Hitt, R. D. Ireland, and R. E. Hoskisson, eds., *Strategic Management: Competitiveness and Globalization* (St. Paul, Minn.: West Publishing, 1995), 856–79.

22. Kenneth F. Iverson with Tom Varian, "Plain Talk," *Inc.,* October 1997, 81-83.

23. Carey Quan Jelernter, "Safeco: Success Depends Partly on Fitting the Mold," *Seattle Times,* 5 June 1986, D8.

24. Bernard Arogyaswamy and Charles M. Byles, "Organizational Culture: Internal and External Fits," *Journal of Management* 13 (1987): 647–59.

25. Paul R. Lawrence and Jay W. Lorsch, *Organization and Environment* (Homewood, Ill.: Irwin, 1969).

26. Scott Kirsner, "Designed for Innovation," *Fast Company* (November 1998): 54, 56.

27. Katrina Brooker, "Can Procter & Gamble Change Its Culture, Protect Its Market Share, and Find the Next Tide?" *Fortune,* 26 April 1999, 146–52.

28. Mary Anne DeVanna and Noel Tichy, "Creating the Competitive Organization of the Twenty-First Century: The Boundaryless Corporation," *Human Resource Management* 29 (Winter 1990): 455–71; and Fred Kofman and Peter M. Senge, "Communities of Commitment: The Heart of Learning Organizations," *Organizational Dynamics* 22, no. 2 (Autumn 1993): 4–23.

29. Paul Roberts, "The Best Interest of the Patient is the Only Interest to be Considered," *Fast Company* (April 1999): 149–62.

30. Marc Ballon, "The Cheapest CEO in America," *Inc.,* October 1997, 53–61.

31. Kotter and Heskett, *Corporate Culture and Performance.*

32. Polly Schneider, "The Renaissance Company," *CIO,* 15 December 1998–1 January 1999, 66–76.

33. Gordon F. Shea, *Practical Ethics* (New York: American Management Association, 1988); Linda K. Treviño, "Ethical Decision Making in Organizations: A Person–Situation Interactionist Model," *Academy of Management Review* 11 (1986): 601–17; and Linda Klebe Treviño and Katherine A. Nelson, *Managing Business Ethics: Straight Talk About How to Do It Right,* 2nd ed. (New York: John Wiley & Sons, Inc. 1999).

34. LaRue Tone Hosmer, *The Ethics of Management,* 2d ed., (Homewood, Ill.: Irwin, 1991).

35. Geanne Rosenberg, "Truth and Consequences," *Working Woman,* July–August 1998, 79–80.

36. Dawn-Marie Driscoll, "Don't Confuse Legal and Ethical Standards," *Business Ethics*, July–August 1996, 44.

37. Eugene W. Szwajkowski, "The Myths and Realities of Research on Organizational Misconduct," in James E. Post, ed., *Research and Corporate Social Performance and Policy*, vol. 9 (Greenwich, Conn.: JAI Press, 1986), 103–22.

38. These incidents are from Hosmer, *The Ethics of Management*.

39. Linda Klebe Treviño, "A Cultural Perspective on Changing and Developing Organizational Ethics," in Richard Woodman and William Pasmore, eds., *Research and Organizational Change and Development*, vol. 4 (Greenwich, Conn.: JAI Press, 1990); Lynn Sharp Paine, "Managing for Organizational Integrity," *Harvard Business Review* (March/April 1994), 106–17.

40. James Weber, "Exploring the Relationship between Personal Values and Moral Reasoning," *Human Relations* 46 (1993): 435–63.

41. L. Kohlberg, "Moral Stages and Moralization: The Cognitive-Developmental Approach," in T. Likona, ed., *Moral Development and Behavior: Theory, Research, and Social Issues* (New York: Holt, Rinehart & Winston, 1976).

42. Hosmer, *The Ethics of Management*.

43. Michael Barrier, "Doing the Right Thing," *Nation's Business,* March 1998, 33–38.

44. "James Burke: The Fine Art of Leadership," an interview with Barbara Ettorre, *Management Review* (October 1996): 13–16; Margaret Kaeter, "The 5th Annual Business Ethics Awards for Excellence in Ethics," *Business Ethics,* November–December 1993, 26–29.

45. Jennifer Bresnahan, "For Goodness Sake," *CIO Enterprise*, Section 2, 15 June 1999, 54–62.

46. David M. Messick and Max H. Bazerman, "Ethical Leadership and the Psychology of Decision Making," *Sloan Management Review* (Winter 1996): 9–22; Dawn-Marie Driscoll, "Don't Confuse Legal and Ethical Standards," *Business Ethics*, July–August 1996, 44.

47. Max B. E. Clarkson, "A Stakeholder Framework for Analyzing and Evaluating Corporate Social Performance," *Academy of Management Review* 20, no. 1 (1995): 92–117; and Linda Klebe Treviño and Katherine A. Nelson, *Managing Business Ethics*, 207.

48. Gwen Kinkead, "In the Future, People Like Me Will Go to Jail," *Fortune*, 24 May 1999, 190–200.

49. Howard Rothman, "A Growing Dilemma," *Business Ethics*, July–August 1996, 18–21.

50. Susan Gaines, "Growing Pains," *Business Ethics,* January–February 1996, 20–23.

51. *Corporate Ethics: A Prime Business Asset* (New York: The Business Round Table, February 1988).

52. Andrew W. Singer, "The Ultimate Ethics Test," *Across the Board*, March 1992, 19–22; Ronald B. Morgan, "Self and Co-Worker Perceptions of Ethics and Their Relationships to Leadership and Salary," *Academy of Management Journal*, 36, no.1 (February 1993): 200–14; Joseph L. Badaracco, Jr. and Allen P. Webb, "Business Ethics: A View From the Trenches," *California Management Review* 37, no. 2 (Winter 1995): 8–28.

53. This discussion is based on Robert J. House, Andre Delbecq, and Toon W. Taris, "Value Based Leadership: An Integrated Theory and an Empirical Test" (Working paper).

54. Barrier, "Doing the Right Thing."

55. Peters and Waterman, In Search of Excellence.

56. "Best Moves of 1995," *Business Ethics*, January–February 1996, 23.

57. Karl E. Weick, "Cognitive Processes in Organizations," in B. M. Staw, ed., *Research in Organizations,* vol. 1 (Greenwich, Conn.: JAI Press, 1979), 42.

58. Patrick E. Murphy and George Enderle, "Managerial Ethical Leadership: Examples Do Matter," *Business Ethics Quarterly* 5, no. 1 (January 1995): 117–28.

59. Bresnahan, "For Goodness Sake."

60. Justin Martin, "New Tricks for an Old Trade," *Across the Board,* June 1992, 40–44.

61. Janet P. Near and Marcia P. Miceli, "Effective Whistle-Blowing," *Academy of Management Review* 20, no. 3 (1995): 679–708.

62. Richard P. Nielsen, "Changing Unethical Organizational Behavior," *Academy of Management Executive* 3 (1989): 123–30.

63. Jene G. James, "Whistle-Blowing: Its Moral Justification," in Peter Madsen and Jay M. Shafritz, eds., *Essentials of Business Ethics* (New York: Meridian Books, 1990), 160–90; Janet P. Near, Terry Morehead Dworkin, and Marcia P. Miceli, "Explaining the Whistle-Blowing Process: Suggestions from Power Theory and Justice Theory," *Organization Science* 4 (1993): 393–411.

64. "Tiny Screws Cause Woes for TVA Whistle-Blower," *The Tennessean*, 21 December 1998, 3B.

65. Beverly Geber, "The Right and Wrong of Ethics Offices," *Training* (October 1995): 102–18.

66. Carolyn Wiley, "The ABC's of Business Ethics: Definitions, Philosophies, and Implementation," *IM* (January–February 1995): 22–27.

67. Carl Anderson, "Values-Based Management," *Academy of Management Executive* 11, no. 4 (1997): 25–46.

68. James Weber, "Institutionalizing Ethics into Business Organizations: A Model and Research Agenda," *Business Ethics Quarterly* 3 (1993): 419–36.

69. Mark Henricks, "Ethics in Action," *Management Review* (January 1995): 53–55; Dorothy Marcic, *Management and the Wisdom of Love* (San Francisco: Jossey-Bass, 1997); Beverly Geber, "The Right and Wrong of Ethics Offices," *Training,* October 1995, 102–18.

70. Susan J. Harrington, "What Corporate America Is Teaching about Ethics," *Academy of Management Executive* 5 (1991): 21–30.

71. Treviño and Nelson, *Managing Business Ethics,* 274–83.

72. Richard W. Judy and Carol D'Amico, *Workforce 2020: Work and Workers in the 21st Century* (Indianapolis, Ind.: Hudson Institute, 1997).

73. Gail Dutton, "Building a Global Brain," *Management Review* (May 1999): 34–38.

74. S. C. Schneider, "National Vs. Corporate Culture: Implications for Human Resource Management," *Human Resource Management* (Summer 1988): 239.

75. Dutton, "Building a Global Brain."

Innovation and Change

CHAPTER 10

A LOOK INSIDE

3M

*W*hen asked about 3M's strategy, CEO L. D. "Desi" DiSimone says, "We're going to do two principal things: be very innovative, and satisfy our customers in all aspects." 3M, a company whose name is synonymous with innovation, has three approaches to new product development: "skunkworks" projects, which are spearheaded by employees and are not overseen by management; traditional development, in which business managers and researchers work together to create new products or improve existing ones; and pacing programs, which consist of a small number of products and technologies the company thinks will produce substantial profits fast and are thus given extra attention and resources. The process works. 3M has achieved its goal of getting 30 percent of sales from products less than four years old so consistently that it is considering raising the bar.

3M also maintains a close connection with customers—company lore tells salespeople to head for the smokestacks, where the end users of products are, rather than the offices where the purchasing department sits. "Major-customer teams" that include representatives from various functions, from R&D to sales, not only look for ways to push existing products but also try to understand customers' unarticulated needs so 3M can develop products to meet them. For example, a new fabric that allows water vapor to pass through but blocks liquids is being used for surgical gowns that protect doctors from patients' blood but don't leave them soaked in their own sweat.

One reason 3M is bubbling over with new ideas and new products is that the culture supports innovation and risk taking. Any employee with a new product or technology idea can always find someone to give advice and moral support. Ideas and knowledge are shared throughout the organization—a new technology that isn't useful in one division may lead to a series of new products in another. All new employees attend a class on risk taking where they're actually encouraged to defy their supervisors. They hear stories of success won despite opposition from the boss—such as how DiSimone himself five times tried to kill the project that became the highly successful Thinsulate. They also hear stories of "failures" that became hot new products—such as the not-very-sticky glue that led to development of the popular Post-it Notes. 3M has remained a highly successful company for nearly a century by supporting a risk-taking, entrepreneurial spirit and by following where its researchers and customers lead.[1]

At 3M, innovation is a primary goal preached by top management and supported throughout the organization. Managers also recognize the importance of staying in touch with customers. Strong cross-functional coordination and communication helps identify customer needs, turn new ideas into new products, and get them to the marketplace fast.

Innovation is not limited to 3M. Today, every organization must change to survive. New discoveries and inventions quickly replace standard ways of doing things. The pace of change is revealed in the fact that the parents of today's college-age students grew up without voice mail, compact discs, video games, debit cards, cellular phones, and laser checkout systems in supermarkets. The idea of communicating instantly with people around the world via the Internet was unimaginable to most people as recently as a decade ago.

PURPOSE OF THIS CHAPTER

This chapter will explore how organizations change and how managers direct the innovation and change process. The next section describes the difference between incremental and radical change, the four types of change—technology, product, structure, people—occurring in organizations, and how to manage change successfully. The organization structure and management approach for facilitating each type of change is then discussed. Management techniques for influencing both the creation and implementation of change are also covered.

INNOVATE OR PERISH: THE STRATEGIC ROLE OF CHANGE

If there is one theme or lesson that emerges from previous chapters, it is that organizations must run fast to keep up with changes taking place all around them. Organizations must modify themselves not just from time to time, but all of the time. Large organizations must find ways to act like small, flexible organizations. Manufacturing firms need to reach out for new computer-integrated manufacturing technology and service firms for new information technology. Today's organizations must poise themselves to innovate and change, not only to prosper but merely to survive in a world of increased competition.[2] Organizations that invest most of their time and resources in maintaining the status quo cannot hope to prosper in today's world of constant change and uncertainty. As illustrated in Exhibit 10.1, a number of environmental forces drive this need for major organizational change. Powerful forces associated with advancing technology, international economic integration, the maturing of domestic markets, and the shift to capitalism in formerly communist regions have brought about a globalized economy that impacts every business, from the largest to the smallest, creating more threats as well as more opportunities. To recognize and manage the threats and take advantage of the opportunities, today's companies are undergoing dramatic changes in all areas of their operations.

As we saw in Chapter 3, many organizations are responding to global forces by adopting self-directed teams and horizontal structures that enhance communication and collaboration, streamlining supply and distribution channels, and overcoming barriers of time and place through e-commerce. Others become involved in joint ventures or consortia to exploit opportunities and extend operations or markets internationally. As described in Chapter 7, some organizations adopt structural innovations such as the network to focus on their core competencies while outside specialists handle other activities. New software programs for information sharing, knowledge management, and enterprise resource planning facilitate the network and help today's businesses keep pace with the rapid changes going on both within and outside the organization. In addition, today's organizations face a need for dramatic strategic and cultural change and for rapid and continuous innovations in technology, services, products, and processes.

Change, rather than stability, is the norm today. Whereas change once occurred incrementally and infrequently, today it is dramatic and constant. A key element of the success of companies such as 3M Corporation, described in the opening case, Starbucks Coffee, and PepsiCo has been their passion for creating change. Former Pepsi CEO Wayne Calloway insisted that the worst rule of

EXHIBIT 10.1   *Forces Driving the Need for Major Organizational Change*

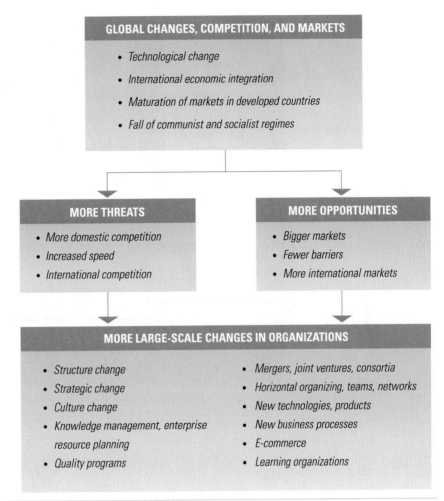

Source: Based on John P. Kotter, *The New Rules: How to Succeed in Today's Post-Corporate World* (New York: The Free Press, 1995).

management is "if it ain't broke, don't fix it." Calloway preached that in today's economy, "if it ain't broke, you might as well break it yourself, because it soon will be."[3]

INCREMENTAL VERSUS RADICAL CHANGE

The changes used to adapt to the environment can be evaluated according to scope—that is, the extent to which changes are incremental or radical for the organization.[4] As summarized in Exhibit 10.2, **incremental change** represents a series of continual progressions that maintain the organization's general equilibrium and often affect only one organizational part. **Radical change**, by contrast, breaks the frame of reference for the organization, often transforming the entire organization. For example, an incremental change is the implementation of sales teams in the marketing department, whereas a radical change is shifting the entire organization from a vertical to a horizontal structure, with all employees who work on specific core processes brought together in teams rather than being separated into functional departments such as marketing, finance, production, and so forth.

EXHIBIT 10.2   *Incremental Versus Radical Change*

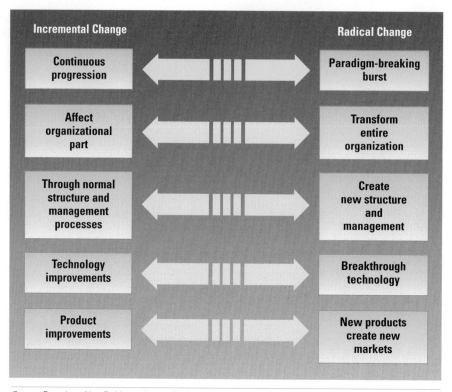

Source: Based on Alan D. Meyer, James B. Goes, and Geoffrey R. Brooks, "Organizations in Disequilibrium: Environmental Jolts and Industry Revolutions," in George Huber and William H. Glick, eds., *Organizational Change and Redesign* (New York: Oxford University Press, 1992), 66–111; and Harry S. Dent, Jr., "Growth through New Product Development," *Small Business Reports* (November 1990): 30–40.

For the most part, incremental change occurs through the established structure and management processes, and it may include technology improvements—such as the introduction of computer-integrated manufacturing—or product improvements—such as Procter & Gamble's addition to Tide detergent of cleaning agents that protect colors and fabrics. Radical change involves the creation of a new structure and management processes. The technology is likely to be breakthrough, and new products thereby created will establish new markets.

As we have just discussed, there is a growing emphasis on the need for radical change because of today's turbulent, unpredictable environment.[5] Indeed, some experts argue that firms must be constantly changing their structures and management processes in response to changing demands. The health-care industry, for example, continues to face tremendous upheaval, and companies likely will have to implement radical change to survive. One example of radical change was the revolution at Motorola that achieved an astounding six sigma quality (only 3.4 mistakes per million parts produced). This level of quality, previously considered impossible, became the new norm. An example of radical change in a service company comes from the traditionally slow-moving insurance industry.

| In Practice 10.1 | Progressive Corporation |

Progressive Corporation has become one of today's most prosperous, fastest-growing auto insurance companies by treating automobile accidents like what they are: emergencies. At the heart of Progressive's breakthrough business performance is the company's Immediate Response program. Progressive has claims representatives available twenty-four hours a day, seven days a week—and they frequently show up at the scene of an accident before the cops arrive, equipped with laptop computers, intelligent software, and the authority to make on-the-spot decisions. The representative inspects the damage, analyzes skid marks and other clues at the scene, interviews witnesses, and consoles the accident victims. Then the agent downloads a claims file and cuts a check on the spot. Claims that once took days or even weeks to settle are often settled in only minutes.

Progressive, which began as a niche player writing policies for high-risk drivers that other companies were reluctant to insure, used to do business like everyone else in the insurance industry. A claim would be assigned to an adjuster who was responsible for interviewing witnesses and the involved parties, inspecting damage, and settling the dispute. Because adjusters worked a traditional nine-to-five schedule, claims often piled up and adjusters found themselves shuffling paper rather than serving clients. Peter Lewis, CEO and son of the founder, reinvented the way Progressive does business to coincide with his beliefs and the values his father instilled in the company: "We're not in the business of auto insurance. We're in the business of reducing the human trauma and economic costs of automobile accidents—in effective and profitable ways."6

Progressive's Immediate Response program broke the traditional rules of auto insurance claims processing and transformed the entire company. Whereas the industry as a whole has run at an underwriting loss over the past several years (meaning they pay out more in claims and expenses than they take in), Progressive has generated underwriting margins of around 8 percent. As CEO Lewis put it, "Before, you had three hundred companies marching in a straight line. Everybody—State Farm, Allstate, Nationwide—did business the same way. Then Progressive broke out of the line and started doing things differently."7

Corporate transformations and turnarounds, such as Larry Bossidy's turnaround of Allied Signal or Lou Gerstner's transformation of IBM, are also considered radical change. A good example of a radical corporate transformation in a small company is Globe Metallurgical, Inc., which was a typical Rust Belt company in the early 1980s: old-fashioned, bureaucratic, slow-moving, and unresponsive to customers. Costs were high and quality was low. When Arden Sims took over as chief executive in 1984, the company was in a death spiral, sure to be run out of business by foreign competition. Over a period of eight years, Sims transformed Globe into today's top source for specialty metals for the chemical and foundry industries worldwide. The transformation involved fundamental changes in management systems, work structures, products, technology, and worker attitudes. Globe became the first small company to win a Malcolm Baldrige National Quality Award.8

STRATEGIC TYPES OF CHANGE

Managers can focus on four types of change within organizations to achieve strategic advantage. These four types of changes are summarized in Exhibit 10.3 as products and services, strategy and structure, culture, and technology. We touched on overall leadership and organizational strategy in Chapter 2 and in the previous chapter on corporate culture. These factors provide an overall context within

EXHIBIT 10.3   *The Four Types of Change Provide a Strategic Competitive Wedge*

Source: Joseph E. McCann, "Design Principles for an Innovating Company," *Academy of Management Executive* 5 (May 1991): 76–93. Used by permission.

which the four types of change serve as a competitive wedge to achieve an advantage in the international environment. Each company has a unique configuration of products and services, strategy and structure, culture, and technologies that can be focused for maximum impact upon the company's chosen markets.[9]

Technology changes are changes in an organization's production process, including its knowledge and skill base, that enable distinctive competence. These changes are designed to make production more efficient or to produce greater volume. Changes in technology involve the techniques for making products or services. They include work methods, equipment, and work flow. For example, in a university, technology changes are changes in techniques for teaching courses. As another example, the British water and sewage company Anglian Water came up with an innovative way to use its existing technologies to devise a water efficiency recycling system called Waterwise, which allows households to use one-third less water. Anglian also adopted new information and knowledge-sharing technology for disseminating technical knowledge throughout the organization.[10]

Product and service changes pertain to the product or service outputs of an organization. New products include small adaptations of existing products or entirely new product lines. New products are normally designed to increase the market share or to develop new markets, customers, or clients. When faced with intense foreign competition in the machine-tool business, Cincinnati Milacron transformed itself into a full-service industrial supplier, providing not only tools but all industrial plastics, fluids, and chemicals. Today, machine tools make up only about one-fourth of Milacron's total revenue base. The new products and services expanded the company's market and customer base, helping the 115-year-old organization survive while many of its counterparts in the machine-tool industry failed.[11]

Strategy and structure changes pertain to the administrative domain in an organization. The administrative domain involves the supervision and management of the organization. These changes include changes in organization structure, strategic management, policies, reward systems, labor relations, coordination devices, management information and control systems, and accounting and budgeting systems. Structure and system changes are usually top-down, that is, mandated by top management, whereas product and technology changes may often come from the bottom up. The structure was changed at Cincinnati Milacron when top executives formed "Wolfpack" teams, groups of engineers, managers, outside suppliers, and customers who work together to develop new products. A system change instituted by management in a university might be a new merit pay plan. Corporate downsizing is another example of top-down structure change.

Culture changes refer to changes in the values, attitudes, expectations, beliefs, abilities, and behavior of employees. Culture changes pertain to changes in how employees think; these are changes in mindset rather than technology, structure, or products. At Globe Metallurgical, the old culture was marked by suspicion and distrust. Managers often dictated changes without consulting workers and sometimes shifted their approaches and policies abruptly. One of the results of Globe's transformation is a new culture that values employee empowerment and involvement, a new respect for management, and a new commitment to quality.

The four types of changes in Exhibit 10.3 are interdependent—a change in one often means a change in another. A new product may require changes in the production technology, or a change in structure may require new employee skills. For example, when Shenandoah Life Insurance Company acquired new computer technology to process claims, the technology was not fully utilized until clerks were restructured into teams of five to seven members that were compatible with the technology. The structural change was an outgrowth of the technology change. In a manufacturing company, engineers introduced robots and advanced manufacturing technologies, only to find that the technology placed greater demands on employees. Upgrading employee skills required a change in wage systems. Organizations are interdependent systems, and changing one part often has implications for other organization elements.

ELEMENTS FOR SUCCESSFUL CHANGE

Regardless of the type or scope of change, there are identifiable stages of innovation, which generally occur as a sequence of events, though innovation stages may overlap.[12] In the research literature on innovation, **organizational change** is considered the adoption of a new idea or behavior by an organization.[13] **Organizational innovation**, in contrast, is the adoption of an idea or behavior that is new to the organization's industry, market, or general environment.[14] The first organization to introduce a new product is considered the innovator, and organizations that copy are considered to adopt changes. For purposes of managing change, however, the terms *innovation* and *change* will be used interchangeably because the **change process** within organizations tends to be identical whether a change is early or late with respect to other organizations in the environment.

Innovations typically are assimilated into an organization through a series of steps or elements. Organization members first become aware of a possible innovation, evaluate its appropriateness, and then evaluate and choose the idea.[15] The required elements of successful change are summarized in Exhibit 10.4. For a change to be successfully implemented, managers must make sure each element occurs in the organization. If one of the elements is missing, the change process will fail.

EXHIBIT 10.4   *Sequence of Elements for Successful Change*

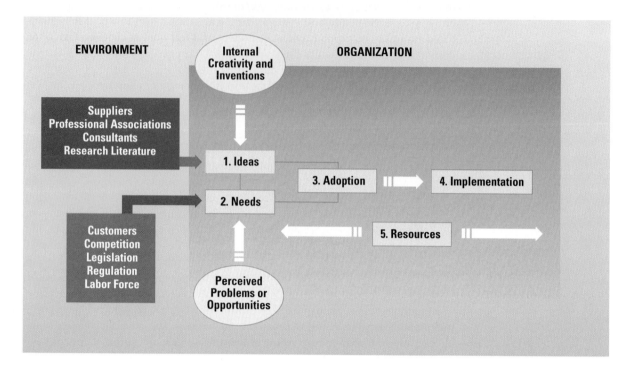

1. *Ideas.* Although creativity is a dramatic element of organizational change, creativity within organizations has not been widely and systematically studied. No company can remain competitive without new ideas; change is the outward expression of those ideas.[16] An idea is a new way of doing things. It may be a new product or service, a new management concept, or a new procedure for working together in the organization. Ideas can come from within or from outside the organization.

2. *Need.* Ideas are generally not seriously considered unless there is a perceived need for change. A perceived need for change occurs when managers see a gap between actual performance and desired performance in the organization. Managers try to establish a sense of urgency so that others will understand the need for change. Sometimes a crisis provides an undoubted sense of urgency. For example, Midwest Contract Furnishings, a small firm that designs and fabricates hotel interiors, faced a crisis when its largest customer, Renaissance Hotels, was sold to Marriott, which did interior designing in-house. Midwest lost 80 percent of its revenues virtually overnight.[17] In many cases, however, there is no crisis, so managers have to recognize a need and communicate it to others.[18] In addition, although many ideas are generated to meet perceived needs, innovative companies encourage the constant development of new ideas that may stimulate consideration of problems or new opportunities.

3. *Adoption.* Adoption occurs when decision makers choose to go ahead with a proposed idea. Key managers and employees need to be in agreement to support the change. For a major organizational change, the decision might require the signing of a legal document by the board of directors. For a small change, adoption might occur with informal approval by a middle manager.

When Ray Kroc was CEO of McDonald's, he made the adoption decision about innovations such as the Big Mac and Egg McMuffin.

4. *Implementation.* Implementation occurs when organization members actually use a new idea, technique, or behavior. Materials and equipment may have to be acquired, and workers may have to be trained to use the new idea. Implementation is a very important step because without it, previous steps are to no avail. Implementation of change is often the most difficult part of the change process. Until people use the new idea, no change has actually taken place.

5. *Resources.* Human energy and activity are required to bring about change. Change does not happen on its own; it requires time and resources, for both creating and implementing a new idea. Employees have to provide energy to see both the need and the idea to meet that need. Someone must develop a proposal and provide the time and effort to implement it.

3M has an unwritten but widely understood rule that its 8,300 researchers can spend up to 15 percent of their time working on any idea of their choosing, without management approval. Most innovations go beyond ordinary budget allocations and require special funding. At 3M, exceptionally promising ideas become "pacing programs" and receive high levels of funding for further development. Some companies use task forces, as described in Chapter 3, to focus resources on a change. Others set up seed funds or venture funds that employees with promising ideas can tap into. Fluke Corporation, which manufactures electronic testing devices, creates teams of workers and gives them a hundred days and $100,000 to generate proposals for new business opportunities.[19]

One point about Exhibit 10.4 is especially important. Needs and ideas are listed simultaneously at the beginning of the change sequence. Either may occur first. Many organizations adopted the computer, for example, because it seemed a promising way to improve efficiency. Today's search for a vaccine against the AIDS virus, on the other hand, was stimulated by a severe need. Whether the need or the idea occurs first, for the change to be accomplished, each of the steps in Exhibit 10.4 must be completed. At the New York law firm of Cadwalader, Wickersham, and Taft, the change process was triggered by a compelling need: improve service and profits or fail.

In Practice 10.2

Cadwalader, Wickersham, and Taft

Only a few years ago, the Wall Street law practice of Cadwalader, Wickersham, and Taft was written off as a has-been. Profits were declining, and important clients were complaining about poor service. The firm consistently failed to win important new projects because of its outdated ways of doing business—for example, in the age of the Internet, Cadwalader, Wickersham, and Taft didn't even have a voice-mail system or emergency photocopying capabilities. Some partners "detected the smell of death" at the 208-year-old firm. When the maintenance crew changed a batch of light bulbs, it set off a rumor that the firm was switching to a lower wattage to save money.

It seemed that Cadwalader, Wickersham, and Taft would go the way of other old-line Wall Street firms and either fold or be swallowed by a younger, stronger, more aggressive firm. However, several young partners began meeting secretly to come up with ideas to revive the company. One major idea was called Project Rightsize, which involved closing money-losing operations and pressuring unproductive partners to leave.

Although group members knew it would be painful, they adopted the idea because they believed it was the only way the firm could survive. Implementation occurred as the change agents took control of the management committee, closed the marginal Palm Beach, Florida, office, cut back an unprofitable branch in Los Angeles, and forced a total of seventeen partners to leave. In addition, the group replaced an outmoded pay system that generated rivalries among partners, revised archaic procedures, and did away with money-losing practices such as maritime finance. Resources invested in the change process included the tremendous amount of time and energy the management committee spent on revising systems and procedures, communicating with other employees, and building a new, dynamic firm.

The changes at Cadwalader, Wickersham, and Taft have not been easy. Notions of loyalty and gentility have eroded in a firm that was once renowned as one of Wall Street's most humane places to work. However, the practice is growing and profitable again. Profits per partner jumped an astounding 22 percent in one recent year. Clients include major investment banks, corporations, and insurance companies, and a number of partners from other top firms have moved to Cadwalader—now considered one of the hottest firms on Wall Street.[20]

TECHNOLOGY CHANGE

In today's business world, any company that isn't constantly developing, acquiring, or adapting new technology will likely be out of business in a few years. However, organizations face a contradiction when it comes to technology change, for the conditions that promote new ideas are not generally the best for implementing those ideas for routine production. An innovative organization is characterized by flexibility, empowered employees, and the absence of rigid work rules.[21] As discussed earlier in this book, an organic, free-flowing organization is typically associated with change and is considered the best organization form for adapting to a chaotic environment.

The flexibility of an organic organization is attributed to people's freedom to create and introduce new ideas. Organic organizations encourage a bottom-up innovation process. Ideas bubble up from middle- and lower-level employees because they have the freedom to propose ideas and to experiment. A mechanistic structure, on the other hand, stifles innovation with its emphasis on rules and regulations, but it is often the best structure for efficiently producing routine products. The challenge for organizations is to create both organic and mechanistic conditions within organizations to achieve both innovation and efficiency. To achieve both aspects of technological change, many organizations use the ambidextrous approach.

THE AMBIDEXTROUS APPROACH

Recent thinking has refined the idea of organic versus mechanistic structures with respect to innovation creation versus innovation utilization. For example, sometimes an organic structure generates innovative ideas but is not the best structure for using those ideas.[22] In other words, the initiation and the utilization of change are two distinct processes. Organic characteristics such as decentralization and employee freedom are excellent for initiating ideas; but these same conditions often make it hard to use a change because employees are less likely to comply. Employees can ignore the innovation because of decentralization and a generally loose structure.

How does an organization solve this dilemma? One approach is for the organization to be **ambidextrous**—to incorporate structures and management processes that are appropriate to both the creation and use of innovation.[23] The organization can behave in an organic way when the situation calls for the initiation of new ideas and in a mechanistic way to implement and use the ideas.

An example of the ambidextrous approach is the Freudenberg-NOK auto-parts factory in Ligonier, Indiana. Shifting teams of twelve, including plant workers, managers, and outsiders, each spend three days creating ideas to cut costs and boost productivity in various sections of the plant. At the end of the three days, team members go back to their regular jobs, and a new team comes in to look for even more improvements. Over a year's time, there are approximately forty of these GROWTTH (Get Rid of Waste Through Team Harmony) teams roaming through the sprawling factory. Management has promised that no one will be laid off as a result of suggestions from GROWTTH teams, which further encourages employees to both create and use innovations.[24]

TECHNIQUES FOR ENCOURAGING TECHNOLOGY CHANGE

Freudenberg-NOK has created both organic and mechanistic conditions in the factory. Some of the techniques used by many companies to maintain an ambidextrous approach are switching structures, separate creative departments, venture teams, and corporate entrepreneurship.

Switching Structures. **Switching structures** means an organization creates an organic structure when such a structure is needed for the initiation of new ideas.[25] Some of the ways organizations have switched structures to achieve the ambidextrous approach are as follows.

- Philips Corporation, a building materials producer based in Ohio, each year creates up to 150 transient teams—made up of members from various departments—to develop ideas for improving Philips products. After five days of organic brainstorming and problem solving, the company reverts to a more mechanistic basis to implement the changes.[26]
- Gardetto's, a family-run snack-food business, sends small teams of workers to Eureka Ranch, where they may engage in a Nerf gun battle to set the tone for fun and freedom, then participate in brainstorming exercises with the idea of generating as many new ideas as possible by the end of the day. Doug Hall, who runs Eureka Ranch, uses cans of baked beans, bags of cookies, and competitors' snack foods to stimulate ideas. After two and a half days, the group returns to the regular organizational structure to put the best of the ideas into action.[27]
- Xerox Corporation's Palo Alto Research Center (PARC) is purposely isolated from the corporation's bureaucracy and is staffed with mavericks not afraid to break the rules. John Seely Brown, Xerox's director of research, encourages his researchers to make trouble and upset conventional thinking. Xerox, which counts on the free thinkers at PARC for new insights, new solutions, and sometimes even entirely new businesses, knows that it is easy for maverick ideas to get trampled in the traditional organization.[28]
- The NUMMI plant, a Toyota subsidiary located in Fremont, California, creates a separate, organically organized cross-functional subunit, called the Pilot

Team, to design production processes for new car and truck models. When the model they are preparing moves into production, workers return to their regular jobs on the shop floor.[29]

Each of these organizations found creative ways to be ambidextrous, establishing organic conditions for developing new ideas in the midst of more mechanistic conditions for implementing and using those ideas.

Creative Departments. In many large organizations the initiation of innovation is assigned to separate **creative departments**.[30] Staff departments, such as research and development, engineering, design, and systems analysis, create changes for adoption in other departments. Departments that initiate change are organically structured to facilitate the generation of new ideas and techniques. Departments that use those innovations tend to have a mechanistic structure more suitable for efficient production. Exhibit 10.5 indicates how one department is responsible for creation and another department implements the innovation.

Raytheon's New Products Center, in operation for thirty years, illustrates how creativity and entrepreneurial spirit can coexist with discipline and controls. The center has been responsible for many technical innovations, including industry-leading combination ovens, which added microwave capabilities to conventional stoves. The New Products Center provides autonomy and freedom for staff to explore new ideas, yet staff must also establish a working relationship with other departments so that innovations meet a genuine need for Raytheon departments.[31]

Venture Teams. **Venture teams** are a recent technique used to give free rein to creativity within organizations. Venture teams are often given a separate location and facilities so they are not constrained by organizational procedures. Dow Chemical created an innovation department that has virtually total license to establish new venture projects for any department in the company. DataCard Corp, which makes products that are critical to the creation of bank cards, ID cards, and smart cards, provides teams with the autonomy and resources to develop start-up business plans, which are then presented to the board of directors for venture funding. At 3M, described in the opening case, venture teams are referred to as *action teams*. An employee with a promising new product idea is allowed to recruit team members from throughout the company. These people may end up running the newly created division if the idea is successful.[32] Action teams and venture teams are kept small so they have autonomy and no bureaucracy emerges.

EXHIBIT 10.5   *Division of Labor Between Departments to Achieve Changes in Technology*

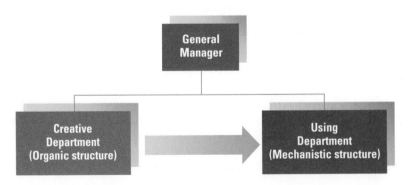

A venture team is like a small company within a large company. Monsanto, Levi Strauss, and Exxon have all used the venture team concept to free creative people from the bureaucracy of a large corporation. Most large companies that have successfully created e-commerce divisions have set them up like venture firms so they have the freedom to explore and develop emerging technologies. For example, Provident American Life & Health CEO Al Clemens set up a separate online company called Health-Axis.com., which became the Web's first full-service insurance agency. The venture was so successful that Provident American eventually shed its bricks-and-mortar operations and moved its entire business into cyberspace.[33] As described in this chapter's Book Mark, large, established organizations have difficulty capitalizing on monumental technological breakthroughs such as the Internet unless they create autonomous units that can focus time and resources on the new technology.

A variation of the venture team concept is the **new-venture fund**, which provides financial resources for employees to develop new ideas, products, or businesses. In order to tap into its employees' entrepreneurial urges, Lockheed Martin allows workers to take up to two years' unpaid leave to explore a new idea, using company labs and equipment and paying company rates for health insurance. If the idea is successful, the corporation's venture fund invests around $250,000 in the start-up company. One successful start-up is Genase, which created an enzyme that "stonewashes" denim.[34]

Corporate Entrepreneurship. Corporate entrepreneurship attempts to develop an internal entrepreneurial spirit, philosophy, and structure that will produce a higher than average number of innovations.[35] Corporate entrepreneurship may involve the use of creative departments and new venture teams as described above, but it also attempts to release the creative energy of all employees in the organization. The most important outcome is to facilitate **idea champions** which go by a variety of names, including advocate, intrapreneur, or change agent. Idea champions provide the time and energy to make things happen. They fight to overcome natural resistance to change and to convince others of the merit of a new idea.[36] Peter Drucker suggests that idea champions need not be within the organization, and that fostering potential idea champions among regular customers can be a highly successful approach.[37] At Anglian Water, every innovation project has a sponsor or champion who is a customer seeking a solution to a specific problem.[38] The importance of the idea champion is illustrated by a fascinating fact discovered by Texas Instruments: When TI reviewed fifty successful and unsuccessful technical projects, it discovered that every failure was characterized by the absence of a volunteer champion. There was no one who passionately believed in the idea, who pushed the idea through all the necessary obstacles to make it work. Texas Instruments took this finding so seriously that now its number one criterion for approving new technical projects is the presence of a zealous champion.[39]

Companies encourage idea champions by providing freedom and slack time to creative people. IBM and General Electric allow employees to develop new technologies without company approval. Known as *bootlegging*, the unauthorized research often pays big dividends. As one IBM executive said, "We wink at it. It pays off. It's just amazing what a handful of dedicated people can do when they are really turned on."[40]

Idea champions usually come in two types. The **technical** or **product champion** is the person who generates or adopts and develops an idea for a

Book Mark 10.0

The Innovator's Dilemma: When New Technologies Cause Great Firms to Fail

By Clayton M. Christensen

In *The Innovator's Dilemma*, Clayton M. Christensen proposes a shocking idea: good management practices can lead to the failure of successful organizations. Christensen argues that it is very difficult for existing successful companies to take full advantage of technological breakthroughs such as the Internet—what he calls "disruptive technologies" because the habits that led to success get in the way. However, he says there is a solution for dealing with disruptive technological change, even though it can't be found in the standard management toolkit. Christensen says managers can harness the power of disruptive forces to lead their companies through these major technological shifts.

PRINCIPLES FOR HARNESSING THE POWER OF DISRUPTIVE TECHNOLOGIES

Managers harness this power by understanding four principles of disruptive change and their implications for action. To achieve successful innovation, organizations:

1. *Align disruptive technologies with the right set of customers.* Successful companies realize that they depend on customers and investors for resources—that is, companies that invest their resources in ways that don't meet customer and shareholder needs don't survive. This makes it almost impossible to exploit an emerging disruptive technology because an organization's established set of customers and shareholders usually don't see a need for the new products. Using financial and human resources to carve out a new customer base for a disruptive technology such as e-commerce means taking resources away from current activities that satisfy existing customers. The only viable option, Christensen suggests, is to create an autonomous organization with a cost-structure that can achieve profits at the low margins characteristic of most disruptive technologies. The new organization can align the disruptive technology with the "right" segment of the market, gradually creating greater customer demand.

2. *Match the size of the organization to the size of the market.* Disruptive technologies allow new markets to emerge, and companies that enter these emerging markets early have significant advantages. However, small markets don't meet the growth needs of large, successful companies. To harness the power of a disruptive technology, therefore, large companies should

delegate responsibility to a small, independent organization, which can best respond to opportunities for growth in a new market.

3. *Recognize failure as a step toward success.* Solid market research and planning are considered hallmarks of good management, but companies that successfully exploit disruptive technologies realize that markets for the emerging technologies may not yet exist and therefore can't be analyzed. Christensen offers a new approach to strategy and planning. Called discovery-based planning, it suggests that managers plan to fail early and often (though inexpensively) as they search for the market for a disruptive technology. Companies learn what works through trial and error and experimentation.

4. *Develop new markets that value the disruptive technologies.* Christensen points out that technology supply may not equal market demand. In their efforts to continuously develop competitively superior products, many companies overshoot what their original customers want, which opens the opportunity for a different approach—usually simpler and cheaper ways of doing business. For example, the old model of bookselling was to build bigger and bigger stores with more and more inventory. When that model reached its limit and reliability and convenience were still inadequate, the door was opened for a company based on a disruptive technology, such as Amazon.com. To exploit disruptive technologies, companies seek to locate or create new markets that value the characteristics of the new technology rather than seeking to find new ways to satisfy mainstream markets.

WHAT'S THE NEXT DISRUPTION?

In the final chapter, Christensen presents a case study of the electric car, which suggests a methodology and a way of thinking that can help managers prepare for the future in any industry. Successful companies often begin their descent into failure, Christensen suggests, by aggressively investing in the products their most profitable customers want. The innovator's challenge is to ensure that disruptive innovations that don't make sense in today's market are taken seriously without putting the needs of present customers at risk.

The Innovator's Dilemma, by Clayton M. Christensen, is published by Harvard Business School Press.

technological innovation and is devoted to it, even to the extent of risking position or prestige. The **management champion** acts as a supporter and sponsor to shield and promote an idea within the organization.[41] The management champion sees the potential application and has the prestige and authority to get it a fair hearing and to allocate resources to it. Technical and management champions often work together because a technical idea will have a greater chance of success if a manager can be found to sponsor it. At Black & Decker, Peter Chaconas is a technical champion. He invented the Piranha circular saw blade, which is a best-selling tool accessory. Next, he invented the Bullet, which is a bit for home power drills and is the first major innovation in this product in almost one hundred years. Chaconas works full time designing products and promoting their acceptance. Randy Blevins, his boss, acts as management champion for Chaconas's ideas.[42]

NEW PRODUCTS AND SERVICES

Many of the concepts described for technology change are also relevant to the creation of new products and services. However, in many ways, new products and services are a special case of innovation because they are used by customers outside the organization. Since new products are designed for sale in the environment, uncertainty about the suitability and success of an innovation is very high.

NEW PRODUCT SUCCESS RATE

Research has explored the enormous uncertainty associated with the development and sale of new products.[43] To understand what this uncertainty can mean to organizations, just consider such flops as RCA's VideoDisc player, which lost an estimated $500 million, or Time Incorporated's *TV-Cable Week*, which lost $47 million. Producing new products that fail is a part of business in all industries. Organizations take the risk because product innovation is one of the most important ways companies adapt to changes in markets, technologies, and competition.[44]

Experts estimate that about 80 percent of new products fail upon introduction and another 10 percent disappear within five years. Considering that it costs $20 million to $50 million to successfully launch a new product, new product development is a risky, high-stakes game for organizations. Nevertheless, more than 25,000 new products appeared in 1998 alone, including more than 5,000 new toys.[45]

A survey some years ago examined two hundred projects in nineteen chemical, drug, electronics, and petroleum laboratories to learn about success rates.[46] To be successful, the new product had to pass three stages of development: technical completion, commercialization, and market success. The findings about success rates are given in Exhibit 10.6. On the average, only 57 percent of all projects undertaken in the R&D laboratories achieved technical objectives, which means all technical problems were solved and the projects moved on to production. Of all projects that were started, however, less than one-third (31 percent) were fully marketed and commercialized. Several projects failed at this stage because production estimates or test market results were unfavorable.

Finally, only 12 percent of all projects originally undertaken achieved economic success. Most of the commercialized products did not earn sufficient returns to cover the cost of development and production. This means that only about one project in eight returned a profit to the company.

EXHIBIT 10.6   *Probability of New Product Success*

	Probability
Technical completion (technical objectives achieved)	.57
Commercialization (full-scale marketing)	.31
Market success (earns economic returns)	.12

Source: Based on Edwin Mansfield, J. Rapaport, J. Schnee, S. Wagner, and M. Hamburger, *Research and Innovation in Modern Corporations* (New York: Norton, 1971), 57.

REASONS FOR NEW PRODUCT SUCCESS

The next question to be answered by research was, "Why are some products more successful than others?" Why did a product such as Frappuccino succeed in the marketplace while those such as Miller Clear Beer and Frito-Lay's lemonade failed? Further studies indicated that innovation success was related to collaboration between technical and marketing departments. Successful new products and services seemed to be technologically sound and also carefully tailored to customer needs.[47] A study called Project SAPPHO examined seventeen pairs of new product innovations, with one success and one failure in each pair, and concluded the following.

1. Successful innovating companies had a much better understanding of customer needs and paid much more attention to marketing.
2. Successful innovating companies made more effective use of outside technology and outside advice, even though they did more work in-house.
3. Top management support in the successful innovating companies was from people who were more senior and had greater authority.

Thus, there is a distinct pattern of tailoring innovations to customer needs, making effective use of technology, and having influential top managers support the project. These ideas taken together indicate that the effective design for new product innovation is associated with horizontal linkage across departments.

HORIZONTAL LINKAGE MODEL

The organization design for achieving new product innovation involves three components—departmental specialization, boundary spanning, and horizontal linkages. These components are similar to the information linkage mechanisms in Chapter 3 and the differentiation and integration ideas in Chapter 4. Exhibit 10.7 illustrates these components in the **horizontal linkage model**.

Specialization. The key departments in new product development are R&D, marketing, and production. The specialization component means that the personnel in all three of these departments are highly competent at their own tasks. The three departments are differentiated from each other and have skills, goals, and attitudes appropriate for their specialized functions.

Boundary Spanning. This component means each department involved with new products has excellent linkage with relevant sectors in the external environment. R&D personnel are linked to professional associations and to colleagues in other R&D departments. They are aware of recent scientific developments. Marketing personnel are closely linked to customer needs. They listen to what customers have to say, and they analyze competitor products and suggestions by

EXHIBIT 10.7   *Horizontal Linkage Model for New Product Innovations*

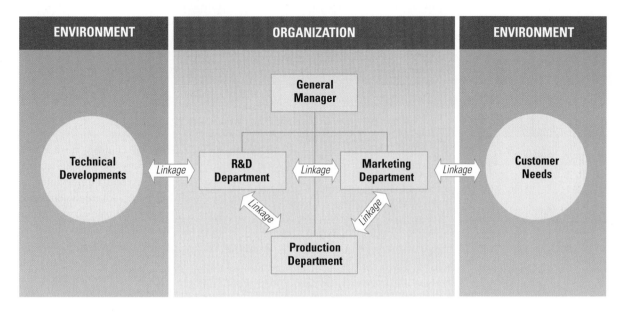

distributors. For example, Kimberly-Clark had amazing success with Huggies Pull-Ups because marketing researchers worked closely with customers in their own homes and recognized the emotional appeal of pull-on diapers for toddlers. By the time competitors caught on, Kimberly-Clark was selling $400 million worth of Huggies annually.[48]

Horizontal Linkages. This component means that technical, marketing, and production people share ideas and information. Research people inform marketing of new technical developments to learn whether the developments are applicable to customers. Marketing people provide customer complaints and information to R&D to use in the design of new products. People from both R&D and marketing coordinate with production because new products have to fit within production capabilities so costs are not exorbitant. The decision to launch a new product is ultimately a joint decision among all three departments.

At General Electric, members of the R&D department have a great deal of freedom to imagine and invent, and then they have to shop their ideas around other departments and divisions, sometimes finding applications for new technologies that are far from their original intentions. As a result, one study shows that of 250 technology products GE undertook to develop over a four-year period, 150 of them produced major applications, far above the U.S. average.[49] IBM's market researchers worked side by side with designers, engineers, and manufacturing personnel, as well as representatives from procurement, logistics, and other departments, to produce IBM's hot-selling Think Pad laptop computer.[50] Famous innovation failures—such as McDonald's Arch Deluxe, the Apple Newton, RJR Nabisco's Premier smokeless cigarettes, and Gerber's Singles, a line of meals for adults—usually violate the horizontal linkage model. Employees fail to connect with customer needs, or internal departments fail to adequately share needs and coordinate with one another.

Companies are increasingly using cross-functional teams for product development to ensure a high level of communication and coordination from the beginning. The functional diversity increases both the amount and the variety of information for new product development, enabling the design of products that meet customer needs and circumventing manufacturing and marketing problems.[51] Kellogg has revised its approach to new product development to improve horizontal collaboration.

Kellogg

When Carlos Gutierrez took over as CEO of Kellogg, he knew the company needed new products to boost profits and revive the struggling cereal company, and he believed that called for a new approach to product development. For years, product development at Kellogg was the exclusive province of marketing, which came up with new ideas and then tossed them over the wall to manufacturing. Over the past couple of decades, the process led to more misses than hits, with products such as Heartwise being taken off the shelves within only a few years.

Now Kellogg is taking a different approach. Employees work in cross-functional teams, with market researchers alongside nutritionists, food scientists, production specialists, and engineers. So far, the approach seems to be working. The company is pumping out twice as many products annually, including some decided hits, such as Raisin Bran Crunch. With thicker, coated flakes that don't get soggy in milk, Raisin Bran Crunch rapidly grabbed nearly 1 percent of the cold cereal market without cutting into sales of Kellogg's traditional Raisin Bran. Another success has been Rice Krispies Treats, a snack-food version of the crunchy marshmallow squares that used to be made only in Mom's kitchen, now including cocoa and peanut butter chocolate varieties.

However, the biggest new product line to come out of Kellogg's improved development process is Ensemble, which includes cereal, frozen entrees, dry pasta, potato chips, and cookies. Kellogg has already gotten approval from the FDA for its claim that the foods reduce cholesterol because they have been enhanced with natural soluble fiber. To reinforce the health pitch, customers will be able to call an 800 number and work with a health coach to devise a personal diet plan. No one yet knows if Ensemble will be a hit in the marketplace, but Gutierrez is betting that Kellogg's new horizontal approach to product development will keep the company turning out products that are tastier, healthier, and more profitable.[52]

Companies such as Kellogg, IBM, and General Electric are using the horizontal linkage model to achieve competitive advantage in today's global marketplace.

ACHIEVING COMPETITIVE ADVANTAGE WITH RAPID PRODUCT INNOVATION

For many companies, creating new products is a critical way to adapt and survive in a rapidly changing environment.[53] Getting new products to market fast and developing products that can compete in a competitive international market are key issues for companies like Xerox, 3M, and Levi Strauss. One authority on time-based competition has said that the old paradigm for success—"provide the most value for the least cost"—has been updated to "provide the most value for the least cost in the least elapsed time."[54]

To gain business, companies are learning to develop new products and services incredibly fast. Whether the approach is called the horizontal linkage model, concurrent engineering, companies without walls, the parallel approach, or simultaneous coupling of departments, the point is the same—get people working together simultaneously on a project rather than in sequence. Many companies are learning to sprint to market with new products.

Hewlett-Packard has made speed a top priority, getting products out the door twice as fast and urging employees to rethink every process in terms of speed. A printer that once took fifty-four months to develop is now on the market in twenty-two. Speed is becoming a major competitive issue and requires the use of cross-functional teams and other horizontal linkages.[55]

Another critical issue is designing products that can compete on a global scale and successfully marketing those products internationally. Companies such as Quaker Oats, Häagen Dazs, and Levi's are trying to improve horizontal communication and collaboration across geographical regions, recognizing that they can pick up winning product ideas from customers in other countries. A new Häagen Dazs flavor, *dulce de leche*, developed primarily for sale in Argentina, has quickly become a favorite in the United States, with sales growing by about 27 percent monthly.[56] Ford has boosted its global competitiveness by using its intranet and global teleconferencing to link car design teams around the world into a single unified group. Black & Decker has also been redesigning its product development process to become a stronger international player. To make global product development faster and more effective, new products are developed by cross-functional project delivery teams, which are answerable to a global business unit team.[57]

Failing to pay attention to global horizontal linkages can hurt companies trying to compete internationally. The Dutch giant Philips Electronics NV was certain its compact disk interactive player called The Imagination Machine would be a hit in the crucial U.S. market, and ultimately, the rest of the world. Five years later, the product, which was promoted as an interactive teaching aid and was so complex it required a thirty-minute sales demonstration, had all but disappeared from the shelves. Marketing employees, salespeople, and major customers had crucial information that would have helped Philips understand the U.S. market, but by the time the executives gathered the information and tried to change course, it was too late. "We should have done things differently," said one Philips executive. "The world isn't as easy as it seems."[58] When companies enter the arena of intense international competition, horizontal coordination across countries is essential to new product development.

STRATEGY AND STRUCTURE CHANGE

The preceding discussion focused on new production processes and products, which are based in the technology of an organization. The expertise for such innovation lies within the technical core and professional staff groups, such as research and engineering. This section turns to an examination of structural and strategy changes.

All organizations need to make changes in their strategies and structures from time to time. In the past, when the environment was relatively stable, most organizations focused on small, incremental changes to solve immediate problems or take advantage of new opportunities. However, over the past decade, companies throughout the world have faced the need to make radical changes in strategy, structure, and management processes to adapt to new competitive demands.[59] Many organizations are cutting out layers of management and decentralizing decision making. There is a strong shift toward more horizontal structures, with teams of front-line workers empowered to make decisions and solve problems on their own. Some companies are breaking totally away from traditional organization forms and shifting toward network strategies and structures, as described in Chapter 7. Others are moving their entire business into cyberspace. Numerous companies are reorganizing and shifting their strategies as the expansion of e-commerce changes the rules. For example, online banking, credit cards, and ATMs are affecting the role of branch banks. Global competition and rapid technological change will likely lead to even greater strategy-structure realignments over the next decade.

These types of changes are the responsibility of the organization's top managers, and the overall process of change is typically different from the process for innovation in technology or new products.

THE DUAL-CORE APPROACH

The dual-core approach compares administrative and technical changes. Administrative changes pertain to the design and structure of the organization itself, including restructuring, downsizing, teams, control systems, information systems, and departmental grouping. Research into administrative change suggests two things. First, administrative changes occur less frequently than do technical changes. Second, administrative changes occur in response to different environmental sectors and follow a different internal process than do technology-based changes.[60] The **dual-core approach** to organizational change identifies the unique processes associated with administrative change.[61]

Organizations—schools, hospitals, city governments, welfare agencies, government bureaucracies, and many business firms—can be conceptualized as having two cores: a technical core and an administrative core. Each core has its own employees, tasks, and environmental domain. Innovation can originate in either core.

The administrative core is above the technical core in the hierarchy. The responsibility of the administrative core includes the structure, control, and coordination of the organization itself and concerns the environmental sectors of government, financial resources, economic conditions, human resources, and competitors. The technical core is concerned with the transformation of raw materials into organizational products and services and involves the environmental sectors of customers and technology.[62]

The findings from research comparing administrative and technical change suggest that a mechanistic organization structure is appropriate for frequent administrative changes, including changes in goals, strategy, structure, control systems, and personnel.[63] For example, administrative changes in policy, regulations, or control systems are more critical than technical changes in many government organizations that are bureaucratically structured. Organizations that successfully adopt many administrative changes often have a larger administrative ratio, are larger in size, and are centralized and formalized compared with organizations that adopt many technical changes.[64] The reason is the top-down implementation of changes in response to changes in the government, financial, or legal sectors of the environment. In contrast, if an organization has an organic structure, lower-level employees have more freedom and autonomy and, hence, may resist top-down initiatives. An organic structure is more often used when changes in organizational technology or products are important to the organization.

The innovation approaches associated with administrative versus technical change are summarized in Exhibit 10.8. Technical change, such as changes in production techniques and innovation technology for new products, is facilitated by an organic structure, which allows ideas to bubble upward from lower- and middle-level employees. Organizations that must adopt frequent administrative changes tend to use a top-down process and a mechanistic structure. For example, policy changes, such as the adoption of tough no-smoking policies by companies like Park Nicollet Medical Center in Minnesota, are facilitated by a top-down approach. Downsizing and restructuring are nearly always managed top down, such as when Raymond Lane, president of Oracle Corp., split the sales force into two teams (one focused on selling database software and the other on selling applications), cut out two levels of management, and placed himself directly in charge of U.S. sales.[65]

The point of the dual-core approach is that many organizations—especially not-for-profit and government organizations—must adopt frequent administrative changes, so a mechanistic structure may be appropriate. For example, research into civil service reform found that the implementation of administrative innovation was extremely difficult in organizations that had an organic technical core. The professional employees in a decentralized agency could resist civil service changes. By contrast, organizations that were considered more bureaucratic in the sense of high formalization and centralization adopted administrative changes readily.[66]

What about business organizations that are normally technologically innovative in bottom-up fashion but suddenly face a crisis and need to reorganize? Or consider a technically innovative, high-tech firm that must reorganize frequently or must suddenly cut back to accommodate changes in production technology or the environment. Technically innovative firms may suddenly have to restructure, reduce the number of employees, alter pay systems, disband teams, or form a new division.[67] The answer is to use a top-down change process. The authority for strategy and structure change lies with top management, who should initiate and

EXHIBIT 10.8   *Dual-Core Approach to Organization Change*

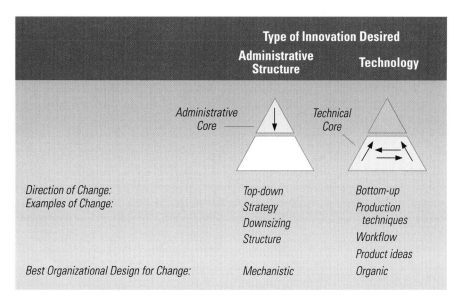

implement the new strategy and structure to meet environmental circumstances. Employee input may be sought, but top managers have the responsibility to direct the change. *Downsizing, restructuring,* and *reorganizing* are common terms for what happens in times of rapid change and global competition. Often, strong top-down changes follow the installation of new top management. For example, when Carol Bartz first arrived at Autodesk, Inc., a leading software company, she introduced a first for the company: a management hierarchy. Autodesk had always been an organic organization, but Bartz believed a more mechanistic approach was needed to revive profits and get the struggling company back on track. She recognized that a top-down change process was needed to develop new goals and strategies and firmly direct the restructuring needed to help Autodesk survive.[68] Changes such as restructuring and downsizing can often be painful for employees, so top managers should move quickly and authoritatively to make both as humane as possible.[69]

Top managers should also remember that top-down change means initiation of the idea occurs at upper levels and is implemented downward. It does not mean that lower-level employees are not educated about the change or allowed to participate in it. Dan Caulfield, founder of Hire Quality Inc., learned the hard way that there are right ways and wrong ways to manage top-down administrative change.

In Practice 10.4

Hire Quality Inc.

Employees laughed when Dan Caulfield stormed through the headquarters of Hire Quality carrying a large waste barrel, snatching Post-it notes off of computer monitors, crumpling spreadsheets, and tossing out reports. But the laughter stopped when he soaked the trash heap with lighter fluid and set it ablaze. Some employees saw months of work go up in flames. One worker even quit the company because of the incident.

Caulfield now realizes that his method of implementing a change to a totally paperless office may have been counterproductive. However, at the time he felt he needed something dramatic to get people to stop using paper and start taking advantage of the $400,000 information technology system he had installed. A job-placement business like Hire Quality is driven by speed and high volume, and Caulfield felt that the tons of paper were getting in the way of performance. The company screens about 35,000 candidates and sends out 3,000 or more résumés a month. There was no way Caulfield could afford the number of staff it would take to handle everything on a paper-only basis. Hire Quality's paperless system includes a massive database that can store information on 200,000 job candidates and be searched by more than 150 possible fields, making it a snap to match candidates with potential jobs. Caulfield also instituted a policy of allowing job candidates to register only electronically, and clients such as FedEx and Bell Atlantic also send job postings electronically. Almost every desk has a scanner so that any paper that comes into the office can be automatically converted to an electronic file.

Caulfield's mistake was that he failed to educate employees and allow them to be involved in the change to a paperless system. Rather than communicating with workers about the importance of switching to electronic files, he assessed fines of a few cents up to a dollar for using the fax machine, making copies, or printing résumés. Employees rebelled against the harsh tactics. Today, Caulfield is trying to tone down his brutal implementation and work gradually to implement the change to a paperless office.[70]

Caulfield recognized that it is the responsibility of top managers to implement administrative changes downward. However, his overly aggressive approach backfired and Caulfield saw the need to educate and communicate with employees. As Carol Bartz at Autodesk puts it, "It's safe to say there are good ways to manage change and bad ways to manage change, and we have to get on the right side of that paradigm".[71]

CULTURE CHANGE

Organizations are made up of people and their relationships with one another. Changes in strategy, structure, technologies, and products do not happen on their own, and changes in any of these areas involve changes in people as well. Employees must learn how to use new technologies, or market new products, or work effectively in a team-based structure.

In a world where any organization can purchase new technology, the motivation, skill, and commitment of employees can provide the competitive edge. Human resource systems can be designed to attract, develop, and maintain an efficient force of employees.

Sometimes achieving a new way of thinking requires a focused change on the underlying corporate culture values and norms. In the last decade, numerous large corporations, including Kodak, IBM, and Ford Motor Company, have undertaken some type of culture change initiative. Changing corporate culture fundamentally shifts how work is done in an organization and generally leads to renewed commitment and empowerment of employees and a stronger bond between the company and its customers.[72]

Some recent trends that generally lead to significant changes in corporate culture are reengineering, the shift to horizontal forms of organizing, and the implementation of total quality management programs, all of which require employees to think in new ways about how work is done.

Organizational development programs also focus on changing old culture values to new ways of thinking, including a learning orientation, greater employee participation and empowerment, and developing a shared companywide vision.

REENGINEERING AND HORIZONTAL ORGANIZATION

Reengineering is a cross-functional initiative involving the radical redesign of business processes to bring about simultaneous changes in culture, structure, and information technology and produce dramatic performance improvements in areas such as customer service, quality, cost, and speed.[73] Reengineering basically means taking a clean-slate approach, pushing aside all the notions of how work is done now and looking at how work can best be designed for optimal performance. The idea is to squeeze out the dead space and time lags in work flows. Such companies as Hoechst Celanese, Union Carbide, BellSouth Telecommunications, and DuPont are among the dozens of companies involved in major reengineering efforts. After reengineering, Union Carbide cut $400 million out of fixed costs in just three years. Hoechst Celanese identified $70 million in cost savings and productivity improvements over a two-year period, without making massive job cuts.[74] Many more organizations have reengineered one or a few specific processes.

Because the focus is on process rather than function, reengineering generally leads to a shift from a vertical organization structure to a horizontal structure as described in Chapter 3. This, in turn, requires major changes in corporate culture and management philosophy. In his book *The Reengineering Revolution*, Michael Hammer refers to people change as "the most perplexing, annoying, distressing, and confusing part" of reengineering.[75] Managers may confront powerful emotions as employees react to rapid, massive change with fear or anger. Top leaders at Jaguar of North America coped with resistance to reengineering by putting their loudest dissenters in charge of solutions and then getting out of the way. They implemented employee suggestions that corrected so many of Jaguar's shortcomings that even the most skeptical dealers accepted that the company truly cared about its employees and its customers.[76]

In the horizontal organization, managers and front-line workers need to understand and embrace the concepts of teamwork, empowerment, and cooperation. Everyone throughout the organization needs to share a common vision and goals so they have a framework within which to make decisions and solve problems. Managers shift their thinking to view workers as colleagues rather than cogs in a wheel; and workers learn to accept not only greater freedom and power, but also the higher level of responsibility—and stress—that comes with it. Mutual trust, risk taking, and tolerance for mistakes become key cultural values in the horizontal organization. Most top managers have little experience dealing with the complexities of human behavior; yet, they should remember that culture changes are crucial to the success of reengineering and the shift to horizontal forms of organization.

TOTAL QUALITY MANAGEMENT

The approach known as **total quality management** infuses quality values throughout every activity within a company. The concept is simple: workers, not managers, are handed the responsibility for achieving standards of quality. No longer are quality control departments and other formal control systems in charge of checking parts and improving quality. Companies train their workers and then trust them to infuse quality into everything they do. The results of TQM programs can be staggering. After noticing that Ford Motor Company cut $40 billion out of its operating budget by adopting quality principles and changing corporate culture, the Henry Ford Health System also instituted a quality program. CEO Gail Warden says of quality programs at Henry Ford and other U.S. health-care institutions, "We have to change the way we practice medicine" to get health-care costs down and remain competitive in the rapidly changing health-care industry.[77]

By requiring organizationwide participation in quality control, TQM requires a major shift in mind-set for both managers and workers. In TQM, workers must be trained, involved, and empowered in a way that many managers at first find frightening. One way in which workers are involved is through **quality circles**, groups of six to twelve volunteer workers who meet to analyze and solve problems.

Another technique of total quality management is known as **benchmarking**, a process whereby companies find out how others do something better than they do and then try to imitate or improve on it. Through research and field trips by small teams of workers, companies compare their products, services, and business practices with those of their competitors and other companies. AT&T, Xerox, DuPont, Kodak, and Motorola are constantly benchmarking.

While the focus of total quality programs is generally on improving quality and productivity, it always involves a significant culture change. Managers should be prepared for this aspect before undertaking quality programs.

THE LEARNING ORGANIZATION

A recent trend is to reduce barriers both within and between organizations and create companies that are focused on knowledge sharing and continuous learning.

As we saw in Chapter 9, one of the key challenges for companies that are shifting to learning organizations is creating an adaptive, learning culture. One method for bringing about this level of culture change is known as **organization development**, which focuses on the human and social aspects of the organization as a way to improve the organization's ability to adapt and solve problems. Organization development (OD) emphasizes the values of human development, fairness, openness, freedom from coercion, and individual autonomy that allows workers to perform the job as they see fit, within reasonable organizational constraints.[78] In the 1970s, OD evolved as a separate field that applied the behavioral sciences in a process of planned organizationwide change, with the goal of increasing organizational effectiveness. Today, the concept has been enlarged to examine how people and groups can change to a learning organization culture in a complex and turbulent environment. Organization development is not a step-by-step procedure to solve a specific problem but a process of fundamental change in the human and social systems of the organization, including organizational culture.[79]

OD uses knowledge and techniques from the behavioral sciences to create a learning environment through increased trust, open confrontation of problems, employee empowerment and participation, knowledge and information sharing, the design of meaningful work, cooperation and collaboration between groups, and the full use of human potential.

OD practitioners believe the best performance occurs by breaking down hierarchical and authoritarian approaches to management. In terms of the competing values effectiveness model described in Chapter 2, OD places high value on internal processes and human relationships. However, consistent with the arguments in the environment and technology chapters, research has shown that the OD approach may not enhance performance or satisfaction in stable business environments and for routine tasks.[80] It is best for organizations that are facing environmental and technological discontinuities and rapid change and that need to become learning organizations. The spirit of what OD tries to accomplish is illustrated in this chapter's Taking the Lead box. The U.S. Department of Agriculture's Animal and Plant Health Inspection Service has used organization development to overcome the problems of bureaucracy and create a culture that supports learning and change.

Shifting organizations toward a learning culture is not easy, but organization development techniques can smooth the process. For example, OD can help managers and employees think in new ways about human relationships, making the transition to more participative management less stressful. At Hewlett-Packard's direct marketing organization, self-confessed "authoritarian" manager Sharon Jacobs used concepts based in organization development to create a better quality of life and participation for employees as well as improve the organization's performance. Spurred by pleas from new staffers who felt constricted by the excessive top-down control, Jacobs is doing her best to let go, to ask her telemarketers for solutions, to listen to the ideas of even lowest-level staff members. Despite the difficulties in the beginning, the new style has resulted in a 40 percent increase in productivity, a rise in employee morale significant enough to warrant a note from HP's president, and a 44 percent decline in the unit's annual attrition rate.[81]

OD CULTURE CHANGE INTERVENTIONS

OD interventions involve training of specific groups or of everyone in the organization. For OD intervention to be successful, senior management in the organization must see the need for OD and provide enthusiastic support for the change. Techniques used by many organizations for improving people skills through OD include the following.

Large Group Intervention. Most early OD activities involved small groups and focused on incremental change. However, in recent years, there has been growing interest in the application of OD techniques to large group settings, which are more attuned to bringing about radical or transformational change in organizations operating in complex environments.[82] The **large group intervention** approach[83] brings together participants from all parts of the organization—often including key stakeholders from outside the organization as well—in an off-site setting to discuss problems or opportunities and plan for change. A large-group intervention might involve fifty to five hundred people and last for several days. The off-site setting limits interference and distractions, enabling participants to focus on new ways of doing things. General Electric's "Work Out" program, an ongoing process of solving problems, learning, and improving, began with large-scale off-site meetings that grew out of Jack Welch's desire to create a "culture of boundarylessness" he felt was critical to learning and growth. Hourly and salaried workers from many different parts of the organization join with customers and suppliers to discuss and solve problems.[84]

Team Building. Team building promotes the idea that people who work together can work as a team. A work team can be brought together to discuss conflicts, goals, the decision-making process, communication, creativity, and leadership. The team can then plan to overcome problems and improve results. Team-building activities are also used in many companies to train task forces, committees, and new product development groups. These activities enhance communication and collaboration and strengthen the cohesiveness of organizational groups and teams.

Interdepartmental Activities. Representatives from different departments are brought together in a mutual location to surface conflict, diagnose its causes, and plan improvement in communication and coordination. This type of intervention has been applied to union–management conflict, headquarters–field office conflict, interdepartmental conflict, and mergers.[85]

In today's world, the work force is becoming more and more diverse, and organizations are constantly adapting to environmental uncertainty and increasing international competition. OD interventions can respond to these new realities as organizations strive to create greater capability for learning and growth.[86]

STRATEGIES FOR IMPLEMENTING CHANGE

This chapter began by looking at incremental versus radical change, the four types of changes managers can use to gain a competitive edge, and the five elements that must be present for any change to succeed—idea, need, adoption, implementation, and resources. In this final section, we are going to briefly discuss the need for strong leadership to support change, resistance to change at the organizational level, and some techniques managers can use to implement change.

LEADERSHIP FOR CHANGE

As the world becomes increasingly complex, the need for change within organizations and the need for leaders who can successfully manage change continues to grow. As we discussed in Chapter 1, coping with rapid change is one of the greatest challenges facing today's organizations. Organizations need to continuously change and adapt in response to a turbulent environment. They need leaders who can clearly recognize the need for change and make it happen, who can develop and communicate a vision for what the organization can be and provide the motivation and guidance to take it there. Leaders who can effect the kind of continuous adaptation needed in today's world recognize that change is painful for employees, and they learn to put themselves in their employees' shoes and develop partnerships that make successful change possible.[87]

Successful change can happen only when employees are willing to devote the time and energy needed to reach new goals as well as endure possible stress and hardship. Having a clearly communicated vision that embodies flexibility and openness to new ideas, methods, and styles sets the stage for a change-oriented organization and helps employees cope with the chaos and tension associated with change.[88] Leaders also build organizationwide commitment by taking

Taking the Lead

U.S. Agriculture Department's Animal and Plant Health Inspection Service

A federal agency might seem an unlikely hotbed of management reform, but that's exactly what the Agriculture Department's Animal and Plant Health Inspection Service (APHIS) has become. A self-designated group of change agents is constantly stirring things up at APHIS, yet far from being seen as troublemakers, these employees are viewed by leaders as crucial to keeping people in the organization active, energized, and empowered. The agency has won a series of Hammer Awards from Vice President Al Gore for its aggressive approach to reinventing government.

According to APHIS Director Lonnie King, in today's difficult world, "the status quo is not acceptable.... You can be the driver, the passenger, or the road kill. We want to be the driver." He and other leaders at APHIS attribute the agency's aptitude for learning and change in part to its organization development (OD) unit. APHIS created the unit to help deal with the problems that were overwhelming federal agencies. For example, Plant Protection and Quarantine workers at Miami International Airport, one of the least desirable work sites within APHIS, wanted to organize into self-directed teams. Yet when the experiment was tried, workers became frustrated and demoralized

because neither they nor their supervisors had the necessary skills. Rather than counting the teamwork experiment a failure, APHIS pumped additional resources into the effort, hiring OD specialists to make it successful.

Since then, the agency's OD unit has continued to grow. OD specialists are now helping the agency coordinate a planning process known as *future search*, to develop a vision and strategy for the future and break down boundaries between functions, divisions, and field offices. APHIS is using OD to create a culture in which change and continuous learning are primary values and where employees have the attitude that "we're all in this together." Rather than cutting OD when resources go down, the agency protects the unit as the best way to help APHIS remain flexible. When managers rated the agency's support services on the degree to which they added value to their operations, OD got one of the highest ratings. According to Dan Stone, head of the unit, "People experienced OD as helping them to solve real problems. When this kind of support is available, people are willing to bite off more. There is a more profound level of change."

Source: James Thompson, "Rogue Workers, Change Agents," *Government Executive*, April 1996, 46–49.

employees through three stages of the change commitment process, illustrated in Exhibit 10.9.[89] In the first stage, preparation, employees hear about the change through memos, meetings, speeches, or personal contact and become aware that the change will directly affect their work. In the second stage, leaders should help employees develop an understanding of the full impact of the change and the positive outcomes of making the change. When employees perceive the change as positive, the decision to implement is made. In the third stage, the true commitment process begins. The installation step, a trial process for the change, gives leaders an opportunity to discuss problems and employee concerns and build commitment to action. In the final stage, institutionalization, employees view the change not as something new but as a normal and integral part of organizational operations.

The pressures on organizations to change will likely increase over the next few decades and leaders must develop the personal qualities, skills, and methods needed to help their companies remain competitive. Indeed, some management experts argue that to survive the upheaval of the early twenty-first century, managers must turn their organizations into *change leaders* by using the present to actually create the future—breaking industry rules, creating new market space, and routinely abandoning outmoded products, services, and processes to free up resources to build the future.[90]

BARRIERS TO CHANGE

Visionary leadership is crucial for change; however, leaders should expect to encounter resistance as they attempt to take the organization through the three stages of the change commitment process. It is natural for people to resist change, and many barriers to change exist at the individual and organizational level.[91]

EXHIBIT 10.9   *Stages of Commitment to Change*

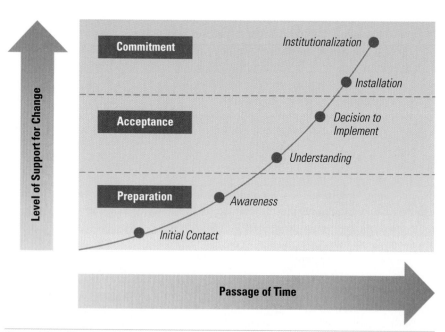

Source: Adapted from Daryl R. Conner, *Managing at the Speed of Change* (New York: Villard Books, 1992), 148. Used with permission.

1. *Excessive focus on costs.* Management may possess the mind-set that costs are all-important and may fail to appreciate the importance of a change that is not focused on costs—for example, a change to increase employee motivation or customer satisfaction.
2. *Failure to perceive benefits.* Any significant change will produce both positive and negative reactions. Education may be needed to help managers and employees perceive more positive than negative aspects of the change. In addition, if the organization's reward system discourages risk-taking, a change process may falter because employees think that the risk of making the change is too high.
3. *Lack of coordination and cooperation.* Organizational fragmentation and conflict often result from the lack of coordination for change implementation. Moreover, in the case of new technology, the old and new systems must be compatible.
4. *Uncertainty avoidance.* At the individual level, many employees fear the uncertainty associated with change. Constant communication is needed so that employees know what is going on and understand how it impacts their jobs.
5. *Fear of loss.* Managers and employees may fear the loss of power and status or even their jobs. In these cases, implementation should be careful and incremental, and all employees should be involved as closely as possible in the change process.

Implementation can typically be designed to overcome many of the organizational and individual barriers to change.

TECHNIQUES FOR IMPLEMENTATION

Top leaders articulate the vision and set the tone, but managers and employees throughout the organization are involved in the process of change. There are a number of techniques that can be used to successfully implement change.

1. *Identify a true need for change.* A careful diagnosis of the existing situation is necessary to determine the extent of the problem or opportunity. If the people affected by the change do not agree with a problem, the change process should not proceed without further analysis and communication among all employees. As mentioned early in the chapter, sometimes a sense of urgency is needed to unfreeze people and make them willing to invest the time and energy to adopt new techniques or procedures.[92] For example, ALLTEL, an information services and telecommunications company, faced both productivity and customer service problems as the company coped with rapid growth in the mid-1990s, but managers found it difficult to convince employees of the need for change. When ALLTEL Technology Center's errors began to mount and the Center almost lost its largest client, GTE, managers used the incident to help establish a sense of urgency. Management and employees began meeting in small groups to talk about the need for change and how they could revise their work to improve the organization.[93]
2. *Find an idea that fits the need.* Finding the right idea often involves search procedures—talking with other managers, assigning a task force to investigate the problem, sending out a request to suppliers, or asking creative people within the organization to develop a solution. The creation of a new idea requires organic conditions. This is a good opportunity to encourage employee participation, because they need the freedom to think about and

explore new options.[94] ALLTEL set up a program called Team Focus to gather input from all employees. In twenty group meetings over a period of two weeks, managers gathered 2,800 suggestions, which they then narrowed down to 170 critical action items that specifically addressed problems that were affecting employee morale and performance.

3. *Get top management support.* Successful change requires the support of top management. Top managers should articulate clear innovation goals. For a single large change, such as a structural reorganization, the president and vice presidents must give their blessing and support. For smaller changes, the support of influential managers in relevant departments is required. The lack of top management support is one of the most frequent causes of implementation failure.[95]

4. *Design the change for incremental implementation.* Sometimes large changes cannot be implemented all at once or employees may feel overwhelmed and resist the change. Recall how Dan Caulfield tried to force employees to shift to a paperless office system overnight but found that he needed to scale back and introduce the new system in a more gradual manner. Likewise, when a large bank in South Carolina installed a complete new $6 million system to computerize processing, it was stunned that the system didn't work very well. The prospect for success of such a large change is improved if the change can be broken into subparts and each part adopted sequentially. Then designers can make adjustments to improve the innovation, and hesitant users who see success can throw support behind the rest of the change program.

5. *Develop plans to overcome resistance to change.* Many good ideas are never used because managers failed to anticipate or prepare for resistance to change by consumers, employees, or other managers. No matter how impressive the performance characteristics of an innovation, its implementation will conflict with some interests and jeopardize some alliances in the organization. To increase the chance of successful implementation, management must acknowledge the conflict, threats, and potential losses perceived by employees. Several strategies can be used by managers to overcome the resistance problem:

   • *Alignment with needs and goals of users.* The best strategy for overcoming resistance is to make sure change meets a real need. Employees in R&D often come up with great ideas that solve nonexistent problems. This happens because initiators fail to consult with the people who use a change. Resistance can be frustrating for managers, but moderate resistance to change is good for an organization. Resistance provides a barrier to frivolous changes or to change for the sake of change. The process of overcoming resistance to change normally requires that the change be good for its users.

   • *Communication and training.* Communication informs users about the need for change and about the consequences of a proposed change, preventing false rumors, misunderstanding, and resentment. In one study of change efforts, the most commonly cited reason for failure was that employees learned of the change from outsiders. Top managers concentrated on communicating with the public and with shareholders, but failed to communicate with the people who would be most intimately involved and most affected by the changes—their own employees.[96] Open communication often gives management an opportunity to explain what steps will be taken to ensure that the change will have no adverse consequences for employees. Training is also needed to help employees understand and cope with their role in the change process.

- *Participation and involvement.* Early and extensive participation in a change should be part of implementation. Participation gives those involved a sense of control over the change activity. They understand it better, and they become committed to successful implementation. One recent study of the implementation and adoption of computer technology at two companies showed a much smoother implementation process at the company that introduced the new technology using a participatory approach.[97] The team-building and large-group intervention activities described earlier can be effective ways to involve employees in a change process.
- *Forcing and coercion.* As a last resort, managers may overcome resistance by threatening employees with loss of jobs or promotions or by firing or transferring them. In other words, management power is used to overwhelm resistance. In most cases, this approach is not advisable because it leaves people angry at change managers, and the change may be sabotaged. However, this technique may be needed when speed is essential, such as when the organization faces a crisis. It may also be required for needed administrative changes that flow from the top down, such as downsizing the work force.[98]

6. *Create change teams.* Throughout, this chapter has discussed the need for resources and energy to make change happen. Separate creative departments, new venture groups, or an ad hoc team or task force are ways to focus energy on both creation and implementation. A separate department has the freedom to create a new technology that fits a genuine need. A task force can be created to see that implementation is completed. The task force can be responsible for communication, involvement of users, training, and other activities needed for change.

7. *Foster idea champions.* One of the most effective weapons in the battle for change is the idea champion. The most effective champion is a volunteer champion who is deeply committed to a new idea. The idea champion sees that all technical activities are correct and complete. An additional champion, such as a manager sponsor, may also be needed to persuade people about implementation, even using coercion if necessary. For example, John Cunningham was the idea champion at Chesebrough-Ponds who developed the polishing pen through which nail polish is applied. Management supporters at Chesebrough-Ponds then solved the implementation problems of manufacturing, packaging, and marketing. Both technical and management champions may break the rules and push ahead even when others are nonbelieving, but the enthusiasm pays off.[99]

SUMMARY AND INTERPRETATION

Organizations face a dilemma. Managers prefer to organize day-to-day activities in a predictable, routine manner. However, change—not stability—is the natural order of things in today's global environment. Thus, organizations need to build in change as well as stability, to facilitate innovation as well as efficiency.

Most change in organizations is incremental, but there is a growing emphasis on the need for radical change. Four types of change—technology, products and services, strategy and structure, and culture—may give an organization a competitive edge, and managers can make certain each of the necessary ingredients for change is present.

For technical innovation, which is of concern to most organizations, an organic structure that encourages employee autonomy works best because it encourages a bottom-up flow of ideas. Other approaches are to establish a separate department charged with creating new technical ideas, establish venture teams, and encourage idea champions. New products and services generally require cooperation among several departments, so horizontal linkage is an essential part of the innovation process.

For changes in strategy and structure, a top-down approach is typically best. These innovations are in the domain of top administrators who take responsibility for restructuring, for downsizing, and for changes in policies, goals, and control systems.

Culture changes are also generally the responsibility of top management. Some recent trends that lead to significant changes in corporate culture are reengineering, the shift to horizontal forms of organizing, and the implementation of total quality management programs, all of which require employees to think in new ways. Organization development (OD) is another process for bringing about culture change by focusing on the development and fulfillment of people to bring about improved performance. OD is particularly useful for companies striving to become learning organizations. All of these approaches typically favor organic conditions that lead to employee participation in decisions, interesting work, and the freedom to initiate ideas to improve their jobs.

Finally, the implementation of change can be difficult. Strong leadership is needed to guide employees through the turbulence and uncertainty and build organizationwide commitment to change. A number of barriers to change exist, including excessive focus on cost, failure to perceive benefits, lack of organizational coordination, and individual uncertainty avoidance and fear of loss. Managers can thoughtfully plan how to deal with resistance to increase the likelihood of success. Techniques that will facilitate implementation are to obtain top management support, implement the change incrementally, align change with the needs and goals of users, include users in the change process through communication and participation, and, in some cases, to force the innovation, if necessary. Change teams and idea champions are also effective.

BRIEFCASE

As an organization manager, keep these guidelines in mind:

1. Facilitate frequent changes in internal technology by adopting an organic organizational structure. Give technical personnel freedom to analyze problems and develop solutions or create a separate organically structured department or venture group to conceive and propose new ideas.
2. Facilitate changes in strategy and structure by adopting a top-down approach. Use a mechanistic structure when the organization needs to adopt frequent administrative changes in a top-down fashion.
3. Work with organization development consultants for large-scale changes in the attitudes, values, or skills of employees, and when shifting to a learning organization culture. Adopt total quality management programs to facilitate change in company culture toward greater quality and productivity.
4. Encourage marketing and research departments to develop linkages to each other and to their environments when new products or services are needed.
5. Make sure every change undertaken has a definite need, idea, adoption, decision, implementation strategy, and resources. Avoid failure by not proceeding until each element is accounted for.
6. Lead employees through the three stages of commitment to change—preparation, acceptance, and commitment—and use techniques to achieve successful implementation. These include obtaining top-management support, implementing the change in a series of steps, assigning change teams or idea champions, and overcoming resistance by actively communicating with workers and encouraging their participation in the change process.

KEY CONCEPTS

ambidextrous approach
benchmarking
change process
creative departments
culture changes
dual-core approach
horizontal linkage model
idea champion
incremental change
large group intervention
management champion
new-venture fund
organization development

organizational change
organizational innovation
product and service changes
quality circles
radical change
reengineering
strategy and structure changes
switching structures
team building
technical or product champion
technology changes
total quality management
venture teams

DISCUSSION QUESTIONS

1. How is the management of radical change likely to differ from the management of incremental change?
2. How are organic characteristics related to changes in technology? To administrative changes?
3. Describe the dual-core approach. How does administrative change normally differ from technology change? Discuss.
4. How might organizations manage the dilemma of needing both stability and change? Discuss.
5. Why do organizations experience resistance to change? What steps can managers take to overcome this resistance?
6. "Bureaucracies are not innovative." Discuss.
7. A noted organization theorist said, "Pressure for change originates in the environment; pressure for stability originates within the organization." Do you agree? Discuss.
8. Of the five elements required for successful change, which element do you think managers are most likely to overlook? Discuss.
9. How do the underlying values of organization development compare to the values underlying other types of change? Why do the values underlying OD make it particularly useful in shifting to a learning organization? Discuss.
10. The manager of R&D for a drug company said only 5 percent of the company's new products ever achieve market success. He also said the industry average is 10 percent and wondered how his organization might increase its success rate. If you were acting as a consultant, what advice would you give him concerning organization structure?
11. Review the stages of commitment to change illustrated in Exhibit 10.9 and the seven techniques for implementing change discussed at the end of the chapter. At which stage of change commitment would each of the seven techniques most likely be used?

CHAPTER 10 WORKBOOK   *Innovation Climate**

In order to examine differences in the level of innovation encouragement in organizations, you will be asked to rate two organizations. You may choose one in which you have worked, or the university. The other should be someone else's workplace, either that of a family member, a friend, or an acquaintance. You will have to interview that person to answer the questions on the next page. You should put your own answers in column A, your interviewee's answers in column B, and what you think would be the ideal in column C. Use a scale of 1 to 5: 1 = don't agree at all to 5 = agree completely.

---

*Adapted by Dorothy Marcic from Susanne G. Scott and Reginald A. Bruce, "Determinants of Innovative Behavior: A Path Model of Individual Innovation in the Workplace," *Academy of Management Journal* 37, no. 3 (1994): 580–607.

INNOVATION MEASURES

Item of Measure	Column A Your Organization	Column B Other Organization	Column C Your Ideal
1. Creativity is encouraged here.★			
2. People are allowed to solve the same problems in different ways.★			
3. I get to pursue creative ideas.#			
4. The organization publicly recognizes and also rewards those who are innovative.#			
5. Our organization is flexible and always open to change.★			
Below score items on the opposite scale: 1 = agree completely to 5 = don't agree at all			
6. The primary job of people here is to follow orders that come from the top.★			
7. The best way to get along here is to think and act like the others.★			
8. This place seems to be more concerned with the status quo than with change.★			
9. People are rewarded more if they don't rock the boat.#			
10. New ideas are great, but we don't have enough people or money to carry them out.#			

Note: ★Starred items indicate the organization's innovation climate.
    # Pound sign items show resource support.

QUESTIONS

1. What comparisons about innovative climates can you make from these two organizations?
2. How might productivity differ between a climate that supports innovation and a climate that does not?

3. For which type of place would you rather work? Why?

Case for Analysis   *Shoe Corporation of Illinois**

Shoe Corporation of Illinois produces a line of women's shoes that sell in the lower-price market for $17.99 to $19.99 per pair. Profits averaged twenty-five cents to thirty cents per pair ten years ago, but according to the president and the controller, labor and materials costs have risen so much in the intervening period that profits today average only fifteen cents to twenty cents per pair.

Production at both the company's plants totals 12,500 pairs per day. The two factories are located within a radius of sixty miles of Chicago: one at Centerville, which produces 4,500 pairs per day, and the other at Meadowvale, which produces 8,000 pairs per day. Company headquarters is located in a building adjacent to the Centerville plant.

It is difficult to give an accurate picture of the number of items in the company's product line. Shoes change in style perhaps more rapidly than any other style product, including garments. This is so chiefly because it is possible to change production processes quickly and because, historically, each company, in attempting to get ahead of competitors, gradually made style changes ever more frequently. At present, including both major and minor style changes, SCI offers 100 to 120 different products to customers each year.

A partial organizational chart, showing the departments involved in this case, appears in Exhibit 1.

COMPETITIVE STRUCTURE OF THE INDUSTRY

Very large general shoe houses, such as International and Brown, carry a line of ladies' shoes and are able to undercut prices charged by Shoe Corporation of Illinois, principally because of the policy in the big companies of producing large numbers of "stable" shoes, such as the plain pump and the loafer. They do not attempt to change styles as rapidly as their smaller competitors. Thus, without constant changes in production processes and sales presentations, they are able to keep costs substantially lower.

Charles F. Allison, the president of Shoe Corporation of Illinois, feels that the only way for a small independent company to be competitive is to change styles frequently, taking advantage of the flexibility of a small organization to create designs that appeal to customers. Thus, demand can be created, and a price set high enough, to make a profit. Allison, incidentally,

appears to have an artistic talent in styling and a record of successful judgments in approving high-volume styles over the years.

Regarding SCI's differences from its large competitors, Allison says:

You see, Brown and International Shoe Company both produce hundreds of thousands of the same pair of shoes. They store them in inventory at their factories. Their customers, the large wholesalers and retailers, simply know their line and send in orders. They do not have to change styles nearly as often as we do. Sometimes I wish we could do that, too. It makes for a much more stable and orderly system. There is also less friction between people inside the company. The sales people always know what they're selling, the production people know what is expected of them. The plant personnel are not shook up so often by someone coming in one morning and tampering with their machine lines or their schedules. The styling people are not shook up so often by the plant saying, "We can't do your new style the way you want it."

To help SCI be even more competitive against larger firms, Allison recently created an e-commerce department. Although his main interest was in marketing over the Internet, he also hoped new technology would help reduce some of the internal friction by giving people an easier way to communicate. He invested in a sophisticated new computer system and hired consultants to set up a company intranet and provide a few days' training to upper and middle managers. Katherine Olsen came on board as director of e-commerce, charged primarily with coordinating Internet marketing and sales. When she took the job, she had visions of one day offering consumers the option of customized shoe designs. However, Olsen was somewhat surprised to learn that most employees still refused to use the intranet even for internal communication and coordination. The process of deciding on new styles, for example, was still handled in the same manner the company had used since the 1970s.

MAJOR STYLE CHANGES

The decision about whether to put a certain style into production requires information from a number

---

*Written by Charles E. Summer. Copyright 1978. Revised with permission.

EXHIBIT 1   *Partial Organization Chart of Shoe Corporation of Illinois*

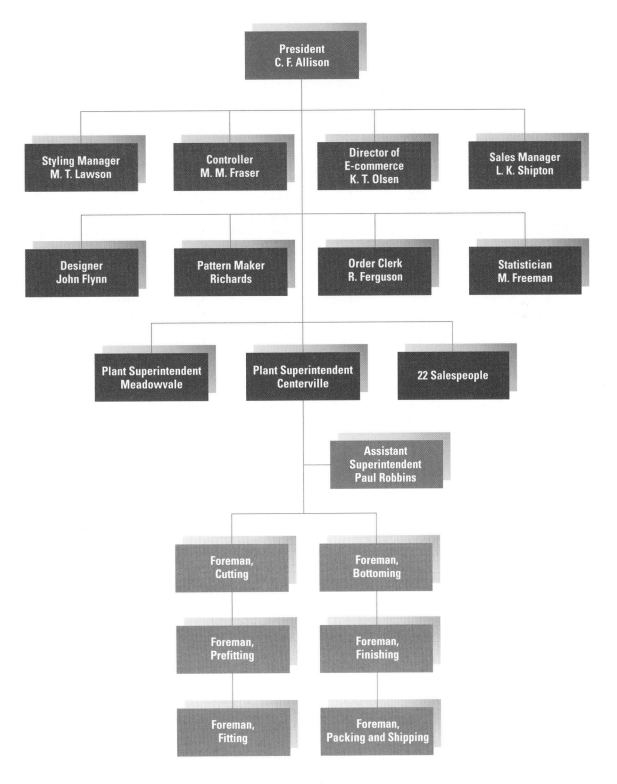

of different people. Here is what typically happens in the company. It may be helpful to follow the organization chart in tracing the procedure.

M. T. Lawson, the style manager, and his designer, John Flynn, originate most of the ideas about shape, size of heel, use of flat sole or heels, and findings (the term used for ornaments attached to, but not part of, the shoes—bows, straps, and so forth). They get their ideas principally from reading style and trade magazines or by copying a top-flight designer. Lawson corresponds with publications and friends in large stores in New York, Rome, and Paris in order to obtain pictures and samples of up-to-the-minute style innovations. Although he uses e-mail occasionally, Lawson prefers telephone contact and receiving drawings or samples by overnight mail. Then, he and Flynn discuss various ideas and come up with design options.

When Lawson decides on a design, he takes a sketch to Allison, who either approves or disapproves it. If Allison approves, he (Allison) then passes the sketch on to Shipton, the sales manager, to find out what lasts (widths) should be chosen. Shipton, in turn, simply forwards the design to Martin Freeman, a statistician in the sales department, who maintains summary information on customer demand for colors and lasts.

To compile this information, Freeman visits sales people twice a year to get their opinions on the colors and lasts that are selling best, and he keeps records of shipments by color and by last. For these needs, he simply totals data that is sent to him by the shipping foreman in each of the two plants.

When Freeman has decided on the lasts and colors, he sends Allison a form that lists the colors and lasts in which the shoe should be produced. Allison, if he approves this list, forwards the information to Lawson, who passes it on to Richards, an expert pattern maker. Richards makes a paper pattern and constructs a prototype in leather and paper, sends this to Lawson, who in turn approves or disapproves it. He forwards any approved prototype to Allison. Allison, if he too approves, notifies Lawson, who takes the prototype to Paul Robbins, assistant to the superintendent of the Centerville plant. Only this plant produces small quantities of new or experimental shoe styles. Such production is referred to as a "pilot run" by executives at the plant.

Robbins then literally carries the prototype through the six production departments of the plant—from cutting to finish—discussing it with each foreman, who in turn works with employees on the machines in having a sample lot of several thousand pairs made.

When the finished lot is delivered by the finishing foreman to the shipping foreman (because of the importance of styling, Allison has directed that each foreman personally deliver styling goods in process to the foreman of the next department), the latter holds the inventory in storage and sends one pair each to Allison and Lawson. If they approve of the finished product, Allison instructs the shipping foreman to mail samples to each of the company's twenty-two sales people throughout the country. Olsen also receives samples, photos, and drawings to post on the Web page and gauge customer interest. Sales people have instructions to take the samples immediately (within one week) to at least ten customers. Orders for already established shoes are normally sent to Ralph Ferguson, a clerk in Shipton's office, who records them and forwards them to the plant superintendents for production. In the case of first orders on new styles, however, sales people have found by experience that Martin Freeman has a greater interest in the success of new "trials," so they rush orders to him by overnight mail, and he in turn places the first orders for a new style in the inter-office mail to the plant superintendents. He then sends off a duplicate of the order, mailed in by the sales people, to Ferguson for entering in his statistical record of all orders received by the company.

Three weeks after the sales people receive samples, Allison requires Ralph Ferguson to give him a tabulation of orders. At that time, he decides whether the sales people and the Web page should push the item and the superintendents should produce large quantities, or whether he will tell them that although existing orders will be produced, the item will be discontinued in a short time.

The procedures outlined here have, according to Allison:

> ...worked reasonably well. The average time from when Lawson decides on a design until we notify the Centerville plant to produce the pilot run is two weeks to a month. Of course, if we could speed that up, it would make the company just that much more secure in staying in the game against the big companies, and in taking sales away from our competitors. There seems to be endless bickering among people around here involved in the styling phase of the business. That's to be expected when you have to move fast—there isn't much time to stop and

observe all of the social amenities. I have never thought that a formal organization chart would be good in this company—we've worked out a customary system here that functions well.

M. T. Lawson, manager of styling, says that within his department all work seems to get out in minimum time; he also states that both Flynn and Richards are good employees and skilled in their work. He mentioned that Flynn had been in to see him twice in the last year:

. . . to inquire about his (Flynn's) future in the company. He is thirty-three years old and has three children. I know that he is eager to make money, and I assured him that over the years we can raise him right along from the $50,000 we are now paying. Actually, he has learned a lot about shoe styles since we hired him from the design department of a fabric company six years ago.

John Flynn revealed that:

I was actually becoming dissatisfied with this job. All shoe companies copy styles—it's generally accepted practice within the industry. But I've picked up a real feel for designs, and several times I've suggested that the company make all its own original styles. We could make SCI a style leader and also increase our volume. When I ask Lawson about this, he says it takes too much time for the designer to create originals—that we have all we can handle to do research in trade magazines and maintain contracts feeding us the results of experts. Beside, he says our styles are standing the test of the marketplace.

"PROJECTS X AND Y"

Flynn also said that he and Martin Freeman had frequently talked about the styling problem. They felt that:

Allison is really a great president, and the company surely would be lost without him. However, we've seen times when he lost a lot of money on bad judgments in styles. Not many times—perhaps six or seven times in the last 18 months. Also, he is, of course, extremely busy as president of the corporation. He must look after everything from financing from the banks to bargaining with the union. The result is that he is sometimes unavailable to do his styling approvals for several days, or even two weeks. In a business like this, that kind of delay can cost money. It also makes him slightly edgy. It tends, at times when he has many other things to

do, to make him look quickly at the styles we submit, or the prototypes Richards makes, or even the finished shoes that are sent for approval by the shipping foreman. Sometimes I worry that he makes two kinds of errors. He simply rubber stamps what we've done, in which sending them to him is simply a waste of time. At other times he makes snap judgments of his own, overruling those of us who have spent so much time and expertise on the shoe. We do think he has good judgment, but he himself has said at times that he wishes he had more time to concentrate on styling and approval of prototypes and final products.

Flynn further explained (and this was corroborated by Freeman) that the two had worked out two plans, which they referred to as "project X" and "project Y." In the first, Flynn created an original design that was not copied from existing styles. Freeman then gave special attention to color and last research for the shoe and recommended a color line that didn't exactly fit past records on consumer purchases—but one he and Flynn thought would provide "great consumer appeal." This design and color recommendation were accepted by Lawson and Allison; the shoe went into production and was one of the three top sellers during the calendar year. The latter two men did not know that the shoe was styled in a different way from the usual procedure.

The result of a second, similar project (Y) was put into production the next year, but this time sales were discontinued after three weeks.

PROBLEM BETWEEN LAWSON AND ROBBINS

Frequently, perhaps ten to twelve times a year, disagreement arises between Mel Lawson, manager of styling, and Paul Robbins, assistant to the superintendent of the Centerville plant. Robbins says that:

The styling people don't understand what it means to produce a shoe in the quantities that we do, and to make the changes in production that we have to. They dream up a style quickly, out of thin air. They do not realize that we have a lot of machines that have to be adjusted, and that some things they dream up take much longer on certain machines than others, thus creating a bottleneck in the production line. If they put a bow or strap in one position rather than others, it may mean we have to keep people idle on later machines while there is a pile-up on the sewing machines on which this complicated little operation is performed. This costs the plant money. Furthermore, there are times when they get the prototype here late, and the foremen and I either have to work overtime or the trial run won't get through in time to have new production runs on new styles, to take the plant capacity liberated by our stopping production on old styles. Lawson doesn't know much about production and sales and the whole company. I think all he does is to bring shoes down here to the plant sort of like a messenger boy. Why should he be so hard to get along with? He isn't getting paid any more than I am, and my position in the plant is just as important as his.

Lawson, in turn says that he has a difficult time getting along with Robbins:

There are many times when Robbins is just unreasonable. I take prototypes to him five or six times a month, and other minor style changes to him six or eight times. I tell him every time that we have problems in getting these ready, but he knows only about the plant, and telling him doesn't seem to do any good. When we first joined the company, we got along all right, but he has gotten harder and harder to get along with.

CERTAIN OTHER PROBLEMS THAT HAVE ARISEN

Ralph Ferguson, the clerk in the sales department who receives orders from sales people and forwards totals for production schedules to the two plant superintendents, has complained that the sales people and Freeman are bypassing him in their practice of sending experimental shoe orders to Freeman. He insists that his job description (one of only two written descriptions in the company) gives him responsibility for receiving all orders throughout the company and for maintaining historical statistics on shipments.

Both the sales people and Freeman, on the other hand, say that before they started the new practice (that is, when Ferguson still received the experimental shoe orders), there were at least eight or ten instances a year when these were delayed from one to three days on Ferguson's desk. They report that Ferguson just wasn't interested in new styles, so the sales people "just started sending them to Freeman." Ferguson acknowledged that there were times of short delay, but there were good reasons for them:

They (sales people and Freeman) are so interested in new designs, colors, and lasts, that they can't understand the importance of a systematic handling of the whole order procedure, including both old and new shoe styles. There must be accuracy. Sure, I give some priority to experimental orders, but sometimes when rush orders for existing company products are piling up, and when there's a lot of planning I have to do to allocate production between Centerville and Meadowvale, I decide which comes first—processing of these, or processing the experimental shoe orders. Shipton is my boss, not the sales people or Freeman. I'm going to insist that these orders come to me.

THE PUSH FOR NEW TECHNOLOGY

Katherine Olsen believes many of these problems could be solved through better use of technology. She has approached Charles Allison several times about the need to make greater use of the expensive and sophisticated computer information systems he had installed. Although Allison always agrees with her, he has so far done nothing to help solve the problem. Olsen thinks the new technology could dramatically improve coordination at SCI:

Everyone needs to be working from the same data at the same time. As soon as Lawson and Flynn come up with a new design, it should be posted on the intranet so all of us can be informed. And everyone needs access to sales and order information, production schedules, and shipping deadlines. If everyone—from Allison down to the people in the production plants—was kept up-to-date throughout the entire process, we wouldn't have all this confusion and bickering. But no one around here wants to give up any control—they all have their own little operations and don't want to share information with anyone else. For example, I sometimes don't even know there's a new style in the works until I get finished samples and photos. No one seems to recognize that one of the biggest advantages of the Internet is to help stay ahead of changing styles. I know that Flynn has a good feel for design, and we're not taking advantage of his abilities. But I also have information and ideas that could help this company keep pace with changes and really stand out from the crowd. I don't know how long we expect to remain competitive using this cumbersome, slow-moving process and putting out shoes that are already behind the times.

Case for Analysis   *Southern Discomfort**

Jim Malesckowski remembers the call of two weeks ago as if he just put down the telephone receiver: "I just read your analysis and I want you to get down to Mexico right away," Jack Ripon, his boss and chief executive officer, had blurted in his ear. "You know we can't make the plant in Oconomo work any-more—the costs are just too high. So go down there, check out what our operational costs would be if we move, and report back to me in a week."

At that moment, Jim felt as if a shiv had been stuck in his side, just below the rib cage. As president of the Wisconsin Specialty Products Division of Lamprey, Inc., he knew quite well the challenge of dealing with high-cost labor in a third-generation, unionized U.S. manufacturing plant. And although he had done the analysis that led to his boss's knee-jerk response, the call still stunned him. There were 520 people who made a living at Lamprey's Oconomo facility, and if it closed, most of them wouldn't have a journeyman's prayer of finding another job in the town of 9,900 people.

Instead of the $16-per-hour average wage paid at the Oconomo plant, the wages paid to the Mexican workers—who lived in a town without sanitation and with an unbelievably toxic effluent from industrial pollution—would amount to about $1.60 an hour on average. That's a savings of nearly $15 million a year for Lamprey, to be offset in part by increased costs for training, transportation, and other matters.

After two days of talking with Mexican government representatives and managers of other companies in the town, Jim had enough information to develop a set of comparative figures of production and shipping costs. On the way home, he started to outline the report, knowing full well that unless some miracle occurred, he would be ushering in a blizzard of pink slips for people he had come to appreciate.

The plant in Oconomo had been in operation since 1921, making special apparel for persons suffering injuries and other medical conditions. Jim had often talked with employees who would recount stories about their fathers or grandfathers working in the same Lamprey company plant—the last of the original manufacturing operations in town.

But friendship aside, competitors had already edged past Lamprey in terms of price and were dangerously close to overtaking it in product quality. Although both Jim and the plant manager had tried to convince the union to accept lower wages, union leaders resisted. In fact, on one occasion when Jim and the plant manager tried to discuss a cell manufacturing approach, which would cross-train employees to perform up to three different jobs, local union leaders could barely restrain their anger. Yet probing beyond the fray, Jim sensed the fear that lurked under the union reps' gruff exteriors. He sensed their vulnerability, but could not break through the reactionary bark that protected it.

A week has passed and Jim just submitted his report to his boss. Although he didn't specifically bring up the point, it was apparent that Lamprey could put its investment dollars in a bank and receive a better return than what its Oconomo operation is currently producing.

Tomorrow, he'll discuss the report with the CEO. Jim doesn't want to be responsible for the plant's dismantling, an act he personally believes would be wrong as long as there's a chance its costs can be lowered. "But Ripon's right," he says to himself. "The costs are too high, the union's unwilling to cooperate, and the company needs to make a better return on its investment if it's to continue at all. It sounds right but feels wrong. What should I do?"

*Doug Wallace, "What Would You Do?" *Business Ethics*, March/April 1996, 52-53. Reprinted with permission from *Business Ethics*, P. O. Box 8439, Minneapolis, MN 55408, 612-879-0695.

NOTES

1. L. D. DiSimone, comments about 3M in "How Can Big Companies Keep the Entrepreneurial Spirit Alive?" *Harvard Business Review* (November-December 1995): 184–85, and Thomas A. Stewart, "3M Fights Back," *Fortune*, 5 February 1996, 94–99.

2. Based on John P. Kotter, *Leading Change* (Boston, Mass.: Harvard Business School Press, 1996), 18–20.

3. Laura Zinn, "Pepsi's Future Becomes Clearer," *Business Week*, 1 February 1993, 74–75; Patricia Sellers, "Pepsi Keeps on Going after No. 1," *Fortune*, 11 March 1991, 61–70.

4. David A. Nadler and Michael L. Tushman, "Organizational Frame Bending: Principles for Managing Reorientation," *Academy of Management Executive* 3 (1989): 194–204; Michael L. Tushman and Charles A. O'Reilly III, "Ambidextrous Organizations: Managing Evolutionary and Revolutionary Change," *California Management Review* 38, No. 4 (Summer 1996): 8–30.

5. William A. Davidow and Michael S. Malone, *The Virtual Corporation* (New York: HarperBusiness, 1992); Gregory G. Dess, Abdul M. A. Rasheed, Kevin J. McLaughlin, and Richard L. Priem, "The New Corporate Architecture," *Academy of Management Executive* 9, no. 3 (1995): 7–20.

6. Chuck Salter, "Progressive Makes Big Claims," *Fast Company*, (November 1998): 177–194.

7. Ibid.

8. Bruce Rayner, "Trial-by-Fire Transformation: An Interview with Globe Metallurgical's Arden C. Sims," *Harvard Business Review* (May–June 1992): 117–29.

9. Joseph E. McCann, "Design Principles for an Innovating Company," *Academy of Management Executive* 5 (May 1991): 76–93.

10. Stuart Crainer and Des Dearlove, "Water Works," *Management Review* (May 1999): 39–43.

11. Anita Lienert, "Jedi Masters and Paradigm Busters," *Management Review* (March, 1998): 11–14.

12. Richard A. Wolfe, "Organizational Innovation: Review, Critique and Suggested Research Directions," *Journal of Management Studies* 31, no. 3 (May 1994): 405–31.

13. John L. Pierce and Andre L. Delbecq, "Organization Structure, Individual Attitudes and Innovation," *Academy of Management Review* 2 (1977): 27–37; Michael Aiken and Jerald Hage, "The Organic Organization and Innovation," *Sociology* 5 (1971): 63–82.

14. Richard L. Daft, "Bureaucratic versus Non-bureaucratic Structure in the Process of Innovation and Change," in Samuel B. Bacharach, ed., *Perspectives in Organizational Sociology: Theory and Research* (Greenwich, Conn.: JAI Press, 1982), 129–66.

15. Alan D. Meyer and James B. Goes, "Organizational Assimilation of Innovations: A Multilevel Contextual Analysis," *Academy of Management Journal* 31 (1988): 897–923.

16. Richard W. Woodman, John E. Sawyer, and Ricky W. Griffin, "Toward a Theory of Organizational Creativity," *Academy of Management Review* 18 (1993): 293–321; Alan Farnham, "How to Nurture Creative Sparks," *Fortune,* 10 January 1994, 94–100.

17. Michael Barrier, "Managing Workers in Times of Change," *Nation's Business* (May 1998): 31-34.

18. John P. Kotter, *Leading Change* (Boston: Harvard University Press, 1996), 20-25, and "Leading Change," *Harvard Business Review* (March–April 1995): 59–67.

19. Eric Matson, "Here, Innovation is No Fluke," *Fast Company* (August–September 1977): 42–44.

20. Paul M. Barrett, "A Once-Stodgy Firm Makes a Flashy Return, But at What Cost?" *The Wall Street Journal*, 17 August 1998, A1, A6.

21. D. Bruce Merrifield, "Intrapreneurial Corporate Renewal," *Journal of Business Venturing* 8 (September 1993): 383–89; Linsu Kim, "Organizational Innovation and Structure," *Journal of Business Research* 8 (1980): 225–45; Tom Burns and G. M. Stalker, *The Management of Innovation* (London: Tavistock Publications, 1961).

22. James Q. Wilson, "Innovation in Organization: Notes toward a Theory," in James D. Thompson, ed., *Approaches to Organizational Design* (Pittsburgh: University of Pittsburgh Press, 1966), 193–218.

23. J. C. Spender and Eric H. Kessler, "Managing the Uncertainties of Innovation: Extending Thompson (1967)," *Human Relations* 48, no. 1 (1995): 35–56; Robert B. Duncan, "The Ambidextrous Organization: Designing Dual Structures for Innovation," in Ralph H. Killman, Louis R. Pondy, and Dennis Slevin, eds., *The Management of Organization*, vol. 1 (New York: North-Holland, 1976), 167–88.

24. James B. Treece, "Improving the Soul of an Old Machine," *Business Week*, 25 October 1993, 134–36.

25. Edward F. McDonough III and Richard Leifer, "Using Simultaneous Structures to Cope with Uncertainty," *Academy of Management Journal* 26 (1983): 727–35.

26. John McCormick and Bill Powell, "Management for the 1990s," *Newsweek*, 25 April 1988, 47–48.

27. Todd Datz, "Romper Ranch," *CIO Enterprise*, Section 2, 15 May 1999, 39–52.

28. Perry Glasser, "Revolutionary Soldiers," *CIO Enterprise*, Section 2, 15 May 1999, 54-60; and John Holusha, "The Case of Xerox PARC," *Strategy & Business*, Issue 10 (First Quarter 1998): 76–82.

29. Paul S. Adler, Barbara Goldoftas, and David I. Levine, "Flexibility Versus Efficiency? A Case Study of Model Changeovers in the Toyota Production System" (Working Paper, School of Business Administration, University of Southern California, Los Angeles, 1996).

30. Judith R. Blau and William McKinley, "Ideas, Complexity, and Innovation," *Administrative Science Quarterly* 24 (1979): 200–19.

31. Rosabeth Moss Kanter, Jeffrey North, Lisa Richardson, Cynthia Ingols, and Joseph Zolner, "Engines of Progress: Designing and Running Entrepreneurial Vehicles in Established Companies: Raytheon's New Product Center, 1969–1989," Journal of Business Venturing 6 (March 1991): 145–63.

32. Russell Mitchell, "Masters of Innovation: How 3M Keeps Its New Products Coming," *Business Week*, 10 April 1989, 58–63.

33. Marcia Stepanek, "Closed, Gone to the Net," *Business Week*, 7 June 1999, 113–116.

34. Phaedra Hise, "New Recruitment Strategy: Ask Your Best Employees to Leave," *Inc.*, July 1997, 2.

35. Daniel F. Jennings and James R. Lumpkin, "Functioning Modeling Corporate Entrepreneurship: An Empirical Integrative Analysis," *Journal of Management* 15 (1989): 485–502.

36. Jane M. Howell and Christopher A. Higgins, "Champions of Technology Innovation," *Administrative Science Quarterly* 35 (1990): 317–41; Jane M. Howell and Christopher A. Higgins, "Champions of Change: Identifying, Understanding, and Supporting Champions of Technology Innovations," *Organizational Dynamics* (Summer 1990): 40–55.

37. Peter F. Drucker, "Change Leaders," *Inc.*, June 1999, 65–72, and Peter F. Drucker, *Management Challenges for the 21st Century* (New York: HarperBusiness, 1999).

38. Crainer and Dearlove, "Water Works."

39. Thomas J. Peters and Robert H. Waterman, Jr., *In Search of Excellence* (New York: Harper & Row, 1982).

40. Ibid., p. 205.

41. Peter J. Frost and Carolyn P. Egri, "The Political Process of Innovation," in L. L. Cummings and Barry M. Staw, eds., *Research in Organizational Behavior*, vol. 13 (New York: JAI Press, 1991), 229–95; Jay R. Galbraith, "Designing the Innovating Organization," *Organizational Dynamics* (Winter 1982): 5–25; Marsha Sinatar, "Entrepreneurs, Chaos, and Creativity—Can Creative People Really Survive Large Company Structure?" *Sloan Management Review* (Winter 1985): 57–62.

42. "Black & Decker Inventory Makes Money for Firm by Just Not 'Doing the Neat Stuff,'" *Houston Chronicle,* 25 December 1987, sec. 3, p. 2.

43. Christopher Power with Kathleen Kerwyn, Ronald Grover, Keith Alexander, and Robert D. Hof, "Flops," *Business Week*, 16 August 1993, 76–82; Modesto A. Maidique and Billie Jo Zirger, "A Study of Success and Failure in Product Innovation: The Case of the U.S. Electronics Industry," *IEEE Transactions in Engineering Management* 31 (November 1984): 192–203.

44. Deborah Dougherty and Cynthia Hardy, "Sustained Product Innovation in Large, Mature Organizations: Overcoming Innovation-to-Organization Problems," *Academy of Management Journal* 39, No. 5 (1996): 1120–1153

45. Cliff Edwards, "Many Products Have Gone Way of the Edsel," *Johnson City Press*, 23 May 1999, 28, 30; Paul Lukas, "The Ghastliest Product Launches," *Fortune*, 16 March 1998, 44; and Robert McMath, *What Were They Thinking? Marketing Lessons I've Learned from Over 80,000 New-Product Innovations and Idiocies* (New York: Times Business, 1998).

46. Edwin Mansfield, J. Rapaport, J. Schnee, S. Wagner, and M. Hamburger, *Research and Innovation in Modern Corporations* (New York: Norton, 1971); Antonio J. Bailetti and Paul F. Litva, "Integrating Customer Requirements into Product Designs," *Journal of Product Innovation Management* (1995): 12: 3–15.

47. Shona L. Brown and Kathleen M. Eisenhardt, "Product Development: Past Research, Present Findings, and Future Directions," *Academy of Management Review* 20, no. 2 (1995): 343–78; F. Axel Johne and Patricia A. Snelson, "Success Factors in Product Innovation: A Selective Review of the Literature," *Journal of Product Innovation Management* 5 (1988): 114–28; Science Policy Research Unit, University of Sussex, *Success and Failure in Industrial Innovation*

(London: Centre for the Study of Industrial Innovation, 1972).

48. Dorothy Leonard and Jeffrey F. Rayport, "Spark Innovation through Empathic Design," *Harvard Business Review* (November–December 1997): 102–13.

49. Amal Kumar Naj, "GE's Latest Invention: A Way to Move Ideas from Lab to Market," *The Wall Street Journal*, 14 June 1990, A1, A99.

50. Ira Sager, "The Man Who's Rebooting IBM's PC Business," *Business Week*, 24 July 1995, 68–72.

51. Shona L. Brown and Kathleen M. Eisenhardt, "Product Development: Past Research, Present Findings, and Future Directions," *Academy of Management Review* 20, no. 2 (1995): 343–78; Dan Dimancescu and Kemp Dwenger, "Smoothing the Product Development Path," *Management Review* (January 1996): 36–41.]

52. Alex Taylor III, "Kellogg Cranks Up Its Idea Machine," *Fortune*, 5 July 1999, 181–182.

53. Kathleen M. Eisenhardt and Behnam N. Tabrizi, "Accelerating Adaptive Processes: Product Innovation in the Global Computer Industry," *Administrative Science Quarterly* 40 (1995): 84–110; and Dougherty and Hardy, "Sustained Product Innovation in Large, Mature Organizations."

54. George Stalk, Jr., "Time and Innovation," *Canadian Business Review*, Autumn 1993, 15–18.

55. Robert D. Hof, "From Dinosaur to Gazelle: HP's Evolution Was Painful but Necessary," *Business Week/Reinventing America*, 1992, 65; Karne Bronikowski, "Speeding New Products to Market," *Journal of Business Strategy* (September–October 1990): 34–37; Brian Dumaine, "How Managers Can Succeed through Speed," *Fortune*, 13 February 1989, 54–59; Otis Port, Zachary Schiller, and Resa W. King, "A Smarter Way to Manufacture," *Business Week*, 30 April 1990, 110–17; Tom Peters, "Time-Obsessed Competition," *Management Review* (September 1990): 16–20.

56. David Leonhardt, "It Was a Hit in Buenos Aires—So Why Not Boise?" *Business Week*, 7 September 1998, 56, 58.

57. Dan Dimancescu and Kemp Dwenger, "Smoothing the Product Development Path," *Management Review*, January 1996, 36–41.

58. Jeffrey A. Trachtenberg, "How Philips Flubbed Its U.S. Introduction of Electronic Product," *The Wall Street Journal*, 28 June 1996, A1.

59. Raymond E. Miles, Henry J. Coleman, Jr., and W. E. Douglas Creed, "Keys to Success in Corporate Redesign," *California Management Review* 37, no. 3 (Spring 1995): 128–45.

60. Fariborz Damanpour and William M. Evan, "Organizational Innovation and Performance: The Problem of 'Organizational Lag,'" *Administrative Science Quarterly*, 29 (1984): 392–409; David J. Teece, "The Diffusion of an Administrative Innovation," *Management Science* 26 (1980): 464–70; John R. Kimberly and Michael J. Evaniski, "Organizational Innovation: The Influence of Individual, Organizational and Contextual Factors on Hospital Adoption of Technological and Administrative Innovation," *Academy of Management Journal* 24 (1981): 689–713; Michael K. Moch and Edward V. Morse, "Size, Centralization, and Organizational Adoption of Innovations," *American Sociological Review* 42 (1977): 716–25; Mary L. Fennell, "Synergy, Influence, and Information in the Adoption of Administrative Innovation," *Academy of Management Journal* 27 (1984): 113–29.

61. Richard L. Daft, "A Dual-Core Model of Organizational Innovation," *Academy of Management Journal* 21 (1978): 193–210.

62. Daft, "Bureaucratic versus Nonbureaucratic Structure"; Robert W. Zmud, "Diffusion of Modern Software Practices: Influence of Centralization and Formalization," *Management Science* 28 (1982): 1421–31.

63. Daft, "A Dual-Core Model of Organizational Innovation"; Zmud, "Diffusion of Modern Software Practices."

64. Fariborz Damanpour, "The Adoption of Technological, Administrative, and Ancillary Innovations: Impact of Organizational Factors," *Journal of Management* 13 (1987): 675–88.

65. Steve Hamm, "Is Oracle Finally Seeing Clearly?" *Business Week*, 3 August 1998, 86–88.

66. Gregory H. Gaertner, Karen N. Gaertner, and David M. Akinnusi, "Environment, Strategy, and the Implementation of Administrative Change: The Case of Civil Service Reform," *Academy of Management Journal* 27 (1984): 525–43.

67. Claudia Bird Schoonhoven and Mariann Jelinek, "Dynamic Tension in Innovative, High Technology Firms: Managing Rapid Technology Change through Organization Structure," in Mary Ann Von Glinow and Susan Albers

Mohrman, eds., *Managing Complexity in High Technology Organizations* (New York: Oxford University Press, 1990), 90–118.

68. Lawrence M. Fisher, "Imposing a Hierarchy on a Gaggle of Techies," *New York Times*, 29 November 1992, F4.

69. David Ulm and James K. Hickel, "What Happens after Restructuring?" *Journal of Business Strategy* (July–August 1990): 37–41; John L. Sprague, "Restructuring and Corporate Renewal: A Manager's Guide," *Management Review* (March 1989): 34–36.

70. Joshua Macht, "Pulp Addiction," *Inc. Technology*, no. 1 (1997): 43–46.

71. Fisher, "Imposing a Hierarchy on a Gaggle of Technies."

72. Benson L. Porter and Warrington S. Parker, Jr., "Culture Change," *Human Resource Management* 31 (Spring–Summer 1992): 45–67.

73. Donna B. Stoddard, Sirkka L. Jarvenpaa, and Michael Littlejohn, "The Reality of Business Reengineering: Pacific Bell's Centrex Provisioning Process," *California Management Review* 38, No. 3 (Spring 1996): 57–76; and Michael Hammer with Steven Stanton, "The Art of Change," *Success* (April 1995): 44A-44H.

74. Thomas A. Stewart, "Reengineering: The Hot New Managing Tool," *Fortune*, 23 August 1993, 41–48; and Brian S. Moskal, "Reengineering without Downsizing," *IW*, 19 February 1996, 23–28.

75. Quoted in Anne B. Fisher, "Making Change Stick," *Fortune*, 17 April 1995, 122.

76. Ibid.

77. Ron Winslow, "Healthcare Providers Try Industrial Tactics to Reduce Their Costs," *The Wall Street Journal*, 3 November 1993, A1, A16.

78. W. Warner Burke, "The New Agenda for Organization Development," in Wendell L. French, Cecil H. Bell, Jr., and Robert A. Zawacki, *Organization Development and Transformation: Managing Effective Change* (Burr Ridge, Ill.: Irwin McGraw-Hill, 2000), 523–35.

79. W. Warner Burke, *Organization Development: A Process of Learning and Changing*, 2nd ed. (Reading, Mass.: Addison-Wesley, 1994); Wendell L. French and Cecil H. Bell, Jr., "A History of Organizational Development," in French, Bell, and Zawacki, *Organization Development and Transformation*, 20–42.

80. Michael Beer and Elisa Walton, "Developing the Competitive Organization: Interventions and Strategies," *American Psychologist* 45 (February 1990): 154–61.

81. Joseph Weber, "Letting Go Is Hard to Do," *Business Week/Enterprise*, 1993, 218–19.

82. French and Bell, "A History of Organization Development."

83. The information on large-group intervention is based on Kathleen D. Dannemiller and Robert W. Jacobs, "Changing the Way Organizations Change: A Revolution of Common Sense," *The Journal of Applied Behavioral Science* 28, No. 4 (December 1992): 48–498; and Barbara B. Bunker and Billie T. Alban, "Conclusion: What Makes Large Group Interventions Effective?" *The Journal of Applied Behavioral Science* 28, No. 4 (December 1992): 570–91; and Marvin R. Weisbord, "Inventing the Future: Search Strategies for Whole System Improvements," in French, Bell, and Zawacki, *Organization Development and Transformation*, 242–50.

84. J. Quinn, "What a Workout!" *Performance* (November 1994): 58–63; and Bunker and Alban, "Conclusion: What Makes Large Group Interventions Effective?"

85. Paul F. Buller, "For Successful Strategic Change: Blend OD Practices with Strategic Management," *Organizational Dynamics* (Winter 1988): 42–55.

86. Jyotsna Sanzgiri and Jonathan Z. Gottlieb, "Philosophic and Pragmatic Influences on the Practice of Organization Development, 1950–2000," *Organizational Dynamics* (Autumn 1992): 57–69.

87. John P. Kotter, *Leading Change* (Boston, Mass.: Harvard Business School Press, 1996); Paul Strebel, "Why Do Employees Resist Change?" *Harvard Business Review* (May–June 1996): 86–92; Michael Beer and Russell A. Eisenstat, "Developing an Organization Capable of Implementing Strategy and Learning," *Human Relations* 49, no. 5 (1996): 597–619.

88. Ronald Recardo, Kathleen Molloy, and James Pellegrino, "How the Learning Organization Manages Change," *National Productivity Review* (Winter 1995/96): 7–13.

89. Based on Daryl R. Conner, *Managing at the Speed of Change* (New York: Villard Books, 1992), 146-60.

90. Drucker, *Management Challenges for the 21st Century*; Tushman and O'Reilly, "Ambidextrous Organizations"; Gary Hamel and C. K. Prahalad, "Seeing the Future First," *Fortune*, 4 September 1994, 64–70; and Linda Yates and Peter Skarzynski, "How Do Companies Get to the Future First?" *Management Review*, (January 1999): 16–22.

91. Based on Carol A. Beatty and John R. M. Gordon, "Barriers to the Implementation of CAD/CAM Systems," *Sloan Management Review* (Summer 1988): 25–33.

92. Kotter, *Leading Change*.

93. Jim Cross, "Back to the Future," *Management Review* (February 1999): 50-54.

94. Richard L. Daft and Selwyn W. Becker, *Innovation in Organizations* (New York: Elsevier, 1978); John P. Kotter and Leonard A. Schlesinger, "Choosing Strategies for Change," *Harvard Business Review* 57 (1979): 106–14.

95. Everett M. Rogers and Floyd Shoemaker, *Communication of Innovations: A Cross Cultural Approach*, 2d ed. (New York: Free Press, 1971); Stratford P. Sherman, "Eight Big Masters of Innovation," *Fortune*, 15 October 1984, 66–84.

96. Peter Richardson and D. Keith Denton, "Communicating Change," *Human Resource Management* 35, no. 2 (Summer 1996): 203–16.

97. Philip H. Mirvis, Amy L. Sales, and Edward J. Hackett, "The Implementation and Adoption of New Technology in Organizations: The Impact on Work, People, and Culture," *Human Resource Management* 30 (Spring 1991): 113–39; Arthur E. Wallach, "System Changes Begin in the Training Department," *Personnel Journal* 58 (1979): 846–48, 872; Paul R. Lawrence, "How to Deal with Resistance to Change," *Harvard Business Review* 47 (January–February 1969): 4–12, 166–76.

98. Dexter C. Dunphy and Doug A. Stace, "Transformational and Coercive Strategies for Planned Organizational Change: Beyond the O. D. Model," *Organizational Studies* 9 (1988): 317–34; Kotter and Schlesinger, "Choosing Strategies for Change."

99. "How Chesebrough-Ponds Put Nail Polish in a Pen," *Business Week*, 8 October 1984: 196–200; Richard L. Daft and Patricia J. Bradshaw, "The Process of Horizontal Differentiation: Two Models," *Administrative Science Quarterly* 25 (1980): 441–56; Alok K. Chakrabrati, "The Role of Champion in Product Innovation," *California Management Review* 17 (1974): 58–62.

Managing Dynamic Processes

Decision-Making Processes

A LOOK INSIDE

White Rose Nursery and Crafts

*S*hortly after arriving in Canada in the early 1950s, Czech-born horticulturist Alexandre Raab opened a small mail-order plant business, selling varieties of roses you couldn't find anywhere else. Thirty-five years later Raab's business, White Rose Nursery and Crafts, had grown to twenty locations and sold $200 million worth of plants, arts-and-crafts supplies, seasonal decorations, and even wicker furniture and school supplies. Faced with a tough choice when none of his children wanted to follow in his footsteps, Raab decided to sell most of his stake in the business to a conglomerate that took the business public a few years later.

Over the next several years, Raab watched in horror as a new management team almost completely destroyed what it had taken practically his entire adult life to build. When sales and profits flattened in the early years of new management—primarily because of an economic recession combined with aggressive competition from new rivals such as Home Depot and arts-and-crafts retailer Michael's—old-time White Rose workers and managers urged executives and directors to be patient. The company was consistently making money they argued (unlike many retailers during the same time period) and there was no need for massive changes in strategy. However, Dean Groussman, hired as CEO in 1995, immediately set a new course for White Rose—he added layers of management, outsourced advertising, and placed inventory management in the hands of managers rather than buyers. Groussman also standardized stores with new layouts and wider aisles, which left less room for the seasonal and sometimes off-the-wall merchandise Raab had been fond of offering customers. To compete with the huge chains, Groussman introduced everyday low pricing, cut back on nursery and seasonal items, and bulked up arts-and-crafts inventory. White Rose's core of loyal customers showed their displeasure by staying away—same-store sales dropped 12 percent the first year and inventory piled up on shelves. Employees weren't happy either—they felt that White Rose's unique, close-knit, casual culture had been replaced with a stiff, inflexible, demoralizing bureaucracy. Almost overnight, it seemed, a $3.4 million profit turned into a $34.3 billion loss. Meanwhile, most of White Rose's competitors in the nursery business were thriving again as economic conditions improved.

After two more years of losses and mounting debts at White Rose, it became clear that Groussman's sincere efforts to transform the company into a booming "twenty-first century organization" had succeeded only in destroying the excitement and spontaneity of the business, driving out talented employees, and leading the company to bankruptcy.[1]

Every organization grows, prospers, or fails as a result of decisions by its managers, and decisions can be risky and uncertain, without any guarantee of success. Decision making must be done amid constantly changing factors, unclear information, and conflicting points of view. Dean Groussman was doing what he believed was right for White Rose Nursery and Crafts, based on market research as well as conventional management thinking. On the other hand, long-time employees were telling him that customers liked White Rose's quirkiness and warned that sudden, massive changes would only erode a solid customer base. New CEO Bill Aziz has made listening to customers and employees a central part of his strategy to revive White Rose. He also decided to cut back on the arts-and-crafts inventory and return to a broader variety, install new computerized inventory management systems, and close down eight Quebec stores to prevent the cash drain. There is no guarantee that Aziz's decisions will succeed, but many insiders believe White Rose is back on the right track.

Many organizational decisions are complete failures. For example, McDonald's Arch Deluxe sandwich, introduced at a cost of $100 million, was axed from the menu after only a few years. Toy makers Mattel and Hasbro both passed on the Ninja Turtles idea in the late 1980s, and the action figures went on to make billions. The decision by previous Toys "R" Us executives to cling to their 1970s-format stores enabled Wal-Mart to overtake the company as the biggest U.S. toy retailer and gave online rivals such as eToys a head start in selling toys over the Internet.[2]

Managers also make many successful decisions every day. Mickey Drexler decided to launch Old Navy, a new kind of discount store, when sales and profits slowed at his Gap stores, and it was an instant success. In less than three years, Gap opened 282 Old Navy stores and sales hit $1 billion. Nokia became a $10 billion leader in the cellular phone and electronics industry because managers at the Finnish company decided to sell off unrelated businesses such as paper, tires, and aluminum and concentrate the company's energy and resources on electronics. Richard Branson, founder of Virgin Airlines, created a whole new retail category when he opened Virgin Bride, a bridal superstore that handles every aspect of wedding planning, from the invitations to the dress and wedding cake.[3]

PURPOSE OF THIS CHAPTER

At any time, an organization may be identifying problems and implementing alternatives for hundreds of decisions. Managers and organizations somehow muddle through these processes.[4] The purpose here is to analyze these processes to learn what decision making is actually like in organizational settings. Decision-making processes can be thought of as the brain and nervous system of an organization. Decision making is the end use of the information and control systems described in Chapters 7 and 8. Decisions are made about organization strategy, structure, innovation, and acquisitions. This chapter explores how organizations can and should make decisions about these issues.

The first section defines decision making. The next section examines how individual managers make decisions. Then several models of organizational decision making are explored. Each model is used in a different organizational situation. The final section in this chapter combines the models into a single framework that describes when and how they should be used and discusses special issues, such as decision mistakes.

DEFINITIONS

Organizational decision making is formally defined as the process of identifying and solving problems. The process contains two major stages. In the **problem identification stage**, information about environmental and organizational conditions is monitored to determine if performance is satisfactory and to diagnose the cause of shortcomings. The **problem solution** stage is when alternative courses of action are considered and one alternative is selected and implemented.

Today, many organizations are using sophisticated information technology systems, as discussed in Chapter 7, to help monitor the environment, detect problems, and quickly develop alternatives. This chapter's Taking the Lead box describes how US West has improved its decision making through the use of information technology.

Organizational decisions vary in complexity and can be categorized as programmed or nonprogrammed.[5] **Programmed decisions** are repetitive and well defined, and procedures exist for resolving the problem. They are well structured because criteria of performance are normally clear, good information is available about current performance, alternatives are easily specified, and there is relative certainty that the chosen alternative will be successful. Examples of programmed decisions include decision rules, such as when to replace an office copy machine, when to reimburse managers for travel expenses, or whether an applicant has sufficient qualifications for an assembly-line job. Many companies adopt rules based on experience with programmed decisions. For example, general pricing rules in the restaurant industry are that food is marked up three times direct cost, beer four times, and liquor six times. A rule for large hotels staffing banquets is to allow one server per thirty guests for a sit-down function and one server per forty guests for a buffet.[6]

Nonprogrammed decisions are novel and poorly defined, and no procedure exists for solving the problem. They are used when an organization has not

Taking the Lead

At US West, Information Is Power

With its massive red, yellow, and green displays and banks of personal computers, US West's network-reliability operations center in Littleton, Colorado, looks like something you'd see on a twenty-third century starship. But this control center is strictly down-to-earth: it's where US West employees constantly monitor the vitality of the phone company's most basic service—the telephone dial tone. Simply by looking at the rows of names and numbers on the eight huge scoreboards, the 700 employees who work in the center can instantly identify problems throughout a 14-state region, see exactly where they're occurring, and know how many people are affected by them. The most severe problems are shaded in red, with less serious outages colored yellow or green. In addition, employees are monitoring other screens, such as continuous feeds from the Weather Channel and from CNN that can help them track events that might cause problems. The Weather Channel, for example, can alert US West employees to storms that might affect phone service. CNN keeps the company in constant touch with breaking news that could affect calling patterns. For example, employees knew immediately about the tragic shooting of students at Columbine High School in the spring of 1999, giving them a head start on preparing for the flood of calls into and out of the region.

Identifying problems is just the first step. US West's control center combines these large-scale scoreboards with small work-group "neighborhoods," in which workers from various functional areas collaborate to solve problems. Every major technical group is represented, from workers who monitor equipment alarms in the field to those who set up new service lines. Because of the wide range of skills and experience, many problems are solved in a matter of minutes.

"Five years ago, we saw all the competition in the telecommunications business coming," says Barbara Anders, one of the center's directors. Top managers decided the best way to compete was to get everyone involved in learning how to best solve problems quickly. That meant putting crucial, real-time data at everyone's fingertips and reorganizing workers into cross-functional teams to tap into their collective knowledge. By making information-sharing central to its operation, US West has empowered its workers to make better and faster decisions.

Source: Based on Ron Lieber, "Information is Everything," *Fast Company,* November 1999, 246–54.

seen a problem before and may not know how to respond. Clear-cut decision criteria do not exist. Alternatives are fuzzy. There is uncertainty about whether a proposed solution will solve the problem. Typically, few alternatives can be developed for a nonprogrammed decision, so a single solution is custom-tailored to the problem.

Many nonprogrammed decisions involve strategic planning, because uncertainty is great and decisions are complex. For example, when he first began his job as CEO of Continental Airlines, Gordon M. Bethune decided to ground forty-one planes, cut more than 4,200 jobs, and abolish cut-rate fares as part of his strategy to make the ailing airline profitable again. Bethune and other top managers had to analyze complex problems, evaluate alternatives, and make a choice about how to pull Continental out of its slump.[7] These and other decisions have proved to be right on target, as Continental has enjoyed renewed profitability and a vastly improved service record.

Particularly complex nonprogrammed decisions have been referred to as "wicked" decisions, because simply defining the problem can turn into a major task. Wicked problems are associated with manager conflicts over objectives and alternatives, rapidly changing circumstances, and unclear linkages among decision elements. Managers dealing with a wicked decision may hit on a solution that merely proves they failed to correctly define the problem to begin with.[8]

Today's managers and organizations are dealing with a higher percentage of nonprogrammed decisions because of the rapidly changing business environment. As outlined in Exhibit 11.1, today's environment has increased both the number and complexity of decisions that have to be made and created a need for new decision-making processes. Managers in rapidly changing Internet-based companies, or e-corporations, for example, often have to make quick decisions based on very limited information. "If your instinct is to wait, ponder, and perfect, then you're dead [in an Internet business]," says Ruthann Quindlen, a partner with Institutional Venture Partners. Jay Walker, founder and vice-president of Priceline.com, believes managers in e-corporations have to focus not on today's problems but on the next generation of problems. For example, Walker and other top managers made the decision to invest resources to hire Rick Braddock, former president of Citicorp, for his skills at managing a billion-dollar company even though Priceline.com was doing only a few million dollars worth of business at the time.[9] Another example is globalization. The trend toward moving production to low-wage countries has managers all over corporate America struggling with ethical decisions concerning working conditions in the Third World and the loss of manufacturing jobs in small American communities. In one Tennessee community where the unemployment rate is 18 percent, six hundred workers recently lost their jobs because most garment manufacturing is now sent overseas.[10]

INDIVIDUAL DECISION MAKING

Individual decision making by managers can be described in two ways. First is the **rational approach**, which suggests how managers should try to make decisions. Second is the **bounded rationality perspective**, which describes how decisions actually have to be made under severe time and resource constraints. The rational approach is an ideal managers may work toward but never reach.

EXHIBIT 11.1   *Decision Making in Today's Environment*

Today's Business Environment

- *Demands more large-scale change via new strategies, reengineering, restructuring, mergers, acquisitions, downsizing, new product or market development, and so on.*

Decisions Made Inside the Organization

- *Are based on bigger, more complex, more emotionally charged issues*
- *Are made more quickly*
- *Are made in a less certain environment, with less clarity about means and outcomes*
- *Require more cooperation from more people involved in making and implementing decisions*

A New Decision-Making Process

- *Is required because no one individual has the information needed to make all major decisions*
- *Is required because no one individual has the time and credibility needed to convince lots of people to implement the decision*
- *Relies less on hard data as a base for good decisions*
- *Is guided by a powerful coalition that can act as a team*
- *Permits decisions to evolve through trial and error and incremental steps as needed*

Source: Adapted from John P. Kotter, *Leading Change* (Boston, Mass.: Harvard Business School Press, 1996), 56. Used with permission.

RATIONAL APPROACH

The rational approach to individual decision making stresses the need for systematic analysis of a problem followed by choice and implementation in a logical step-by-step sequence. The rational approach was developed to guide individual decision making because many managers were observed to be unsystematic and arbitrary in their approach to organizational decisions. Although the rational model is an "ideal" not fully achievable in the real world of uncertainty, complexity, and rapid change highlighted in Exhibit 11.1, the model does help managers think about decisions more clearly and rationally. Managers should use systematic procedures to make decisions whenever possible. When managers have a deep understanding of the rational decision-making process, it can help them make better decisions even when there is a lack of clear information. The authors of a recent book on decision making use the example of the U.S. Marines, who have a reputation for handling complex problems quickly and decisively. However, the Marines are trained to quickly go through a series of mental routines that help them analyze the situation and take action.[11]

According to the rational approach, decision making can be broken down into eight steps, as illustrated in Exhibit 11.2.[12]

EXHIBIT 11.2   *Steps in the Rational Approach to Decision Making*

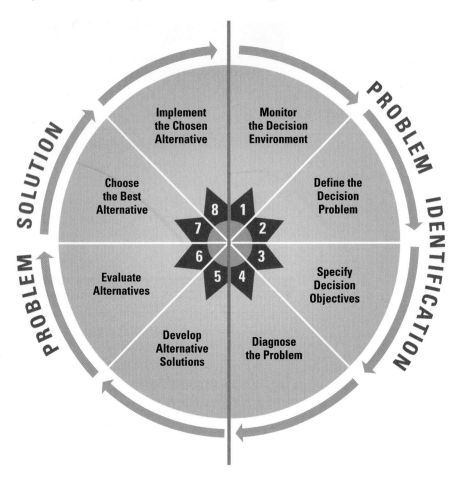

1. *Monitor the decision environment.* In the first step, a manager monitors internal and external information that will indicate deviations from planned or acceptable behavior. He or she talks to colleagues and reviews financial statements, performance evaluations, industry indices, competitors' activities, and so forth. For example, during the pressure-packed five-week Christmas season, Linda Koslow, general manager of Marshall Fields's Oakbrook, Illinois, store, checks out competitors around the mall, eyeing whether they are marking down merchandise. She also scans printouts of her store's previous day's sales to learn what is or is not moving.[13]

2. *Define the decision problem.* The manager responds to deviations by identifying essential details of the problem: where, when, who was involved, who was affected, and how current activities are influenced. For Koslow, this means defining whether store profits are low because overall sales are less than expected or because certain lines of merchandise are not moving as expected.

3. *Specify decision objectives.* The manager determines what performance outcomes should be achieved by a decision.

4. *Diagnose the problem.* In this step, the manager digs below the surface to analyze the cause of the problem. Additional data may be gathered to facilitate

this diagnosis. Understanding the cause enables appropriate treatment. For Koslow at Marshall Fields, the cause of slow sales may be competitors' marking down of merchandise or Marshall Fields's failure to display hot-selling items in a visible location.

5. *Develop alternative solutions.* Before a manager can move ahead with a decisive action plan, he or she must have a clear understanding of the various options available to achieve desired objectives. The manager may seek ideas and suggestions from other people. Koslow's alternatives for increasing profits could include buying fresh merchandise, running a sale, or reducing the number of employees.

6. *Evaluate alternatives.* This step may involve the use of statistical techniques or personal experience to assess the probability of success. The merits of each alternative are assessed as well as the probability that it will reach the desired objectives.

7. *Choose the best alternative.* This step is the core of the decision process. The manager uses his or her analysis of the problem, objectives, and alternatives to select a single alternative that has the best chance for success. At Marshall Fields, Koslow may choose to reduce the number of staff as a way to meet the profit goals rather than increase advertising or markdowns.

8. *Implement the chosen alternative.* Finally, the manager uses managerial, administrative, and persuasive abilities and gives directions to ensure that the decision is carried out. The monitoring activity (step 1) begins again as soon as the solution is implemented. For Linda Koslow, the decision cycle is a continuous process, with new decisions made daily based on monitoring her environment for problems and opportunities.

The first four steps in this sequence are the problem identification stage, and the next four steps are the problem solution stage of decision making, as indicated in Exhibit 11.2. All eight steps normally appear in a manager's decision, although each step may not be a distinct element. Managers may know from experience exactly what to do in a situation, so one or more steps will be minimized. The following case illustrates how the rational approach is used to make a decision about a personnel problem.

In Practice 11.1

Alberta Manufacturing

1. *Monitor the decision environment.* It is Monday morning, and Joe DeFoe, one of Alberta's most skilled cutters, is absent again.

2. *Define the decision problem.* This is the sixth consecutive Monday DeFoe has been absent. Company policy forbids unexcused absenteeism, and DeFoe has been warned about his excessive absenteeism on the last three occasions. A final warning is in order but can be delayed, if warranted.

3. *Specify decision objectives.* DeFoe should attend work regularly and establish the production and quality levels of which he is capable. The time period for solving the problem is two weeks.

4. *Diagnose the problem.* Discreet discussions with DeFoe's co-workers and information gleaned from DeFoe indicate that DeFoe has a drinking problem. He apparently uses Mondays to dry out from weekend benders. Discussion with other company sources confirms that DeFoe is a problem drinker.

5. *Develop alternative solutions.* (1) Fire DeFoe. (2) Issue a final warning without comment. (3) Issue a warning and accuse DeFoe of being alcoholic to let him know you

are aware of his problem. (4) Talk with DeFoe to see if he will discuss his drinking. If he admits he has a drinking problem, delay the final warning and suggest that he enroll in Alberta's new employee assistance program for help with personal problems, including alcoholism. (5) Talk with DeFoe to see if he will discuss his drinking. If he does not admit he has a drinking problem, let him know that the next absence will cost him his job.

6. *Evaluate alternatives.* The cost of training a replacement is the same for each alternative. Alternative 1 ignores cost and other criteria. Alternatives 2 and 3 do not adhere to company policy, which advocates counseling where appropriate. Alternative 4 is designed for the benefit of both DeFoe and the company. It might save a good employee if DeFoe is willing to seek assistance. Alternative 5 is primarily for the benefit of the company. A final warning might provide some initiative for DeFoe to admit he has a drinking problem. If so, dismissal might be avoided, but further absences will no longer be tolerated.

7. *Choose the best alternative.* DeFoe does not admit that he has a drinking problem. Choose alternative 5.

8. *Implement the chosen alternative.* Write up the case and issue the final warning.[14]

In the preceding case, issuing the final warning to Joe DeFoe was a programmable decision. The standard of expected behavior was clearly defined, information on the frequency and cause of DeFoe's absence was readily available, and acceptable alternatives and procedures were described. The rational procedure works best in such cases, when the decision maker has sufficient time for an orderly, thoughtful process. Moreover, Alberta Manufacturing had mechanisms in place to implement the decision, once made.

When decisions are nonprogrammed, ill defined, and piling on top of one another, the individual manager should still try to use the steps in the rational approach, but he or she often will have to take shortcuts by relying on intuition and experience. Deviations from the rational approach are explained by the bounded rationality perspective.

BOUNDED RATIONALITY PERSPECTIVE

The point of the rational approach is that managers should try to use systematic procedures to arrive at good decisions. When organizations are facing little competition and are dealing with well-understood issues, managers generally use rational procedures to make decisions.[15] Yet research into managerial decision making shows managers often are unable to follow an ideal procedure. In today's competitive environment, decisions often must be made very quickly. Time pressure, a large number of internal and external factors affecting a decision, and the ill-defined nature of many problems make systematic analysis virtually impossible. Managers have only so much time and mental capacity and, hence, cannot evaluate every goal, problem, and alternative. The attempt to be rational is bounded (limited) by the enormous complexity of many problems. There is a limit to how rational managers can be. For example, an executive in a hurry may have a choice of fifty ties on a rack but will take the first or second one that matches his suit. The executive doesn't carefully weigh all fifty alternatives because the short amount of time and the large number of plausible alternatives would be overwhelming. The manager simply selects the first tie that solves the problem and moves on to the next task.

Large organizational decisions are not only too complex to fully comprehend, but many other constraints impinge on the decision maker, as illustrated in Exhibit 11.3. The circumstances are ambiguous, requiring social support, a shared perspective on what happens, and acceptance and agreement. For example, in a study of the decision making surrounding the Cuban missile crisis, the executive committee in the White House knew a problem existed but was unable to specify exact goals and objectives. The act of discussing the decision led to personal objections and finally to the discovery of desired objectives that helped clarify the desired course of action and possible consequences.[16] In addition, personal constraints—such as decision style, work pressure, desire for prestige, or simple feelings of insecurity—may constrain either the search for alternatives or the acceptability of an alternative. All of these factors constrain a perfectly rational approach that should lead to an obviously ideal choice.[17] Recent research on the importance of personal decision style is discussed in Book Mark 11.0. Even seemingly simple decisions, such as selecting a job on graduation from college, can quickly become so complex that a bounded rationality approach is used. Graduating students have been known to search for a job until they have two or three acceptable job offers, at which point their search activity rapidly diminishes. Hundreds of firms may be available for interviews, and two or three job offers are far short of the maximum number that would be possible if students made the decision based on perfect rationality.

The bounded rationality perspective is often associated with intuitive decision processes. In **intuitive decision making**, experience and judgment rather than sequential logic or explicit reasoning are used to make decisions.[18] Intuition is not arbitrary or irrational because it is based on years of practice and hands-on

EXHIBIT 11.3   *Constraints and Trade-offs During Nonprogrammed Decision Making*

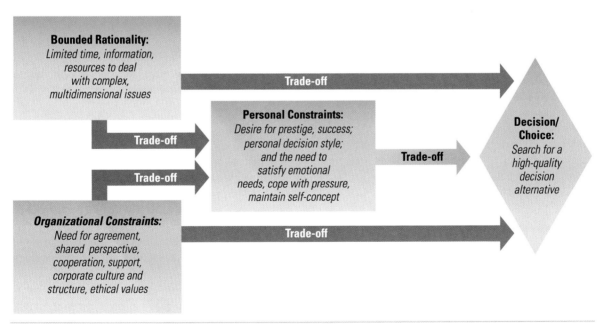

Source: Adapted from Irving L. Janis, *Crucial Decisions* (New York: Free Press, 1989); and A. L. George, *Presidential Decision Making in Foreign Policy: The Effective Use of Information and Advice* (Boulder, Colo.: Westview Press, 1980).

experience, often stored in the subconscious. When managers use their intuition based on long experience with organizational issues, they more rapidly perceive and understand problems, and they develop a gut feeling or hunch about which alternative will solve a problem, speeding the decision-making process.[19] Indeed, many universities are offering courses in creativity and intuition so business students can learn to understand and rely on these processes.

In a situation of great complexity or ambiguity, previous experience and judgment are needed to incorporate intangible elements at both the problem identification and problem solution stages.[20] A study of manager problem finding showed that thirty of thirty-three problems were ambiguous and ill defined.[21] Bits and scraps of unrelated information from informal sources resulted in a pattern in the

$\mathcal{B}$ook $\mathcal{M}$ark 11.0

Have You Read This Book?

The Dynamic Decisionmaker

By Michael J. Driver, Kenneth R. Brousseau, and Philip L. Hunsaker

The Dynamic Decisionmaker discusses the thought processes and decision styles managers use when making decisions. The authors develop a model based on two decision factors that combine into five decision styles.

TWO KEY FACTORS

The basic decision style model presented by the authors is based on two decision elements—the amount of information used in making a decision (called information use) and the number of alternatives considered (called focus). With respect to information use, managers may be maximizers or satisficers. The maximizer wants as much relevant information as possible before making a decision; the satisficer, in contrast, is a fast-action person who wants just enough information to get on with the decision.

Moreover, some decision makers are unifocused, which means they look at the problem with the idea of coming up with a single solution. Others are multifocused, wanting to develop a variety of options and related pros and cons before deciding.

FIVE DECISION STYLES

The underlying elements can appear in various combinations to form five decision making styles.

The **decisive style** is satisficing and unifocused. This style uses minimum information and perhaps a single alternative to solve a problem quickly. Attention quickly shifts to the next problem.

The **flexible style** is satisficing and multifocused. This style moves fast also but often changes focus, interpreting information to see multiple alternatives.

The **hierarchic style** is maximizing and unifocused. This style uses lots of information and analysis to create a detailed, specific solution to a problem. This style exerts control with emphasis on quality and perfection to reach the "best" solution.

The **integrative style** is maximizing and multifocused. Lots of information is collected but is used to develop many possible solutions. Emphasis is on creativity and exploration and on openness to new options.

The **systemic style** is the most complex of all. This style is both multifocused and unifocused and prefers maximum information while looking at different perspectives and alternative solutions. This style sees the big picture and handles complex decisions well.

CONCLUSION

Learning one's personal style and the style of co-workers will increase a manager's effectiveness as a leader and in interpersonal relationships. For example, a supervisor and employee may have a "style clash." A multifocused manager is seen by a unifocused subordinate as wishy-washy, and the unifocused subordinate is seen by the manager as having tunnel vision.

While the authors suggest there is no best style, people should adapt their style to the decision. Managers fail not because they make wrong decisions but because they use the wrong style for the situation—deciding too quickly and impulsively, gathering too much information, or postponing action too long.

The Dynamic Decisionmaker by Michael J. Driver, Kenneth R. Brousseau, and Phillip L. Hunsaker is published by Ballinger.

manager's mind. The manager could not "prove" a problem existed but knew intuitively that a certain area needed attention. A too simple view of a complex problem is often associated with decision failure,[22] and research shows managers are more likely to respond intuitively to a perceived threat to the organization than to an opportunity.[23]

Intuitive processes are also used in the problem solution stage. A survey found that executives frequently made decisions without explicit reference to the impact on profits or to other measurable outcomes.[24] As we saw in Exhibit 11.3, many intangible factors—such as a person's concern about the support of other executives, fear of failure, and social attitudes—influence selection of the best alternative. These factors cannot be quantified in a systematic way, so intuition guided the choice of a solution. Managers may make a decision based on what they sense to be right rather than on what they can document with hard data.

Patrizio Bertelli, CEO of Prada, has transformed the family business into a European fashion powerhouse by making good intuitive decisions—some of which seem inexplicable to his industry colleagues. Even though Bertelli's decisions often seem to come from "out of the blue," they are actually based on a depth of experience, knowledge, and understanding developed over many years in the fashion business. Another example is Jodie Foster, who is known for making good decisions based on gut instinct at her production company, Egg Pictures. Foster made her movie debut at the age of eight, and her manager–mother involved her in almost all decision making regarding roles, script changes, and so forth. "She understands Hollywood almost mathematically," said one producer.[25] Thus, intuition may be thought of as "recognition" because when managers develop a depth of experience and knowledge in a particular area, problem recognition and problem solution often come almost effortlessly as a recognition of information that has largely been forgotten by the conscious mind.[26]

However, managers may walk a fine line between two extremes: on the one hand, making arbitrary decisions without careful study and on the other, relying obsessively on numbers and rational analysis.[27] Remember that the bounded rationality perspective and the use of intuition applies mostly to nonprogrammed decisions. The novel, unclear, complex aspects of nonprogrammed decisions mean hard data and logical procedures are not available. A study of executive decision making found that managers simply could not use the rational approach for nonprogrammed decisions, such as when to buy a CT scanner for an osteopathic hospital or whether a city had a need for and could reasonably adopt an enterprise resource planning system.[28] In those cases, managers had limited time and resources, and some factors simply couldn't be measured and analyzed. Trying to quantify such information could cause mistakes because it may oversimplify decision criteria. When Michael Eisner was president of Paramount Pictures, he learned to rely on intuition for making nonprogrammed decisions. His decision approach was astonishingly successful at Paramount and, more recently, at Disney.

In Practice 11.2

Paramount Pictures Corporation

When Barry Diller and Michael Eisner went to the movies, it wasn't for entertainment. They were checking audience reaction on one of their new movies. Barry Diller was chairman and Michael Eisner was president of Paramount Pictures Corporation.

Some of Paramount's successes under their leadership were *Indiana Jones and the Temple of Doom*, *Raiders of the Lost Ark*, *An Officer and a Gentleman*, *Trading Places*, *48 Hours*, *Flashdance*, and *Terms of Endearment*. A major reason for the string of hits was the excellent choice of films. Paramount decision makers were attuned to the tastes of eighteen- to twenty-four-year olds, who count most. Paramount had also gotten into other ventures, such as selling its films to Showtime. And *Entertainment Tonight*, Paramount's entertainment-news TV show, was also hugely successful.

Why was Paramount so successful at selecting films? Diller and Eisner claim they relied on gut reaction when picking films or other projects. Their tastes were shaped while they were executives at ABC, where they were responsible for the "Movie of the Week." Their experience paid off. Columbia Pictures, then a division of Coca-Cola, used market research to identify what people want to see. "We don't use Coca-Cola type research. We think it's junk," said Eisner. He thinks about what he likes, not what the public likes. "If I ask Miss Middle America if she wants to see a movie about religion, she'll say yes. If I say, 'Do you want to see a movie about sex,' she'll say no. But she'll be lying."

Experience is so important, Eisner said, because "you tend not to make the same mistakes twice." Eisner and Diller made their share of mistakes, and they frequently disagreed about the right path. They hammered out the best decision and combined their intuition through intense arguments. One bomb was *The Keep*, which ran for only three weeks. *Flashdance* went the other way because no one realized it would be a smash. The experience of both successes and failures helped Diller and Eisner develop an intuition for projects the public wanted.

Eisner's remarkable success led to his selection as president of Disney. After he took over, Disney's studio, Touchstone, moved from last place to being a top studio in the industry. Eisner's intuitive decision skills have made two studios successful, an incredible record in an unpredictable business.[29]

ORGANIZATIONAL DECISION MAKING

Organizations are composed of managers who make decisions using both rational and intuitive processes; but organization-level decisions are not usually made by a single manager. Many organizational decisions involve several managers. Problem identification and problem solution involve many departments, multiple viewpoints, and even other organizations, which are beyond the scope of an individual manager.

The processes by which decisions are made in organizations are influenced by a number of factors, particularly the organization's own internal structures as well as the degree of stability or instability of the external environment.[30] Research into organization-level decision making has identified four types of organizational decision-making processes: the management science approach, the Carnegie model, the incremental decision process model, and the garbage can model.

MANAGEMENT SCIENCE APPROACH

The **management science approach** to organizational decision making is the analog to the rational approach by individual managers. Management science came into being during World War II.[31] At that time, mathematical and statistical techniques were applied to urgent, large-scale military problems that were beyond the ability of individual decision makers. Mathematicians, physicists, and operations researchers used systems analysis to develop artillery trajectories, anti-submarine strategies, and bombing strategies such as salvoing (discharging multiple shells simultaneously). Consider the problem of a battleship trying to sink an enemy ship several miles away. The calculation for aiming the battleship's guns should consider distance, wind speed, shell size, speed and direction of both ships, pitch and roll of the firing ship, and curvature of the earth. Methods for performing such calculations using trial and error and intuition are not accurate, take far too long, and may never achieve success.

This is where management science came in. Analysts were able to identify the relevant variables involved in aiming a ship's guns and could model them with the use of mathematical equations. Distance, speed, pitch, roll, shell size, and so on could be calculated and entered into the equations. The answer was immediate, and the guns could begin firing. Factors such as pitch and roll were soon measured mechanically and fed directly into the targeting mechanism. Today, the human element is completely removed from the targeting process. Radar picks up the target, and the entire sequence is computed automatically.

Management science yielded astonishing success for many military problems. This approach to decision making diffused into corporations and business schools, where techniques were studied and elaborated. Today, many corporations have assigned departments to use these techniques. The computer department develops quantitative data for analysis. Operations research departments use mathematical models to quantify relevant variables and develop a quantitative representation of alternative solutions and the probability of each one solving the problem. These departments also use such devices as linear programming, Bayesian statistics, PERT charts, and computer simulations.

Management science is an excellent device for organizational decision making when problems are analyzable and when the variables can be identified and measured. Mathematical models can contain a thousand or more variables, each one relevant in some way to the ultimate outcome. Management science techniques have been used to correctly solve problems as diverse as finding the right spot for a church camp, test marketing the first of a new family of products, drilling for oil, and radically altering the distribution of telecommunications services.[32] Other problems amenable to management science techniques are the scheduling of airline employees, ambulance technicians, telephone operators, and turnpike toll collectors.[33] The SABRE Group, perhaps best known for its travel reservations system, is one of the largest users of the management science approach.

In Practice 11.3   The SABRE Group

The SABRE Group, which began as a system for keeping track of reservations for American Airlines, is today made up of a number of companies providing operations research and information technology solutions to a wide variety of organizations. SABRE has won several awards for its innovative use of management science techniques, including its yield management system for American Airlines. American operates more than 4,000 flights per day, each offering multiple-fare classes, and begins taking reservations 330 days prior to each departure. The job of yield management is to forecast demand by inventory class and optimize the decision of whether to sell the most tickets at a lower price to those customers who book early or wait and charge higher prices for tickets to those customers who book at the last minute. SABRE has estimated that the use of its computer-based system generates almost $1 billion in annual incremental revenue for American Airlines.

Another problem for companies such as airlines is scheduling. For a large carrier such as American, scheduling is an extremely complex problem with thousands of decision constraints and millions of variables. Some of those variables include where to fly, how often to serve a specific market, what time of day to fly, what type of aircraft to assign to each route, and what flights to designate as through-flights. Working with American, SABRE designed a system that relies on sophisticated forecasting models and optimization models that make these complex decisions. The system added millions of dollars to American's bottom line each year and SABRE has now succeeded in selling it to such airlines as Delta, Lufthansa, Swissair, Northwest, Air France, US Air, and Air New Zealand.[34]

The SABRE Group continues to explore the many ways in which management science techniques can be used to help businesses adapt to new demands and shifts in operational methods.

Management science can accurately and quickly solve problems that have too many explicit variables for human processing. This system is at its best when applied to problems that are analyzable, are measurable, and can be structured in a logical way. Increasingly sophisticated computer technology and software programs are allowing the expansion of management science to cover a broader range of problems than ever before. For example, GE Capital Mortgage Insurance Company used management science techniques to improve the decision making of loss management representatives, who have to decide whether the company can "cure" loans for customers who have stopped making payments or whether it will have to recommend foreclosure on the loan. By creating a sophisticated decision-making software program called Loss Mitigation Optimizer that analyzes and measures relevant variables, GE Capital Mortgage Insurance improved its cure rates from 30 percent of cases to more than 50 percent, while representatives were taking 30 to 50 percent less time per deal. Savings jumped dramatically, to about $8,000 per case, resulting in a savings of $115 million in net income over an eighteen–month period.[35]

Management science has also produced many failures.[36] In recent years, many banks have begun using computerized scoring systems to rate those applying for credit, but some argue that human judgment is needed to account for extenuating circumstances. In one case, a member of the Federal Reserve Board, the agency that sets interest rates and regulates banks, was denied a Toys "R" Us credit card based on his computerized score.[37] One problem with the management science approach is that quantitative data are not rich and do not convey tacit knowledge, as discussed in Chapter 7. Informal cues that indicate the existence of problems have to be sensed on a more personal basis by managers.[38] The most sophisticated mathematical analyses are of no value if the important factors cannot be quantified and included in the model. Such things as competitor reactions, consumer "tastes," and product "warmth" are qualitative dimensions. In these situations, the role of management science is to supplement manager decision making. Quantitative results can be given to managers for discussion and interpretation along with their informal opinions, judgment, and intuition. The final decision can include qualitative factors as well as quantitative calculations.

CARNEGIE MODEL

The **Carnegie model** of organizational decision making is based on the work of Richard Cyert, James March, and Herbert Simon, who were all associated with Carnegie-Mellon University.[39] Their research helped formulate the bounded rationality approach to individual decision making as well as provide new insights about organization decisions. Until their work, research in economics assumed that business firms made decisions as a single entity, as if all relevant information were funneled to the top decision maker for a choice. Research by the Carnegie group indicated that organization-level decisions involved many managers and that a final choice was based on a coalition among those managers. A **coalition** is an alliance among several managers who agree about organizational goals and problem priorities.[40] It could include managers from line departments, staff specialists, and even external groups, such as powerful customers, bankers, or union representatives.

Management coalitions are needed during decision making for two reasons. First, organizational goals are often ambiguous, and operative goals of departments are often inconsistent. When goals are ambiguous and inconsistent, managers disagree about problem priorities. They must bargain about problems and build a coalition around the question of which problems to solve.

The second reason for coalitions is that individual managers intend to be rational but function with human cognitive limitations and other constraints, as described earlier. Managers do not have the time, resources, or mental capacity to identify all dimensions and to process all information relevant to a decision. These limitations lead to coalition-building behavior. Managers talk to each other and exchange points of view to gather information and reduce ambiguity. People who have relevant information or a stake in a decision outcome are consulted. Building a coalition will lead to a decision that is supported by interested parties.

The process of coalition formation has several implications for organizational decision behavior. First, decisions are made to satisfice rather than to optimize problem solutions. **Satisficing** means organizations accept a "satisfactory" rather than a maximum level of performance, enabling them to achieve several goals simultaneously. In decision making, the coalition will accept a solution that is perceived as satisfactory to all coalition members. Second, managers are concerned with immediate problems and short-run solutions. They engage in what Cyert and March called problemistic search.[41] **Problemistic search** means managers look around in the immediate environment for a solution to quickly resolve a problem. Managers don't expect a perfect solution when the situation is ill defined and conflict-laden. This contrasts with the management science approach, which assumes that analysis can uncover every reasonable alternative. The Carnegie model says search behavior is just sufficient to produce a satisfactory solution and that managers typically adopt the first satisfactory solution that emerges. Third, discussion and bargaining are especially important in the problem identification stage of decision making. Unless coalition members perceive a problem, action will not be taken. The decision process described in the Carnegie model is summarized in Exhibit 11.4.

The Carnegie model points out that building agreement through a managerial coalition is a major part of organizational decision making. This is especially true at upper management levels. Discussion and bargaining are time consuming, so search procedures are usually simple and the selected alternative satisfices rather than optimizes problem solution. When problems are programmed—are clear and have been seen before—the organization will rely on previous procedures and routines. Rules and procedures prevent the need for renewed coalition formation and political bargaining. Nonprogrammed decisions, however, require bargaining and conflict resolution.

One of the best and most visible coalition builders of recent years was former President George Bush, who would seek a broad-based coalition at the start of an important decision process. During the decision process regarding the

EXHIBIT 11.4   *Choice Processes in the Carnegie Model*

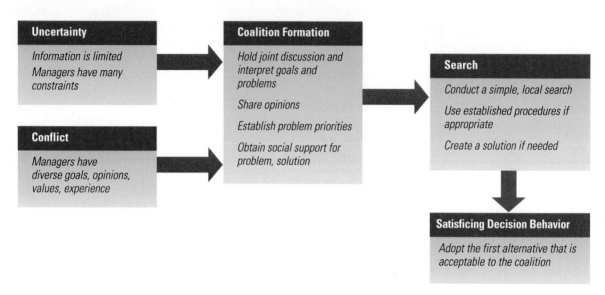

Uncertainty

*Information is limited
Managers have many
constraints*

Conflict

*Managers have
diverse goals, opinions,
values, experience*

Coalition Formation

*Hold joint discussion and
interpret goals and
problems*

Share opinions

Establish problem priorities

*Obtain social support for
problem, solution*

Search

Conduct a simple, local search

*Use established procedures if
appropriate*

Create a solution if needed

Satisficing Decision Behavior

*Adopt the first alternative that is
acceptable to the coalition*

Persian Gulf War, President Bush kept up a barrage of personal calls and visits to world leaders to gain agreement for his vision of forcing Saddam Hussein from Kuwait and for shaping a "new world order."[42]

Organizations suffer when managers are unable to build a coalition around goals and problem priorities, as illustrated by the case of Encyclopaedia Britannica.

In Practice 11.4

Encyclopaedia Britannica

For most of its 231-year history, the *Encyclopaedia Britannica* was viewed as an illustrious repository of cultural and historical knowledge—almost a national treasure. Generations of students and librarians relied on the Britannica—but that was before CD-ROMs and the Internet became the study tools of choice. Suddenly, the thirty-two-volume collection of encyclopedias, stretching four feet on a bookshelf and costing as much as a personal computer, seemed destined to fade into history.

When Swiss-based financier Joseph Safra bought Britannica, he discovered one of the reasons. For nearly a decade, managers had bickered over goals and priorities. Some top executives believed the company needed to invest more in electronic media, but others supported Britannica's traditional direct-to-home sales force. Eventually, the company's Compton unit, a CD-ROM pioneer now being used by millions of consumers, was sold, leaving Britannica without any presence in the new market. In the 1980s, Microsoft had approached Britannica to develop a CD-ROM encyclopedia; when it didn't work out, Microsoft went with Funk & Wagnalls and developed Encarta. Microsoft arranged to have Encarta preinstalled on PCs, so the CD-ROM was essentially free to new PC buyers. When Britannica finally came out with its CD-ROM version, however, it was priced at a staggering $1,200. The squabbling among managers, owners, and editors about product development, pricing, distribution, and other important decisions contributed to the company's decline.

The first step in Safra's turnaround strategy was to install a new top management team, led by chief executive Don Yannias, one of Safra's long-time advisors. The team immediately coalesced around the important problem of establishing a presence in the world of electronic media and rushed out a series of new products, including a revamped graphics-intensive CD-ROM package, a complete online subscription service, and an Internet search engine that filters out marginal Web pages and offers users what Britannica editors think are the most useful sites. The company dropped Britannica's prices to be more competitive and did away with the direct-to-home sales force in favor of selling through bookstores, super chains, and online. But the online subscription fee of $85 a year was not well-received in the Internet world. In October 1999, Britannica stunned both followers and critics by posting the entire encyclopedia on the Internet—for free. Britannica took the gamble that it would come out ahead by selling advertising on its Web site. Initial response was highly favorable, suggesting that the gamble might pay off.

Encyclopedia Britannica has an unimpeachable reputation, and is now hoping to use that advantage online, where sources are often hard to verify. "We want to become the most trusted source of information, learning, and knowledge in the online environment," said Jorge Cauz, senior vice-president of marketing at Britannica.com, Inc., the Internet arm of the company.

Britannica's sales to schools and libraries remain strong, but industry experts say that the Web site is the key to recapturing Britannica's key market—parents who invest in their children's future.[43]

The Carnegie model is particularly useful at the problem identification stage. However, a coalition of key department managers is also important for smooth implementation of a decision, particularly a major reorganization. Top executives at Britannica realize the importance of building coalitions for decision making to keep the company moving forward. When top managers perceive a problem or want to make a major decision, they need to reach agreement with other managers to support the decision.[44]

INCREMENTAL DECISION PROCESS MODEL

Henry Mintzberg and his associates at McGill University in Montreal approached organizational decision making from a different perspective. They identified twenty-five decisions made in organizations and traced the events associated with these decisions from beginning to end.[45] Their research identified each step in the decision sequence. This approach to decision making, called the **incremental decision process model**, places less emphasis on the political and social factors described in the Carnegie model, but tells more about the structured sequence of activities undertaken from the discovery of a problem to its solution.[46]

Sample decisions in Mintzberg's research included choosing which jet aircraft to acquire for a regional airline, developing a new supper club, developing a new container terminal in a harbor, identifying a new market for a deodorant, installing a controversial new medical treatment in a hospital, and firing a star announcer.[47] The scope and importance of these decisions are revealed in the length of time taken to complete them. Most of these decisions took more than a year, and one-third of them took more than two years. Most of these decisions were nonprogrammed and required custom-designed solutions.

One discovery from this research is that major organization choices are usually a series of small choices that combine to produce the major decision. Thus, many organizational decisions are a series of nibbles rather than a big bite. Organizations move through several decision points and may hit barriers along the way. Mintzberg called these barriers *decision interrupts*. An interrupt may mean an organization has to cycle back through a previous decision and try something new. Decision loops or cycles are one way the organization learns which alternatives will work. The ultimate solution may be very different from what was initially anticipated.

The pattern of decision stages discovered by Mintzberg and his associates is shown in Exhibit 11.5. Each box indicates a possible step in the decision sequence. The steps take place in three major decision phases: identification, development, and selection.

Identification Phase. The identification phase begins with *recognition*. Recognition means one or more managers become aware of a problem and the need to make a decision. Recognition is usually stimulated by a problem or an opportunity. A problem exists when elements in the external environment change or when internal performance is perceived to be below standard. In the case of firing a radio announcer, comments about the announcer came from listeners, other announcers, and advertisers. Managers interpreted these cues until a pattern emerged that indicated a problem had to be dealt with.

The second step is *diagnosis*, which is where more information is gathered if needed to define the problem situation. Diagnosis may be systematic or informal, depending upon the severity of the problem. Severe problems do not have time for extensive diagnosis; the response must be immediate. Mild problems are usually diagnosed in a more systematic manner.

Development Phase. The development phase is when a solution is shaped to solve the problem defined in the identification phase. The development of a solution takes one of two directions. First, *search* procedures may be used to seek out alternatives within the organization's repertoire of solutions. For example, in the case of firing a star announcer, managers asked what the radio station had done the last time an announcer had to be let go. To conduct the search, organization participants may look into their own memories, talk to other managers, or examine the formal procedures of the organization.

The second direction of development is to *design* a custom solution. This happens when the problem is novel so that previous experience has no value. Mintzberg found that in these cases, key decision makers have only a vague idea of the ideal solution. Gradually, through a trial-and-error process, a custom-designed alternative will emerge. Development of the solution is a groping, incremental procedure, building a solution brick by brick.

Selection Phase. The selection phase is when the solution is chosen. This phase is not always a matter of making a clear choice among alternatives. In the case of custom-made solutions, selection is more an evaluation of the single alternative that seems feasible.

Evaluation and choice may be accomplished in three ways. The *judgment* form of selection is used when a final choice falls upon a single decision maker, and the choice involves judgment based upon experience. In analysis, alternatives are evaluated on a more systematic basis, such as with management science techniques. Mintzberg found that most decisions did not involve systematic analysis and evaluation of alternatives. *Bargaining* occurs when selection involves a group of decision makers. Each decision maker may have a different stake in the outcome, so conflict emerges. Discussion and bargaining occur until a coalition is formed, as in the Carnegie model described earlier.

When a decision is formally accepted by the organization, *authorization* takes place. The decision may be passed up the hierarchy to the responsible hierarchical

EXHIBIT 11.5   *The Incremental Decision Process Model*

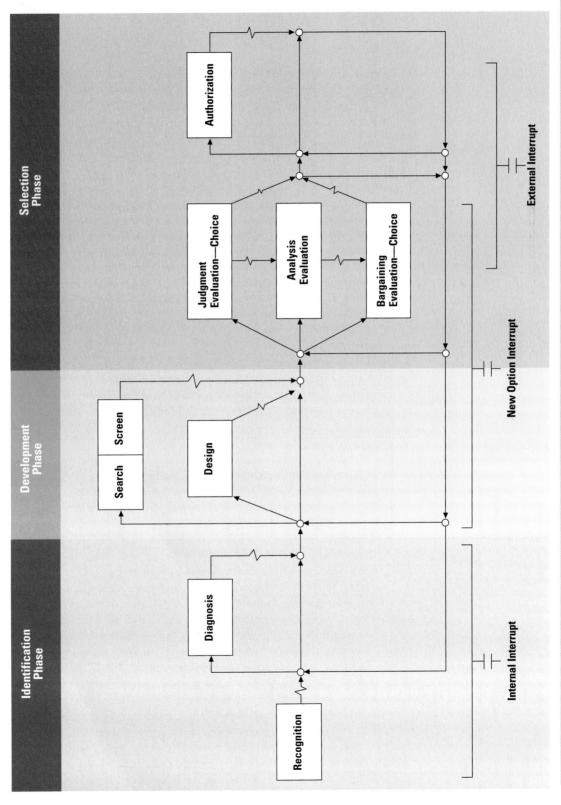

Source: Adapted and reprinted from "The Structure of Unstructured Decision Processes" by Henry Mintzberg, Duru Raisinghani, and André Théorêt, published in *Administrative Science Quarterly* 21, no. 2 (1976): 266, by permission of *The Administrative Science Quarterly.* Copyright ©1976 Cornell University.

level. Authorization is often routine because the expertise and knowledge rest with the lower decision makers who identified the problem and developed the solution. A few decisions are rejected because of implications not anticipated by lower-level managers.

Dynamic Factors. The lower part of the chart in Exhibit 11.5 shows lines running back toward the beginning of the decision process. These lines represent loops or cycles that take place in the decision process. Organizational decisions do not follow an orderly progression from recognition through authorization. Minor problems arise that force a loop back to an earlier stage. These are decision interrupts. If a custom-designed solution is perceived as unsatisfactory, the organization may have to go back to the very beginning and reconsider whether the problem is truly worth solving. Feedback loops can be caused by problems of timing, politics, disagreement among managers, inability to identify a feasible solution, turnover of managers, or the sudden appearance of a new alternative. For example, when a small Canadian airline made the decision to acquire jet aircraft, the board authorized the decision, but shortly after, a new chief executive was brought in who canceled the contract, recycling the decision back to the identification phase. He accepted the diagnosis of the problem but insisted upon a new search for alternatives. Then a foreign airline went out of business and two used aircraft became available at a bargain price. This presented an unexpected option, and the chief executive used his own judgment to authorize the purchase of the aircraft.[48]

Because most decisions take place over an extended period of time, circumstances change. Decision making is a dynamic process that may require a number of cycles before a problem is solved. An example of the incremental process and cycling that can take place is illustrated in Gillette's decision to create a new razor.

Gillette Company

The Gillette Company uses incremental decision making to perfect the design of razors such as the Sensor and the new Mach3. While searching for a new idea to increase sales in Gillette's mature shaving market, researchers at the company's British research lab came up with a bright idea to create a razor with three blades to produce a closer, smoother, more comfortable shave (recognition and diagnosis). Ten years later, the Mach3 reached the market, after thousands of shaving tests, numerous design modifications, and a development and tooling cost of $750 million.

The technical demands of building a razor with three blades that would follow a man's face and also be easy to clean had several blind alleys. Engineers first tried to find established techniques (search, screen), but none fit the bill. Eventually a prototype called Manx was built (design), and in shaving tests it "beat the pants off" Gillette's Sensor Excel, the company's best-selling razor at the time. However, Gillette's CEO insisted that the razor had to have a radically new blade edge so the razor could use thinner blades (internal interrupt), so engineers began looking for new technology that could produce a stronger blade (search, screen). Eventually, the new edge, known as DLC for diamond-like carbon coating, would be applied atom by atom with chipmaking technology (design). The next problem was manufacturing (diagnosis), which required an entirely new process to handle the complexity of the triple-bladed razor (design). Although the board gave the go-ahead to develop manufacturing equipment (judgment, authorization), some members became concerned because the new blades, which are three times stronger than stainless steel, would last longer and cause Gillette to sell fewer cartridges (internal interrupt). The board eventually made the decision to continue with the new blades, which would have a blue indicator strip that would fade to white and signal when it's time for a new cartridge. The board gave final approval for production of the Mach3 to begin in the fall of 1997.

The new razor was introduced in the summer of 1998 and began smoothly sliding off shelves. Gillette expects to recover its huge investment in record time. Now Gillette is starting the process of searching for the next shaving breakthrough all over again, using new technology that can examine a razor blade at the atomic level and high-speed video that can capture the act of cutting a single whisker. The company will move ahead in increments to create its next major shaving product, projected for release in 2006.[49]

At Gillette, the identification phase occurred because executives were aware of the need for a new razor and became alert to the idea of using three blades to produce a closer shave. The development phase was characterized by the trial-and-error custom design leading to the Mach3. During the selection phase, certain approaches were found unacceptable, causing Gillette to cycle back and redesign the razor, including using thinner, stronger blades. Advancing once again to the selection phase, the Mach3 passed the judgment of top executives and board members, and manufacturing and marketing budgets were quickly authorized. This decision took more than a decade, finally reaching completion in the summer of 1998.

THE LEARNING ORGANIZATION

At the beginning of this chapter, we discussed how the rapidly changing business environment is creating greater uncertainty for decision makers. Organizations that are particularly affected by this trend include Internet-based companies as well as those companies shifting to the learning organization concept. These organizations are marked by a tremendous amount of uncertainty at both the problem identification and problem solution stages. Two approaches to decision making have evolved to help managers cope with this uncertainty and complexity. One approach is to combine the Carnegie and incremental process models just described. The second is a unique approach called the garbage can model.

COMBINING THE INCREMENTAL PROCESS AND CARNEGIE MODELS

The Carnegie description of coalition building is especially relevant for the problem identification stage. When issues are ambiguous, or if managers disagree about problem severity, discussion, negotiation, and coalition building are needed. Once agreement is reached about the problem to be tackled, the organization can move toward a solution.

The incremental process model tends to emphasize the steps used to reach a solution. After managers agree on a problem, the step-by-step process is a way of trying various solutions to see what will work. When problem solution is unclear, a trial-and-error solution may be designed.

The two models do not disagree with one another. They describe how organizations make decisions when either problem identification or solution is uncertain. The application of these two models to the stages in the decision process is illustrated in Exhibit 11.6. When both parts of the decision process are highly uncertain simultaneously, which is often the case in learning organizations, the organization is in an extremely difficult position. Decision processes in that situation may be a combination of Carnegie and incremental process models, and this combination may evolve into a situation described in the garbage can model.

GARBAGE CAN MODEL

The **garbage can model** is one of the most recent and interesting descriptions of organizational decision processes. It is not directly comparable to the earlier models, because the garbage can model deals with the pattern or flow of multiple decisions within organizations, whereas the incremental and Carnegie models focus on how a single decision is made. The garbage can model helps you think of the whole organization and the frequent decisions being made by managers throughout.

Organized Anarchy. The garbage can model was developed to explain the pattern of decision making in organizations that experience extremely high uncertainty, such as the growth and change required in a learning organization. Michael Cohen, James March, and Johan Olsen, the originators of the model, called the highly uncertain conditions an **organized anarchy**, which is an extremely organic organization.[50] Organized anarchies do not rely on the normal vertical hierarchy of authority and bureaucratic decision rules. They are caused by three characteristics:

1. *Problematic preferences.* Goals, problems, alternatives, and solutions are ill defined. Ambiguity characterizes each step of a decision process.
2. *Unclear, poorly understood technology.* Cause-and-effect relationships within the organization are difficult to identify. An explicit database that applies to decisions is not available.
3. *Turnover.* Organizational positions experience turnover of participants. In addition, employees are busy and have only limited time to allocate to any one problem or decision. Participation in any given decision will be fluid and limited.

The organized anarchy describes organizations characterized by rapid change and a collegial, nonbureaucratic environment. No organization fits this extremely organic circumstance all the time, although learning organizations and today's Internet-based companies may experience it much of the time.

EXHIBIT 11.6   *Learning Organization Decision Process When Problem Identification and Problem Solution Are Uncertain*

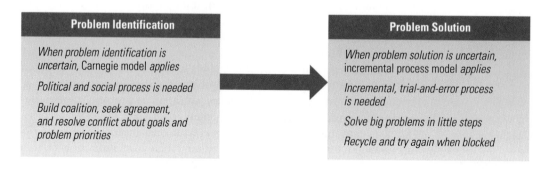

Many organizations will occasionally find themselves in positions of making decisions under unclear, problematic circumstances. The garbage can model is useful for understanding the pattern of these decisions.

Streams of Events. The unique characteristic of the garbage can model is that the decision process is not seen as a sequence of steps that begins with a problem and ends with a solution. Indeed, problem identification and problem solution may not be connected to each other. An idea may be proposed as a solution when no problem is specified. A problem may exist and never generate a solution. Decisions are the outcome of independent streams of events within the organization. The four streams relevant to organizational decision making are as follows:

1. *Problems.* Problems are points of dissatisfaction with current activities and performance. They represent a gap between desired performance and current activities. Problems are perceived to require attention. However, they are distinct from solutions and choices. A problem may lead to a proposed solution or it may not. Problems may not be solved when solutions are adopted.

2. *Potential solutions.* A solution is an idea somebody proposes for adoption. Such ideas form a flow of alternative solutions through the organization. Ideas may be brought into the organization by new personnel or may be invented by existing personnel. Participants may simply be attracted to certain ideas and push them as logical choices regardless of problems. Attraction to an idea may cause an employee to look for a problem to which the idea can be attached and, hence, justified. The point is that solutions exist independent of problems.

3. *Participants.* Organization participants are employees who come and go throughout the organization. People are hired, reassigned, and fired. Participants vary widely in their ideas, perception of problems, experience, values, and training. The problems and solutions recognized by one manager will differ from those recognized by another manager.

4. *Choice opportunities.* Choice opportunities are occasions when an organization usually makes a decision. They occur when contracts are signed, people are hired, or a new product is authorized. They also occur when the right mix of participants, solutions, and problems exists. Thus, a manager who happened to learn of a good idea may suddenly become aware of a problem to which it applies and, hence, can provide the organization with a choice opportunity. Match-ups of problems and solutions often result in decisions.

With the concept of four streams, the overall pattern of organizational decision making takes on a random quality. Problems, solutions, participants, and choices all flow through the organization. In one sense, the organization is a large garbage can in which these streams are being stirred, as illustrated in Exhibit 11.7. When a problem, solution, and participant happen to connect at one point, a decision may be made and the problem may be solved; but if the solution does not fit the problem, the problem may not be solved. Thus, when viewing the organization as a whole and considering its high level of uncertainty, one sees problems arise that are not solved and solutions tried that do not work. Organization decisions are disorderly and not the result of a logical, step-by-step sequence. Events may be so ill defined and complex that decisions, problems, and solutions act as independent events. When they connect, some problems are solved, but many are not.[51]

EXHIBIT 11.7   *Illustration of Independent Streams of Events in the Garbage Can Model of Decision Making*

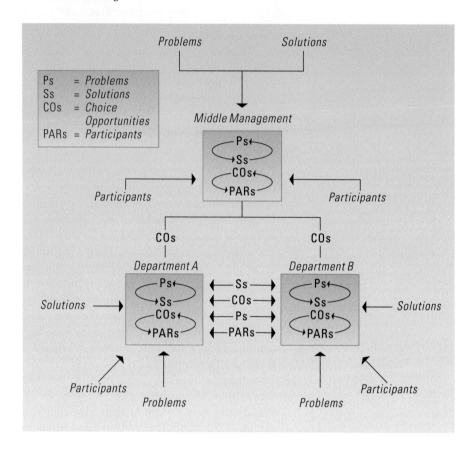

Consequences. Four consequences of the garbage can decision process for organizational decision making are as follows:

1. *Solutions may be proposed even when problems do not exist.* An employee may be sold on an idea and may try to sell it to the rest of the organization. An example was the adoption of computers by many organizations during the 1970s. The computer was an exciting solution and was pushed by both computer manufacturers and systems analysts within organizations. The computer did not solve any problems in those initial applications. Indeed, some computers caused more problems than they solved.

2. *Choices are made without solving problems.* A choice such as creating a new department may be made with the intention of solving a problem; but, under conditions of high uncertainty, the choice may be incorrect. Moreover, many choices just seem to happen. People decide to quit, the organization's budget is cut, or a new policy bulletin is issued. These choices may be oriented toward problems but do not necessarily solve them.

3. *Problems may persist without being solved.* Organization participants get used to certain problems and give up trying to solve them; or participants may not know how to solve certain problems because the technology is unclear. A university in Canada was placed on probation by the American Association of

University Professors because a professor had been denied tenure without due process. The probation was a nagging annoyance that the administrators wanted to remove. Fifteen years later, the nontenured professor died. The probation continues because the university did not acquiesce to the demands of the heirs of the association to reevaluate the case. The university would like to solve the problem, but administrators are not sure how, and they do not have the resources to allocate to it. The probation problem persists without a solution.

4. *A few problems are solved.* The decision process does work in the aggregate. In computer simulation models of the garbage can model, important problems were often resolved. Solutions do connect with appropriate problems and participants so that a good choice is made. Of course, not all problems are resolved when choices are made, but the organization does move in the direction of problem reduction.

The effects of independent streams and the rather chaotic decision processes of the garbage can model can be seen in the production of the classic film *Casablanca*.

Casablanca

The public flocked to see *Casablanca* when it opened in 1942. The film won Academy Awards for best picture, best screenplay, and best director, and is recognized today by film historians and the public alike as a classic. But up until the filming of the final scene, no one involved in the production of the now-famous story even knew how it was going to end.

Everybody Comes to Rick's wasn't a very good play, but when it landed on Hal Wallis's desk at Warner Brothers, Wallis spotted some hot-from-the-headlines potential, purchased the rights, and changed the name to *Casablanca* to capitalize on the geographical mystique the story offered. A series of negotiations led to casting Humphrey Bogart as Rick, even though studio chief Jack Warner questioned his romantic appeal. The casting of Ingrid Bergman as Ilsa was largely by accident. A fluke had left an opening in her usually booked schedule. The screenplay still wasn't written.

Filming was chaotic. Writers made script changes and plot revisions daily. Actors were unsure of how to develop their characterizations, so they just did whatever seemed right at the time. For example, when Ingrid Bergman wanted to know which man should get most of her on-screen attention, she was told, "We don't know yet—just play it, well . . . in between." Scenes were often filmed blindly with no idea of how they were supposed to fit in the overall story. Amazingly, even when it came time to shoot the climactic final scene, no one involved in the production seemed to know who would "get the girl"; a legend still persists that two versions were written. During filming, Bogart disagreed with director Michael Curtiz's view that Rick should kiss Ilsa good-bye, and Hal Wallis was summoned to mediate. Because the cast received their scripts only hours before filming began, they couldn't remember their lines, causing continual delays.

Some industry analysts predicted disaster, but the haphazard process worked. Ingrid Bergman plays it "in between" just right. Bogart's characterization of Rick is perfect. The tale of love and glory and heartbreaking romance couldn't have been told better than it was in *Casablanca*. In addition, fortuitous circumstances outside the studio contributed to the film's commercial success. Just eighteen days before the premiere on Thanksgiving Day, 1942, the Allies invaded North Africa and fought the Battle of Casablanca. Then, when the film opened nationwide, President Franklin D. Roosevelt and Prime Minister Winston Churchill presided over the Casablanca Conference, a historical coincidence that was clearly a boon to the film, helping to push its initial gross to $3.7 million.[52]

The production of *Casablanca* was not a rational process that started with a clear problem and ended with a logical solution. Many events occurred by chance and were intertwined, which characterizes the garbage can model. Everyone from the director to the actors continuously added to the stream of new ideas to the story. Some solutions were connected to emerging problems: the original script arrived just when Hal Wallis was looking for topical stories; and Bergman was surprisingly available to be cast in the role of Ilsa. The actors (participants) daily made personal choices regarding characterization that proved to be perfect for the story line. Other events that contributed to *Casablanca*'s success were not even connected to the film—for example, the invasion of North Africa only eighteen days before the premiere. Overall, the production of *Casablanca* had a random, chancy flavor that is characteristic of the garbage can model. As evidenced by the film's huge success and continuing popularity after more than fifty years, the random, garbage can decision process did not hurt the film or the studio.

The garbage can model, however, doesn't always work—in the movies or in organizations. A similar haphazard process during the filming of *Waterworld* led to the most expensive film in Hollywood history and a decided box-office flop for Universal Pictures.[53]

CONTINGENCY DECISION-MAKING FRAMEWORK

This chapter has covered several approaches to organizational decision making, including management science, the Carnegie model, the incremental decision process model, and the garbage can model. It has also discussed rational and intuitive decision processes used by individual managers. Each decision approach is a relatively accurate description of the actual decision process, yet all differ from each other. Management science, for example, reflects a different set of decision assumptions and procedures than does the garbage can model.

One reason for having different approaches is that they appear in different organizational situations. The use of an approach is contingent on the organization setting. Two characteristics of organizations that determine the use of decision approaches are (1) problem consensus and (2) technical knowledge about the means to solve those problems.[54] Analyzing organizations along these two dimensions suggests which approach will be used to make decisions.

PROBLEM CONSENSUS

Problem consensus refers to the agreement among managers about the nature of a problem or opportunity and about which goals and outcomes to pursue. This variable ranges from complete agreement to complete disagreement. When managers agree, there is little uncertainty—the problems and goals of the organization are clear, and so are standards of performance. When managers disagree, organization direction and performance expectations are in dispute, creating a situation of high uncertainty. One example of problem uncertainty occurred at Wal-Mart stores regarding the issue of parking-lot patrols. Some managers presented evidence that golf-cart patrols significantly reduced auto theft, assault, and other crimes in the stores' lots, as well as increased business because they encouraged more night-time shopping. While these managers argued that the patrols should be used, others believed the patrols were not needed and were too expensive, emphasizing that parking-lot crime was a society issue rather than a store issue.[55]

Problem consensus tends to be low when organizations are differentiated, as described in Chapter 4. Recall that uncertain environments cause organizational departments to differentiate from one another in goals and attitudes to specialize in specific environmental sectors. This differentiation leads to disagreement and conflict about organizational goals and problem priorities. When differentiation among departments or divisions is high, managers must make a special effort to build coalitions during decision making.

Problem consensus is especially important for the problem identification stage of decision making. When problems are clear and agreed on, they provide clear standards and expectations for performance. When problems are not agreed on, problem identification is uncertain and management attention must be focused on gaining agreement about goals and priorities.

TECHNICAL KNOWLEDGE ABOUT SOLUTIONS

Technical knowledge refers to understanding and agreement about how to solve problems and reach organizational goals. This variable can range from complete agreement and certainty to complete disagreement and uncertainty about cause-effect relationships leading to problem solution. One example of low technical knowledge occurred at PepsiCo's 7-Up division. Managers agreed on the problem to be solved—they wanted to increase market share from 6 percent to 7 percent. However, the means for achieving this increase in market share were not known or agreed on. A few managers wanted to use discount pricing in supermarkets. Other managers believed they should increase the number of soda fountain outlets in restaurants and fast-food chains. A few other managers insisted that the best approach was to increase advertising through radio and television. Managers did not know what would cause an increase in market share. Eventually, the advertising judgment prevailed at 7-Up, but it did not work very well. The failure of its decision reflected 7-Up's low technical knowledge about how to solve the problem.

When means are well understood, the appropriate alternatives can be identified and calculated with some degree of certainty. When means are poorly understood, potential solutions are ill defined and uncertain. Intuition, judgment, and trial and error become the basis for decisions.

CONTINGENCY FRAMEWORK

Exhibit 11.8 describes the **contingency decision-making framework**, which brings together the two dimensions of problem consensus and technical knowledge about solutions. Each cell represents an organizational situation that is appropriate for the decision-making approaches described in this chapter.

Cell 1. In cell 1 of Exhibit 11.8, rational decision procedures are used because problems are agreed on, and cause-effect relationships are well understood so there is little uncertainty. Decisions can be made in a computational manner. Alternatives can be identified and the best solution adopted through analysis and calculations. The rational models described earlier in this chapter, both for individuals and for the organization, are appropriate when problems and the means for solving them are well defined.

Cell 2. In cell 2, there is high uncertainty about problems and priorities, so bargaining and compromise are used to reach consensus. Tackling one problem might mean the organization must postpone action on other issues. The

EXHIBIT 11.8   *Contingency Framework for Using Decision Models*

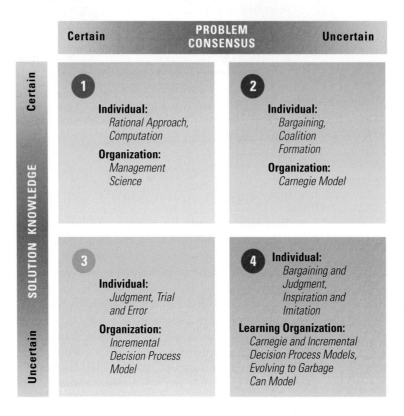

priorities given to respective problems are decided through discussion, debate, and coalition building.

Managers in this situation should use broad participation to achieve consensus in the decision process. Opinions should be surfaced and discussed until compromise is reached. The organization will not otherwise move forward as an integrated unit. In the case of Wal-Mart, managers will discuss conflicting opinions about the benefits and costs of parking-lot patrols.

The Carnegie model applies when there is dissension about organizational problems. When groups within the organization disagree, or when the organization is in conflict with constituencies (government regulators, suppliers, unions), bargaining and negotiation are required. The bargaining strategy is especially relevant to the problem identification stage of the decision process. Once bargaining and negotiation are completed, the organization will have support for one direction.

Cell 3. In a cell 3 situation, problems and standards of performance are certain, but alternative technical solutions are vague and uncertain. Techniques to solve a problem are ill defined and poorly understood. When an individual manager faces this situation, intuition will be the decision guideline. The manager will rely on past experience and judgment to make a decision. Rational, analytical approaches are not effective because the alternatives cannot be identified and calculated. Hard facts and accurate information are not available.

The incremental decision process model reflects trial and error on the part of the organization. Once a problem is identified, a sequence of small steps enables the organization to learn a solution. As new problems arise, the organization may recycle back to an earlier point and start over. Eventually, over a period of months or years, the organization will acquire sufficient experience to solve the problem in a satisfactory way. Solving the engineering and manufacturing problems for the Mach3 razor, described earlier, is an example of a cell 3 situation. Gillette engineers had to use trial and error to develop an efficient manufacturing process.

The situation in cell 3, of senior managers agreeing about problems but not knowing how to solve them, occurs frequently in business organizations. If managers use incremental decisions in such situations, they will eventually acquire the technical knowledge to accomplish goals and solve problems.

Cell 4. The situation in cell 4, characterized by high uncertainty about both problems and solutions is difficult for decision making. An individual manager making a decision under this high level of uncertainty can employ techniques from both cell 2 and cell 3. The manager can attempt to build a coalition to establish goals and priorities and use judgment or trial and error to solve problems. Additional techniques, such as inspiration and imitation, also may be required. **Inspiration** refers to an innovative, creative solution that is not reached by logical means. **Imitation** means adopting a decision tried elsewhere in the hope that it will work in this situation.

For example, in one university, accounting department faculty were unhappy with their current circumstances but could not decide on the direction the department should take. Some faculty members wanted a greater research orientation, whereas others wanted greater orientation toward business firms and accounting applications. The disagreement about goals was compounded because neither group was sure about the best technique for achieving its goals. The ultimate solution was inspirational on the part of the dean. An accounting research center was established with funding from Big Five accounting firms. The funding was used to finance research activities for faculty interested in basic research and to provide contact with business firms for other faculty. The solution provided a common goal and unified people within the department to work toward that goal.

When an entire organization is characterized by high uncertainty regarding both problems and solutions, as in e-corporations and learning organizations, elements of the garbage can model will appear. Managers may first try techniques from both cells 2 and 3, but logical decision sequences starting with problem identification and ending with problem solution will not occur. Potential solutions will precede problems as often as problems precede solutions. In this situation, managers should encourage widespread discussion of problems and idea proposals to facilitate the opportunity to make choices. Eventually, through trial and error, the organization will solve some problems.

SPECIAL DECISION CIRCUMSTANCES

In a highly competitive world beset by global competition and rapid change, decision making seldom fits the traditional rational, analytical model. To cope in today's world, managers must learn to make decisions fast, especially in high-velocity environments, to learn from decision mistakes, and to avoid escalating commitment to an unsatisfactory course of action.

HIGH-VELOCITY ENVIRONMENTS

In some industries today, the rate of competitive and technological change is so extreme that market data is either unavailable or obsolete, strategic windows open and shut quickly, perhaps within a few months, and the cost of a decision error is company failure. Recent research has examined how successful companies make decisions in these **high-velocity environments**, especially to understand whether organizations abandon rational approaches or have time for incremental implementation.[56]

Comparing successful with unsuccessful decisions in high-velocity environments suggests the following guidelines.

- Successful decision makers track information in real time to develop a deep and intuitive grasp of the business. Two to three intense meetings per week with all key players are usual. Decision makers track operating statistics about cash, scrap, backlog, work in process, and shipments to constantly feel the pulse of what is happening. Unsuccessful firms were more concerned with future planning and forward-looking information, with only a loose grip on immediate happenings.

- During a major decision, successful companies began immediately to build multiple alternatives. Implementation may run in parallel before finally settling on a final choice. Slow-decision companies developed only a single alternative, moving to another only after the first one failed.

- Fast, successful decision makers sought advice from everyone and depended heavily on one or two savvy, trusted colleagues as counselors. Slow companies were unable to build trust and agreement among the best people.

- Fast companies involved everyone in the decision and tried for consensus; but if consensus did not emerge, the top manager made the choice and moved ahead. Waiting for everyone to be on board created more delays than warranted. Slow companies delayed decisions to achieve a uniform consensus.

- Fast, successful choices were well integrated with other decisions and the overall strategic direction of the company. Less successful choices considered the decision in isolation from other decisions; the decision was made in the abstract.[57]

When speed matters, a slow decision is as ineffective as the wrong decision. As we discussed in Chapter 10, speed is a crucial competitive weapon in a growing number of industries, and companies can learn to make decisions fast. Managers must be plugged into the pulse of the company, must seek consensus and advice, and then be ready to take the risk and move ahead. When Deborah Triant, CEO and president of Check Point Software Technologies, has to make a fast decision about a complex problem, she asks everyone she knows for an opinion, but then she trusts her intuition and experience to make the decision and move forward.[58]

DECISION MISTAKES AND LEARNING

Organizational decisions produce many errors, especially when made under high uncertainty. Managers simply cannot determine or predict which alternative will solve a problem. In these cases, the organization must make the decision—and take the risk—often in the spirit of trial and error. If an alternative fails, the organization can learn from it and try another alternative that better fits the situation. Each failure provides new information and learning. The point for managers is to move ahead with the decision process despite the potential for mistakes. "Chaotic action is preferable to orderly inaction."[59]

In many cases, managers have been encouraged to instill a climate of experimentation, even foolishness, to facilitate creative decision making. If one idea fails, another idea should be tried. Failure often lays the groundwork for success, as when technicians at 3M developed Post-it Notes based on a failed product— a not-very-sticky glue. Companies such as PepsiCo believe that if all their new products succeed, they're doing something wrong, not taking the necessary risks to develop new markets.[60]

Only by making mistakes can managers and organizations go through the process of **decision learning** and acquire sufficient experience and knowledge to perform more effectively in the future. Robert Townsend, who was president at Avis Corporation, gives the following advice:

> Admit your mistakes openly, maybe even joyfully. Encourage your associates to do likewise by commiserating with them. Never castigate. Babies learn to walk by falling down. If you beat a baby every time he falls down, he'll never care much for walking.
>
> My batting average on decisions at Avis was no better than a .333. Two out of every three decisions I made were wrong. But my mistakes were discussed openly and most of them corrected with a little help from my friends.[61]

ESCALATING COMMITMENT

A much more dangerous mistake is to persist in a course of action when it is failing. Research suggests that organizations often continue to invest time and money in a solution despite strong evidence that it is not working. Two explanations are given for why managers **escalate commitment** to a failing decision. The first is that managers block or distort negative information when they are personally responsible for a negative decision. They simply don't know when to pull the plug. In some cases, they continue to throw good money after bad even when a strategy seems incorrect and goals are not being met.[62] An example of this distortion is the reaction at Borden when the company began losing customers following its refusal to lower prices on dairy products. When the cost of raw milk dropped, Borden hoped to boost the profit margins of its dairy products, convinced that customers would pay a premium for the brand name. Borden's sales plummeted as low-priced competitors mopped up, but top executives stuck with their premium pricing policy for almost a year. By then, the company's dairy division was operating at a severe loss.[63]

As another example, consider the increasing investment of the Canadian Imperial Bank of Commerce in the ill-fated Canary Wharf project, an $8 billion development in London's remote Docklands area. CIBC had already lent over $1 billion for Canary Wharf to the now-failed Olympia & York Developments Ltd. and its subsidiaries. Despite loads of negative information that led CEO Al Flood to pronounce Canary Wharf a project that "would not meet our lending criteria today," CIBC turned around and invested an additional $36 million in the project. Flood said the move was designed to "protect our investment . . . and try to make the project work."[64] These additional millions now seem like a terrible choice.

A second explanation for escalating commitment to a failing decision is that consistency and persistence are valued in contemporary society. Consistent managers are considered better leaders than those who switch around from one course of action to another. Even though organizations learn through trial and error, organizational norms value consistency. These norms may result in a course of action being maintained, resources being squandered, and learning being inhibited. Emphasis on consistent leadership was partly responsible for the Long Island Lighting Company's refusal to change course in the construction of the Shoreham Nuclear Power Plant, which was eventually abandoned—after an investment of more than $5 billion—without ever having begun operation. Shoreham's cost was estimated at $75 million when the project was announced in 1966, but by the time a construction permit was granted, LILCO had already spent $77 million. Opposition to nuclear power was growing. Critics continued to decry the huge sums of money being pumped into Shoreham. Customers complained that LILCO was cutting back on customer service and maintenance of current operations. Shoreham officials, however, seemed convinced that they would triumph in the end; their response to criticism was, "If people will just wait until the end, they are going to realize that this is a hell of an investment."

The end came in 1989, when a negotiated agreement with New York led LILCO to abandon the $5.5 billion plant in return for rate increases and a $2.5 billion tax write-off. By the time Governor Mario Cuomo signed an agreement with the company, LILCO had remained firmly committed to a losing course of action for more than twenty-three years.[65]

Failure to admit a mistake and adopt a new course of action is far worse than an attitude that encourages mistakes and learning. Based on what has been said about decision making in this chapter, one can expect companies to be ultimately successful in their decision making by adopting a learning approach toward solutions. They will make mistakes along the way, but they will resolve uncertainty through the trial-and-error process.

SUMMARY AND INTERPRETATION

The single most important idea in this chapter is that most organizational decisions are not made in a logical, rational manner. Most decisions do not begin with the careful analysis of a problem, followed by systematic analysis of alternatives, and finally implementation of a solution. On the contrary, decision processes are characterized by conflict, coalition building, trial and error, speed, and mistakes. Managers operate under many constraints that limit rationality; hence, intuition and hunch often are the criteria for choice.

Another important idea is that individuals make decisions, but organizational decisions are not made by a single individual. Organizational decision making is a social process. Only in rare circumstances do managers analyze problems and find solutions by themselves. Many problems are not clear, so widespread discussion and coalition building take place. Once goals and priorities are set, alternatives to achieve those goals can be tried. When a manager does make an individual decision, it is often a small part of a larger decision process. Organizations solve big problems through a series of small steps. A single manager may initiate one step but should be aware of the larger decision process in which it is embedded.

The greatest amount of conflict and coalition building occurs when problems are not agreed on. Priorities must be established to indicate which goals are important and what problems should be solved first. If a manager attacks a problem other people do not agree with, the manager will lose support for the solution to be implemented. Thus, time and activity should be spent building a coalition in the problem identification stage of decision making. Then the organization can move toward solutions. Under conditions of low technical knowledge, the solution unfolds as a series of incremental trials that will gradually lead to an overall solution.

The most novel description of decision making is the garbage can model. This model describes how decision processes can seem almost random in highly organic organizations such as learning organizations. Decisions, problems, ideas, and people flow through organizations and mix together in various combinations. Through this process, the organization gradually learns. Some problems may never be solved, but many are, and the organization will move toward maintaining and improving its level of performance.

Finally, many organizations must make decisions with speed, which means staying in immediate touch with operations and the environment. Moreover, in an uncertain world, organizations will make mistakes, and mistakes made through trial and error should be encouraged. Encouraging trial-and-error increments facilitates organizational learning. On the other hand, an unwillingness to change from a failing course of action can have serious negative consequences for an organization. Norms for consistency and the desire to prove one's decision correct can lead to continued investment in a useless course of action.

BRIEFCASE

As an organization manager, keep these guidelines in mind:

1. Adopt decision processes to fit the organizational situation.
2. Use a rational decision approach—computation, management science—when a problem situation is well understood.
3. Use a coalition-building approach when organizational goals and problem priorities are in conflict. When managers disagree about priorities or the true nature of the problem, they should discuss and seek agreement about priorities. The Carnegie model emphasizes the need for building a coalition and maintaining agreement about goals and problems.
4. Take risks and move the company ahead by increments when a problem is defined but solutions are uncertain. Try solutions step-by-step to learn whether they work.
5. Apply both the Carnegie model and the incremental process model in a situation with high uncertainty about both problems and solutions. Decision making may also employ garbage can procedures. Move the organization toward better performance by proposing new ideas, spending time working in important areas, and persisting with potential solutions.
6. Track real-time information, build multiple alternatives simultaneously, and try to involve everyone—but move ahead anyway when making decisions in a high-velocity environment.
7. Do not persist in a course of action that is failing. Some actions will not work out if uncertainty is high, so encourage organizational learning by readily trying new alternatives. Seek information and evidence that indicates when a course of action is failing, and allocate resources to new choices rather than to unsuccessful ventures.

KEY CONCEPTS

bounded rationality perspective
Carnegie model
coalition
contingency decision-making framework
decision learning
escalating commitment
garbage can model
high-velocity environment
imitation
incremental decision process model
inspiration
intuitive decision making

management science approach
nonprogrammed decisions
organizational decision making
organized anarchy
problem consensus
problem identification
problem solution
problemistic search
programmed decisions
rational approach
satisficing
technical knowledge

DISCUSSION QUESTIONS

1. A professional economist once told his class, "An individual decision maker should process all relevant information and select the economically rational alternative." Do you agree? Why or why not?
2. Why is intuition used in decision making?
3. The Carnegie model emphasizes the need for a political coalition in the decision-making process. When and why are coalitions necessary?
4. What are the three major phases in Mintzberg's incremental decision process model? Why might an organization recycle through one or more phases of the model?
5. An organization theorist once told her class, "Organizations never make big decisions. They make small decisions that eventually add up to a big decision." Explain the logic behind this statement.
6. Why would managers in high-velocity environments worry more about the present than the future? Discuss.
7. How does problem consensus affect decision making processes in an organization?
8. Describe the four streams of events in the garbage can model of decision making. Why are they considered to be independent?
9. Are there decision-making situations in which managers should be expected to make the "correct" decision? Are there situations in which decision makers should be expected to make mistakes? Discuss.
10. Why are decision mistakes usually accepted in organizations but penalized in college courses and exams that are designed to train managers?

CHAPTER 11 WORKBOOK   *Decision Styles**

Think of some recent decisions that have influenced your life. Choose two significant decisions that you made and two decisions that other people made. Fill out the following table, using Exhibit 11.8 to determine decision styles.

*Adapted by Dorothy Marcic from "Action Assignment" in Jennifer M. Howard and Lawrence M. Miller, *Team Management*, Miller Consulting Group, 1994, p. 205.

Your decisions	Approach used	Advantages and disadvantages	Your recommended decision style
1.			
2.			
Decisions by others			
1.			
2.			

QUESTIONS

1. How can a decision approach influence the outcome of the decision? What happens when the approach fits the decision? When it doesn't fit?

2. How can you know what approach is best?

Case for Analysis   *Cracking the Whip**

Harmon Davidson stared dejectedly at the departing figure of his management survey team leader. Their meeting had not gone well. Davidson had relayed to Al Pitcher complaints about his handling of the survey. Pitcher had responded with adamant denial and unveiled scorn.

Davidson, director of headquarters management, was prepared to discount some of the criticism as resentment of outsiders meddling with "the way we've always done business," exacerbated by the turbulence of continual reorganization. But Davidson could hardly ignore the sheer volume of complaints or his high regard for some of their sources.

"Was I missing danger signals about Pitcher from the start?" Davidson asked himself. "Or was I just giving a guy I didn't know a fair chance with an inherently controversial assignment?"

With his division decimated in the latest round of downsizing at the Department of Technical Services (DTS) earlier that year, Davidson had been asked to return to the headquarters management office after a five-year hiatus. The director, Walton Drummond, had abruptly taken early retirement.

One of the first things Davidson had learned about his new job was that he would be responsible for a comprehensive six-month survey of the headquarters management structure and processes. The DTS Secretary had promised the survey to the White House as a prelude to the agency's next phase of management reform. Drummond had already picked the five-person survey team consisting of two experienced management analysts, a promising younger staff member, an intern, and Pitcher, the team leader. Pitcher was fresh from the Treasury Department, where he had participated in a similar survey. But having gone off after retirement for an extended

* This case was prepared by David Hornestay and appeared in *Government Executive*, August 1998, 45–46, as part of a series of case studies examining workplace dilemmas confronting federal managers. Reprinted by permission of *Government Executive*.

mountain-climbing expedition in Asia, Drummond was unavailable to explain his survey plans or any understandings he had reached with Pitcher.

Davidson had been impressed with Pitcher's energy and motivation. He worked long hours, wrote voluminously if awkwardly, and was brimming with the latest organizational theory. Pitcher had other characteristics, however, that were disquieting. He seemed uninterested in DTS's history and culture and was paternalistic toward top managers, assuming they were unsophisticated and unconcerned about modern management.

A series of pre-survey informational briefings for headquarters office heads conducted by Davidson and Pitcher seemed to go swimmingly. Pitcher deferred to his chief on matters of philosophy and confined his remarks to schedule and procedures. He closed his segment on a friendly note, saying, "If we do find opportunities for improvement, we'll try to have recommendations for you."

But the survey was barely a week old when the director of management received his first call from an outraged customer. It was the assistant secretary for public affairs, Erin Dove, and she was not speaking in her usual upbeat tones. "Your folks have managed to upset my whole supervisory staff with their comments about how we'll have to change our organization and methods," she said. "I thought you were going through a fact-finding study. This guy Pitcher sounds like he wants to remake DTS headquarters overnight. Who does he think he is?"

When Davidson asked him about the encounter with public affairs, Pitcher expressed puzzlement that a few summary observations shared with supervisors in the interest of "prompt informal feedback" had been interpreted as such disturbing conclusions. "I told them we'll tell them how it fix it," he reassured his supervisor.

"Listen, Al," Davidson remonstrated gently. "These are very accomplished managers who aren't used to being told they have to fix anything. This agency's been on a roll for years, and the need for reinvention isn't resonating all that well yet. We've got to collect and analyze the information and assemble a convincing case for change, or we'll be spinning our wheels. Let's hold off on the feedback until you and I have reviewed it together."

But two weeks later, technology development director Phil Canseco, an old and treasured colleague, was on Davidson's doorstep looking as unhappy as Erin Dove had sounded on the phone. "Harmon, buddy, I think you have to rein in this survey team a bit," he said. "Several managers who were scheduled for survey interviews were working on a 24-hour turnaround to give a revised project budget to the Appropriations subcommittee that day. My deputy says Pitcher was all put out about postponing interviews and grumbled about whether we understood the new priorities. Is he living in the real world?"

Canseco's comments prompted Davidson to call a few of his respected peers who had dealt with the survey team. With varying degrees of reluctance, they all criticized the team leader and, in some cases, team members, as abrasive and uninterested in the rationales offered for existing structure and processes.

And so Davidson marshaled all of his tact for a review with the survey team leader. But Pitcher was in no mood for either introspection or reconsideration. He took the view that he had been brought in to spearhead a White House-inspired management improvement initiative in a glamour agency that had never had to think much about efficiency. He reminded Davidson that even he had conceded that managers were due some hard lessons on this score. Pitcher didn't see any way to meet his deadline except by adhering to a rigorous schedule, since he was working with managers disinclined to cooperate with an outsider pushing an unpopular exercise. He felt Davidson's role was to hold the line against unwarranted criticisms from prima donnas trying to discredit the survey.

Many questions arose in Davidson's mind about the survey plan and his division's capacity to carry it out. Had they taken on too much with too little? Had the right people been picked for the survey team? Had managers and executives, and even the team, been properly prepared for the survey?

But the most immediate question was whether Al Pitcher could help him with these problems.

Until the 1980s, Aliesha was a well-reputed, somewhat sleepy State Teachers College located on the outer fringes of a major metropolitan area. Then with the rapid expansion of college enrollments, the state converted Aliesha to a four-year state college (and the plans called for its becoming a state university with graduate work and perhaps even with a medical school in the 1990s). Within ten years, Aliesha grew from 1,500 to 9,000 students. Its budget expanded even faster than the enrollment, increasing twentyfold during that period.

The only part of Aliesha that did not grow was the original part, the teachers college; there enrollment actually went down. Everything else seemed to flourish. In addition to building new four-year schools of liberal arts, business, veterinary medicine, and dentistry, Aliesha developed many community service programs. Among them were a rapidly growing evening program, a mental-health clinic, and a speech therapy center for children with speech defects—the only one in the area. Even within education one area grew—the demonstration high school attached to the old teachers college. Even though it enrolled only 300 students, this high school was taught by the leading experts in teacher education and was considered the best high school in the whole area.

Then in 1986, the budget was suddenly cut quite sharply by the state legislature. At the same time the faculty demanded and got a fairly hefty raise in salary. It was clear that something had to give—the budget deficit was much too great to be covered by ordinary cost reductions. When the faculty committee sat down with the president and the board of trustees,

two candidates for abandonment emerged after long and heated wrangling: the speech therapy program and the demonstration high school. Both cost about the same—and both were extremely expensive.

The speech therapy clinic, everyone agreed, addressed itself to a real need and one of high priority. But—and everyone had to agree as the evidence was overwhelming—it did not do the job. Indeed it did such a poor, sloppy, disorganized job that pediatricians, psychiatrists, and psychologists hesitated to refer their patients to the clinic. The reason was that the clinic was a college program run to teach psychology students rather than to help children with serious speech impediments.

The opposite criticism applied to the high school. No one questioned its excellence and the impact it made on the education students who listened in on its classes and on many young teachers in the area who came in as auditors. But what need did it fill? There were plenty of perfectly adequate high schools in the area.

"How can we justify," asked one of the psychologists connected with the speech clinic, "running an unnecessary high school in which each child costs as much as a graduate student at Harvard?"

"But how can we justify," asked the dean of the school of education, himself one of the outstanding teachers in the demonstration high school, "a speech clinic that has no results even though each of its patients costs the state as much as one of our demonstration high school students, or more?"

*Peter F. Drucker, *Management Cases* (New York: Harper's College Press, 1977), 23–24.

NOTES

1. Sean Silcoff, "Where Have all the Dollars Gone?" *Canadian Business*, 12 March 1999, 48–52.

2. Bruce Horovitz and Gary Strauss, "Fast-Food Icon Wants Shine Restored to Golden Arches," *USA Today*, 1 May 1998, 1B, 2B; "Tickling a Child's Fancy," *The Tennessean*, 6 February 1997, 1E, 4E; and Katrina Brooker, "Toys Were Us," *Fortune*, 27 September 1999, 145–148.

3. Nina Munk, "Gap Gets It," *Fortune*, 3 August 1998, 68–82; and Linda Yates and Peter Skarzynski, "How Do Companies Get to the Future First?" *Management Review*, January 1999, 16–22.

4. Charles Lindblom, "The Science of 'Muddling Through,'" *Public Administration Review* 29 (1954): 79–88.

5. Herbert A. Simon, *The New Science of Management Decision* (Englewood Cliffs, N.J.: Prentice-Hall, 1960), 1–8.

6. Paul J. H. Schoemaker and J. Edward Russo, "A Pyramid of Decision Approaches," *California Management Review* (Fall 1993): 9–31.

7. Wendy Zellner, "Back to Coffee, Tea, or Milk?" *Business Week*, 3 July 1995, 52–56.

8. Michael Pacanowsky, "Team Tools for Wicked Problems," *Organizational Dynamics* 23, no. 3 (Winter 1995): 36–51.

9. Polly LaBarre, ed., "Leaders.com," (Unit of One column), *Fast Company*, June 1999, 95–112.

10. Doug Wallace, "What Would You Do? Southern Discomfort," *Business Ethics*, March/April 1996, 52–53; Renee Elder, "Apparel Plant Closings Rip Fabric of Community's Employment," *The Tennessean,* 3 November 1996, 1E.

11. Karen Dillon, "The Perfect Decision," (an interview with John S. Hammond and Ralph L. Keeney), *Inc.* October 1998, 74–78; and John S. Hammond and Ralph L. Keeney, *Smart Choices: A Practical Guide to Making Better Decisions* (Boston, Mass.: Harvard Business School Press, 1998).

12. Earnest R. Archer, "How to Make a Business Decision: An Analysis of Theory and Practice," *Management Review* 69 (February 1980): 54–61; Boris Blai, "Eight Steps to Successful Problem Solving," *Supervisory Management* (January 1986): 7–9.

13. Francine Schwadel, "Christmas Sales' Lack of Momentum Test Store Managers' Mettle," *The Wall Street Journal*, 16 December 1987, 1.

14. Adapted from Archer, "How to Make a Business Decision," 59–61.

15. James W. Dean, Jr., and Mark P. Sharfman, "Procedural Rationality in the Strategic Decision-Making Process," *Journal of Management Studies* 30 (1993): 587–610.

16. Paul A. Anderson, "Decision Making by Objection and the Cuban Missile Crisis," *Administrative Science Quarterly* 28 (1983): 201–22.

17. Irving L. Janis, *Crucial Decisions: Leadership in Policymaking and Crisis Management* (New York: The Free Press, 1989); Paul C. Nutt, "Flexible Decision Styles and the Choices of Top Executives," *Journal of Management Studies* 30 (1993): 695–721.

18. Herbert A. Simon, "Making Management Decisions: The Role of Intuition and Emotion," *Academy of Management Executive* 1 (February 1987): 57–64; Daniel J. Eisenberg, "How Senior Managers Think," *Harvard Business Review* 62 (November-December 1984): 80–90.

19. Sefan Wally and J. Robert Baum, "Personal and Structural Determinants of the Pace of Strategic Decision Making," *Academy of Management Journal* 37, no. 4 (1994): 932–56; Orlando Behling and

Norman L. Eckel, "Making Sense Out of Intuition," *Academy of Management Executive* 5, no. 1 (1991): 46–54.

20. Thomas F. Issack, "Intuition: An Ignored Dimension of Management," *Academy of Management Review* 3 (1978): 917–22.

21. Marjorie A. Lyles, "Defining Strategic Problems: Subjective Criteria of Executives," *Organizational Studies* 8 (1987): 263–80; Marjorie A. Lyles and Ian I. Mitroff, "Organizational Problem Formulation: An Empirical Study," *Administrative Science Quarterly* 25 (1980): 102–19.

22. Marjorie A. Lyles and Howard Thomas, "Strategic Problem Formulation: Biases and Assumptions Embedded in Alternative Decision-Making Models," *Journal of Management Studies* 25 (1988): 131–45.

23. Susan E. Jackson and Jane E. Dutton, "Discerning Threats and Opportunities," *Administrative Science Quarterly* 33 (1988): 370–87.

24. Ross Stagner, "Corporate Decision-Making: An Empirical Study," *Journal of Applied Psychology* 53 (1969): 1–13.

25. Lauren Goldstein, "Prada Goes Shopping," *Fortune*, 27 September 1999, 207–10; and Suzanna Andrews, "Calling the Shots," *Working Woman*, November 1995, 30–35, 90.

26. Michael L. Ray and Rochelle Myers, *Creativity in Business* (Garden City, New Jersey: Doubleday, 1986).

27. Ann Langley, "Between 'Paralysis By Analysis' and 'Extinction By Instinct,'" *Sloan Management Review* (Spring 1995): 63–76.

28. Paul C. Nutt, "Types of Organizational Decision Processes," *Administrative Science Quarterly* 29 (1984): 414–50.

29. "How Paramount Keeps Turning Out Winners," *Business Week,* 11 June 1984, 148–151; Ron Grover, "Michael Eisner's Hit Parade," *Business Week*, 1 February 1988, 27.

30. Nandini Rajagopalan, Abdul M. A. Rasheed, and Deepak K. Datta, "Strategic Decision Processes: Critical Review and Future Decisions," *Journal of Management* 19 (1993): 349–84; Paul J. H. Schoemaker, "Strategic Decisions in Organizations: Rational and Behavioral Views," *Journal of Management Studies* 30 (1993): 107–29; Charles J. McMillan, "Qualitative Models of Organizational Decision Making," *Journal of Management Studies* 5 (1980): 22–39; Paul C. Nutt, "Models for Decision

Making in Organizations and Some Contextual Variables Which Stimulate Optimal Use," *Academy of Management Review* 1 (1976): 84–98.

31. Hugh J. Miser, "Operations Analysis in the Army Air Forces in World War II: Some Reminiscences," *Interfaces* 23 (September-October 1993): 47–49; Harold J. Leavitt, William R. Dill, and Henry B. Eyring, *The Organizational World* (New York: Harcourt Brace Jovanovich, 1973), chap. 6.

32. Stephen J. Huxley, "Finding the Right Spot for a Church Camp in Spain," *Interfaces* 12 (October 1982): 108–14; James E. Hodder and Henry E. Riggs, "Pitfalls in Evaluating Risky Projects," *Harvard Business Review* (January-February 1985): 128–35.

33. Edward Baker and Michael Fisher, "Computational Results for Very Large Air Crew Scheduling Problems," *Omega* 9 (1981): 613–18; Jean Aubin, "Scheduling Ambulances," *Interfaces* 22 (March-April, 1992): 1–10.

34. Thomas M. Cook, "SABRE Soars," *OR/MS Today*, June 1998, 26–35.

35. Anna Muoio, "Decisions, Decisions," (Unit of One column), *Fast Company*, October 1998, 93–101; also see Brian Palmer, "Click Here for Decisions," *Fortune*, 10 May 1999, 153–56, for information on decision making software.

36. Harold J. Leavitt, "Beyond the Analytic Manager," *California Management Review* 17 (1975): 5–12; C. Jackson Grayson, Jr., "Management Science and Business Practice," *Harvard Business Review* 51 (July-August 1973): 41–48.

37. David Wessel, "A Man Who Governs Credit Is Denied a Toys 'R' Us Card," *The Wall Street Journal*, 14 December 1995, B1.

38. Richard L. Daft and John C. Wiginton, "Language and Organization," *Academy of Management Review* (1979): 179–91.

39. Based on Richard M. Cyert and James G. March, *A Behavioral Theory of the Firm* (Englewood Cliffs, N.J.: Prentice-Hall, 1963); and James G. March and Herbert A. Simon, *Organizations* (New York: Wiley, 1958).

40. William B. Stevenson, Joan L. Pearce, and Lyman W. Porter, "The Concept of 'Coalition' in Organization Theory and Research," *Academy of Management Review* 10 (1985): 256–68.

41. Cyert and March, *Behavioral Theory of the Firm*, 120–22.

42. Ann Reilly Dowd, "How Bush Decided," *Fortune*, 11 February 1991, 45–46.

43. Richard A. Melcher, "Dusting Off the *Britannica*," *Business Week*, 20 October 1997, 143–46; Johnathan Gaw, "Encyclopaedica Britannica Takes Risk, Now Free on Web," *Seattle Times*, 19 October 1999, posted on Internet. Copyright 1999 The Seattle Times Company.

44. Lawrence G. Hrebiniak, "Top-Management Agreement and Organizational Performance," *Human Relations* 35 (1982): 1139–58; Richard P. Nielsen, "Toward a Method for Building Consensus during Strategic Planning," *Sloan Management Review* (Summer 1981): 29–40.

45. Based on Henry Mintzberg, Duru Raisinghani, and André Théorêt, "The Structure of 'Unstructured' Decision Processes," *Administrative Science Quarterly* 21 (1976): 246–75.

46. Lawrence T. Pinfield, "A Field Evaluation of Perspectives on Organizational Decision Making," *Administrative Science Quarterly* 31 (1986): 365–88.

47. Mintzberg, et al, "The Structure of 'Unstructured' Decision Processes."

48. Ibid., 270.

49. William C. Symonds with Carol Matlack, "Gillette's Edge," *Business Week*, 19 January 1998, 70–77; and William C. Symonds, "Would You Spend $1.50 for a Razor Blade?" *Business Week*, 27 April 1998, 46.

50. Michael D. Cohen, James G. March, and Johan P. Olsen, "A Garbage Can Model of Organizational Choice," *Administrative Science Quarterly* 17 (March 1972): 1–25; Michael D. Cohen and James G. March, *Leadership and Ambiguity: The American College President* (New York: McGraw-Hill, 1974).

51. Michael Masuch and Perry LaPotin, "Beyond Garbage Cans: An AI Model of Organizational Choice," *Administrative Science Quarterly* 34 (1989): 38–67.

52. David Krouss, "Casablanca," *Sky*, November 1992, 82–91

53. Thomas R. King, "Why 'Waterworld,' with Costner in Fins, Is Costliest Film Ever," *The Wall Street Journal*, 31 January 1995, A1.

54. Adapted from James D. Thompson, *Organizations in Action* (New York: McGraw-Hill, 1967), chap. 10; and McMillan, "Qualitative Models of Organizational Decision Making," 25.

55. Louise Lee, "Courts Begin to Award Damages to Victims of Parking-Area Crime," *The Wall Street Journal*, 23 April 1997, A1, A8.

56. L. J. Bourgeois III and Kathleen M. Eisenhardt, "Strategic Decision Processes in High Velocity

Environments: Four Cases in the Microcomputer Industry," *Management Science* 34 (1988): 816–35.

57. Kathleen M. Eisenhardt, "Speed and Strategic Course: How Managers Accelerate Decision Making," *California Management Review* (Spring 1990): 39–54.

58. Anna Muoio, "Decisions, Decisions."

59. Karl Weick, T*he Social Psychology of Organizing,* 2d ed. (Reading, Mass.: Addison-Wesley, 1979), 243.

60. Christopher Power with Kathleen Kerwin, Ronald Grover, Keith Alexander, and Robert D. Hof, "Flops," *Business Week*, 16 August 1993, 76-82.

61. Robert Townsend, *Up the Organization* (New York: Knopf, 1974), 115.

62. Helga Drummond, "Too Little Too Late: A Case Study of Escalation in Decision Making," *Organization Studies* 15, no. 4 (1994): 591–607; Joel Brockner, "The Escalation of Commitment to a Failing Course of Action: Toward Theoretical Progress," *Academy of Management Review* 17 (1992): 39–61; Barry M. Staw and Jerry Ross, "Knowing When to Pull the Plug," *Harvard Business Review* 65 (March-April 1987): 68–74; Barry M. Staw, "The Escalation of Commitment to a Course of Action," *Academy of Management Review* 6 (1981): 577–87.

63. Elizabeth Lesly, "Why Things Are So Sour at Borden," *Business Week*, 22 November 1993, 78–85.

64. Shona McKay, "When Good People Make Bad Choices," *Canadian Business*, February 1994, 52–55.

65. Jerry Ross and Barry M. Staw, "Organizational Escalation and Exit: Lessons from the Shoreham Nuclear Power Plant," *Academy of Management Journal* 36 (1993): 701–32.

Conflict, Power, and Politics

A LOOK INSIDE

Pacific Medical Center

oger Simpson, head of the largest radiology group in the San Francisco area, had worked at Pacific Medical Center for more than fifteen years when Pacific was acquired by a huge, for-profit healthcare corporation. Like other healthcare professionals, Simpson and members of his group had long provided radiology services for other hospitals in the region, including Pacific's biggest local competitor. However, Adam Schiff, the hospital's new administrator, who came in with a goal of strengthening Pacific as a for-profit business, quickly issued an ultimatum, not only to radiologists but to pathologists and emergency room doctors as well: practice only at Pacific or leave. The new rules threw healthcare professionals into severe conflict with hospital administrators. The doctors saw themselves as independent practitioners, while administrators viewed doctors as part of the hospital's assets. Although many other hospital-based doctor groups eventually gave in to Schiff's demands, Simpson and his group made the decision to fight. The forty-five members of the group, five of whom practice nearly full-time at Pacific, say they have tried to hash out a compromise, but Schiff insisted that the doctors who practiced at Pacific must break off totally from the group.

The conflict between Schiff and Simpson illustrates a power struggle that is going on all over America as large, for-profit corporations take control of more and more hospitals. Traditionally, hospitals would give an exclusive contract to a radiology or pathology group in return for an agreement that the group would staff the hospital twenty-four hours a day year-round. However, doctors were also free to forge similar relationships with other hospitals and clinics, as long as they met their obligations to each one. Schiff's demands, according to Paul Ginsburg, president for the Center for Studying Health System Change, are "a reflection of the shifting market power from physicians to hospitals." While Simpson and members of his group have continued to practice at their outpatient facility and at other hospitals and clinics in addition to Pacific, the chief of physician services has made it clear that the doctors will ultimately have to make a choice."[1]

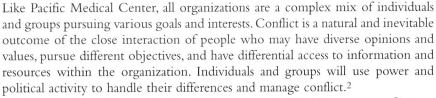

Like Pacific Medical Center, all organizations are a complex mix of individuals and groups pursuing various goals and interests. Conflict is a natural and inevitable outcome of the close interaction of people who may have diverse opinions and values, pursue different objectives, and have differential access to information and resources within the organization. Individuals and groups will use power and political activity to handle their differences and manage conflict.[2]

Too much conflict can be harmful to an organization. However, conflict can also be a positive force because it challenges the status quo, encourages new ideas and approaches, and leads to change.[3] Some degree of conflict occurs in all human relationships—between friends, romantic partners, and teammates as well as between parents and children, teachers and students, and bosses and employees. Conflict is not necessarily a negative force; it results from the normal interaction of varying human interests. Within organizations, individuals and groups frequently have different interests and goals they wish to achieve through the organization. In learning organizations, which encourage a democratic push and pull of ideas, the forces of conflict, power, and politics may be particularly evident. Managers in all organizations regularly deal with conflict and struggle with decisions about how to get the most out of employees, enhance job satisfaction and team identification, and realize high organizational performance.

PURPOSE OF THIS CHAPTER

This chapter will discuss the nature of conflict and the use of power and political tactics to manage and reduce conflict among individuals and groups. The notion of conflict has appeared in previous chapters. In Chapter 3, we talked about horizontal linkages such as task forces and teams that encourage collaboration among functional departments. Chapter 4 introduced the concept of differentiation, which means that different departments pursue different goals and may have different attitudes and values. Chapter 9 discussed the emergence of subcultures, and in Chapter 11, coalition building was proposed as one way to resolve disagreements among departments.

The first sections of this chapter explore the nature of intergroup conflict, characteristics of organizations that contribute to conflict, and the use of a political versus a rational model of organization to manage conflicting interests. Subsequent sections examine individual and organizational power, the vertical and horizontal sources of power for managers and other employees, and how power is used to attain organizational goals. The latter part of the chapter looks at politics, which is the application of power and authority to achieve desired outcomes. We will also discuss some tactics managers can use to enhance collaboration among people and departments.

WHAT IS INTERGROUP CONFLICT?

Intergroup conflict requires three ingredients: group identification, observable group differences, and frustration. First, employees have to perceive themselves as part of an identifiable group or department.[4] Second, there has to be an observable group difference of some form. Groups may be located on different floors of the building, members may have gone to different schools, or members may work in different departments. The ability to identify oneself as a part of one group and to observe differences in comparison with other groups is necessary for conflict.[5]

The third ingredient is frustration. Frustration means that if one group achieves its goal, the other will not; it will be blocked. Frustration need not be severe and only needs to be anticipated to set off intergroup conflict. Intergroup conflict will appear when one group tries to advance its position in relation to other groups. **Intergroup conflict** can be defined as the behavior that occurs among organizational groups when participants identify with one group and perceive that other groups may block their group's goal achievement or expectations.[6] Conflict means that groups clash directly, that they are in fundamental opposition. Conflict is similar to competition but more severe. **Competition** means rivalry among groups in the pursuit of a common prize, while conflict presumes direct interference with goal achievement.

Intergroup conflict within organizations can occur horizontally—across departments—or vertically—between different levels of the organization.[7] For example, the production department of a manufacturing company may have a dispute with quality control because new quality procedures reduce production efficiency. Teammates may argue about the best way to accomplish tasks and achieve goals. Workers may clash with bosses about new work methods, reward systems, or job assignments. Another typical source of conflict is between groups such as unions and management or franchise owners and headquarters. Franchise owners for McDonald's, Taco Bell, Burger King, and KFC have clashed with headquarters because of the increase of company-owned stores in neighborhoods that compete directly with franchisees. The FedEx pilots' union has fought with the company over wage increases, working hours, and control over scheduling. Conflict can also occur between different divisions or business units. For example, a conflict emerged between the two sides of Andersen Worldwide—Andersen Consulting (management consulting) and Arthur Andersen (accounting services)—because the two groups found themselves going after the same business.[8]

WHY CONFLICT EXISTS

Some specific organizational characteristics can generate conflict. These **sources of intergroup conflict** are goal incompatibility, differentiation, task interdependence, and limited resources. These characteristics of organizational relationships are determined by the contextual factors of environment, size, technology, strategy and goals, and organizational structure, which have been discussed in previous chapters. These characteristics, in turn, help shape the extent to which a rational model of behavior versus a political model of behavior is used to accomplish objectives.

Goal Incompatibility. Goal incompatibility is probably the greatest cause of intergroup conflict in organizations.[9] The goals of each department reflect the specific objectives members are trying to achieve. The achievement of one department's goals often interferes with another department's goals. University police, for example, have a goal of providing a safe and secure campus. They can achieve their goal by locking all buildings on evenings and weekends and not distributing keys. Without easy access to buildings, however, progress toward the science department's research goals will proceed slowly. On the other hand, if scientists come and go at all hours and security is ignored, police goals for security will not be met. Goal incompatibility throws the departments into conflict with each other.

The potential for conflict is perhaps greater between marketing and manufacturing than between other departments because the goals of these two departments are frequently at odds. Exhibit 12.1 shows examples of goal conflict between typical marketing and manufacturing departments. Marketing strives to increase the breadth of the product line to meet customer tastes for variety. A broad product line means short production runs, so manufacturing has to bear higher costs.[10] Other areas of goal conflict are quality, cost control, and new products. Goal incompatibility exists among departments in most organizations.

Differentiation. Differentiation was defined in Chapter 4 as "the differences in cognitive and emotional orientations among managers in different functional departments." Functional specialization requires people with specific education, skills, attitudes, and time horizons. For example, people may join a sales department because they have ability and aptitude consistent with sales work. After becoming members of the sales department, they are influenced by departmental norms and values.

EXHIBIT 12.1   *Marketing–Manufacturing Areas of Potential Goal Conflict*

Goal Conflict	MARKETING versus MANUFACTURING	
	Operative goal is customer satisfaction	**Operative goal is production efficiency**
Conflict Area	**Typical Comment**	**Typical Comment**
1. Breadth of product line	"Our customers demand variety."	"The product line is too broad—all we get are short, uneconomical runs."
2. New product introduction	"New products are our lifeblood."	"Unnecessary design changes are prohibitively expensive."
3. Product scheduling	"We need faster response. Our lead times are too long."	"We need realistic customer commitments that don't change like wind direction."
4. Physical distribution	"Why don't we ever have the right merchandise in inventory?"	"We can't afford to keep huge inventories."
5. Quality	"Why can't we have reasonable quality at lower cost?"	"Why must we always offer options that are too expensive and offer little customer utility?"

Source: Based on Benson S. Shapiro, "Can Marketing and Manufacturing Coexist?" *Harvard Business Review* 55 (September–October 1977): 104–14; and Victoria L. Crittenden, Lorraine R. Gardiner, and Antonie Stam, "Reducing Conflict Between Marketing and Manufacturing," *Industrial Marketing Management* 22 (1993): 299–309.

Departments or divisions within an organization often differ in values, attitudes, and standards of behavior, and these cultural differences lead to conflicts.[11] Consider an encounter between a sales manager and an R&D scientist about a new product:

> The sales manager may be outgoing and concerned with maintaining a warm, friendly relationship with the scientist. He may be put off because the scientist seems withdrawn and disinclined to talk about anything other than the problems in which he is interested. He may also be annoyed that the scientist seems to have such freedom in choosing what he will work on. Furthermore, the scientist is probably often late for appointments, which, from the salesman's point of view, is no way to run a business. Our scientist, for his part, may feel uncomfortable because the salesman seems to be pressing for immediate answers to technical questions that will take a long time to investigate. All the discomforts are concrete manifestations of the relatively wide differences between these two men in respect to their working and thinking styles. . . .[12]

Cultural differences can be particularly acute in the case of mergers or acquisitions. Employees in the acquired company may have completely different work styles and attitudes, and a "we against them" attitude can develop. One reason for the failure of many mergers is that although managers can integrate financial and production technologies, they have difficulty integrating the unwritten norms and values that have an even greater impact on company success.[13] The Taking the Lead box describes how GE Plastics overcame cultural differences after acquiring rival Borg-Warner Chemicals.

Task Interdependence. Task interdependence refers to the dependence of one unit on another for materials, resources, or information. As described in Chapter 5 on technology, pooled interdependence means little interaction; sequential interdependence means the output of one department goes to the next department; and reciprocal interdependence means departments mutually exchange materials and information.[14]

Generally, as interdependence increases, the potential for conflict increases.[15] In the case of pooled interdependence, units have little need to interact. Conflict is at a minimum. Sequential and reciprocal interdependence require employees to spend time coordinating and sharing information. Employees must communicate frequently, and differences in goals or attitudes will surface. Conflict is especially likely to occur when agreement is not reached about the coordination of services to each other. Greater interdependence means departments often exert pressure for a fast response because departmental work has to wait on other departments.[16]

Limited Resources. Another major source of conflict involves competition between groups for what members perceive as limited resources.[17] Organizations

Taking the Lead

GE Plastics/Borg-Warner

GE Plastics, with headquarters in Pittsfield, Massachusetts, recognized the importance of team building, but it took on new urgency after the company purchased a long-time rival, Borg-Warner Chemicals, based in Parkersville, West Virginia. The acquisition gave GE Plastics a real boost in technical and manufacturing strength, new products, and domestic and international marketing facilities. However, the two former competitors had very different corporate cultures. Borg-Warner had a paternalistic atmosphere and a group of loyal, older employees who wanted to stay put in Parkersville. In contrast to this familylike atmosphere, GE Plastics was described as youthful, aggressive, a little tougher, and a little colder than Borg-Warner.

Many Borg-Warner employees still considered GE "the competition" and didn't feel like a part of the company—and what's more, they weren't sure they wanted to. Executives considered team-building activities they had used in the past—rowing events, donkey races, wilderness experiences—and realized what they really needed was an event that would make a lasting impression on employees while serving a larger purpose and creating something of enduring value. The decision was made that employees would renovate five nonprofit facilities, using many of GE's materials, borrowing equipment when possible, and purchasing other supplies and tools in the local community. Teams were carefully formed to give employees a chance to meet and work with new people, to combine executives

with lower-level workers, and, above all, to mix former Borg-Warner employees with GE workers. In one twelve-hour day, thirty teams completely renovated the run-down Copley Family YMCA, located in a low-income San Diego neighborhood riddled with gangs and drugs. Together they scraped and painted walls, cleaned graffiti, laid tile, replaced windows, landscaped the grounds, and even restored a twenty-year-old mural covering a two-story outer wall.

The teams had arrived at the site ready to compete with one another, but as the day wore on they noticed something different about this team-building exercise—they wanted *all* the teams to win, and any team that finished its project first gladly pitched in to help others. The final effect on the community was impressive, but what was most phenomenal was the impact on employees. The event proved to be the turning point in the integration of GE Plastics and Borg-Warner employees. After a day of pounding nails and painting walls, they shed their rivalries to become teammates working toward a common cause they all felt proud of. As one former Borg-Warner worker said, " . . . any questions I had about whether or not this was the kind of company I wanted to work for were gone, absolutely. For us to be able to pull this off and to want to do this really made all the difference."

Source: David Bollier, "Building Corporate Loyalty While Rebuilding the Community," *Management Review* (October 1996): 17–22.

have limited money, physical facilities, staff resources, and human resources to share among departments. In their desire to achieve goals, groups want to increase their resources. This throws them into conflict. Managers may develop strategies, such as inflating budget requirements or working behind the scenes, to obtain a desired level of resources. Resources also symbolize power and influence within an organization. The ability to obtain resources enhances prestige. Departments typically believe they have a legitimate claim on additional resources. However, exercising that claim results in conflict. For example, in almost every organization, conflict occurs during the annual budget exercise, often creating political activity.

Rational Versus Political Model. The sources of intergroup conflict are listed in Exhibit 12.2. The degree of goal incompatibility, differentiation, interdependence, and conflict over limited resources determines whether a rational or political model of behavior is used within the organization to accomplish goals. When goals are in alignment, there is little differentiation, departments are characterized by pooled interdependence, and resources seem abundant, managers can use a **rational model** of organization, as outlined in Exhibit 12.2. As with the rational approach to decision making described in Chapter 11, the rational model of organization is an "ideal" that is not fully achievable in the real world, though managers strive to use rational processes whenever possible. In the rational organization, behavior is not random or accidental. Goals are clear and choices are made in a logical way. When a decision is needed, the goal is defined, alternatives are identified, and the choice with the highest probability of success is selected. The rational model is also characterized by centralized power and control, extensive information systems, and an efficiency orientation.[18] The opposite view of organizational processes is the **political model**, also described in Exhibit 12.2. When differences are great, organization groups have separate interests, goals, and values. Disagreement and conflict are normal, so power and influence are needed to reach decisions. Groups will engage in the push and pull of debate to decide goals and reach decisions. Information is ambiguous and

EXHIBIT 12.2   *Sources of Conflict and Use of Rational Versus Political Model*

Sources of Potential Intergroup Conflict	When Conflict is Low, Rational Model Describes Organization		When Conflict is High, Political Model Describes Organization
• Goal incompatibility	Consistent across participants	Goals	Inconsistent, pluralistic within the organization
• Differentiation	Centralized	Power and control	Decentralized, shifting coalitions and interest groups
• Task interdependence	Orderly, logical, rational	Decision process	Disorderly, result of bargaining and interplay among interests
• Limited resources	Norm of efficiency	Rules and norms	Free play of market forces; conflict is legitimate and expected
	Extensive, systematic, accurate	Information	Ambiguous; information used and withheld strategically

incomplete. The political model particularly describes organizations that strive for democracy and participation in decision making by empowering workers. Purely rational procedures do not work in democratic organizations, such as learning organizations.

Both rational and political processes are normally used in organizations. In most organizations, neither the rational model nor the political model characterizes things fully, but each will be used some of the time. Managers may strive to adopt rational procedures but will find that politics is needed to accomplish objectives. The political model means managers learn to acquire, develop, and use power to accomplish objectives.

INDIVIDUAL VERSUS ORGANIZATIONAL POWER

In popular literature, power is often described as a personal characteristic, and a frequent topic is how one person can influence or dominate another person.[19] You probably recall from an earlier management or organizational behavior course that managers have five sources of personal power.[20] *Legitimate power* is the authority granted by the organization to the formal management position a manager holds. *Reward power* stems from the ability to bestow rewards—promotion, raise, pat on the back—to other people. The authority to punish or recommend punishment is called *coercive power. Expert power* derives from a person's higher skill or knowledge about the tasks being performed. The last one, *referent power*, derives from personal characteristics such that people admire the manager and want to be like or identify with the manager out of respect and admiration. Each of these sources may be used by individuals within organizations.

Power in organizations, however, is often the result of structural characteristics.[21] Organizations are large, complex systems that contain hundreds, even thousands, of people. These systems have a formal hierarchy in which some tasks are more important regardless of who performs them. In addition, some positions have access to greater resources, or their contribution to the organization is more critical. Thus, the important power processes in organizations reflect larger organizational relationships, both horizontal and vertical, and organizational power usually is vested in the position, not in the person.

POWER VERSUS AUTHORITY

Power is an intangible force in organizations. It cannot be seen, but its effect can be felt. Power is often defined as the potential ability of one person (or department) to influence other persons (or departments) to carry out orders[22] or to do something they would not otherwise have done.[23] Other definitions stress that power is the ability to achieve goals or outcomes that power holders desire.[24] The achievement of desired outcomes is the basis of the definition used here: **Power** is the ability of one person or department in an organization to influence other people to bring about desired outcomes. It is the potential to influence others within the organization but with the goal of attaining desired outcomes for power holders. Book Mark 12.0 offers some guidelines for increasing your power and ability to influence others.

Power exists only in a relationship between two or more people, and it can be exercised in either vertical or horizontal directions. The source of power often derives from an exchange relationship in which one position or department provides scarce or valued resources to other departments. When one person is dependent on another person, a power relationship emerges in which the person with the resources has greater power.[25] When power exists in a relationship, the power holders can achieve compliance with their requests. For example, the following outcomes are indicators of power in an organization:

- Obtain a larger increase in budget than other departments.
- Obtain above-average salary increases for subordinates.

Book Mark 12.0

Have You Read This Book?

The 48 Laws of Power

By Robert Greene and Joost Elffers

In *The 48 Laws of Power*, Robert Greene and Joost Elffers attempt to elucidate the "timeless essence of power" by looking at examples spanning three thousand years of history. They distill some of the thoughts of power brokers from the past, including Niccolo Machiavelli, whose classic *The Prince* told sixteenth-century noblemen how to acquire and use power, often through means of deception and manipulation. Like Machiavelli, the authors do not see deception as evil or immoral but as a basic element in most human relationships. They emphasize that the quest for power is an amoral game that requires the ability to look at circumstances rather than good and evil. To be a master player, you also need to be a master psychologist—an understanding of others' hidden motives is the greatest piece of knowledge you can have.

SAMPLE POWER LAWS

The "48 laws" offer basic guidelines for how to subtly play the power game and increase power and influence over others. Laws such as "Conceal Your Intentions," and "Get Others to Do the Work for You, But Always Take the Credit" are interspersed with less duplicitous guidelines, including some that can be useful to managers in many situations:

Law 9: Win through your actions, never through argument. The authors emphasize that the resentment and ill will you may stir up through argument will last longer than any momentary change of opinion in your opponent. It is much more powerful to get others to agree with you through your actions, without saying a word.

Law 18: Do not build fortresses to protect yourself–isolation is dangerous. Managers need to build coalitions, allying

themselves with others, in order to truly have power. Although a fortress may seem like the safest protection when "enemies are everywhere," Greene and Elffers emphasize that isolation exposes you to more dangers by cutting you off from valuable information and making you an easy target.

Law 47: Do not go past the mark you aimed for; in victory, learn when to stop. Too many people become arrogant and overconfident when they achieve a victory, causing them to push past the goal they originally aimed for. Doing so, the authors point out, will cause you to make more enemies than you defeat. "Do not allow success to go to your head.... Set a goal, and when you reach it, stop."

Law 48: Assume formlessness. Rather than taking a form for your enemies to attack, Greene and Elffers advise that you keep yourself adaptable and on the move. "The best way to protect yourself is to be as fluid and formless as water; never bet on stability or lasting order. Everything changes."

IT'S ALL IN THE GAME

This book constantly reminds the reader that power is a game. It advises that you play the power game as a "civilized war," always taking the indirect route rather than appearing power hungry. As the authors put it: "Outwardly, you must seem to respect the niceties, but inwardly, unless you are a fool, you learn quickly to be prudent, and to do as Napoleon advised: Place your iron hand inside a velvet glove."

The 48 Laws of Power by Robert Greene and Joost Elffers is published by Viking.

- Obtain production schedules that are favorable to your department.
- Get items on the agenda at policy meetings.[26]

People throughout the organization can exercise power to achieve desired outcomes. Back in 1994, when the Discovery Channel wanted to extend its brand beyond cable television, Tom Hicks began pushing for a focus on the emerging Internet. Even though Discovery's CEO favored exploring interactive television, Hicks organized a campaign that eventually persuaded the CEO to focus instead on Web publishing, indicating that Hicks had power within the organization. Today, Hicks runs Discovery Channel Online. The key to success, he says, is "to consider your personal ambitions separately from your strategic goals for the company."[27]

The concept of formal authority is related to power but is narrower in scope. **Authority** is also a force for achieving desired outcomes, but only as prescribed by the formal hierarchy and reporting relationships. Three properties identify authority:

1. *Authority is vested in organizational positions.* People have authority because of the positions they hold, not because of personal characteristics or resources.
2. *Authority is accepted by subordinates.* Subordinates comply because they believe position holders have a legitimate right to exercise authority.[28] Even though Jim Heard and Gregg Trueman founded Buoyant Company and served as CEO and president respectively, they learned that employees did not accept their authority to make critical decisions. Staff members were aligned with three top managers who had been hired to handle the day-to-day hands-on work of the company. Staffers accepted the authority of these managers because they worked with them on a daily basis; therefore, they supported the managers' decisions over those of the two co-owners.[29].
3. *Authority flows down the vertical hierarchy.*[30] Authority exists along the formal chain of command, and positions at the top of the hierarchy are vested with more formal authority than are positions at the bottom.

Organizational power can be exercised upward, downward, and horizontally in organizations. Formal authority is exercised downward along the hierarchy and is the same as vertical power and legitimate power. In the following sections, we will examine vertical and horizontal sources of power for employees throughout the organization.

VERTICAL SOURCES OF POWER

All employees along the vertical hierarchy have access to some sources of power. Although a large amount of power is typically allocated to top managers by the organization structure, employees throughout the organization often obtain power disproportionate to their formal positions and can exert influence in an upward direction. There are four major sources of vertical power: formal position, resources, control of decision premises, and network centrality.[31]

Formal Position. Certain rights, responsibilities, and prerogatives accrue to top positions. People throughout the organization accept the legitimate right of top managers to set goals, make decisions, and direct activities. Thus, the power from formal position is sometimes called legitimate power.[32] Senior managers often use symbols and language to perpetuate their legitimate power. For example, Adam Schiff, administrator of Pacific Medical Center, described in the opening case, symbolized his formal power by issuing a newsletter with his photo on the cover and airing a 24-hour-a-day video in the rooms to welcome patients and announce that "we don't waste dollars."

The amount of power provided to middle managers and lower-level participants can be built into the organization's structural design. The allocation of power to middle managers and staff is important because power enables employees to be productive. When job tasks are nonroutine, and when employees participate in self-directed teams and problem-solving task forces, this encourages employees to be flexible and creative and to use their own discretion. Allowing people to make their own decisions increases their power. Power is also increased when a position encourages contact with high-level people. Access to powerful people and the development of a relationship with them provide a strong base of influence.[33] For example, in some organizations a secretary to the vice-president has more power than a department head because the secretary has access to the senior executive on a daily basis.

The logic of designing positions for more power assumes that an organization does not have a limited amount of power to be allocated among high-level and low-level employees. The total amount of power in an organization can be increased by designing tasks and interactions along the hierarchy so everyone has more influence. If the distribution of power is skewed too heavily toward the top, research suggests the organization will be less effective.[34]

Resources. Organizations allocate huge amounts of resources. Buildings are constructed, salaries are paid, and equipment and supplies are purchased. Each year, new resources are allocated in the form of budgets. These resources are allocated downward from top managers. Top managers often own stock, which gives them property rights over resource allocation. However, in many of today's organizations, employees throughout the organization also share in ownership, which increases their power. At St. Luke's, a London advertising agency, the company is owned entirely by its employees, from the CEO down to the janitors.

In most cases, top managers control the resources and, hence, can determine their distribution. Resources can be used as rewards and punishments, which are also sources of power. Resource allocation also creates a dependency relationship. Lower-level participants depend on top managers for the financial and physical resources needed to perform their tasks. Top management can exchange resources in the form of salaries, personnel, promotion, and physical facilities for compliance with the outcomes they desire.

Control of Decision Premises and Information. Control of **decision premises** means that top managers place constraints on decisions made at lower levels by specifying a decision frame of reference and guidelines. In one sense, top managers make big decisions, whereas lower-level participants make small decisions. Top management decides which goal an organization will try to achieve, such as increased market share. Lower-level participants then decide how the goal is to be reached. In one company, top management appointed a committee to select a new marketing vice president. The CEO provided the committee with detailed qualifications that the new vice president should have. He also selected people to serve on the committee. In this way, the CEO shaped the decision premises within which the marketing vice president would be chosen. Top manager actions and decisions such as these place limits on the decisions of lower-level managers and thereby influence the outcome of their decisions.[35]

The control of information can also be a source of power. Managers in today's organizations recognize that information is a primary business resource and that by controlling what information is collected, how it is interpreted, and how it is shared, they can influence how decisions are made.[36] In many of today's companies, especially in learning organizations, information is openly and broadly shared, which increases the power of people throughout the organization.

However, top managers generally have access to more information than do other employees. This information can be released as needed to shape the decision outcomes of other people. In one organization, Clark, Ltd., the senior manager controlled information given to the board of directors and thereby influenced the board's decision to purchase a large computer system.[37] The board of directors had formal authority to decide from which company the computer would be purchased. The management services group was asked to recommend which of six computer manufacturers should receive the order. Jim Kenny was in charge of the management services group, and Kenny disagreed with other managers about which computer to purchase. As shown in Exhibit 12.3, other managers had to go through Kenny to have their viewpoints heard by the board. Kenny shaped the board's thinking to select the computer he preferred by controlling information given to them.

Middle managers and lower-level employees may also have access to information that can increase their power. A secretary to a senior executive can often control information that other people want and will thus be able to influence those people. Top executives also depend on people throughout the organization for information about problems or opportunities. Middle managers or lower-level

EXHIBIT 12.3   *Information Flow for Computer Decision at Clark Ltd.*

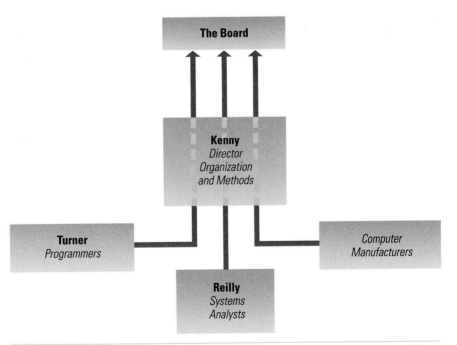

Source: Andrew M. Pettigrew, *The Politics of Organizational Decision-Making* (London: Tavistock, 1973), 235, with permission.

employees may manipulate the information they provide to top managers in order to influence decision outcomes.

Network Centrality. Network centrality means being centrally located in the organization and having access to information and people that are critical to the company's success. Top executives often increase their power by surrounding themselves with a network of loyal subordinates and using the network to learn about events throughout the organization.[38] They can use their central positions to build alliances and wield substantial power in the organization.

Middle managers and lower-level employees have more power when their jobs are related to current areas of concern or opportunity. When a job pertains to pressing organizational problems, power is more easily accumulated. David Shoenfeld, who is now senior vice-president for worldwide marketing, customer service, and corporate communications at FedEx, increased his power by being central to solving an organizational problem. When pilots threatened to go on strike, Shoenfeld believed the best approach was to warn customers up front on the company's Web site. The strike that had crippled archrival UPS had warned FedEx managers about the dangers of letting customers be caught by surprise. Shoenfeld's idea of openly sharing information with customers on a regular basis through a daily "Pilot Negotiation Update" helped FedEx maintain the trust of its customers.[39] Lower-level employees may also increase their network centrality by becoming knowledgeable and expert about certain activities or by taking on difficult tasks and acquiring specialized knowledge that makes them indispensable to managers above them. People who show initiative, work beyond what is expected, take on undesirable but important projects, and show interest in learning about the company and industry often find themselves with influence. Physical location also helps because some locations are in the center of things. Central location lets a person be visible to key people and become part of important interaction networks.

When she took a job as manager of employee communications at Xerox, Cindy Casselman used the idea of network centrality to increase her power and accomplish a goal.

In Practice 12.1

Xerox

When Cindy Casselman first began working at Xerox headquarters, she noticed that company communications weren't so good. Most of the company's employees would read about a big acquisition or a drop in earnings in the newspaper before they ever heard about it from the company. Even though Casselman wanted to change that by developing an intranet site that would be a haven of free speech and open information, she had very little formal authority. Still, she formed a makeshift budget to explore ideas, got the grudging approval of her direct supervisor, and put together a volunteer team that she called the Sanctioned Covert Operation (SCO).

Casselman knew that many people inside Xerox would feel threatened by her idea rather than energized by it. Thus, she began recruiting allies by emphasizing the benefits that would accrue to whomever she was talking to at the time. For example, to a manager at Xerox Business Services, Casselman presented the WebBoard as a place to test virtual reality delivery of documents; to a worker in the information management division, she sold it as a place to showcase a new technology architecture he had developed for the company. By positioning her idea in different ways to different people, blending her goals with the goals of others, Casselman gradually built a network of allies all around the huge corporation.

On Xerox Teamwork Day, Xerox Chairman and CEO Paul Allaire proudly described the company's newest internal communications tool—the WebBoard. Today, thanks to Casselman and the SCO team, 85,000 Xerox employees can visit this lively intranet site to read up-to-the-minute news about internal developments, talk with other workers, and generally stay connected with what's going on in the company. Casselman herself has been promoted to executive assistant to the head of corporate research and technology. "The WebBoard raised my profile and proved that I could follow through on an ambitious project and form the relationships needed to support the project," Casselman says. "It definitely helped me win my new job."[40]

Even though Cindy Casselman had little formal power and authority, she surrounded herself with a network of people who supported her idea for a company intranet. Casselman developed sufficient network centrality to accomplish her goal.

HORIZONTAL SOURCES OF POWER

Horizontal power pertains to relationships across departments. All vice-presidents are usually at the same level on the organization chart. Does this mean each department has the same amount of power? No. Horizontal power is not defined by the formal hierarchy or the organization chart. Each department makes a unique contribution to organizational success. Some departments will have greater say and will achieve their desired outcomes, whereas others will not. For example, Charles Perrow surveyed managers in several industrial firms.[41] He bluntly asked, "Which department has the most power?" among four major departments: production, sales and marketing, research and development, and finance and accounting. Partial survey results are given in Exhibit 12.4. In most firms, sales had the greatest power. In a few firms, production was also quite powerful. On average, the sales and production departments were more powerful than R&D and finance, although substantial variation existed. Differences in the amount of horizontal power clearly occurred in those firms. Today, e-commerce departments and information services departments have growing power in many organizations.

Horizontal power is difficult to measure because power differences are not defined on the organization chart. However, some initial explanations for departmental power differences, such as those shown in Exhibit 12.4, have been found. The theoretical concept that explains relative power is called strategic contingencies.[42]

STRATEGIC CONTINGENCIES

Strategic contingencies are events and activities both inside and outside an organization that are essential for attaining organizational goals. Departments involved with strategic contingencies for the organization tend to have greater power. Departmental activities are important when they provide strategic value by solving problems or crises for the organization. For example, if an organization faces an intense threat from lawsuits and regulations, the legal department will gain power and influence over organizational decisions because it copes with such a threat. If product innovation is the key strategic issue, the power of R&D can be expected to be high.

The strategic contingency approach to power is similar to the resource dependence model described in Chapters 4 and 5. Recall that organizations try to reduce

EXHIBIT 12.4   *Ratings of Power Among Departments in Industrial Firms*

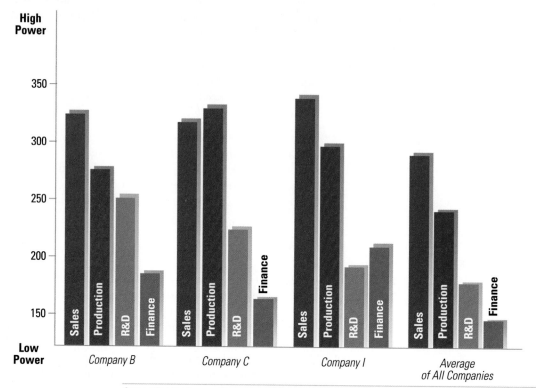

Source: Charles Perrow, "Departmental Power and Perspective in Industrial Firms," in Mayer N. Zald, ed., *Power in Organizations* (Nashville, Tenn.: Vanderbilt University Press, 1970), 64.

dependency on the external environment. The strategic contingency approach to power suggests that the departments most responsible for dealing with key resource issues and dependencies in the environment will become most powerful.

POWER SOURCES

Jeffrey Pfeffer and Gerald Salancik, among others, have been instrumental in conducting research on the strategic contingency theory.[43] Their findings indicate that a department rated as powerful may possess one or more of the characteristics illustrated in Exhibit 12.5.[44] In some organizations these five **power sources** overlap, but each provides a useful way to evaluate sources of horizontal power.

Dependency. Interdepartmental dependency is a key element underlying relative power. Power is derived from having something someone else wants. The power of department A over department B is greater when department B depends on A.[45]

Many dependencies exist in organizations. Materials, information, and resources may flow between departments in one direction, such as in the case of sequential task interdependence (Chapter 6). In such cases, the department receiving resources is in a lower power position than the department providing them. The number and strength of dependencies are also important. When seven or eight departments must come for help to the engineering department, for example, engineering is in a strong power position. In contrast, a department that depends on many other departments is in a low power position.

EXHIBIT 12.5   *Strategic Contingencies That Influence Horizontal Power Among Departments*

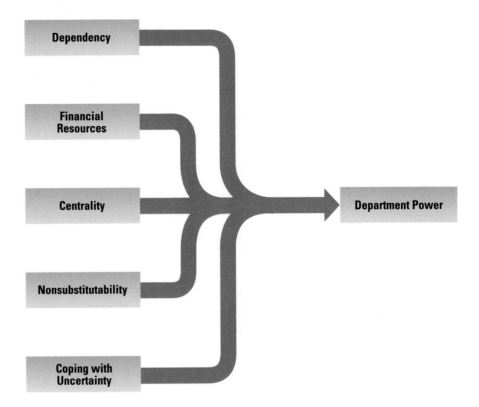

In a cigarette factory, one might expect that the production department would be more powerful than the maintenance department, but this was not the case in a cigarette plant near Paris.[46] The production of cigarettes was a routine process. The machinery was automated and production jobs were small in scope. Production workers were not highly skilled and were paid on a piece-rate basis to encourage high production. On the other hand, the maintenance department required skilled workers. These workers were responsible for repair of the automated machinery, which was a complex task. They had many years of experience. Maintenance was a craft because vital knowledge to fix machines was stored in the minds of maintenance personnel.

Dependency between the two groups was caused by unpredictable assembly line breakdowns. Managers could not remove the breakdown problem; consequently, maintenance was the vital cog in the production process. Maintenance workers had the knowledge and ability to fix the machines, so production managers became dependent on them. The reason for this dependence was that maintenance managers had control over a strategic contingency—they had the knowledge and ability to prevent or resolve work stoppages.

Financial Resources. There's a new golden rule in the business world: "The person with the gold makes the rules."[47] Control over various kinds of resources, and particularly financial resources, is an important source of power in organizations. Money can be converted into other kinds of resources that are needed by other departments. Money generates dependency; departments that provide financial resources have something other departments want. Departments that generate income for an organization have greater power. The survey of industrial firms reported in Exhibit 12.4 showed sales as the most powerful unit in most of those firms. Sales had power because salespeople find customers and sell the product, thereby removing an important problem for the organization. The sales department ensures the inflow of money. An ability to provide financial resources also explains why certain departments are powerful in other organizations, such as universities.

In Practice12.2

University of Illinois

You might expect budget allocation in a state university to be a straightforward process. The need for financial resources can be determined by such things as the number of undergraduate students, the number of graduate students, and the number of faculty in each department.

In fact, resource allocation at the University of Illinois is not clear-cut. The University of Illinois has a relatively fixed resource inflow from state government. Beyond that, important resources come from research grants and the quality of students and faculty. University departments that provide the most resources to the university are rated as having the most power. Some departments have more power because of their resource contribution to the university. Departments that generate large research grants are more powerful because research grants contain a sizable overhead payment to university administration. This overhead money pays for a large share of the university's personnel and facilities. The size of a department's graduate student body and the national prestige of the department also add to power. Graduate students and national prestige are nonfinancial resources that add to the reputation and effectiveness of the university.

How do university departments use their power? Generally, they use it to obtain even more resources from the rest of the university. Very powerful departments receive university resources, such as graduate student fellowships, internal research support, and summer faculty salaries, far in excess of their needs based on the number of students and faculty.[48]

As shown in the example of the University of Illinois, power accrues to departments that bring in or provide resources that are highly valued by an organization. Power enables those departments to obtain more of the scarce resources allocated within the organization. "Power derived from acquiring resources is used to obtain more resources, which in turn can be employed to produce more power—the rich get richer."[49]

Centrality. **Centrality** reflects a department's role in the primary activity of an organization.[50] One measure of centrality is the extent to which the work of the department affects the final output of the organization. For example, the production department is more central and usually has more power than staff groups (assuming no other critical contingencies). Centrality is associated with power because it reflects the contribution made to the organization. The corporate finance department of an investment bank generally has more power than the stock research department. By contrast, in the manufacturing firms described in Exhibit 12.4, finance tends to be low in power. When the finance department has the limited task of recording money and expenditures, it is not responsible for obtaining critical resources or for producing the products of the organization.

Nonsubstitutability. Power is also determined by **nonsubstitutability**, which means that a department's function cannot be performed by other readily available resources. Nonsubstitutability increases power. If an employee cannot be easily replaced, his or her power is greater. If an organization has no alternative sources of skill and information, a department's power will be greater. This can be the case when management uses outside consultants. Consultants might be used as substitutes for staff people to reduce the power of staff groups.

The impact of substitutability on power was studied for programmers in computer departments.[51] When computers were first introduced, programming was a rare and specialized occupation. People had to be highly qualified to enter the profession. Programmers controlled the use of organizational computers because they alone possessed the knowledge to program them. Over a period of about ten years, computer programming became a more common activity. People could be substituted easily, and the power of programming departments dropped.

The power of computer programming departments increased again as organizations battled the "Y2K problem." Most large corporations use computer systems that were programmed thirty years ago to deal only in two-digit dates, which convert the year 2000 into 00, throwing the entire system out of whack. The complex conversion process had to be done manually, and programmers with the skills to handle the conversion became highly prized.

Coping with Uncertainty. The chapters on environment and decision making described how elements in the environment can change swiftly and can be unpredictable and complex. In the face of uncertainty, little information is available to managers on appropriate courses of action. Departments that cope with this uncertainty will increase their power.[52] Just the presence of uncertainty does not provide power; reducing the uncertainty on behalf of other departments will. When market research personnel accurately predict changes in demand for new products, they gain power and prestige because they have reduced a critical uncertainty. Forecasting is only one technique for **coping with uncertainty**. Sometimes uncertainty can be reduced by taking quick and appropriate action after an unpredictable event occurs.

Three techniques that departments can use to cope with critical uncertainties are (1) obtaining prior information, (2) prevention, and (3) absorption.[53] *Obtaining prior information* means a department can reduce an organization's uncertainty by forecasting an event. Departments increase their power through *prevention* by predicting and forestalling negative events. *Absorption* occurs when a department takes action after an event to reduce its negative consequences. In the following case, the industrial relations department increased its power by absorbing a critical uncertainty. It took action after the event to reduce uncertainty for the organization.

In Practice 12.3   Crystal Manufacturing

Although union influence has been declining in recent years, unions are still actively seeking to extend their membership to new organizations. A new union is a crucial source of uncertainty for many manufacturing firms. It can be a countervailing power to management in decisions concerning wages and working conditions.

In 1998, the workers in Crystal Manufacturing Company voted to become part of the Glassmakers Craft Union. Management had been aware of union organizing activities, but it had not taken the threat seriously. No one had acted to forecast or prevent the formation of a union.

The presence of the union had potentially serious consequences for Crystal. Glassmaking is a delicate and expensive manufacturing process. The float-glass process cannot be shut down even temporarily except at great expense. A strike or walkout would mean financial disaster. Therefore, top management decided that establishing a good working relationship with the union was critically important.

The industrial relations department was assigned to deal with the union. This department was responsible for coping with the uncertainties created by the new union. The industrial relations group quickly developed expertise in union relationships. It became the contact point on industrial relations matters for managers throughout the organization. Industrial relations members developed a network throughout the organization and could bypass the normal chain of command on issues they considered important. Industrial relations had nearly absolute knowledge and control over union relations.

In Crystal Manufacturing Company, the industrial relations unit coped with the critical uncertainty by absorption. It took action to reduce the uncertainty after it appeared. This action gave the unit increased power.

Horizontal power relationships in organizations change as strategic contingencies change. For example, in recent years, giant retailers such as Wal-Mart and Winn-Dixie have increased their power over magazine publishers by refusing to sell issues that contain cover photos or stories that might be objectionable to some customers. Some magazine publishers have agreed to provide advance copies so retailers can spot controversial material ahead of time and decline the issue. "If you don't let them know in advance," one circulation director said, "they will delist the title and never carry it again." These demands from powerful retailers are creating new uncertainties and strategic issues for magazine publishers such as Hearst Corp., Miller Publishing Group, and Time Warner, which has so far refused to provide preview copies.[54]

POLITICAL PROCESSES IN ORGANIZATIONS

Politics, like power, is intangible and difficult to measure. It is hidden from view and is hard to observe in a systematic way. Two recent surveys uncovered the following reactions of managers toward political behavior.[55]

1. Most managers have a negative view toward politics and believe that politics will more often hurt than help an organization in achieving its goals.
2. Managers believe political behavior is common to practically all organizations.
3. Most managers think political behavior occurs more often at upper rather than lower levels in organizations.
4. Political behavior arises in certain decision domains, such as structural change, but is absent from other decisions, such as handling employee grievances.

Based on these surveys, politics seems more likely to occur at the top levels of an organization and around certain issues and decisions. Moreover, managers do not approve of political behavior. The remainder of this chapter explores more fully what is political behavior, when it should be used, the type of issues and decisions most likely to be associated with politics, and some political tactics that may be effective.

DEFINITION

Power has been described as the available force or potential for achieving desired outcomes. *Politics* is the use of power to influence decisions in order to achieve those outcomes. The exercise of power and influence has led to two ways to define politics—as self-serving behavior or as a natural organizational decision process. The first definition emphasizes that politics is self-serving and involves activities that are not sanctioned by the organization.[56]

In this view, politics involves deception and dishonesty for purposes of individual self-interest and leads to conflict and disharmony within the work environment. This dark view of politics is widely held by laypeople. Recent studies have shown that workers who perceive this kind of political activity at work within their companies often have related feelings of anxiety and job dissatisfaction. Studies also support the belief that inappropriate use of politics is related to low employee morale, inferior organizational performance, and poor decision making.[57] This view of politics explains why managers in the surveys described above did not approve of political behavior.

Although politics can be used in a negative, self-serving way, the appropriate use of political behavior can serve organizational goals.[58] The second view sees politics as a natural organizational process for resolving differences among organizational interest groups.[59] Politics is the process of bargaining and negotiation that is used to overcome conflicts and differences of opinion. In this view, politics is very similar to the coalition-building decision processes defined in Chapter 11 on decision making.

The organization theory perspective views politics as described in the second definition—as a normal decision-making process. Politics is simply the activity through which power is exercised in the resolution of conflicts and uncertainty. Politics is neutral and is not necessarily harmful to the organization. The formal definition of organizational politics is as follows: **organizational politics** involves activities to acquire, develop, and use power and other resources to obtain the preferred outcome when there is uncertainty or disagreement about choices.[60]

Political behavior can be either a positive or a negative force. Politics is the use of power to get things accomplished—good things as well as bad. Uncertainty and conflict are natural and inevitable, and politics is the mechanism for reaching agreement. Politics includes informal discussions that enable participants to arrive at consensus and make decisions that otherwise might be stalemated or unsolvable.

WHEN IS POLITICAL ACTIVITY USED?

Politics is a mechanism for arriving at consensus when uncertainty is high and there is disagreement over goals or problem priorities. Recall the rational versus political models described in Exhibit 12.2. The political model is associated with conflict over goals, shifting coalitions and interest groups, ambiguous information, and uncertainty. Thus, political activity tends to be most visible when managers confront nonprogrammed decisions, as discussed in Chapter 11, and is related to the Carnegie model of decision making. Because managers at the top of an organization generally deal with more nonprogrammed decisions than do managers at lower levels, more political activity will appear. Moreover, some issues are associated with inherent disagreement. Resources, for example, are critical for the survival and effectiveness of departments, so resource allocation often becomes a political issue. "Rational" methods of allocation do not satisfy participants. Three

domains of political activity (areas in which politics plays a role) in most organizations are structural change, management succession, and resource allocation.

Structural reorganizations strike at the heart of power and authority relationships. Reorganizations such as those discussed in Chapter 3 change responsibilities and tasks, which also affects the underlying power base from strategic contingencies. For these reasons, a major reorganization can lead to an explosion of political activity.[61] Managers may actively bargain and negotiate to maintain the responsibilities and power bases they have.

Organizational changes such as hiring new executives, promotions, and transfers have great political significance, particularly at top organizational levels where uncertainty is high and networks of trust, cooperation, and communication among executives are important.[62] Hiring decisions can generate uncertainty, discussion, and disagreement. Managers can use hiring and promotion to strengthen network alliances and coalitions by putting their own people in prominent positions.

The third area of political activity is resource allocation. Resource allocation decisions encompass all resources required for organizational performance, including salaries, operating budgets, employees, office facilities, equipment, use of the company airplane, and so forth. Resources are so vital that disagreement about priorities exists, and political processes help resolve the dilemmas.

USING POWER, POLITICS, AND COLLABORATION

One theme in this chapter has been that power in organizations is not primarily a phenomenon of the individual. It is related to the resources departments command, the role departments play in an organization, and the environmental contingencies with which departments cope. Position and responsibility more than personality and style determine a manager's influence on outcomes in the organization.

Power is used through individual political behavior, however. Individual managers seek agreement about a strategy to achieve their departments' desired outcomes. Individual managers negotiate decisions and adopt tactics that enable them to acquire and use power. In addition, managers develop ways to increase cooperation and collaboration within the organization to reduce damaging conflicts.

To fully understand the use of power within organizations, it is important to look at both structural components and individual behavior.[63] Although the power comes from larger organizational forms and processes, the political use of power involves individual-level activities. This section briefly summarizes tactics that managers can use to increase the power base of their departments, political tactics they can use to achieve desired outcomes, and tactics for increasing collaboration. These tactics are summarized in Exhibit 12.6.

TACTICS FOR INCREASING POWER

Four **tactics for increasing power** are as follows:

1. *Enter areas of high uncertainty.* One source of departmental power is to cope with critical uncertainties.[64] If department managers can identify key uncertainties and take steps to remove those uncertainties, the department's power base will be enhanced. Uncertainties could arise from stoppages on an assembly line, from the needed quality of a new product, or from the inability to predict a demand for new services. Once an uncertainty is identified, the

EXHIBIT 12.6   *Power and Political Tactics in Organizations*

Tactics for Increasing the Power Base	Political Tactics for Using Power	Tactics for Enhancing Collaboration
1. Enter areas of high uncertainty.	1. Build coalitions.	1. Create integration devices.
2. Create dependencies.	2. Expand networks.	2. Use confrontation and negotiation.
3. Provide resources.	3. Control decision premises.	3. Schedule intergroup consultation.
4. Satisfy strategic contingencies.	4. Enhance legitimacy and expertise.	4. Practice member rotation.
	5. Make preferences explicit, but keep power implicit.	5. Create superordinate goals.

department can take action to cope with it. By their very nature, uncertain tasks will not be solved immediately. Trial and error will be needed, which is to the advantage of the department. The trial-and-error process provides experience and expertise that cannot easily be duplicated by other departments.

2. *Create dependencies.* Dependencies are another source of power.[65] When the organization depends on a department for information, materials, knowledge, or skills, that department will hold power over the others. This power can be increased by incurring obligations. Doing additional work that helps out other departments will obligate the other departments to respond at a future date. The power accumulated by creating a dependency can be used to resolve future disagreements in the department's favor. An equally effective and related strategy is to reduce dependency on other departments by acquiring necessary information or skills. For example, information technology departments have created dependencies in many organizations because of the rapid changes in this area. Employees in other departments depend on the information technology unit to master complex software programs, changing use of the Internet, and other advances so that they will have the information they need to perform effectively.

3. *Provide resources.* Resources are always important to organizational survival. Departments that accumulate resources and provide them to an organization in the form of money, information, or facilities will be powerful. For example, In Practice 12.2 described how university departments with the greatest power are those that obtain external research funds for contributions to university overhead. Likewise, sales departments are powerful in industrial firms because they bring in financial resources.

4. *Satisfy strategic contingencies.* The theory of strategic contingencies says that some elements in the external environment and within the organization are especially important for organizational success. A contingency could be a critical event, a task for which there are no substitutes, or a central task that is interdependent with many others in the organization. An analysis of the organization and its changing environment will reveal strategic contingencies. To the extent that contingencies are new or are not being satisfied, there is room for a department to move into those critical areas and increase its importance and power.

In summary, the allocation of power in an organization is not random. Power is the result of organizational processes that can be understood and predicted. The abilities to reduce uncertainty, increase dependency on one's own department, obtain resources, and cope with strategic contingencies will all enhance a department's power. Once power is available, the next challenge is to use it to attain helpful outcomes.

POLITICAL TACTICS FOR USING POWER

The use of power in organizations requires both skill and willingness. Many decisions are made through political processes because rational decision processes do not fit. Uncertainty or disagreement is too high. **Political tactics for using power** to influence decision outcomes include the following:

1. *Build coalitions.* Coalition building means taking the time to talk with other managers to persuade them to your point of view.[66] Most important decisions are made outside formal meetings. Managers discuss issues with each other and reach agreements on a one-to-one basis. Effective managers are those who huddle, meeting in groups of twos and threes to resolve key issues.[67] An important aspect of coalition building is to build good relationships. Good interpersonal relationships are built on liking, trust, and respect. Reliability and the motivation to work with others rather than exploit others are part of coalition building.[68]

2. *Expand networks.* Networks can be expanded (1) by reaching out to establish contact with additional managers and (2) by co-opting dissenters. The first approach is to build new alliances through the hiring, transfer, and promotion process. Placing in key positions people who are sympathetic to the outcomes of the department can help achieve departmental goals.[69] On the other hand, the second approach, co-optation, is the act of bringing a dissenter into one's network. One example of co-optation involved a university committee whose membership was based on promotion and tenure. Several female professors who were critical of the tenure and promotion process were appointed to the committee. Once a part of the administrative process, they could see the administrative point of view and learned that administrators were not as evil as suspected. Co-optation effectively brought them into the administrative network.[70]

3. *Control decision premises.* To control decision premises means to constrain the boundaries of a decision. One technique is to choose or limit information provided to other managers. A common method is simply to put your department's best foot forward, such as selectively presenting favorable criteria. A variety of statistics can be assembled to support the departmental point of view. A university department that is growing rapidly and has a large number of students can make claims for additional resources by emphasizing its growth and large size. Such objective criteria do not always work, but they are a valuable step.

   Decision premises can be further influenced by limiting the decision process. Decisions can be influenced by the items put on an agenda for an important meeting or even by the sequence in which items are discussed.[71] Items discussed last, when time is short and people want to leave, will receive less attention than those discussed early. Calling attention to specific problems and suggesting alternatives also will affect outcomes. Stressing a specific problem to get it—rather than problems not relevant to your department— on the agenda is an example of agenda setting.

4. *Enhance legitimacy and expertise.* Managers can exert the greatest influence in areas in which they have recognized legitimacy and expertise. If a request is within the task domain of a department and is consistent with the department's

vested interest, other departments will tend to comply. Members can also identify external consultants or other experts within the organization to support their cause.[72] For example, a financial vice-president in a large retail firm wanted to fire the director of human resource management. She hired a consultant to evaluate the human resource management projects undertaken to date. A negative report from the consultant provided sufficient legitimacy to fire the director, who was replaced with a director loyal to the financial vice-president.

5. *Make preferences explicit, but keep power implicit.* If managers do not ask, they seldom receive. Political activity is effective only when goals and needs are made explicit so the organization can respond. Managers should bargain aggressively and be persuasive. An assertive proposal may be accepted because other managers have no better alternatives. Moreover, an explicit proposal will often receive favorable treatment because other alternatives are ambiguous and less well defined. Effective political behavior requires sufficient forcefulness and risk taking to at least try to achieve desired outcomes.

   The use of power, however, should not be obvious.[73] If one formally draws upon his or her power base in a meeting by saying, "My department has more power, so the rest of you have to do it my way," the power will be diminished. Power works best when it is used quietly. To call attention to power is to lose it. Explicit claims for power are made by the powerless, not by the powerful. People know who has power. There is substantial agreement on which departments are more powerful. Explicit claims to power are not necessary and can even harm the department's cause.

When using any of the preceding tactics, recall that most people feel self-serving behavior hurts rather than helps an organization. If managers are perceived to be throwing their weight around or are perceived to be after things that are self-serving rather than beneficial to the organization, they will lose respect. On the other hand, managers must recognize the relational and political aspect of their work. It is not sufficient to be rational and technically competent. Politics is a way to reach agreement. When managers ignore political tactics, they may find themselves failing without understanding why. This happened to Jeff Glover, a new manager with a firm in California's Silicon Valley.

In Practice 12.4

Halifax Business Machines

Jeff Glover was promoted to group leader at Halifax Business Machines because of his reputation as a well-respected technical specialist. Glover was interested in medical applications of the electronic business machines manufactured by his company. After visiting a hospital several times during his wife's illness, he developed specifications for a new piece of medical equipment. It was a clever modification of one of Halifax's existing products, and Glover's bosses were enthusiastic. They gave him permission to work half time on the new product and asked for cooperation from appropriate people in engineering, marketing, and manufacturing to develop a prototype.

A month after the project began, Glover was told that the engineer assigned to the project had to reduce his time to only five hours a week. Then Glover discovered that the manufacturing engineer who was supposed to do cost estimates was temporarily reassigned to a small crisis in a New York plant. Three days later, Glover was hit with the most damaging blow. His boss said that marketing had redone the market potential analysis and found the projected market was only one-fifth the size originally forecast. The project would have to be stopped immediately. Glover was furious. He resigned at the end of the day.

A few weeks later, Glover learned from a friend that the sales manager had immediately disliked Glover's idea when it was proposed. He didn't want his people to develop new knowledge about hospitals and medical purchasing practices. He had gotten one of his people to develop pessimistic numbers about market potential and had suggested to top management that time not be wasted on Glover's project.[74]

Glover's problem was that he naively assumed the logic and technical merits of his proposed machine would carry the day. He ignored political relationships, especially with the sales manager. He did not take the time to build a network of support for the project among key managers. He should have devoted more time to building a coalition and enhancing the legitimacy of his proposal, perhaps with his own market research.

TACTICS FOR ENHANCING COLLABORATION

Power and political tactics are important means for getting things done within organizations. Most organizations today have at least moderate interunit conflict. An additional approach in many organizations is to overcome conflict by stimulating cooperation and collaboration among departments to support the attainment of organizational goals. **Tactics for enhancing collaboration** include the following:

1. *Create integration devices.* As described in Chapter 3, teams, task forces, and project managers who span the boundaries between departments can be used as integration devices. Bringing together representatives from conflicting departments in joint problem-solving teams is an effective way to enhance collaboration because representatives learn to understand each other's point of view.[75] Sometimes a full-time integrator is assigned to achieve cooperation and collaboration by meeting with members of the respective departments and exchanging information. The integrator has to understand each group's problems and must be able to move both groups toward a solution that is mutually acceptable.[76]

   As an outgrowth of teams and task forces, many organizations today are restructuring into permanent multidisciplinary, self-directed work teams focused on horizontal process rather than function. At Saturn Corporation, teams of about fifteen employees handle everything from production schedules and new car quality to budgeting and hiring new workers.[77] Teams and task forces reduce conflict and enhance cooperation because they integrate people from different departments. Integration devices can also be used to enhance cooperation between labor and management, as the example of Aluminum Company of America and the International Association of Machinists illustrates.

In Practice 12.5   Aluminum Company of America/International Association of Machinists

When representatives from the International Association of Machinists (IAM) approached David Groetsch, president of a division of Aluminum Company of America (Alcoa) and offered to help create a new work system, Groetsch immediately agreed to give it a try. Alcoa managers joined union leaders for a week-long course at the union's school in Maryland, where they learned how to set up a labor–management partnership and spur productivity. Working together, labor and management studied everything from the history of high performance systems to new accounting methods to help measure them. Following the course, the union sent experts free of charge to help union leaders and managers from manufacturing to marketing create teams and joint-decision-making councils.

The IAM is at the forefront of a revolutionary change in the relationship between labor and management. After decades of suspicion about company-sponsored teams, many unions are now actively embracing the concept of partnership. According to Groetsch, relationships on the shop floor at Alcoa have improved because each side better understands the other's concerns. "The days of 1950s-style table-banging aren't gone yet," says Laborers' President Arthur C. Coia, whose union is also involved in cooperative ventures.[78] However, the use of integration devices is dramatically improving cooperative relationships between labor and management.

Labor-management teams, which are designed to increase worker participation and provide a cooperative model for union–management problems, are increasingly being used at companies such as Goodyear, Ford Motor Company, and Xerox. In the steel industry, companies such as USX and Wheeling-Pittsburgh Steel Corp. have signed pacts that give union representatives seats on the board.[79] Although unions continue to battle over traditional issues such as wages, these integration devices are creating a level of cooperation that many managers would not have believed possible just a few years ago.

2. *Use confrontation and negotiation.* **Confrontation** occurs when parties in conflict directly engage one another and try to work out their differences. **Negotiation** is the bargaining process that often occurs during confrontation and that enables the parties to systematically reach a solution. These techniques bring appointed representatives from the departments together to work out a serious dispute.

    Confrontation and negotiation involve some risk. There is no guarantee that discussions will focus on a conflict or that emotions will not get out of hand. However, if members are able to resolve the conflict on the basis of face-to-face discussions, they will find new respect for each other, and future collaboration becomes easier. The beginnings of relatively permanent attitude change are possible through direct negotiation.

    For example, one technique used by companies is to have each department head meet face-to-face once a month with each of the other department heads and list what he or she expects from that department. After discussion and negotiation, department heads sign off on their commitment to perform the services on the list. The regular contact develops managers' skills as well as their desire to work out conflicts and solve problems among themselves.[80]

    Confrontation is successful when managers engage in a "win-win" strategy. Win-win means both departments adopt a positive attitude and strive to resolve the conflict in a way that will benefit each other.[81] Ron Shapiro and Mark Jankowski, who negotiate deals for star athletes, suggest that each side should clearly identify, in descending order of importance, what it truly wants out of the negotiation and then try to do the same thing for the other side, eventually determining how the two sides' interests mesh.[82] If the negotiations deteriorate into a strictly win-lose strategy (each group wants to defeat the other), the confrontation will be ineffective. Top management can urge group members to work toward mutually acceptable outcomes. The differences between win-win and win-lose strategies of negotiation are shown in Exhibit 12.7. With a win-win strategy—which includes defining the problem as mutual, communicating openly, and avoiding threats—understanding can be changed while the dispute is resolved.

One type of negotiation, used to resolve a disagreement between workers and management, is referred to as **collective bargaining**. The bargaining process is usually accomplished through a union and results in an agreement that specifies each party's responsibilities for the next two to three years. Union–management negotiations are currently underway at several major U.S. airlines, including US Airways, TWA, Northwest, Delta, and United.[83]

3. *Schedule intergroup consultation.* When conflict is intense and enduring, and department members are suspicious and uncooperative, managers can bring in a third-party consultant to work with the groups. This process, sometimes called *workplace mediation*, is a strong intervention to reduce conflict because it involves bringing the disputing parties together and allowing each side to present its version of "reality." The technique has been developed by such psychologists as Robert Blake, Jane Mouton, and Richard Walton.[84]

Department members attend a workshop, which may last for several days, away from day-to-day work problems. This approach is similar to the OD approach described in Chapter 10 on innovation and change. The steps typically associated with an intergroup training session are as follows:

a. The conflicting groups are brought into a training setting with the stated goal of exploring mutual perceptions and relationships.

b. The conflicting groups are then separated, and each group is invited to discuss and make a list of its perceptions of itself and the other group.

c. In the presence of both groups, group representatives publicly share the perceptions of self and other that the groups have generated, and the groups are obligated to remain silent. The objective is simply to report to the other group as accurately as possible the images that each group has developed in private.

d. Before any exchange takes place, the groups return to private sessions to digest and analyze what they have heard; there is great likelihood that the representatives' reports have revealed to each group discrepancies between its self-image and the image the other group holds of it.

EXHIBIT 12.7   *Negotiating Strategies*

Win-Win Strategy	Win-Lose Strategy
1. Define the conflict as a mutual problem.	1. Define the problem as a win-lose situation.
2. Pursue joint outcomes.	2. Pursue own group's outcomes.
3. Find creative agreements that satisfy both groups.	3. Force the other group into submission.
4. Use open, honest, and accurate communication of group's needs, goals, and proposals.	4. Use deceitful, inaccurate and misleading communication of group's needs, goals, and proposals.
5. Avoid threats (to reduce the other's defensiveness).	5. Use threats (to force submission).
6. Communicate flexibility of position.	6. Communicate high commitment (rigidity) regarding one's position.

Source: Adapted from David W. Johnson and Frank P. Johnson, *Joining Together: Group Theory and Group Skills* (Englewood Cliffs, N.J.: Prentice-Hall, 1975), 182–83.

    e. In public session, again working through representatives, each group shares with the other what discrepancies it has uncovered and the possible reasons for them, focusing on actual, observable behavior.

    f. Following this mutual exposure, a more open exploration is permitted between the two groups on the now-shared goal of identifying further reasons for perceptual distortions.

    g. A joint exploration is then conducted of how to manage future relations in such a way as to encourage cooperation among groups.[85]

    Intergroup consultation can be quite demanding for everyone involved. It is fairly easy to have conflicting groups list perceptions and identify discrepancies. However, exploring their differences face-to-face and agreeing to change is more difficult. If handled correctly, these sessions can help department employees understand each other much better and lead to improved attitudes and better working relationships for years to come.

4. *Practice member rotation.* Rotation means individuals from one department can be asked to work in another department on a temporary or permanent basis. The advantage is that individuals become submerged in the values, attitudes, problems, and goals of the other department. In addition, individuals can explain the problems and goals of their original departments to their new colleagues. This enables a frank, accurate exchange of views and information.

    Rotation works slowly to reduce conflict but is very effective for changing the underlying attitudes and perceptions that promote conflict.[86]

5. *Create shared mission and superordinate goals.* Another strategy is for top management to create a shared mission and establish superordinate goals that require cooperation among departments.[87] As discussed in Chapter 9, organizations with strong, adaptive cultures, where employees share a larger vision for their company, are more likely to have a united, cooperative workforce. Recent studies have shown that when employees from different departments see that their goals are linked together, they will openly share resources and information.[88] To be effective, superordinate goals must be substantial, and employees must be granted the time to work cooperatively toward those goals. The reward system can also be redesigned to encourage the pursuit of the superordinate goals rather than departmental subgoals.

    Perhaps the most powerful superordinate goal is company survival. If an organization is about to fail and jobs will be lost, groups forget their differences and try to save the organization. The goal of survival has improved relationships among groups in meat packing plants and auto supply firms that have been about to go out of business. At Harley-Davidson Inc., internal relationships as well as union-management relationships dramatically improved after top executives made it clear that the company was facing extinction. Harley-Davidson now applies the concept of self-directed work teams from the shop floor to the executive suite, and the workers closest to the job have the authority and responsibility to do their jobs as they see fit. In addition, all workers attend eighty hours of training, which includes training in communication and conflict resolution. The company negotiated agreements with its two unions, the International Association of Machinists and Aerospace Workers and the United Paperworkers International, to share a commitment to making Harley a high-performance organization. The new level of cooperation helped the company weather the turbulence and rise again to the pinnacle of American business success.[89]

SUMMARY AND INTERPRETATION

The most important point of this chapter is that conflict, power, and politics are natural outcomes of organizing. Differences in goals, backgrounds, and tasks are necessary for organizational excellence, but these differences can throw groups into conflict. Managers use power and politics to manage and resolve conflict. Two views of organization were presented. The rational model of organization assumes that organizations have specific goals and that problems can be logically solved. The other view, the political model of organization, is the basis for much of the chapter. This view assumes that the goals of an organization are not specific or agreed upon. Departments have different values and interests, so managers come into conflict. Decisions are made on the basis of power and political influence. Bargaining, negotiation, persuasion, and coalition building decide outcomes.

The chapter also discussed the vertical and horizontal sources of power. Vertical sources of power include formal position, resources, control of decision premises, and network centrality. In general, managers at the top of the organizational hierarchy have more power than people at lower levels. However, positions all along the hierarchy can be designed to increase the power of employees. As organizations face increased competition and environmental uncertainty, top executives are finding that increasing the power of middle managers and lower-level employees can help the organization be more competitive. Research into horizontal power processes has revealed that certain characteristics make some departments more powerful than others. Such factors as dependency, resources, and nonsubstitutability determine the influence of departments.

Managers can use political tactics such as coalition building, expanded networks, and control of decision premises to help departments achieve desired outcomes. Many people distrust political behavior, fearing that it will be used for selfish ends that benefit the individual but not the organization. However, politics is often needed to achieve the legitimate goals of a department or organization. Three areas in which politics often play a role are structural change, management succession, and resource allocation because these are areas of high uncertainty. Although conflict and political behavior are natural and can be used for beneficial purposes, managers also strive to enhance collaboration so that conflict between groups does not become too strong. Tactics for enhancing collaboration include integration devices, confrontation and negotiation, intergroup consultation, member rotation, and shared mission and superordinate goals.

BRIEFCASE

As an organization manager, keep these guidelines in mind:

1. Recognize that some interdepartmental conflict is natural and can benefit the organization. Associate the organizational design characteristics of goal incompatibility, differentiation, task interdependence, and resource scarcity with greater conflict among groups. Expect to devote more time and energy to resolving conflict in these situations.

2. Understand and use the vertical sources of power in organizations, including formal position, resources, control of decision premises and information, and network centrality. Also be aware of the less visible, but equally important, horizontal power relationships that come from the ability of a department to

deal with strategic contingencies that confront the organization. Increase the horizontal power of a department by increasing involvement in strategic contingencies.

3. Expect and allow for political behavior in organizations. Politics provides the discussion and clash of interests needed to crystallize points of view and to reach a decision. Build coalitions, expand networks, control decision premises, enhance legitimacy, and make preferences explicit to attain desired outcomes.

4. Use the rational model of organization when alternatives are clear, when goals are defined, and when managers can estimate the outcomes accurately. In these circumstances, coalition building, cooptation, or other political tactics are not needed and will not lead to effective decisions.

5. If conflict becomes too strong, use tactics for enhancing collaboration, including integration devices, confrontation, intergroup consultation, member rotation, and superordinate goals. Select the techniques that fit the organization and the conflict.

KEY CONCEPTS

authority
centrality
collective bargaining
competition
confrontation
coping with uncertainty
decision premises
domains of political activity
intergroup conflict
labor-management teams
negotiation
network centrality

nonsubstitutability
organizational politics
political model
political tactics for using power
power
power sources
rational model
sources of intergroup conflict
strategic contingencies
tactics for enhancing collaboration
tactics for increasing power

DISCUSSION QUESTIONS

1. Briefly describe how differences in tasks, personal background, and training lead to conflict among groups. How does task interdependence lead to conflict among groups?

2. Discuss why some conflict is considered beneficial to organizations.

3. In a learning organization, are decisions more likely to be made using the rational or political model of organization? Discuss.

4. What is the difference between power and authority? Is it possible for a person to have formal authority but no real power? Discuss.

5. Explain how control over decision premises gives power to a person.

6. In Exhibit 12.4, research and development has greater power in company B than in the other firms. Discuss possible strategic contingencies that give R&D greater power in this firm.

7. State University X receives 90 percent of its financial resources from the state and is overcrowded with students. It is trying to pass regulations to limit student enrollment. Private University Y receives 90 percent of its income from student tuition and has barely enough students to make ends meet. It is actively recruiting students for next year. In which university will students

have greater power? What implications will this have for professors and administrators? Discuss.

8. Do you believe it is possible to increase the total amount of power in an organization by delegating power to employees? Explain.

9. The engineering college at a major university brings in three times as many government research dollars as does the rest of the university combined. Engineering appears wealthy and has many professors on full-time research status. Yet, when internal research funds are allocated, engineering gets a larger share of the money, even though it already has substantial external research funds. Why would this happen?

10. Which do you believe would have a greater long-term impact on changing employee attitudes toward increased collaboration—intergroup consultation or confrontation and negotiation? Discuss.

CHAPTER 12 WORKBOOK *How Do You Handle Conflict?*

Think of some disagreements you have had with a friend, relative, manager, or co-worker. Then indicate how frequently you engage in each of the following described behaviors. For each item, select the number that represents the behavior you are *most likely* to exhibit. There are no right or wrong answers. Respond to all items using the scale. The responses from 1 to 7 are

Scale

Always	Very often	Often	Sometimes	Seldom	Very seldom	Never
1	2	3	4	5	6	7

____ 1. I blend my ideas to create new alternatives for resolving a disagreement.

____ 2. I shy away from topics that are sources of disputes.

____ 3. I make my opinion known in a disagreement.

____ 4. I suggest solutions that combine a variety of viewpoints.

____ 5. I steer clear of disagreeable situations.

____ 6. I give in a little on my ideas when the other person also gives in.

____ 7. I avoid the other person when I suspect that he or she wants to discuss a disagreement.

____ 8. I integrate arguments into a new solution from the issues raised in a dispute.

____ 9. I will go 50-50 to reach a settlement.

____ 10. I raise my voice when I'm trying to get the other person to accept my position.

____ 11. I offer creative solutions in discussions of disagreements.

____ 12. I keep quiet about my views in order to avoid disagreements.

____ 13. I give in if the other person will meet me halfway.

____ 14. I downplay the importance of a disagreement.

____ 15. I reduce disagreements by making them seem insignificant.

* From "How Do You Handle Conflict?" in Robert E. Quinn, et al., *Becoming a Master Manager* (New York: Wiley, 1990), 221–23. Used with permission.

_____ 16. I meet the other person at a midpoint in our differences.

_____ 17. I assert my opinion forcefully.

_____ 18. I dominate arguments until the other person understands my position.

_____ 19. I suggest we work together to create solutions to disagreements.

_____ 20. I try to use the other person's ideas to generate solutions to problems.

_____ 21. I offer trade-offs to reach solutions in disagreements.

_____ 22. I argue insistently for my stance.

_____ 23. I withdraw when the other person confronts me about a controversial issue.

_____ 24. I sidestep disagreements when they arise.

_____ 25. I try to smooth over disagreements by making them appear unimportant.

_____ 26. I insist my position be accepted during a disagreement with the other person.

_____ 27. I make our differences seem less serious.

_____ 28. I hold my tongue rather than argue with the other person.

_____ 29. I ease conflict by claiming our differences are trivial.

_____ 30. I stand firm in expressing my viewpoints during a disagreement.

Scoring and Interpretation: Three categories of conflict-handling strategies are measured in this instrument: solution-oriented, nonconfrontational, and control. By comparing your scores on the following three scales, you can see which of the three is your preferred conflict-handling strategy.

To calculate your three scores, add the individual scores for the items and divide by the number of items measuring the strategy. Then subtract each of the three mean scores from seven.

Solution-oriented: Items 1, 4, 6, 8, 9, 11, 13, 16, 19, 20, 21 (Total = 11)
Nonconfrontational: Items 2, 5, 7, 12, 14, 15, 23, 24, 25, 27, 28, 29 (Total = 12)
Control: Items 3, 10, 17, 18, 22, 26, 30 (Total = 7)

Solution-oriented strategies tend to focus on the problem rather than on the individuals involved. Solutions reached are often mutually beneficial, with neither party defining himself or herself as the winner and the other party as the loser.

Nonconfrontational strategies tend to focus on avoiding the conflict by either avoiding the other party or by simply allowing the other party to have his or her way. These strategies are used when there is more concern with avoiding a confrontation than with the actual outcome of the problem situation.

Control strategies tend to focus on winning or achieving one's goals without regard for the other party's needs or desires. Individuals using these strategies often rely on rules and regulations in order to win the battle.

QUESTIONS

1. Which strategy do you find easiest to use? Most difficult? Which do you use more often?
2. How would your answers have differed if the other person was a friend, family member, or co-worker?
3. What is it about the conflict situation or strategy that tells you which strategy to use in dealing with a conflict situation?

Case for Analysis   *The Daily Tribune**

The *Daily Tribune* is the only daily newspaper serving a six-county region of eastern Tennessee. Even though its staff is small and it serves a region of mostly small towns and rural areas, the *Tribune* has won numerous awards for news coverage and photojournalism from the Tennessee Press Association and other organizations.

Rick Arnold became news editor almost fifteen years ago. He has spent his entire career with the *Tribune* and feels a great sense of pride that it has been recognized for its journalistic integrity and balanced coverage of issues and events. The paper has been able to attract bright, talented young writers and photographers thanks largely to Rick's commitment and his support of the news staff. In his early years, the news room was a dynamic, exciting place to work—reporters thrived on the fast pace and the chance to occasionally "scoop" the major daily paper in Knoxville.

But times have changed at the *Daily Tribune*. Over the past five years or so, the advertising department has continued to grow, both in terms of staff and budget, while the news department has begun to shrink. "Advertising pays the bills," publisher John Fisher reminded everyone at this month's managers' meeting. "Today, advertisers can go to direct mail, cable television, even the Internet, if they don't like what we're doing for them."

Rick has regularly clashed with the advertising department regarding news stories that are critical of major advertisers, but the conflicts have increased dramatically over the past few years. Now, Fisher is encouraging greater "horizontal collaboration," as he calls it, asking that managers in the news department and the ad department consult with one another regarding issues or stories that involve the paper's major advertisers. The move was prompted in part by a growing number of complaints from advertisers about stories they deemed unfair. "We print the news," Fisher said, "and I understand that sometimes we've got to print things that some people won't like. But we've got to find ways to be more advertiser-friendly. If we work together, we can develop strategies that both present good news coverage and serve to attract more advertisers."

Rick left the meeting fuming, and he didn't fail to make his contempt for the new "advertiser-friendly" approach known to all, including the advertising manager Fred Thomas, as he headed down the hallway back to the newsroom. Lisa Lawrence, his managing editor, quietly agreed but pointed out that advertisers were readers too, and the newspaper had to listen to all its constituencies. "If we don't handle this carefully, we'll have Fisher and Thomas in here dictating to us what we can write and what we can't." Lawrence has worked with Rick since he first came to the paper, and even though the two have had their share of conflicts, the relationship is primarily one of mutual respect and trust. "Let's just be careful," she emphasized. "Read the stories about big advertisers a little more carefully, make sure we can defend whatever we print, and it will all work out. I know this blurring of the line between advertising and editorial rubs you the wrong way, but Thomas is a reasonable man. We just need to keep him in the loop."

Late that afternoon, Rick received a story from one of his corresponding reporters that had been in the works for a couple of days. East Tennessee Healthcorp (ETH), which operated a string of health clinics throughout the region, was closing three of its rural clinics because of mounting financial woes. The reporter, Elisabeth Fraley, who lived in one of the communities, had learned about the closings from her neighbor, who worked as an accountant for ETH, before the announcement had been made just this afternoon. Fraley had written a compelling human-interest story about how the closings would leave people in two counties with essentially no access to health care, while clinics in larger towns that didn't really need them were being kept open. She had carefully interviewed both former patients of the clinics as well as ETH employees, including the director of one of the clinics and two high-level managers at the corporate office, and she had carefully documented her sources. After this morning's meeting, Rick knew he should run the story by Lisa Lawrence, since East Tennessee Healthcorp was one of the Tribune's biggest advertisers, but Lawrence had left for the day. And he simply couldn't bring himself to consult with the advertising department—that political b.s. was for Lawrence to handle. If he held the story for Lawrence's approval, it wouldn't make the Sunday edition. His only other option was to write a brief story simply reporting the closings and

*This case was inspired by G. Pascal Zachary, "Many Journalists See a Growing Reluctance to Criticize Advertisers," *The Wall Street Journal*, 6 February 1992, A1, A9; and G. Bruce Knecht, "Retail Chains Emerge as Advance Arbiters of Magazine Content," *The Wall Street Journal*, 22 October 1997, A1, A13.

leaving out the human interest aspect. Rick was sure the major papers from Knoxville and other nearby cities would have the report in their Sunday papers, but none of them would have the time to develop as comprehensive and interesting an account as Fraley had presented. With a few quick strokes of the pen to make some minor editorial changes, Rick sent the story to production.

When he arrived at work the next day, Rick was called immediately to the publisher's office. He knew it was bad news for Fisher to be in on a Sunday. After some general yelling and screaming, Rick learned that tens of thousands of copies of the Sunday paper had been destroyed and a new edition printed. The advertising manager had called Fisher at home in the wee hours of Sunday morning and informed him of the ETH story, which was appearing the same day the corporation was running a full page ad touting its

service to the small towns and rural communities of East Tennessee.

"The story's accurate, and I assumed you'd want to take advantage of a chance to scoop the big papers," Rick began, but Fisher cut his argument short with his favorite line: "When you assume," he screamed, "you make an ass out of you and me. You could have just reported the basic facts without implying that the company doesn't care about the people of this region. The next time something like this happens, you'll find yourself and your reporters standing in the unemployment line!"

Rick had heard it before, but somehow this time he almost believed it. "What happened to the days when the primary purpose of a newspaper was to present the news?" Rick mumbled. "Now, it seems we have to dance to the tune played by the ad department."

Case for Analysis   *Pierre Dux**

Pierre Dux sat quietly in his office considering the news. A third appointment to regional management had been announced and, once again, the promotion he had expected had been given to someone else. The explanations seemed insufficient this time. Clearly, this signaled the end to his career at INCO. Only one year ago, the company president had arrived at Dux's facility with national press coverage to publicize the success of the innovation he had designed and implemented in the management of manufacturing operations. The intervening year had brought improved operating results and further positive publicity for the corporation but a string of personal disappointments for Pierre Dux.

Four years earlier, the INCO manufacturing plant had been one of the least productive of the thirteen facilities operating in Europe. Absenteeism and high employee turnover were symptoms of the low morale among the work group. These factors were reflected in mediocre production levels and the worst quality record in INCO. Pierre Dux had been in his current position one year and had derived his only satisfaction from the fact that these poor results might have been worse had he not instituted minor reforms in organizational communication. These allowed workers and supervisors to vent their concerns and frustrations. Although nothing substantial had changed during that first year, operating results had stabilized, ending a period of rapid decline. But this "honeymoon" was ending. The expectation of significant change was growing, particularly among workers who had been vocal in expressing their dissatisfaction and suggesting concrete proposals for change.

The change process, which had begun three years before, had centered on a redesign of production operations from a single machine-paced assembly line to a number of semi-autonomous assembly teams. Although the change had been referred to as the INCO "Volvo project" or "INCO's effort at Japanese-style management," it had really been neither of these. Rather, it had been the brainchild of a group of managers, led by Dux, who believed that both productivity and working conditions in the plant could be improved through a single effort. Of course, members of the group had visited other so-called "innovative production facilities," but the new work groups and job classifications had been designed with the particular products and technology at INCO in mind.

After lengthy discussions among the management group, largely dedicated to reaching agreement on the general direction that the new project would take, the actual design began to emerge. Equally lengthy discussions (often referred to as negotiations) with members of the workforce, supervisors, and representatives of the local unions were part of the design process. The first restructuring into smaller work groups was tried in an experimental project that received tentative approval from top management in INCO headquarters and a "wait and see" response from the union. The strongest initial resistance had come from the plant engineers. They were sold neither on the new structure nor on the process of involving the workforce in the design of operating equipment and production methods. Previously, the engineering group had itself fulfilled these functions, and it felt the problems now present were a result of a lack of skill among employees or managerial unwillingness to make the system work.

The experiment was staffed by volunteers supported by a few of the better trained workers in the plant. The latter were necessary to ensure a start-up of the new equipment, which had been modified from the existing technology on the assembly line.

The initial experiment met with limited success. Although the group was able to meet the productivity levels of the existing line within a few weeks, critics of the new plan attributed the minor success to the unrepresentative nature of the experimental group or the newness of the equipment on which they were working. However, even this limited success attracted the attention of numerous people at INCO headquarters and in other plants. All were interested in visiting the new "experiment." Visits soon became a major distraction, and Dux declared a temporary halt to permit the project to proceed, although this produced some muttering at headquarters about his "secretive" and "uncooperative" behavior.

Because of the experiment's success, Dux and his staff prepared to convert the entire production

*This case was prepared by Michael Brimm, Associate Professor of INSEAD. It is intended to be used as a basis for class discussion rather than to illustrate either effective or ineffective handling of an administrative situation. Copyright © 1983 INSEAD Foundation, Fontainebleau, France. Revised 1987.

operation to the new system. The enthusiasm of workers in the plant grew as training for the changeover proceeded. In fact, a group of production workers asked to help with the installation of the new equipment as a means of learning more about its operation.

Dux and his staff were surprised at the difficulties encountered at this phase. Headquarters seemed to drag their feet in approving the necessary funding for the changeover. Even after the funding was approved, there was a stream of challenges to minor parts of the plan. "Can't you lay the workers off during the changeover?" "Why use workers on overtime to do the changeover when you could hire temporary workers more cheaply?" These criticisms reflected a lack of understanding of the basic operating principles of the new system, and Dux rejected them.

The conversion of the entire assembly line to work groups was finally achieved, with the local management group making few concessions from their stated plans. The initial change and the first days of operation were filled with crisis. The design process had not anticipated many of the problems that arose with full scale operations. However, Dux was pleased to see managers, staff, and workers clustered together at the trouble areas, fine-tuning the design when problems arose. Just as the start-up finally appeared to be moving forward, a change in product specifications from a headquarters group dictated additional changes in the design of the assembly process. The new change was handled quickly and with enthusiasm by the workforce.

While the period was exhausting and seemingly endless to those who felt responsible for the change, the new design took only six months to reach normal operating levels (one year had been forecast as the time needed to reach that level—without the added requirement for a change in product specification).

Within a year, Dux was secure that he had a major success on his hands. Productivity and product quality measures for the plant had greatly improved. In this relatively short period his plant had moved from the worst, according to these indicators, to the third most productive in the INCO system. Absenteeism had dropped only slightly, but turnover had been reduced substantially. Morale was not measured formally but was considered by all members of the management team to be greatly improved. Now, after three years of full operations, the plant was considered the most productive in the entire INCO system.

Dux was a bit surprised when no other facility in INCO initiated a similar effort or called upon him for help. Increases of the early years had leveled off, with the peak being achieved in the early part of year three. Now the facility seemed to have found a new equilibrium. The calm of smoother operations had been a welcome relief to many who had worked so hard to launch the new design. For Dux it provided the time to reflect on his accomplishment and think about his future career.

It was in this context that he considered the news that he had once again been bypassed for promotion to the next level in the INCO hierarchy.

NOTES

1. This example is based on an incident reported in Monica Langley, "Columbia Tells Doctors at Hospital to End Their Outside Practice," *The Wall Street Journal*, 2 May 1997, A1, A6.

2. Lee G. Bolman and Terrence E. Deal, *Reframing Organizations: Artistry, Choice, and Leadership* (San Francisco: Jossey-Bass, 1991).

3. Paul M. Terry, "Conflict Management," *The Journal of Leadership Studies* 3, No. 2 (1996), 3–21; and Kathleen M. Eisenhardt, Jean L. Kahwajy, and L. J. Bourgeois III, "How Management Teams Can Have a Good Fight," *Harvard Business Review* (July–August 1997): 77–85.

4. Clayton T. Alderfer and Ken K. Smith, "Studying Intergroup Relations Imbedded in

Organizations," *Administrative Science Quarterly* 27 (1982): 35–65.

5. Muzafer Sherif, "Experiments in Group Conflict," *Scientific American* 195 (1956): 54–58; Edgar H. Schein, *Organizational Psychology*, 3d ed. (Englewood Cliffs, N.J.: Prentice-Hall, 1980).

6. M. Afzalur Rahim, "A Strategy for Managing Conflict in Complex Organizations," *Human Relations* 38 (1985): 81–89; Kenneth Thomas, "Conflict and Conflict Management," in M. D. Dunnette, ed., *Handbook of Industrial and Organizational Psychology* (Chicago: Rand McNally, 1976); Stuart M. Schmidt and Thomas A. Kochan, "Conflict: Toward Conceptual

Clarity," *Administrative Science Quarterly* 13 (1972): 359–70.

7. L. David Brown, "Managing Conflict among Groups," in David A. Kolb, Irwin M. Rubin, and James M. McIntyre, eds., *Organizational Psychology: A Book of Readings* (Englewood Cliffs, N.J.: Prentice-Hall, 1979), 377–89; Robert W. Ruekert and Orville C. Walker, Jr., "Interactions between Marketing and R&D Departments in Implementing Different Business Strategies," *Strategic Management Journal* 8 (1987): 233–48.

8. Amy Barrett, "Indigestion at Taco Bell," *Business Week,* 14 December 1994, 66–67; Greg Burns, "Fast-Food Fight," *Business Week,* 2 June 1997, 34–36; and Nicole Harris, "Flying into a Rage," *Business Week,* 27 April 1998; David Whitford, "Arthur, Arthur," *Fortune,* 10 November 1997, 1690–178; and Elizabeth MacDonald and Joseph B. White, "How Consulting Issue is Threatening to Rend Andersen Worldwide," *The Wall Street Journal,* 4 February 1998, A1, A10.

9. Thomas A. Kochan, George P. Huber, and L. L. Cummings, "Determinants of Intraorganizational Conflict in Collective Bargaining in the Public Sector," *Administrative Science Quarterly* 20 (1975): 10–23.

10. Victoria L. Crittenden, Lorraine R. Gardiner, and Antonie Stam, "Reducing Conflict between Marketing and Manufacturing," *Industrial Marketing Management* 22 (1993): 299–309; Benson S. Shapiro, "Can Marketing and Manufacturing Coexist?" *Harvard Business Review* 55 (September-October 1977): 104–14.

11. Eric H. Neilsen, "Understanding and Managing Intergroup Conflict," in Jay W. Lorsch and Paul R. Lawrence, eds., *Managing Group and Intergroup Relations* (Homewood, Ill.: Irwin and Dorsey, 1972), 329–43; Richard E. Walton and John M. Dutton, "The Management of Interdepartmental Conflict: A Model and Review," *Administrative Science Quarterly* 14 (1969): 73–84.

12. Jay W. Lorsch, "Introduction to the Structural Design of Organizations," in Gene W. Dalton, Paul R. Lawrence, and Jay W. Lorsch, eds., *Organization Structure and Design* (Homewood, Ill.: Irwin and Dorsey, 1970), 5.

13. Morty Lefkoe, "Why So Many Mergers Fail," *Fortune,* 20 June 1987, 113–14; Afsaneh Nahavandi and Ali R. Malekzadeh, "Acculturation in Mergers and Acquisitions," *Academy of Management Review* (1988): 79–90.

14. James D. Thompson, *Organizations in Action* (New York: McGraw-Hill, 1967), 54–56.

15. Walton and Dutton, "Management of Interdepartmental Conflict."

16. Joseph McCann and Jay R. Galbraith, "Interdepartmental Relationships," in Paul C. Nystrom and William H. Starbuck, eds., *Handbook of Organizational Design,* vol. 2 (New York: Oxford University Press, 1981), 60–84.

17. Roderick M. Cramer, "Intergroup Relations and Organizational Dilemmas: The Role of Categorization Processes," in L. L. Cummings and Barry M. Staw, eds., *Research in Organizational Behavior,* vol. 13 (New York: JAI Press, 1991), 191–228; Neilsen, "Understanding and Managing Intergroup Conflict"; Louis R. Pondy, "Organizational Conflict: Concepts and Models," *Administrative Science Quarterly* 12 (1968): 296–320.

18. Jeffrey Pfeffer, *Power in Organizations* (Marshfield, Mass.: Pitman, 1981).

19. Examples are Robert Greene and Joost Elffers, *The 48 Laws of Power* (New York: Viking, 1999); Jeffrey J. Fox, *How to Become CEO* (New York: Hyperion, 1999).

20. John R. P. French, Jr., and Bertram Raven, "The Bases of Social Power," in *Group Dynamics,* D. Cartwright and A. F. Zander, eds. (Evanston, Ill.: Row Peterson, 1960), 607–23.

21. Ran Lachman, "Power from What? A Reexamination of Its Relationships with Structural Conditions," *Administrative Science Quarterly* 34 (1989): 231–51; Daniel J. Brass, "Being in the Right Place: A Structural Analysis of Individual Influence in an Organization," *Administrative Science Quarterly* 29 (1984): 518–39.

22. Robert A. Dahl, "The Concept of Power," *Behavioral Science* 2 (1957): 201–15.

23. W. Graham Astley and Paramjit S. Sachdeva, "Structural Sources of Intraorganizational Power: A Theoretical Synthesis," *Academy of Management Review* 9 (1984): 104–13; Abraham Kaplan, "Power in Perspective," in Robert L. Kahn and Elise Boulding, eds., *Power and Conflict in Organizations* (London: Tavistock, 1964), 11–32.

24. Gerald R. Salancik and Jeffrey Pfeffer, "The Bases and Use of Power in Organizational Decision-Making: The Case of the University," *Administrative Science Quarterly* 19 (1974): 453–73.

25. Richard M. Emerson, "Power-Dependence Relations," *American Sociological Review* 27 (1962): 31–41.

26. Rosabeth Moss Kanter, "Power Failure in Management Circuits," *Harvard Business Review* (July-August 1979): 65–75.

27. Michael Warshaw, "The Good Guy's Guide to Office Politics," *Fast Company* (April–May 1998): 157–78.

28. A. J. Grimes, "Authority, Power, Influence, and Social Control: A Theoretical Synthesis," *Academy of Management Review* 3 (1978): 724–35.

29. Russ Baker, "Edged Out," *Inc.,* August 1998, 69–77.

30. Astley and Sachdeva, "Structural Sources of Intraorganizational Power."

31. Jeffrey Pfeffer, *Managing with Power: Politics and Influence in Organizations* (Boston: Harvard Business School Press, 1992).

32. Robert L. Peabody, "Perceptions of Organizational Authority," *Administrative Science Quarterly* 6 (1962): 479.

33. Richard S. Blackburn, "Lower Participant Power: Toward a Conceptual Integration," *Academy of Management Review* 6 (1981): 127–31.

34. Kanter, "Power Failure in Management Circuits," 70.

35. Jeffrey Pfeffer, *Power in Organizations* (Marshfield, Mass.: Pitman, 1981).

36. Erik W. Larson and Jonathan B. King, "The Systemic Distortion of Information: An Ongoing Challenge to Management," *Organizational Dynamics* 24, no. 3 (Winter 1996): 49–61; Thomas H. Davenport, Robert G. Eccles, and Lawrence Prusak, "Information Politics," *Sloan Management Review* (Fall 1992): 53–65.

37. Andrew M. Pettigrew, *The Politics of Organizational Decision-Making* (London: Tavistock, 1973).

38. Astley and Sachdeva, "Structural Sources of Intraorganizational Power"; Noel M. Tichy and Charles Fombrun, "Network Analysis in Organizational Settings," *Human Relations* 32 (1979): 923–65.

39. Eryn Brown, "9 Ways to Win on the Web," *Fortune,* 24 May 1999, 112–25.

40. Warshaw, "The Good Guy's Guide to Office Politics."

41. Charles Perrow, "Departmental Power and Perspective in Industrial Firms," in Mayer N. Zald, ed., *Power in Organizations* (Nashville, Tenn.: Vanderbilt University Press, 1970), 59–89.

42. D. J. Hickson, C. R. Hinings, C. A. Lee, R. E. Schneck, and J. M. Pennings, "A Strategic Contingencies Theory of Intraorganizational Power," *Administrative Science Quarterly* 16 (1971): 216–29; Gerald R. Salancik and Jeffrey Pfeffer, "Who Gets Power—and How They Hold onto It: A Strategic-Contingency Model of Power," *Organizational Dynamics* (Winter 1977): 3–21.

43. Pfeffer, *Managing with Power*; Salancik and Pfeffer, "Who Gets Power"; C. R. Hinings, D. J. Hickson, J. M. Pennings, and R. E. Schneck, "Structural Conditions of Intraorganizational Power," *Administrative Science Quarterly* 19 (1974): 22–44.

44. Carol Stoak Saunders, "The Strategic Contingencies Theory of Power: Multiple Perspectives," *Journal of Management Studies* 27 (1990): 1–18; Warren Boeker, "The Development and Institutionalization of Sub-Unit Power in Organizations," *Administrative Science Quarterly* 34 (1989): 388–510; Irit Cohen and Ran Lachman, "The Generality of the Strategic Contingencies Approach to Sub-Unit Power," *Organizational Studies* 9 (1988): 371–91.

45. Emerson, "Power-Dependence Relations."

46. Michel Crozier, *The Bureaucratic Phenomenon* (Chicago: University of Chicago Press, 1964).

47. Pfeffer, *Managing with Power.*

48. Jeffrey Pfeffer and Gerald Salancik, "Organizational Decision-Making as a Political Process: The Case of a University Budget," *Administrative Science Quarterly* (1974): 135–51.

49. Salancik and Pfeffer, "Bases and Use of Power in Organizational Decision-Making," 470.

50. Hickson, et al., "Strategic Contingencies Theory."

51. Pettigrew, *Politics of Organizational Decision-Making.*

52. Hickson, et al., "Strategic Contingencies Theory."

53. Ibid.

54. G. Bruce Knecht, "Retail Chains Emerge as Advance Arbiters of Magazine Content," *The Wall Street Journal*, 22 October 1997, A1, A13.

55. Jeffrey Gantz and Victor V. Murray, "Experience of Workplace Politics," *Academy of Management Journal* 23 (1980): 237–51; Dan L. Madison, Robert W. Allen, Lyman W. Porter, Patricia A. Renwick, and Bronston T. Mayes, "Organizational Politics: An Exploration of Managers' Perception," *Human Relations* 33 (1980): 79–100.

56. Gerald R. Ferris and K. Michele Kacmar, "Perceptions of Organizational Politics," *Journal of Management* 18 (1992): 93–116; Parmod Kumar and Rehana Ghadially, "Organizational Politics and its Effects on Members of Organizations," *Human Relations* 42 (1989): 305–14; Donald J. Vredenburgh and John G. Maurer, "A Process Framework of Organizational Politics," *Human Relations* 37 (1984): 47–66; Gerald R. Ferris, Dwight D. Frink, Maria Carmen Galang, Jing Zhou, Michele Kacmar, and Jack L. Howard, "Perceptions of Organizational Politics: Prediction, Stress-Related Implications, and Outcomes," *Human Relations* 49, no. 2 (1996): 233–66.

57. Ferris, et. al., "Perceptions of Organizational Politics: Prediction, Stress-Related Implications, and Outcomes"; John J. Voyer, "Coercive Organizational Politics and Organizational Outcomes: An Interpretive Study," *Organization Science* 5, no. 1 (February 1994): 72–85; James W. Dean, Jr., and Mark P. Sharfman, "Does Decision Process Matter? A Study of Strategic Decision-Making Effectiveness," *Academy of Management Journal* 39, no. 2 (1996): 368–96.

58. Jeffrey Pfeffer, *Managing With Power: Politics and Influence in Organizations* (Boston, Mass.: Harvard Business School Press, 1992).

59. Amos Drory and Tsilia Romm, "The Definition of Organizational Politics: A Review," *Human Relations* 43 (1990): 1133–54; Vredenburgh and Maurer, "A Process Framework of Organizational Politics."

60. Pfeffer, *Power in Organizations,* p. 70.

61. Madison, et al., "Organizational Politics"; Jay R. Galbraith, *Organizational Design* (Reading, Mass.: Addison-Wesley, 1977).

62. Gantz and Murray, "Experience of Workplace Politics"; Pfeffer, *Power in Organizations.*

63. Daniel J. Brass and Marlene E. Burkhardt, "Potential Power and Power Use: An Investigation of Structure and Behavior," *Academy of Management Journal* 38 (1993): 441–70.

64. Hickson, et al., "A Strategic Contingencies Theory."

65. Pfeffer, *Power in Organizations.*

66. Ibid.

67. V. Dallas Merrell, *Huddling: The Informal Way to Management Success* (New York: AMACON, 1979).

68. Vredenburgh and Maurer, "A Process Framework of Organizational Politics."

69. Ibid.

70. Pfeffer, *Power in Organizations.*

71. Ibid.

72. Ibid.

73. Kanter, "Power Failure in Management Circuits"; Pfeffer, *Power in Organizations.*

74. Based on John P. Kotter, "How to Win Friends and Influence Comanagers," *Canadian Business,* October 1985, 29–30, 100–107.

75. Robert R. Blake and Jane S. Mouton, "Overcoming Group Warfare," *Harvard Business Review* (November–December 1984): 98–108.

76. Blake and Mouton, "Overcoming Group Warfare"; Paul R. Lawrence and Jay W. Lorsch, "New Management Job: The Integrator," *Harvard Business Review* 45 (November–December 1967): 142–51.

77. David Woodruff, "Saturn: Labor's Love Lost?" *Business Week,* 8 February 1993, 122–24; David Woodruff, James Treece, Sunita Wadekar Bhargava, and Karen Lowry, "Saturn," *Business Week,* 17 August 1992, 87–91.

78. Aaron Bernstein, "Look Who's Pushing Productivity," *Business Week,* 7 April 1997, 72–75.

79. Ibid.

80. Wilson Harrell, "Inspire Action—What Really Motivates Your People to Excel?" *Success,* September 1995, 100.

81. Robert R. Blake, Herbert A. Shepard, and Jane S. Mouton, *Managing Intergroup Conflict in Industry* (Houston: Gulf Publishing, 1964); and Doug Stewart, "'Expand the Pie Before You Divvy It Up,'" *Smithsonian,* November 1997, 78-90.

82. Ron Shapiro and Mark Jankowski, with James Dale, *The Power of Nice—How to Negotiate So Everyone Wins, Especially You!* (John Wiley & Sons, 1998).

83. Kenneth Labich, "Fasten Your Seat Belts," *Fortune,* 10 May 1999, 114–18.

84. Robert R. Blake and Jane S. Mouton, "Overcoming Group Warfare"; Schein, *Organizational Psychology*; Blake, Shepard, and Mouton, *Managing Intergroup Conflict in Industry*; Richard E. Walton, *Interpersonal Peacemaking: Confrontation and Third-Party Consultations* (Reading, Mass.: Addison-Wesley, 1969).

85. Mark S. Plovnick, Ronald E. Fry, and W. Warner Burke, *Organizational Development* (Boston: Little,

Brown, 1982), 89–93; Schein, *Organizational Psychology,* 177–78, reprinted by permission of Prentice-Hall, Inc.

86. Neilsen, "Understanding and Managing Intergroup Conflict"; Joseph McCann and Jay R. Galbraith, "Interdepartmental Relations."

87. Neilsen, "Understanding and Managing Intergroup Conflict"; McCann and Galbraith, "Interdepartmental Relations"; Sherif et al., *Intergroup Conflict and Cooperation.*

88. Dean Tjosvold, Valerie Dann, and Choy Wong, "Managing Conflict between Departments to Serve Customers," *Human Relations* 45 (1992): 1035–54.

89. Gina Imperato, "Harley Shifts Gears," *Fast Company* (June–July 1997): 104–13.

Contemporary Trends in Organization Design

CHAPTER 13

A LOOK INSIDE

Kalahari Bushmen

For hundreds of years, the Kalahari Bushmen were nomadic hunters and foragers in the harsh, unpredictable Southern African desert. The Bushmen developed the skills to find water during a drought, to live on reptiles and plants in the absence of game, and to fashion bows and arrows from limited sources. They traveled in bands bound together by ties of kinship and friendship. Their mobility and few possessions enabled Bushmen to switch easily to more successful bands, in this way capitalizing on success wherever it was found over a wide geographical area. The flexible band system was enhanced by values of equality, sharing, and gift giving. A hunter's kill would be used to feed neighbors, who would later reciprocate. Gift giving meant that useful artifacts and utensils were widely shared. Hunting camps had grass huts facing the center of a circle where the cooking hearths were hubs of continuous discussion and social exchanges. The Bushmen also bonded through a deep culture in their camps of shared mythology, stories, and dances.

Enter civilization. In recent years, exposure to material wealth has fostered a transformation. Bushmen now accumulate possessions, which hamper mobility, forcing a lifestyle shift from foraging to farming. A new community structure has evolved, with families living in separate, permanent huts. Entrances are located for privacy, and hearths have been moved inside. Survival skills have deteriorated, with bows and arrows produced only for curio shops. Without sharing and communication, a hierarchy of authority—the chief—is used to resolve disputes. Tension and conflicts have increased, and the tribe's ability to handle drought and disaster today is nonexistent. No longer are there shared stories and mythology that bind the tribespeople into a community and transfer knowledge of the traditional skills and abilities that enabled the Bushmen to thrive in an unpredictable environment.[1]

The emerging herder-farmer society resembles a bureaucracy that excels in a stable, safe environment, leaving the Bushmen vulnerable to sudden environmental changes. The hunter-forager society resembles today's entrepreneurial and learning organization, based on little hierarchy, equality of rewards, shared culture and knowledge, and a flowing, adaptable structure designed to seize opportunities and handle crises.

Many organizations in industrialized societies have evolved toward bureaucratic forms, as discussed in Chapter 8. However, in the face of complex, shifting environments, these organizations no longer work. The hunter-forager society of the Kalahari Bushmen is a metaphor for the learning organization that many companies want to become. Chapter 1 presented an overview of the characteristics of a learning organization, and throughout this book we have examined ways in which organizations are transforming themselves into fluid learning systems. Chapter 3 discussed trends toward greater cross-functional information sharing and the shift toward the horizontal organization in which teams of employees are organized around core work processes. In Chapter 5, we looked at how organizations are increasingly thinking of themselves as part of a larger ecosystem and developing relationships that make the whole system stronger. Chapter 7 discussed the trend toward knowledge sharing, which attempts to promote a kind of open dialogue and storytelling similar to that once common to the Kalahari Bushmen. Other chapters have examined how organizations are changing their technologies, strategies, and cultures to support increased learning, knowledge sharing, and adaptability.

PURPOSE OF THIS CHAPTER

This chapter brings together many of the ideas touched on throughout the book and discusses some of the contemporary trends that are having an effect as organizations cope with tremendous upheaval and struggle through the transition to a new century. We will first describe the enormous impact of globalization on today's companies and discuss how managers can help their organizations achieve excellence in this highly competitive environment. The chapter will then look at specific organization designs for global advantage. Subsequent sections will examine the trend toward empowerment, which is essential for a learning organization on both the domestic and global scale, and how managers can help lead the transformation to a learning organization. Finally, the chapter will discuss coping with organizational decline and the impact of top leadership on organizational performance.

THE GLOBAL ENVIRONMENT

As recently as twenty years ago, many organizations remained insulated from foreign competition. However, the rapid changes of the 1980s and 1990s have led to the development of a highly competitive global economy where worldwide events that change rapidly and unpredictably are forcing companies in all industries to rethink their approach to organization design. Extraordinary advancements in communications and technology have created a new, highly competitive global landscape for organizations. Products can be made and sold anywhere in the world, communications are instant, and product development and life cycles are shorter than ever before. Technology is rapidly replacing manual labor, and the ability to create and leverage knowledge is becoming more important than the control of capital assets.[2]

It is hard to deny the impact of these changes. A college student in Austin, Texas, can sit at her computer and communicate instantly with someone in Japan or South America, research a class project at the Library of Congress in Washington, D. C., and order products made by a company in Germany and have them delivered to her door in a matter of days. Burger King is owned by a British firm, and McDonald's sells hamburgers on every continent except Antarctica. France's Alcatel recently purchased DSC Communications Corp., with headquarters in Texas, and U.S.-based Chrysler merged with Germany's Daimler-Benz. So-called American companies such as General Motors, Exxon, and Coca-Cola rely on international business for a substantial portion of their sales and profits. For example, Whirlpool Corp.'s Brazilian affiliates contributed $78 million to 1997 earnings, compared to only an $11 million operating profit for the parent company, based in Benton Harbor, Michigan.[3]

No company is isolated from global influence. Newly industrialized countries such as Korea, Taiwan, and Spain are fast-growing and rapidly becoming industrialized. Their companies produce low-cost, high-quality commodities and are moving into high-value items such as automobiles and high-technology electronic goods. The shift toward market economies in China, India, eastern Europe, and the former Soviet republics is producing more sources of goods, potential new markets, and, to some extent, an unpredictable future about how these countries will affect the global economy.[4] Even more uncertainty is being created by international trading blocs such as the North American Free Trade Agreement (NAFTA), the Association of Southeast Asian Nations (ASEAN), and the European Union, which have significantly reduced tariffs and barriers to trade. These power blocs will continue to reshape the world economy and will likely mean the end of U.S. domination of international trade policy.

For organizations, these events create tremendous economic volatility: No one knows whether oil will cost fifteen or thirty dollars a barrel next year. Likewise, currency values fluctuate based on inflation, trade balances, and capital investments over which no single country has control. Products we buy today, such as an IBM PC or Black & Decker appliance, may include components from a dozen nations. No company or country can provide global economic leadership; every company and country is subordinate to larger economic forces.

No wonder we've seen the dramatic restructuring of traditional industries in the United States through leveraged buyouts, mergers, and breakups. These companies were striving for greater efficiency within an increasingly turbulent and competitive international environment. In addition, rapidly growing industries such as information technology and biotechnology are fostering a new industrial revolution. People who grew up feeling comfortable and secure working for a manufacturing firm appreciate just how elusive stability and security are in the new world order.

ATTRIBUTES OF ORGANIZATIONAL EXCELLENCE

There are a number of ways in which organizations are coping with the reality of increased global competitiveness. One book that is concerned with how companies can remain competitive in a changing environment, *Built to Last: Successful Habits of Visionary Companies,* argues that there are certain "timeless fundamentals" that help companies achieve and sustain long-term organizational excellence.[5] Other publications, such as *The New Pioneers,* which spotlights companies that are thriving in today's turbulent environment, and *The Horizontal Organization,* about how companies are organizing work around core processes, have also added new understanding about organizational excellence.[6] Some of the major ideas about excellence are summarized in Exhibit 13.1. They are organized into four categories: strategic orientation, top management, organization design, and corporate culture.

1. *Strategic Orientation.* Four characteristics identified in corporate research pertain to an organization's strategic orientation:

   - Being close to the customer
   - Providing fast response
   - Having a clear business focus and goals
   - Establishing interorganizational linkages

   Excellent organizations are customer driven. Organizations are increasingly looking at customers as their most important stakeholders, and a dominant value is satisfying customer needs.[7] For example, John Chambers, CEO

EXHIBIT 13.1   *Factors Associated with Organization Excellence*

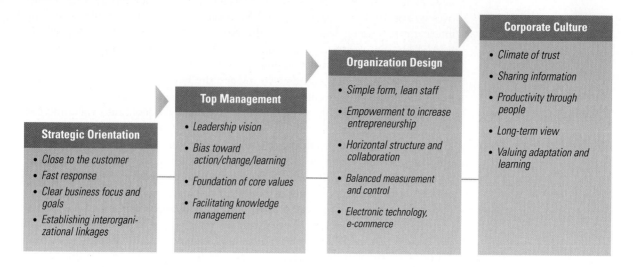

of Cisco Systems, spends about 55 percent of his time with customers and receives voice-mail updates every night (365 nights a year) on key clients.[8] As we saw in Chapter 7, many organizations are using information technology to stay close to the customer, such as by tracking customer preferences in a database or providing a Web page where customers can get detailed information about products and services and send e-mail messages directly to company representatives.

A fast response means that successful companies respond quickly to problems and opportunities. In learning organizations, for example, information is widely shared so that all employees can act quickly on problems and opportunities. Successful organizations lead rather than follow. They take chances. Employees are encouraged to experiment, which leads to continuous improvement. Chapter 10 discussed how some companies set up seed funds for employees with promising ideas for new products or technologies in order to encourage creativity and spur innovation.

Moreover, to sustain excellence, companies need to have a clear focus and goals, as discussed in Chapter 2. They know that to be successful, they should do what they do best. At Gerber, for example, the motto is "Babies are our business . . . our only business." Kodak, Coca-Cola, and Nokia have sold off unrelated product lines to focus their energies on the core business.

Establishing interorganizational linkages is a fourth key characteristic of excellent organizations. As described in Chapter 5, interorganizational relationships are becoming critical to the success of most organizations in a world of rapidly changing technology and growing global competition. In learning organizations, strategy actually emerges from collaboration with other companies, which may include suppliers, customers, and even competitors. Interorganizational linkages can help companies exploit new technologies, develop products faster, and serve larger markets. Cisco's partnership with Microsoft to develop a technology that makes networks more intelligent enabled them to get the product out and build the market faster for both organizations.[9]

2. *Top Management.* Management techniques and processes are another dimension of excellent organizations. Four elements related to managers are part of a highly successful company:

- Leadership vision
- A bias toward action, change, and learning
- Promoting a foundation of core values
- Facilitating knowledge management

To achieve and maintain excellence, an organization needs a special kind of leadership vision that provides leadership of the organization, not just leadership within the organization. Leaders must provide a vision of what the organization can be and what it stands for; they give employees a sense of direction, shared purpose, and meaning that persists despite changes in product line or manager turnover.

Managers and employees in excellent organizations are also poised for constant change and learning. They are oriented toward action—they don't talk problems to death before making decisions or creating solutions. In learning organizations, all employees are constantly working with each other and with customers to find new and better ways of doing things. Successful companies "do it, try it, fix it." The decision philosophy at PepsiCo., for example, is "Ready, Fire, Aim."[10]

Yet decisions are not based on thin air: top managers support and promote a core ideology that permeates organizational life and guides all decision making. The best companies, like Johnson & Johnson, Wal-Mart, and 3M, are guided by values and a sense of purpose that go beyond just making money. For example, the well-known Johnson & Johnson Credo, the code of ethics that tells employees what to care about and in what order, puts profits dead last—yet the company has never lost money since going public in 1944.[11] At McDonald's no exceptions are made to the core values of quality, service, cleanliness, and value; yet in other areas, employees are free to experiment, to be flexible, and to take risks in ways that can help the company reach its goals.

Another characteristic of successful organizations is that top managers recognize knowledge as a key corporate asset and work to facilitate the sharing of knowledge across the organization and the creation of new knowledge, as described in Chapter 7. KPMG Peat Marwick's interactive computer system, called Knowledge Manager, enables each consultant to draw on the knowledge and experience of 75,000 KPMG professionals around the world. Besides locating explicit knowledge about client experiences, proposals, methodologies, and best practices, consultants can use Knowledge Manager to post a request for help on a specific project and get immediate feedback from other consultants, who share their own experiences and know-how. Consultants arrive at deeper insights by communicating back and forth about problems.[12]

3. *Organization Design.* Excellent organizations are characterized by five design attributes:

- Simple form and lean staff
- Empowerment to increase entrepreneurship
- Horizontal structure and collaboration
- A balance between financial and nonfinancial measures of performance
- The use of electronic technology and e-commerce

Simple form and lean staff means that the underlying form and systems of excellent organizations are elegantly simple and few personnel are in staff positions. There is little bureaucracy. Large companies are divided into small divisions for simplicity and adaptability.

In addition, employees are given the autonomy and information needed to make decisions and take action without the approval of management. *Empowerment* of employees, which will be discussed in detail later in this chapter, is essential to the constant change and learning that mark successful companies. Creativity and innovation by employees at all levels are encouraged and rewarded, and organizational units are kept small to create a sense of belonging and shared problem solving.

Excellent organizations foster high levels of horizontal communication and collaboration. Some, particularly learning organizations, shift to horizontal structures that emphasize collaborative teams of employees organized around core processes, as described in Chapter 3. Others use cross-functional teams, task forces, and project managers to encourage horizontal communication and collaboration.

Successful organizations also measure more than the bottom line, recognizing that excellence depends on a diverse set of competencies and values. Balancing financial and nonfinancial measures provides a better picture of the company's performance and also helps managers align all employees toward key strategic goals.[13] As discussed in Chapter 8, companies such as Amoco Corporation and Nationwide Financial Services are using the balanced scorecard approach to link employee goals and activities to strategy. The balanced scorecard provides a new way to look at what drives the success of the organization and recognizes the importance of key competencies such as knowledge retention, customer satisfaction, and innovation and change. One study found that companies that carefully track these "soft" competencies along with "hard" data like financial performance and operating efficiency were more successful over the long term.[14]

Finally, today's successful organizations are making effective use of electronic technology and e-commerce, as described in Chapter 7 and throughout this book. Competitive companies such as Charles Schwab set up autonomous e-commerce divisions that are not constrained by the bureaucracy or competing needs of the traditional organization. Others use electronic technology to tie together distinct, autonomous companies into a network organization, or to link far-flung global divisions for greater collaboration and speed. Some scholars have suggested that twenty-first century organizations may come to resemble amoebas—collections of workers connected electronically who are divided into ever-changing teams that can best exploit the organization's unique resources, capabilities, and core competencies.[15] As described in this chapter's Taking the Lead box, two young advertising executives used new ideas about organization design to redefine what it means to be an ad agency.

4. *Corporate Culture.* Companies throughout the United States and Canada are discovering that employee commitment is a vital component of organization success. Excellent companies manage to harness employee energy and enthusiasm. They do so by:

- Creating a climate of trust
- Sharing information
- Encouraging productivity through people

- Taking a long-term view
- Valuing adaptation and learning

A climate of trust is necessary so that employees can deal openly and honestly with one another. Collaboration across departments requires trust. Managers and workers must trust one another to work together in joint problem solving. At Ford Motor Company, where workers were historically suspicious of management, a new climate of trust has led to increased productivity and reduced costs.[16]

Rather than using information to control employees, managers in excellent organizations look for ways to open channels of communication so that ideas flow in all directions. Successful companies want employees to have complete information so they can act quickly. In addition, sharing information on such things as financial performance and operational measures enhances trust. At Springfield Remanufacturing, top managers open the financial books to workers, explain what the numbers mean, and show how individual jobs affect the company's bottom line. Whole Foods Markets also shares detailed financial and performance information with every employee and even allows interested employees to review salary information on other employees and top executives. As CEO John Mackey puts it, "If you're trying to create a high-trust organization, an organization where people are all-for-one and one-for-all, you can't have secrets."[17]

Productivity through people simply means that everyone must participate. Rank-and-file workers are considered the root of quality and productivity. People are empowered to participate in production, marketing, and

Taking the Lead

Host Universal

Robin Smith always loved the advertising business, but hated the ad-*agency* business. He felt that most agencies were overstaffed and inefficient, and he knew from experience that many good ideas got lost in bureaucratic paper shuffling. He began dreaming of a new kind of organization that would focus all its energies on developing innovative solutions for clients. Rather than running an agency full of employees, this organization would contract work out to small ad hoc teams that offered the best combination of talent for each particular project.

Even though he knew the idea of a virtual ad agency might be considered insane in the industry, Smith contacted a former colleague at ad agency Leo Burnett and talked him into joining the adventure. Two years later, Smith and his partner Steven Hess had built a network of thirty-five creative professionals—art directors, writers, producers, and so forth—and formed them into idea teams for some eighty different advertising projects for clients such as Kellogg, the Body Shop, and British Telecom. Host Universal itself consists only of Smith and Hess; everyone

else is a freelance professional, hired on a project-by-project basis. Smith and Hess work to put the right combination of people together for each project. Then, the team works directly for and is paid directly by the client. Host Universal takes a percentage off the top for finding clients and matching them with the right team.

Interestingly, Host Universal is getting a lot of business from the big-agency world that Smith and Hess left behind. Former employer Leo Burnett hired Host to develop concepts for a new Kellogg product. DDB Needham Worldwide in Dusseldorf asked the company to put together a team for a Volkswagen campaign. The small-scale, team-based approach enables Host to take on numerous projects at once and get them done quickly because each team is staffed with the people who can produce the best ideas for each situation. "We create links between people," Hess says. "We give people the chance to create great ideas very quickly with other great people."

Source: Based on Keith H. Hammonds, "This Virtual Agency Has Big Ideas," *Fast Company* (November 1999): 70–72.

new product improvements. Conflicting ideas are encouraged rather than suppressed. The ability to move ahead through consensus preserves the sense of trust, increases motivation, and facilitates both innovation and efficiency.

Another lesson from successful companies is the importance of taking a long-term view. Organizational success is not built in a day. Successful companies realize they must invest in training employees and commit to employees for the long term. Career paths are designed to give employees broad backgrounds rather than rapid upward mobility.

Finally, excellent companies emphasize cultural values that encourage adaptation and learning rather than stability and control. Recall from Chapter 1 and Chapter 9 that one of the most important components of a learning organization is a strong culture that encourages adaptation to a changing environment. For all successful organizations, culture plays a crucial role because it determines whether employees cling to outmoded ways of doing things or search for new and better approaches. Procter & Gamble CEO Durk Jager, for example, has recognized the importance of culture in reviving the company. Jager is attempting to get employees to forget about "how things have always been done" and come up with bold, risky new ideas for the company's future. His efforts to instill values that encourage adaptation are an important part of Jager's plan for getting P&G back on track.[18]

The ideas summarized in Exhibit 13.1 are important, but they may not always translate into short-term success. Some research suggests that organizations that have these characteristics often go through periods of lower performance.[19] A preponderance of these characteristics, however, can help organizations adapt and evolve as the environment changes and thus sustain a long-term commitment to excellence. Book Mark 13.0 offers additional ideas for how companies can change and thrive over the long term.

The attributes of organizational excellence can help companies compete internationally as well as at home. Organizations also take other steps to become more competitive on a global basis. In the following section, we will discuss specific design options that can enhance global competitiveness.

DESIGNS FOR THE GLOBAL ARENA

Companies today must think globally or get left behind. The distinctions between foreign and domestic organizations are becoming increasingly blurred, and the world is rapidly becoming a single global marketplace. Global trade has tripled over the past twenty-five years. The global environment represents a huge potential market for companies. International expansion can lead to greater profits, efficiency, and responsiveness. Of course, no company can become a global giant overnight. The change from domestic to international usually occurs through stages of development, similar to the life cycle described in Chapter 8.

STAGES OF INTERNATIONAL DEVELOPMENT

Exhibit 13.2 summarizes the four stages many companies go through as they evolve toward full-fledged global operations.[20] In stage one, the **domestic stage**, the company is domestically oriented, but managers are aware of the global environment and may want to consider initial foreign involvement to expand production volume. Market potential is limited and is primarily in the home country. The structure of the company is domestic, typically functional or divisional, and initial foreign sales are handled through an export department. The details of freight forwarding, customs problems, and foreign exchange are handled by outsiders.

In stage two, the **international stage**, the company takes exports seriously and begins to think multidomestically. **Multidomestic** means competitive issues in each country are independent of other countries; the company deals with each country individually. The concern is with international competitive positioning compared with other firms in the industry. At this point, an international division has replaced the export department, and specialists are hired to handle sales, service, and warehousing abroad. Multiple countries are identified as a potential market.

$\mathcal{B}$ook $\mathcal{M}$ark 13.0

Have You Read This Book?

The Living Company

By Arie de Geus

Arie de Geus argues that companies survive the upheavals of change and competition over the long haul by focusing on people rather than material assets. Although most major corporations survive for only about forty years, there are some remarkable organizations that have withstood the test of centuries. The author studied twenty-seven companies scattered throughout North America, Europe, and Japan that range in age from 100 to 700 years, including W. R. Grace, Kodak, Mitsui, DuPont, and Siemens. These *living companies*, he says, have a personality that allows them to "evolve harmoniously." In his book, *The Living Company*, de Geus suggests that "the amount that people care, trust, and engage themselves at work" has a direct effect on the bottom line, as well as the most direct effect of any factor on a company's expected lifespan. How do leaders get people to care about the organization and engage themselves fully at work?

LEADERSHIP IN A LIVING COMPANY

Leaders in living companies set priorities that allow people to grow as part of a community held together by trust and common values. Four priorities are:

- *A commitment to people before assets.* The traditional management priorities are inverted, so that leaders value employees rather than buildings, equipment, or other material resources.
- *Loosening controls and giving people space to develop new ideas.* Leaders put a respect for innovation before a devotion to rules, policies, and procedures. Employees in living companies have the freedom to take risks without fear of punishment for failures.

- *Organizing for learning.* "Birds that flock learn faster," de Geus says. "So do organizations that encourage flocking behavior." These companies encourage interaction and collaboration among creative, curious employees so that they can learn together and create new organizational knowledge. Living companies also invest heavily in training programs that bring together people from diverse backgrounds and disciplines.
- *Putting the perpetuation of the human community before all other concerns.* In living companies, employees are bound together by strong bonds of shared values, mutual trust, sharing, and caring. They understand that in exchange for their effort and commitment, the company will help them develop their potential and give them opportunities for continuous learning and growth.

CONCLUSION

In today's companies, where knowledge is the key corporate asset, the concept of putting people first and giving them opportunities to think and learn together becomes even more critical. Although profitability is important, de Geus points out that a single-minded focus on profits can kill a company. To cope with the fundamental changes that occur over long periods of time, companies must become learning organizations—they manage change by changing themselves.

The Living Company, by Arie de Geus, is published by Harvard Business School Press.

EXHIBIT 13.2   *Four Stages of International Evolution*

	I. Domestic	II. International	III. Multinational	IV. Global
Strategic Orientation	Domestically oriented	Export-oriented multidomestic	Multinational	Global
Stage of Development	Initial foreign involvement	Competitive positioning	Explosion	Global
Structure	Domestic structure, plus export department	Domestic structure, plus international division	Worldwide geographic, product	Matrix, transnational
Market Potential	Moderate, mostly domestic	Large, multidomestic	Very large, multinational	Whole world

Source: Based on Nancy J. Adler, *International Dimensions of Organizational Behavior* (Boston: PWS–Kent, 1991), 7–8; and Theodore T. Herbert, "Strategy and Multinational Organization Structure: An Interorganizational Relationships Perspective," *Academy of Management Review* 9 (1984): 259–71.

In stage three, the **multinational stage**, the company has extensive experience in a number of international markets and has established marketing, manufacturing, or research and development facilities in several foreign countries. The organization obtains a large percentage of revenues from sales outside the home country. Explosion occurs as international operations take off, and the company has business units scattered around the world along with suppliers, manufacturers, and distributors.

The fourth and ultimate stage is the **global stage**, which means the company transcends any single country. The business is not merely a collection of domestic industries; rather, subsidiaries are interlinked to the point where competitive position in one country significantly influences activities in other countries.[21] Truly **global companies** no longer think of themselves as having a single home country, and, indeed, have been called "stateless" corporations.[22] This represents a new and dramatic evolution from the multinational company of the 1960s and 1970s.

Global companies operate in truly global fashion, and the entire world is their marketplace. Organization structure at this stage can be extremely complex and often evolves into an international matrix or transnational model, which will be discussed later in this chapter.

Global companies such as Royal Dutch/Shell, Unilever, and Matsushita Electric may operate in forty to seventy-five countries. The structural problem of holding together this huge complex of subsidiaries scattered thousands of miles apart is immense. Before turning to a discussion of specific structures, let's briefly consider two additional approaches to international activity, international alliances and global teams.

INTERNATIONAL STRATEGIC ALLIANCES

Strategic alliances are perhaps the hottest way to get involved in international operations. Typical alliances include licensing, joint ventures, and consortia.[23] Licensing agreements are frequently entered into by manufacturing firms to capitalize on the diffusion of new technology quickly and inexpensively while getting the advantage of lucrative worldwide sales. For example, Merck, Eli Lilly, and

Bayer cross-license their newest drugs to one another to support industrywide innovation and advertising and offset the high fixed costs of research and distribution.[24] **Joint ventures** are separate entities created with two or more active firms as sponsors. This is another growing approach to sharing development and production costs and penetrating new markets. Joint ventures may be with either customers or competitors.[25] Caterpillar Inc. and Mitsubishi Heavy Industries Ltd. established a joint venture that allowed Caterpillar to manufacture and sell in Japan and helped Mitsubishi expand its export markets. Manufacturers often seek joint ventures to distribute new technologies and products through another country's distribution channels and markets.

The agreement between Toyota and General Motors to construct a Chevrolet Nova plant in California was Toyota's way of distributing its technology to the United States. Texas Instruments sought long-term alliances with its biggest customers in Japan, including Sony, to gain subsidiaries in Japan. Over time, TI bought out Sony's share and ended up with four major plants in Japan producing semiconductors for the rest of TI's worldwide operations.[26]

Given the expense of new technology, **consortia** of organizations are likely to be the wave of the future. Rather than one-on-one competition among individual firms, groups of independent companies—suppliers, customers, and even competitors—will join together to share skills, resources, costs, and access to one another's markets.

Managers must learn to cooperate as well as compete.[27] For example, Airbus Industrie is a European consortium of businesses backed by the governments of Germany, France, the United Kingdom, and Spain to produce commercial aircraft. Airbus successfully competes with Boeing and has even stolen some market share from the U.S. company in recent years. Consortia are often used in other parts of the world, such as the *keiretsu* families of corporations in Japan, described in Chapter 5. In Korea, these interlocking company arrangements are called *choebol*.

A type of consortia, called the *virtual organization*, is increasingly being used in the United States and offers a promising avenue for worldwide competition in the future. The virtual organization is a continually evolving group of companies that unite to exploit specific opportunities or attain specific strategic advantages and then disband when objectives are met. A company may be involved in multiple alliances at any one time. Some U.S. executives believe shifting to a consortia or virtual approach is the best way for U.S. companies to remain competitive in the global marketplace.[28]

GLOBAL WORK TEAMS

The reality of today's business world as a global work environment has led many companies to establish global work teams to expand their products and operations into international markets.[29] **Global teams**, also called *transnational teams*, are work groups made up of multinational members whose activities span multiple countries. For example, Heineken formed the European Production Task Force, a thirteen-member team representing five countries, to wrestle with the question of how the company's production facilities throughout Europe could best be configured to cope with the challenges of the twenty-first century.[30] Global teams have been used in various ways. Some, such as Heineken's, help organizations achieve global efficiencies by developing regional or worldwide cost advantages and standardizing designs and operations. Other global teams help their companies be more locally responsive by meeting the needs of different regional markets, consumer preferences, and political and legal systems. A third primary use of global teams is to contribute to continuous organizational learning and adaptation on a global level.[31] The most advanced use of global teams involves simultaneous contributions in all of these strategic areas.

Global work teams bring unique problems to the concept of teamwork. Team leaders and members must learn to accommodate one another's cultural values and backgrounds and work together smoothly, usually in conditions of rapid change. One model for global team effectiveness, called the GRIP model, suggests that teams focus on developing common understanding in four critical areas: goals, relationships, information, and work processes, thus enabling the team to "get a grip" on its collaborative work at a very high level.[32] The need for and use of global work teams is likely to grow. Teams that effectively blend their varied backgrounds and interests into a teamwork culture focused on serving the organization's international goals can significantly enhance a company's global competitiveness.

STRUCTURAL DESIGNS FOR GLOBAL OPERATIONS

As we discussed in Chapter 3, an organization's structure must fit its situation by providing sufficient information processing for coordination and control while focusing employees on specific functions, products, or geographic regions. Organization design for international structure follows a similar logic, with special interest on global versus local strategic opportunities.

MODEL FOR GLOBAL VERSUS LOCAL OPPORTUNITIES

A major strategic issue for firms venturing into the international domain is whether (and when) to use a globalization rather than a multidomestic strategy. The **globalization strategy** means that product design and advertising strategy are standardized throughout the world.[33] For example, the Japanese took business away from Canadian and American companies by developing similar high-quality, low-cost products for all countries. The Canadian and American companies incurred higher costs by tailoring products to specific countries. Black & Decker became much more competitive internationally when it standardized its line of power hand tools. Other products, such as Coca-Cola and Levi jeans, are naturals for globalization, because only advertising and marketing need to be tailored for different regions.

A **multidomestic strategy** means that competition in each country is handled independently of competition in other countries. Thus, a multidomestic strategy would encourage product design, assembly, and marketing tailored to the specific needs of each country. Some companies have found that their products do not thrive in a single global market. The French do not drink orange juice for breakfast, and laundry detergent is used to wash dishes, not clothes, in parts of Mexico. Parker Pen experienced a disaster when it reduced from five hundred to one hundred pen styles because the different styles were valued in different countries.

The model in Exhibit 13.3 illustrates how organization design and international strategy fit the needs of the environment.[34] Companies can be characterized by whether their product and service lines have potential for globalization, which means advantages through worldwide standardization. Companies that sell diverse products or services across many countries have a globalization strategy.

EXHIBIT 13.3   *Model to Fit Organization Structure to International Advantages*

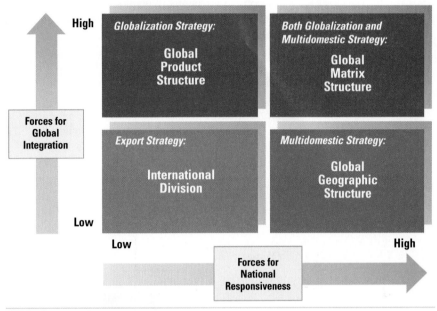

Source: Roderick E. White and Thomas A. Poynter, "Organizing for Worldwide Advantage," *Business Quarterly* (Summer 1989): 84–89. Adapted by permission of *Business Quarterly,* published by the Western Business School, the University of Western Ontario, London, Ontario, Canada.

On the other hand, some companies have products and services appropriate for a multidomestic strategy, which means local–country advantages through differentiation and customization.

As indicated in Exhibit 13.3, when forces for both global integration and national responsiveness in many countries are low, simply using an international division with the domestic structure is an appropriate way to handle international business. For some industries, however, technological, social, or economic forces may create a situation in which selling standardized products worldwide provides a basis for competitive advantage. For example, the introduction of transistors and integrated circuits for the design and production of products such as televisions and radios meant companies could achieve global economies by standardizing these products worldwide. In these cases, a global product structure is appropriate. This structure provides product managers with authority to handle their product lines on a global basis and enables the company to take advantage of a unified global marketplace. In other cases, a company can gain competitive advantages through national responsiveness—by responding to unique needs in the various countries in which it does business. For example, people in different countries have very different expectations regarding personal care products such as deodorant or toothpaste. For companies in these industries, a worldwide geographic structure is appropriate. Each country or region will have subsidiaries modifying products and services to fit that locale.

In many instances, companies will need to respond to both global and local opportunities simultaneously, in which case the global matrix structure can be used. Part of the product line may need to be standardized globally, and other parts tailored to the needs of local countries. Let's discuss each of the structures in Exhibit 13.3 in more detail.

INTERNATIONAL DIVISION

As companies begin to explore international opportunities, they typically start with an export department that grows into an **international division**. The international division has a status equal to the other major departments or divisions within the company and is illustrated in Exhibit 13.4. The international division has its own hierarchy to handle business (licensing, joint ventures) in various countries, selling the products and services created by the domestic divisions, opening subsidiary plants, and in general moving the organization into more sophisticated international operations.

Although functional structures are often used domestically, they are less frequently used to manage a worldwide business.[35] Lines of functional hierarchy running around the world would extend too long, so some form of product or geographical structure is used to subdivide the organization into smaller units. Firms typically start with an international department and, depending on their strategy, later use product or geographic divisional structures.

EXHIBIT 13.4   *Domestic Hybrid Structure with International Division*

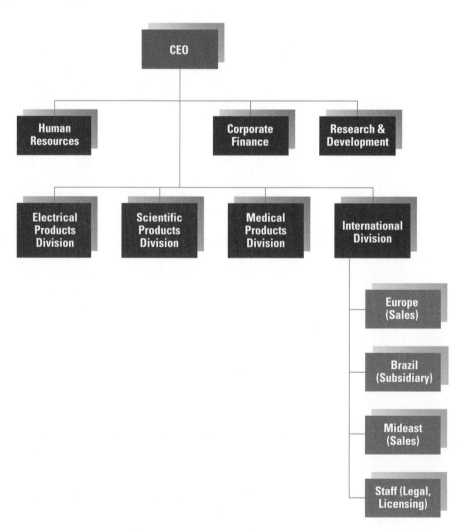

GLOBAL PRODUCT DIVISION STRUCTURE

In a **global product structure**, the product divisions take responsibility for global operations in their specific product area. Each product division can organize for international operations as it sees fit. Each division manager is responsible for planning, organizing, and controlling all functions for the production and distribution of its products for any market around the world. The product-based structure works best when a division handles products that are technologically similar and can be standardized for marketing worldwide. As we saw in Exhibit 13.3, the global product structure works best when the company has opportunities for worldwide production and sale of standard products for all markets, thus providing economies of scale and standardization of production, marketing, and advertising.

Eaton Corporation has used a form of worldwide product structure, as illustrated in Exhibit 13.5. In this structure, the automotive components group, industrial group, and so on are responsible for manufacture and sale of products worldwide. The vice-president of international is responsible for coordinators in each region, including a coordinator for Japan, Australia, South America, and northern Europe. The coordinators find ways to share facilities and improve production and delivery across all product lines sold in their region. These coordinators provide the same function as integrators described in Chapter 3.

EXHIBIT 13.5   *Partial Global Product Structure Used by Eaton Corporation*

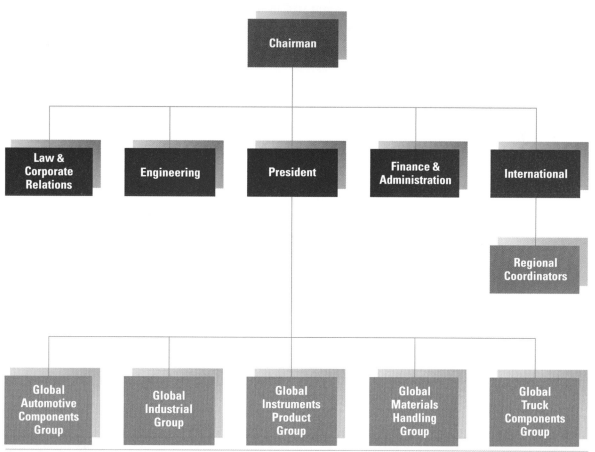

Source: Based on *New Directions in Multinational Corporate Organization* (New York: Business International Corp., 1981).

The product structure is great for standardizing production and sales around the globe, but it also has problems. Often the product divisions do not work well together, competing instead of cooperating in some countries; and some countries may be ignored by product managers. The solution adopted by Eaton Corporation of using country coordinators who have a clearly defined role is a superb way to overcome these problems.

GLOBAL GEOGRAPHIC DIVISION STRUCTURE

A worldwide regional organization divides the world into regions, each of which reports to the CEO. Each region has full control of functional activities in its geographical area. Companies that use this **global geographic structure** tend to have mature product lines and stable technologies. They find low-cost manufacturing within countries as well as different needs across countries for marketing and sales. Strategically, this structure can exploit many opportunities for regional or locally based competitive advantages.[36]

The problems encountered by senior management using a global geographic structure result from the autonomy of each regional division. For example, it is difficult to do planning on a global scale—such as new product R&D—because each division acts to meet only the needs of its region. New domestic technologies and products can be difficult to transfer to international markets because each division thinks it will develop what it needs. Likewise, it is difficult to rapidly introduce products developed offshore into domestic markets; and there is often duplication of line and staff managers across regions. Companies such as Dow Chemical find ways to take advantage of the geographic structure while overcoming these problems.

| **In Practice 13.1** | Dow Chemical |

For several years, Dow Chemical used a geographic structure of the form illustrated in Exhibit 13.6. First, Dow Europe developed its own manufacturing, sales, and technical

EXHIBIT 13.6   *Global Geographic Division Structure*

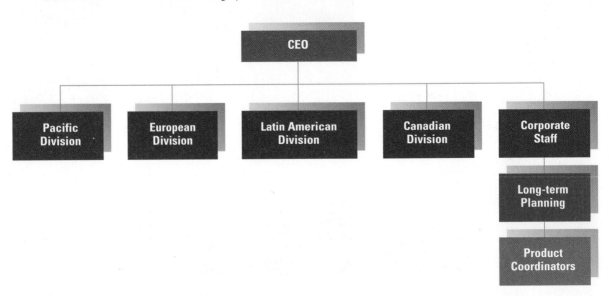

services that became an autonomous division. Subsequently the Pacific and Latin American areas developed as regional entities also, as did Canadian operations. Dow handled the problems of coordination across regions by creating a corporate-level product department to provide long-term planning and worldwide product coordination and communication. It used six corporate product directors, each of whom had been a line manager with overseas experience. The product directors are essentially staff coordinators, but they have authority to approve large capital investments and to move manufacturing of a product from one geographic location to another to best serve corporate needs. With this structure, Dow maintains its focus on each region and achieves coordination for overall planning, savings in administrative staff, and manufacturing and sales efficiency.[37]

GLOBAL MATRIX STRUCTURE

We've discussed how Eaton used a global product division structure and found ways to coordinate across worldwide divisions. Dow Chemical used a global geographic division structure and found ways to coordinate across geographical regions. Each of these companies emphasized a single dimension. Recall from Chapter 3 that a matrix structure provides a way to achieve vertical and horizontal coordination simultaneously along two dimensions. Matrix structures used by multinational corporations are similar to those described in Chapter 3, except that geographical distances for communication are greater and coordination is more complex.

The matrix works best when pressure for decision making balances the interests of both product standardization and geographical localization and when coordination to share resources is important. An excellent example of a **global matrix structure** that has worked extremely well is ABB, an electrical equipment corporation headquartered in Zurich.

In Practice 13.2

Asea Brown Boveri (ABB)

ABB, which employs more than 200,000 people worldwide and has annual revenues of $29 billion, has given new meaning to the notion of "being local worldwide." ABB owns 1,300 subsidiary companies, divided into 5,000 profit centers located in 140 countries. ABB's average plant has fewer than 200 workers and most of the company's 5,000 profit centers contain only forty to fifty people, meaning almost everyone stays close to the customer. For many years, ABB used a complex global matrix structure similar to Exhibit 13.7 to achieve worldwide economies of scale combined with local flexibility and responsiveness.

At the top are the chief executive officer and an international committee of eight top managers, who hold frequent meetings around the world. Along one side of the matrix are sixty-five or so business areas located worldwide, into which ABB's products and services are grouped. Each business area leader is responsible for handling business on a global scale, allocating export markets, establishing cost and quality standards, and creating mixed-nationality teams to solve problems. For example, the leader for power transformers is responsible for twenty-five factories in sixteen countries.

Along the other side of the matrix is a country structure; ABB has more than one hundred country managers, most of them citizens of the country in which they work. They run national companies and are responsible for local balance sheets, income statements, and career ladders. The German president, for example, is responsible for 36,000

EXHIBIT 13.7   *Global Matrix Structure*

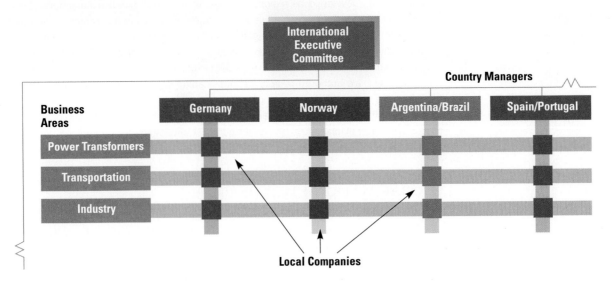

people across several business areas that generate annual revenues in Germany of more than $4 billion.

The matrix structure converges at the level of the 1,300 local companies. The presidents of local companies report to two bosses—the business area leader, who is usually located outside the country, and the country president, who runs the company of which the local organization is a subsidiary.

ABB's philosophy is to decentralize things to the lowest levels. Global managers are generous, patient, and multilingual. They must work with teams made up of different nationalities and be culturally sensitive. They craft strategy and evaluate performance for people and subsidiaries around the world. Country managers, by contrast, are regional line managers responsible for several country subsidiaries. They must cooperate with business area managers to achieve worldwide efficiencies and the introduction of new products. Finally, the presidents of local companies have both a global boss—the business area manager—and a country boss, and they learn to coordinate the needs of both.[38]

ABB is a large, successful company that has achieved the benefits of both product and geographic organizations through this matrix structure. However, over the past several years, as ABB has faced increasingly complex competitive issues, leaders have been transforming the company toward something called the *transnational model.*

TRANSNATIONAL MODEL

The **transnational model** of organization structure goes beyond the global matrix to apply the concept of the learning organization to a huge, international corporation. The transnational model of organization is essentially the learning organization extended to the international arena. It is useful for large, multinational companies with subsidiaries in many countries that try to exploit both global and local advantages, and perhaps technological superiority, rapid innovation, and global knowledge sharing. While the matrix is effective for handling two issues (product and geographic), dealing with multiple, interrelated, competitive issues requires a more complex form of organization and structure.

The transnational model represents the most current thinking about the kind of structure needed by complex global organizations such as N. V. Philips, illustrated in Exhibit 13.8. Headquartered in the Netherlands, Philips has operating units in sixty countries and is typical of global companies, such as Heinz, Unilever, or Procter & Gamble.[39]

The units in Exhibit 13.8 are far-flung. Achieving coordination, a sense of participation and involvement by subsidiaries, and a sharing of information, new technologies, and customers requires a complex and multidimensional form of structure. For example, a global corporation like Philips is so large that size itself is a problem when coordinating global operations. In addition, some subsidiaries may become so large that they no longer fit a narrow strategic role assigned to them by headquarters. While being part of a large organization, they also need autonomy for themselves and need to have impact on other parts of the organization.

The transnational model is much more than just an organization chart. It is a state of mind, a set of values, a shared desire to make a worldwide learning system work, and an idealized organization structure for effectively managing such a system. The transnational model cannot be given a precise definition, but the following characteristics distinguish it from and move it beyond a matrix structure.[40]

1. *The transnational model differentiates into many centers of different kinds.* Like the global matrix structure, the transnational model strives to achieve global competitiveness through both global integration and national responsiveness. However, the matrix structure had a single headquarters, a single center of control for each country, and a single center for each product line. The transnational operates on a principle of "flexible centralization." A transnational may centralize some functions in one country, some in another, yet decentralize still other functions among its many geographically dispersed operations. An R&D center may be centralized in Holland and a purchasing center located in Sweden, while financial accounting responsibilities are decentralized to operations in many countries. A unit in Hong Kong may be responsible for coordinating activities across Asia, while activities for all other countries are coordinated by a large division headquarters in London.

2. *Subsidiary managers initiate strategy and innovations that become strategy for the corporation as a whole.* In traditional structures, managers have a strategic role only for their division. In a transnational, various centers and subsidiaries can shape the company from the bottom up because there is no notion of a single headquarters, no clear top-down corporate level responsibility. Managers at all levels in any country have authority to develop creative responses and initiate programs in response to emerging local trends, then disperse their innovations worldwide. Transnational companies recognize that different parts of the organization possess different capabilities. In addition, environmental demands and opportunities vary from country to country, and exposing the whole organization to this broader range of environmental stimuli can trigger greater learning and innovation. By ensuring that the entire organization has access to the combined knowledge, abilities, and intellectual

EXHIBIT 13.8   *International Organizational Units and Interlinkages Within N.V. Phillips*

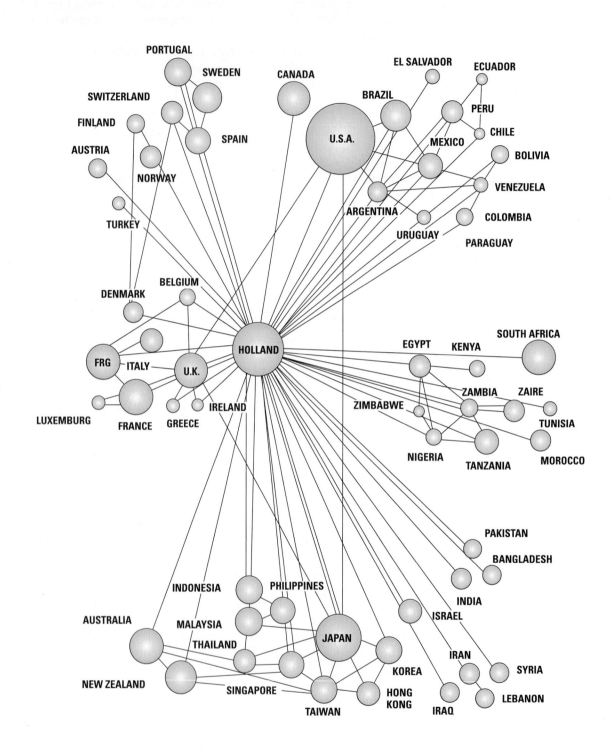

Source: Sumantra Ghoshal and Christopher A. Bartlett, "The Multinational Corporation as an Interorganizational Network," *Academy of Management Review* 15 (1990): 605. Used by permission.

capacities of all divisions and all employees, transnationals engage in continuous worldwide learning and knowledge sharing.

3. *Unification and coordination are achieved through corporate culture, shared vision and values, and management style rather than through the vertical hierarchy.* The transnational is essentially a horizontal structure. It is diverse, extended, and exists in a fluctuating environment so that standard rules, procedures, and close supervision are not appropriate. The very nature of the transnational organization dramatically expands the difficulty of unifying and coordinating operations. To achieve unity and coordination, organization leaders build a context of shared vision, values, and perspectives among managers, who in turn cascade these elements down through all parts of the organization. For example, people are often promoted by rotation through different jobs, divisions, and countries. Moreover, long experience with the company is highly valued because these people have been strongly socialized into the corporate culture. Experience plus rotation through different divisions and regions means that people share corporate culture and values sufficient for unity of purpose.

4. *Alliances are established with other company parts and with other companies.* Although resources and functions are widely dispersed, the transnational may integrate them through strong interdependencies. A world-scale production plant in Singapore may depend on world-scale component plants in Australia, Mexico, and Germany; major sales subsidiaries, in turn, depend on Singapore for finished products. In addition, each part of the organization can serve as an independent catalyst, bringing together unique elements with synergistic potential, perhaps other firms or subsidiaries from different countries, to improve its performance. These alliances may include joint ventures, cooperation with governments, and licensing arrangements.

Taken together, these characteristics facilitate organizational learning and knowledge sharing on a broad, global scale. Although the transnational model is truly a complex and "messy" way to conceptualize organization structure, it is becoming increasingly relevant for large, global firms that treat the whole world as their playing field and do not have a single country base. The autonomy of organizational parts gives strength to smaller units and allows the firm to take advantage of rapid change and competitive opportunities. Managers follow their own instincts, using worldwide resources to achieve their local objectives. Strategy is the result of action in the sense that company parts seek to improve on their own rather than waiting for a strategy from the top. Indeed, each part of the company must be aware of the whole organization so its local actions will complement and enhance other company parts.

To achieve the advantages of the transnational model, a broad range of people throughout the organization must develop the capacity for strategic thinking and strategic action. People are not constrained by rigid rules or hierarchies but are instead empowered to think, experiment, develop creative responses, and take action.

THE TREND TOWARD EMPOWERMENT

The shift to the learning organization, on both the domestic and international level, goes hand in hand with the recent trend toward empowering employees throughout the organization. Whether we are talking about self-directed teams

(Chapter 3), organic management processes and systems (Chapter 4), or participative cultures (Chapter 9), the attempts to diffuse and share power throughout the organization are widespread. The notion of giving employees the power, freedom, and information to make decisions and participate fully in the organization is called **empowerment**.[41]

In an environment characterized by intense global competition and new technology, many top managers believe that giving up centralized control will promote speed, flexibility, and decisiveness. Indeed, fully 74 percent of CEOs report that they are more participatory, more consensus-oriented, and rely more on communication than on command in today's global environment. They are finding less value in being dictatorial, autocratic, or imperial.[42] The trend is clearly toward moving power out of the executive suite and into the hands of employees. This trend can be seen in a variety of manufacturing and service industries, including some of the best known companies in the world, such as Hewlett-Packard, Southwest Airlines, Boeing, General Electric, and Caterpillar.[43]

REASONS FOR EMPOWERMENT

Why are so many organizations empowering workers and what advantages do these organizations achieve? One study suggests three primary reasons firms adopt empowerment: (1) as a strategic imperative to improve products or services; (2) because other firms in their industry are doing so (recall from Chapter 5 how firms tend to imitate similar organizations in the same environment); and (3) to create a unique learning organization with superior performance capabilities. Of the three reasons, the most compelling in terms of durability and success is the third—to create a learning organization that becomes the basis of sustainable competitive advantage.[44] Empowerment is essential for learning organizations because it unleashes the potential and creativity of all employees, allowing them to experiment and learn and giving them the freedom to act on their knowledge and understanding. In today's world, where competitive advantage relies increasingly on ideas and innovation, an empowered work force is critical to organizational success. People create and share knowledge because they want to—these activities can't be forced out of employees or supervised in the traditional sense.[45]

Empowerment provides a basis of sustainable competitive advantage in several ways. For one thing, empowerment *increases* the total amount of power in the organization. Many managers mistakenly believe power is a zero-sum game, which means they must give up power in order for someone else to have more. Not true. Both research and the experience of managers indicate that delegating power from the top creates a bigger power pie, so that everyone has more power.[46] Ralph Stayer, CEO of Johnsonville Foods, believes a manager's strongest power comes from committed workers: "Real power comes from giving it up to others who are in a better position to do things than you are."[47] The manager who gives away power gets commitment and creativity in return. Employees find ways to use their knowledge and abilities to make good things happen. Front-line workers often have a better understanding than do managers of how to improve a work process, satisfy a customer, or solve a production problem. In addition, employees are more likely to be committed to a decision or course of action when they are closely involved in the decision-making process.[48] Management's fear of power loss is the biggest barrier to empowerment of employees; however, by understanding they will actually gain power, delegation should be easy. For example, at Fastenal, a highly successful company that sells 49,000 different kinds of fasteners, from hex nuts to pin bolt drive anchors, CEO Bob Kierlin constantly pushes management-level decision making down to entry-level positions. Kierlin believes empowering his workers has been the primary reason for the company's rapid growth, record profits, and high shareholder returns. "Just believe in people, give them a chance to make decisions, take risks, and work hard," is Kierlin's philosophy of management.[49]

Empowerment also increases employee motivation. Research indicates that individuals have a need for *self-efficacy*, which is the capacity to produce results or outcomes, to feel they are effective. Increasing employee power heightens motivation for task accomplishment because people improve their own effectiveness, choosing how to do the task and using their creativity.[50] Most people come into the organization with the desire to do a good job, and empowerment enables them to release the motivation already there. Their reward is a sense of personal mastery and competence. Giving employees the power to actively affect outcomes led to a 100 percent increase in productivity at Monarch Marking Systems.

<table>
<tr><td>**In Practice 13.3**</td><td>Monarch Marking Systems</td></tr>
</table>

When Jerry Schlaegel and Steve Schneider first rolled out a new empowerment program at Monarch Marking Systems, a manufacturer of bar coding and price marking machines, some employees flat-out refused to participate. They'd seen too many similar programs do nothing but waste their time.

This time, however, managers decided to try a new approach. Rather than initiating an open-ended process of giving workers more decision-making authority, Schlaegel and Schneider decided to give employees specific problems and charge them with not only creating a solution, but also implementing it. They told workers, "Go make it happen, then tell us about it." Some teams rapidly achieved results—one found a way to reduce the number of job categories from 120 to only 32 through cross-training; another synchronized the changing of paper rolls in a label-making line to cut set-up time by 25 percent. However, the team charged with coming up with a more efficient assembly process for a hand-held bar code reader at first rebelled, assuming this was another exercise in coming up with ideas that never turned into action. Top managers called them into a conference room, laid out the problem, and gave the team a deadline for implementing their own solution.

Seeing that top managers truly expected them to produce final results, not just ideas, the group quickly began talking about ways to solve the problem. They all knew, for example, that building a two-pound product on a mechanical conveyor belt was ridiculous—they could stand around a work station and simply pass the product by hand. People could easily talk to one another, and those who got ahead could help out if anyone else was falling behind. Ultimately, the team reduced the square footage of their assembly area 70 percent, cut work-in-progress inventory by $127,000, doubled productivity, and reduced past-due shipments 90 percent.

Worker enthusiasm and motivation at Monarch dramatically increased once employees saw the results of their own creativity and hard work. "We're not just pieces of equipment anymore," said employee Effie Winters. "My input means something."[51]

Truly empowering workers means not only giving employees the responsibility to come up with ideas and make decisions, but also allowing them to take action. By replacing an open-ended "empowerment" initiative with a system that gave employees a chance to really make a difference, managers at Monarch increased employees' self-efficacy and thus their inner motivation, enabling the company to tap into the knowledge and creativity of all employees.

Another benefit from empowerment is that it may help companies retain good employees—and their knowledge. Companies that effectively empower employees often have uncommonly low turnover rates. Hewlett-Packard's turnover of engineers is only 3 percent, against an industry norm of 7 to 8 percent.[52] People stay with companies where they feel appreciated and where their knowledge and actions can make a difference.

ELEMENTS OF EMPOWERMENT

Empowering employees means giving them four elements that enable them to act more freely to accomplish their jobs: information, knowledge, power, and rewards.[53]

1. *Employees receive information about company performance.* In companies where employees are fully empowered, such as Semco S/A, Brazil's largest manufacturer of marine and food processing equipment, no information is secret. At Semco, every employee has access to the books and any other information, including executive salaries. To show they're serious about sharing information, Semco management works with the labor union that represents its workers to train employees—even messengers and cleaning people—to read balance sheets and cash flow statements.

2. *Employees have knowledge and skills to contribute to company goals.* Companies use various approaches to training to give employees the knowledge and skills they need to personally contribute to company performance in an empowered environment. At Ashton Photo, a volume producer of prints for professional photographers, more experienced employees are expected to educate new ones about how to read financial statements and understand how their actions and performance affect company finances. CIBC uses individual development planning guides to provide workers with a clear target of what competencies they need to develop. Fourteen Employee Development Centers across Canada provide consultants to assist employees in using learning resources to meet their goals.[54] Xerox gives its workers what the company calls "line of sight" training, in which employees familiarize themselves with how their jobs fit into upstream and downstream activities. The training helps empowered employees make better decisions that support other workers and contribute to the organization's goals.[55]

3. *Employees have the power to make substantive decisions.* Many of today's most competitive companies are giving workers the power to influence work procedures and organizational direction through quality circles and self-directed work teams. At Ashton Photo, teams of workers schedule their own workloads and have the freedom to determine how to best serve customers. Each worker has a key to the building and is able to schedule his or her work time as the production schedule warrants. Teams of workers at a Lucent Technologies factory in Mt. Olive, New Jersey, are continually altering the production process and even the product design. Although management establishes a list of working principles, teams have the freedom to make day-to-day decisions and take action within those guidelines.[56]

4. *Employees are rewarded based on company performance.* Two of the ways in which organizations can reward employees financially based on company performance are through profit sharing and employee stock ownership plans (ESOPs). At W. L. Gore & Associates, makers of Gore-Tex, compensation takes three forms—salary, profit sharing, and an associates stock ownership program.[57]

EMPOWERMENT APPLICATIONS

Many of today's organizations are implementing empowerment programs, but they are empowering workers to varying degrees. At some companies, empowerment means encouraging employee input while managers maintain final authority for decisions; at others it means giving front-line workers almost complete power to make decisions and exercise initiative and imagination.[58] At Nordstrom (a department store chain), for example, employees are given the following guidelines: "Rule No. 1: Use your good judgment in all situations. There will be no additional rules."[59]

Exhibit 13.9 shows a continuum of empowerment, from a situation where front-line workers have no discretion (for example, a traditional assembly line) to full empowerment, where workers actively participate in determining organizational strategy. Current methods of empowering workers fall along this continuum. When employees are fully empowered, they are given decision-making authority and control over how they do their own jobs, as well as the power to influence and change such areas as organizational goals, structures, and reward systems. An example is when self-directed teams are given the power to

EXHIBIT 13.9   *The Empowerment Continuum*

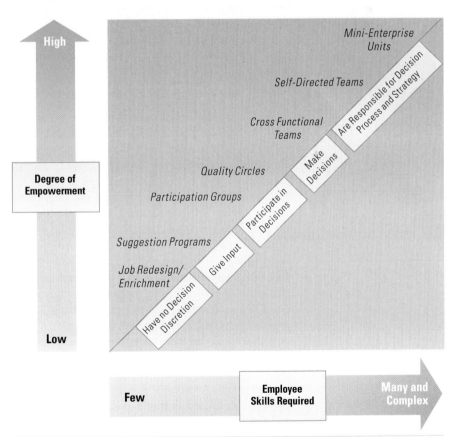

Source: Based on Robert C. Ford and Myron D. Fottler, "Empowerment: A Matter of Degree," *Academy of Management Executive* 9, no. 3 (1995): 21–31; Lawrence Holpp, "Applied Empowerment," *Training* (February 1994): 39–44; and David P. McCaffrey, Sue R. Faerman, and David W. Hart, "The Appeal and Difficulties of Participative Systems," *Organization Science* 6, no. 6 (November–December 1995): 603–27.

hire, discipline, and dismiss team members and to set compensation rates. One example is W. L. Gore and Associates. The company, which operates with no titles, hierarchy, or any of the conventional structures associated with a company of its size, has remained highly successful and profitable under this empowered system for more than thirty years. The culture emphasizes teamwork, mutual support, freedom, motivation, independent effort, and commitment to the total organization rather than to narrow jobs or departments.[60]

Empowerment programs are difficult to implement in established organizations because they destroy hierarchies and upset the familiar balance of power. A study of *Fortune* 1000 companies found that the empowerment practices that have diffused most widely are those that redistribute power and authority the least, for example, quality circles and other types of participation groups and job enrichment and redesign.[61] Managers may have difficulty giving up power and authority; and although workers like the increased freedom, they may balk at the added responsibility freedom brings. Most organizations begin with small steps and gradually increase employee empowerment. For example, at Recyclights, a small Minneapolis-based company that recycles fluorescent lights, CEO Keith Thorndyke first gave employees control of their own tasks. As employee skills grew and they developed a greater interest in how their jobs fit into the total picture, Thorndyke recognized that workers also wanted to help shape corporate goals rather than having a plan handed down to them as a finished package.[62]

The trend toward empowering lower-level workers is likely to grow, with more companies moving up the continuum of empowerment shown in Exhibit 13.9.

LEADING THE CHANGE TOWARD LEARNING ORGANIZATIONS

Empowering workers is a key step toward becoming a fluid, adaptable learning organization that can thrive in a world of rapid change. Many organization leaders cite change as the most common problem they face.[63] Today's business world is characterized by globalization, intense competition, instantaneous communications, and surprise. Small events may have huge consequences that are difficult or impossible to predict. Today's best organization leaders recognize that the organization has to keep pace with what is happening in the external environment. As Jack Welch, chairman and CEO of General Electric, once stated, "When the rate of change outside exceeds the rate of change inside, the end is in sight."[64]

Organizations respond to external changes in many ways. For example, many organizations are adopting new organizational forms that include less hierarchy and more self-directed teams or dynamic network structures that can bring together the best combination of people and resources to remain competitive. In general, the trend is away from vertical structures that create distance between managers and workers toward horizontal structures focused on core work processes. A related shift is a concern for giving employees more responsibility and authority for decision making, and a stronger interest in corporate values and culture. Some companies are transforming themselves into *learning organizations,* which emphasize equality, strong cultural values, and a flowing, adaptable structure designed to seize opportunities, handle crises, and remain competitive in a volatile environment.

TRANSFORMATIONAL LEADERSHIP

One important question is what kind of people can lead an organization through major change, such as the shift to a learning organization? One type of leadership that has a substantial impact on organizations is transformational leadership.

Transformational leaders are characterized by the ability to bring about change, innovation, and entrepreneurship. Transformational leaders motivate followers to not just follow them personally but to believe in the vision of corporate transformation, to recognize the need for revitalization, to sign on for the new vision, and to help institutionalize a new organizational process.[65]

Throughout previous chapters, we have discussed the need for large-scale changes in organizations—whether to implement a new corporate culture or self-directed team structure, grow to a new stage in the life cycle, or expand internationally. A massive change such as the transition to a learning organization involves a fundamental transformation of mission, structure, culture, management processes, and political systems of an organization to provide a new level of organizational learning capability and knowledge sharing. Transformational leadership will be increasingly important in all industries A transformational leader can take the organization through these major changes by successfully achieving the following three activities:[66]

1. *Create a compelling vision.* In a recent survey of 1,450 executives from a dozen global firms, the ability to "articulate a tangible vision, values, and strategy" was considered the most important competency for global leaders to have.[67] The vision of a desired future state communicates that the organization must break free of previous patterns and that old structures, processes, and activities are no longer useful. By spreading the vision throughout the organization, the transformational leader focuses the organization's learning efforts so that they increase the firm's competitive advantage. A *compelling vision* is one in which all organization members can believe. They understand the vision and they support it. Alfred P. West, founder and CEO of SEI Investments, transformed his company into a learning organization by spreading his vision of a new kind of financial services company, in which all work is performed by self-organized and self-directed teams who work directly with customers. West's vision includes the values of equality, freedom, responsibility, and dedication to serving customers.[68] Although leaders should involve managers and employees throughout the organization through task forces or other mechanisms, they alone are ultimately responsible for initiating a new vision.

2. *Mobilize commitment.* For the transformation to succeed, there must be a shared commitment to the new vision and mission. Leaders build a coalition, as described in Chapters 11 and 12, to guide the transformation process and work to develop a sense of teamwork among the group. The coalition should include people from all levels of the organization who can engage the commitment of others and successfully guide the transformation process. Mechanisms such as off-site meetings and the large-scale intervention approach described in Chapter 9 can get people together to discuss the new vision and how to achieve it.

   At Siemens Rolm, a U.S. telecommunications business owned by Siemens AG of Germany, six hundred managers attended a three-day institute and then went back and mobilized commitment to the new vision in their own units.[69] Large scale, discontinuous change requires special commitment, or it will be resisted as inconsistent with traditional organizational goals and activities.

3. *Empower employees.* Giving employees the power and knowledge to act on the vision is critical. This means getting rid of obstacles such as strict, unnecessary rules and regulations, rigid hierarchies, and policies and procedures that limit and constrain employees. People are empowered with knowledge, resources, and discretion to make things happen. Leaders work hard to support and develop mechanisms that allow and encourage people to actively participate in the organization. They provide opportunities for workers to learn and share their experience and understanding, which increases commitment. Transformational leaders view people as the organization's primary resource and work to unleash the potential of each employee. Rather than relying on hierarchical control, leaders motivate and align people around the vision through webs of relationships that promote learning and knowledge transfer. In the transformation of Bethlehem Steel's Sparrows Point, Maryland, division, management changed from a traditional command-and-control style to a new model that actively involved employees at all levels of the company in making and implementing important decisions. By tapping into the knowledge and emotional commitment of employees through empowerment, Bethlehem Steel leaders revitalized the Sparrows Point division.[70]

4. *Institutionalize a culture of change.* This is the follow-through stage that makes changes stick. Old and outmoded values, traditions, and mind-sets are permanently replaced by values of risk taking, adaptation, learning, and knowledge sharing. A culture of change recognizes that competitive advantage is a shifting concept and that the organization must constantly be moving forward. Leaders use symbols, stories, language, and other mechanisms described in Chapter 9 to help change organizational culture. For a learning organization, they attempt to instill practices and values that help employees be comfortable with the reality of constant change and the need for continuous experimentation and learning. A long time period, perhaps several years, may be needed for leaders to bring about this type of culture change. The transformational leader must be persistent to move the organization toward a new way of doing and thinking. The new system may alter power and status and revise interaction patterns. New executives may be hired who display values and behaviors appropriate for the new order of things. The new system is then institutionalized and made permanent.

One example of a leader with transformational qualities is Mary Ann Byrnes of Corsair Communications.

In Practice 13.4   Corsair Communications Inc.

Like big defense contractors everywhere, California-based TRW was forced to find commercial applications for many of its products. One good prospect, developed by the top-secret ESL division, was a technology for identifying the source of electronic transmissions, which had significant commercial potential for inhibiting fraudulent cellular telephone use. Corsair Communications was created as a spinoff company, to be owned 20 percent by TRW, 60 percent by venture capitalists, and 20 percent by its employees. When Mary Ann Byrnes was hired as CEO, Corsair already had a product (although it was far from perfected), a multimillion-dollar contract with a cellular carrier, and a group of first-rate engineers. Everything was in place to build the new business except the glue that would hold it together.

Byrnes knew she had to teach a group of government contract engineers, who were accustomed to working what one called a "10%-of-the-day kind of job," to compete as entrepreneurs. Byrnes's vision was to create a culture that communicated a sense of shared responsibility and destiny—of everyone pulling together to serve the customer and sharing in the success or failure. She started by allowing workers to make the decisions they would have to live with—for example, out of a group of sixty engineers, Byrnes had to pick thirty, so she allowed the engineers themselves to decide who would stay and who would go. Later, she let those who stayed help select the new vice-president of engineering. She set up cross-functional teams that work face-to-face with customers and began sharing all information with employees. Companywide pizza lunches enhance information sharing as well as team spirit. The sense of ownership and shared destiny is strengthened because employees themselves own part of the company.

Corsair's culture has become its major competitive weapon. By trusting employees, Byrnes created an environment that motivates them to get the job done. For example, when engineers told Byrnes they would need six months to solve one particular technical problem, she took them at their word and told them to get to work. At ESL, managers had insisted they do it in six weeks, and the problem *never* got solved. At Corsair, the engineers made their six-month deadline, and subsequent goals have been met even earlier than projected.

Byrnes's skill as a transformational leader has not gone unrecognized. In June 1999, she was named chairman of the board of directors. Kevin Compton, former chairman, said, "Mary Ann has been an essential part of Corsair's success over the last five years." Thomas Meyer, who had been chief operating officer, was promoted to CEO. Byrnes and other executives view these top-management changes as a way to capitalize on the success of the past few years and strengthen Corsair's competitive advantage for the future.[71]

As in the case of Corsair, transformational leaders often emerge during times of crisis or rapid change. Mary Ann Byrnes used the qualities of transformational leadership to help set the company on course to becoming a learning organization.

ASSESSING THE IMPACT OF TOP LEADERSHIP

Top leaders are responsible for changing their organizations to help them stay competitive as environmental conditions change. How are today's leaders doing in this important role? Some interesting research relates to two important issues concerning the leadership of organizations: whether top management can truly have an impact on organizational performance and how executive turnover affects organizations.

EXPERIMENTS WITH TOP-MANAGEMENT TEAMS

In recent years, top executives have begun experimenting with the idea of top-management teams, based partly on the notion that a broader range of skills, experiences, and knowledge can help the organization better recognize and respond to threats or opportunities in the environment and make the necessary changes in the organization.

The makeup of the top-management group is believed to affect the development of organizational capability and the ability to exploit strategic opportunities and bring about periodic revitalization. A team provides a range of aptitudes and skills to deal with complex organizational situations. The configuration of the top management team is believed by many researchers to be more important for organizational success than the personality characteristics of the CEO. For example, the size, diversity, attitudes, and skills of the team affect patterns of communication and collaboration, which in turn affect company performance.[72]

The emerging focus on top-management teams is more realistic in some ways than focusing on individual leadership. In a complex environment, a single leader cannot do all things. An effective team has a better chance of identifying and implementing a successful strategy, of providing an accurate interpretation of the environment, and of developing internal capability based on empowered employees and a shared mind-set. Without a capable and effectively interacting top-management team, a company cannot adapt readily in a shifting environment.

The idea of a top-management team is powerful, but many times executives become quite frustrated by their efforts to operate as a team.[73] The companies that have been most successful in using top-management teams focus on real, specific problems that require a collective effort to solve. For example, at Texas Instruments during the mid-1980s, a top-management team focused on the company's declining calculator business. The market for calculators was in turmoil as customers shifted toward greater use of personal computers. The group used its combined skills and abilities to better understand the market and lead the company through a potential crisis.[74]

Four significant issues that can prevent top-management teams from providing effective leadership are fragmentation, intense conflict, the emergence of groupthink, and inadequate capabilities of one or more top executives.[75] The most damaging problem may be *fragmentation,* which means the top-management team is not a team at all, but rather a group of executives each pursuing his or her own agenda. This can lead to the negative use of political activity, as discussed in Chapter 12. In addition, *conflict* that is too strong or becomes focused on personal rather than organizational issues can seriously limit team effectiveness. However, the complete suppression of conflict is also detrimental to performance because it can lead to *groupthink,* in which members agree, for the sake of harmony and cohesion, to decisions that prove to be unsound. Top-management teams need to engage in serious debate to reach sound decisions. Finally, when one or more team members do not perform effectively or engage in shortsighted thinking and behavior, the team and the company can suffer.

An effective top-management team is a balancing act, as is an effective organization. The top executive still plays a critical role as leader of the team and is largely responsible for its effectiveness. Considering that no one manager can do it alone in today's complex world, bringing unity of purpose to the top-management team may be the most important challenge a top executive faces. In the following sections, we discuss how changes in top management affect organizations.

SUCCESSION AND ADAPTATION

One finding from succession research is that, for an organization as a whole, periodic management turnover is a form of organizational adaptation. In organizations characterized by turbulent environments, the turnover of organizational leaders is greater.[76] Such organizations are more difficult to manage, so new energy and vitality are needed on a frequent basis. Software retailer Egghead, Inc. has gone through four CEOs in an effort to find a leader with the right skills to revive the company.[77]

Top manager turnover also allows an organization to cope with new contingencies. The selection of a new chief executive may reflect the need for a specific skill or specialization.[78] For example, if the dominant issue confronting an organization is financing mergers, choosing a finance person as chief executive gives priority to financial activities. Historically, CEO backgrounds have changed with business conditions. Early in this century, large firms were controlled by people who came up through manufacturing. In the middle decades, sales and marketing people were more frequently selected as chief executive officers. In the 1980s and 1990s, finance personnel became increasingly dominant.[79] The major issues confronting business organizations were first manufacturing technology, then sales, and then finance. Today, organizations are looking primarily for top leaders who have a track record of being change leaders. Companies in a volatile environment need a CEO who can shake things up and keep the company moving forward.

Turnover every few years can have a positive effect. If a chief executive and top management team serve too long, say over ten years, organizational stagnation may begin. New executives are not coming in to provide fresh energy, new strategies, or expertise for new environmental situations.

One example of how management succession is used for adaptation is IBM, which was described in the case that opened this textbook. Recall from that case in Chapter 1 that IBM was a tradition-bound, stagnating corporation that many analysts thought might not survive. The firm was clearly not adapting to its turbulent international environment and the rapidly changing computer industry. That all changed with the appointment of new top executives, led by CEO Lou Gerstner, who could bring new blood and an orientation to change and adaptation. Gerstner, along with hand-picked sidekicks who followed him from his previous job, immediately began shaking things up at Big Blue. As a result, IBM became a sizzling leader in the world of e-commerce and the stock price quadrupled.[80]

SUCCESSION AND PERFORMANCE

In recent years, companies such as Delta Airlines, Unisys, Times Mirror, and Borland International had turnover at the top. Turnover at the top is of particular interest to organization studies because the CEO has a pervasive impact on an organization. In addition, there are often symbolic aspects connected with CEO succession, and turnover at the top may be associated with firm decline and eventual transformation.[81]

Athletic Team Performance. One type of organization that can help answer the question of whether manager turnover influences performance is an athletic team. The coach is the top manager of the team, and coaches are regularly replaced in both college and professional sports. Several studies have analyzed coaching changes to see whether they lead to an improvement in performance. The general finding is that manager (coach) turnover does not lead to improved performance unless the new coach is exceptionally competent.[82] If the coach has prior experience and has brought about improvements in other teams, then the coach can make a difference. However, most manager replacements do not lead to improved performance.

Another finding from those studies is that performance leads to turnover.[83] Teams with poor records experience greater succession because a poor record often leads to the firing of the old coach. Firing the previous coach serves as a symbol that the team is trying to improve. The term **ritual scapegoating** describes how turnover signals to fans and others that efforts are being made to improve the team's performance record.[84] Corporations also use ritual scapegoating, in the sense that poor performance causes turnover.[85] For example, the board fired the CEO at Allegheny to signal to stockholders and the press that it was attempting to make changes that would correct ethical problems and improve performance.

Corporations and Performance. A corporation is much larger and more diverse than an athletic team. Can the chief executive make a difference to performance in a corporate setting? Several studies of chief executive turnover have been conducted, including a sample of 167 corporations studied over a twenty-year period, 193 manufacturing companies, a large sample of Methodist churches, and retail firms in the United Kingdom.[86] These studies found that leader succession was associated with improved profits and stock prices and, in the case of churches, by improved attendance, membership, and donations. It was also found that performance was improved by good economic conditions and industry circumstances, but the chief executive officer had impact beyond these environmental factors. Overall, when research has been carefully done, there has been a finding that leadership succession explains 20 percent to 45 percent of the variance in an organization's outcomes.[87]

An interesting corollary is that the importance of chief executives means turnover in some cases may lead to poorer performance. In a study of managerial succession in local newspapers, when the founder who created and developed the organization left, performance dropped. In the early stages of the organizational life cycle, an organization depends heavily on the special skills of its founder. A new top manager is unable to achieve the same level of performance.[88]

A realistic interpretation of these findings is the conclusion that corporate performance is the result of many factors. General economic and industry conditions outside the control of the chief executive do affect sales and net earnings. However, outcomes under the control of executive strategy—such as net profit—are influenced by the chief executive. In addition, the chief executive can bring new energy for change and adaptation. By using symbolic action, a new CEO can begin a process of culture change and affect the direction and performance of the organization.

MANAGING ORGANIZATIONAL DECLINE

One reality facing leaders today is that the dramatic changes in the economy and the associated adjustments needed within the organization may cause or even require a phase of decline. Despite the booming U.S. economy in recent years, all around us we see evidence that some organizations have stopped growing and many are declining. Some organizations have gotten out of sync with the environment and are having a hard time competing in the world of e-commerce, for example. Others have had to cut large numbers of employees to reduce operating costs and fend off global competition. For example, Earnest W. Deavenport Jr., chairman and CEO of Eastman Chemical Company, recently announced the organization's first round of companywide layoffs as part of a dramatic cost-cutting plan designed to help the company survive in the increasingly competitive chemicals industry.[89]

In this section we will examine the causes of organizational decline and discuss a model of decline stages that can help managers understand and effectively deal with decline.

DEFINITION AND CAUSES

The term **organizational decline** is defined as a condition in which a substantial, absolute decrease in an organization's resource base occurs over a period of time.[90] Organizational decline is often associated with environmental decline in the sense that an organization's domain experiences either a reduction in size (such as shrinkage in customer demand or erosion of a city's tax base) or a reduction in shape (for example, a shift in customer demand).

Several factors can cause organizational decline. As we discussed in Chapter 5, organizations progress through a life cycle and have to regularly go through periods of revitalization. Sometimes organizations do not make the necessary changes as they grow older, and the company's ability to adapt to its environment deteriorates. Organizational decline may follow a long period of success because the organization becomes attached to practices and structures that worked in the past.[91] As we saw in Chapter 9, the cultural values that led to success often become institutionalized, and companies have a hard time breaking out of these outmoded ways of thinking.

Another factor is that organizations become vulnerable to shifts in consumer tastes or in the economic health of the larger community. *Vulnerability* reflects an organization's strategic inability to prosper in its environment. This often happens to young, small organizations that are not yet established. Larger, mature organizations also become vulnerable because they are unable to define the correct strategy to fit the environment. Merrill Lynch, for example, is playing catch-up because managers chose to emphasize increased traditional services rather than develop an e-commerce division when the environment changed due to the rapid rise of Internet business.

Organizations also become vulnerable because of *environmental decline* or *increased competition*. Environmental decline refers to reduced energy and resources available to support an organization. When the environment has less capacity to support organizations, the organization has to either scale down operations or shift to another domain.[92] For example, banks, real estate firms, oil service firms, and many other organizations found the total resource base in the Southwest declining after oil prices dropped. Companies had to divide up a shrinking pie, so several of them inevitably declined.

Increased global competition is also influencing many companies to scale down operations and cut back personnel as they strive for lean, nimble organizations. As discussed earlier, large companies have become bloated with too many administrative and support personnel and find that they need to slim down to remain competitive. Firms such as Procter & Gamble, American Home Products Corp., Sara Lee, and Bank One have all experienced major layoffs, arguing that cutbacks are necessary in an era of cutthroat competition.[93]

A MODEL OF DECLINE STAGES

Based on an extensive review of organizational decline research, a model of decline stages has been proposed and is summarized in Exhibit 13.10. This model suggests that decline, if not managed properly, can move through five stages resulting in organizational dissolution.[94]

1. *Blinded stage.* The first stage of decline is the internal and external changes that threaten long-term survival and may require the organization to tighten up. The organization may have excess personnel, cumbersome procedures, or lack of harmony with customers. Leaders often miss the signals of decline at this point, and the solution is to develop effective scanning and control systems that indicate when something is wrong. With timely information, alert leaders can bring the organization back to top performance.

2. *Inaction stage.* The second stage of decline is called inaction, in which denial occurs despite signs of deteriorating performance. Leaders may try to persuade employees that all is well. Creative accounting may make things look well during this period. The solution is for leaders to recognize decline and take prompt action to realign the organization with the environment. Leadership actions can include new problem-solving approaches, increasing decision-making participation, and encouraging expression of dissatisfaction to learn what is wrong.

EXHIBIT 13.10   *Stages of Decline and the Widening Performance Gap*

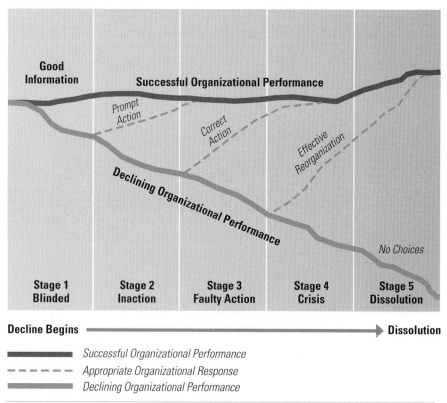

Source: Reprinted from "Decline in Organizations: A Literature Integration and Extension," by William Weitzel and Ellen Jonsson, published in *Administrative Science Quarterly*, Vol. 34 (1), March 1989, by permission of *Administrative Science Quarterly*.

3. *Faulty action.* In the third stage, the organization is facing serious problems, and indicators of poor performance cannot be ignored. Failure to adjust to the declining spiral at this point can lead to organizational failure. Leaders are forced by severe circumstances to consider major changes. Actions may involve retrenchment, including downsizing personnel. Leaders should reduce employee uncertainty by clarifying values and providing information. A major mistake at this stage decreases the organization's chance for a turnaround.

4. *The crisis stage.* In stage four, the organization still has not been able to deal with decline effectively and is facing a panic. The organization may experience chaos, efforts to go back to basics, sharp changes, and anger. It is best for an organization to prevent a stage-four crisis, and the only solution is major reorganization. The social fabric of the organization is eroding, and dramatic action, such as replacing top administrators, and revolutionary changes in structure, strategy, and culture, are necessary. Downsizing may be severe.

5. *Dissolution.* This stage of decline is irreversible. The organization is suffering loss of markets and reputation, the loss of its best personnel, and capital depletion. The only available strategy is to close down the organization in an orderly fashion and reduce the separation trauma of employees.

The following example of a once venerable law firm shows how failure to respond appropriately to signs of decline can lead to disaster.

In Practice 13.5

Mudge, Rose, Guthrie, Alexander & Ferdon

As the remaining partners in the New York law firm that once counted Richard Nixon among its members met to consider a plan of dissolution, the firm's problems had long been widely known in legal circles. Mudge's leaders failed to recognize the first signals of decline (blinded stage) as the firm gradually lost touch with customers and with changes in the law world. The company culture promoted the genteel, passive approach of the 1950s and 1960s and failed to develop partners who understood the need to hustle and retain business in the competitive legal world of the 1990s. Top leaders never even met with executives of Cigna Life Insurance Co., one of their top clients, which ultimately bolted for a more aggressive competitor.

As signs of trouble grew, executives responded with inaction. Unproductive partners were kept on, draining profits and morale, because the executive committee couldn't agree on what to do. Finally, the firm added a number of strong young partners in the areas of litigation, real estate, and white-collar defense, but when these partners later met to air their grievances over the firm's operations, executives responded with faulty action—supporting the weaker partners and trying to strengthen a paternalistic corporate culture that no longer worked. At the crisis stage, leaders were unable to make the revolutionary changes in structure, strategy, and culture that could turn the company around.

The departure of top-performing partners and significant clients sapped what strength remained in the 126-year-old firm. With little loyalty among partners or clients and with its reputation virtually destroyed, the only option for the organization was dissolution. As one partner put it: "You can't hold together something that no longer exists."[95]

As this example shows, properly managing organizational decline is necessary if an organization is to avoid dissolution. Leaders have a responsibility to detect the signs of decline, acknowledge them, implement necessary action, and reverse course.

SUMMARY AND INTERPRETATION

This chapter integrates ideas from throughout the book and covers several important topics concerning contemporary trends in organization design. All firms are facing significant global forces that demand new approaches to organization design and management. Managers can develop a number of characteristics that contribute to long-term organizational excellence. This chapter examined attributes of strategic orientation, top management, organization design, and corporate culture that are usually found in excellent companies.

Many companies are developing overseas operations to take advantage of global markets. One way companies get involved globally is through international strategic alliances, such as joint ventures or consortia of independent organizations that share resources and access to one another's markets. Global work teams are increasingly being used to help companies expand their operations internationally.

Organizations typically evolve through four stages, beginning with a domestic orientation, shifting to an international orientation, then a multinational orientation, and finally to a global orientation that sees the whole world as a potential market. Organizations initially use an export department, then an international division, and finally develop into a worldwide geographic or product structure. Huge global firms may use a matrix or transnational form of structure.

A global product structure is typically best when a company has many opportunities for globalization, which means products can be standardized and sold worldwide. A global geographic structure is used when a company's products and services have local country advantages, which means they will do best when tailored to local needs and cultures. When an international company must succeed on two dimensions—global and local—simultaneously, the matrix structure is appropriate. When global companies compete on multiple dimensions simultaneously, requiring worldwide learning and knowledge sharing, they may evolve toward a transnational model, which is a global learning organization. Employee empowerment is essential to learning organizations on both the domestic and international level. Managers empower employees by giving them four elements they need to act freely: information, knowledge, power, and rewards.

When a company needs to change toward a learning organization, a transformational leader is needed to create a vision, mobilize commitment and empower employees to help achieve it, and institutionalize a culture of change. Top leaders are responsible for recognizing the need for change and helping to implement it. Recent research has explored the impact of top-management teams and turnover on organizations. Turnover at the top brings new energy and perspectives for organizational leadership. Succession also provides new skills to cope with changing environmental conditions and may symbolize a new organizational direction. Top leadership often changes when an organization suffers a period of decline. Top leaders are responsible for recognizing the causes and stages of decline and getting the organization back on track.

BRIEFCASE

As an organization manager, keep these guidelines in mind:

1. Implement strategies for achieving internal company characteristics that contribute to long-term organizational excellence. Remember that the company's strategic orientation, top-management characteristics, organization design, and corporate culture strongly influence company success.

2. Choose a global product structure when the organization can gain competitive advantages through a globalization strategy (global integration). Choose a global geographic structure when the company has advantages with a multidomestic strategy (national responsiveness). Use an international division when the company is primarily domestic and has only a few international operations.

3. Develop international strategic alliances, such as licensing, joint ventures, and consortia, as fast and inexpensive ways to become involved in international sales and operations.

4. Implement a matrix structure when the forces for global integration and national responsiveness are about equal. Move to a transnational model when the organization is responding to many global forces simultaneously and needs to promote worldwide learning and knowledge sharing.

5. When the organization needs to change toward a learning organization, act as a transformational leader by creating a compelling vision, mobilizing commitment, empowering workers, and institutionalizing a culture of change.

6. Encourage periodic top management succession to ensure a flow of fresh energy and ideas into the upper ranks. Adapt to specific problems by bringing needed skills and experience into the chief executive position. Remember that executive succession is typically associated with improved organizational performance.

7. Be aware of the causes of organizational decline and do not ignore signs of deteriorating performance. Take swift action to prevent the firm from reaching the final stages of decline.

KEY CONCEPTS

consortia	international division
domestic stage	international stage
empowerment	joint ventures
global companies	multidomestic
global geographic structure	multidomestic strategy
global matrix structure	multinational stage
global product structure	organizational decline
global stage	ritual scapegoating
global teams	transformational leaders
globalization strategy	transnational model

DISCUSSION QUESTIONS

1. What are the consequences to an organization if no single company or country is able to dominate global commerce?
2. Of the eighteen characteristics associated with long-term organizational excellence, which three do you think are of primary importance for today's companies? Explain.
3. Under what conditions should an organization consider adopting a global product structure as opposed to a global geographic structure?
4. Why do you think firms join strategic alliances? Would they be better served to go it alone in international operations? Explain.
5. When would an organization consider using a global matrix structure? How does the global matrix differ from the domestic matrix structure described in Chapter 3?
6. Compare the description of the transnational model in this chapter to the elements of the learning organization described in Chapter 1. Do you think the transnational model seems workable in a huge global firm? Discuss.
7. Why is the empowerment of employees essential for the creation of a learning organization?
8. How might top-management succession be used for adaptation or ritual scapegoating? Explain.
9. Do you see any conflict between the concept of an individual transformational leader and the current emphasis on the importance of top-management teams? Discuss.
10. Why do you think top leaders often ignore or deny the signs of deteriorating performance, thus allowing the firm to decline? Discuss.

CHAPTER 13 WORKBOOK   *Creating a Learning Organization**

Imagine you are working in the ideal learning organization. What would it be like and how is that different from a recent work experience you have had (or your experience in the "job" of student)? What keeps your workplace from becoming more learning oriented? Complete the following table:

*Adapted by Dorothy Marcic from "Defining Your Learning Organization," in Peter Senge, et al., *The Fifth Discipline Fieldbook* (New York: Doubleday, 1994): 50–52.

What are aspects of the ideal learning organization?	What are behaviors for this aspect?	What would be the result of these behaviors?	What are blocks to achieving these?	How would I know if progress has been made?
1. (Example): Employees feel what they do has some meaning.	They display energy and enthusiasm when they work.	The team is more motivated and new ideas are generated.	There is a lack of clarity on how tasks help fulfill the overall mission.	Employees talk about how they are fulfilling an important mission.
2.				
3.				
4.				
5.				
6.				

FURTHER WORK

1. Choose the three aspects that are the most compelling to you and the organization.
2. How can the organization achieve these? What are the major blocks?
3. *Optional:* Form groups and compare your table and the three aspects you chose with those of other students. Are there some common themes? What is most important in creating a learning organization? What are reasons for not having a learning organization—what are the blocks?

"To make money and have fun." W. L. Gore

THE FIRST DAY ON THE JOB

Bursting with resolve, Jack Dougherty, a newly minted M.B.A. from the College of William and Mary, reported to his first day at W. L. Gore & Associates on July 26, 1976. He presented himself to Bill Gore, shook hands firmly, looked him in the eye, and said he was ready for anything.

Jack was not ready, however, for what happened next. Gore replied, "That's fine, Jack, fine. Why don't you look around and find something you'd like to do?" Three frustrating weeks later he found that something: trading in his dark blue suit for jeans, he loaded fabric into the mouth of a machine that laminated the company's patented GORE-TEX®[1] membrane to fabric. By 1982, Jack had become responsible for all advertising and marketing in the fabrics group. This story is part of the folklore of W. L. Gore & Associates.

Today the process is more structured. Regardless of the job for which they are hired, new Associates[2] take a journey through the business before settling into their own positions. A new sales Associate in the fabrics division may spend six weeks rotating through different areas before beginning to concentrate on sales and marketing. Among other things the newcomer learns is how GORE-TEX fabric is made, what it can and cannot do, how Gore handles customer complaints, and how it makes its investment decisions.

Anita McBride related her early experience at W. L. Gore & Associates this way: Before I came to Gore, I had worked for a structured organization. I came here, and for the first month it was fairly structured because I was going through training and this is what we do and this is how Gore is and all of that. I went to Flagstaff for that training. After a month I came down to Phoenix and my sponsor said, "Well, here's your office; it's a wonderful office," and "Here's your desk," and walked away. And I thought, "Now what do I do?" You know, I was waiting for a memo or something, or a job description. Finally after another month I was so frustrated, I felt, "What have I gotten myself into?" And so I went to my sponsor and I said, "What the heck do you want from me? I need something from you." And he said, "If you don't know what you're supposed to do, examine your commitment, and opportunities."

COMPANY BACKGROUND

W. L. Gore & Associates was formed by the late Wilbert L. Gore and his wife in 1958. The idea for the business sprang from his personal, organizational, and technical experiences at E. I. DuPont de Nemours, and, particularly, his discovery of a chemical compound with unique properties. The compound, now widely know as GORE-TEX, has catapulted W. L. Gore & Associates to a high ranking on the *Forbes* 1998 list of the 500 largest private companies in the United States, with estimated revenues of more than $1.1 billion. The company's avant-garde culture and people management practices resulted in W. L. Gore being ranked as the seventh best company to work for in America by *Fortune* in a January 1998 article.

Wilbert Gore was born in Meridian, Idaho, near Boise in 1912. By age six, according to his own account, he was an avid hiker in the Wasatch Mountain Range in Utah. In those mountains, at a church camp, he met Genevieve, his future wife. In 1935, they got married—in their eyes, a partnership. He would make breakfast and Vieve, as everyone called her, would make lunch. The partnership lasted a lifetime.

He received both a bachelor of science in chemical engineering in 1933 and a master of science in physical chemistry in 1935 from the University of Utah. He began his professional career at American Smelting and Refining in 1936. He moved to Remington Arms Company in 1941 and then to E. I. DuPont de Nemours in 1945. He held positions as research supervisor and head of operations research. While at DuPont, he worked on a team to develop applications for polytetrafluoroethylene, referred to as PTFE in the scientific community and known as "Teflon" by DuPont's consumers. (Consumers know it under other names from other companies.) On this team Wilbert Gore, called Bill by everyone, felt a sense of excited commitment, personal fulfillment,

---

1 GORE-TEX is a registered trademark of W. L. Gore & Associates.
2. In this case the word "Associate" is used and capitalized because in W. L. Gore & Associates' literature the word is always used instead of employees and is capitalized. In fact, case writers were told that Gore "never had 'employees'—always 'Associates.'"

Prepared by Frank Shipper, Department of Management and Marketing, Franklin P. Perdue School of Business, Salisbury State University and Charles C. Manz, Nirenberg Professor of Business Leadership, School of Management, University of Massachusetts. Used with permission.

and self-direction. He followed the development of computers and transistors and felt that PTFE had the ideal insulating characteristics for use with such equipment.

He tried many ways to make a PTFE-coated ribbon cable without success. A breakthrough came in his home basement laboratory while he was explaining the problem to his nineteen year old son Bob. The young Gore saw some PTFE sealant tape made by 3M and asked his father, "Why don't you try this tape?" Bill then explained that everyone knew that you cannot bond PTFE to itself. Bob went on to bed.

Bill Gore remained in his basement lab and proceeded to try what everyone knew would not work. At about 4:00 A.M. he woke up his son, waving a small piece of cable around and saying excitedly, "It works, it works." The following night father and son returned to the basement lab to make ribbon cable coated with PTFE. Because the breakthrough idea came from Bob, the patent for the cable was issued in Bob's name.

For the next four months Bill Gore tried to persuade DuPont to make a new product—PTFE-coated ribbon cable. By this time in his career Bill Gore knew some of the decision makers at DuPont. After talking to a number of them, he came to realize that DuPont wanted to remain a supplier of raw materials and not a fabricator.

Bill and his wife, Vieve, began discussing the possibility of starting their own insulated wire and cable business. On January 1, 1958, their wedding anniversary, they founded W. L. Gore & Associates. The basement of their home served as their first facility. After finishing dinner that night, Vieve turned to her husband of twenty-three years and said, "Well, let's clear up the dishes, go downstairs, and get to work."

Bill Gore was forty-five years old with five children to support when he left DuPont. He put aside a career of seventeen years, and a good, secure salary. To finance the first two years of the business, he and Vieve mortgaged their house and took $4,000 from savings. All their friends told them not to do it.

The first few years were rough. In lieu of salary, some of their employees accepted room and board in the Gore home. At one point eleven Associates were living and working under one roof. One afternoon, while sifting PTFE powder, Vieve received a call from the City of Denver's water department. The caller indicated that he was interested in the ribbon cable, but wanted to ask some technical questions. Bill was out running some errands. The caller asked for the product manager. Vieve explain that he was out at the moment. Next he asked for the sales manager and finally, the president. Vieve explained that they were also out. The caller became outraged and hollered, "What kind of company is this anyway?" With a little diplomacy the Gores were able eventually to secure an order for $100,000. This order put the company on a profitable footing and it began to take off.

W. L. Gore & Associates continued to grow and develop new products, primarily derived from PTFE. Its best-known product would become GORE-TEX fabric. In 1986, Bill Gore died while backpacking in the Wind River Mountains of Wyoming. He was then Chairman of the Board. His son Bob continued to occupy the position of president. Vieve remained as the only other officer, secretary-treasurer.

COMPANY PRODUCTS

In 1998 W. L. Gore & Associates has a fairly extensive line of high-tech products that are used in a variety of applications, including electronic, waterproofing, industrial filtration, industrial seals, and coatings.

Electronic & Wire Products

Gore electronic products have been found in unconventional places where conventional products will not do—in space shuttles, for example, where Gore wire and cable assemblies withstand the heat of ignition and the cold of space. In addition, they have been found in fast computers, transmitting signals at up to 93 percent of the speed of light. Gore cables have even gone underground, in oil-drilling operations, and underseas, on submarines that require superior microwave signal equipment and no-fail cables that can survive high pressure. The Gore electronic products division has a history of anticipating future customer needs with innovative products. Gore electronic products have been well received in industry for their ability to last under adverse conditions. For example, Gore has become, according to Sally Gore, leader in Human Resources and Communications, " . . . . one of the largest manufacturers of ultrasound cable in the world, the reason being that Gore's electronic cables' signal transmission is very, very accurate and it's very thin and extremely flexible and has a very, very long flex life. That makes it ideal for things like ultrasound and many medical electronic applications."

Medical Products

The medical division began on the ski slopes of Colorado. Bill was skiing with a friend, Dr. Ben Eiseman of Denver General Hospital. As Bill Gore told the story: "We were just to start a run when I absentmindedly pulled a small tubular section of GORE-TEX out of my pocket and looked at it. 'What is that stuff?' Ben asked. So I told him about its properties. 'Feels great,' he said. 'What do you use it for?' 'Got no idea,' I said. 'Well give it to me,' he said, 'and I'll try it in a vascular graft on a pig.' Two weeks later, he called me up. Ben was pretty excited. 'Bill,' he said, 'I put it in a pig and it works. What do I do now?' I told him to get together with Pete Cooper in our Flagstaff plant, and let them figure it out." Not long after, hundreds of thousands of people throughout the world began walking around with GORE-TEX vascular grafts.

GORE-TEX-expanded PTFE proved to be an ideal replacement for human tissue in many situations. In patients suffering from cardiovascular disease the diseased portion of arteries has been replaced by tubes of expanded PTFE—strong, biocompatible structures capable of carrying blood at arterial pressures. Gore has a strong position in this product segment. Other Gore medical products have included patches that can literally mend broken hearts by sealing holes, and sutures that allow for tissue attachment and offer the surgeon silk-like handling coupled with extreme strength. In 1985, W. L. Gore & Associates won Britain's Prince Philip Award for Polymers in the Service of Mankind. The award recognized especially the lifesaving achievements of the Gore medical products team.

Two recently developed products by this division are a new patch material that is intended to incorporate more tissue into the graft more quickly and GORE™ RideOn®3 Cable System for bicycles. According to Amy LeGere of the medical division, "All the top pro riders in the world are using it. It was introduced just about a year ago and it has become an industry standard." This product had a positive cash flow very soon after its introduction. Some Associates who were also outdoor sports enthusiasts developed the product and realized that Gore could make a great bicycle cable that would have 70 percent less friction and need no lubrication. The Associates maintain that the profitable development, production, and marketing of such specialized niche products are possible because of the lack of bureaucracy and associated overhead, Associate commitment, and the use of product champions.

Industrial Products

The output of the industrial products division has included sealants, filter bags, cartridges, clothes, and coatings. Industrial filtration products, such as GORE-TEX filter bags, have reduced air pollution and recovered valuable solids from gases and liquids more completely than alternatives—and they have done so economically. In the future they may make coal-burning plants completely smoke free, contributing to a cleaner environment. The specialized and critical applications of these products, along with Gore's reputation for quality, have had a strong influence on industrial purchasers.

This division has developed a unique joint sealant—a flexible cord of porous PTFE—that can be applied as a gasket to the most complex shapes, sealing them to prevent leakage of corrosive chemicals, even at extreme temperature and pressure. Steam valves packed with GORE-TEX have been sold with a lifetime guarantee, provided the valve is used properly. In addition, this division has introduced Gore's first consumer product—GLIDE®4—a dental floss. "That was a product that people knew about for a while and they went the route of trying to persuade industry leaders to promote the product, but they didn't really pursue it very well. So out of basically default almost, Gore decided, Okay they're not doing it right. Let's go in ourselves. We had a champion, John Spencer, who took that and pushed it forward through the dentist's offices and it just skyrocketed. There were many more people on the team but it was basically getting that one champion who focused on that product and got it out. They told him it 'Couldn't be done,' 'It's never going to work,' and I guess that's all he needed. It was done and it worked," said Ray Wnenchak of the industrial products division. Amy LeGere added, "The champion worked very closely with the medical people to understand the medical market like claims and labeling so that when the product came out on the market it would be consistent with our medical products. And that's where, when we cross divisions, we know whom to work with and with whom we combine forces so that the end result takes the strengths of all of our different teams." As of 1998,

3 GORE RideOn is a registered trademark of W.L. Gore & Associates.

4 GLIDE is a registered trademark of W.L. Gore & Associates.

GLIDE has captured a major portion of the dental floss market and the mint flavor is the largest selling variety in the U.S. market based on dollar volume.

Fabric Products

The Gore fabrics division has supplied laminates to manufacturers of foul weather gear, ski wear, running suits, footwear, gloves, and hunting and fishing garments. Firefighters and U.S. Navy pilots have worn GORE-TEX fabric gear, as have some Olympic athletes. The U.S. Army adopted a total garment system built around a GORE-TEX fabric component. Employees in high-tech clean rooms also wear GORE-TEX garments.

GORE-TEX membrane has 9 billion pores randomly dotting each square inch and is feather light. Each pore is 700 times larger than a water vapor molecule, yet thousands of times smaller than a water droplet. Wind and water cannot penetrate the pores, but perspiration can escape.

As a result, fabrics bonded with GORE-TEX membrane are waterproof, windproof, and breathable. The laminated fabrics bring protection from the elements to a variety of products—from survival gear to high-fashion rainwear. Other manufacturers, including 3M, Burlington Industries, Akzo Nobel Fibers, and DuPont, have brought out products to compete with GORE-TEX fabrics. Earlier, the toughest competition came from firms that violated the patents on GORE-TEX. Gore successfully challenged them in court. In 1993, the basic patent on the process for manufacturing ran out. Nevertheless, as Sally Gore explained, "... what happens is you get an initial process patent and then as you begin to create things with this process you get additional patents. For instance we have patents protecting our vascular graft, different patents for protecting GORE-TEX patches, and still other patents protecting GORE-TEX industrial sealants and filtration material. One of our patent attorneys did a talk recently, a year or so ago, when the patent expired and a lot of people who were saying, Oh, golly, are we going to be in trouble! We would be in trouble if we didn't have any patents. Our attorney had this picture with a great big umbrella, sort of a parachute, with Gore under it. Next he showed us lots of little umbrellas scattered all over the sky. So you protect certain niche markets and niche areas, but indeed competition increases as your initial patents expire." Gore, however, has continued to have a commanding position in the active wear market.

To meet the needs of a variety of customer needs, Gore introduced a new family of fabrics in the 1990s (Exhibit 13.11). The introduction posed new challenges. According to Bob Winterling," ... we did such a great job with the brand GORE-TEX that we actually have hurt ourselves in many ways. By that I mean it has been very difficult for us to come up with other new brands, because many people didn't even know Gore. We are the GORE-TEX company. One thing we decided to change about Gore four or five years ago was instead of being the GORE-TEX company we wanted to become the Gore company and that underneath the Gore company we had an umbrella of products that fall out of being the great Gore company. So it was a shift in how we positioned GORE-TEX. Today GORE-TEX is stronger than ever as it's turned out, but now we've ventured

EXHIBIT 13.11   *Gore's Family of Fabrics*

Brand Name	Activity/Conditions	Breathability	Water Protection	Wind Protection
GORE-TEX®	rain, snow, cold, windy	very breathable	waterproof	windproof
Immersion™ technology	for fishing and paddle sports	very breathable	waterproof	windproof
Ocean technology	for offshore and coastal sailing	very breathable	waterproof	windproof
Windstopper®	cool/cold, windy	very breathable	no water resistance	windproof
Gore Dryloft™	cold, windy, light precipitation	extremely breathable	water resistant	windproof
Activent™	cool/cold, windy, light precipitation	extremely breathable	water resistant	windproof

into such things as WindStopper®[5] fabric that is very big in the golf market. It could be a sweater or a fleece piece or even a knit shirt with the WindStopper behind it or closer to your skin and what it does is it stops the wind. It's not waterproof; it's water resistant. What we've tried to do is position the Gore name and beneath that all of the great products of the company."

W. L. GORE & ASSOCIATES APPROACH TO ORGANIZATION AND STRUCTURE

W. L. Gore & Associates has never had titles, hierarchy, or any of the conventional structures associated with enterprises of its size. The titles of president and secretary-treasurer continue to be used only because they are required by the laws of incorporation. In addition, Gore has never had a corporatewide mission or code of ethics statement nor has Gore ever required or prohibited business units from developing such statements for themselves. Thus, the Associates of some business units who have felt a need for such statements have developed them on their own. When questioned about this issue, one Associate stated, "The company belief is that (1) its four basic operating principles cover ethical practices

---

5 WindStopper is a registered trademark of W.L. Gore & Associates.

required of people in business; (2) it will not tolerate illegal practices." Gore's management style has been referred to as unmanagement. The organization has been guided by Bill's experiences on teams at DuPont and has evolved as needed.

For example, in 1965 W. L. Gore & Associates was a thriving company with a facility on Paper Mill Road in Newark, Delaware. One Monday morning in the summer, Bill Gore was taking his usual walk through the plant. All of a sudden he realized that he did not know everyone in the plant. The team had become too big. As a result, he established the practice of limiting plant size to approximately two hundred Associates. Thus was born the expansion policy of "Get big by staying small." The purpose of maintaining small plants was to accentuate a close-knit atmosphere and encourage communication among Associates in a facility.

At the beginning of 1998 W. L. Gore & Associates consisted of over forty-five plants worldwide with approximately seven thousand Associates. In some cases, the plants are grouped together on the same site (as in Flagstaff, Arizona, with ten plants). Overseas, Gore's manufacturing facilities are located in Scotland, Germany, China, and the company has two joint ventures in Japan (see Exhibit 13.12). In addition, it has sales facilities located in fifteen other countries. Gore

EXHIBIT 13.12   *International Locations of W.L. Gore & Associates*

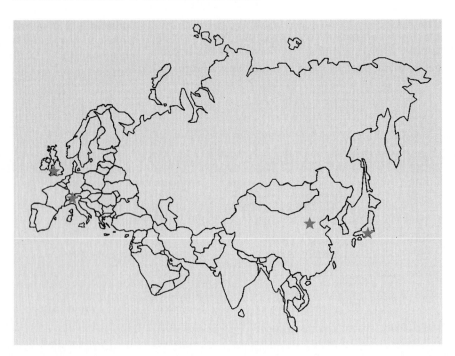

manufactures electronic, medical, industrial, and fabric products. In addition, it has numerous sales offices worldwide including Eastern Europe and Russia.

THE LATTICE ORGANIZATION

W. L. Gore & Associates has been described not only as unmanaged, but also as unstructured. Bill Gore referred to the structure as a lattice organization (see Exhibit 13.13). The characteristics of this structure are:

1. Direct lines of communication—person to person—no intermediary
2. No fixed or assigned authority
3. Sponsors, not bosses
4. Natural leadership defined by followership
5. Objectives set by those who must "make them happen"
6. Tasks and functions organized through commitments

The structure within the lattice is complex and evolves from interpersonal interactions, self commitment to group-known responsibilities, natural leadership, and group-imposed discipline. Bill Gore once explained the structure this way: "Every successful organization has an underground lattice. It's where the news spreads like lightning, where people can go around the organization to get things done." An analogy might be drawn to a structure of constant cross area teams—the equivalent of quality circles going on all the time. When a puzzled interviewer told Bill that he was having trouble understanding how planning and accountability worked, Bill replied with a grin: "So am I. You ask me how it works? Every which way."

The lattice structure has not been without its critics. As Bill Gore stated, "I'm told from time to time that a lattice organization can't meet a crisis well because it takes too long to reach a consensus when there are no bosses. But this isn't true. Actually, a lattice by its very nature works particularly well in a crisis. A lot of useless effort is avoided because there is no rigid management hierarchy to conquer before you can attack a problem."

The lattice has been put to the test on a number of occasions. For example, in 1975, Dr. Charles Campbell of the University of Pittsburgh reported that a GORE-TEX arterial graft had developed an aneurysm. If the bubble-like protrusion continued to expand, it would explode.

EXHIBIT 13.13   *The Lattice Structure*

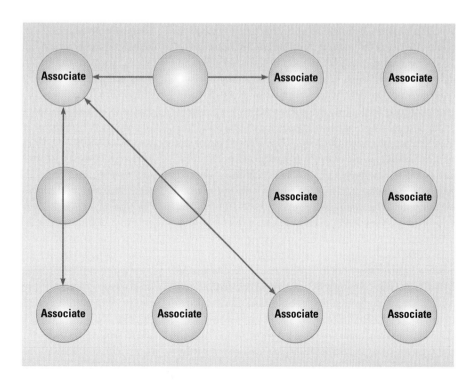

Obviously, this life-threatening situation had to be resolved quickly and permanently. Within only a few days of Dr. Campbell's first report, he flew to Newark to present his findings to Bill and Bob Gore and a few other Associates. The meeting lasted two hours. Dan Hubis, a former policeman who had joined Gore to develop new production methods, had an idea before the meeting was over. He returned to his work area to try some different production techniques. After only three hours and twelve tries, he had developed a permanent solution. In other words, in three hours a potentially damaging problem to both patients and the company was resolved. Furthermore, Hubis's redesigned graft went on to win widespread acceptance in the medical community.

Eric Reynolds, founder of Marmot Mountain Works Ltd. of Grand Junction, Colorado, and a major Gore customer, raised another issue: "I think the lattice has its problems with the day-to-day nitty-gritty of getting things done on time and out the door. I don't think Bill realizes how the lattice system affects customers. I mean, after you've established a relationship with someone about product quality, you can call up one day and suddenly find that someone new to you is handling your problem. It's frustrating to find a lack of continuity." He went on to say: "But I have to admit that I've personally seen at Gore remarkable examples of people coming out of nowhere and excelling."

When Bill Gore was asked if the lattice structure could be used by other companies, he answered: "No. For example, established companies would find it very difficult to use the lattice. Too many hierarchies would be destroyed. When you remove titles and positions and allow people to follow who they want, it may very well be someone other than the person who has been in charge. The lattice works for us, but it's always evolving. You have to expect problems." He maintained that the lattice system worked best when it was put in place in start-up companies by dynamic entrepreneurs.

Not all Gore Associates function well in this unstructured work environment, especially initially. For those accustomed to a more structured work environment, there can be adjustment problems. As Bill Gore said: "All our lives most of us have been told what to do, and some people don't know how to respond when asked to do something—and have the very real option of saying no—on their job. It's the new Associate's responsibility to find out what he or she can do for the good of the operation." The vast majority of the new Associates, after some initial floundering, have adapted quickly.

Others, especially those who require more structured working conditions, have found that Gore's flexible workplace is not for them. According to Bill for those few, "It's an unhappy situation, both for the Associate and the sponsor. If there is no contribution, there is no paycheck."

As Anita McBride, an Associate in Phoenix, noted: "It's not for everybody. People ask me do we have turnover, and yes we do have turnover. What you're seeing looks like utopia, but it also looks extreme. If you finally figure the system, it can be real exciting. If you can't handle it, you gotta go. Probably by your own choice, because you're going to be so frustrated." Overall, the Associates appear to have responded positively to the Gore system of unmanagement and unstructure. And the company's lattice organization has proven itself to be good for it from a bottom-line perspective. Bill estimated the year before he died that "the profit per Associate is double" that of DuPont.

FEATURES OF W. L. GORE'S CULTURE

Outsiders have been struck by the degree of informality and humor in the Gore organization. Meetings tend to be only as long as necessary. As Trish Hearn, an Associate in Newark, Delaware, said, "No one feels a need to pontificate." Words such as "responsibilities" and "commitments" are commonly heard, whereas words such as "employees," "subordinates," and "managers" are taboo in the Gore culture. This is an organization that has always taken what it does very seriously, without its members taking themselves too seriously.

For a company of its size, Gore has always had a very short organizational pyramid. As of 1995 the pyramid consists of Bob Gore, the late Bill Gore's son, as president and Vieve, Bill Gore's widow, as secretary-treasurer. He has been the chief executive officer for more than twenty years. No second-in-command or successor has been designated. All the other members of the Gore organization were, and continue to be, referred to as Associates.

Some outsiders have had problems with the idea of no titles. Sarah Clifton, an Associate at the Flagstaff facility, was being pressed by some outsiders as to what her title was. She made one up and had it printed on some business cards: SUPREME COMMANDER (see Exhibit 13.14). When Bill Gore learned what she did, he loved it and recounted the story to others.

EXHIBIT 13.14   *The Supreme Commander*

Leaders, Not Managers

Within W. L. Gore & Associates, the various people who take lead roles are thought of as being leaders, not managers. Bill Gore described in an internal memo the kinds of leadership and the role of leadership as follows:

1. The Associate who is recognized by a team as having a special knowledge, or experience (for example, this could be a chemist, computer expert, machine operator, salesman, engineer, lawyer). This kind of leader gives the team *guidance in a special area.*
2. The Associate the team looks to for coordination of individual activities in order to achieve the agreed upon objectives of the team. The role of this leader is to persuade team members to *make the commitments* necessary for success (commitment seeker).
3. The Associate who proposes necessary objectives and activities and seeks agreement and team *consensus on objectives.* This leader is perceived by the team members as having a good grasp of how the objectives of the team fit in with the broad objective of the enterprise. This kind of leader is often also the "commitment seeking" leader in 2 above.
4. The leader who evaluates relative contribution of team members (in consultation with other sponsors), and reports these contribution evaluations to a compensation committee. This leader may also participate in the compensation committee on relative contribution and pay and *reports changes in compensation* to individual Associates. This leader is then also a compensation sponsor.
5. *Product specialists* who coordinate the research, manufacturing, and marketing of one product type within a business, interacting with team leaders and individual Associates who have com-

mitments regarding the product type. They are respected for their knowledge and dedication to their products.
6. *Plant leaders* who help coordinate activities of people within a plant.
7. *Business leaders* who help coordinate activities of people in a business.
8. *Functional leaders* who help coordinate activities of people in a "functional" area.
9. *Corporate leaders* who help coordinate activities of people in different businesses and functions and who try to promote communication and cooperation among all Associates.
10. *Entrepreneuring Associates* who organize new teams for new businesses, new products, new processes, new devices, new marketing efforts, new or better methods of all kinds. These leaders invite other Associates to "sign up" for their project.

It is clear that leadership is widespread in our lattice organization and that it is continually changing and evolving. The situation that leaders are frequently *also* sponsors should not imply that these are different activities and responsibilities.

Leaders are not authoritarians, managers of people, or supervisors who tell us what to do or forbid us to do things; nor are they "parents" to whom we transfer our own self-responsibility. However, they do often advise us of the consequences of actions we have done or propose to do. Our actions result in contributions, or lack of contribution, to the success of our enterprise. Our pay depends on the magnitude of our contributions. This is the basic discipline of our lattice organization.

Egalitarian and Innovative

Other aspects of the Gore culture have been aimed at promoting an egalitarian atmosphere, such as parking lots with no reserved parking spaces except for customers and disabled workers or visitors; dining areas—only one in each plant—set up as focal points for Associate interaction. As Dave McCarter of Phoenix explained: "The design is no accident. The lunchroom in Flagstaff has a fireplace in the middle. We want people to like to be here." The location of a plant is also no accident. Sites have been selected on the basis of transportation access, a nearby university, beautiful surroundings, and climate appeal. Land cost has never been a primary consideration. McCarter justified the selection by stating: "Expanding is not costly in the long run. The loss of money is what you make happen by stymieing people into a box."

Bob Gore is a champion of Gore culture. As Sally Gore related, "We have managed surprisingly to maintain our sense of freedom and our entrepreneurial spirit. I think what we've found is that we had to develop new ways to communicate with Associates because you can't communicate with six thousand people the way that you can communicate with five hundred people. It just can't be done. So we have developed a newsletter that we didn't have before. One of the most important communication mediums that we developed, and this was Bob Gore's idea, is a digital voice exchange which we call our Gorecom. Basically everyone has a mailbox and a password. Lots of companies have gone to e-mail and we use e-mail, but Bob feels very strongly that we're very much an oral culture and there's a big difference between cultures that are predominantly oral and predominantly written. Oral cultures encourage direct communication, which is, of course, something that we encourage."

In rare cases an Associate "is trying to be unfair," in Bill's own words. In one case the problem was chronic absenteeism and in another, an individual was caught stealing. "When that happens, all hell breaks loose," said Bill Gore. "We can get damned authoritarian when we have to."

Over the years, Gore & Associates has faced a number of unionization drives. The company has neither tried to dissuade Associates from attending an organizational meeting nor retaliated when flyers were passed out. As of 1995, none of the plants has been organized. Bill believed that no need existed for third-party representation under the lattice structure. He asked the question, "Why would Associates join a union when they own the company? It seems rather absurd."

Commitment has long been considered a two-way street. W. L. Gore & Associates has tried to avoid layoffs. Instead of cutting pay, which in the Gore culture would be disastrous to morale, the company has used a system of temporary transfers within a plant or cluster of plants and voluntary layoffs. Exhibit 13.17 in the back contains excerpts of interviews with two Gore Associates that further indicate the nature of the culture and work environment at W. L. Gore and Associates.

W. L. GORE & ASSOCIATES SPONSOR PROGRAM

Bill Gore knew that products alone did not a company make. He wanted to avoid smothering the company in thick layers of formal "management." He felt that hierarchy stifled individual creativity. As the company grew, he knew that he had to find a way to assist new people and to follow their progress. This was particularly important when it came to compensation. W. L. Gore & Associates developed its "sponsor" program to meet these needs.

When people apply to Gore, they are initially screened by personnel specialists. As many as ten

EXHIBIT 13.15   *Growth of Gore's Sales vs. Gross Domestic Product*

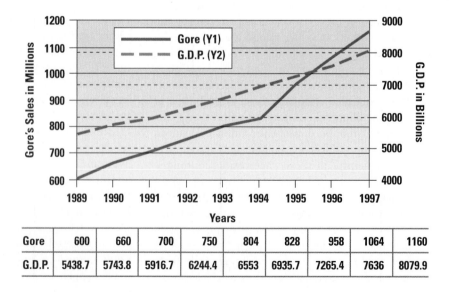

	1989	1990	1991	1992	1993	1994	1995	1996	1997
Gore	600	660	700	750	804	828	958	1064	1160
G.D.P.	5438.7	5743.8	5916.7	6244.4	6553	6935.7	7265.4	7636	8079.9

references might be contacted on each applicant. Those who meet the basic criteria are interviewed by current Associates. The interviews have been described as rigorous by those who have gone through them. Before anyone is hired, an Associate must agree to be his or her sponsor. The sponsor is to take a personal interest in the new Associate's contributions, problems, and goals, acting as both a coach and an advocate. The sponsor tracks the new Associate's progress, helping and encouraging, dealing with weaknesses, and concentrating on strengths. Sponsoring is not a short-term commitment. All Associates have sponsors and many have more than one. When individuals are hired initially, they are likely to have a sponsor in their immediate work area. If they move to another area, they may have a sponsor in that work area. As Associates' commitments change or grow, they may acquire additional sponsors. Because the hiring process looks beyond conventional views of what makes a good Associate, some anomalies have occurred. Bill Gore proudly told the story of "a very young man" of 84 who walked in, applied, and spent five very good years with the company. The individual had thirty years of experience in the industry before joining Gore. His other Associates had no problems accepting him, but the personnel computer did. It insisted that his age was 48. The individual success stories at Gore have come from diverse backgrounds.

An internal memo by Bill Gore described three roles of sponsors:

1. *Starting sponsor*—a sponsor who helps a new Associate get started on a first job, or a present Associate get started on a new job.
2. *Advocate sponsor*—a sponsor who sees that an Associate's accomplishments are recognized.
3. *Compensation sponsor*—a sponsor who sees to it that an Associate is fairly paid for contributions to the success of the enterprise.

A single person can perform any one or all three kinds of sponsorship. Quite frequently, a sponsoring Associate is a good friend and it is not unknown for two Associates to sponsor each other.

COMPENSATION PRACTICES

Compensation at W. L. Gore & Associates has taken three forms: salary, profit sharing, and an Associates' Stock Ownership Program (ASOP).[6] Entry-level

salary has been in the middle for comparable jobs. According to Sally Gore: "We do not feel we need to be the highest paid. We never try to steal people away from other companies with salary. We want them to come here because of the opportunities for growth and the unique work environment." Associates' salaries have been reviewed at least once a year and more commonly twice a year. The reviews are conducted by a compensation team at each facility, with sponsors for the Associates acting as their advocates during the review process. Prior to meeting with the compensation committee, the sponsor checks with customers or Associates familiar with the person's work to find out what contribution the Associate has made. The compensation team relies heavily on this input. In addition, the compensation team considers the Associate's leadership ability and willingness to help others develop to their fullest.

Profit sharing follows a formula based on economic value added (EVA). Sally Gore had the following to say about the adoption of a formula, "It's become more formalized and in a way, I think that's unfortunate because it used to be a complete surprise to receive a profit share. The thinking of the people like Bob Gore and other leaders was that maybe we weren't using it in the right way and we could encourage people by helping them know more about it and how we made profit-share decisions. The fun of it before was people didn't know when it was coming and all of a sudden you could do something creative about passing out checks. It was great fun and people would have a wonderful time with it. The disadvantage was that Associates then did not focus much on, 'What am I doing to create another profit share?' By using EVA as a method of evaluation for our profit share, we know at the end of every month how much EVA was created that month. When we've created a certain amount of EVA, we then get another profit share. So everybody knows and everyone says, 'We'll do it in January,' so it is done. Now Associates feel more part of the happening to make it work. What have you done? Go make some more sales calls, please! There are lots of things we can do to improve our EVA and everybody has a responsibility to do that." Every month EVA is calculated and every Associate is informed. John Mosko of electronic products commented, " . . . (EVA) lets us know where we are on the path to getting one (a profit share). It's very critical—every Associate knows."

---

6 Similar legally to an ESOP (Employee Stock Ownership Plan). Again, Gore simply has never allowed the word "employee" in any of its documentation.

Annually, Gore also buys company stock equivalent to a fixed percent of the Associates' annual incomes, placing it in the ASOP retirement fund. Thus, an Associate can become a stockholder after being at Gore for a year. Gore's ASOP ensures Associates participate in the growth of the company by acquiring ownership in it. Bill Gore wanted Associates to feel that they themselves are owners. One Associate stated, "This is much more important than profit sharing." In fact, some long-term Associates (including a twenty-five-year veteran machinist) have become millionaires from the ASOP.

W. L. GORE & ASSOCIATES' GUIDING PRINCIPLES AND CORE VALUES

In addition to the sponsor program, Bill Gore articulated four guiding principles:

1. Try to be fair.
2. Encourage, help, and allow other Associates to grow in knowledge, skill, and scope of activity and responsibility.
3. Make your own commitments, and keep them.
4. Consult with other Associates before taking actions that may be "below the water line."

The four principles have been referred to as Fairness, Freedom, Commitment, and Waterline. The *waterline* terminology is drawn from an analogy to ships. If someone pokes a hole in a boat above the water line, the boat will be in relatively little real danger. If someone, however, pokes a hole below the water line, the boat is in immediate danger of sinking. "Water line" issues must be discussed across teams and plants before decisions are made.

The operating principles were put to a test in 1978. By this time word about the qualities of GORE-TEX fabric was being spread throughout the recreational and outdoor markets. Production and shipment had begun in volume. At first a few complaints were heard. Next some of the clothing started coming back. Finally, much of the clothing was being returned. The trouble was that the GORE-TEX fabric was leaking. Waterproofing was one of the major properties responsible for GORE-TEX fabric's success. The company's reputation and credibility were on the line.

Peter W. Gilson, who led Gore's fabrics division recalled: "It was an incredible crisis for us at that point. We were really starting to attract attention; we were taking off—and then this." In the next few months, Gilson and a number of his Associates made a number of those below-the-water line decisions.

First, the researchers determined that oils in human sweat were responsible for clogging the pores in the GORE-TEX fabric and altering the surface tension of the membrane. Thus, water could pass through. They also discovered that a good washing could restore the waterproof property. At first this solution, known as the "Ivory Snow solution," was accepted. A single letter from "Butch," a mountain guide in the Sierras, changed the company's position. Butch described what happened while he was leading a group: "My parka leaked and my life was in danger." As Gilson noted, "That scared the hell out of us. Clearly our solution was no solution at all to someone on a mountain top." All the products were recalled. Gilson remembered: "We bought back, at our own expense, a fortune in pipeline material— anything that was in the stores, at the manufacturers, or anywhere else in the pipeline."

In the meantime, Bob Gore and other Associates set out to develop a permanent fix. One month later, a second-generation GORE-TEX fabric had been developed. Gilson, furthermore, told dealers that if a customer ever returned a leaky parka, they should replace it and bill the company. The replacement program alone cost Gore roughly $4 million.

The popularity of GORE-TEX outerwear took off. Many manufacturers now make numerous pieces of apparel such as parkas, gloves, boots, jogging outfits, and wind shirts from GORE-TEX laminate. Sometimes when customers are dissatisfied with a garment, they return them directly to Gore. Gore has always stood behind any product made of GORE-TEX fabric. Analysis of the returned garments found that the problem was often not the GORE-TEX fabric. The manufacturer, " . . . had created a design flaw so that the water could get in here or get in over the zipper and we found that when there was something negative about it, everyone knew it was GORE-TEX. So we had to make good on products that we were not manufacturing. We now license the manufacturers of all our GORE-TEX fabric products. They pay a fee to obtain a license to manufacture GORE-TEX products. In return we oversee the manufacture and we let them manufacture only designs that we are sure are guaranteed to keep you dry, that really will work. Then it works for them and for us—a win-win for them as well as for us," according to Sally Gore.

To further ensure quality, Gore & Associates has its own test facility including a rain room for garments made from GORE-TEX. Besides a rain/storm test all garments must pass abrasion and washing machine tests. Only the garments that pass these tests will be licensed to display the GORE-TEX label.

RESEARCH AND DEVELOPMENT

Like everything else at Gore, research and development has always been unstructured. Even without a formal R&D department, the company has been issued many patents, although most inventions have been held as proprietary or trade secrets. For example, few Associates are allowed to see GORE-TEX being made. Any Associate can, however, ask for a piece of raw PTFE (known as a silly worm) with which to experiment. Bill Gore believed that all people had it within themselves to be creative.

One of the best examples of Gore inventiveness occurred in 1969. At the time, the wire and cable division was facing increased competition. Bill Gore began to look for a way to straighten out the PTFE molecules. As he said, "I figured out that if we ever unfold those molecules, get them to stretch out straight, we'd have a tremendous new kind of material." He thought that if PTFE could be stretched, air could be introduced into its molecular structure. The result would be greater volume per pound of raw material with no effect on performance. Thus, fabricating costs would be reduced and profit margins would be increased. Going about this search in a scientific manner, Bob Gore heated rods of PTFE to various temperatures and then slowly stretched them. Regardless of the temperature or how carefully he stretched them, the rods broke.

Working alone late one night after countless failures, Bob in frustration stretched one of the rods violently. To his surprise, it did not break. He tried it again and again with the same results. The next morning Bob demonstrated his breakthrough to his father, but not without some drama. As Bill Gore recalled: "Bob wanted to surprise me so he took a rod and stretched it slowly. Naturally, it broke. Then he pretended to get mad. He grabbed another rod and said, 'Oh, the hell with this,' and gave it a pull. It didn't break—he'd done it." The new arrangement of molecules not only changed the wire and cable division, but led to the development of GORE-TEX fabric.

Bill and Vieve did the initial field-testing of GORE-TEX fabric the summer of 1970. Vieve made a hand-sewn tent out of patches of GORE-TEX fabric. They took it on their annual camping trip to the Wind River Mountains in Wyoming. The very first night in the wilderness, they encountered a hail storm. The hail tore holes in the top of the tent, and the bottom filled up like a bathtub from the rain. Undaunted, Bill Gore stated: "At least we knew from all the water that the tent was waterproof. We just needed to make it stronger, so it could withstand hail."

Gore Associates have always been encouraged to think, experiment, and follow a potentially profitable idea to its conclusion. At a plant in Newark, Delaware, Fred L. Eldreth, an Associate with a third-grade education, designed a machine that could wrap thousands of feet of wire a day. The design was completed over a weekend. Many other Associates have contributed their ideas through both product and process breakthroughs.

Even without an R&D department, innovation and creativity continue at a rapid pace at Gore & Associates. The year before he died, Bill Gore claimed that "the creativity, the number of patent applications and innovative products is triple" that of DuPont.

DEVELOPMENT OF GORE ASSOCIATES

Ron Hill, an Associate in Newark, noted that Gore "will work with Associates who want to advance themselves." Associates have been offered many in-house training opportunities, not only in technical and engineering areas but also in leadership development. In addition, the company has established cooperative education programs with universities and other outside providers, picking up most of the costs for the Gore Associates. The emphasis in Associate development, as in many parts of Gore, has always been that the Associate must take the initiative.

MARKETING APPROACHES AND STRATEGY

Gore's business philosophy incorporates three beliefs and principles: (1) that the company can and should offer the best-valued products in the markets and market segments where it chooses to compete, (2) that buyers in each of its markets should appreciate the caliber and performance of the items it manufactures, and (3) that Gore should become a leader with unique expertise in each of the product categories where it competes. To achieve these outcomes, the company's approach to marketing (it has no formally organized marketing department) is based on the following principles:

1. Marketing a product requires a leader, or *product champion*. According to Dave McCarter: "You marry your technology with the interests of your champions, since you've got to have champions for all these things no matter what. And that's the key element within our company. Without a product champion you can't do much anyway, so it is individually driven. If you get people interested in a particular market or a particular product for the marketplace, then there is no stopping them." Bob Winterling of the Fabrics Division elaborated further on the role and importance of the product champion.

> The product champion is probably the most important resource we have at Gore for the introduction of new products. You look at that bicycle cable. That could have come out of many different divisions of Gore, but it really happened because one or two individuals said, "Look, this can work. I believe in it; I'm passionate about it; and I want it to happen." And the same thing with GLIDE floss. I think John Spencer in this case—although there was a team that supported John, let's never forget that—John sought the experts out throughout the organization. But without John making it happen on his own, GLIDE floss would never have come to fruition. He started with a little chain of drug stores here, Happy Harry's I think, and we put a few cases in and we just tracked the sales and that's how it all started. Who would have ever believed that you could take what we would have considered a commodity product like that, sell it direct for $3–5 apiece. That is so unGorelike it's incredible. So it comes down to people and it comes down to the product champion to make things happen.

2. *A product champion is responsible for marketing the product through commitments with sales representatives.* Again, according to Dave McCarter: "We have no quota system. Our marketing and our sales people make their own commitments as to what their forecasts have been. There is no person sitting around telling them that is not high enough, you have to increase it by 10 percent, or whatever somebody feels is necessary. You are expected to meet your commitment, which is your forecast, but nobody is going to tell you to

change it. . . . There is no order of command, no chain involved. These are groups of independent people who come together to make unified commitments to do something and sometimes when they can't make those agreements . . . you may pass up a marketplace, . . . but that's OK, because there's much more advantage when the team decides to do something."

3. *Sales Associates are on salary, not commission.* They participate in the profit sharing and ASOP plans in which all other Associates participate. As in other areas of Gore, individual success stories have come from diverse backgrounds. Dave McCarter related another success of the company relying on a product champion as follows:

> I interviewed Sam one day. I didn't even know why I was interviewing him actually. Sam was retired from AT&T. After twenty-five years, he took the golden parachute and went down to Sun Lakes to play golf. He played golf a few months and got tired of that. He was selling life insurance. I sat reading the application; his technical background interested me. . . . He had managed an engineering department with six hundred people. He'd managed manufacturing plants for AT&T and had a great wealth of experience at AT&T. He said, "I'm retired. I like to play golf but I just can't do it every day so I want to do something else. Do you have something around here I can do?" I was thinking to myself, "This is one of these guys I would sure like to hire but I don't know what I would do with him." The thing that triggered me was the fact that he said he sold insurance and here is a guy with a high degree of technical background selling insurance. He had marketing experience, international marketing experience. So, the bell went off in my head that we were trying to introduce a new product into the marketplace that was a hydrocarbon leak protection cable. You can bury it in the ground and in a matter of seconds it could detect a hydrocarbon like gasoline. I had a couple of other guys working on the product who hadn't been very successful with marketing it. We were having a hard time finding a customer. Well, I thought that kind of product would be like selling insurance. If you think about it, why should you protect

your tanks? It's an insurance policy that things are not leaking into the environment. That has implications, big time monetary. So, actually, I said, "Why don't you come back Monday? I have just the thing for you." He did. We hired him; he went to work, a very energetic guy. Certainly a champion of the product, he picked right up on it, ran with it single handed... .

Now it's a growing business. It certainly is a valuable one too for the environment. In the implementation of its marketing strategy, Gore has relied on cooperative and word-of-mouth advertising. Cooperative advertising has been especially used to promote GORE-TEX fabric products. These high-dollar, glossy campaigns include full-color ads and dressing the sales force in GORE-TEX garments. A recent slogan used in the ad campaigns has been, "If it doesn't say GORE-TEX, it's not." Some retailers praise the marketing and advertising efforts as the best. Leigh Gallagher, managing editor of *Sporting Goods Business* magazine, describes Gore & Associates marketing as "unbeatable."

Gore has stressed cooperative advertising because the Associates believe positive experiences with any one product will carry over to purchases of other and more GORE-TEX fabric products. Apparently, this strategy has paid off. When the Grandoe Corporation introduced GORE-TEX gloves, its president, Richard Zuckerwar, noted: "Sports activists have had the benefit of GORE-TEX gloves to protect their hands from the elements. . . . With this handsome collection of gloves . . . you can have warm, dry hands without sacrificing style." Other clothing manufacturers and distributors who sell GORE-TEX garments include Apparel Technologies, Lands End, Austin Reed, Hudson Trail Outfitters, Timberland, Woolrich, North Face, L. L. Bean, and Michelle Jaffe.

The power of these marketing techniques extends beyond consumer products. According to Dave McCarter: "In the technical end of the business, company reputation probably is most important. You have to have a good reputation with your company." He went on to say that without a good reputation, a company's products would not be considered seriously by many industrial customers. In other words, the sale is often made before the representative calls. Using its marketing strategies Gore has been very successful in securing a market leadership position in a number of

areas, ranging from waterproof outdoor clothing to vascular grafts. Its market share of waterproof, breathable fabrics is estimated to be 90 percent.

ADAPTING TO CHANGING ENVIRONMENTAL FORCES

Each of Gore's divisions has faced from time to time adverse environmental forces. For example, the fabric division was hit hard when the fad for jogging suits collapsed in the mid-1980's. The fabric division took another hit from the recession of 1989. People simply reduced their purchases of high-end athletic apparel. By 1995, the fabric division was the fastest-growing division of Gore again.

The electronic division was hit hard when the mainframe computer business declined in the early 1990s. By 1995, that division was seeing a resurgence for its products partially because that division had developed some electronic products for the medical industry. As can be seen, not all the forces have been negative.

The aging population of America has increased the need for health care. As a result, Gore has invested in the development of additional medical products and the medical division is growing.

W. L. GORE & ASSOCIATES' FINANCIAL PERFORMANCE

As a closely held private corporation, W. L. Gore has kept its financial information as closely guarded as proprietary information on products and processes. It has been estimated that Associates who work at Gore own 90 percent of the stock. According to Shanti Mehta, an Associate, Gore's returns on assets and sales have consistently ranked it among the top 10 percent of the *Fortune* 500 companies. According to another source, W. L. Gore & Associates has been doing just fine by any financial measure. For thirty-seven straight years (from 1961 to 1997) the company has enjoyed profitability and positive return on equity. The compounded growth rate for revenues at W. L. Gore & Associates from 1969 to 1989 was more than 18 percent, discounted for inflation.[7] In 1969, total sales were about $6 million, by 1989, the figure was $600 million. As should be expected with the increase in size, the percentage increase in sales has slowed over the last seven years (Exhibit 13.16). The company projects

---

7 In comparison, only 11 of the 200 largest companies in the *Fortune* 500 had positive ROE each year from 1970 to 1988 and only 2 other companies missed a year. The revenue growth rate for these 13 companies was 5.4 percent, compared with 2.5 percent for the entire *Fortune* 500.

sales to reach $1.4 billion in 1998. Gore financed this growth without long-term debt unless it made sense. For example, "We used to have some industrial revenue bonds where, in essence, to build facilities the government allows banks to lend you money tax free. Up to a couple of years ago we were borrowing money through industrial revenue bonds. Other than that, we are totally debt free. Our money is generated out of the operations of the business, and frankly we're looking for new things to invest in. I know that's a challenge for all of us today," said Bob Winterling. *Forbes* magazine estimates Gore's operating profits for 1993, 1994, 1995, 1996, and 1997 to be $120, $140, $192, $213, and $230 million, respectively (Exhibit 13.16). Bob Gore predicts that the company will reach $2 billion in sales by 2001.

Recently, the company purchased Optical Concepts Inc., a laser, semiconductor technology company, of Lompoc, California. In addition, Gore & Associates is investing in test-marketing a new product, guitar strings, that was developed by its Associates.

When asked about cost control, Sally Gore had the following to say:

> You have to pay attention to cost or you're not an effective steward of anyone's money, your own or anyone else's. It's kind of interesting, we started manufacturing medical products in 1974 with the vascular graft and it built from there. The Gore vascular graft is the Cadillac or BMW

or the Rolls Royce of the business. There is absolutely no contest, and our medical products division became very successful. People thought this was Mecca. Nothing had ever been manufactured that was so wonderful. Our business expanded enormously, rapidly out there (Flagstaff, Arizona) and we had a lot of young, young leadership. They spent some time thinking they could do no wrong and that everything they touched was going to turn to gold.

They have had some hard knocks along the way and discovered it wasn't as easy as they initially thought it was. And that's probably good learning for everyone somewhere along the way. That's not how business works. There's a lot of truth in that old saying that you learn more from your failures than you do your successes. One failure goes a long way toward making you say, Oh, wow!

ACKNOWLEDGMENTS

Many sources were helpful in providing background material for this case. The most important sources of all were the W.L. Gore Associates, who generously shared their time and viewpoints about the company. They provided many resources, including internal documents and added much to this case through sharing their personal experiences as well as ensuring that the case accurately reflected the Gore company and culture.

EXHIBIT 13.16   *Operating and Net Profits of W.L. Gore & Associates*

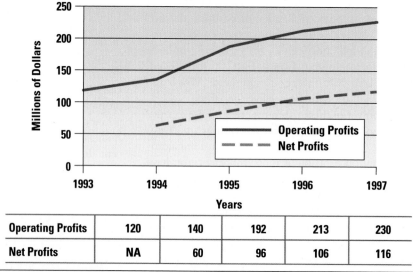

	1993	1994	1995	1996	1997
Operating Profits	120	140	192	213	230
Net Profits	NA	60	96	106	116

Data from *Forbes* Magazine's Annual Report on the 500 Largest Private Companies in the U.S.

EXHIBIT 13.17   *Excerpts from Interviews with Associates*

EXCERPTS FROM INTERVIEWS WITH ASSOCIATES

The first excerpt is from an Associate that was formerly with IBM and has been with Gore for two years:

Q. What is the difference between being with IBM and Gore?

A. I spent twenty-four years working for IBM, and there's a big difference. I can go ten times faster here at Gore because of the simplicity of the lattice organization. Let me give you an example. If I wanted to purchase chemicals at IBM (I am an industrial chemist), the first thing I would need to do is get accounting approval, then I would need at least two levels of managers' approval, then a secretary to log in my purchase and the purchase order would go to Purchasing where it would be assigned a buyer. Some time could be saved if you were willing to "walk" the paperwork through the approval process, but even after computerizing the process, it typically would take one month from the time you initiated the purchase requisition till the time the material actually arrived. Here they have one simple form. Usually, I get the chemicals the next day and a copy of the purchase order will arrive a day or two after that. It happens so fast. I wasn't used to that.

Q. Do you find that a lot more pleasant?

A. Yeah, you're unshackled here. There's a lot less bureaucracy that allows you to be a lot more productive. Take Lab Safety, for example. In my lab at IBM, we were cited for not having eyewash taped properly. The first time, we were cited for not having a big enough area taped off. So we taped off a bigger area. The next week the same eyewash was cited again, because the area we taped off was three inches too short in one direction. We retaped it and the following week, it got cited again for having the wrong color tape. Keep in mind that the violation was viewed as serious as a pail of gasoline next to a lit Bunsen burner. Another time I had the dubious honor of being selected the functional safety representative in charge of getting the function's labs ready for a Corporate Safety Audit. (The function was a third level in the pyramidal organization—(1) department, (2) project, and (3) function). At the same time I was working on developing a new surface mount package. As it turned out, I had no time to work on development, and the function spent a lot of time and money getting ready for the Corporate Auditors who in the end never showed. I'm not belittling the importance of safety, but you really don't need all that bureaucracy to be safe.

The second interview is with an Associate who is a recent engineering graduate:

Q. How did you find the transition coming here?

A. Although I never would have expected it to be, I found my transition coming to Gore to be rather challenging. What attracted me to the company was the opportunity to "be my own boss" and determine my own commitments. I am very goal oriented, and enjoy taking a project and running with it—all things that you are able to do, and encouraged to do within the Gore culture. Thus, I thought, a perfect fit!

However, as a new Associate, I really struggled with where to focus my efforts—I was ready to make my own commitments, but to what?! I felt a strong need to be sure that I was working on something that had value, something that truly needed to be done. While I didn't expect to have the "hottest" project, I did want to make sure that I was helping the company to 'make money' in some way.

At the time, though, I was working for a plant that was pretty typical of what Gore was like when it was originally founded—after my first project (which was designed to be a 'quick-win'—a project with meaning, but one that had a definite end point), I was told "Go find something to work on." While I could have found something, I wanted to find something with at least a small degree of priority! Thus, the whole process of finding a project was very frustrating for me—I didn't feel that I had the perspective to make such a choice, and ended up in many conversations with my sponsor about what would be valuable. . . .

EXHIBIT 13.17   *Excerpts from Interviews with Associates (continued)*

In the end, of course, I did find that project—and it did actually turn out to be a good investment for Gore. The process to get there, though, was definitely trying for someone as inexperienced as I was—so much ground would have been gained by suggesting a few projects to me and then letting me choose from that smaller pool.

What's really neat about the whole thing, though, is that my experience has truly made a difference. Due in part to my frustrations, my plant now provides college grads with more guidance on their first several projects. (This guidance obviously becomes less and less critical as each Associate grows within Gore.) Associates still are choosing their own commitments, but they're doing so with additional perspective, and the knowledge that they are making a contribution to Gore—which is an important thing within our culture. As I said, though, it was definitely rewarding to see that the company was so responsive, and to feel that I had helped to shape someone else's transition!

REFERENCES

Aburdene, Patricia, and John Nasbitt, *Re-inventing the Corporation*, New York: Warner Books, 1985.

Angrist, S. W. "Classless Capitalists," *Forbes*, 9 May 1983, 123–24.

Franlesca, L. "Dry and Cool," *Forbes*, 27 August 1984, 126.

Hoerr, J. "A Company Where Everybody Is the Boss," *Business Week*, 15 April 1985, 98.

Levering, Robert, *The 100 Best Companies to Work for in America*, See the chapter on W. L. Gore & Associates, Inc., New York: Signet, 1985.

McKendrick, Joseph. "The Employees as Entrepreneur," *Management World* (January 1985): 12–13.

Milne, M. J. "The Gorey Details," *Management Review* (March 1985): 16–17.

Posner, B. G. "The First Day on the Job," *Inc.*, June 1986, 73–75.

Price, Debbie M. "GORE-TEX style." *Baltimore Sun*, 20 April 1997, 1D & 4D.

Price, Kathy, "Firm Thrives Without Boss," *AZ Republic*, 2 February 1986.

Rhodes, Lucien, "The Un-manager," *Inc.*, August 1982, 34.

Simmons, J. "People Managing Themselves: Un-management at W. L. Gore Inc.," *The Journal for Quality and Participation*, December 1987, 14–19.

"The Future Workplace," *Management Review* (July 1986): 22–23.

Trachtenberg, J. A. "Give Them Stormy Weather," *Forbes*, 24 March 1986, 172–74.

Ward, Alex. "An All-Weather Idea," *The New York Times Magazine*, 10 November 1985, Sec. 6.

Weber, Joseph. "No Bosses. And Even 'Leaders' Can't Give Orders," *Business Week*, 10 December 1990, 196–97.

"Wilbert L. Gore," *Industry Week*, 17 October 1983, 48–49.

NOTES

1. David K. Hurst, "Cautionary Tales from the Kalahari: How Hunters Become Herders (and May Have Trouble Changing Back Again)," *Academy of Management Executive* 3, no. 5 (1991): 74–86.

2. R. Duane Ireland and Michael A. Hitt, "Achieving and Maintaining Strategic Competitiveness in the 21st Century: The Role of Strategic Leadership," *Academy of Management Executive* 13, No. 1 (1999): 43–57.

3. Ian Katz, "Whirlpool: In the Wringer," *Business Week*, 14 December 1998, 83–85.

4. Cesare R. Mainardi, Martin Salia, and Muir Sanderson, "Label of Origin: Made on Earth," *Strategy & Business*, Issue 15 (Second Quarter, 1999): 42–53.

5. James C. Collins and Jerry I. Porras, *Built to Last: Successful Habits of Visionary Companies* (New York: HarperBusiness, 1994).

6. Thomas Petzinger, Jr., *The New Pioneers: The Men and Women Who Are Transforming the Workplace and Marketplace* (New York: Simon & Schuster, 1999); Frank Ostroff, *The Horizontal Organization: What the Organization of the Future Looks Like and How It Delivers Value to Customers* (New York: Oxford University Press, 1999).

7. Oren Harari, "You're Not in Business to Make a Profit," *Management Review* (July 1992): 53–55.

8. John A. Byrne, "The Corporation of the Future," *Business Week*, 31 August 1998, 102–106.

9. Byrne, "The Corporation of the Future."

10. Amy Dunkin, "Pepsi's Marketing Magic: Why Nobody Does It Better," *Business Week*, 10 February 1986, 52–57.

11. James C. Collins, "Building Companies to Last"; Brian O'Reilly; "J&J Is on a Roll," *Fortune*, 26 December 1994, 178-91.

12. Stephanie Stahl, "Hire on One, Get 'Em All," *Information Week*, 20 March 1995, 120–24.

13. James V. Koch and Richard J. Cebula, "In Search of Excellent Management," *Journal of Management Studies* 31, no. 5 (September 1994); 681–99; Robert S. Kaplan and David P. Norton, "Using the Balanced Scorecard as a Strategic Management System," *Harvard Business Review* (January–February 1996); 75–85.

14. Brian McWilliams, "The Measure of Success," *Across the Board* (February 1996): 16–20; John H. Lingle and William A. Schiemann, "From Balanced Scorecard to Strategic Gauges: Is Measurement Worth It?" *Management Review* (March 1996): 56–61.

15. Ireland and Hitt, "Achieving and Maintaining Strategic Competitiveness in the 21st Century."

16. Neil Templin, "A Decisive Response to Crisis Brought Ford Enhanced Productivity," *The Wall Street Journal*, 15 December 1992, A1, A8.

17. "My Life is an Open Book," *Inc.,* 20th Anniversary Issue, 1999, 30–31; Jeffrey Pfeffer, "Seven Practices of Successful Organizations," in Wendell L. French, Cecil H. Bell, Jr., and Robert A. Zawacki, *Organization Development and Transformation: Managing Effective Change* (Burr Ridge, Ill.: Irwin McGraw-Hill, 2000), 494–514; Charles Fishman, "Whole Foods is All Teams," *Fast Company* (April–May 1996): 102–09.

18. Katrina Brooker, "Can Procter & Gamble Change Its Culture, Protect Its Market Share, and Find the Next Tide?" *Fortune*, 26 April 1999, 146–52.

19. Michael A. Hitt and R. Duane Ireland, "Peters and Waterman Revisited: The Unended Quest for Excellence," *Academy of Management Executive* 1 (1987): 91–98.

20. Based heavily on Nancy J. Adler, *International Dimensions of Organizational Behavior*, 2d ed. (Boston: PWS-Kent, 1991); Theodore T. Herbert, "Strategy and Multinational Organizational Structure: An Interorganizational Relationships Perspective," *Academy of Management Review* 9 (1984): 259–71; Laura K. Rickey, "International Expansion—U.S. Corporations: Strategy, Stages of Development and Structure," (Unpublished manuscript, Vanderbilt University, 1991.)

21. Michael E. Porter, "Changing Patterns of International Competition," *California Management Review* 28 (Winter 1986): 9–40.

22. William J. Holstein, "The Stateless Corporation;" *Business Week*, 14 May 1990, 98–115.

23. David Lei and John W. Slocum, Jr., "Global Strategic Alliances: Payoffs and Pitfalls," *Organizational Dynamics* (Winter 1991): 17–29.

24. Ibid.

25. Stratford Sherman, "Are Strategic Alliances Working?" *Fortune*, 21 September 1992, 77–78; David Lei, "Strategies for Global Competition," *Long-Range Planning* 22 (1989): 102–09.

26. Lei, "Strategies For Global Competition."

27. Kathryn Rudie Harrigan, "Managing Joint Ventures: Part I," *Management Review* (February 1987): 24–41.

28. Kevin Kelly and Otis Port, with James Treece, Gail DeGeorge, and Zachary Schiller, "Learning from Japan," *Business Week*, 27 January 1992, 52–60; Dess, Rasheed, McLaughlin, and Priem, "The New Corporate Architecture."

29. Mary O'Hara-Devereaux and Robert Johansen, *Globalwork: Bridging Distance, Culture & Time* (San Francisco: Jossey-Bass, 1994).

30. Charles C. Snow, Scott A. Snell, Sue Canney Davison, and Donald C. Hambrick, "Use Transnational Teams to Globalize Your Company," *Organizational Dynamics* 24, no. 4 (Spring 1996): 50–67.

31. Ibid.

32. Mary O'Hara-Devereaux and Robert Johansen, *Globalwork: Bridging Distance, Culture & Time,* 227–28.

33. Kenichi Ohmae, "Managing in a Borderless World," *Harvard Business Review* (May-June 1989): 152–61.

00

34. Sumantra Ghoshal and Nitin Nohria, "Horses for Courses: Organizational Forms for Multinational Corporations," *Sloan Management Review* (Winter 1993): 23–35; Roderick E. White and Thomas A. Poynter, "Organizing for Worldwide Advantage," *Business Quarterly* (Summer 1989): 84–89.

35. John D. Daniels, Robert A. Pitts, and Marietta J. Tretter, "Strategy and Structure of U.S. Multinationals: An Exploratory Study," *Academy of Management Journal* 27 (1984): 292–307.

36. *New Directions in Multinational Corporate Organization* (New York: Business International Corporation, 1981).

37. Ibid.

38. William Taylor, "The Logic of Global Business: An Interview with ABB's Percy Barnevik," *Harvard Business Review* (March–April 1991): 91–105; Carla Rappaport, "A Tough Swede Invades the U.S.," *Fortune*, 29 January 1992, 76–79; Raymond E. Miles and Charles C. Snow, "The New Network Firm: A Spherical Structure Built on a Human Investment Philosophy," *Organizational Dynamics* (Spring 1995): 5–18; Manfred F. R. Kets de Vries, "Making a Giant Dance," *Across the Board* (October 1994): 27–32.

39. Sumantra Ghoshal and Christopher A. Bartlett, "The Multinational Corporation as an Interorganizational Network," *Academy of Management Review* 15 (1990): 603–25.

40. Christopher A. Bartlett and Sumantra Ghoshal, *Managing Across Borders: The Transnational Solution* (Boston, Mass.: Harvard Business School Press, 1998).

41. Edwin P. Hollander and Lynn R. Offermann, "Power and Leadership in Organizations," *American Psychologist* 45 (February 1990): 179–89.

42. Thomas A. Stewart, "New Ways to Exercise Power," *Fortune*, 6 November 1989, 52–64; Thomas A. Stewart, "CEOs See Clout Shifting," *Fortune*, 6 November 1989, 66.

43. Frank Shipper and Charles C. Manz, "Employee Self-Management without Formally Designated Teams: An Alternative Road to Empowerment," *Organizational Dynamics* (Winter 1992): 48–61; Bob Filipczak, "Ericsson General Electric: The Evolution of Empowerment," *Training*, September 1993, 21–27.

44. David E. Bowen and Edward E. Lawler III, "Empowering Service Employees," *Sloan Management Review* (Summer 1995): 73–84.

45. W. Chan Kim and Renée Mauborgne, "Fair Process: Managing in the Knowledge Economy," *Harvard Business Review* (July–August 1997): 65–75.

46. Arnold S. Tannenbaum and Robert S. Cooke, "Organizational Control: A Review of Studies Employing the Control Graph Method," in Cornelius J. Lamners and David J. Hickson, eds., *Organizations Alike and Unlike* (Boston: Rutledge and Keegan Paul, 1980), 183–210.

47. Stewart, "New Ways to Exercise Power."

48. David P. McCaffrey, Sue R. Faerman, and David W. Hart, "The Appeal and Difficulties of Participative Systems," *Organization Science* 6, no. 6 (November–December 1995): 603–27.

49. Richard Teitelbaum, "Who is Bob Kierlin–And Why Is He So Successful?" *Fortune*, 8 December 1997, 245–48.

50. Jay A. Conger and Rabindra N. Kanungo, "The Empowerment Process: Integrating Theory and Practice," *Academy of Management Review* 13 (1988): 471–82.

51. Thomas Petzinger, Jr., "Forget Empowerment, This Job Requires Constant Brainpower," (The Front Lines column), *The Wall Street Journal*, 17 October 1997, B12.

52. Barbara Ettorre, "The Empowerment Gap: Hype vs. Reality," *Management Review*, (July–August 1997): 10–14.

53. David E. Bowen and Edward E. Lawler III, "Empowering Service Employees," *Sloan Management Review* (Summer 1995): 73–84.

54. Ettorre, "The Empowerment Gap"; "Empowerment: Myth or Reality," Address by Michèle Darling, executive vice-president, Human Resources, CIBC, Delivered to the Human Resources Professionals Association of Ontario, Toronto, Canada, February 14, 1996, from *Vital Speeches of the Day*, May 15, 1996, 474–78.

55. Gordon Brockhouse, "Can This Marriage Succeed?" *Canadian Business*, October 1992, 128–35; Bowen and Lawler, "Empowering Service Employees."

56. Ettorre, "The Empowerment Gap"; Thomas Petzinger, Jr., "How Lynn Mercer Manages a Factory That Manages Itself," (The Front Lines column), *The Wall Street Journal*, 7 March 1997, B11.

57. Shipper and Manz, "An Alternative Road to Empowerment."

58. Robert C. Ford and Myron D. Fottler,

"Empowerment: A Matter of Degree," *Academy of Management Executive* 9, no. 3 (1995): 21–31.

59. Jeffrey Pfeffer, "Producing Sustainable Competitive Advantage Through the Effective Management of People," *Academy of Management Executive* 9, no. 1 (1995): 55–69.

60. Robert C. Ford and Myron D. Fottler, "Empowerment: A Matter of Degree."

61. David P. McCaffrey, Sue R. Faerman, and David W. Hart, "The Appeal and Difficulties of Participative Systems," *Organization Science* 6, no. 6 (November–December 1995): 603–27.

62. Michael Barrier, "The Changing Face of Leadership," *Nation's Business* (January 1995): 41–42.

63. Eileen Davis, "What's On American Managers' Minds?" *Management Review* (April, 1995): 14–20.

64. Quoted in *Inc.*, March 1995, 13.

65. Bernard M. Bass, *Bass & Stogdill's Handbook of Leadership: Theory, Research, and Managerial Applications*, 3d ed. (New York: Free Press, 1990); Joseph Seltzer and Bernard M. Bass, "Transformational Leadership: Beyond Initiation and Consideration," *Journal of Management* 16 (1990): 693–703; and J. Bruce Tracey and Timothy R. Hinkin, "How Transformational Leaders Lead in the Hospitality Industry," *International Journal of Hospitality Management* 15, No. 2 (1996), 165-76.

66. Based on R. Duane Ireland, "Achieving and Maintaining Strategic Competitiveness in the 21st Century: The Role of Strategic Leadership," *Academy of Management Executive* 13, No. 1 (1999), 43–57; Noel M. Tichy and David O. Ulrich, "The Leadership Challenge—A Call for the Transformational Leader," *Sloan Management Review* 26 (Fall 1984), 59–64, and John P. Kotter, *Leading Change*, (Boston, Mass.: Harvard Business School Press, 1996), 20–25.

67. Ireland and Hitt, "Achieving and Maintaining Strategic Competitiveness in the 21st Century."

68. Scott Kirsner, "Every Day, It's a New Place," *Fast Company* (April–May 1998): 130–34.

69. Gillian Flynn, "On Track to a Comeback," *Personnel Journal* (February 1996): 58–69.

70. Kim and Mauborgne, "Fair Process."

71. Alessandra Bianchi, "Mission Improbable," *Inc.* September 1996, 69–75; and press release from Corsair Communications, June 2, 1999, posted on company's Web site: www.corsair.com.

72. Ken G. Smith, Ken A. Smith, Judy D. Olian,

Henry P. Sims, Jr., Douglas P. O'Bannon, and Judith A. Scully, "Top Management Team Demography and Process: The Role of Social Integration and Communication," *Administrative Science Quarterly* 39 (1994): 412–38.

73. Jon R. Katzenbach, "The Myth of the Top Management Team," *Harvard Business Review* (November–December 1997): 83–91.

74. Katzenbach, "The Myth of the Top Management Team."

75. This discussion is based on Donald C. Hambrick, "Fragmentation and the Other Problems CEOs Have with Their Top Management Teams," *California Management Review* 37, no. 3 (Spring 1995): 110–27.

76. Gerald R. Salancik, Barry M. Staw, and Louis R. Pondy, "Administrative Turnover as a Response to Unmanaged Organizational Interdependence," *Academy of Management Journal* 23 (1980): 422–37; Jeffrey Pfeffer and William L. Moore, "Average Tenure of Academic Department Heads: The Effects of Paradigm, Size, and Departmental Philosophy," *Administrative Science Quarterly* 25 (1980): 387–406.

77. John Helyar and Joann S. Lublin, "The Portable CEO: Do You Need an Expert on Widgets to Head a Widget Company?" *The Wall Street Journal,* 21 January 1998, A1, A10.

78. Jeffrey Pfeffer and Gerald R. Salancik, "Organizational Context and the Characteristics and Tenure of Hospital Administrators," *Academy of Management Journal* 20 (1977): 74–88.

79. Neil Fligstein, "The Intraorganizational Power Struggle: Rise of Finance Personnel to Top Leadership in Large Corporations, 1919–1979," *American Sociological Review* 52 (1987): 44–58.

80. Helyar and Lublin, "The Portable CEO."

81. Idalene F. Kesner and Terrence C. Sebora, "Executive Succession: Past, Present & Future," *Journal of Management* 20, no. 2 (1994): 327–72.

82. Jeffrey Pfeffer and Alison Davis-Blake, "Administrative Succession and Organizational Performance: How Administrator Experience Mediates the Succession Effect," *Academy of Management Journal* 29 (1986): 72–83; Michael Patrick Allen, Sharon K. Panian, and Roy E. Lotz, "Managerial Succession and Organizational Performance: A Recalcitrant Problem Revisited," *Administrative Science Quarterly* 24 (1979): 167–80; M. Craig Brown, "Administrative Succession and Organizational Performance: The Succession

Effect," *Administrative Science Quarterly* 27 (1982): 1–16.

83. David R. James and Michael Soref, "Profit Constraints on Managerial Autonomy: Managerial Theory and the Unmaking of the Corporation President," *American Sociological Review* 46 (1981): 1–18; Oscar Grusky, "Managerial Succession and Organizational Effectiveness," *American Journal of Sociology* 69 (1963): 21–31.

84. Brown, "Administrative Succession and Organizational Performance"; William Gamson and Norman Scotch, "Scapegoating in Baseball," *American Journal of Sociology* 70 (1964): 69–72.

85. J. Richard Harrison, David L. Torres, and Sal Kukalis, "The Changing of the Guard: Turnover and Structural Change in the Top-Management Positions," *Administrative Science Quarterly* 33 (1988): 211–32.

86. Stanley Lieberson and James F. O'Connor, "Leadership and Organizational Performance: A Study of Large Corporations," *American Sociological Review* 37 (1972): 119; Nan Weiner and Thomas A. Mahoney, "A Model of Corporate Performance as a Function of Environmental, Organizational, and Leadership Influences," *Academy of Management Journal* 24 (1981): 453–70; Jonathan E. Smith, Kenneth P. Carson, and Ralph A. Alexander, "Leadership: It Can Make a Difference," *Academy of Management Journal* 27 (1984): 765–76; Alan Berkeley Thomas, "Does Leadership Make a Difference to Organizational Performance?" *Administrative Science Quarterly* 33 (1988): 388–400.

87. David V. Day and Robert G. Lord, "Executive Leadership and Organizational Performance: Suggestions for a New Theory and Methodology," *Journal of Management* 14 (1988): 453–64.

88. Glenn E. Carroll, "Dynamics of Publishers Succession in Newspaper Organizations," *Administrative Science Quarterly* 29 (1984): 93–113.

89. Dawn Davenport, "Eastman To Eliminate 1,200 Jobs," *Johnson City Press*, 19 October 1999, 1.

90. Kim S. Cameron, Myung Kim, and David A. Whetten, "Organizational Effects of Decline and Turbulence," *Administrative Science Quarterly* 32 (1987), 222–40.

91. Danny Miller, "What Happens After Success: The Perils of Excellence," *Journal of Management Studies* 31, No. 3 (May 1994), 325–58.

92. Kim S. Cameron and Raymond Zammuto, "Matching Managerial Strategies to Conditions of Decline," *Human Resources Management* 22 (1983): 359–75; Leonard Greenhalgh, Anne T. Lawrence, and Robert I. Sutton, "Determinants of Workforce Reduction Strategies in Declining Organizations," *Academy of Management Review* 13 (1988): 241–54.

93. Matt Murray, "Amid Record Profits, Companies Continue to Lay Off Employees," *The Wall Street Journal*, 4 May 1995, A1, A6.

94. William Weitzel and Ellen Jonsson, "Reversing the Downward Spiral: Lessons from W. T. Grant and Sears Roebuck," *Academy of Management Executive* 5 (1991): 7–21; William Weitzel and Ellen Jonsson, "Decline in Organizations: A Literature Integration and Extension," *Administrative Science Quarterly* 34 (1989): 91–109.

95. Amy Stevens and Edward Felsenthal, "Mudge Rose To Vote Today on Dissolution," *The Wall Street Journal*, 2 October 1995, B1, B6.

Integrative Cases

INTRODUCTION

It was 7:50 on Monday morning. Frank Questin, Product Engineering Manager at Custom Chip, Inc. was sitting in his office making a TO DO list for the day. From 8:00 to 9:30 A.M., he would have his weekly meeting with his staff of engineers. After the meeting, Frank thought he would begin developing a proposal for solving what he called "Custom Chip's manufacturing documentation problem"—inadequate technical information regarding the steps to manufacture many of the company's products. Before he could finish his TO DO list, he answered a phone call from Custom Chip's human resource manager, who asked him about the status of two overdue performance appraisals and reminded him that this day marked Bill Lazarus's fifth-year anniversary with the company. Following this call, Frank hurried off to the Monday morning meeting with his staff.

Frank had been Product Engineering Manager at Custom Chip for fourteen months. This was his first management position, and he sometimes questioned his effectiveness as a manager. Often he could not complete the tasks he set out for himself due to interruptions and problems brought to his attention by others. Even though he had not been told exactly what results he was supposed to accomplish, he had a nagging feeling that he should have achieved more after these fourteen months. On the other hand, he thought maybe he was functioning pretty well in some of his areas of responsibility given the complexity of the problems his group handled and the unpredictable changes in the semiconductor industry—changes caused not only by rapid advances in technology, but also by increased foreign competition and a recent downturn in demand.

COMPANY BACKGROUND

Custom Chip, Inc. was a semiconductor manufacturer specializing in custom chips and components used in radars, satellite transmitters, and other radio frequency devices. The company had been founded in 1977 and had grown rapidly with sales exceeding $25 million in 1986. Most of the company's 300 employees were located in the main plant in Silicon Valley, but overseas manufacturing facilities in Europe and the Far East were growing in size and importance. These overseas facilities assembled the less complex, higher volume products. New products and the more complex ones were assembled in the main plant. Approximately one-third of the assembly employees were in overseas facilities.

While the specialized products and markets of Custom Chip provided a market niche that had thus far shielded the company from the major downturn in the semiconductor industry, growth had come to a standstill. Because of this, cost reduction had become a high priority.

THE MANUFACTURING PROCESS

Manufacturers of standard chips have long production runs of a few products. Their cost per unit is low and cost control is a primary determinant of success. In contrast, manufacturers of custom chips have extensive product lines and produce small production runs of special applications. Custom Chip, Inc., for example, manufactured over 2000 different products in the last five years. In any one quarter the company might schedule 300 production runs for different products, as many as one-third of which might be new or modified products that the company had not made before. Because they must be efficient in designing and manufacturing many product lines, all custom chip manufacturers are highly dependent on their engineers. Customers are often first concerned with whether Custom Chip can design and manufacture the needed product *at all;* second, with whether they can deliver it on time; and only third, with cost.

After designing a product, there are two phases to the manufacturing process. (See Exhibit 1.) The first is wafer fabrication. This is a complex process in which circuits are etched onto the various layers added to a silicon wafer. The number of steps that the wafer goes through plus inherent problems in controlling various chemical processes make it very difficult to meet the exacting specifications required for the final wafer. The wafers, which are typically "just a few" inches in diameter when the fabrication process is complete, contain hundreds, sometimes thousands, of tiny identical die. Once the wafer has been tested and sliced up to produce these die, each die will be used as a circuit component.

If the completed wafer passes the various quality tests, it moves on to the assembly phase. In assembly,

EXHIBIT 1   *Manufacturing Process*

Pre-production
- *Application engineers design and produce prototype*
- *Product engineers translate design into manufacturing instructions*

Production
- *Wafer fabrication*

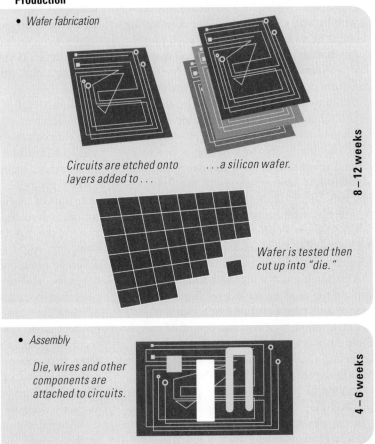

Circuits are etched onto layers added to . . .

. . . a silicon wafer.

Wafer is tested then cut up into "die."

8 – 12 weeks

- *Assembly*

Die, wires and other components are attached to circuits.

4 – 6 weeks

the die from the wafers, very small wires and other components are attached to a circuit in a series of precise operations. This finished circuit is the final product of Custom Chip, Inc.

Each product goes through many independent and delicate operations, and each step is subject to operator or machine error. Due to the number of steps and tests involved, the wafer fabrication takes eight to twelve weeks and the assembly process takes four to six weeks. Because of the exacting specifications, products are rejected for the slightest flaw. The likelihood that every product starting the run will make it through all of the processes and still meet specifications is often quite low. For some products,

average yield[1] is as low as 40 percent, and actual yields can vary considerably from one run to another. At Custom Chip, the average yield for all products is in the 60 to 70 percent range.

Because it takes so long to make a custom chip, it is especially important to have some control of these yields. For example, if a customer orders one thousand units of a product and typical yields for that product average 50 percent, Custom Chip will schedule a starting batch of 2,200 units. With this approach, even if the yield falls as low as 45.4 percent

---

1. Yield refers to the ratio of finished products that meet specifications relative to the number that initially entered the manufacturing process.

(45.4 percent of 2,200 is 1,000) the company can still meet the order. If the actual yield falls below 45.4 percent, the order will not be completed in that run, and a very small, costly run of the item will be needed to complete the order. The only way the company can effectively control these yields and stay on schedule is for the engineering groups and operations to cooperate and coordinate their efforts efficiently.

ROLE OF THE PRODUCT ENGINEER

The product engineer's job is defined by its relationship to application engineering and operations. The applications engineers are responsible for designing and developing prototypes when incoming orders are for new or modified products. The product engineer's role is to translate the application engineering group's design into a set of manufacturing instructions, then to work alongside manufacturing to make sure that engineering-related problems get solved. The product engineers' effectiveness is ultimately measured by their ability to control yields on their assigned products. The organization chart in Exhibit 2 shows the engineering and operations departments. Exhibit 3 summarizes the roles and objectives of manufacturing, application engineering, and product engineering.

The product engineers estimate that 70 to 80 percent of their time is spent in solving day-to-day manufacturing problems. The product engineers have cubicles in a room directly across the hall from the manufacturing facility. If a manufacturing supervisor has a question regarding how to build a product during a run, that supervisor will call the engineer assigned to that product. If the engineer is available, he or she will go to the manufacturing floor to help answer the question. If the engineer is not available, the production run may be stopped and the product put aside so that other orders can be manufactured. This results in delays and added costs. One reason that product engineers are consulted is that documentation—the instructions for manufacturing the product—is unclear or incomplete.

The product engineer will also be called if a product is tested and fails to meet specifications. If a product fails to meet test specifications, production stops, and the engineer must diagnose the problem and attempt to find a solution. Otherwise, the order for that product may be only partially met. Test failures are a very serious problem, which can result in considerable cost increases and schedule delays for customers. Products do not test properly for many reasons, including operator errors, poor materials, a

EXHIBIT 2   *Custom Chip, Inc., Partial Organization Chart*

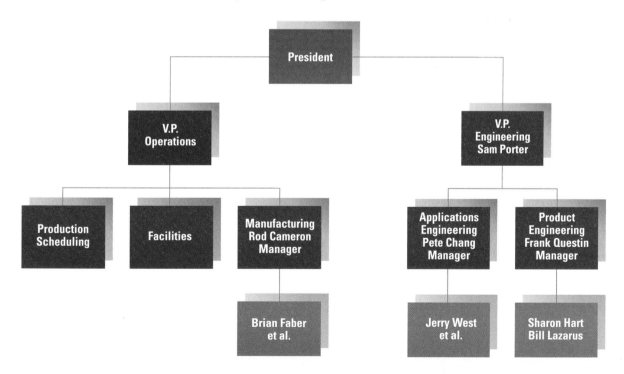

EXHIBIT 3   *Developmental Roles and Objectives*

Department	Role	Primary Objective
Applications Engineering	Designs and develops prototypes for new or modified products	Satisfy customer needs through innovative designs
Product Engineering	Translates designs into manufacturing instructions and works alongside manufacturing to solve "engineering related" problems	Maintain and control yields on assigned products
Manufacturing	Executes designs	Meet productivity standards and time schedules

design that is very difficult to manufacture, a design that provides too little margin for error, or a combination of these.

On a typical day, the product engineer may respond to half a dozen questions from the manufacturing floor, and two to four calls to the testing stations. When interviewed, the engineers expressed a frustration with this situation. They thought they spent too much time solving short-term problems, and, consequently, they were neglecting other important parts of their jobs. In particular, they felt they had little time in which to:

*   **Coordinate with applications engineers during the design phase.** The product engineers stated that their knowledge of manufacturing could provide valuable input to the applications engineer. Together they could improve the manufacturability and thus, the yields of the new or modified product.
*   **Engage in yield improvement projects.** This would involve an in-depth study of the existing process for a specific product in conjunction with an analysis of past product failures.
*   **Accurately document the manufacturing steps for their assigned products, especially for those that tend to have large or repeat orders.** They said that the current state of the documentation is very poor. Operators often have to build products using only a drawing showing the final circuit, along with a few notes scribbled in the margins. While experienced operators and supervisors may be able to work with this information, they often make incorrect guesses and assumptions. Inexperienced operators may not be able to proceed with certain products because of this poor documentation.

WEEKLY MEETING

As manager of the product engineering group, Frank Questin had eight engineers reporting to him, each responsible for a different set of Custom Chip products. According to Frank:

> When I took over as manager, the product engineers were not spending much time together as a group. They were required to handle operation problems on short notice. This made it difficult for the entire group to meet due to constant requests for assistance from the manufacturing area.
>
> I thought that my engineers could be of more assistance and support to each other if they all spent more time together as a group, so one of my first actions as a manager was to institute a regularly scheduled weekly meeting. I let the manufacturing people know that my staff would not respond to requests for assistance during the meeting.

The meeting on this particular Monday morning followed the usual pattern. Frank talked about upcoming company plans, projects, and other news that might be of interest to the group. He then provided data about current yields for each product and commended those engineers who had maintained or improved yields on most of their products. This initial phase of the meeting lasted until about 8:30 A.M. The remainder of the meeting was a meandering discussion of a variety of topics. Since there was no agenda, engineers felt comfortable in raising issues of concern to them.

The discussion started with one of the engineers describing a technical problem in the assembly of one of his products. He was asked a number of questions and given some advice. Another engineer raised the topic of a need for new testing equipment and described a test unit he had seen at a recent demonstration. He claimed the savings in labor and improved yields from this machine would allow it to pay for itself in less than nine months. Frank immediately replied that budget limitations made such a purchase unfeasible, and the discussion moved into another area. They briefly discussed the increasing inaccessibility of the applications engineers, then talked about a few other topics.

In general, the engineers valued these meetings. One commented that:

> The Monday meetings give me a chance to hear what's on everyone's mind and to find out about and discuss companywide news. It's hard to reach any conclusions because the meeting is a freewheeling discussion. But I really appreciate the friendly atmosphere with my peers.

COORDINATION WITH APPLICATIONS ENGINEERS

Following the meeting that morning, an event occurred that highlighted the issue of the inaccessibility of the applications engineers. An order of 300 units of custom chip 1210A for a major customer was already overdue. Because the projected yield of this product was 70 percent, they had started with a run of 500 units. A sample tested at one of the early assembly points indicated a major performance problem that could drop the yield to below 50 percent. Bill Lazarus, the product engineer assigned to the 1210A, examined the sample and determined that the problem could be solved by redesigning the wiring. Jerry West, the applications engineer assigned to that product category, was responsible for revising the design. Bill tried to contact Jerry, but he was not immediately available, and didn't get back to Bill until later in the day. Jerry explained that he was on a tight schedule trying to finish a design for a customer who was coming into town in two days, and could not get to "Bill's problem" for a while.

Jerry's attitude that the problem belonged to product engineering was typical of the applications engineers. From their point of view there were a number of reasons for making the product engineers' needs for assistance a lower priority. In the first place, applications engineers were rewarded and acknowledged primarily for satisfying customer needs through designing new and modified products. They got little recognition for solving manufacturing problems. Second, applications engineering was perceived to be more glamorous than product engineering because of opportunities to be credited with innovative and groundbreaking designs. Finally, the size of the applications engineering group

had declined over the past year, causing the workload on each engineer to increase considerably. Now they had even less time to respond to the product engineers' requests.

When Bill Lazarus told Frank about the situation, Frank acted quickly. He wanted this order to be in process again by tomorrow, and he knew manufacturing was also trying to meet this goal. He walked over to see Pete Chang, head of applications engineering (see the Organizational Chart in Exhibit 2). Meetings like this with Pete to discuss and resolve interdepartmental issues were common.

Frank found Pete at a workbench talking with one of his engineers. He asked Pete if he could talk to him in private, and they walked to Pete's office.

Frank: We've got a problem in manufacturing in getting out an order of 1210As. Bill Lazarus is getting little or no assistance from Jerry West. I'm hoping you can get Jerry to pitch in and help Bill. It should take no more than a few hours of his time.

Pete: I do have Jerry on a short leash trying to keep him focused on getting out a design for Teletronics. We can't afford to show up empty-handed at our meeting with them in two days.

Frank: Well, we are going to end up losing one customer in trying to please another. Can't we satisfy everyone here?

Pete: Do you have an idea?

Frank: Can't you give Jerry some additional support on the Teletronics design?

Pete: Let's get Jerry in here to see what we can do.

Pete brought Jerry back to the office, and together they discussed the issues and possible solutions. When Pete made it clear to Jerry that he considered the problem with the 1210As a priority, Jerry offered to work on the 1210A problem with Bill. He said, "This will mean I'll have to stay a few hours past 5:00 this evening, but I'll do what's required to get the job done."

Frank was glad he had developed a collaborative relationship with Pete. He had always made it a point to keep Pete informed about activities in the product engineering group that might affect the applications engineers. In addition, he would often chat with Pete informally over coffee or lunch in the company cafeteria. This relationship with Pete made Frank's job easier. He wished he had the same rapport with Rod Cameron, the manufacturing manager.

COORDINATION WITH MANUFACTURING

The product engineers worked closely on a day-to-day basis with the manufacturing supervisors and workers. The problems between these two groups stemmed from an inherent conflict between their objectives (see Exhibit 3). The objective of the product engineers was to maintain and improve yields. They had the authority to stop production of any run that did not test properly. Manufacturing, on the other hand, was trying to meet productivity standards and time schedules. When a product engineer stopped a manufacturing run, he was possibly preventing the manufacturing group from reaching its objectives.

Rod Cameron, the current manufacturing manager, had been promoted from his position as a manufacturing supervisor a year ago. His views on the product engineers:

> The product engineers are perfectionists. The minute a test result looks a little suspicious they want to shut down the factory. I'm under a lot of pressure to get products out the door. If they pull a few $50,000 orders off the line when they are within a few days of reaching shipping, I'm liable to miss my numbers by $100,000 that month.
>
> Besides that, they are doing a lousy job of documenting the manufacturing steps. I've got a lot of turnover, and my new operators need to be told or shown exactly what to do for each product. The instructions for a lot of our products are a joke.

At first, Frank found Rod very difficult to deal with. Rod found fault with the product engineers for many problems and sometimes seemed rude to Frank when they talked. For example, Rod might tell Frank to "make it quick, I haven't got much time." Frank tried not to take Rod's actions personally, and through persistence was able to develop a more amicable relationship with him. According to Frank:

> Sometimes, my people will stop work on a product because it doesn't meet test results at that stage of manufacturing If we study the situation, we might be able to maintain yields or even save an entire run by adjusting the manufacturing procedures. Rod tries to bully me into changing my engineers' decisions. He yells at me or criticizes the competence of my people, but I don't allow his temper or ravings to influence my best judgment in a situation My strategy in dealing with Rod is to try not to respond defensively to him. Eventually he cools down, and we can have a reasonable discussion of the situation.

Despite this strategy, Frank could not always resolve his problems with Rod. On these occasions, Frank took the issue to his own boss, Sam Porter, the vice-president in charge of engineering. However, Frank was not satisfied with the support he got from Sam. Frank said:

> Sam avoids confrontations with the operations VP. He doesn't have the influence or clout with the other VPs or the president to do justice to engineering's needs in the organization.

Early that afternoon, Frank again found himself trying to resolve a conflict between engineering and manufacturing. Sharon Hart, one of his most effective product engineers, was responsible for a series of products used in radars—the 3805A-3808A series. Today she had stopped a large run of 3806As. The manufacturing supervisor, Brian Faber, went to Rod Cameron to complain about the impact of this stoppage on his group's productivity. Brian felt that yields were low on that particular product because the production instructions were confusing to his operators, and that even with clearer instructions, his operators would need additional training to build it satisfactorily. He stressed that the product engineer's responsibility was to adequately document the production instructions and provide training. For these reasons, Brian asserted that product engineering, and not manufacturing, should be accountable for the productivity loss in the case of these 3806As.

Rod called Frank to his office, where he joined the discussion with Sharon, Brian, and Rod. After listening to the issues, Frank conceded that product engineering had responsibility for documenting and training. He also explained, even though everyone was aware of it, that the product engineering group had been operating with reduced staff for over a year now, so training and documentation were lower priorities. Because of this staffing situation, Frank suggested that manufacturing and product engineering work together and pool their limited resources to solve the documentation and training problem. He was especially interested in using a few of the long-term experienced workers to assist in training newer workers. Rod and Brian opposed his suggestion. They did not want to take experienced operators off of the line because it would decrease productivity. The meeting ended when Brian stormed out, saying that Sharon had better get the 3806As up and running again that morning.

Frank was particularly frustrated by this episode with manufacturing. He knew perfectly well that his group had primary responsibility for documenting the manufacturing steps for each product. A year ago he told Sam Porter that the product engineers needed to update and standardize all of the documentation for manufacturing products. At that time, Sam told Frank that he would support his efforts to develop the documentation, but would not increase his staff. In fact, Sam had withheld authorization to fill a recently vacated product engineering slot. Frank was reluctant to push the staffing issue because of Sam's adamance about reducing costs. "Perhaps," Frank thought, "if I develop a proposal clearly showing the benefits of a documentation program in manufacturing and detailing the steps and resources required to implement the program, I might be able to convince Sam to provide us with more resources." But Frank could never find the time to develop that proposal. And so he remained frustrated.

LATER IN THE DAY

Frank was reflecting on the complexity of his job when Sharon came to the doorway to see if he had a few moments. Before he could say "Come in," the phone rang. He looked at the clock. It was 4:10 P.M. Pete was on the other end of the line with an idea he wanted to try out on Frank, so Frank said he could call him back shortly. Sharon was upset, and told him that she was thinking of quitting because the job was not satisfying for her.

Sharon said that although she very much enjoyed working on yield improvement projects, she could find no time for them. She was tired of the applications engineers acting like "prima donnas," too busy to help her solve what they seemed to think were mundane day-to-day manufacturing problems. She also thought that many of the day-to-day problems she handled wouldn't exist if there was enough time to document manufacturing procedures to begin with.

Frank didn't want to lose Sharon, so he tried to get into a frame of mind where he could be empathetic to her. He listened to her and told her that he could understand her frustration in this situation. He told her the situation would change as industry conditions improved. He told her that he was pleased that she felt comfortable in venting her frustrations with him, and he hoped she would stay with Custom Chip.

After Sharon left, Frank realized that he had told Pete that he would call back. He glanced at the TO DO list he had never completed, and realized that he hadn't spent time on his top priority—developing a proposal relating to solving the documentation problem in manufacturing. Then, he remembered that he had forgotten to acknowledge Bill Lazarus' fifth year anniversary with the company. He thought to himself that his job felt like a roller coaster ride, and once again he pondered his effectiveness as a manager.

THE COMPANY

Between 1993 and 1997, Microsoft Corporation continued its historically dramatic growth. Revenue more than quadrupled from $2.75 billion in 1993 to $11.36 billion in 1997, reflecting a compounded annual growth rate over 43 percent. Net income likewise grew from $708 million to $3.45 billion over the same period.[1] Asset levels rose from $3.8 billion in 1993 to $14.4 billion in 1997, while the number of employees increased to approximately 25,000 worldwide. The company's continued success in the development and marketing of operating systems and personal productivity applications software drove most of this growth. Microsoft's MS/DOS and Windows 3.1 operating system together with its MS Office Suite of personal productivity applications had commanding shares in their respective segments.[2]

The rapid growth generated by Microsoft's success, however, began to create coordination, management, and legal problems. Coordination problems surfaced in the form of delays in the software rewrites and product introductions. Windows 95, for instance, was introduced over one year after the original roll-out date.[3] Management of the company's various projects also grew more complex and unwieldy. In fact, between 1982 and 1992, Microsoft went through a series of presidents until William "Bill" Gates ultimately decided to create an Office of the President in which three senior executives would jointly hold the post.[4] Lastly, legal problems cropped up as government officials from the Antitrust Division of the U.S. Department of Justice began investigating whether Microsoft's dominant market position was an impediment to competition in certain segments of the computer software market. In fact, in mid-1995, the Justice Department successfully blocked Microsoft from pursuing its planned acquisition of rival software maker Intuit on the grounds that such an action would consolidate too much market power and consequently reduce market competition within the product segment.[5]

In response to these challenges, Gates introduced a number of incremental structural and organizational changes. The coordination problems were partially addressed by continued enhancement of the company's internal communication capabilities. Microsoft used a number of formal and informal methods for facilitating information flows such as frequent project team meetings, internal newsletters, and prodigious e-mail usage. As noted previously, Gates created the Office of the President to be shared by the three chief operating heads: Michael Maples, who headed the applications systems business; Steve Ballmer, who headed the operating systems business; and Francis Gaudette, Microsoft's chief financial officer.[6] In May of 1995, this group was augmented by Pete Higgins, head of desktop applications, and Nathan Myhrvold, head of advanced technology.[7] By creating the senior committee, Gates freed himself from supervising daily operations in order to focus on broader strategic concerns. Lastly, in terms of the antitrust issues, Microsoft retreated from the proposed merger with Intuit.[8]

Further structural adjustments were made as the three divisions under Maples, Higgins, and Myhrvold were reorganized into two groups. Maples would continue to oversee the Platforms Group, while Higgins and Myhrvold would jointly run the Applications and Content Group. Microsoft's other two divisions were the Sales and Support Group, which continued to manage customer relationships, and the Operations Group, which supervised the manufacturing and delivery of products.[9]

INTERNET

The Internet is a global network of computer servers providing an alternate communications platform for the private, public, and government sectors. The term *Internet* was coined in the early 1980s as university researchers developed a common computing language to link a loose collection of networks called the Arpanet.[10] The Arpanet, a 1960s product of the Department of Defense, evolved into a research tool to promote data sharing and the remote access of supercomputers among researchers in the United States.[11]

The boom in inexpensive personal computers and network-ready servers in the 1980s allowed many companies and universities to join the rapidly growing Internet.[12] By the early 1990s, rapid innovations gave rise to the World Wide Web, which allowed users to navigate the Internet with "point-and-click" ease.[13] In 1993, Mosaic, the first Web

*This case was prepared by Richard D. Freedman, Eduardo Olbes and Sharon Simon, New York University, Leonard N. Stern School of Business. Revised September 1999. © 1997 by Richard Freedman. Reprinted by permission.

browser, provided a user-friendly interface to the Internet.[14]

During this period, the growth in the use of the Internet soared. Between 1987 and 1997, the number of Internet hosts grew from 10,000 to over 5 million.[15] In 1993, traffic on the Internet expanded at a 341,634 percent annual rate.[16] By 1996, analysts estimated that more than 20 million people used the Internet regularly.[17] Growth has been so rapid that the Internet is believed to have doubled in size every year since 1988.[18] Studies also suggest that more than $1 billion per year changes hands at Internet shopping malls.[19]

In order to meet this growing demand, a number of companies such as Cisco Systems, Sun Microsystems, Netscape Communications, and Oracle Corporation made significant investments in developing and marketing hardware and software applications for the Internet.[20] Microsoft, on the other hand, initially questioned the Internet's commercial viability and therefore postponed committing significant resources for research and development of Internet-friendly applications.

As the Internet's popularity continued to grow, industry analysts began to forecast the possibility that the Internet could supersede Windows as the de facto operating system for personal computers.[21] The principal concern was the fact that competing firms were developing systems, such as Sun Microsystem's NC computer, that could operate without the industry-standard Windows operating system or other resident applications. Instead, these so-called network computers would be linked to the Internet via high-speed servers in a central location and would operate like PCs.[22] By concentrating computing power and software applications in a central computer, many of the costs and hassles of operating in a PC environment would be significantly reduced.

Development of such a scenario would free consumers from the need to purchase operating systems or software applications. Instead, consumers could rely on the applications and operating systems resident in the servers of their online service provider. As a result, Microsoft's cash-generating capabilities would be severely diminished, since the licensing and sale of the company's operating system and personal productivity applications account for the majority of its revenues. Microsoft's principal business of developing operating systems and personal productivity applications would be seriously compromised.[23]

THE RESPONSE

During the mid-1990s, much of Gates's attention was focused on the development and launch of Windows 95, a new operating system developed to replace Microsoft's popular Windows 3.1 system.[24] With its 15 million lines of computer code, Windows 95 was billed as the operating system that would finally give the PC the ease of use associated with Apple's Macintosh System.[25] Analysts expected Microsoft to take in $1 billion on Windows 95 upgrades in year one alone.[26]

In the midst of Windows 95 development, a small band of programmers at Microsoft led by Steven Sinofsky campaigned for the company to articulate a more deliberate strategy for developing Internet-based applications. Sinofsky, one of Gates's technical assistants, sparked an interest in the Internet during a company recruiting visit to Cornell in early 1994. He was surprised to note the popularity of e-mail and the Internet among the students and faculty of the university.[27]

Together with programmer J. Allard, Sinofsky began peppering Gates and his technical staff with e-mail messages about the Internet and its potential commercial promise.[28] Both men pointed to the rapidly growing popularity of the Internet with both private and corporate users. In fact, by 1994, analysts estimated that there were some 21,700 commercial Web sites, up from only 9,000 in 1991.[29] Sinofsky and Allard were alarmed at the possibility that Microsoft, which at this point was almost entirely focused on the rewrite of the Windows operating system, might miss the significance of this dramatic development in information technology. Sinofsky was determined to focus management's attention on this issue despite the fact that the technological implications for Microsoft's own operating system and applications software business were still unclear.

After two months of incessant drum beating, senior executives from Microsoft convened for an executive retreat to focus on the Internet. Retreats were commonly used at Microsoft to help executives focus on specific issues and challenges. Gates and his top executives reviewed documents prepared by Sinofsky outlining the critical issues. A second retreat followed during which Gates penned a memo outlining the company's first shades of a formal—albeit tepid—commitment to the Internet. Gates wrote, "We want to and will invest resources to be a leader in

Internet support."[30] During the months that followed, however, the intense focus on Windows 95 and Windows NT, which was designed specifically for the corporate market, derailed much of the initial momentum.

By May 1995, with work on Windows 95 rapidly approaching completion, Gates issued a memo declaring the Internet as the "most important single development" since the advent of the personal computer.[31] Benjamin J. Slivka, who was the project leader for Microsoft Explorer, an Internet browser developed to compete with Netscape Communication's Navigator, followed up with his own memo suggesting that an Internet-based platform could potentially supersede Windows as the de facto operating system for the personal computer.[32] This memo was notable because it was one of the first formal, public acknowledgments from Microsoft's senior management of the fundamental threat presented by the Internet. This realization prompted another round of brainstorming sessions for Gates and his colleagues.

On August 24, 1995, after a delay of more than one year, Microsoft officially launched Windows 95. Analysts and industry players alike confirmed the success of the operating system's introduction.[33] While corporate customers generally postponed purchases of the new system in anticipation of the Windows NT operating system, most retail consumers and original equipment manufacturers adopted Windows 95 as the de facto standard.

The success of Windows 95 notwithstanding, on November 16, 1995, Goldman Sachs & Co., the New York investment bank, withdrew Microsoft from its recommended purchase list due to concerns that the company did not have an adequate strategy for coping with the Internet.[34] Despite multiple memos and brainstorming sessions, the company had failed to articulate a comprehensive and convincing response to the threat presented by the Internet.

Subsequent to the ratings downgrade, Steve Ballmer, Microsoft's executive vice president, adamantly pushed for the company to solidify its strategic plans. December 7, 1995, was the deadline set for the announcement of Microsoft's wide-ranging Internet strategy, which called for browsers, Web servers, consumer and content applications, and the Microsoft Network (a new proprietary online service provider), among others. In front of an estimated 300 analysts and reporters, Bill Gates announced that Microsoft was "hard-core about the Internet."[35]

INTERNET STRATEGY

Microsoft's vision regarding the Internet extended beyond the immediate competitive threat it presented to the company's virtual monopoly in operating systems and applications software. Gates believed that the Internet would be the principal communications platform of the future, just as the MS/DOS and Windows operating systems are today's dominant platform for personal computing.[36] The Internet offered a cost-effective medium for capturing, analyzing, and transmitting millions of bits of information. Specifically, however, the Internet was a powerful tool for collecting information on consumer practices and behavior. Gates believed that the company that could cost-effectively collect, sift through, and capitalize on information such as purchasing habits, product interests, and hobbies would attain a significant competitive advantage.[37] Consequently, capturing and controlling the key interfaces for the Internet became a critical aspect of the company's overall strategy.[38]

Microsoft announced its intention to develop a broad array of Internet-related applications and software. The company began positioning itself in most of the Web-related market segments by using a variety of tactics from joint ventures and acquisitions to internally funded research and development. As of fiscal year 1996, the company had a cash balance in excess of $8 billion that was available to fund its various initiatives.[39] On the hardware segment, Microsoft entered into a joint venture with Intel Corporation, Hewlett-Packard, and Compaq in order to develop the NetPC, an Internet PC computer that would be positioned against the NC computer from Sun Microsystems, Oracle, and IBM. The NetPC would make use of both Intel's microprocessor and Microsoft's operating system.[40]

For the software market, Microsoft has allocated significant resources for developing applications for corporate Intranets. An Intranet is similar to the Internet, but it includes networked computers within a single company. Microsoft believes that control of this particular market segment is critical since Intranet applications will act effectively as the de facto operating system for networked computers. The company has also made an effort to transform many of its more popular personal productivity products into Intranet-friendly applications. For example, in 1997 the company introduced Office 97, an upgrade of its widely popular MS Office Suite. Office 97 includes an interface with the World Wide Web.[41]

What Microsoft is unable to create in-house, it attempts to buy. Within one and a half years, Microsoft either acquired or entered into joint ventures with UUNET Technologies Inc., Vermeer Technologies Inc., Colusa Software Inc., eShop Inc., and Electric Gravity Inc.[42] Licensing of software and advanced technology was also frequently used. Notable among its recent deals was Microsoft's licensing agreement with chief rival Sun Microsystems for the use of Sun's Java computing language.[43]

For the content segment of the market, Microsoft has embarked on a number of joint ventures with established players in the media, publishing, and telecommunications industry in order to create content for display through a variety of interactive devices. These initiatives included computer equipment, television, and printed publications. For example, to address the needs in the consumer segment of the content market, Microsoft worked with Dreamworks SKG to develop a line of 3-D computer games.[44] Dreamworks provided the creative talent for the venture while Microsoft furnished technical expertise. Microsoft also has allocated a significant portion of its cash reserves to purchase fledgling content development firms. For the business segment of the content market, Microsoft's principal efforts focused on the development of MSNBC, a 24-hour business news channel distributed both via cable networks and the Internet.[45] MSNBC is a joint venture with General Electric's NBC television subsidiary.[46]

While preparing the launch of Windows 95, Microsoft's programmers were also putting the finishing touches on the company's new proprietary online service provider, the Microsoft Network (MSN).[47] The principal business of an online service provider is to provide subscribers access to the Internet. America Online (AOL), CompuServe, and Prodigy were among the first companies to actively package and market Internet access.[48] Microsoft began development of MSN in December 1992, in part due to the success of AOL, which rapidly became the world's largest proprietary online service provider.

RESULTS

Jeffrey Katzenberg, principal of Dreamworks SKG, noted, "I cannot think of one corporation that has had this kind of success and after twenty years, just stopped and decided to reinvent itself from the ground up. What they are doing is decisive, quick, breathtaking.[49] A Microsoft employee adds that Bill Gates has taken a booming $11 billion company with 25,000 employees and turned the "battleship around as if it were a PT boat."[50]

Within a one-year period, Gates and his team achieved what many industry analysts said was impossible. Essentially, Microsoft took what was the world's largest and most prolific operating software and personal productivity application developer and transformed it into a dominant Internet-focused company with significant ventures in the hardware, software, and content segments of the market. In fiscal year 1996, total sales revenues grew 46 percent from $5.96 billion in 1995 to $8.67 billion.[51] Net income grew over 40 percent from $1.5 billion to $2.2 billion.[52] Perhaps even more telling about the company's future are its plans to dramatically raise its investment in new technologies. Over the next year alone, the company will deploy its financial resources to fund over $2.0 billion worth of research and development, which is almost half of the total $4.4 billion that it has spent over its twenty-two-year history. Employment applications are still flooding in at a rate of 15,000 per month, giving Microsoft the enviable advantage of picking from the best and the brightest.

GOVERNMENT AND COMPETITOR REACTIONS

By packaging MSN together with Windows 95, Microsoft intended to create a system whose features would be seamlessly blended together. While the product was delivered on schedule in November 1995, an antitrust investigation by the Justice Department ultimately forced the company to reassess its approach. The principal issue investigated by the government was whether Microsoft's packaging plan would constitute an unfair advantage over its competitors.[53] While no formal charges were filed during the investigation, Microsoft moved to adjust aspects of its original plan in order to address some of the government's concerns.

In October 1997, Microsoft again came under government scrutiny for tying its Internet browser, known as Internet Explorer (IE), to the upgraded version of Windows 95. The Justice Department sued Microsoft for "trying to use its overwhelming dominance in computer operating systems to compete unfairly in the browser market."[54] Microsoft considers Windows 95 to be an integrated program, which means that a wide variety of features are built into the software. The company was requiring computer manufacturers to install IE as a condition of licensing Windows 95 on new PCs. As such, computers that come with Windows 95 preinstalled would automatically have the IE icon on the desktop. Further,

> [s]worn statements from computer manufacturers … show exactly how Microsoft ruthlessly used its control over what appears on the PC desktop as the means to displace Netscape's Navigator with its own Internet Explorer browser. Although 'end-users' were free to adapt their desktops, the computer manufacturers had to ensure, as a condition of their Windows license, that when a machine was switched on for the first time the desktop had every icon on it that Microsoft decreed. Faced with the threat…that they would lose their Windows license and thus their business if they removed the IE icon, PC makers all meekly fell into line.[55]

In December 1997, the government ordered Microsoft to offer PC manufacturers the choice of whether to include IE on the system. Microsoft responded by offering PC manufacturers two alternatives to the combined Windows and IE system: (1) an outdated version of Windows that predated IE, or (2) a version of Windows with IE disabled. The problem with the second option was that the software would not function properly without IE fully activated. Neither option was accepted by any OEM (original equipment manufacturers).

The government was outraged by Microsoft's response. Since Windows is the de facto standard for operating systems, the government maintained that Microsoft was "using its near-monopoly in operating system software to restrict competition in the market for Internet browsing software, where its main competitor is Netscape Communications Corporation."[56] Microsoft, on the other hand, maintained that Windows and IE had become a single integrated product. In addition, Microsoft feared that government interference would hamper the company's strategy of blending Internet capabilities into all of its new products.[57]

In addition to complaints from the government and Windows licensees, Microsoft's competitors in the software arena have actively voiced concerns about the company's growing market power. Both Netscape and Sun Microsystems "have suggested that Microsoft's aggressive tactics in the software marketplace border on the tyrannical."[58] Netscape, the current leader for Internet browsers with a 60 percent market share, has steadily been losing ground, and attributes its losses to Microsoft's policy of bundling IE with the Windows operating system.

Until January 1998, Microsoft continued to insist that IE and Windows were so intricately integrated that Windows simply could not operate without IE. In order to avoid being found in contempt of court, however, Microsoft ultimately gave in to government demands by agreeing to make Windows available with the Internet browser icon hidden or partially removed from the computer desktop. A moderately knowledgeable consumer can easily install the icon on the desktop.

ADDRESSING GOVERNMENT CONCERNS

Throughout the 1970s and 1980s, while in its infancy, Microsoft had no need to be concerned with government matters. Rapidly increasing market power, however, has caused the government to pay attention to the now large corporation. While Gates maintains that he has done nothing more than remain responsive to consumer demands, the company's ability to influence industry standards has led to intense government scrutiny. Specifically, the Justice Department fears that Microsoft's control of industry standards could impede innovation, leaving competing technologies little chance to survive. Too much government interference, however, could have potentially devastating effects on Microsoft's strategy.

In 1996 Gates began to hire lobbyists, including Washington lawyer Jack Krumholtz, in order to defend his company against government attacks. "We've increased our [political giving] efforts in response to the very concerted campaign by our competitors to use the government against us rather than to compete in the marketplace," says Krumholtz.[59] Until recently, the company made few political contributions and preferred to lobby in Washington through the Business Software Alliance—an industry trade group whose mission is "to advocate free and open world trade for legitimate business software"[60]—and its own law firm, Preston Gates Ellis & Rouvelas Meeds.

Even Gates himself has begun to spend more time in government matters. Although he rarely visits Capitol Hill, Microsoft's chief executive has been inviting more and more politicians to both the company's corporate headquarters and his private home. Microsoft has also increased its campaign contributions. In 1996, for example, the company donated $236,784 to candidates for office, as compared to only $105,484 just two years earlier.[61]

PUBLIC RELATIONS

As Microsoft's market power has increased since its humble beginnings, the company's tremendous success has coincided with a shift in Gates's image as a 'quintessential nerd' to one who uses brute force to dominate the marketplace, stifling innovation by controlling industry standards. Indeed, "Microsoft has been able to crush competitors—eliminating competition and perhaps innovation, which could harm consumers."[62] To further promote this negative image, it has been said that Microsoft has taken a "combative stance" in government courtroom confrontations, during which the company, "usually so sure footed, has appeared at times to be throwing a temper tantrum, picking fights with a federal judge and the Justice Department."[63]

In a campaign beginning in March 1998, Bill Gates became a celebrity endorser for a line of golf clubs. The campaign consisted of a television commercial and print advertisement, and featured Gates as an enthusiastic new golf player. Gates added his role as an endorser to his resume "at a time when he seems to be engaged in a frenetic series of activities intended to change perceptions of him as a rapacious cyber capitalist bent on dominating the information industry."[64] Corporate identity and brand image consultant Clay Timon commended the move, stating, "It will make [Gates] seem human after all."[65] In additional public relations activities, Gates paid tribute to the Wright brothers at *Time* magazine's seventy-fifth anniversary party, presented a $640,000 gift to the New York Library, and visited a sixth grade class.

STRUCTURE

Microsoft's Internet-focused strategy had dramatic implications for both the company and its employees. New product groups were formed and divisions were reorganized in order to focus on a variety of product initiatives. As previously noted, Microsoft was organized into four main business groups: (1) the Platforms Products Group; (2) the Applications and Content Product Group; (3) the Sales and Support Group; and (4) the Operations Group.[66] In February 1996, both the Platforms Products Group and the Applications and Content Product Group were reorganized in conjunction with company's efforts to enhance its Internet capabilities.

The Platforms Group, headed by Group Vice-President Paul Maritz, was organized into three divisions: (1) the Personal and Business Division (which develops and markets applications such as Windows 3.x, Windows 95, Windows NT, and the BackOffice applications, etc.); (2) the Consumer Devices and Public Networks Division (hand-held devices, set-top boxes, etc.); and (3) the Internet Platforms Division (focusing on Web browsers, shell and multimedia technology, developer tools, online service commerce technology, etc.).[67]

The Applications and Content Product Group, run by Group Vice-Presidents Nathan Myhrvold and Pete Higgins, was likewise reorganized into three divisions. The Desktop Applications Division focuses on personal productivity and consumer applications (e.g., Microsoft Office).[68] The Interactive Media Division develops online and CD-ROM based versions of consumer and business software while overseeing development of content for MSN. The Advanced Technology and Research Division focuses emerging technologies such as speech recognition and artificial intelligence.[69]

The Sales and Support Group, headed by EVP Ballmer, is responsible for "building long-term business relationships with customers."[70] This group is structured to focus on three customer types: end users, organizations, and original equipment manufacturers (OEMs).

The Operations Group, headed by EVP and COO Bob Herbold, is responsible for managing business operations. This includes processing, manufacturing and delivering finished goods, licenses, subscriptions and overall business planning.[71]

In reorganizing the Platforms Products Group and the Applications and Content Product Group, Microsoft was able to capitalize on its loosely structured team approach to software development. Teams of software developers and marketers frequently are used to develop specific software applications. Because the team concept is so pervasive, management was readily able to reshape both business groups by adding and eliminating product teams according to management's assessment of their strategic value. A variety of new units were created to focus on discrete aspects of the company's overall Internet strategy.

Microsoft was reorganized again in early 1998. The move placed three product groups under Paul Maritz, group vice-president for Platforms and Operations. The groups are: (1) Personal and Business Systems, (2) Consumer Platforms, and (3) Applications and Tools. The move shifted responsibility for Internet Explorer into the Personal and Business Systems Group, which is the unit that develops and markets Windows. David Readerman, a financial analyst at Nationsbanc Montgomery Securities Inc., supports the move, stating that "Internet Explorer is an integrated product. You better integrate the reporting responsibilities." The reorganization came less than one month after the company agreed to make Windows available without the Internet Explorer icon present on the desktop. Due to this timing, it has been said that the move "is certain to raise eyebrows in light of the Microsoft Corporation's antitrust battle with the United States Government."[72]

THE TRIAL

In June 1998, the federal Court of Appeals overturned the government's December order for Microsoft to separate its browser from Windows. The court ruled that Judge Jackson, the presiding judge in the antitrust trial, "had erred 'substantively' by acting as if judges should try to 'oversee product design.'"[73] The court went on to say that "instead of being harmed ... consumers benefited that every company does what Microsoft has been accused of doing." AOL announced in November 1998 that it was acquiring Netscape and joining with Sun Microsystems "to build an Internet service company that could rival Microsoft and IBM."[75] Microsoft's lead counsel, William H. Neukom, declared, "This proposed deal pulls the rug out from under the government. It proves indisputably that no company can control the supply of technology."[76] Judge Jackson appeared to agree to some extent, stating that "this new alliance 'might be a very significant change in the playing field.'"[77]

Two of the twenty-six witnesses in the antitrust trial, both economists from the Massachusetts Institute of Technology (MIT), are of particular interest. Franklin M. Fisher described Microsoft's behavior in the Internet software business as "predatory." He stated that Microsoft stifled competition and innovation and posed a substantial threat of harm to consumers.[78] Asserting that Microsoft is a monopoly, Fisher cited Microsoft's dominance of PC operating systems, its power to raise prices at will, and the existence of barriers to competitors attempting to enter the market.[79] However, when asked if consumers were being harmed by Microsoft, he stated, "On balance, I would think the answer was no, up to this point."[80] Richard L. Schmalensee, dean of the Sloan School of Management at MIT, stated that Microsoft does not hold a monopoly in operating system software, and that, in fact, it faces "vicious and serious competitors."[81] He cited Linux, a free operating system, and the Palm Pilot as examples of "significant" threats. However, when asked if the Palm Pilot posed a "significant" threat today, Schmalensee admitted it didn't. "As it stands, it is not a significant competitor. It is a germ of a potential

competitor."[82] Thus, the government further supported its case that Microsoft is a monopoly. In a recent interview, Bill Gates said, "Even with all the great people we have, we face probably more intense competition now than ever before. Only in a courtroom can somebody say, 'Hey, Linux is a serious competitor,' and the press laughs in a way that makes the judge think, O.K., that must be a false statement, that must be posturing."[83] In fact, 17 percent of servers used Linux in 1998, up from 6 percent in 1997.[84] And, when Red Hat, a leading distributor of Linux, made an initial offering in August 1999, its shares more than tripled by the close of trading despite recent market corrections of high-technology stocks, indicating that the market believes in the potential for Linux to become a commercial competitor to Microsoft's Windows NT.[85]

There is little question that Microsoft has been aggressive in its marketing efforts. Intent on controlling the look of the Windows boot-up screen, Microsoft offers desktop space as an incentive for partners and a method of keeping them in line. After learning that some PC manufacturers were reconfiguring the boot-up screen, Microsoft executives discussed how to make that more difficult. Although no solutions were available for Windows 95, they resolved to "do something to make this hard" in Windows 98.[86] Hewlett-Packard was displeased with Microsoft's refusal to let them customize the startup sequence. In a memo to Microsoft, they said, "From a consumer perspective, we are hurting our industry. ... If we had a choice of another supplier, based on your actions, I assure you that you would not be our supplier of choice."[87] In March 1996, AOL signed an agreement with Netscape to license its browser. When, on the very next day, Microsoft offered to feature AOL in Windows 95 in exchange for an agreement limiting AOL's distribution and promotion of Netscape, AOL capitulated to Microsoft's demands.[88]

Within Microsoft, the phrase *hard core* is often used to describe their position with respect to competitors and their corporate culture. Being "hard core" means preferring a fight to a compromise. One former Microsoft insider says, that "the peer pressure [at Microsoft] is to push, to boast of being hard core; so a Gates negotiation is more a head-on competition than an opportunity for both sides to win."[89] This attitude comes through in Microsoft's dealings with the government, which have been described as arrogant. In an early settlement negotiation, "Gates exclaimed, 'You give me any seat at the table'—he mentioned Linux ... and Java, a computer language created by Sun Microsystems, a Microsoft foe—'and I can blow away Microsoft!' "[90]

With witness testimony complete and closing arguments expected in the fall, Professor Nicholas Economides of the Stern School of Business believes a settlement is unlikely. The government is heartened by Microsoft's poor presentation of its case and is now likely to ask for very severe remedies, including a breakup of Microsoft.[91] Microsoft had thought that it would lose some in the trial but win everything on appeal. However, Judge Jackson has decided to separate a findings-of-fact ruling from a conclusions-of-law ruling, making Microsoft less certain of its chances of winning everything on appeal and increasing the incentive for Microsoft to settle. In secret meetings with the government as recently as June 1999, Microsoft has submitted three different draft versions of a proposed settlement, but the government has rejected these as unsatisfactory.[92] Bill Gates says he has long wanted a settlement. "The stumbling block … was that he [Bill Gates] couldn't go back to the government for permission each time he wanted to add a new feature…. 'You have to have a business left when you settle,'" he said.[93] However, Gates sees the trial as bad for Microsoft, no matter what the outcome. "The costs to the company and the taxpayers have been huge. The last thing any company wants is to be sued by the government."[94] So why didn't Gates settle the case before it went to trial? A settlement, though practical, would have meant a compromise resulting in loss of control over his company's intellectual property.[95]

RECENT PRODUCT DEVELOPMENTS

Despite the ongoing antitrust trial, Microsoft continues to integrate new features into the Windows operating system. In July 1999, Microsoft announced plans to more tightly integrate digital-music and photography technology as well as adding online services to Windows. The finished product will be the successor to Windows 98 and is expected to be released in 2000. Although Windows currently includes some digital-music and photography technologies, many users prefer products from competitors such as RealNetworks, which currently holds a wide lead in the market.[96] Microsoft has also formally abandoned its original vision statement, created by Bill Gates in 1975 (A computer on every desk and in every home) in favor of a new vision (Empower people through great software anytime, anyplace, and on any device.).[97] This new statement expands the original vision to include Internet-based software and services and non-PC devices such as handheld computers and TV set-top boxes.[98]

In an interesting turnaround, Microsoft is calling for open standards for instant messaging, a medium dominated by AOL. Instant messaging is possibly the fastest growing communications medium in history. "AOL says its three instant-messaging services have nearly 80 million users, and crossed the 50 million mark in less than two and a half years—compared with five years for the Internet and 13 years for television."[99] AOL has responded to competition from Microsoft, Yahoo!, and Prodigy by blocking access to its network. AOL is concerned that the unauthorized software could disrupt the quality of its service.[100]

CONCLUSION

Bill Gates still says that rivals should pay more attention to their own businesses and less time obsessing about Microsoft's competitive position. After all, the technology markets are fast paced, and there are no guarantees that Microsoft will remain the industry leader. In fact, it has been said that the Justice Department "faces an extraordinary challenge in keeping … in step with the fast-changing Internet software market and Microsoft's quickly shifting tactics."[101] However, there is little opposition to the point that Microsoft virtually owns the future of computing. In fact, it has been said that if Gates can extend Microsoft's dominance to the Internet browser realm, "the little software company he co-founded in 1975 could come to dominate the nexus of computing and communications well into the twenty-first century."[102]

Microsoft has dominated during the 1990s. Only thirteen years after its IPO, Microsoft has the largest market capitalization in the world and represents 3.9 percent of the S&P 500 Index.[103] In July 1999, Microsoft announced the financial results for fiscal year 1999: $19.75 billion in revenue, a 29 percent increase over FY1998 and EPS of $1.42, a 69 percent increase compared to FY1998.[104] Microsoft stock has enjoyed an annualized return of more than 68 percent over the last five years as compared to 21.37 percent for the S&P 500 and 23.05 percent for the NASDAQ Composite Index over the same period.[105]

Gates once said, "You don't have to have a lot of political protection to be allowed to innovate."[106] However, Microsoft has begun to take its political problems more seriously by hiring top lobbyists and substantially increasing campaign contributions to both major parties.

Around the time that the trial adjourned, he [Bill Gates] appeared before the Senate's Joint Economic Committee to talk about the future of the Information Age. A year earlier, after testifying matter-of-factly before the Judiciary Committee, he had rushed from the hearing room. This time he replied graciously to even the dimmest questions. "You've raised an interesting issue," he said repeatedly, and then he worked the room, bestowing, "Hi, nice to see ya" handshakes on senators. It was as if Gates now understood that Microsoft, like the software that had made him rich, needed an upgrade.[107]

NOTES

1. http://www.microsoft.com.
2. Hingorani, Sanjiv G. and Sheela Chandrashekhara, "Microsoft Corporation—The Renaissance at Redmond: From DOS to the Web," Furman Selz LLC, August 1996.
3. Staff, Windows 95, *Business Week*, August 1995.
4. Lohr, Steve, "Three Named to Microsoft's Top Management," *The New York Times*, 5/22/95.
5. Staff, *The New York Times*, 5/7/95.
6. Lohr, Steve, "Three Named to Microsoft's Top Management."
7. Ibid.
8. Staff, *The New York Times*, 5/7/95.
9. Lohr, Steve, "Three Named to Microsoft's Top Management."
10. http://www.PBS.org/internet/history.
11. http://www.PBS.org/internet/history.
12. http://www.PBS.org/internet/history.
13. http://www.PBS.org/internet/history.
14. http://www.PBS.org/internet/history.
15. http://www.economist.com/surveys/internet/intro.html.
16. http://www.PBS.org/internet/history.
17. http://www.economist.com/surveys/internet/intro.html.
18. http://www.economist.com/surveys/internet/intro.html.
19. http://www.PBS.org/internet/history.
20. Flynn, Mary Kathleen, "The Battle for the Net," *US News and World Report*, 12/18/95.
21. Cortese, Amy, "Win 95 Lose 96," *Business Week*, 12/18/95.
22. Reinhardt, Andy, "Intel Inside the Net," *Business Week*, 11/18/96.
23. Hingorani and Chandrashekhara, "Microsoft Corporation—The Renaissance at Redmond."
24. Rebello, Kathy, "Inside Microsoft: The Untold Story of How the Internet Forced Bill Gates to Reverse Course," *Business Week*, 7/15/96.
25. Staff, Windows 95, *Business Week*, August 1995.
26. Ibid.
27. Rebello, "Inside Microsoft."
28. Ibid.
29. Ibid.
30. Ibid.
31. Ibid.
32. Cortese, Amy, "Win 95 Lose 96."
33. Hingorani, and Chandrashekhara, "Microsoft Corporation—The Renaissance at Redmond."
34. Rebello, "Inside Microsoft."
35. Flynn, "The Battle for the Net."
36. Hafner, Katie, "Microsoft Century," *Newsweek*, 12/2/96.
37. Ibid.
38. Gleick, James, "Making Microsoft Safe for Capitalism," *The New York Times Magazine*, 11/5/95.
39. Annual Report—Fiscal Year 1996, Microsoft Corporation.
40. Reinhardt, "Intel Inside the Net."
41. Rebello, "Microsoft's Suite Spot," *Business Week*, 11/25/96.
42. Hingorani, and Chandrashekhara, "Microsoft Corporation—The Renaissance at Redmond."
43. Flynn, "The Battle for the Net."
44. Hingorani, and Chandrashekhara, "Microsoft Corporation—The Renaissance at Redmond."
45. Ibid.
46. Ibid.
47. Rebello, "Inside Microsoft."
48. Hingorani, and Chandrashekhara, "Microsoft Corporation—The Renaissance at Redmond."
49. Rebello, "Inside Microsoft."
50. Ibid.
51. Annual Report—Fiscal Year 1996, Microsoft Corporation.
52. Ibid.
53. Markoff, John, "US Won't Challenge Microsoft Network Before Its Debut," *The New York Times*, 8/5/95.
54. Brinkley, Joel, "Microsoft Gives in to a Federal Order on Internet Browser," *The New York Times*, 1/23/98.
55. _____, "Microsoft is Fighting its Competitors and the Justice Department Tooth and Nail. Is it Driven by Strategy or Nature?" *The Economist*, 1/31/98, p. 65.

56. Lohr, Steve, and John Markoff, "Why Microsoft is Taking a Hard Line With the Government," *The New York Times*, 1/12/98, p. D1.

57. Hamm, Steve, Amy Cortese, and Susan Garland, "Microsoft's Future," *Business Week*, 1/19/98, p. 58.

58. Westneat, Danny, and James Grimaldi, "Gates to Testify: Will Star Power Work on Senate? Meek Lessons Suggested for Microsoft Chief," *The Seattle Times*, 3/1/98, p A1.

59. Yang, Catherine, Amy Borrus, Susan Garland and Steve Hamm, "Microsoft Goes Low-Tech in Washington," *Business Week*, 12/22/97.

60. http://www.bsa.org/info/aboutbsa/html.

61. Yang, Borrus, Garland, and Hamm, "Microsoft Goes Low-Tech in Washington."

62. Lohr and Markoff, "Why Microsoft is Taking a Hard Line With the Government."

63. Ibid.

64. Elliot, Stuart "Bill Gates is Tiger Woods? Well, He's Doing a Commercial," *The New York Times*, 3/6/98, p. D5.

65. Ibid.

66. Hingorani and Chandrashekhara, "Microsoft Corporation—The Renaissance at Redmond."

67. Ibid.

68. Ibid.

69. Ibid.

70. Ibid.

71. Ibid.

72. Markoff, John, "Microsoft Shifts Web Unit to Windows Group," *The New York Times*, 2/6/98, p. D3.

73. Auletta, Ken, "Hard Core," *The New Yorker*, 8/16/99, p. 45.

74. Ibid.

75. Ibid., p. 61.

76. Ibid.

77. Ibid.

78. Lohr, Steve, "Point and Counterpoint in the Microsoft Trial," *The New York Times*, 6/28/99.

79. Auletta, "Hard Core," p. 62.

80. Ibid.

81. Brinkley, Joel, "Microsoft's Final Witness Asked to Rebut U.S. Case," *The New York Times*, 6/23/99.

82. Auletta, "Hard Core," p. 62.

83. Ibid., p. 67.

84. Richtel, Matt, "Share Price More Than Triples in Red Hat's Public Offering," *The New York Times*, 8/12/99.

85. Ibid.

86. Auletta, "Hard Core," p. 48.

87. Ibid., p. 49.

88. Ibid., p. 55.

89. Ibid., p. 57.

90. Ibid., p. 44.

91. http://www.economics.about.com/library/weekly/aa060199.htm.

92. Auletta, "Hard Core," p. 66.

93. Ibid., p. 68.

94. Ibid., p. 69.

95. Ibid.

96. Bank, David, "Microsoft Plans to Integrate More Products into Windows," *The Wall Street Journal*, 7/26/99.

97. Bank, David, and Don Clark, "Microsoft Broadens Vision Statement To Go Beyond the PC-Centric World," *The Wall Street Journal*, 7/23/99.

98. Ibid.

99. Clark, Don, "Web Rivals Attempt to Open Up AOL's Instant Message Service, *The Wall Street Journal*, 7/26/99.

100. Ibid.

101. Lohr, Steve, "US Facing Lightning Technology Shifts in Microsoft Case," *The New York Times*, 3/30/98, p. D1.

102. Hamm, Steve, Amy Cortese and Susan Garland, "Microsoft's Future," Business Week, 1/19/98, p. 58.

103. Browning, E.S., "Will Tech Stocks' Surge End With the Decade?" *The Wall Street Journal*, 8/23/99.

104. http://www.microsoft.com/msft/earn.htm.

105. http://www.moneycentral.msn.com/investor/charts.

106. Auletta, Ken "Hard Core," *The New Yorker*, 8/16/99, p. 58.

107. Ibid., p. 69.

Integrative Case 3.1 *Littleton Manufacturing (A)*

Rule #1 for business organizations: People, not structure, make a business work or fail. Blindly following organizational concepts that have worked elsewhere is a sure way to waste talent and get poor results. Organizational change alone achieves nothing, while dedicated people can make any structure work. This doesn't mean that organizational changes shouldn't happen. But design any changes to get the most out of people in the company's unique circumstances. Top management should never dictate change as a cure-all to avoid facing fundamental problems.

> Quotation from the *Harvard Business Review*
> (title and author uncited) posted on the wall of
> Bill Larson, Plant Manager of
> Littleton Manufacturing

On June 21, 1990, Paul Winslow, the director of human resources at Littleton Manufacturing, was told by his boss, Bill Larson, to put together a team of employees to address a number of issues that Larson thought were hurting Littleton's bottom line. Winslow's assignment had come about as a result of his making a presentation on those problems to Larson. Larson had then met with his executive staff, and he and Winslow had subsequently gone to the plant's Quality Steering Committee to discuss what to do. They decided to form a Human Resources Process Improvement Team (PIT) to prioritize the issues and propose a corrective course of action. Winslow, who had been at the plant for seventeen years, had been asked by Larson to chair the PIT.

The Quality Steering Committee decided that the PIT should include two representatives each from Sales and Marketing, Fabrication, and Components. Two managers from each of these areas were chosen, including Dan Gordon, the Fabrication Manufacturing Manager, and Phil Hanson, the Components Manufacturing Manager. There were no supervisors or hourly employees on the team.

At the first meeting, the PIT discussed the six widely recognized problem areas that Winslow had identified to Larson. Each member's assignment for the next meeting, on June 28, was to prioritize the issues and propose an action plan.

THE PROBLEMS

A course in management and organizational studies carried out by students at a nearby college had started the chain of events that led to the formation of the Human Resources PIT. In late 1989, Winslow was approached by a faculty member at a local college who was interested in using Littleton as a site for a field-project course. Because of ongoing concerns about communication at the plant by all levels, Winslow asked that the students assess organizational communication at Littleton. Larson gave his approval, and in the spring of 1990 the students carried out the project, conducting individual and group interviews with employees at all levels of the plant.

Winslow and his staff combined the results of the students' assessment with the results of an in-house survey done several years earlier. The result was the identification of six problem areas that they thought were critical for the plant to address:

* Lack of organizational unity
* Lack of consistency in enforcing rules and procedures
* Supervisor's role poorly perceived
* Insufficient focus on Littleton's priorities
* Change is poorly managed
* Lack of a systematic approach to training

THE COMPANY

Littleton Manufacturing, located in rural Minnesota, was founded in 1925. In 1942, Littleton was bought by Brooks Industries, a major manufacturer of domestic appliances and their components. At that time, Littleton manufactured custom-made and precision-machined components from special metals for a variety of industries.

In 1983, through the purchase of a larger competitor, Frühling, Inc., Brooks was able to increase its domestic market share from 8 percent to about 25 percent. Brooks then decided to have only one facility produce the components that were used in most of the products it made in the United States. The site chosen was Littleton Manufacturing. To do this,

* By David E. Whiteside, organizational development consultant. This case was written at Lewiston-Auburn College of the University of Southern Maine with the cooperation of management, solely for the purpose of stimulating student discussion. Data are based on field research; all events are real, although the names of organizations, locations, and individuals have been disguised. Faculty members in nonprofit institutions are encouraged to reproduce this case for distribution to their students without charge or written permission. All other rights reserved jointly to the author and the North American Case Research Association (NACRA). Copyright © 1994 by the *Case Research Journal* and David E. Whiteside.

Brooks added a whole new business (Components) to Littleton's traditional activity. To accommodate the new line, a building of 80,000 square feet was added to the old Littleton plant, bringing the total to 220,000 square feet of plant space. Because of the addition of this new business, Littleton went from 150 employees in 1984 to 600 in 1986. In mid-1990, there were about 500 employees.

The older part of the plant (the Fabrication side) manufactured its traditional custom-made products and sold them to a variety of industrial customers. It also supplied the newer side of the plant (the Components side) with a variety of parts that were further processed and used to make electrical components. These components were used by all other Brooks plants in the assembly of domestic appliances that were sold worldwide. About 95 percent of the products made on the Components side of the plant originated on the Fabrication side.

The plant was also headquarters for Brooks Industries' sales and marketing department, known as the "commercial group," which had worldwide sales responsibilities for products made by the Fabrication side. These included international and domestic sales of products to several industries, including the semiconductor, consumer electronics, and nuclear furnace industry. This group marketed products made not only by Littleton Manufacturing but also those made by Brooks's other fourteen plants, all located in the United States.

Bill Larson, the plant manager, reported to the executive vice president of manufacturing of Brooks, whose corporate office was in Chicago, Illinois. Larson met once a month with his boss and the other plant managers. Reporting directly to Larson were six functional line managers and the manager of the Quality Improvement System (QIS). This group of seven managers, known as the "staff," met weekly to plan and discuss how things were going. (See Exhibit 1 for an organizational chart.)

In December 1989, there were 343 hourly and 125 salaried employees at the plant. About 80 percent of the work force was under 45. Seventy-seven percent were male, and 23 percent were female. Seventy-six percent had been at the plant 10 years or less. All of the hourly workers were represented by the Teamsters union.

THE FINANCIAL PICTURE

Brooks Industries

Brooks was the second largest producer of its kind of domestic appliances in the United States. Its three core business units were commercial/industrial, consumer, and original equipment manufacturing. The major U.S. competitors for its domestic appliances were Eagleton, Inc., and Universal Appliances, Inc. In the United States, Eagleton's market share was 47 percent; Brooks had about 23 percent; and Universal Appliances and a number of small companies had the remaining 30 percent. However, U.S. manufacturers

EXHIBIT 1 *Littleton Manufacturing Organizational Chart (Littleton Manufacturing)*

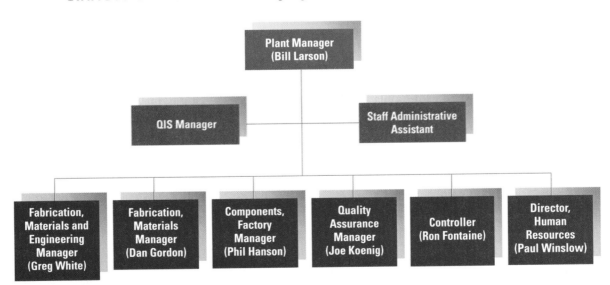

were facing increasing competition, primarily based on lower prices, from companies in Asia and eastern Europe.

In 1989, Brooks's sales declined 4 percent, and in 1990, they declined another 5 percent, to $647 million. Their 1989 annual report contained the following statement about the company's financial condition: "There was fierce competition . . . which led to a decline in our share of a stable market and a fall in prices, resulting in a lower level of sales. . . . With sales volume showing slower growth, we failed to reduce our costs proportionately and there was underutilization of capacity." In May 1990, after announcing unexpected first-quarter losses, Brooks started a corporationwide efficiency drive, including planned layoffs of 16 percent of its work force, a corporate restructuring, and renewed emphasis on managerial accountability for bottom-line results.

Because of its worsening financial condition, for the past few years Brooks had been reducing the resources available to Littleton. For example, Larson's budget for salaries had been increased by only 4 percent each year for the past several years. As a result, supervisors and middle managers complained strongly that recent salary increases had been too little and that plant salaries were too low. They also felt that the forced-ranking performance appraisal system used by the plant, which was based on a bell curve, did not reward good performance adequately. One middle manager commented: "All we get now for good performance is a card and a turkey." In April 1990, the company cut Littleton's capital budget by half and stipulated that any new project involving nonessential items had to have a one-year payback.

In addition, in both 1988 and 1989 Brooks had charged the Littleton plant around $300,000 for various services provided, such as technical support, but in 1990 this charge was increased by $1 million. Many of the Littleton plant managers felt that this was done to help offset Brooks's deteriorating financial condition and were frustrated by it. Indicating that he thought Brooks was using Littleton as a cash cow, one staff member said, "The more profitable we get, the more corporate will charge us."

Many managers, especially those on the Fabrication side, felt that even though they had made money for the plant, corporate's increase in charges nullified their success and hard work. A number of managers on the Fabrication side also feared that if their operation did not do well financially, the company might close it down.

In discussing the increasing lack of resources available from corporate and the plant's own decline in profits, Larson said: "There needs to be a change in the way people here think about resources. They have to think more in terms of efficiency." He was proud of the fact that the company had achieved its goal of reducing standard costs by 1 percent for each of the past three years and that in 1990 cost reductions would equal 5 percent of production value. He thought that if the company reduced the number of reworks, costs could be lowered by another 20 to 30 percent.

LITTLETON MANUFACTURING

The Fabrication and the Components operations at Littleton Manufacturing were managed as cost centers by Brooks while the commercial group was a profit center. (A *profit center* is part of an organization that is responsible for accumulating revenues as well as costs. A *cost center* is an organizational division or unit of activity in which accounts are maintained containing direct costs for which the center's head is responsible.) In 1989 and 1990, the Fabrication side of Littleton had done well in terms of budgeted costs, while the Components side had incurred significant losses for both years.

Littleton's net worth increased from $319,000 in 1989 to $3,094,000 in 1990 due to the addition of a new Fabrication-side product that was sold on the external market and had required no additional assets or resources. In 1990, sales for the plant as a whole were $41,196,000, with an operating profit of 3.7 percent, down from 7.3 percent in 1989. Larson estimated that the current recession, which was hurting the company, would lower sales in 1991 by 10 percent. Exhibit 2 presents an operating statement for Littleton Manufacturing from 1988 to 1990.

THE QUALITY IMPROVEMENT SYSTEM

In 1985, corporate mandated a total quality management effort, the Quality Improvement System (QIS), which replaced the quality circles that the plant had instituted in 1980. Posted throughout the plant was a Quality Declaration, which had been developed by Larson and his staff. It read:

> We at Littleton Manufacturing are dedicated to achieving lasting quality. This means that each of us must understand and meet the requirements of our customers and co-workers. We all must continually strive for improvement and error-free work in all we do—in every job . . . on time . . . all the time.

EXHIBIT 2   *Littleton Manufacturing Operating Profit Statement*

	1988	1989	1990
Fabrication			
Sales	$16,929	$18,321	$19,640
Direct costs	11,551	11,642	11,701
Contribution margin	5,378	6,679	7,939
% of sales	31.8%	36.5%	40.4%
All other operating costs	4,501	4,377	4,443
Operating profit	877	2,301	3,496
% to sales	5.2%	12.6%	17.8%
Components			
Sales	$20,468	$15,590	$21,556
Direct costs	16,049	10,612	18,916
Contribution margin	4,419	4,978	2,640
% of sales	21.6%	31.9%	12.2%
All other operating costs	4,824	4,797	4,628
Operating profit	(405)	180	(1,988)
% to sales	-2.0%	1.2%	-9.2%
Total Littleton Manufacturing			
Sales	$37,397	$33,911	41,196
Direct Costs	27,599	22,254	30,617
Contribution margin	9,788	11,656	10,579
% to sales	26.2%	34.4%	25.7%
All other operating costs	9,326	9,175	9,071
Operating profit	472	2,482	1,508
% to sales	1.3%	7.3%	3.7%

Note: Changes in Operating Profit from year to year are posted to retained earnings (net worth) account on the corporate balance sheet. It must be noted, however, that the balance sheet figures include the impact of headquarters, national organization changes, and extraordinary income from other operations, which are not reflected on the operating profit statement shown above.

Source: Controller, Littleton Manufacturing.

Bill Larson was enthusiastic about QIS. He saw QIS as a total quality approach affecting not just products but all of the plant's processes, one that would require a long-term effort at changing the culture at the plant. He felt that QIS was already reaping benefits in terms of significant improvements in quality, and that the system had also greatly helped communication at the plant.

In the QIS all employees were required to participate in Departmental Quality Teams (DQTs) that met in groups of six to twelve every two weeks for at least an hour to identify ways to improve quality. Most hourly employees were on only one DQT; middle managers were, on average, on three DQTs. Some managers were on as many as six. The results of each team's efforts were exhibited in graphs and charts by their work area and updated monthly. There were about sixty teams in the plant.

The leader from each Departmental Quality Team, a volunteer, served also as a member of a Quality Improvement Team (QIT), whose goals were to support the DQTs and help them link their goals to the company's goals. QITs consisted of six to eight people; each was chaired by a member of the executive staff. These staff members, along with Bill Larson, composed the Quality Steering Committee (QSC) for the plant. The QSC's job was to oversee the direction and implementation of the Quality Improvement System for the plant and to coordinate with corporate's quality improvement programs. The QSC also sometimes formed corrective action teams to work on special projects. Unlike DQTs, which were composed of employees from a single department or work area, corrective action teams had members from different functions or departments. By 1986, there were nine corrective action teams, but by 1989, none were functioning. When asked about them, Winslow said, "I'm not sure what happened to them. They just sort of died out."

Larson and most managers believed that the QIS had improved quality. On most of its Fabrication products, the company competed on the basis of quality and customer service, and the vice-president of sales and marketing thought that their quality was the best in the industry. In 1988 and 1989, the plant won several Brooks awards for quality and was publicly cited by a number of customers for quality products.

Hourly employees in general also thought that QIS had improved quality, although they were less enthusiastic about the system than management. A number of hourly employees complained that since participation was mandatory, many groups were held back by unmotivated members. They thought participation should be voluntary. Another complaint was that there was inadequate training for group leaders, with the result that some groups were not productive.

In the spring of 1990, the company decided that the QIS effort was "stagnating" and that DQTs should be changed to include members from different departments. It was thought that this would improve communication and coordination between departments and lead to further improvements in quality, productivity, and on-time delivery. DQTs became known is IDQTs (Interdepartmental Quality Teams). IDQTs were scheduled to begin in November 1990. In addition, the company decided to begin Process Improvement Teams (PITs), which would focus on various ongoing processes at the plant, such as budgeting and inventory management. A PIT, composed of managers from different functions, would not be ongoing but only last as long as it took to achieve its particular goals.

HOW DIFFERENT LEVELS PERCEIVED THE PROBLEMS

In order to choose the issues to tackle first and to devise a tentative plan for addressing them, Winslow reflected on the background information he had on the six problem areas that he and his staff had identified on the basis of their own analysis and the students' assessment of organizational communication.

A Lack of Organizational Unity

People often talked about "this side of the wall and that side of the wall" in describing the plant. They were referring to the wall separating the newer, Components side and the older, Fabrication side of the plant. (Some parts of the Fabrication side had been built in the twenties.) The Components side was brighter, cleaner, and more open, and, in summer, it was cooler. In comparing the two sides one manager said, "At the end of the shift in Fabrication, you come out looking like you've been through the wringer." On the whole, the equipment in the Components side was also newer, with most of it dating from the 1970s and 1980s and some of it state-of-the-art machinery that was developed at the plant. Much of the equipment on the Fabrication side went back to the 1950s and 1960s. These differences in age meant that, in general, the machinery on the Fabrication side required more maintenance.

It was generally agreed that Components jobs were cleaner and easier, and allowed more social interaction. On the Fabrication side many of the machines could run only two to three hours before needing attention, whereas on the Components side the machines might run for days without worker intervention. On the Fabrication side, because of the placement of the machines and the need for frequent maintenance, people tended to work more by themselves and to "be on the go all the time." It was not uncommon for senior hourly employees in Fabrication to request a transfer to Components.

Hourly workers described Components as "a country club" compared to the Fabrication side. Many attributed this to how the different sides were managed. Enforcement of rules was more lax on the Components side. For example, rules requiring safety shoes and goggles were not as strictly enforced, and some operators were allowed to eat on the job.

One Human Resources staff member described Components supervisors as "laid-back about sticking to the rules" and those in Fabrication as "sergeants." He saw the manufacturing manager of Fabrication, Dan Gordon, as having a clear vision of what he wanted for the Fabrication side and a definite plan on how to get there. He also saw Gordon as keeping a tight rein on his supervisors and holding them accountable. The same Human Resources employee described the factory manager of Components, Phil Hanson, as dealing with things as they came up—as more reactive. Hanson allowed his supervisors more freedom and did not get involved on the floor unless there was a problem. When there was a problem, however, he reacted strongly and swiftly. For example, to combat a recent tendency for employees to take extended breaks, he had begun posting supervisors outside of the bathrooms right before and after scheduled breaks.

Bill Larson attributed the differences in the two sides "to the different performance and accountability needs dictated by their business activities and by the corporate office." Components met the internal production needs of Brooks by supplying all of the other Brooks plants with a product that they, in turn, used to manufacture a household product that sold in the millions each year. Fabrication, however, had to satisfy the needs of a variety of industrial customers while competing on the open market. Larson felt that Fabrication had to have a more entrepreneurial ethic than Components because "Fabrication lives or dies by how they treat their customers—they have to woo them and interact well with them," whereas Components had a ready-made market.

Larson also thought that some of the differences were due to the fact that the plant was "held prisoner by what goes on in corporate." Although the corporate office set financial targets for both sides of the plant, it exercised more control over the financial and productivity goals of the Components side because no other Brooks plant was in the Fabrication business and Brooks understood the Components business much better. In addition, corporate was dependent on the Components side for the standardized parts—primarily wire coils—used in many of its finished products. The Components side produced as many as 2 million of some of these small parts a day.

Larson also indicated that the requirements for the number of workers on the two sides of the plant were different. For example, depending on what business was like for each side, the overtime requirements could vary. Hourly employees on the side of the plant that had more overtime felt the side that was working less was getting "easier" treatment. Larson knew that the overtime disparity was due to need, not preferential treatment of one side over the other, but as he put it: "You can talk your head off, but you're not going to be able to explain it to them to their satisfaction. So that causes a lot of frustration among the ranks down there."

The Manager of QIS traced the differences between the Fabrication side and the Components side to the consolidation at Littleton of all of Brooks's production of wire coils needed for its domestic appliances after Brooks bought Frühling, Inc., in 1984. Most of the upper managers hired to start the Components business were brought in from Frühling, and, as he put it, "They had a different way of doing things. It wasn't a tightly run ship." He said that some of the old managers at the plant wondered about the wisdom of bringing in managers from a company that had not been successful. People asked, "Why use them here? They must have been part of what was wrong." One Fabrication manager added that the manager brought in to start the Components business, Bob Halperin, had the view: "We're going to start a new business here and do whatever is necessary to make it run and to hell with Littleton Manufacturing policies." Also, when the new Components business was started, its manager reported directly to the Brooks corporate office and not to the plant manager. In 1986 the structure was changed so that the factory manager of Components reported to the Littleton Manufacturing plant manager.

A union steward at the plant attributed some of the differences between the two sides to the fact that the work force on the Components side tended to be younger and had more women with young children (67 percent of the hourly women in the plant worked in Components). The demands of raising children, he thought, resulted in the women needing to take more time off from work. One of the Fabrication supervisors thought that since the supervisors on the Components side were younger, they expected more from management and were more outspoken, especially about how much an hour they should be paid. A number of these supervisors had also been brought in from Frühling, and were not originally from Littleton.

Lack of Consistency in Enforcing Rules and Procedures

A major complaint of both hourly and salaried workers was the inconsistent application of policies and procedures. Although most people mentioned the differences from one side of the plant to the other, there were also differences from one department to another. As the chief union steward put it, "This is the number one problem here—nobody is the same!" Some Components supervisors were letting people take longer breaks and going for breaks earlier than they were supposed to. Some supervisors allowed hourly employees to stand around and talk for a while before getting them to start their machines. In some departments on the Components side, employees were allowed to gather in the bathrooms and "hang out" anywhere from five to twenty minutes before quitting time. The chief steward cited an example where, contrary to previous policy, some workers on the Components side were allowed to have radios. "When people on the Fabrication side found out," he said, "they went wild."

Some other examples of inconsistencies cited by employees were as follows:

1. Fighting in the plant was supposed to result in automatic dismissal, but the Human Resources administrator recalled two incidents of fighting where the people involved were not disciplined.
2. Another incident that had been much discussed throughout the plant involved an employee who was "caught in a cloud of marijuana smoke" by his supervisor. Since the supervisor did not observe the man smoking but just smelled the marijuana, the person was only given a written warning. One manager said, "We need to take a stand on these things. We need to make a statement. That way we would gain some respect." Describing the same incident, another manager said, "It makes us close to thinking we're giving them (hourly employees) the key to the door."
3. Several people also mentioned the case of a mother who claimed she missed work several times because of doctor's appointments for her children and was suspended for three days, which they compared with the case of an operator who also missed work several times, and was suspected of drug or alcohol abuse, but was not disciplined.

In discussing differences in the enforcement of safety regulations throughout the plant, the administrator of plant safety and security said that when he confronted people who were wearing sneakers, often they would just say they forgot to wear their safety shoes. He said, "If I had to punish everyone, I'd be punishing 50 to 100 people a day."

There were also differences in absenteeism for the two sides of the plant. Absenteeism on the Components side was around 2.2 percent, whereas it was slightly less than 1 percent on the Fabrication side. Some attributed this to a looser enforcement of the rules governing absenteeism by supervisors on the Components side.

Winslow had tried to estimate the annual cost of failure to enforce the rules governing starting and stopping work. His estimate was that the plant was losing $2,247.50 per day, for a total of $539,400 a year. Winslow's memo detailing how he arrived at his overall estimate had been part of his presentation to Larson; it is included as Exhibit 3. Although Winslow had not said so in the memo, he later estimated that 70 percent of the total loss occurred on the Components side of the plant.

Supervisors complained that when they tried to discipline subordinates, they often did not feel confident of backing by management. They referred to incidents where they had disciplined hourly employees only to have their decisions changed by management or the Human Resources department. One supervisor told of an incident in which he tried to fire someone in accordance with what he thought was company policy, but the termination was changed to a suspension. He was told he had been too harsh. In a subsequent incident he had another decision overruled and was told he had been too lenient. He said, "We feel our hands are tied; we're not sure what we can do." Supervisors' decisions that were changed were usually communicated directly to the union by the Human Resources department. In these instances, the supervisors felt they wound up with "egg on their face."

Winslow attributed some of these problems to a lack of communication regarding the company's policies and procedures. He thought that if the supervisors understood company policy better, their decisions would not need to be changed so frequently. There was no Human Resources policy manual, for example, although the work rules were contained in the union contract.

Dan Gordon disagreed with the view that these problems were a result of the supervisors' lack of understanding of the plant's policies and procedures. He claimed: "Ninety-nine percent of the supervisors know the policies but they lack the skills and willingness to enforce them. Just like a police officer needs to be trained to read a prisoner his rights, the supervisors need to be taught to do their jobs." He thought that in some of the cases where a supervisor's decision was changed, the supervisor had made a mistake in following the proper disciplinary procedure. Then, when the supervisor's decision was overturned, no explanation was provided, so the supervisor would be left with his or her own erroneous view of what happened.

The Human Resources administrator thought that some of the supervisors were reluctant to discipline or confront people because "They're afraid to

EXHIBIT 15.7 *Modern Versus Post-Modern Organization Paradigms*

MEMORANDUM

From: Paul Winslow, Director of Human Resources

To: Bill Larson

Subject: Estimated Cost of Loss of Manufacturing Time

Date: 6/18/90

Loss of Manufacturing Time*

(Based on 348 Hourly Employees)

Delay at start of shift	10 Minutes × 25% (87) =	14.50 hours
Wash-up before AM break	5 Minutes × 75% (261) =	21.75 hours
Delayed return from break	10 Minutes × 50% (174) =	29.00 hours
Early wash up—Lunch	avg. 10 Minutes × 50% (174) =	29.00 hours
Daily return from Lunch	10 Minutes × 25% (87) =	14.50 hours
Early wash-up before PM break	5 Minutes × 75% (261) =	21.75 hours
Delayed return from break	10 Minutes × 50% (174) =	29.00 hours
Early wash up—end of shift	5 Minutes × 75% (261) =	65.25 hours
	Total =	224.75 hours/day

Cost: 224.75 × Avg. $10 hr. = $2,247.50/day

     240 days × $2,247.50 = $539,400.00/year

*1. Does not include benefits.
 2. Does not include overtime abuses.
 3. Does not include instances of employees exiting building while punched in.

---

hurt people's feelings and want to stay on their good side."

Supervisor's Role Is Poorly Perceived

On the first shift in Fabrication there were about 70 hourly workers and 7 supervisors, and in Components there were about 140 hourly workers and 11 supervisors. Supervisors were assisted by group leaders, hourly employees who were appointed by the company and who received up to an extra 10 cents an hour.

All levels of the plant were concerned about the role of supervisors. "Supervisors feel like a nobody," said one senior manager. In the assessment of organizational communication done by the students, hourly employees, middle managers, and supervisors all reported that supervisors had too much to do and that this limited their effectiveness. A typical observation by one hourly employee was: "The supervisors can't be out on the floor because of meetings and paperwork. They have a tremendous amount of things on their mind. . . . The supervisor has become a paperboy, which prevents him from being able to do his job." In speaking about how busy the supervisors were and how they responded to suggestions by hourly employees, another hourly person said, "The supervisor's favorite word is 'I forgot.'"

Supervisors also wanted more involvement in decision making. "You will! You will! You will!" is the way one supervisor characterized the dominant decision-making style of managers at the plant. He thought that most managers expected supervisors to just do what they were told to do. "We have a lot of responsibility but little authority," was how another supervisor put it. Many supervisors felt that they were ordered to do things by their managers, but when something went wrong, they were blamed.

Another factor contributing to the low morale of supervisors was a perceived lack of the resources that they felt were necessary to do a good job. Many complained that they were often told there was no money to make changes to improve things. They also complained of too few engineering, housekeeping, and maintenance personnel. Some supervisors thought there were too few supervisors on the second and third shifts. They thought this resulted in inadequate supervision and allowed some hourly workers to "goof off," since the employees knew when these few supervisors would and would not be around.

The combination of these factors—job overload, too much paperwork, lack of authority, not enough involvement in decision making, lack of resources to make changes, inadequate training, and few rewards—made it difficult to find hourly people at the plant who would accept an offer to become a supervisor.

In discussing the role of supervisors, Larson said, "We don't do a good job of training our supervisors. We tell them what we want and hold them accountable, but we don't give them the personal tools for them to do what we want them to do. They need to have the confidence and ability to deal with people and to hold them accountable without feeling badly." He continued by praising one supervisor who he thought was doing a good job. In particular, Larson felt, this supervisor's subordinates knew what to expect from him. This person had been a chief petty officer in the Navy for many years, and Larson thought this had helped him feel comfortable enforcing rules. Reflecting on this, he said, "Maybe we should just look for people with military backgrounds to be supervisors."

Insufficient Focus on Littleton's Priorities

The phrase "insufficient focus on Littleton's priorities" reflected two concerns expressed by employees. First, there was a lack of understanding of Littleton's goals. Second, there was a questioning of the plant's commitment to these goals. However, various levels saw these matters differently.

Although the plant had no mission statement, senior managers said that they thought that they understood Littleton's priorities. A typical senior management description of the plant's goals was, "To supply customers with quality products on time at the lowest possible cost in order to make a profit."

Each year, Larson and the executive staff developed a four-year strategic plan for Littleton. Sales and marketing would first project the amounts and types of products that they thought they could sell. Then manufacturing would look at the machine and labor capabilities of the plant. The sales projections and capabilities were then adjusted as necessary. Throughout the process, goals were set for improving quality and lowering costs. Larson then took the plan to Brooks for revision and/or approval. Next, Larson turned the goals in the strategic plan into specific objectives for each department. These departmental objectives were used to set measurable objectives for each executive staff member. These then formed the basis for annual performance appraisals. Because of this process, all of the executive staff felt that they knew what was expected of them and how their jobs contributed to achieving the company's goals.

At the same time, both senior and middle managers thought there was insufficient communication and support from corporate headquarters. They mentioned not knowing enough about corporate's long-term plans for the company. A number of the managers on the Fabrication side wondered about corporate's commitment to the Fabrication business. They thought that if their operation did not do well financially, the company might end it. In discussing the status of the Fabrication side of the plant, Gordon said that Brooks considered it a "noncore business." The Quality Assurance manager felt that corporate was not providing enough support and long-term direction for the QIS. Winslow was concerned about the lack of consistency in corporate's Human Resources policies and felt that he did not have enough say in corporate Human Resources planning efforts.

All levels below the executive staff complained that they did not have a good understanding of Littleton's own long-range goals. Some middle managers thought there was a written, long-range plan for the company but others disagreed. One member of the executive staff reported that as far as he knew, the entire strategic plan was seen only by the executive staff, although some managers would see the portions of it that concerned their departments. He also reported that the strategic plan was never discussed at operations review meetings. Most hourly employees said that they relied on the grapevine for information about "the big picture." In discussing the flow of information at the plant, one union steward said, "Things get lost in the chain of command." He said he got more than 80 percent of his information from gossip on the floor.

The primary mechanism used to communicate Littleton's goals and the plant's status with regard to achieving them was the operations review meeting held once a month by the plant manager, to which all salaried employees were ostensibly invited. At these meetings, usually attended by about eighty people, the plant manager provided figures on how closely the plant had hit selected business indicators. At one recent and typical meeting, for example, the Manager of QIS described various in-place efforts to improve quality. Bill Larson then reviewed "the numbers." He presented data on budgeted versus actual production, variances between budgeted and actual manufacturing costs, profits, the top ten products in sales, standard margins on various products, shipments of products, information on backlogs, and the top ten customers.* When he asked for questions at the end of his presentation, there were none.

The students' organizational assessment reported that all levels appreciated the intent of the operations review meetings, but there were a number of concerns. Everyone interviewed wanted more two-way communication but thought the size and format of the meetings inhibited discussion. Middle managers thought the meetings focused too much on what had happened and not enough on the future. As one manager said: "It's like seeing Lubbock in the rearview mirror. We want to know where we're going—not where we've been. We want to know what's coming up, how it's going to affect our department, and what we can do to help." Others, including some of the executive staff, complained about the difficulty of understanding the financial jargon. Some hourly employees interviewed did not know there were operations review meetings, and others did not know what was discussed at them.

A number of middle managers in manufacturing thought that having regular departmental meetings would improve communication within their departments. They also said that they would like to see minutes of the executive staff meetings.

When interviewed by the students for their assessment of organizational communication, a number of middle managers, supervisors, and hourly workers thought the company was not practicing what it preached with regard to its stated goals. A primary goal

was supposed to be a quality product; however, they reported that there was too much emphasis on "hitting the numbers," or getting the required number of products shipped, even if there were defects. They said this especially occurred toward the end of the month when production reports were submitted. One worker's comment reflected opinions held by many hourly employees: "Some foremen are telling people to push through products that are not of good quality. This passes the problem from one department to another and the end result is a lousy product. They seem too interested in reaching the quota and getting the order out on time rather than quality. It's a big problem because when the hourly workers believe that quality isn't important, they start not to care about their work. They pass it on to the next guy, and the next guy gets mad."

The perception by a number of hourly workers that their suggestions to improve quality were not responded to because of a lack of money also resulted in their questioning the company's commitment to quality.

Change Is Poorly Managed

Most of the employees interviewed by the students thought there were too many changes at the plant and that the numerous changes resulted in confusion.

1. QIS was initiated in 1985.
2. In 1986, 100 hourly employees were laid off.
3. In 1984, there were 154 managers; in 1990, there were 87 managers.
4. In 1989, corporate initiated a restructuring that changed the reporting relationships of several senior managers.
5. In 1989, as part of QIS, the plant began using statistical process control techniques and began efforts to attain ISO certification. (ISO is an internationally recognized certification of excellence.)
6. In 1989, a new production and inventory control system was introduced, with the help of a team of outside consultants who were at the plant for almost a year studying its operations.
7. In 1990, the Components side reorganized its production flow.

A number of complaints were voiced about the effect of all the changes. People felt that some roles and

---

*At Littleton, the manufacturing, engineering, and accounting departments estimated the standard labor costs for making each of the plant's products and a budget was prepared based on those estimates. The budgeted costs were plant goals. A variance is the difference between actual and standard costs. A variance could be positive (less than) or negative (greater than) with respect to the budgeted costs.

responsibilities were not clear. There was a widespread belief that the reasons for changes were not communicated well enough and that people found out about changes affecting them too late. In addition, many were uncertain how long a new program, once started, would be continued. Larson thought that many hourly employees were resistant to the changes being made because they thought the changes would require more work for them and they were already "running all the time." One union steward observed, "There's never a gradual easing in of things here." A middle manager said: "We're mandated for speed. We pride ourselves on going fast. We rush through today to get to tomorrow."

Larson thought the culture of the plant was gradually changing due to the implementation of QIS, but he noted that a lot of time had to be spent giving the employees reasons for changes.

Dan Gordon thought the plant needed to "communicate change in a single voice." He said that Larson's style was to leave it to the staff to tell others about upcoming changes. He commented, "By the time it gets to the last person, it's lost something." He felt that Larson needed to communicate changes to those on lower levels in person.

The QIS manager thought that Brooks did not provide enough resources and support for changes at the plant. In explaining his view of corporate's approach to change, he said, "Step one is to not give much. Step two is to not give anything. Step three is they take what's left away." Another middle manager commented, "We're always being asked to do more with less, but the requirements by corporate don't get cut back."

A frequently mentioned example of change that was frustrating to many people was the introduction of the Manufacturing Assisted Production and Inventory Control System (MAPICS) in 1989. MAPICS was a computerized system that was supposed to keep track of materials, productivity, and labor efficiency. Theoretically, it tracked orders from time of entry to payment of the bill, and one could find out where an order was at any point in the system by calling it up on a computer. However, the system was time consuming (data had to be entered manually by the supervisors), and was not as well suited to the Fabrication side of the plant as it was to the Components side, where production was more standardized. One senior manager commented, "MAPICS was sold as the savior for the supervisors, and the company was supposed to get all of the data

it needed. But it's never happened. It's only half-installed, and there are systems problems and input problems." Recently, there had been some question as to whether MAPICS was giving an accurate inventory count.

Hourly workers felt put upon by the way in which changes were made. One person said, "We were all of a sudden told to start monitoring waste and then all of a sudden we were told to stop." Another said, "One day the MAPICS room is over here, and then the next day it's over there. They also put a new system in the stock room, and we didn't know about it." Many resented the outside consultants that had been brought in by corporate, reporting that they did not know why the consultants were brought in or what they were doing. They feared that the consultants' recommendations might result in layoffs.

Hourly people felt that a lot of their information about upcoming changes came through the grapevine. "Rumors fly like crazy" is the way one hourly person described communication on the floor. Another said, "The managers don't walk through the plant much. We only see them when things are going bad."

In discussing communication about changes, one middle manager said: "It's a standing joke. The hourly know what's going to happen before we do." One steward said, "Lots of times, you'll tell the supervisor something that's going to happen and they will be surprised. It raises hell with morale and creates unstable working conditions. But nine out of ten times it's true."

Hourly workers also felt that they were not involved enough in management decisions about changes to be made. One hourly worker said, "They don't ask our input. We could tell them if something is not going to work. They should keep us informed. We're not idiots."

Lack of a Systematic Approach to Training

The company had carried out a well-regarded training effort when employees were hired to begin the Components side of the plant and when the QIS program was started. In addition, every two years each employee went through refresher training for the QIS. There was no other formal company training or career development at the plant.

Hourly employees and supervisors in particular complained about the lack of training. One hourly employee expressed the predominant view: "When you start work here, it's sink or swim." In discussing the promotion of supervisors, the chief union steward said he did not know how people got to be a supervisor and that as far as he knew there was no training that one had to have to become a supervisor.

When they were hired, new hourly and salaried employees attended an orientation session in which they were informed about benefits, attendance policies, their work schedule, parking regulations, and safety issues. After the orientation session, further training for new salaried employees was left up to individual departments. Standard practice was for the department supervisor to assign the hourly person to an experienced hourly operator for one-on-one job training for two weeks. Winslow expressed some of his reservations about this approach by commenting, "You don't know if the department is assigning the best person to train the new employee or if they always use the same person for training."

The Human Resources department had no separate training budget. Individual departments, however, did sometimes use their money for training and counted the money used as a variance from their budgeted goals. The training that did occur with some regularity tended to be technical training for maintenance personnel.

When asked to explain why there was not more training, Winslow replied, "We would like to do more but we haven't been able to because of the cost and manpower issues." For example, in 1986 Winslow's title was manager of training and development, and he had been responsible for the training program for all of the new employees hired to begin the Components unit. After the initial training was completed, he requested that the plant provide ongoing training for Components operators. However, his request was turned down by Larson, who did not want to spend the money. Winslow also recalled the over 160 hours he had spent the previous year developing a video training package for hourly workers in one part of the Components side of the plant. He said that the program had been piloted, but when it came time to send people through the training course, production management was unwilling to let people take time off the floor.

Winslow also cited a lack of support from corporate as a factor in the plant's sporadic training efforts. At one time Brooks had employed a director of training for its plants, but in 1987, the person left and the company never hired anyone to replace him. Now, Brooks had no training department; each plant was expected to provide its own training. The training

Brooks did provide, according to Winslow, was for the "promising manager" and was purchased from an outside vendor.

TOP MANAGEMENT

As he sat in his office thinking about what to do, Winslow knew that any plan would have to be acceptable to Larson, Gordon, and Hanson—the plant manager and the two factory managers—and he spent some time thinking about their management styles.

Bill Larson was in his late forties, had a B.S. in mechanical engineering, and had started at Littleton in 1970. He had been plant manager since 1983. His direct reports considered him bright, analytical, and down to earth. When asked once how he would describe himself to someone who didn't know him, he said, "I keep my emotions out of things. I can remember when I was in the Army, standing at attention in my dress blues at the Tomb of the Unknown Soldier. People would come up a foot from my face and look me in the eye and try to get me to blink. But I was able to remove myself from that. I wouldn't even see it." He added that he had built most of his own home and repaired his own equipment, including the diesels on a cabin cruiser he used to own. Being raised on a farm in the rural Midwest, he said he learned at an early age how to repair equipment with baling wire to keep it going.

Although Larson was considered accessible by the executive staff, he rarely got out on the floor to talk to people. Many managers saw him as a "numbers" man who readily sprinkled his conversations about the plant with quantitative data about business indicators, variances, budgeted costs, etc. In referring to his discomfort discussing personal things, he somewhat jokingly said about himself, "I can talk on the phone for about thirty-five seconds and then I can't talk any longer."

In describing his own management style, Larson said, "I like to support people and get them involved. I like to let them know what I am thinking and what they need to accomplish. I like to let ideas come from them. I want them to give me recommendations, and if I feel they're O.K., I won't change them. They need to be accountable, but I don't want them to feel I'm looking over their shoulder. I don't want to hamper their motivation." He estimated that 40 percent of his job responsibility consisted of managing change.

Dan Gordon, who was 38, had been at Littleton for fifteen years and had been manufacturing manager of Fabrication for seven years. In describing himself, he said, "I'm a stickler for details, and I hate to not perform well. My superiors tell me I'm a Theory X manager and that I have a 'strong' personality—that I can intimidate people."

In speaking about how much he communicated with hourly employees, Gordon said that he didn't do enough of it, adding that "Our platters are all so loaded, we don't spend as much time talking to people as we should." He said he seldom walked through the plant and never talked to hourly workers one-on-one. Once a year, though, he met formally with all the hourly employees on the Fabrication side to have an operations review meeting like the salaried people had in order to discuss what the plant was doing, profits, new products, etc. "The hourly people love it," he reported.

Reflecting on why he didn't communicate more with hourly workers, Gordon said, "Since the accounting department's data depends, in part, on our data collection, a lot of my time is eaten up with this. Maybe I'm too busy with clerical activities to be more visible." He based his management decisions on documented data and regularly studied the financial and productivity reports issued by the accounting department. He said he would like to see the supervisors go around in the morning to just talk to people but acknowledged that they had too many reports to fill out and too many meetings to attend.

When asked to explain what one needed to do to succeed as a manager at Littleton, Gordon answered, "You have to get things done. Bill Larson wants certain things done within a certain time span. If you do this, you'll succeed."

Phil Hanson, in his early fifties, had been at Littleton for seven years. He was hired as materials manager for Components and was promoted to Components factory manager in mid-1989. Phil estimated that he spent 50 percent of his time on the factory floor talking to people. He felt it gave him a better insight as to what was going on at the plant and created trust. He thought that too many of the managers at the plant were "office haunts"—they felt it was beneath them to talk with hourly workers. It appeared to other managers that Hanson often made decisions based on what he learned in informal conversations with hourly employees. He tried to delegate as much as he could to his managers. When asked what a manager had to do to succeed there, he said, "You have to be a self-starter and make things happen."

Winslow remembered how a few years ago, when he was manager of training and development, the executive staff had gone to one of those management development workshops where you find out about your management style. All of the staff had scored high on the authoritarian end of the scale.

This triggered a memory of a recent debate in which he had passed along a suggestion by his staff to the executive staff to "do something nice for the workers on the floor." To celebrate the arrival of summer, his staff wanted the company to pay for buying hamburgers, hot dogs, and soft drinks so the workers could have a cookout during their lunch break. Those on the executive staff who resisted the idea cited the "jelly bean theory of management." As one manager explained it, "If you give a hungry bear jelly beans, you can keep it happy and get it to do what you want. But watch out when you run out of jelly beans! You're going to have a helluva angry bear to deal with!" The jelly bean argument carried the day, and the cookout was not held.

RECOMMENDATION TIME

As Winslow turned on the computer to write down his recommendations concerning the six problem areas, he recalled how Larson had reacted when the students made their presentation on organizational communication at Littleton. After praising the students' efforts, Larson had said, in an offhanded way, "This mainly confirms what we already knew. Most of this is not a surprise." Winslow was hopeful that now some of these issues would be addressed.

One potential sticking point, he knew, was the need for the meetings that would be necessary to discuss the problems and plan a strategy. People were already strapped for time and complaining about the number of meetings. Yet unless they took time to step back and look at what they were doing, nothing would change.

On a more hopeful note, he recalled that Larson had been impressed when the Human Resources staff emphasized in their presentation to him that these issues were impacting Littleton's bottom line. Winslow felt that the decline in sales and profits at Brooks, the increasing domestic and foreign competition, the current recession, and declining employee morale made it even more important that the issues be dealt with. People at all levels of the plant were starting to worry about the possibility of more layoffs.

Integrative Case 3.2   Littleton Manufacturing (B)*

Winslow met with his staff to develop a list of proposed corrective actions. Exhibit 1 is the memo that Winslow sent, in June 1990, to the Human Resources PIT, outlining suggested corrective actions. (The action steps were not prioritized.)

The PIT did not meet to discuss what to do about the six issues identified by the Human Resources department until the middle of September. The first issue the PIT decided to address was the inconsistent application of disciplinary policies and procedures. They chose this issue first because they thought that if this could be improved, many of the other issues would be resolved as well.

The PIT decided to first find out how well supervisors understood the work rules and the extent to which they had different interpretations of them. To do this they developed a quiz covering Littleton's twenty-eight work rules and gave the quiz to all supervisors. One question, for example, was "If you came in and found an employee who had just dozed off at his/her workstation, what would you do?" The supervisor then had to choose from several alternatives. This question was followed by "If you came in and found an employee away from the job and asleep on top of some packing materials, what would you do?" Again, there was a choice of several responses. After taking the exam, the answers were discussed and the correct answer explained by Winslow and the Human Resources staff. The results revealed to the PIT that there was much less knowledge of these rules and how to apply them than management had expected.

The PIT then theorized that a number of supervisors were not comfortable with confronting employees about their failure to follow the company's policies and procedures, especially the wearing of safety shoes and goggles. They decided to seek the assistance of an outside consultant to help them develop a training program for the supervisors. However, on September 1, 1991, as a continuation of its "efficiency drive," Brooks had imposed a freeze on salaries and a reduction in travel, and prohibited the use of outside consultants at all of its plants. When Winslow asked Bill Larson for approval to hire the consultant, he was reminded that because of the freeze they would have to do the training in-house.

As a consequence, Winslow began a series of meetings with union stewards and supervisors—called "Sup and Stew" meetings—to discuss what the work rules were, different interpretations of them, and how violations of work rules should be handled. For scheduling reasons, it was planned so that half of the supervisors and the stewards would attend each meeting. These meetings were held biweekly for over a year. Winslow believed that the meetings were helping to clarify and support the role of the supervisors and were beginning to have a positive effect on the enforcement of policies and procedures.

In 1991, because the plants that bought the wire coils made by Components had excess finished goods inventory, Brooks shut them down for a month during the Christmas holidays, leading Littleton to eliminate 125 positions from the Components side for the same month, to reduce production. "If we hadn't," Winslow said, "we would have had a horrendous amount of inventory." The employees filling those positions had, in general, less seniority than their counterparts from Fabrication, and no one from the Fabrication side was laid off. A few of the more senior employees from the Components side were hired to work on the Fabrication side. At the time of the layoffs, business on the Fabrication side was "booming." In January, the plant started rehiring the laid-off workers, and by the end of June, all of them had been rehired.

In November 1991, Bill Larson learned that he had cancer, and in June, 1992, he died. Because of Larson's illness, the lack of resources, and time pressures, there was no formal attempt to address any of the issues identified by Winslow other than inconsistent enforcement of policies and procedures.

The new plant manager, Bob Halperin, took over in the fall of 1992; Halperin had been managing another Brooks plant in the south for three years. One of the reasons he was chosen was his familiarity with Littleton. He had been at Littleton as an industrial engineer from 1973 to 1980, when he left to manage another facility. In 1984 he was sent back to Littleton to start and manage Components. He held

* By David E. Whiteside, organizational development consultant. This case was written at Lewiston-Auburn College of the University of Southern Maine with the cooperation of management, solely for the purpose of stimulating student discussion. Data are based on field research; all events are real, although the names of organizations, locations, and individuals have been disguised. Faculty members in nonprofit institutions are encouraged to reproduce this case for distribution to their students without charge or written permission. All other rights reserved jointly to the author and the North American Case Research Association (NACRA). Copyright © 1994 by the *Case Research Journal* and David E. Whiteside.

EXHIBIT 1   *Memorandum from Paul Winslow to Human Resources*

MEMORANDUM

From: Paul Winslow, Director of Human Resources

To: Human Resources Process Improvement Team

Subject: Proposed Corrective Actions

Date: 6/14/90

Lack of Organizational Unity

1. Use job shadowing or rotation to help people understand each other's jobs, e.g., do this across functions.
2. Reformat the Operations Review meetings, e.g., have a program committee.
3. Have a smaller group forum, e.g., have supervisors from the two sides meet.
4. Provide teamwork training for salaried employees.

Lack of Consistency in Enforcing Rules and Procedures

1. Hold meetings with department managers and supervisors to discuss how to enforce policies and procedures. Have these led by Bill Larson.
2. Develop a policy and procedures review and monitoring system.

Supervisor's Role Poorly Perceived

1. Have department managers meet with supervisors to determine priorities or conflicts between priorities.
2. Have supervisory training for all manufacturing supervisors.
3. Time assessment. (How is their time being spent?)

Insufficient Focus on Littleton's Priorities

1. Use the in-house newsletter to communicate priorities.
2. Develop an internal news sheet.
3. Have a question box for questions to be answered at Operations Review meetings.
4. Have a restatement of Littleton's purpose (do at Operations Review).
5. Have an Operations Review for hourly workers.
6. Use payroll stuffers to communicate information about goals.
7. Hold department meetings; have the manager of the department facilitate the meeting.

Lack of a Systematic Approach to Training

1. Establish annual departmental training goals.
2. Link training goals to organizational priorities.
3. Have a systematic approach to training the hourly work force.
4. Have a training plan for each salaried employee.
5. Have an annual training budget.

Change Is Poorly Managed

1. Provide training in managing change.
2. Communicate changes.

HR Dept.

6/90

this position for four years before leaving to manage the plant in the southern United States.

Shortly after Halperin arrived, Winslow acquainted him with the problem areas defined the previous year, gave him a copy of the (A) case, and met with him to discuss the issues. At that time, although Winslow felt that progress had been made on having more consistent enforcement of policies and procedures from one side of the plant to the other, he did not feel much had changed with regard to the other issues. With the exception of the Sup and Stew meetings, none of the specific action steps recommended by him and his staff had been implemented.

In the fall of 1995, Bill Sanko, president of XEL Communications, Inc., strolled around in the new 115,000-square-foot facility with its spacious conference rooms and computer-based skills training center, into which the company had just moved. Their former facility had been a 53,000-square-foot building that just could not accommodate XEL's growth. During the upcoming round of strategic planning sessions, Bill wondered how XEL and its management team would decide to grapple with the two-edged sword of rapid growth. Would it be possible for XEL to maintain its entrepreneurial culture while it experienced rapid growth? Would it find the resources necessary to sustain growth without harming its culture? From where?

XEL COMMUNICATIONS, INC.

XEL Communications, Inc.[1]—located in the outskirts of Denver, Colorado—designed and manufactured various telecommunications products for a number of companies—primarily large U.S. telephone operating companies. Originally a division within GTE headed by Bill Sanko, it was in the process of being closed when Bill and a few key managers persuaded GTE to sell the division to them. In July 1984, Sanko and fellow managers signed a letter of intent to buy the division from GTE. Two months later, the bill of sale was signed, and XEL Communications, Inc., became an independent company. Ironically, GTE remained as one of XEL's major customer accounts.

In terms of overall financial performance, XEL was profitable. Its revenues increased from $16.8 million in 1992 to $23.6 million in 1993 and $52.3 million in 1994—over a threefold increase in three years. In 1996, XEL employed approximately 300 people.

XEL designed and manufactured more than 300 individual products that enabled network operators to upgrade existing infrastructures and cost effectively enhance the speed and functionality of their networks while reducing operating expenses and overhead costs. The firm's products provided access to telecommunications services and automated monitoring and maintenance of network performance, and extended the distance over which network operators were able to offer their services.[2] For example, XEL produced equipment that "conditioned" existing lines to make them acceptable for business use

and sold products that facilitated the transmission of data and information over phone lines. Driving the need for XEL's products was the keen interest in electronic data transference: "Businesses are more and more dependent on the transfer of information," Bill Sanko noted. In addition, more businesses, including XEL, were operating by taking and filling orders through electronic data exchanges. Instead of dialing into inside salespeople, businesses often accessed databases directly.

One of XEL's strengths was its ability to adapt one manufacturer's equipment to another's. XEL provided the bits and pieces of telecommunications equipment to the "network," allowing the smooth integration of disparate transmission pieces. XEL also sold central office transmission equipment and a full range of mechanical housings, specialty devices, power supplies, and shelves.

In 1995, XEL began developing a hybrid fiber/ cable broadband modem for use by cable television firms seeking to provide enhanced data communication services over their network facilities. Cable modems were one of the hottest new products in telecommunications. The devices would enable computers to send and receive information about one hundred times faster than standard modems used with phone lines. Given that 34 million homes had personal computers, cable modems were seen as a surefire way to exploit the personal-computer (PC) boom and the continuing convergence of computers and television. Media analysts estimated that cable modem users would rise to 11.8 million by the end of 2005 from a handful in 1996.[3]

"Business customers and their changing telecommunications needs drive the demand for XEL's products. That, in turn, presents a challenge to the company," said Sanko. Sanko cited the constant stream of new products developed by XEL—approximately two per month—as the driving force behind the growth. Throughout the industry, product lifecycle times were getting even shorter. Before the breakup of the Bell System in 1984, transmission

*This case was prepared by Professors Robert P. McGowan and Cynthia V. Fukami, Daniels College of Business, as a basis for classroom discussion rather than to illustrate either effective or ineffective handling of an administrative situation. Copyright © 1995 by the authors: © 1997 by the Case Center, Daniels College of Business, University of Denver. Published by South-Western College Publishing.

For information regarding this and other CaseNet® cases, please visit CaseNet® on the World Wide Web at **casenet.thomson.com**.

switches and other telecommunications devices enjoyed a thirty- to forty-year life. In 1995, with technology moving so fast, XEL's products had about a three-year to five-year life.

XEL sold products to all of the Regional Bell Operating Companies (RBOCs), as well as such companies as GTE and Centel. Railroads, with their own telephone networks, were also customers. In addition to its domestic business, products were sold in Canada, Mexico, and Central and South America.[4] XEL's field salespeople worked with engineers to satisfy client requests for specific services. Over a period of time, the salespeople developed a rapport with these engineers, providing XEL with new product leads.

With all the consolidations and ventures in telecommunications, those who watched the industry often concluded that the overall market would become more difficult. Sanko believed, however, that "out of change comes opportunity. The worst-case scenario would be a static situation. Thus, a small company, fast to respond to customer needs and able to capitalize on small market niches, will be successful. Often, a large company like AT&T will forsake a smaller market and XEL will move in. Also, XEL's size allows it to design a project in a very short time."

Sanko watched federal legislation keenly. The recently signed Telecommunications Act of 1996, which removed numerous barriers to competition, had clearly changed the rules of the game. Consequently, said Sanko, "we need to expand our market and be prepared to sell to others as the regulatory environment changes." The recent joint venture between Time-Warner and US West also signaled that telephone and cable companies would be pooling their resources to provide a broader array of information services. As for the future, Sanko saw "a lot of opportunities we can't even now imagine."

THE XEL VISION

A feature that set XEL apart from other companies was its strong, healthy corporate culture. Developing a culture of innovation and team decision making was instrumental in providing the results XEL prided itself on.[5] An early attempt to define culture in a top-down fashion was less successful than the management team had hoped,[6] so the team had embarked on a second journey to determine what their core values were and what they would like the company to look like in five years. The team had then gone off-site for several days and finalized the XEL Vision

statement (Exhibit 1). By the summer of 1987, the statement had been signed by members of the senior team and been hung up by the bulletin board. Employees were not required to sign the statement, but were free to do so when each was ready.

Julie Rich, vice-president of human resources, described the management team's approach to getting the rest of the organization to understand as well as become comfortable with the XEL Vision: "Frequently, organizations tend to take a combination top-down/bottom-up approach in instituting cultural change. That is, the top level will develop a statement about values and overall vision. They will then communicate it down to the bottom level and hope that results will percolate upward through the middle levels. Yet it is often the middle level of management which is most skeptical, and they will block it or resist change. We decided to take a 'cascade' approach in which the process begins at the top and gradually cascades from one level to the next so that the critical players are slowly acclimated to the process. We also did a number of other things— including sending a copy of the vision statement to the homes of the employees and dedicating a section of the company newspaper to communicate what key sections of the vision mean from the viewpoint of managers and employees."

The vision statement became a living symbol of the XEL culture and the degree to which XEL embraced and empowered its employees. When teams or managers made decisions, they routinely brought out the XEL Vision document so workers might consult various parts of the statement to help guide and direct decisions. According to Julie, the statement was used to help evaluate new products, emphasize quality (a specific XEL strategic objective was to be the top quality vendor for each product), support teams, and drive the performance-appraisal process.

The XEL Vision was successfully implemented as a key first step; but it was far from being a static document. Key XEL managers continually revisited the statement to ensure that it became a reflection of where they wanted to go, not where they had been. Julie believed this regular appraisal was a large factor in the success of the vision. "Our values are the key," Julie explained, "They are strong, they are truly core values, and they are deeply held." Along with the buy-in process, the workers also saw that the managers experimented with the statement, which reflected the strong entrepreneurial nature of XEL's founders—a common bond that they all shared. They

EXHIBIT 1   *The XEL Vision*

> **XEL will become the leader** in our selected telecommunications markets through innovation in products and services. Every XEL product and service will be rated Number One by our customers.
>
> **XEL will set the standards** by which our competitors are judged. We will be the best, most innovative, responsive designer, manufacturer and provider of quality products and services as seen by customers, employees, competitors, and suppliers.*
>
> **We will insist upon the highest quality from everyone in every task.**
>
> **We will be an organization where each of us is a self-manager who will:**
> - initiate action, commit to, and act responsibly in achieving objectives
> - be responsible for XEL's performance
> - be responsible for the quality of individual and team output
> - invite team members to contribute based on experience, knowledge and ability
>
> **We will:**
> - be ethical and honest in all relationships
> - build an environment where creativity and risk taking is promoted
> - provide challenging and satisfying work
> - ensure a climate of dignity and respect for all
> - rely on interdepartmental teamwork, communications and cooperative problem solving to attain common goals**
> - offer opportunities for professional and personal growth
> - recognize and reward individual contribution and achievement
> - provide tools and services to enhance productivity
> - maintain a safe and healthy work environment
>
> **XEL will be profitable and will grow** in order to provide both a return to our investors and rewards to our team members.
>
> **XEL will be an exciting and enjoyable place to work while we achieve success.**
>
> *Responsiveness to customers' new product needs as well as responding to customers' requirements for emergency delivery requirements have been identified as key strategic strengths. Therefore, the vision statement has been updated to recognize this important element.
> **The importance of cooperation and communication was emphasized with this update of the Vision Statement.

were not afraid of risk, or of failure, and this spirit was reinforced in all employees through the vision itself, as well as through the yearly process of revisiting the statement. Once a year, Bill Sanko sat with all employees and directly challenged (and listened to direct challenges to) the XEL Vision. From 1987 to 1995, only two relatively minor additions had altered the original statement.

WHICH PATH TO CHOOSE

When the 1995 annual strategic planning process got underway, XEL was in good shape on any one of a number of indicators. Profits were growing, new products were being developed, the culture and vision of the company were strong, employee morale was high, and the self-directed work teams were achieving exceptional quality.[7] Rapid growth, however, was also presenting a challenge. Would it be possible for XEL to maintain its entrepreneurial culture in the face of rapid growth? Could they sustain their growth without harming their culture? Would they find the resources necessary to sustain the growth? From where?

As the strategic planning retreat progressed, three options seemed apparent to the team. First, they could stay the course and remain privately held. Second, they could initiate a public offering of stock. Third, they could seek a strategic partnership. Which would be the right choice for XEL?

STAYING THE COURSE

The most obvious option was to do nothing. Bill Sanko indicated that the management team did not favor staying the course and remaining privately held. "We had a venture capitalist involved who, after being with us for ten years, wanted out. In addition, the founders—ourselves—also wanted out from a financial standpoint. You also have to understand that one of the original founders, Don Donnelly, had passed away; and his estate was looking to make his investment more liquid. So, there were a lot things that converged at the same time."

Once they determined they would not remain privately held, Bill mentioned that the decision boiled down to two main avenues: XEL would do an initial public offering and go public, or it would find a strategic partner. "To guide us in this process, we decided to retain the services of an outside party; we talked to about a dozen investment houses. In October 1994, we decided to hire Alex Brown, a long-time investment house out of Baltimore. What we liked about this firm was that they had experience with doing both options—going public or finding a partner."

GOING PUBLIC

One avenue open to XEL was initiating a public offering of stock. Alex Brown advised them of the pluses and minuses of this option. Sanko reviewed their recommendations:

The plus side for XEL doing an initial public offering was that technology was really hot about this time [October 1994]. In addition, we felt that XEL would be valued pretty highly in the market. The downside of going public was that XEL was really not a big firm, and institutional investors usually like doing offerings of firms that generate revenues of over $100 million. Another downside was that you had to deal with analysts, and their projections become your plan, which really turned me off. Also, shareholders want a steady and predictable rate of return. Technology stocks are not steady—there are frequent ups and downs in this marketplace—caused by a number of factors, such as a major telecommunications company deciding not

to upgrade at the last minute or Congress considering sweeping regulatory changes. Finally, Alex Brown felt that the stock would have traded thinly. This, coupled with SEC restrictions on trading, made the option of going public less desirable.

STRATEGIC PARTNERSHIP

After taking these factors into account, Sanko said,

. . . we decided to take the third path and look for a potential partner. But you have to also note that there was always the first option available as a safety valve. We could not do anything and stay the way we were. That's the nice thing about all of this. We were not under any pressure to go public or seek a partner. We could also wait and do one of these things later on. So, we had the luxury of taking our time.

In terms of finding a potential partner, there were certain key items that we wanted Alex Brown to consider in helping us in this process. The first was that we, management, wanted to remain with XEL. We had really grown XEL as a business and were not interested in going off and doing something else. The second key item was that we were not interested in being acquired by someone who was interested in consolidating our operations with theirs, closing this facility and moving functions from here to there. To us, this would destroy the essence of XEL. The third item was that we wanted a partner that would bring something to the table but would not try to micromanage our business.

THE CASE AGAINST STRATEGIC PARTNERSHIP

In the 1990s, "merger mania" swept the United States. In the first nine months of 1995, the value of all announced mergers and acquisitions reached $248.5 billion, surpassing the record full year volume of $246.9 billion reached in 1988. This volume occurred in the face of strong evidence that over the past thirty-five years, mergers and acquisitions had hurt organizations more than they had helped.[8] Among the reasons for failure in mergers and acquisitions were the following:

- Inadequate due diligence
- Lack of strategic rationale
- Unrealistic expectations of possible synergies
- Paying too much
- Conflicting corporate cultures
- Failure to move quickly to meld the two companies

Nevertheless, there had been successful mergers and acquisitions. Most notably, small and mid-sized deals had been found to have a better chance for success. Michael Porter argued that the best acquisitions were "gap-filling," that is, a deal in which one company bought another to strengthen its product line or expand its territory, including globally. Anslinger and Copeland argued that successful acquisitions were more likely when preacquisition managers were kept in their positions, big incentives were offered to top-level executives so that their net worths were on the line, and the holding company was kept flat (that is, the business was kept separate from other operating units and retained a high degree of autonomy).[9]

More often than not, however, the deal was won or lost after it was done. Bad post-merger planning and integration could doom the acquisition. "While there is clearly a role for thoughtful and well-conceived mergers in American business, all too many don't meet that description."[10]

CHOOSING A PARTNER

"With these issues in mind, Alex Brown was able to screen out possible candidates," said Sanko. "In January, 1995, this plan was presented to our board of directors for approval, and by February, we had developed the 'book' about XEL that was to be presented to these candidates. We then had a series of meetings with the candidates in the conference room at our new facility. The interesting aside on these meetings was that, often, senior management from some of these firms didn't know what pieces of their business that they still had or had gotten rid of. We did not see this as a good sign."

One of the firms with which XEL met was Gilbert Associates, based in Reading, Pennsylvania. Gilbert Associates was founded in the 1940s as an engineering and construction firm, primarily in the area of power plants. They embarked on a strategy of reinventing themselves by divesting their energy-related companies and becoming a holding company whose subsidiaries operated in the high-growth markets of telecommunications and technical services. Gilbert also owned a real estate management-and-development subsidiary. After due diligence and due deliberation, Gilbert was chosen by the management team as XEL's strategic partner. The letter of intent was signed on October 5, 1995, and the deal was closed on October 27, 1995. Gilbert paid $30 million in cash.[11]

Why was Gilbert chosen as the partner from among six or seven suitors? Not because they made the highest bid. XEL was attracted to Gilbert by three factors: (1) Gilvert's long-term strategy to enter the telecommunications industry, (2) its intention of keeping XEL as a separate, autonomous company, and (3) its willingness to pay cash (as opposed to stock or debt). "It was a clean deal," said Sanko.

The deal was also attractive because it was structured with upside potential. XEL was given realistic performance targets for the next three years. If these targets were achieved, and Sanko had every expectation that they would be, approximately $6-$8 million would be earned. Gilbert did not place a cap on the upside.

In spite of the attractive financial package, more was necessary to seal the deal. "At the end of the day," said Sanko, "culture, comfort, and trust—those were more important than money." It was important to XEL's board that Gilbert presented a good fit. Sanko was encouraged because he felt comfortable with Gilbert's chief executive officer. Vice president of Human Resources, Julie Rich, also noted, "The management team was to remain intact. Gilbert recognized that the XEL Vision was part of our success and our strength. They wanted to keep it going."

As one way of gaining confidence in Gilbert, Bill Sanko personally spoke with the CEOs of other companies Gilbert had recently acquired. In these conversations, Sanko was assured that Gilbert would keep its promises.

Timothy S. Cobb, chair, president, and CEO of Gilbert Associates, commented at the time of the acquisition: "This transaction represented the first clear step toward the attainment of our long-term strategy of focusing on the higher margin areas of telecommunications and technical services. XEL's superior reputation for quality throughout the industry, its innovative design and manufacturing capabilities, and its focus on products aimed at the emerging information highway markets, will serve us well as we seek to further penetrate this important segment of the vast communications market."[12]

Mr. Cobb continued, "We see long-term growth opportunities worldwide for XEL's current proprietary and Original Equipment Manufacturer [OEM] products as well as for the powerful new products being developed. These products fall into two families: (1) fiber optic network interfaces designed specifically to meet the needs of telephone companies, interexchange carriers (e.g., AT&T, Sprint,

MCI), and specialized network carriers installing fiber-optic facilities, and (2) a hybrid fiber/cable broadband modem for use by cable television firms seeking to provide enhanced data communications services over their network facilities. Going forward, we expect to leverage Gilbert's knowledge and relationships with the RBOCs to significantly increase sales to those important customers, while also utilizing our GAI-Tronics subsidiary's established international sales organization to further penetrate the vast global opportunities which exist. As a result, revenues from Gilbert Associates' growing telecommunications segment could represent over half of our total revenues by the end of 1996."

Timothy Cobb had come to Gilbert from Ameritech, an RBOC which covered the midwestern United States. He had been president of GAI-Tronics Corporation, an international supplier of industrial communication equipment, a subsidiary of Gilbert, prior to his appointment as Gilbert's CEO.

Bill Sanko offered, "When all the dust had settled, the one firm that we really felt good about was Gilbert. . . . Gilbert is an interesting story in itself. Ironically, they had contacted us in August, 1994, based on the advice of their consultant who had read about us in an *Inc.* magazine article. Unfortunately, at the time, they did not have the cash to acquire us since they were in the process of selling off one of their divisions. In the intervening period, Gilbert Associates divested itself of one of its companies, Gilbert/Commonwealth. This sale provided needed funds for the acquisition of XEL."

Once Sanko was confident that the deal would go, but before the letter of intent was signed, the pending acquisition was announced to the management team, and a general meeting was held with all employees. SEC regulations prohibited sharing particular information (and common sense seconded this directive), but Sanko and his associates felt it was important to keep employees informed before the letter was signed.

During the meeting, Sanko told the employees that the board was "seriously considering" an offer. Sanko assured the employees that the suitor was not a competitor, and that he felt that the suitor was a good fit in culture and values. Sanko reiterated that this partnership would give XEL the resources it needed to grow. Questions were not allowed because of SEC regulations. Employees left the meeting concerned and somewhat nervous, but members of the management team and Julie Rich

were positioned in the audience and made themselves available to talk.

During the closing of the deal, Sanko held another general meeting, attended by Timothy Cobb, where more detailed information was shared with employees. Managers had been informed in a premeeting so that they would be prepared to meet with their teams directly following the general meeting.

Employees wanted to know about Gilbert. They wanted to know simple information, such as where Gilbert was located and what businesses it was in. They also wanted to know strategic plans, such as whether Gilbert had plans to consolidate manufacturing operations. Finally, they wanted to know about the near future of XEL—they wanted to know if their benefits would change, if they would still have profit sharing, and if the management team would stay in place. "We have a track record of being open," says Sanko. "Good news or bad is always shared. This history stemmed much of the rumor mill."

In the next few weeks, Tim Cobb returned to hold a series of meetings with the management team and with a focus group of thirty employees representing a cross-section of the organization. Cobb also met with managers and their spouses at an informal reception. Sanko wanted to ease the management team into the realization that they were now part of a larger whole in Gilbert. He asked Cobb to make the same presentation to XEL that he was currently making to stockholders throughout the country—a presentation that emphasized the role XEL would play in the long-term strategy of Gilbert.

GOING FORWARD

The human resource systems remained in place with no changes. The management bonus system would change slightly because it included stock options, which were no longer available. XEL's internal advisory board, the "management team," remained intact, but XEL's external advisory board was disbanded. Bill Sanko reported to Gilbert's chairman.

XEL's strategic plan was to follow the process it already had in place, and which was not unlike Gilbert's. The cycle did not change: Gilbert expected XEL's next strategic plan in early November 1996.

XEL's strategic objectives also remained the same. Nothing was put on hold. Plans were still in place to penetrate Brazil, Mexico, and South America.[13] Sanko hoped to capitalize on the synergies of Gilbert's existing international distribution network. XEL met with Gilbert's international representatives to see if this was an avenue for XEL to gain a more rapid presence in South America. Finally, XEL was planning to move into Radio Frequency (RF) engineering and manufacturing, potentially opening the door for wireless support.

Whether XEL would grow depended on the success of these new ventures. In 1996, slight growth was forecasted. But if these new markets really took off, Julie Rich was concerned about hiring enough people in Colorado when the labor market was approaching full employment. Julie considered more creative ways of attracting new hires: for example, by offering more flexible scheduling, or by hiring unskilled workers and training them internally. A new U.S. Department of Education grant to test computer-based training systems was being implemented. Nevertheless, employment was strong in the Denver metro area in 1996, and migration to Colorado had slowed. It would be a challenge to staff XEL if high growth became the business strategy.

Approximately six weeks after the acquisition, Sanko noted that few changes had taken place. Now that they were a publicly held company, there was a great deal more interest in meeting quarterly numbers. "If there has been a change," said Sanko, "it is that there is more attention to numbers." Julie Rich noted that there had been no turnover in the six-week period following the acquisition. She took this calm in the workforce as a sign that things were going well so far.

One reason things went well was that the management team had all worked for GTE prior to the spin-off of XEL. Having all worked for a large public company, they did not experience a terrible culture shock when the Gilbert acquisition took place. Time would tell if the remaining XEL employees would feel the same way.

As Sanko awaited Cobb's upcoming visit, he wondered how to prepare for the event and for the year ahead. He wondered whether XEL would attempt new ventures into RF technology, or how the planned fiber/cable broadband modem would progress. He wondered whether Gilbert's experience in selling in South America would prove valuable for XEL's international strategy. In addition, he wondered how he could encourage XEL and its employees to become members of Gilbert's "team." Would XEL's vision survive the new partnership?

Finally, according to one study of CEO turnover after acquisition, 80 percent of acquired CEOs left their companies by the sixth year after the acquisition, but 87 percent of those who did leave, did so within two years. The key factor in their turnover was post-acquisition autonomy.[14] After nearly twelve years as the captain of his own ship, Sanko wondered what his own future, and the future of the XEL management team, would hold.

NOTES

1. For additional information on XEL Communications, Inc., and the key strategic issues facing XEL, see "XEL Communications, Inc. (A)" by McGowan and Fukami, 1995.
2. *PR Newsletter*, 5 October 1995.
3. Menezes, Bill, "Modern Times," *Rocky Mountain News*, 28 April 1996.
4. *PR Newswire*, 5 October 1995.
5. Sheridan, John, "America's Best Plants: XEL Communications," *Industry Week*, 16 October 1995.
6. See McGowan and Fukami, XEL Communications, Inc. (A) for a larger discussion of corporate culture at XEL.
7. Sheridan, John, "America's Best Plants: XEL Communications," *Industry Week*, 16 October 1995.
8. Zweig, Philip, "The Case Against Mergers," *Business Week*, 30 October 1995.
9. Anslinger, Patricia and Thomas Copeland, "Growth Through Acquisitions: A Fresh Look," *Harvard Business Review* (January-February 1996).
10. Zweig, "The Case Against Mergers."
11. Bunn, Dina, "XEL to be Sold in $30 Million Deal," *Rocky Mountain News*, 27 October 1995.
12. *PR Newswire*, 5 October 1995.
13. For more information on XEL's global penetration, see McGowan and Allen, "XEL Communications (B): Going Global."
14. Stewart, Kim A. "After the Acquisition: A Study of Turnover of Chief Executives of Target Companies," Doctoral Dissertation, University of Houston, 1992.

The National Bank of San Francisco operates seven branches that receive deposits and make loans to both businesses and individual depositors. Deposits have grown from $14 million to $423 million within the past twenty years, and the directors have opened more branches as population and business activity in the Bay area have increased.

The Bank has generally been characterized by aggressive marketing including give-away promotions for new deposits and extremely competitive interest rates on loans. President E. F. Wellington has prided himself on his ability to appoint entrepreneurial branch managers and loan officers who have pushed new business development.

In response to a question at a board meeting two years ago concerning a noticeable rate of increase in operating and overhead expenses, Wellington announced that he would undertake a study of ways the bank might lower, or at least hold the line on, these costs.

Shortly thereafter, he called in James Nicholson, one of his two assistants, described the general problem of reducing costs, and told him that the bank had reached the size where it needed someone to devote full time to operating methods and facilities. He said that he had talked this matter over with Ms. Simmons, manager of personnel, and that both of them had agreed "that you would be ideal for this position." He also explained that Ms. Simmons would be simultaneously promoted to vice-president and put in charge of all equipment purchases, the maintenance of all bank buildings, and personnel relations. "Simmons and I feel that you might have a permanent advisory committee made up of one person from each branch, and that such a group can be really effective in deciding on ways to utilize our banking buildings and equipment, and our people, more effectively. Unless you have some objection, each of the branch managers will appoint a representative to meet with you regularly."

Within three months of the original reference to the subject at the directors' meeting, Simmons had been promoted to vice-president, Nicholson received the title of manager of personnel and equipment planning, and all branch managers had appointed, at Wellington's request, an employee to what became known as the "systems committee." At the present time, two years later, the committee appears to have taken its work seriously, as evidenced by:

1. a record of regular meetings held over a period of eighteen months;
2. the transcripts of those meetings and exhibits, which show that all seven committee members entered the discussions;
3. seventeen recommendations in writing, supported by a total of 1,800 pages of research data and reasoning;
4. the fact that meetings often lasted four to five hours, extending after working hours; and
5. the statements of all seven members of the committee to the effect that they enjoyed the work, felt that they were accomplishing something for the bank, and had personally enjoyed being on the committee with the other members.

All members have also expressed their high regard for Jim Nicholson and feel that he has done a good job.

The seventeen recommendations cover such matters as salary scales, a policy on days off for personal business, a policy on central purchasing of janitorial supplies, and a recommendation that certain models of personal computers and software be adopted uniformly in all branches.

OFFICE SPACE AND FURNISHINGS

About a year ago, both Simmons and Nicholson had made inspection trips to the branches and had come to the conclusion that there was much wasted space in branch offices and that this situation had been brought about principally because office personnel and clerical personnel had been, over a period of years, buying equipment—such as desks, telephone stands, and extra tables—that pleased them personally but that, in many instances, was also "too large and expensive" for what the bank needed to keep up its public appearance. In addition, loan officers in some branches had succeeded in having the managers construct walls for unnecessary private offices. Nicholson had obtained the services of the bank's architect and also of systems engineers from two large equipment manufacturers; together they made a "general estimate, to be confirmed by further fact-finding" that the bank could save $80,000 a year over a thirty-year period if (1) furniture were to be standardized with functional equipment that was modest in design but

* Written by Charles E. Summer. Copyright 1978. Used with permission.

met the essential requirements of dignity for the branches and if (2) henceforth, only branch managers could have private offices.

Before the meeting of the systems committee last week, Simmons expressed concern to Nicholson that his committee had not taken up these two problems.

> Your committee could have done some real research on these questions. I hope that you will put them on the agenda right away and agree, let's say in six months, on standard layouts and equipment. You and I both know, for instance, that the loan officers at San Mateo and Menlo Park have entirely too much space, should not be in those large offices, and perhaps should have three standard pieces of equipment—a desk, chair, and small bookcase. There should be no telephone stands like those that were purchased there last year for $90 each.

RELATIONS WITH BRANCH MANAGERS

Branch managers have been kept informed of the committee's general work over the eighteen-month period. Most managers selected a loan officer (assistant manager) to represent them, and these officers made a real effort to let their managers know what was going on. Dick May, representative of the Burlingame branch, reports that he has been spending at least an hour a week with his boss telling him what the committee is doing and asking for his ideas. Janice Strickland of the Market Street branch says that she has been able to confer briefly with her boss about once a week on the subjects the committee is working on. Other members report that they, too, have been able to keep their managers informed and that the latter exhibit a good deal of interest in the committee's work. In all cases except Burlingame, however, representatives say that their managers quite naturally do not have the time to go into the details of committee recommendations and that they, the managers, have not been particularly aggressive or enthusiastic about putting any of these recommendations into effect.

The committee has talked about the best way to get its recommendations adopted. Dick May claims that his manager is ready to put many of them into effect immediately and that it is up to each representative to convince his or her own manager. All others say they believe that the president should issue the recommendations as instructions over his signature. The reason given by Strickland is typical:

> We're convinced that the recommendations are best for the bank, but the managers just won't buy

them. The only way to get the managers to carry them out is to have Mr. Wellington lay them out as official and let it be known that they are going to be put into effect. Of course, they would have to be acknowledged as being drawn up by the Department of Personnel and Equipment, with some advice from our committee.

James Nicholson reported in his own weekly meeting with the president that it looked as if it is going to be "rather touchy" to get managers to accept the recommendations. Mr. Wellington thereupon stated that his own knowledge of the committee recommendations was rather sketchy, even though he had discussed them in part with Nicholson each week for a year. He therefore decided to call a meeting of all branch managers and committee members at the same time so that he and everyone concerned could be acquainted in detail with them. This meeting took place one week ago.

INFORMAL COMMENTS OF BRANCH MANAGERS

Most of the branch managers dropped in to the officers' dining room for lunch before the meeting. After the usual banter, the conversation naturally drifted onto the proposals of the systems committee.

> Sure hope my secretary likes those new computers. I can't spell, and if Sally left I'd be sunk.

> So what, Karen, you always talk better than you write.

> Say, I sure hated to come in here this afternoon. Ever since Smedley Scott became president of Menlo Laboratories I've been trying to convince him to do all his banking with us. Had to break a date with him, and in my office, too. If we start spending all our time buying mops, our development program goes out the window.

> How are you making out with your two (officer) trainees, Carl? I have a smart one coming right along, but she won't be happy under the proposed salary schedule.

> The best employee we have came from the credit department a year ago. He sure gets around. Tennis matches, hospital drives, U.N. meetings; always on the go. I thought of him when I read that proposal for days off. How do you decide when a guy like that is working? Granted his work gets behind sometimes. That's better than drawing pay for just sitting at his desk. I get a kick out of bringing a

young employee like that along. And he is building a lot of good will for the bank in my area.

Well, I kind of like that days-off rule. It would save a lot of complaints and conversation about grandfather's weak heart.

It might be just fine for you, Tyson, but not so good for Ann. Why not let each manager decide? After all, each of us is paid to run our branch in the best interests of the bank, and we wouldn't be in our present positions if we weren't doing it. What do you think, Oscar?

Guess I have longer service than any of the rest of you. It will be thirty-nine years in September. But I'd say there isn't a manager who doesn't run his branch just as though it was his own business.

And the record is not bad either. Deposits are going up and the bank is making money.

It's making money that counts. (This from a manager of one of the slower-growing branches.)

I heard from somebody about a year ago that the committee was going to study office space and equipment and that someone figured they could save $1 million over a period of years. But apparently they didn't get around to that.

Don't worry. We're building a real base for the future. By the way, did you see the latest report on Zenith Radio?

Just before the meeting with the systems committee, Simmons called Jim Nicholson into her office to have a brief discussion of the recommendations. The two read over the list of seventeen final recommendations; then Nicholson explained briefly the reasons why each recommendation was made and how it would help the bank to reduce costs.

THE MEETING OF THE COMMITTEE AND BRANCH MANAGERS

The meeting started at 2 P.M. and was scheduled to last until 5 P.M., but actually ran over until 6 P.M. The committee, branch managers, Wellington, and Simmons were present. Wellington opened the meeting by stating that its purpose was to study the committee recommendations and, it was hoped, to arrive at a decision on whether they should be accepted and put into effect.

In fact, however, after a reading of the seventeen recommendations, the entire meeting was taken up by a discussion of the first two recommendations.

1. It is recommended that the following pay scales be adopted for clerical and nonofficer personnel in all branches. (This was followed by a list of positions and grades—the bank had had some uniformity before, but the recommendations specified absolute uniformity and also changed some of the classifications, thus meaning, for instance, that head tellers would in the future receive more than head bookkeepers, whereas both had received the same in the past.)

2. Employees should be allowed two days per year off with pay for miscellaneous personal business, such days to be granted at the discretion of managers. Because of the possibility of abuse of this privilege, days in excess of two must be taken without pay. This limitation does not apply to sickness or death in the immediate family.

In the discussion, the branch managers found a great many points on which (a) they disagreed among themselves, and (b) they agreed among themselves but disagreed with the committee. For instance, they all agreed that uniformity was in the interest of the bank but disagreed on many of the salary scales and classifications. On this point, they cited many instances in which one competent employee would feel hurt if the scales were arranged in the way the committee recommended.

The committee members had talked confidentially among themselves before the meeting and agreed that Jim Nicholson must be the one to present the findings and, by and large, the one to defend them. This plan was carried out, and after the meeting, the president remarked to Jim that

> the combined thinking of the managers, with all of their experience, made quite an impression on Simmons and me. We have confidence in you, and you know that, but I can't help but wonder if your committee really worked out the "best" recommendation for all on this salary matter. If you had, why couldn't you convince the managers instead of raising all of the criticism?

Yesterday, Wellington and Simmons met to consider the recommendations privately. Simmons again expressed the same idea that Wellington passed on to Nicholson, wondering out loud whether the committee should be sent back to do more research on the recommendations. Both were concerned that two years had elapsed since the committee was established without any recommendations having been accepted and put into effect.

The Audubon Zoo was the focus of national concern in the early 1970s, with well-documented stories of animals kept in conditions that were variously termed an "animal ghetto,"[1] "the New Orleans antiquarium," and even "an animal concentration camp."[2] In 1971, the Bureau of Governmental Research recommended a $5.6 million zoo improvement plan to the Audubon Park Commission and the City Council of New Orleans. The local *Times Picayune* commented on the new zoo: "It's not going to be quite like the Planet of the Apes situation in which the apes caged and studied human beings but something along those broad general lines."[3] The new zoo confined people to bridges and walkways while the animals roamed amidst grass, shrubs, trees, pools, and fake rocks. The gracefully curving pathways, generously lined with luxuriant plantings, gave the visitor a sense of being alone in a wilderness, although crowds of visitors might be only a few yards away.

THE DECISION

The Audubon Park Commission launched a $5.6 million development program, based on the Bureau of Governmental Research plan for the zoo, in March 1972. A bond issue and a property tax dedicated to the zoo were put before the voters on November 7, 1972. When it passed by an overwhelming majority, serious discussions began about what should be done. The New Orleans City Planning Commission finally approved the master plan for the Audubon Park Zoo in September 1973. But the institution of the master plan was far from smooth.

The Zoo Question Goes Public

Over two dozen special interests were ultimately involved in choosing whether to renovate/expand the existing facilities or move to another site. Expansion became a major community controversy. Some residents opposed the zoo expansion, fearing "loss of green space" would affect the secluded character of the neighborhood. Others opposed the loss of what they saw as an attractive and educational facility.

Most of the opposition came from the zoo's affluent neighbors. Zoo Director John Moore ascribed the criticism to "a select few people who have the money and power to make a lot of noise." He went on to say "[T]he real basis behind the problem is that the neighbors who live around the edge

of the park have a selfish concern because they want the park as their private back yard." Legal battles over the expansion plans continued until early 1976. At that time, the 4th Circuit Court of Appeals ruled that the expansion was legal.[3] An out-of-court agreement with the zoo's neighbors (the Upper Audubon Association) followed shortly.

Physical Facilities

The expansion of the Audubon Park Zoo took it from fourteen to fifty-eight acres. The zoo was laid out in geographic sections: the Asian Domain, World of Primates, World's Grasslands, Savannah, North American Prairie, South American Pampas, and Louisiana Swamp, according to the zoo master plan developed by the Bureau of Governmental Research. Additional exhibits included the Wisner Discovery Zoo, Sea Lion exhibit, and Flight Cage. Exhibit 1 is a map of the new zoo.

PURPOSE OF THE ZOO

The main outward purpose of the Audubon Park Zoo was entertainment. Many of the promotional efforts of the zoo were aimed at creating an image of the zoo as an entertaining place to go. Obviously, such a campaign was necessary to attract visitors to the zoo. Behind the scenes, the zoo also preserved and bred many animal species, conducted research, and educated the public. The mission statement of the Audubon Institute is given in Exhibit 2.

NEW DIRECTIONS

A chronology of major events in the life of the Audubon Zoo is given in Exhibit 3. One of the first significant changes made was the institution of an admission charge in 1972. Admission to the zoo had been free to anyone prior to the adoption of the renovation plan. Ostensibly, the initial purpose behind instituting the admission charge was to prevent vandalism,[4] but the need for additional income was also apparent. Despite the institution of and increases in admission charges, attendance increased dramatically (see Exhibit 4).

* By Claire J. Anderson, Old Dominion University, and Caroline Fisher, Loyola University, New Orleans. © 1993, 1991, 1989, 1987, Claire J. Anderson and Caroline Fisher. This case was designed for classroom discussion only, not to depict effective or ineffective handling of administrative situations.

EXHIBIT 1   *The Audubon Park Zoo*

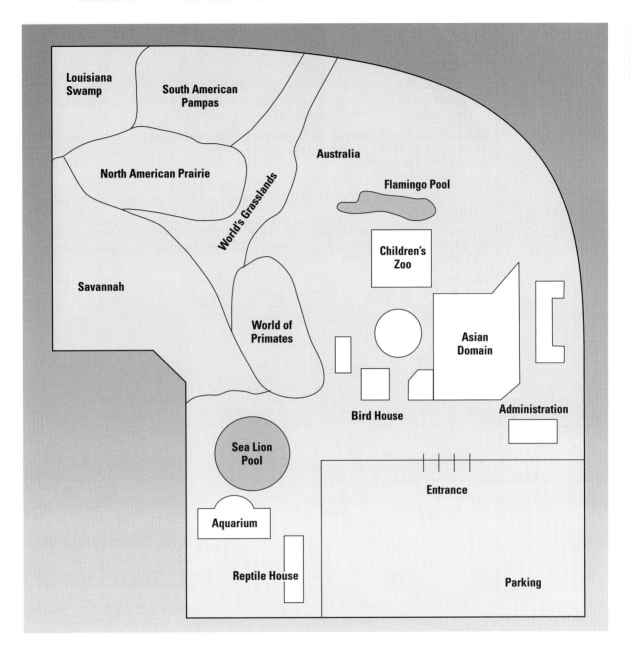

OPERATIONS

Friends of the Zoo

The Friends of the Zoo was formed in 1974 and incorporated in 1975 with four hundred members. The stated purpose of the group was to increase support and awareness of the Audubon Park Zoo. Initially, the Friends of the Zoo tried to increase interest in and commitment to the zoo, but its activities increased dramatically over the following years to where it was involved in funding, operating, and governing the zoo.

The Friends of the Zoo had a 24-member governing board. Yearly elections were held for six members of the board, who served four-year terms. The board oversaw the policies of the zoo and set guidelines for memberships, concessions, fund raising, and

EXHIBIT 2   *Audubon Institute Mission Statement*

The mission of the Audubon Institute is to cultivate awareness and appreciation of life and the earth's resources and to help conserve and enrich our natural world. The Institute's primary objectives toward this are:

Conservation: To participate in the global effort to conserve natural resources by developing and maintaining captive stocks of endangered plants, animals and marine life, and by cooperating with related projects in the wild.

Education: To impart knowledge and understanding of the interaction of nature and man through programs, exhibits, and publications and to encourage public participation in global conservation efforts.

Research: To foster the collection and dissemination of scientific information that will enhance the conservation and educational objectives of the facilities of the Audubon Institute.

Economics: To ensure long-range financial security by sound fiscal management and continued development, funding through creative means that encourage corporate, foundation, and individual support.

Leadership: To serve as a model in the civic and professional communities. To foster a spirit of cooperation, participation, and pride.

Source: The Audubon Institute

EXHIBIT 3   *Chronology of Major Events for the Zoo*

1972	Voters approved a referendum to provide tax dollars to renovate and expand the Zoo. The first Zoo-To-Do was held. An admission charge was instituted.
1973	The City Planning Commission approved the initial master plan for the Audubon Park Zoo calling for $3.4 million for upgrading. Later phases called for an additional $2.1 million.
1974	Friends of the Zoo formed with 400 members to increase support and awareness of the Zoo.
1975	Renovations began with $25 million public and private funds; 14 acres to be expanded to 58 acres.
1976	The Friends of the Zoo assumed responsibility for concessions.
1977	John Moore went to Albuquerque; Ron Forman took over as Park and Zoo director.
1980	First full-time education staff assumed duties at the Zoo.
1981	Contract signed allowing New Orleans Steamboat Company to bring passengers from downtown to the Park.
1981	Delegates from the American Association of Zoological Parks and Aquariums ranked the Audubon Zoo as one of the top three zoos of its size in America.
1981	Zoo accredited.
1982	The Audubon Park Commission reorganized under Act 352, which required the Commission to contract with a non-profit organization for the daily management of the Park.
1985	The Zoo was designated as a Rescue Center for Endangered and Threatened Plants.
1986	Voters approved a $25 million bond issue for the Aquarium.
1988	The Friends of the Zoo became The Audubon Institute.
1990	The Aquarium of the Americas opened in September.

Source: The Audubon Institute.

EXHIBIT 4 *Admission Charges*

	ADMISSION CHARGES	
Year	**Adult**	**Child**
1972	$0.75	$0.25
1978	1.00	0.50
1979	1.50	0.75
1980	2.00	1.00
1981	2.50	1.25
1982	3.00	1.50
1983	3.50	1.75
1984	4.00	2.00
1985	4.50	2.00
1986	5.00	2.50
1987	5.50	2.50
1988	5.50	2.50
1989	6.00	3.00
1990	6.50	3.00
1991	7.00	3.25

	ADMISSION	
Year	**Number of Paid Admissions**	**Number of Member Admissions**
1972	163,000	
1973	310,000	
1974	345,000	
1975	324,000	
1976	381,000	
1977	502,000	
1978	456,000	
1979	561,000	
1980	707,000	
1981	741,000	
1982	740,339	78,950
1983	835,044	118,665
1984	813,025	128,538
1985	856,064	145,020
1986	916,865	187,119
1987	902,744	193,926
1988	899,181	173,313
1989	711,709	239,718
1990	725,469	219,668

Source: The Audubon Institute

marketing. Actual policy making and operations were controlled by the Audubon Park Commission, however, which set zoo hours, admission prices, and so forth.

Through its volunteer programs, the Friends of the Zoo staffed many of the zoo's programs. Members of the Friends of the Zoo served as "edZOOcators," education volunteers who were specially trained to conduct interpretive educational programs, and "Zoo Area Patrollers," who provided general information at the zoo and helped with crowd control. Other volunteers assisted in the commissary, the Animal Health

Care Center and Wild Bird Rehabilitation Center or helped with membership, public relations, graphics, clerical work, research, or horticulture.

In 1988, the name of the Friends of the Zoo was changed to the Audubon Institute to reflect its growing interest in activities beyond the zoo alone. It planned to promote the development of other facilities and manage these facilities once they were a reality.

Fund Raising. The Audubon Park Zoo and the Friends of the Zoo raised funds through five major types of activities: Friends of the Zoo membership, concessions, "Adopt an Animal," "Zoo-To-Do," and capital fund drives. Zoo managers from around the country came to the Audubon Park Zoo for tips on fund raising.

Membership. Membership in the Friends of the Zoo was open to anyone. The membership fees increased over the years as summarized in Exhibit 5, yet the number of members increased steadily from the original 400 members in 1974 to 38,000 members in 1990, but declined to 28,000 in 1992. Membership allowed free entry to the Audubon Park Zoo and many other zoos around the United States. Participation in Zoobilations (annual members–only evenings at the zoo) and the many volunteer programs described earlier were other benefits of membership.

Expanding membership required a special approach to marketing the zoo. Chip Weigand, director of marketing for the zoo, stated,

> . . . [I]n marketing memberships we try to encourage repeat visitations, the feeling that one can visit as often as one wants, the idea that the zoo changes from visit to visit and that there are good reasons to make one large payment or donation for a membership card, rather than paying for each visit. . . . [T]he overwhelming factor is a good zoo that people want to visit often, so that a membership makes good economical sense.

Results of research on visitors to the zoo are contained in Exhibits 6 and 7.

In 1985, the zoo announced a new membership designed for business, the Audubon Zoo Curator Club, with four categories of membership: bronze, $250; silver, $500; gold, $1,000; and platinum, $2,500 and more.

Concessions. The Friends of the Zoo took over the Audubon Park Zoo concessions for refreshments and gifts in 1976 through a public bidding process. The concessions were run by volunteer members of the Friends of the Zoo and all profits went directly to the zoo. Before 1976, concession rentals brought in $1,500 in a good year. Profits from operation of the concessions by the Friends of the Zoo brought in $400,000 a year by 1980 and almost $700,000 in profits in 1988. In 1993, FOTZ was considering leasing the concessions to a third-party vendor.

Adopt an Animal. Zoo Parents paid a fee to "adopt" an animal, the fee varying with the animal chosen. Zoo Parents' names were listed on a large sign inside the zoo. They also had their own annual celebration, Zoo Parents Day.

EXHIBIT 5   *Membership Fees and Membership*

Year	Family Membership Fees	Individual Membership Fees	Number of Memberships
1979	$20	$10	1,000
1980	20	10	7,000
1981	20	10	11,000
1982	25	15	18,000
1983	30	15	22,000
1984	35	20	26,000
1985	40	20	27,000
1986	45	25	28,616
1987	45	25	29,318
1988	45	25	33,314
1989	49	29	36,935
1990	49	29	38,154

Source: The Audubon Institute

EXHIBIT 6   *Respondent Characteristics of Zoo Visitors According to Visitation Frequency (in %)*

Number of Zoo visits over past two years Respondent Characteristic	Four or More	Two or Three	One or None	Never Visited Zoo
Age				
Under 27	26	35	31	9
27 to 35	55	27	15	3
36 to 45	48	32	11	9
46 to 55	18	20	37	25
Over 55	27	29	30	14
Marital status				
Married	41	28	20	11
Not married	30	34	24	13
Children at home				
Yes	46	30	15	9
No	34	28	27	12
Interested in visiting New Orleans Aquarium				
Very, with emphasis	47	26	18	9
Very, without emphasis	45	24	23	12
Somewhat	28	37	14	11
Not too	19	32	27	22
Member of Friends of the Zoo				
Yes	67	24	6	4
No, but heard of it	35	30	24	12
Never heard of it	25	28	35	13
Would you be interested in joining FOTZ (non-members only)?				
Very/somewhat	50	28	14	8
No/don't know	33	29	26	12

Source: The Audubon Institute

Zoo-To-Do. Zoo-To-Do was an annual black-tie fund raiser held with live music, food and drink, and original, high-class souvenirs, such as posters or ceramic necklaces. Admission tickets, limited to 3,000 annually, were priced starting at $100 per person. A raffle was conducted in conjunction with the Zoo-To-Do, with raffle items varying from an opportunity to be zoo curator for a day to the use of a Mercedes-Benz for a year. Despite the rather stiff price, the Zoo-To-Do was a popular sellout every year. Local restaurants and other businesses donated most of the necessary supplies, decreasing the cost of the affair. In 1985, the Zoo-To-Do raised almost $500,000 in one night, more money than any other nonmedical fund-raiser in the county.[5]

Advertising
The Audubon Zoo launched impressive marketing campaigns in the 1980s. The zoo received ADDY awards from the New Orleans Advertising Club year after year.[6] In 1986, the film *Urban Eden*, produced by Alford Advertising and Buckholtz Productions Inc. in New Orleans, finished first among fifty entries in the "documentary films, public relations" category of the Eighth Annual Houston International Film Festival. The first-place Gold Award recognized the film for vividly portraying Audubon Zoo as a conservation, rather than a confining, environment.

During the same year, local television affiliates of ABC, CBS and NBC produced independent TV spots using the theme: "One of the World's Greatest Zoos Is in Your Own Back Yard...Audubon Zoo!" Along with some innovative views of the Audubon Zoo being in someone's "backyard," local news anchor personalities enjoyed "monkeying around" with the animals, and the zoo enjoyed some welcome free exposure.[7]

In 1993 the marketing budget was over $800,000, including group sales, public relations, advertising, and special events. Not included in this budget was

EXHIBIT 7   *Relative Importance of Seven Reasons as to Why Respondent Does Not Visit the Zoo More Often (in %)*

Reason (Closed Ended)	Very Imp. w/ Emphasis	Very Imp. w/o Emphasis	Somewhat Important	Unimportant
The distance of the Zoo's location from where you live	7	11	21	60
The cost of a Zoo visit	4	8	22	66
Not being all that interested in Zoo animals	2	12	18	67
The parking problems on weekends	7	11	19	62
The idea that you get tired of seeing the same exhibits over and over	5	18	28	49
It's too hot during summer months	25	23	22	30
Just not having the idea occur to you	8	19	26	48

Source: The Audubon Institute

EXHIBIT 8   *1991 Marketing Budget*

Marketing

General and Administrative	$ 30,900
Sales	96,300
Public Relations	109,250
Advertising	304,800
Special Events	157,900
TOTAL	699,150

Advertising

Media	$244,000
Production	50,000
Account Service	10,800
TOTAL	$304,800

Public Relations

Education, Travel, and Subscriptions	$ 5,200
Printing and Duplicating	64,000
Professional Services	15,000
Delivery and Postage	3,000
Telephone	1,250
Entertainment	2,000
Supplies	16,600
Miscellaneous	2,200
TOTAL	$109,250

Special Events

General and Administrative	$ 27,900
LA Swamp Fest	35,000
Earthfest	25,000
Ninja Turtle Breakfast	20,000
Jazz Search	15,000
Fiesta Latina	10,000
Crescent City Cats	10,000
Other Events	15,000
TOTAL	$157,900

Source: The Audubon Institute

developmental fund raising or membership. Percentage breakdowns of the marketing budget can be found in Exhibit 8.

The American Association of Zoological Parks and Aquariums reported that most zoos find the majority of their visitors live within a single population center in close proximity to the park.[8] Thus, to sustain attendance over the years, zoos must attract the same visitors repeatedly. A large number of the zoo's promotional programs and special events were aimed at just that.

Progress was slow among non-natives. For example, Simon & Schuster, a reputable publishing firm, in its 218-page [Frommer's] 1983–84 Guide to New Orleans, managed only a three-word allusion to a "very nice zoo." A 1984 study found that only 36 percent of the visitors were tourists, and even this number was probably influenced to some extent by an overflow from the World's Fair.

Promotional Programs

The Audubon Park Zoo and the Friends of the Zoo conducted a multitude of very successful promotional programs. The effect was to have continual parties and celebrations going on, attracting a variety of people to the zoo (and raising additional revenue). Exhibit 9 lists the major annual promotional programs conducted by the zoo.

In addition to these annual promotions, the zoo scheduled concerts of well-known musicians, such as Irma Thomas, Pete Fountain, The Monkeys, and Manhattan Transfer, and other special events throughout the year. As a result, a variety of events occurred each month.

Many educational activities were conducted all year long. These included (1) a junior zoo keeper program for seventh and eighth graders, (2) a student intern program for high school and college students, and (3) a ZOOmobile that took live animals to such locations as special education classes, hospitals, and nursing homes.

Admission Policy

The commission recommended the institution of an admission charge. Arguments generally advanced against such a charge held that it results in an overall decline in attendance and a reduction of nongate revenues. Proponents held that gate charges control vandalism, produce greater revenues, and result in increased public awareness and appreciation of the

EXHIBIT 9   *Selected Audubon Park Zoo Promotional Programs*

Month	Activity
March	**Louisiana Black Heritage Festival.** A two-day celebration of Louisiana's Black history and its native contributions through food, music, and arts and crafts.
March	**Earth Fest.** The environment and our planet are the focus of this fun-filled and educational event. Recycling, conservation displays, and puppet shows.
April	**Jazz Search.** This entertainment series is aimed at finding the best new talent in the area with the winners featured at the New Orleans Jazz & Heritage Festival.
April	**Zoo-To-Do for kids.** At this "pint-sized" version of the Zoo-To-Do, fun and games abound for kids.
May	**Zoo-To-Do.** Annual black tie fundraiser featuring over 100 of New Orleans' finest restaurants and three music stages.
May	**Irma Thomas Mother's Day Concert.** The annual celebration of Mother's Day with a buffet.
August	**Lego Invitational.** Architectural firms turn thousands of Lego pieces into original creations.
September	**Fiesta Latina.** Experience the best the Hispanic community has to offer through music, cuisine, and arts and crafts.
October	**Louisiana Swamp Festival.** Cajun food, music, and crafts highlight this four-day salute to Louisiana's bayou country; features hands-on contact with live swamp animals.
October	**Boo at the Zoo.** This annual Halloween extravaganza features games, special entertainment, trick or treat, a haunted house, and the Zoo's Spook Train.

Source: The Audubon Institute

facility. In the early 1970s, no major international zoo failed to charge admission, and 73 percent of the 125 zoos in the United States charged admission.

The commission argued that there is no such thing as a free zoo; someone must pay. If the zoo is tax-supported, then locals carry a disproportionate share of the cost. At the time, neighboring Jefferson Parish was growing by leaps and bounds and surely would bring a large, nonpaying [constituency] to the new zoo. Further, since most zoos are tourist attractions, tourists should pay since they contribute little to the local tax revenues.

The average yearly attendance for a zoo may be estimated using projected population figures multiplied by a "visitor generating factor." The average visitor generating factor of fourteen zoos similar in size and climate to the Audubon Zoo was 1.34, with a rather wide range from a low of 0.58 in the cities of Phoenix and Miami to a high of 2.80 in Jackson, Mississippi.

Attracting More Tourists and Other Visitors

A riverboat ride on the romantic paddle wheeler Cotton Blossom took visitors from downtown New Orleans to the zoo. Originally, the trip began at a dock in the French Quarter, but it was later moved to a dock immediately adjacent to New Orleans's newest attraction, the Riverwalk, a Rouse development, on the site of the 1984 Louisiana World Exposition. Not only was the riverboat ride great fun, it also lured tourists and conventioneers from the downtown attractions of the French Quarter and the new Riverwalk to the zoo, some six miles upstream. A further allure of the riverboat ride was a return trip to downtown on the New Orleans Streetcar, one of the few remaining trolley cars in the United States. The Zoo Cruise not only drew more visitors but also generated additional revenue through landing fees paid by the New Orleans Steamboat Company and [helped keep] traffic out of uptown New Orleans.[9]

FINANCIAL

The zoo's ability to generate operating funds has been ascribed to the dedication of the Friends of the Zoo, continuing increases in attendance, and creative special events and programs. A history of adequate operating funds allowed the zoo to guarantee capital donors that their gifts would be used to build and maintain top-notch exhibits. A comparison of the 1989 and 1990 Statements of Operating Income and Expense for the Audubon Institute is in Exhibit 10.

Capital Fund Drives

The Audubon Zoo Development Fund was established in 1973. Corporate/Industrial support of the zoo has

EXHIBIT 10   *The Audubon Institute, Inc. The Audubon Park and Zoological Garden Statement of Operating Income and Expenses*

	1989	1990 (ZOO)	1990 (AQUARIUM)
Operating Income			
Admissions	$ 2,952,000	$ 3,587,000	$3,664,000
Food and Gift Operations	2,706,000	3,495,500	711,000
Membership	1,476,000	1,932,000	2,318,000
Recreational Programs	410,000	396,000	0
Visitor Services	246,000	218,000	0
Other	410,000	32,000	650,000
TOTAL INCOME	$8,200,000	$9,660,500	$7,343,000
Operating Expenses			
Maintenance	$ 1,394,000	$ 1,444,000	$ 1,316,000
Educational/Curatorial	2,296,000	2,527,500	2,783,000
Food and Gift Operations	1,804,000	2,375,000	483,000
Membership	574,000	840,000	631,000
Recreational	328,000	358,000	362,000
Marketing	410,000	633,000	593,000
Visitor Services	574,000	373,000	125,000
Administration	820,000	1,110,000	1,050,000
TOTAL EXPENSES	$8,200,000	$9,660,500	$7,343,000

been very strong—many corporations have under-written construction of zoo displays and facilities. A partial list of major corporate sponsors is in Exhibit 11. A sponsorship was considered to be for the life of the exhibit. The development department operated on a 12 percent overhead rate, which meant 88 cents of every dollar raised went toward the projects. By 1989, the master plan for development was 75 per-cent complete. The fund-raising goal for the zoo in 1989 was $1,500,000.

MANAGEMENT

The Zoo Director

Ron Forman, Audubon Zoo director, was called a "zoomaster extraordinaire" and was described by the press as a "cross between Doctor Doolittle and the Wizard of Oz," as a "practical visionary," and as "seri-ous, but with a sense of humor."[10] A native New Orleanian, . . . Forman quit an MBA program to join the city government as an administrative assistant and found himself doing a business analysis project on the Audubon Park. Once the city was committed to a new zoo, Forman was placed on board as an assistant to the zoo director, John Moore. In early 1977, Moore gave up the battle between the "animal peo-ple" and the "people people,"[11] and Forman took over as park and zoo director.

Forman was said to bring an MBA-meets-menagerie style to the zoo, which was responsible for

transforming it from a public burden into an almost completely self-sustaining operation. The result not only benefited the citizens of the city but also added a major tourist attraction to the economically troubled city of the 1980s.

Staffing

The zoo used two classes of employees, civil service, through the Audubon Park Commission, and non-civil service. The civil service employees included the curators and zoo keepers. They fell under the juris-diction of the city civil service system but were paid out of the budget of the Friends of the Zoo. Employees who worked in public relations, advertis-ing, concessions, fund raising, and so on were hired through the Friends of the Zoo and were not part of the civil service system. See Exhibit 12 for further data on staffing patterns.

THE ZOO IN THE LATE 1980s

A visitor to the new Audubon Park Zoo could quickly see why New Orleanians were so proud of their zoo. In a city that was termed among the dirti-est in the nation, the zoo was virtually spotless. This was a result of adequate staffing and the clear pride of both those who worked at and those who visited the zoo. One of the first points made by volunteers guid-ing school groups was that anyone seeing a piece of trash on the ground must pick it up.[12] A 1986 city poll showed that 93 percent of the citizens surveyed

EXHIBIT 11   *Major Corporate Sponsors*

Amoco Foundation	Louisiana Coca-Cola Bottling Company, Ltd.
American Express	Louisiana Land and Exploration Company
Anheuser-Busch, Inc.	Martin Marietta Manned Space Systems
Arthur Andersen and Company	McDonald's Operators of New Orleans
J. Aron Charitable Foundation, Inc.	Mobil Foundation, Inc.
Bell South Corporation	National Endowment for the Arts
BP America	National Science Foundation
Chevron USA, Inc.	Ozone Spring Water
Conoco, Inc.	Pan American Life Insurance Company
Consolidated Natural Gas Corporation	Philip Morris Companies Inc.
Entergy Corporation	Shell Companies Foundation, Inc.
Exxon Company, USA	Tenneco, Inc.
Freeport-McMoRan, Inc.	Texaco USA
Host International, Inc.	USF&G Corporation
Kentwood Spring Water	Wendy's of New Orleans, Inc.

Source: The Audubon Institute

EXHIBIT 12   *Employee Structure*

Year	Number of Paid Employees	Number of Volunteers
1972	36	
1973	49	
1974	69	
1975	90	
1876	143	
1977	193	
1978	184	
1979	189	
1980	198	
1981	245	
1982	305	
1983	302	56
1984	419	120
1985	454	126
1986	426	250
1987	431	300
1988	462	310
1989	300	270
1990	450	350

Source: The Audubon Institute

gave the zoo a high approval rating—an extremely high rating for any public facility.

Kudos came from groups outside the local area as well. Delegates from the American Association of Zoological Parks and Aquariums ranked the Audubon Park Zoo as one of the three top zoos of its size in America. In 1982, the American Association of Nurserymen gave the zoo a Special Judges Award for its use of plant materials. In 1985, the Audubon Park Zoo received the Phoenix Award from the Society of American Travel Writers for its achievements in conservation, preservation, and beautification.

By 1987, the zoo was virtually self-sufficient. The small amount of money received from government grants amounted to less than 10 percent of the budget. The master plan for the development of the zoo was 75 percent complete, and the reptile exhibit was scheduled for completion in the fall. The organization had expanded with a full complement of professionals and managers. (See Exhibit 13 for the organizational structure of the zoo.)

While the zoo made great progress in fifteen years, all was not quiet on the political front. In a court battle, the city won over the state on the issue of who wielded ultimate authority over Audubon Park and Zoo. Indeed, the zoo benefited from three friendly mayors in a row, starting with Moon Landrieu, who championed the new zoo, to Ernest "Dutch" Morial, to Sidney Barthelemy who threw his support to both the zoo and the aquarium proposal championed by Ron Forman.

THE FUTURE

New Directions for the Zoo

Zoo Director Ron Forman demonstrated that zoos have almost unlimited potential. A 1980 New Orleans magazine article cited some of Forman's ideas, ranging from a safari train to a breeding center for rare animals. The latter has an added attraction as a potential money-maker since an Asiatic lion cub, for example, sells for around $10,000. This wealth of ideas was important because expanded facilities and programs are required to maintain attendance at any public attraction. The most ambitious of Forman's ideas was for an aquarium and riverfront park to be located at the foot of Canal Street.

Although the zoo enjoyed political support in 1992, New Orleans was still suffering from a high unemployment rate and a generally depressed economy resulting from the slump in the oil industry. Some economists predicted the beginning of a

EXHIBIT 13 *Audubon Park Commission*

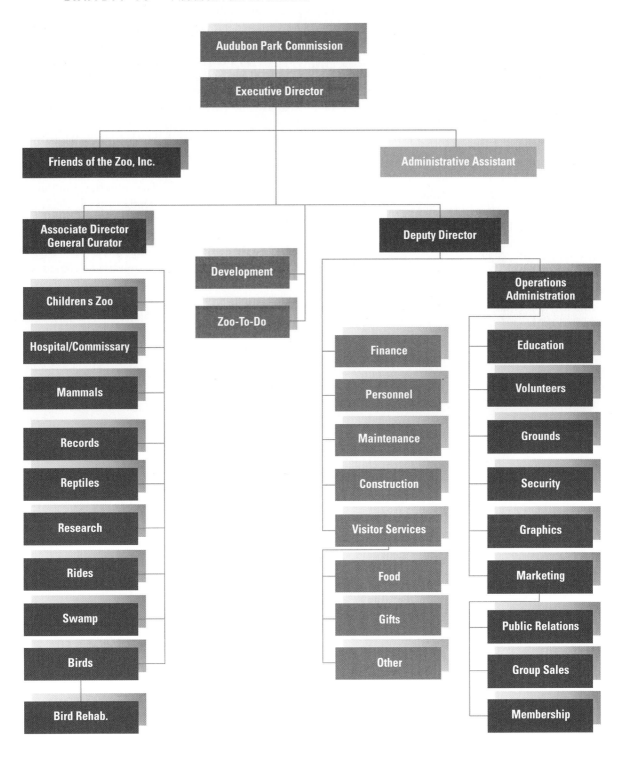

gradual turnaround in 1988, but any significant improvement in the economy was still forecasted to be years away in 1993. (A few facts about New Orleans are given in Exhibit 14.) In addition, the zoo operated in a city where many attractions competed for the leisure dollar of citizens and visitors. The Audubon Zoological Garden had to vie with the French Quarter, Dixieland jazz, the Superdome, and even the greatest of all attractions in the city—Mardi Gras.

The New Orleans Aquarium

In 1986, Forman and a group of supporters proposed the development of an aquarium and riverfront park to the New Orleans City Council. In November 1986, the electorate voted to fund an aquarium and a riverfront park by a 70 percent margin—one of the largest margins the city has ever given to any tax proposal. Forman[13] hailed this vote of confidence from the citizens as a mandate to build a world-class aquarium that would produce new jobs, stimulate the local economy, and create an educational resource for the children of the city.

The Aquarium of the Americas opened in September 1990. The $40 million aquarium project was located providing a logical pedestrian link for visitors between [major] attractions of the Riverwalk and the Jax Brewery, a shopping center in the French Quarter. Management of the aquarium was placed under the Audubon Institute, the same organization that ran the Audubon Zoo. A feasibility study prepared by Harrison Price Company[14] projected a probable 863,000 visitors by the year 1990, with 75 percent of the visitors coming from outside the metropolitan area. That attendance figure was reached in only four months and six days from the grand opening. Attendance remained strong through 1992, after a slight drop from the initial grand opening figures.

Meanwhile, the zoo had its own future to plan. The new physical facilities and professional care paid off handsomely in increased attendance and new animal births. But the zoo could not expand at its existing location because of lack of land within the city. Forman and the zoo considered several alternatives.

EXHIBIT 14   *A Few Facts About the New Orleans MSA*

Population	1,324,400
Households	489,900
Median Age	30.8 years
Median Household EBI	$29,130
Average Temperature	70 degrees
Average Annual Rainfall	63 inches
Average Elevation	5 feet below sea level
Area	363.5 square miles
	199.4 square miles of land

Major Economic Activities

Tourism (5 million visitors per year)
Oil and Gas Industry
The Port of New Orleans (170 million tons of cargo/year)

Taxes

State Sales Tax	4.0%
Parish (County) Sales Tax	5.0% (Orleans)
State Income Tax	2.1–2.6% on first $20,000
	3.0–3.5% on next $30,000
	6.0% on $51,000 and over

Parish property tax of 126.15 mills (Orleans) is based on 10% of appraised value over $75,000 homestead exemption.

Source: Sales and Marketing Management. South Central Bell Yellow Pages, 1991.

One was little "neighborhood" zoos to be located all over the city. A second was a special survival center, a separate breeding area to be located outside the city boundaries where land was available.

Forman presented . . . plans for a project called Riverfront 2000, which included expansion of the aquarium, the Woldenberg Riverfront Park, a species survival center, an arboretum, an insectarium, a natural history museum, and a further expansion of the zoo. With the zoo running smoothly, the staff seemed to need new challenges to tackle, and the zoo needed new facilities or programs to continue to increase attendance.

NOTES

1. Millie Ball, "The New Zoo of '82," *Dixie Magazine, Sunday Times Picayune,* 24 June 1979.
2. Merikaye Presley, "Neighbors Objecting to Audubon Zoo Expansion Project in Midst of Work," *Times Picayune*, 30 March 1975, p. A3.
3. "Zoo Expansion Is Ruled Illegal," *Times Picayune*, 20 January 1976.
4. "Society Seeks Change at Zoo," *Times Picayune*, 29 April 1972, p. D25.
5. "Zoo Thrives Despite Tough Times in New Orleans," *Jefferson Business*, August 1985, p. A1.
6. Ibid.
7. Sharon Donovan, "New Orleans Affiliates Monkey Around for Zoo," *Advertising Age*, 17 March 1986.
8. Karen Sausmann, ed., *Zoological Park and Aquarium Fundamentals* (Wheeling, W. Va.: American Association of Zoological Parks and Aquariums, 1982), p. 111.
9. Diane Luope, "Riverboat Rides to Zoo Are Planned," *Times Picayne*, 30 November 1981, p. A17.
10. Steve Brooks, "Don't Say 'No Can Do' to Audubon Zoo Chief," *Jefferson Business*, 5 May 1986, p. 1
11. Ross Yuchey, "No Longer Is Heard a Discouraging Word at the Audubon Zoo," *New Orleans*, August 1980, p. 53.
12. Ibid., p. 49.
13. At the Zoo, Winter 1987.
14. Feasibility Analysis and Conceptual Planning for a Major Aquarium Attraction, prepared for the City of New Orleans, March 1985.

REFERENCES

Beaulieu, Lovell. "It's All Happening at the Zoo," *The Times Picayune*, Sunday, January 28, 1978.

Ball, Millie. "The New Zoo of '82," *Dixie Magazine, Sunday Times Picayune,* June 24, 1978.

Brooks, Steve. "Don't Say 'No Can Do' to Audubon Zoo Chief," *Jefferson Business*, May 5, 1986.

Bureau of Governmental Research, City of New Orleans. Audubon Park Zoo Study, Part I, Zoo Improvement Plan. August 1971. New Orleans: Bureau of Governmental Research.

Bureau of Governmental Research, City of New Orleans. Audubon Park Zoo Study, Part II, An Operational Analysis. August 1971 New Orleans: Bureau of Governmental Research.

Donovan, S. "The Audubon Zoo: A Dream Come True," *New Orleans*, May 1986, pp. 52–66.

Feasibility Analysis and Conceptual Planning for a Major Aquarium Attraction, prepared for the City of New Orleans, March 1985.

Forman, R., J. Logsdon and J. Wilds. Audubon Park: An Urban Eden, 1985, New Orleans: The Friends of the Zoo.

Poole, Susan. *Frommer's 1983–84 Guide to New Orleans*, 1983, New York: Simon & Schuster.

Sausmann, K., ed., *Zoological Park and Aquarium Fundamentals*, 1982, Wheeling, West Virginia: American Association of Zoological Parks and Aquariums.

Yuckey, R. "No Longer Is Heard a Discouraging Word at the Audubon Zoo," *New Orleans*, August, 1980, pp. 49–60.

Zuckerman, S., ed., *Great Zoos of the World*, (Colorado: Westview Press, 1980).

In 1960, Bill Dowling, a "machine-tool set-up man" for a large auto firm, became so frustrated with his job that he quit to form his own business. The manufacturing operation consisted of a few general-purpose metal working machines that were set up in Dowling's garage. Space was such a constraint that it controlled the work process. For example, if the cutting press was to be used with long stock, the milling machines would have to be pushed back against the wall and remain idle. Production always increased on rain-free, summer days since the garage doors could be opened and a couple of machines moved out onto the drive. Besides Dowling, who acted as salesman, accountant, engineer, president, manufacturing representative, and working foreman, members of the original organization were Eve Sullivan, who began as a part-time secretary and payroll clerk; and Wally Denton, who left the auto firm with Bill. The work force was composed of part-time "moonlighters," full-time machinists for other firms, who were attracted by the job autonomy that provided experience in setting up jobs and job processes, where a high degree of ingenuity was required.

The first years were touch and go, with profits being erratic. Gradually the firm began to gain a reputation for being ingenious at solving unique problems and for producing a quality product on, or before, deadlines. The "product" consisted of fabricating dies for making minor component metal parts for automobiles and a specified quantity of the parts. Having realized the firm was too dependent on the auto industry and that sudden fluctuations in auto sales could have a drastic effect on the firm's survival, Dowling began marketing their services toward manufacturing firms not connected with the auto industry. Bids were submitted for work that involved legs for vending machines, metal trim for large appliances, clamps and latches for metal windows, and display racks for small power hand tools.

As Dowling Flexible Metals became more diversified, the need for expansion forced the company to borrow building funds from the local bank, which enabled construction of a small factory on the edge of town. As new markets and products created a need for increasingly more versatile equipment and a larger work force, the plant has since expanded twice until it is now three times its original size.

In 1980, Dowling Flexible Metals hardly resembles the garage operation of the formative years. The firm now employs approximately thirty full-time journeymen and apprentice machinists, a staff of four engineers that were hired about three years ago, and a full-time office secretary subordinate to Eve Sullivan, the office manager. The rapid growth has created problems that in 1980 have not been resolved. Bill Dowling, realizing his firm is suffering from growing pains, has asked you to "take a look at the operation and make recommendations as to how things could be run better." You begin the consulting project by interviewing Dowling, other key people in the firm, and workers out in the shop who seem willing to express their opinions about the firm.

BILL DOWLING, OWNER-PRESIDENT

"We sure have come a long way from that first set-up in my garage. On a nice day we would get everything all spread out in the drive and then it would start pouring cats and dogs—so we would have to move back inside. It was just like a one-ring circus. Now it seems like a three-ring circus. You would think that with all that talent we have here and all the experience, things would run smoother. Instead, it seems I am putting in more time than ever and accomplishing a whole lot less in a day's time.

"It's not like the old days. Everything has gotten so complicated and precise in design. When you go to a customer to discuss a job you have to talk to six kids right out of engineering school. Every one of them has a calculator—they don't even carry slide rules anymore—and all they can talk is fancy formulas and how we should do our job. It just seems I spend more time with customers and less time around the shop than I used to. That's why I hired the engineering staff—to interpret specifications, solve engineering problems, and draw blueprints. It still seems all the problems are solved out on the shop floor by guys like Walt and Tom, just like always. Gene and the other engineers are necessary, but they don't seem to be working as smoothly with the guys on the floor as they should.

"One of the things I would like to see us do in the future is to diversify even more. Now that we have the capability, I am starting to bid jobs that require the computerized milling machine process

* This case was prepared by Floyd G. Willoughby, Oakland University, Rochester, MI. © by Floyd G. Willoughby. Reprinted by permission.

tape. This involves devising a work process for milling a part on a machine and then making a computer process tape of it. We can then sell copies of the tape just like we do dies and parts. These tapes allow less-skilled operators to operate complicated milling machines without the long apprenticeship of a tradesman. All they have to do is press buttons and follow the machine's instructions for changing the milling tools. Demand is increasing for the computerized process tapes.

"I would like to see the firm get into things like working with combinations of bonded materials such as plastics, fiberglass, and metals. I am also starting to bid jobs involving the machining of plastics and other materials beside metals."

WALLY DENTON, SHOP FOREMAN, FIRST SHIFT

"Life just doesn't seem to be as simple as when we first started in Bill's garage. In those days he would bring a job back and we would all gather 'round and decide how we were going to set it up and who would do it. If one of the 'moonlighters' was to get the job, either Bill or I would lay the job out for him when he came in that afternoon. Now, the customers' ideas get processed through the engineers and we, out here in the shop, have to guess just exactly what the customer had in mind.

"What some people around here don't understand is that I am a partner in this business. I've stayed out here in the shop because this is where I like it and it's where I feel most useful. When Bill isn't here, I'm always around to put out fires. Between Eve, Gene, and myself we usually make the right decision.

"With all this diversification and Bill spending a lot of time with customers, I think we need to get somebody else out there to share the load."

THOMAS MCNULL, SHOP FOREMAN, SECOND SHIFT

"In general, I agree with Wally that things aren't as simple as they used to be, but I think, given the amount of jobs we are handling at any one time, we run the ship pretty smoothly. When the guys bring problems to me that require major job changes, I get Wally's approval before making the changes. We haven't had any difficulty in that area.

"Where we run into problems is with the engineers. They get the job when Bill brings it back. They decide how the part should be made and by what process, which in turn pretty much restricts

what type of dies we have to make. Therein lies the bind. Oftentimes we run into a snag following the engineers' instructions. If it's after five o'clock, the engineers have left for the day. We, on the second shift, either have to let the job sit until the next morning or solve the problem ourselves. This not only creates bad feeling between the shop personnel and the engineers, but it makes extra work for the engineers because they have to draw up new plans.

"I often think we have the whole process backwards around here. What we should be doing is giving the job to the journeymen—after all, these guys have a lot of experience and know-how—then give the finished product to the engineers to draw up. I'll give you an example. Last year we got a job from a vending machine manufacturer. The job consisted of fabricating five sets of dies for making those stubby little legs for vending machines, plus five hundred of the finished legs. Well, the engineers figured the job all out, drew up the plans, and sent it out to us. We made the first die to specs, but when we tried to punch out the leg on the press, the metal tore. We took the problem back to the engineers, and after the preliminary accusations of who was responsible for the screw up, they changed the raw material specifications. We waited two weeks for delivery of the new steel, then tried again. The metal still tore. Finally, after two months of hassle, Charlie Oakes and I worked on the die for two days and finally came up with a solution. The problem was that the shoulders of the die were too steep for forming the leg in just one punch. We had to use two punches (see Exhibit 1). The problem was the production process, not the raw materials. We spent four months on that job and ran over our deadline. Things like that shouldn't happen."

CHARLIE OAKES, JOURNEYMAN APPRENTICE

"Really, I hate to say anything against this place because it is a pretty good place to work. The pay and benefits are pretty good and because it is a small shop our hours can be somewhat flexible. If you have a doctor's appointment you can either come in late or stay until you get your time in or punch out and come back. You can work as much overtime as you want to.

"The thing I'm kind of disappointed about is that I thought the work would be more challenging. I'm just an apprentice, but I've only got a year to go in my program before I can get my journeyman's card, and I think I should be handling more jobs on my own. That's why I came to work here. My Dad

EXHIBIT 1   *Two-Stage Production Process*

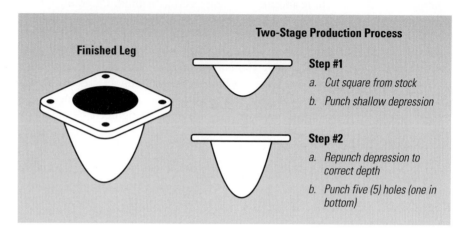

was one of the original 'moonlighters' here. He told me about how interesting it was when he was here. I guess I just expected the same thing."

GENE JENKINS, CHIEF ENGINEER

"I imagine the guys out in the shop have already told you about 'The Great Vending Machine Fiasco.' They'll never let us forget that. However, it does point out the need for better coordination around here. The engineers were hired as engineers, not as draftsmen, which is just about all we do. I'm not saying we should have the final say on how the job is designed, because there is a lot of practical experience out in that shop; but just as we haven't their expertise neither do they have ours. There is a need for both, the technical skill of the engineers and the practical experience of the shop.

"One thing that would really help is more information from Bill. I realize Bill is spread pretty thin but there are a lot of times he comes back with a job, briefs us, and we still have to call the customer about details because Bill hasn't been specific enough or asked the right questions of the customer. Engineers communicate best with other engineers. Having an engineering function gives us a competitive advantage over our competition. In my opinion, operating as we do now, we are not maximizing that advantage.

"When the plans leave here we have no idea what happens to those plans once they are out in the shop. The next thing we know, we get a die or set of dies that doesn't even resemble the plans we sent out in the shop. We then have to draw up new plans to fit the dies. Believe me, it's not only discouraging, but it really makes you wonder what your job is around

here. It's embarrassing when a customer calls to check on the status of the job and I have to run out in the shop, look up the guy handing the job, and get his best estimate of how the job is going.

EVE SULLIVAN, OFFICE MANAGER

"One thing is for sure, life is far from dull around here. It seems Bill is either dragging in a bunch of plans or racing off with the truck to deliver a job to a customer.

"Really, Wally and I make all the day-to-day decisions around here. Of course, I don't get involved in technical matters. Wally and Gene take care of those, but if we are short-handed or need a new machine, Wally and I start the ball rolling by getting together the necessary information and talking to Bill the first chance we get. I guess you could say that we run things around here by consensus most of time. If I get a call from a customer asking about the status of a job, I refer the call to Gene because Wally is usually out in the shop.

"I started with Bill and Wally twenty years ago, on a part-time basis, and somehow the excitement has turned into work. Joan, the office secretary, and I handle all correspondence, bookkeeping, payroll, insurance forms, and everything else besides run the office. It's just getting to be too hectic—I just wish the job was more fun, the way it used to be."

Having listened to all concerned, you returned to Bill's office only to find him gone. You tell Eve and Wally that you will return within one week with you recommendations.

EXHIBIT 2   *Dowling Flexible Metals Organizational Chart*

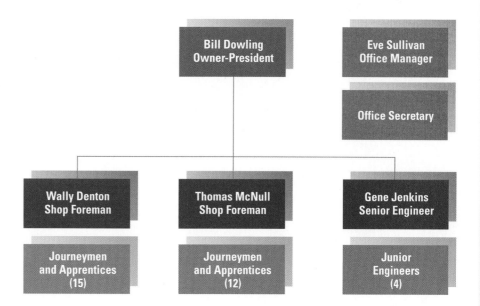

Glossary

adaptability/entrepreneurial culture a culture characterized by strategic focus on the external environment through flexibility and change to meet customer needs.

administrative principles a closed systems management perspective that focuses on the total organization and grows from the insights of practitioners.

ambidextrous approach a characteristic of an organization that can behave both in an organic and a mechanistic way.

analyzability a dimension of technology in which work activities can be reduced to mechanical steps and participants can follow an objective, computational procedure to solve problems.

analyzer a business strategy that seeks to maintain a stable business while innovating on the periphery.

authority a force for achieving desired outcomes that is prescribed by the formal hierarchy and reporting relationships.

balanced scorecard a comprehensive management control system that balances traditional financial measures with operational measures relating to an organization's critical success factors.

benchmarking process whereby companies find out how others do something better than they do and then try to imitate or improve on it.

boundary spanning roles activities that link and coordinate an organization with key elements in the external environment.

bounded rationality perspective how decisions are made when time is limited, a large number of internal and external factors affect a decision, and the problem is ill-defined.

buffering roles activities that absorb uncertainty from the environment.

bureaucracy an organizational framework marked by rules and procedures, specialization and division of labor, hierarchy of authority, technically qualified personnel, separate position and incumbent, and written communications and records.

bureaucratic control the use of rules, policies, hierarchy of authority, written documentation, standardization, and other bureaucratic mechanisms to standardize behavior and assess performance.

bureaucratic culture a culture that has an internal focus and a consistency orientation for a stable environment.

bureaucratic organization a perspective that emphasizes management on an impersonal, rational basis through such elements as clearly defined authority and responsibility, formal recordkeeping, and uniform application of standard rules.

Carnegie model organizational decision making involving many managers and a final choice based on a coalition among those managers.

centrality a trait of a department whose role is in the primary activity of an organization.

centralization refers to the level of hierarchy with authority to make decisions.

change process the way in which changes occur in an organization.

charismatic authority based in devotion to the exemplary character or heroism of an individual and the order defined by him or her.

clan control the use of social characteristics, such as corporate culture, shared values, commitments, traditions, and beliefs, to control behavior.

clan culture a culture that focuses primarily on the involvement and participation of the organization's members and on rapidly changing expectations from the external environment.

closed system a system that is autonomous, enclosed, and not dependent on its environment.

coalition an alliance among several managers who agree through bargaining about organizational goals and problem priorities.

coercive forces external pressures such as legal requirements exerted on an organization to adopt structures, techniques, or behaviors similar to other organizations.

collaborative network an emerging perspective whereby organizations allow themselves to become dependent on other organizations to increase value and productivity for all.

collective bargaining the negotiation of an agreement between management and workers.

collectivity stage the life cycle phase in which an organization has strong leadership and begins to develop clear goals and direction.

communities of practice made up of individuals who are informally bound to one another through exposure to a similar set of problems and a common pursuit of solutions.

competing values approach a perspective on organizational effectiveness that combines diverse indicators of performance that represent competing management values.

competition rivalry between groups in the pursuit of a common prize.

computer-integrated manufacturing (CIM) computer systems that link together manufacturing components, such as robots, machines, product design, and engineering analysis.

confrontation a situation in which parties in conflict directly engage one another and try to work out their differences.

consortia groups of firms that venture into new products and technologies.

contextual dimensions traits that characterize the whole organization, including its size, technology, environment, and goals.

contingency a theory meaning one thing depends on other things; the organization's situation dictates the correct management approach.

contingency decision-making framework a perspective that brings together the two organizational dimensions of problem consensus and technical knowledge about solutions.

continuous process production a completely mechanized manufacturing process in which there is no starting or stopping.

cooptation occurs when leaders from important sectors in the environment are made part of an organization.

coping with uncertainty a source of power for a department that reduces uncertainty for other departments by obtaining prior information, prevention, and absorption.

craft technology technology characterized by a fairly stable stream of activities but in which the conversion process is not analyzable or well-understood.

creative departments organizational departments that initiate change, such as research and development, engineering, design, and systems analysis.

culture the set of values, guiding beliefs, understandings, and ways of thinking that is shared by members of an organization and is taught to new members as correct.

culture changes changes in the values, attitudes, expectations, beliefs, abilities, and behavior of employees.

culture strength the degree of agreement among members of an organization about the importance of specific values.

data the input of a communication channel.

data mining software that uses sophisticated decision-making processes to search raw data for patterns and relationships that may be significant.

data warehousing the use of a huge database that combines all of an organization's data and allows users to access the data directly, create reports, and obtain answers to "what-if" questions.

decision learning a process of recognizing and admitting mistakes that allows managers and organizations to acquire the experience and knowledge to perform more effectively in the future.

decision premises constraining frames of reference and guidelines placed by top managers on decisions made at lower levels.

decision support system a system that enables managers at all levels of the organization to retrieve, manipulate, and display information from integrated data bases for making specific decisions.

defender a business strategy that seeks stability or even retrenchment rather than innovation or growth.

departmental grouping a structure in which employees share a common supervisor and resources, are jointly responsible for performance, and tend to identify and collaborate with each other.

dialogue a group communication process aimed at creating a culture based on collaboration, trust, and commitment to shared goals.

differentiation the cognitive and emotional differences among managers in various functional departments of an organization and formal structure differences among these departments.

direct interlock a situation that occurs when a member of the board of directors of one company sits on the board of another.

divisional grouping a grouping in which people are organized according to what the organization produces.

divisional structure the structuring of the organization according to individual products, services, product groups, major projects, or profit centers; also called product structure or strategic business units.

domain an organization's chosen environmental field of activity.

domains of political activity areas in which politics plays a role. Three domains in organizations are structural change, management succession, and resource allocation.

domestic stage the first stage of international development in which a company is domestically oriented while managers are aware of the global environment.

dual-core approach an organizational change perspective that identifies the unique processes associated with administrative change compared to those associated with technical change.

e-commerce any commercial activity that takes place by digital processes over a computer network; the exchange of money and products is replaced or enhanced by the exchange of information from one computer to another.

effectiveness the degree to which an organization realizes its goals.

efficiency the amount of resources used to produce a unit of output.

elaboration stage the organizational life cycle phase in which the red tape crisis is resolved through the development of a new sense of teamwork and collaboration.

electronic data interchange (EDI) the linking of organizations through computers for the transmission of data without human interference.

electronic libraries databases of specific types of information and knowledge that can be "checked out" and re-used by others.

empowerment power sharing; the delegation of power or authority to subordinates.

engineering technology technology in which there is substantial variety in the tasks performed, but the activities are usually handled on the basis of established formulas, procedures and techniques.

enterprise resource planning (ERP) sophisticated computerized systems that collect, process, and provide information about a company's entire enterprise, including order processing, product design, purchasing, inventory, manufacturing, distribution, human resources, receipt of payments, and forecasting of future demand.

entrepreneurial stage the life cycle phase in which an organization is born and its emphasis is on creating a product and surviving in the marketplace.

escalating commitment persisting in a course of action when it is failing; occurs because managers block or distort negative information and because consistency and persistence are valued in contemporary society.

ethical dilemma one in which each alternative choice or behavior seems undesirable because of a potentially negative ethical consequence.

ethics the code of moral principles and values that governs the behavior of a person or group with respect to what is right or wrong.

ethics committee a group of executives appointed to oversee company ethics.

ethics ombudsperson a single manager who serves as the corporate conscience.

executive information system (EIS) interactive systems that help top managers monitor and control organizational operations by processing and presenting data in usable form.

explicit knowledge formal, systematic knowledge that can be codified, written down, and passed on to others in documents or general instructions.

external adaptation the manner in which an organization meets goals and deals with outsiders.

extranet an extension of a company's intranet that gives access to key partners, suppliers, or customers.

focus an organization's dominant perspective value, which may be internal or external.

focus strategy a strategy in which an organization concentrates on a specific regional market or buyer group.

formalization the degree to which an organization has rules, procedures, and written documentation.

formalization stage the phase in an organization's life cycle involving the installation and use of rules, procedures, and control systems.

functional grouping the placing together of employees who perform similar functions or work processes or who bring similar knowledge and skills to bear.

functional matrix a structure in which functional bosses have primary authority and product or project managers simply coordinate product activities.

functional structure the grouping of activities by common function.

garbage can model model that describes the pattern or flow of multiple decision within an organization.

general environment includes those sectors that may not directly affect the daily operations of a firm but will indirectly influence it.

generalist an organization with a wide niche or domain.

global company a company that no longer thinks of itself as having a home country.

global geographic structure a form in which an organization divides its operations into world regions, each of which reports to the CEO.

global matrix structure a form of horizontal linkage in an international organization in which both product and functional structures (horizontal and vertical) are implemented simultaneously.

global product structure a form in which product divisions take responsibility for global operations in their specific product areas.

global stage the stage of international development in which the company transcends any one country.

global teams work groups made up of multinational members whose activities span multiple countries; also called transnational teams.

globalization strategy the standardization of product design and advertising strategy throughout the world.

goal approach an approach to organizational effectiveness that is concerned with output and whether the organization achieves its output goals.

Hawthorne Studies a series of experiments on worker productivity begun in 1924 at the Hawthorne plant of Western Electric Company in Illinois; attributed employees' increased output to managers' better treatment of them during the study.

heroes organizational members who serve as models or ideals for serving cultural norms and values.

high-velocity environments industries in which competitive and technological change is so extreme that market data is either unavailable or obsolete, strategic windows open and shut quickly, and the cost of a decision error is company failure.

horizontal grouping the organizing of employees around core work processes rather than by function, product, or geography.

horizontal linkage the amount of communication and coordination that occurs horizontally across organizational departments.

horizontal linkage model a model of the three components of organizational design needed to achieve new product innovation: departmental specialization, boundary spanning, and horizontal linkages.

horizontal structure a structure that virtually eliminates both the vertical hierarchy and departmental boundaries by organizing teams of employees around core work processes, the end-to-end work, information, and material flows that provide value directly to customers.

human relations model an organizational model that incorporates the values of an internal focus and a flexible structure.

hybrid structure a structure that combines characteristics of various structural approaches (functional, divisional, geographical, horizontal) tailored to specific strategic needs.

idea champions organizational members who provide the time and energy to make things happen; sometimes called "advocates," "intrapreneurs," and "change agents."

imitation the adoption of a decision tried elsewhere in the hope that it will work in the present situation.

incremental change a series of continual progressions that maintain an organization's general equilibrium and often affect only one organizational part.

incremental decision process model a model that describes the structured sequence of activities undertaken from the discovery of a problem to its solution.

indirect interlock a situation that occurs when a director of one company and a director of another are both directors of a third company.

information that which alters or reinforces understanding.

information reporting systems the most common form of management information system, these computerized systems provide managers with reports that summarize data and support day-to-day decision making.

inspiration an innovative, creative solution that is not reached by logical means.

institutional environment norms and values from stakeholders (customers, investors, boards, government etc.) that organizations try to follow in order to please stakeholders.

institutional perspective an emerging view that holds that under high uncertainty, organizations imitate others in the same institutional environment.

institutional similarity the emergence of common structures, management approaches, and behaviors among organizations in the same field.

integration the quality of collaboration between departments of an organization.

integrator a position or department created solely to coordinate several departments.

intensive technologies a variety of products or services provided in combination to a client.

interdependence the extent to which departments depend on each other for resources or materials to accomplish their tasks.

intergroup conflict behavior that occurs between organizational groups when participants identify with one group and perceive that other groups may block their group's goal achievement or expectations.

interlocking directorate a formal linkage that occurs when a member of the board of directors of one company sits on the board of another company.

internal integration a state in which organization members develop a collective identity and know how to work together effectively.

internal process approach an approach that looks at internal activities and assesses effectiveness by indicators of internal health and efficiency.

internal process model an organizational model that reflects the values of internal focus and structural control.

international division a division that is equal in status to other major departments within a company and has its own hierarchy to handle business in various countries.

international stage the second stage of international development, in which the company takes exports seriously and begins to think multidomestically.

Internet an amorphous, rapidly growing web of computer networks around the world; enables individuals and businesses to rapidly share information on a global basis.

interorganizational relationships the relatively enduring resource transactions, flows, and linkages that occur among two or more organizations.

intranet a private companywide information network that uses the communications protocols and standards of the Internet but is accessible only to people within the company.

intuitive decision making the use of experience and judgment rather than sequential logic or explicit reasoning to solve a problem.

job design the assignment of goals and tasks to be accomplished by employees.

job enlargement the designing of jobs to expand the number of different tasks performed by an employee.

job enrichment the designing of jobs to increase responsibility, recognition, and opportunities for growth and achievement.

job rotation moving employees from job to job to give them a greater variety of tasks and alleviate boredom.

job simplification the reduction of the number and difficulty of tasks performed by a single person.

joint optimization the goal of the sociotechnical systems approach, which states that an organization will function best only if its social and technical systems are designed to fit the needs of one another.

joint venture a separate entity for sharing development and production costs and penetrating new markets that is created with two or more active firms as sponsors.

knowledge a conclusion drawn from information that has been linked to other information and compared to what is already known.

knowledge management the efforts to systematically find, organize, and make available a company's intellectual capital and to foster a culture of continuous learning and knowledge sharing so that organizational activities build on existing knowledge.

knowledge mapping projects that identify where knowledge is located in an organization and how to access it.

labor management teams a cooperative approach designed to increase worker participation and provide a cooperative model for union-management problems.

language slogans, sayings, metaphors, or other expressions that convey a special meaning to employees.

large group intervention an approach that brings together participants from all parts of the organization (and may include outside stakeholders as well) to discuss problems or opportunities and plan for change.

large-batch production a manufacturing process characterized by long production runs of standardized parts.

learning histories a written narrative of a specific major event or project, based on the recollections of everyone who participated and designed to understand how critical decisions were made and problems were solved.

learning organization an organization in which everyone is engaged in identifying and solving problems, enabling the organization to continuously experiment, improve, and increase its capability.

legends stories of events based in history that may have been embellished with fictional details.

legitimacy the general perspective that an organization's actions are desirable, proper, and appropriate within the environment's system of norms, values, and beliefs.

level of analysis in systems theory, the subsystem on which the primary focus is placed; four levels of analysis normally characterize organizations.

liaison role the function of a person located in one department who is responsible for communicating and achieving coordination with another department.

life cycle a perspective on organizational growth and change that suggests organizations are born, grow older, and eventually die.

long-linked technology the combination within one organization of successive stages of production, with each stage using as its inputs the production of the preceding stage.

low-cost leadership a strategy that tries to increase market share by emphasizing low cost compared to competitors.

management champion a manager who acts as a supporter and sponsor of a technical champion to shield and promote an idea within the organization.

management control systems the formalized routines, reports, and procedures that use information to maintain or alter patterns in organizational activity.

management information system a system that generally contains comprehensive data about all transactions within an organization.

management science approach organizational decision making that is the analog to the rational approach by individual managers.

managerial ethics principles that guide the decisions and behaviors of managers with regard to whether they are morally right or wrong.

market control a situation that occurs when price competition is used to evaluate the output and productivity of an organization.

mass customization the use of computer-integrated systems and flexible work processes to enable companies to mass produce a variety of products or services designed to exact customer specification.

matrix structure a strong form of horizontal linkage in which both product and functional structures (horizontal and vertical) are implemented simultaneously.

mechanistic an organization system marked by rules, procedures, a clear hierarchy of authority, and centralized decision making.

mediating technology the provision of products or services that mediate or link clients from the external environment and allow each department to work independently.

meso theory a new approach to organization studies that integrates both micro and macro levels of analysis.

mimetic forces under conditions of uncertainty, the pressure to copy or model other organizations that appear successful in the environment.

mission the organization's reason for its existence.

mission culture a culture that places emphasis on a clear vision of the organization's purpose and on the achievement of specific goals.

multidomestic company a company that deals with competitive issues in each country independent of other countries.

multidomestic strategy one in which competition in each country is handled independently of competition in other countries.

multifocused grouping a structure in which an organization embraces structural grouping alternatives simultaneously.

multinational stage the stage of international development in which a company has marketing and production facilities in many countries and more than one-third of its sales outside its home country.

myths stories that are consistent with the values and beliefs of the organization but are not supported by facts.

negotiation the bargaining process that often occurs during confrontation and enables the parties to systematically reach a solution.

network centrality top managers increase their power by locating themselves centrally in an organization and surrounding themselves with loyal subordinates.

network organization structure an organization structure that disaggregates major functions into separate companies that are coordinated by a small headquarters organization.

networking linking computers within or between organizations.

new-venture fund a fund that provides financial resources to employees to develop new ideas, products, or businesses.

niche a domain of unique environmental resources and needs.

nonprogrammed decisions novel and poorly defined, these are used when no procedure exists for solving the problem.

nonroutine technology technology in which there is high task variety and the conversion process is not analyzable or well understood.

nonsubstitutability a trait of a department whose function cannot be performed by other readily available resources.

normative forces pressures to adopt structures, techniques, or management processes because they are considered by the community to be up-to-date and effective.

official goals the formally stated definition of business scope and outcomes the organization is trying to achieve; another term for **mission**.

open system a system that must interact with the environment to survive.

open systems model an organizational model that reflects a combination of external focus and flexible structure.

operative goals descriptions of the ends sought through the actual operating procedures of the organization; these explain what the organization is trying to accomplish.

organic an organization system marked by free-flowing, adaptive processes, an unclear hierarchy of authority, and decentralized decision making.

organization theory a macro approach to organizations that analyzes the whole organization as a unit.

organizational behavior a micro approach to organizations that focuses on the individuals within organizations as the relevant units for analysis.

organizational change the adoption of a new idea or behavior by an organization.

organizational decision making the organizational process of identifying and solving problems.

organizational decline a condition in which a substantial, absolute decrease in an organization's resource base occurs over a period of time.

organizational development a behavioral science field devoted to improving performance through trust, open confrontation of problems, employee empowerment and participation, the design of meaningful work, cooperation between groups, and the full use of human potential.

organizational ecosystem a system formed by the interaction of a community of organizations and their environment, usually cutting across traditional industry lines.

organizational environment all elements that exist outside the boundary of the organization and have the potential to affect all or part of the organization.

organizational form an organization's specific technology, structure, products, goals, and personnel.

organizational goal a desired state of affairs that the organization attempts to reach.

organizational innovation the adoption of an idea or behavior that is new to an organization's industry, market, or general environment.

organizational politics activities to acquire, develop, and use power and other resources to obtain one's preferred outcome when there is uncertainty or disagreement about choices.

organizations social entities that are goal-directed, deliberately structured activity systems linked to the external environment.

organized anarchy extremely organic organizations characterized by highly uncertain conditions.

paradigm a shared mind-set that represents a fundamental way of thinking, perceiving, and understanding the world.

personnel ratios the proportions of administrative, clerical and professional support staff.

political model a definition of an organization as being made up of groups that have separate interests, goals, and values in which power and influence are needed to reach decisions.

political tactics for using power these include build coalitions, expand networks, control decision premises, enhance legitimacy and expertise, and make preferences explicit while keeping power implicit.

pooled interdependence the lowest form of interdependence among departments, in which work does not flow between units.

population a set of organizations engaged in similar activities with similar patterns of resource utilization and outcomes.

population ecology model a perspective in which the focus is on organizational diversity and adaptation within a community or population or organizations.

power the ability of one person or department in an organization to influence others to bring about desired outcomes.

power sources there are five sources of horizontal power in organizations: dependency, financial resources, centrality, nonsubstitutability, and the ability to cope with uncertainty.

problem consensus the agreement among managers about the nature of problems or opportunities and about which goals and outcomes to pursue.

problem identification the decision-making stage in which information about environmental and organizational conditions is monitored to determine if performance is satisfactory and to diagnose the cause of shortcomings.

problem solution the decision-making stage in which alternative courses of action are considered and one alternative is selected and implemented.

problemistic search occurs when managers look around in the immediate environment for a solution to resolve a problem quickly.

product and service changes changes in an organization's product or service outputs.

product matrix a variation of the matrix structure in which project or product managers have primary authority and functional managers simply assign technical personnel to projects and provide advisory expertise.

programmed decisions repetitive and well-defined procedures that exist for resolving problems.

prospector a business strategy characterized by innovation, risk taking, seeking out new opportunities, and growth.

quality circles groups of six to twelve volunteer workers who meet to analyze and solve problems.

radical change a breaking of the frame of reference for an organization, often creating a new equilibrium because the entire organization is transformed.

rational approach a process of decision making that stresses the need for systematic analysis of a problem followed by choice and implementation in a logical sequence.

rational goal model an organizational model that reflects values of structural control and external focus.

rational-legal authority based on employees' belief in the legality of rules and the right of those in authority to issue commands.

rational model a description of an organization characterized by a rational approach to decision making, extensive and reliable information systems, central power, a norm of optimization, uniform values across groups, little conflict, and an efficiency orientation.

reactor a business strategy in which environmental threats and opportunities are responded to in an ad hoc fashion.

reasons organizations grow growth occurs because it is an organizational goal; it is necessary to attract and keep quality managers; or it is necessary to maintain economic health.

reciprocal interdependence the highest level of interdependence, in which the output of one operation is the input of a second, and the output of the second operation is the input of the first (for example, a hospital).

reengineering a cross-functional initiative involving the radical redesign of business processes to bring about simultaneous changes in organization structure, culture, and information technology and produce dramatic performance improvements.

resource-based approach an organizational perspective that assesses effectiveness by observing how successfully the organization obtains, integrates, and manages valued resources.

resource dependence a situation in which organizations depend on the environment but strive to acquire control over resources to minimize their dependence.

retention the preservation and institutionalization of selected organizational forms.

rites and ceremonies the elaborate, planned activities that make up a special event and often are conducted for the benefit of an audience.

ritual scapegoating the functioning of manager turnover as a sign that the organization is trying to improve.

role a part in a dynamic social system that allows an employee to use his or her discretion and ability to achieve outcomes and meet goals.

routine technology technology characterized by little task variety and the use of objective, computational procedures.

rule of law that which arises from a set of codified principles and regulations that describe how people are required to act, are generally accepted in society, and are enforceable in the courts.

satisficing the acceptance by organizations of a satisfactory rather than a maximum level of performance.

scientific management a classical approach that claims decisions about organization and job design should be based on precise, scientific procedures.

sectors subdivisions of the external environment that contain similar elements.

selection the process by which organizational variations are determined to fit the external environment; variations that fail to fit the needs of the environment are "selected out" and fail.

sequential interdependence a serial form of interdependence in which the output of one operation becomes the input to another operation.

service technology technology characterized by simultaneous production and consumption, customized output, customer participation, intangible output, and being labor intensive.

simple-complex dimension the number and dissimilarity of external elements relevant to an organization's operation.

small-batch production a manufacturing process, often custom work, that is not highly mechanized and relies heavily on the human operator.

social responsibility management's obligation to make choices and take action so that the organization contributes to the welfare and interest of society as well as itself.

sociotechnical systems approach an approach that combines the needs of people with the needs of technical efficiency.

sources of intergroup conflict factors that generate conflict, including goal incompatibility, differentiation, task interdependence, and limited resources.

specialist an organization that has a narrow range of goods or services or serves a narrow market.

stable-unstable dimension the state of an organization's environmental elements.

stakeholder any group within or outside an organization that has a stake in the organization's performance.

stakeholder approach also called the constituency approach, this perspective assesses the satisfaction of stakeholders as an indicator of the organization's performance.

stories narratives based on true events that are frequently shared among organizational employees and told to new employees to inform them about an organization.

strategic contingencies events and activities inside and outside an organization that are essential for attaining organizational goals.

strategy the current set of plans, decisions, and objectives that have been adopted to achieve the organization's goals.

strategy and structure changes changes in the administrative domain of an organization, including structure, policies, reward systems, labor relations, coordination devices, management information control systems, and accounting and budgeting.

structural dimensions descriptions of the internal characteristics of an organization indicating whether stability or flexibility is the dominant organizational value.

structure the formal reporting relationships, groupings, and systems of an organization.

struggle for existence a principle of the population ecology model that holds that organizations are engaged in a competitive struggle for resources and fighting to survive.

subcultures cultures that develop within an organization to reflect the common problems, goals, and experiences that members of a team, department, or other unit share.

subsystems divisions of an organization that perform specific functions for the organization's survival; organizational subsystems perform the essential functions of boundary spanning, production, maintenance, adaptation, and management.

switching structures an organization creates an organic structure when such a structure is needed for the initiation of new ideas.

symbol something that represents another thing.

symptoms of structural deficiency signs of the organizational structure being out of alignment, including delayed or poor-quality decision making, failure to respond innovatively to environmental changes, and too much conflict.

system a set of interacting elements that acquires inputs from the environment, transforms them, and discharges outputs to the external environment.

tacit knowledge knowledge that is based on personal experience, intuition, rules of thumb, and judgment and cannot be easily codified and passed on to others in written form.

tactics for enhancing collaboration techniques such as integration devices, confrontation and negotiation, intergroup consultation, member rotation, and shared mission and superordinate goals that enable groups to overcome differences and work together.

tactics for increasing power these include entering areas of high uncertainty, creating dependencies, providing resources, and satisfying strategic contingencies.

task a narrowly defined piece of work assigned to a person.

task environment sectors with which the organization interacts directly and that have a direct effect on the organization's ability to achieve its goals.

task force a temporary committee composed of representatives from each department affected by a problem.

team building activities that promote the idea that people who work together can work together as a team.

teams permanent task forces often used in conjunction with a full-time integrator.

technical champion a person who generates or adopts and develops an idea for a technological innovation and is devoted to it, even to the extent of risking position or prestige; also called product champion.

technical complexity the extent of mechanization in the manufacturing process.

technical knowledge understanding and agreement about how to solve problems and reach organizational goals.

technology the tools, techniques, and actions used to transform organizational inputs into outputs.

technology changes changes in an organization's production process, including its knowledge and skills base, that enable distinctive competence.

total quality management an organizational approach in which workers, not managers, are handed the responsibility for achieving standards of quality.

traditional authority based in the belief in traditions and the legitimacy of the status of people exercising authority through those traditions.

transaction processing systems (TPS) automation of the organization's routine, day-to-day business transactions.

transformational leadership the ability of leaders to motivate followers to not just follow them personally but to believe in the vision of organizational transformation, to recognize the need for revitalization, to commit to the new vision, and to help institutionalize a new organizational process.

transnational model a form of horizontal organization that has multiple centers, subsidiary managers who initiate strategy and innovations for the company as a whole, and unity and coordination achieved through corporate culture and shared vision and values.

uncertainty occurs when decision makers do not have sufficient information about environmental factors and have a difficult time predicting external changes.

values-based leadership a relationship between a leader and followers that is based on strongly shared values that are advocated and acted upon by the leader.

variation appearance of new organizational forms in response to the needs of the external environment; analogous to mutations in biology.

variety in terms of tasks, the frequency of unexpected and novel events that occur in the conversion process.

venture teams a technique to foster creativity within organizations in which a small team is set up as its own company to pursue innovations.

vertical information system the periodic reports, written information, and computer-based communications distributed to managers.

vertical linkages communication and coordination activities connecting the top and bottom of an organization.

whistle-blowing employee disclosure of illegal, immoral, or illegitimate practices on the part of the organization.

Name Index

Corporate Name Index

A

A.T. Kearney, 96
AccountingNet, 150
Acumin, 207
AES Corporation, 13
Agfa-Gevart Group, 175
Airbus Industrie, 169, 491
Alcatel, 482
Albany Ladder Company, 96
Alberta Manufacturing, 406
Allied Signal, 355
Allstate Insurance, 137, 152, 204, 255, 301, 355
ALLTEL, 379–380
Aluminum Company of America, 464–465
American Airlines, 411
America Online, 13, 100, 149, 179, 324
American Express Corporation, 57
American Home Products Corp., 513
American Hospital Supply Corporation, 247
American Standard Companies, 91
Amoco Corp., 175, 301, 486
AMP, 175
Andersen Consulting, 443
Andersen Windows, 10
Andersen Worldwide, 443
Anglian Water Services, 262, 356, 363
Anheuser-Busch, 129, 173, 280
Apple Computer, 100, 149, 151, 285, 286, 287, 289, 367
Archer-Daniels-Midland, 11
Arthur Andersen, 443
Asea Brown Boveri Ltd. (ABB), 283, 297, 497–498
Ashton Photo, 504
Associated Builders and Contractors Inc., 245
AT&T, 23, 111, 130, 136, 151, 169, 173, 178, 179, 374
Atlanta Braves, 52
Atlantic Group, 133
Autodesk, Inc, 372
Avis Corporation, 60, 429
Axiom Corp., 320

B

Baker & Taylor Books, 11
Baldwin Locomotive, 179
Bank One, 318, 513
Bantam, 129
Barnes & Noble, 129, 130, 150, 178, 249
BASFAG, 11
Bayer, 491
Bell Emergis, 301
BellSouth Telecommunications, 373
Bergen Brunswig, 248
Bertelsmann AG, 7, 129, 150
Best Buy, 130
Bethlehem Steel, 22, 508
Biogen, Inc., 287–288
Black & Decker, 365, 369, 492
Blue Bell Creameries, 97–98
BMW, 207
Boeing, 92, 152, 169, 207, 281, 326, 331, 502
Boise Cascade Corporation, 222
Bombardier, 152
Booz, Allen & Hamilton, Inc., 169
Borden, 429
Borders, 249
Borg-Warner Chemicals, 444, 445–446
Borien, 177
Borland International, 511
Boston Edison Company, 204–205
Bouyant Company, 449
Bridgestone, 177
Bristol-Myers Squibb Company, 293
British Airways, 60
British Telecom, 136, 169
Brothers Coffee, 59–60
Buckman Laboratories, 28
Burger King, 443, 482

C

Cable and Wireless, 130
Cadence Design Systems Inc., 262
Cadwalader, Wickersham, and Taft, 359–360
Canadian Imperial Bank of Commerce, 429
Canadair, 152

Capital Protection Insurance Services, 212–213
Cardinal Health, 248
Carrefour, 133, 135
Caterpillar Inc., 287, 491, 502
CBS Records, 133
Cementos Mexicanos (Cemex), 8, 30–31, 54
Centex, 292
Centrobe, 96
Certified Transmission Rebuilders, 329
Charles Schwab Corporation, 182, 260, 486
Check Point Software Technologies, 428
Chesebrough-Ponds Inc., 257, 381
Chevron, 10, 23
Chiron, 283
Chrysler Corporation, 89, 482
CHS Electronics, 134
Ciba-Geigy, 264
Cincinnati Milacron, 356, 357
Circuit City, 166
Cisco Systems, 29–30, 54, 89, 165, 167, 173, 244, 250, 254, 484
Citicorp, 399
CKS Group, 149
Clark, Ltd., 452
Coca-Cola, 13, 132, 133, 135, 137, 280, 292, 410, 482, 484
Coldwell Banker, 152
Coleco Industries, 137
Columbia/HCA Healthcare Corp., 11, 330
Columbus Mills, 299–300
Comcast Communications, 173
Commercial Casework, 90
Compaq Computer Corporation, 115, 183
Continental Airlines, 399
Corning, 175
Corsair Communications Inc., 508–509
Crescendo Communications, 165
Crystal Manufacturing, 457–458
Cummins, 177
Custom Foot, 207

D

Daimler-Benz, 482
DaimlerChrysler, 10, 89, 177

$\mathcal{S}$ubject Index

P 12. What is an organisation

— MWt loschonung for NM

LL SWL P 281 — Scaler